Navigating strategic possibilities

ENDORSEMENTS

The richness of this book is evident, with a breadth, depth and scope that is commendable ... It covers a vast array of contemporary and relevant themes in the realm of strategy and would serve as a valuable addition to the 21st century management practitioner's strategy toolkit.

The title aptly represents the content of the book and demarcates the overarching topic of strategy adequately. Overall, the purpose as set out is believed to be achieved in terms of "... multiple contemporary strategy perspectives and practices ..." and "... stimulating new strategic thinking ..."

The book is structured quite well, appropriately organised, logical and coherent, appropriately taking the reader on a journey from Strategic leadership → Strategy formulation → Multiple futures → Strategy execution → Strategy renewal and innovation. The construction is sound, well written, argued and synthesised. Augmenting the learnings with reflection questions, cases and application tools makes it an excellently rounded-off resource.

In a book of this scope, integrating various themes into a cohesive whole, is challenging but it has been skilfully done in a way that will be appealing and understood by the target audience.

Dr Cobus Oosthuizen, Dean: Business School, Milpark Education

The book is well-written and covers important aspects of strategy formulation and implementation with due attention to context. I am particularly impressed with the approach to leadership, which differs from standard strategy texts. The focus on 'humans' in the organisation doing strategy to achieve the organisation's goals is a welcome and much-needed approach.

My sense is that this book can serve as a 'manual' for practitioners to improve their strategy execution abilities. If students use this book they should be well prepared to master strategy in the workplace.

Hester Nienaber, Research Professor at the Department of Business Management, Unisa

Up till now, most authors in the field of strategy have been focusing on describing the content of strategy and strategy concepts. Whilst this is required and necessary, this practice has left students somewhat bewildered, in that they now had to sort out for themselves as to how one should use the theory of strategy to develop a practical process of strategy. Managers were forced to rely on consultants who could reduce the complexity of strategy development for them. The authors of *Navigating Strategic Possibilities* have succeeded in integrating the theory of strategy development with the practical process of strategy development. Very few other authors have been able to do so.

The focus on leadership as a point of departure makes a clear statement of the job of the strategic leaders of the organisation as to where strategy fits in. Explaining the different kinds of strategic thinking adds more value to the chapter! The authors have also integrated the latest learnings of *avant garde* authors, such as Alexander Osterwalder, Ash Maurya, and Kim and Mauborgne, into the process. A further pro of the book is the focus on the role of strategy in the life of the business entrepreneur! In addition, the use of scenarios in strategy development adds tremendous value to an already very useful textbook. This book should not only become the standard textbook at business schools, but should be read by every middle, senior and executive manager!

Johan Burger, Director, NTU-SBF Centre for African Studies, Nanyang Business School, Nanyang Technological University

While there are many strategic management books, most of these focus on the strategic management process. What makes this book different is its very strong focus on the building blocks of strategic management, rather than on the process. It puts leadership at the core, which is a fundamental shift in approach, and includes strong sections on the business model and scenario planning – vital aspects of modern strategy-making that are generally neglected in mainstream strategic management books. While it addresses the widely accepted theoretical aspects of strategy-making, it also introduces many new tools, frameworks and practical exercises that enhance the fundamental material. The book is very comprehensive, and could present a very useful resource for academics and postgraduate students in this field.

Peet Venter, Professor of Strategy at the Graduate School of Business Leadership (SBL), Unisa

Navigating strategic possibilities

Strategy Formulation and Execution Practices to Flourish

Marius Ungerer, Gerard Ungerer and Johan Herholdt

kr publishing

2016

First published in 2016

ISBN: 978-1-86922-623-7
ISBN: 978-1-86922-624-4 (ePDF)

Published by KR Publishing
P O Box 3954
Randburg
2125
Republic of South Africa

Tel: (011) 706-6009
Fax: (011) 706-1127
E-mail: orders@knowres.co.za
Website: www.kr.co.za

Typesetting, layout and design: Cia Joubert, cia@knowres.co.za Cover
design: Marlene de Villiers, marlene@knowres.co.za
Editing: Jill Bishop, jill.bishop@absamail.co.za
Proofreading: Valda Strauss: valda@global.co.za
Project management: Cia Joubert, cia@knowres.co.za
Index created with: TExtract – www.Texyz.com

ACKNOWLEDGEMENTS

We want to thank the team from Knowledge Resources Publishing for making this book a reality. Your professionalism is acknowledged and appreciated.

We want to acknowledge past MBA students from USB (2008–2015) as valuable co-creators of strategic management tools and applications as reflected in different parts of this book. Your contributions to strategy practice building are valued.

We are indebted to our families, who are always willing to support us. Thank you.

We acknowledge the blessings we are privileged to receive from our Creator.

Our peer reviewers provided us with knowledgeable feedback and caused us to change our text in crucial places – we thank you.

TABLE OF CONTENTS

List of figures

List of tables

ABOUT THE AUTHORS

Prof. Marius Ungerer is a core faculty member of the University of Stellenbosch Business School (USB) where he conducts research and teaches strategic management, leadership and change management for postgraduate degree programmes like MBA, MPhil in Management Coaching and PGD in Leadership. He is also an annual visiting academic to the University of Johannesburg and Nagoya University of Commerce and Business, Japan.

Dr. Gerard Ungerer is a digital enterprise strategist and industrial engineer who is passionate about competitive strategy, business models, digital start-ups, technology, innovation and management. He has been involved in several strategy consulting projects, has developed more than 10 conceptual strategy tools that can be used to guide people's strategic thinking, innovation and problem solving processes, and by applying the principles of business model innovation, his team prevailed as category winners in an international innovation challenge.

Johan Herholdt is a management thinker and an experienced author of more than 10 books (five as editor) and various book chapters. He is an expert facilitator, concentrating on individual and team coaching, discourse processes and dialogics, as well as systemic problem-solving.

INTRODUCTION

Purpose of the book

This book utilises multiple contemporary strategy perspectives and practices to give leaders and strategy practitioner's deep insights into the dynamics and optionalities involved in developing good and robust strategies. The core of the book is about stimulating new strategic thinking and action to enhance the competitiveness of a firm.

View on business strategy

Strategy is seen as the collective, emerging pattern – based on strategic choices – an organisation consciously exhibits and executes over time to ensure its sustainable endurance by differentiating itself in unique ways to create and add value for stakeholders. Strategy is about navigating the competitive business landscape. It explains how an organisation intends to move forward and how it intends to advance the interests of stakeholders. Strategy formulation and execution are therefore an organic emergent learning process of people relating on a shared future in a specific context which they have the power to influence.

Core focus

Navigating strategic possibilities involves the invention and re-invention of an organisation. Strategic leadership, as a part of this navigation journey, is an integral guiding force of the strategic choices an organisation makes to fulfil its aspirations. In this book, the key strategic choices related to the competitive advantage and positioning of an organisation are presented in an integrated strategic architecture perspective, and the following seven strategic architecture building blocks are discussed:

- Strategic leadership as a key capacity that gives life, meaning and on-going momentum to the strategy of an organisation.
- The development of views on the external and internal strategic landscape and context of an organisation.
- Strategy formulation and development which include a menu of strategic options and choices to consider.
- The development of multiple futures perspectives for an organisation.
- Strategy execution practices to make strategy a lived reality for stakeholders.
- Strategy renewal and innovation practices to refresh the strategy on a continuous basis.
- Entrepreneurial leadership and strategy practices to foster both entrepreneurship and intrapreneurship.

The future holds an abundance of possibilities for those aware enough to spot them. The strategy navigation tools contained in this book provide the identification and execution tools needed to flourish in the future.

This book complements the book *Crystallising the Strategic Business Landscape* by the same authors.

| | Focus of this book |
| | ↓ |

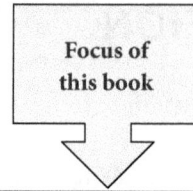

CRYSTALLISING THE STRATEGIC BUSINESS LANDSCAPE	NAVIGATING STRATEGIC POSSIBILITIES
Strategy analysis	**Strategy Formulation and Execution**
What is our current reality? **External Global, Macro, Industry and Customer analysis** • **Market opportunities** • **Market threats** **Internal analysis** • **Resource strengths** • **Resource weaknesses** **Utilising strategy analysis tools and problem-solving approaches**	**What are our future strategic choices?** **What are our aspirations?** **What should we be doing?** **How can we change to make these aspirations a reality?** **How do we execute successfully?**

Who can benefit from this book?

The book is for strategy practitioners and leaders taking up their strategy role in analysing external and internal contexts. The focus is on practice-based applications informed by theoretical perspectives. If you want to understand **how** to do a thorough strategic analysis, this book is for you.

We welcome feedback

Readers who want to share their experiences and development of applying the strategic analysis practices and suggest alternative application approaches are welcome to send such feedback to joherholdt@gmail.com. We welcome all feedback.

Important note by the authors

This book with a focus on **strategy formulation** is part of a series of two books on the topic of **strategic management**. The first book, which was published in February 2016, focuses on **strategy analysis** to complement this book.

Chapter 1

Strategic leadership

"A leader is a dealer in hope." – Napoleon Bonaparte[1]

"Before you are a leader, success is all about growing yourself. When you become a leader, success is all about growing others." – Jack Welch[2]

LEARNING OBJECTIVES

This chapter introduces the topic of strategic leadership as a variable of organisational success or failure. We support the view of Phil Rosenzweig that leadership and culture "are perhaps better understood as attributions based on performance rather than causes of performance"[3]. This chapter covers the topic of ethics in strategic management and presents virtuous leadership as a practice to foster sound moral decision-making, and provide guidance for leadership modelling or setting positive examples. At the end of this chapter, you will be able to use the following perspectives and tools to develop your own strategic leadership capacity:

- Understand the dynamic context of business and the implications for leaders.
- Describe different ways to lead in a VUCA world to build organisational agility.
- Explain the rationale for the different strategic thinking departure points.
- Describe what strategy is, what it is not and how it is changing.
- Outline the role of strategic leadership in an organisation.
- Explain the concept of strategic architecture and how it fits with strategy.
- Value and apply business ethics and virtuous leadership as part of strategic leadership.

INTRODUCTION

This chapter is about strategic leadership, ethical aspects related to strategy and virtuous leadership as a sound example of virtue- and values-based leadership practice. In this chapter we show how strategic leadership gives life, meaning and focus to the strategic management processes.

Strategic leadership is an organisational capacity that should be spread wide and deep in organisations, as it can never only be the exclusive task of a few executives at the "top" of the organisation. In this chapter, we therefore highlight the need for distributed values-based leadership capacity as a crucial part of managing in the twenty-first century.

Figure 1.1 positions strategic leadership thinking and practices, business ethics through virtuous leadership (chapter 1) and entrepreneurial thinking and practices (chapter 9) as the foundation for launching strategic management processes such as: external and internal analysis and synthesis[4], strategy formulation (chapter 2–3), exploring multiple futures (chapter 4), strategy execution (chapter 5) and strategy renewal and innovation (chapter 6–8). In this it is acknowledged that strategic management processes can only become an organisational reality through the involvement of many organisational actors and collaborators who all contribute their strategic leadership thinking and capabilities to explore and act on possibilities.

Remember the words of Rumelt:[5] "strategy cannot be a useful concept if it is a synonym for success. Nor can it be a useful tool if it is confused with ambition, determination, inspirational leadership, and innovation".

Strategic success is not based on a single cause, but is the result of various variables interacting in a virtuous way. Two strategic variables that contribute hugely to strategic success are (1) the ability of leaders to choose the winners from amongst the many available strategic options and (2) the ability to consistently execute these strategic choices in an excellent way.[6] Jim Collins[7] once said that: "Greatness is not a matter of circumstances. Greatness, it turns out, is largely a matter of conscious choice."

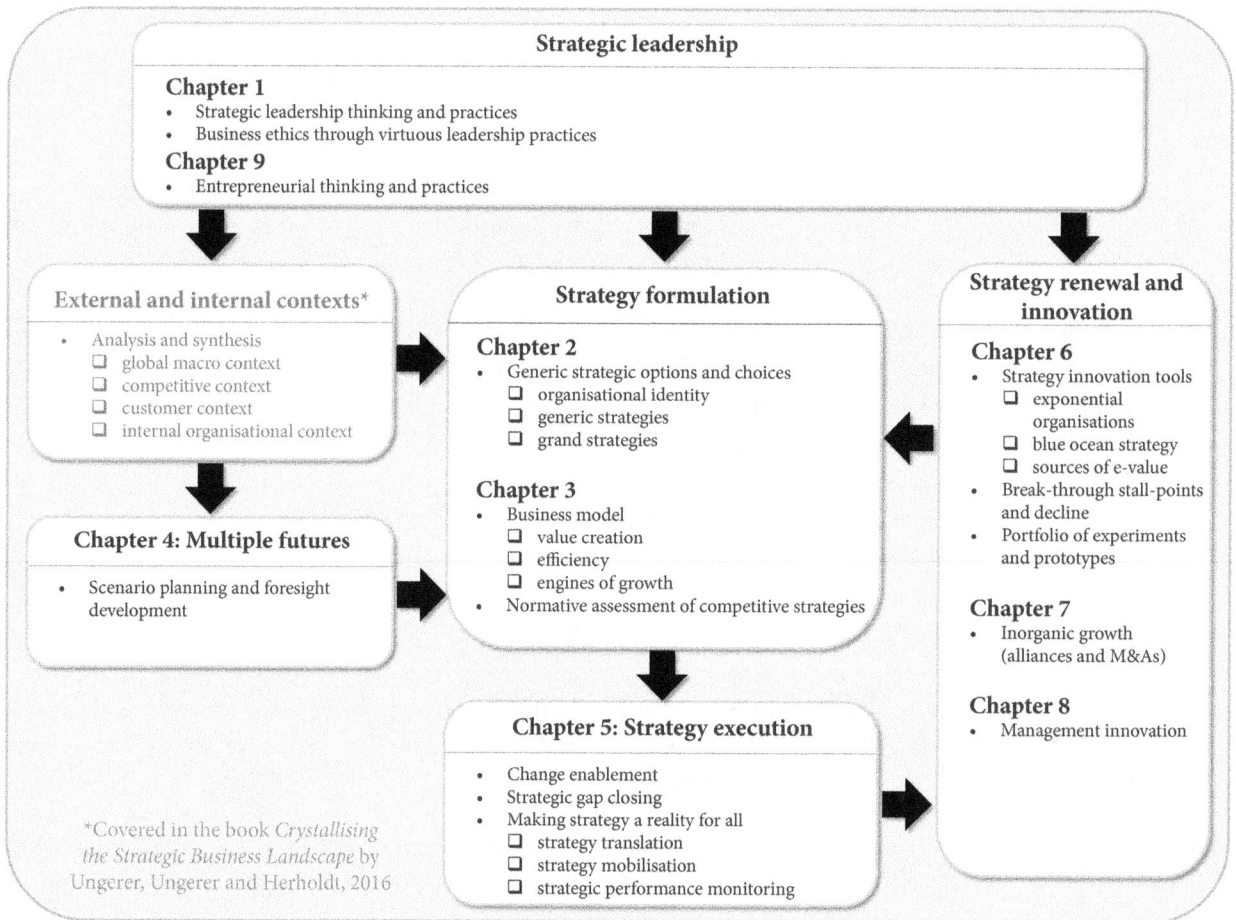

Strategic leadership

Chapter 1
- Strategic leadership thinking and practices
- Business ethics through virtuous leadership practices

Chapter 9
- Entrepreneurial thinking and practices

External and internal contexts*
- Analysis and synthesis
  - global macro context
  - competitive context
  - customer context
  - internal organisational context

Strategy formulation

Chapter 2
- Generic strategic options and choices
  - organisational identity
  - generic strategies
  - grand strategies

Chapter 3
- Business model
  - value creation
  - efficiency
  - engines of growth
- Normative assessment of competitive strategies

Strategy renewal and innovation

Chapter 6
- Strategy innovation tools
  - exponential organisations
  - blue ocean strategy
  - sources of e-value
- Break-through stall-points and decline
- Portfolio of experiments and prototypes

Chapter 7
- Inorganic growth (alliances and M&As)

Chapter 8
- Management innovation

Chapter 4: Multiple futures
- Scenario planning and foresight development

Chapter 5: Strategy execution
- Change enablement
- Strategic gap closing
- Making strategy a reality for all
  - strategy translation
  - strategy mobilisation
  - strategic performance monitoring

*Covered in the book *Crystallising the Strategic Business Landscape* by Ungerer, Ungerer and Herholdt, 2016

Figure 1.1: The strategic architecture landscape

In the next part of this chapter we discuss the context strategic leaders operate in today as well as the concepts "strategic thinking", "strategy-making", "strategic leadership" and "strategic architecture". This is followed by a perspective on ethics in strategic management and virtuous leadership practices.

THE CONTEXT

The world we live in today is characterised by experts as a so-called VUCA environment, which represents features of Volatility, Uncertainty, Complexity and Ambiguity.[8] The last decade was even labelled by *Time* magazine as "the decade from hell"[9].

Volatility is the nonpredictability of changes and the speed, magnitude and nature of these changes. Uncertainty is associated with our difficulty in making future-orientated forecasts and decisions, especially if they are based on what we know about past issues and events. This impedes our capacity to predict and prepare for the future. Complexity relates to the fact that most problems have multiple causes and mitigating factors that are difficult to understand. This adds to the strain of decision-making. Ambiguity represents the lack of clarity and the difficulty of ascertaining the causes of patterns and events and identifying the "who, what, where, how and why" associated with what is happening around us. This relative chaotic, turbulent, disruptive and fast-changing environment has become a permanent condition and reality, as well as the "new normal", for organisations at the beginning of the twenty-first century.[10] The VUCA world realities are not only influencing how we do business in future; they also impact on how we lead in an ever-changing, dynamic context.

Experts[11] indicate that the above context requires a skill-set from leaders that reflects aspects such as personal agility, complex and adaptive thinking abilities and innovative and critical thinking skills. In a VUCA world "leaders must make continuous shifts in people, process, technology, and structure. This requires flexibility and quickness in decision-making".[12] The focus is on creating adaptive institutions that can learn and change fast in an economical way continuously.[13] Examples of firms with this adaptive ability are Apple, Google, 3M, Unilever, Amazon and Naspers. The departure point is:

> "you can say, "It's a very tough world", or you can say, "It's a world that's changing fast" … Two and-a-half billion more people will be added to the planet between now and 2050, of which 2 billion will be added in developing countries. The digital revolution, the shift in consumer spending, all this suggests that companies have to reinvent the way they do business."[14]

Other skills that assist leaders to thrive in a VUCA world are self-awareness about how to leverage personal strengths and compensate consciously for weaknesses through partnering with others; an openness to engage with change to understand more and develop clarity about opportunities and threats; the development of knowledge and an understanding of their organisation beyond their own functional or business line domains; the ability to work collaboratively on challenges; and an ability to learn fast in a constantly changing environment.[15] The capacity to enable the development of "just-in-time" solutions as a flexible response to changes is part of the future requirements for leaders.[16] Risk scanning by all functions and levels to deliberately widen and deepen this activity is part of risk management and creates a greater anticipation of potential disruptive changes.[17] The more risk-scanning processes and interactions are diverse and devolved, the higher the possibility that they will generate useable knowledge and understanding to inform strategising activities. Later in this chapter we also explore leadership styles and approaches such as values-based leadership, authentic leadership and responsible leadership that resonate with a VUCA context (see Virtuous leadership).

It also needs to be highlighted that business is not the victim of VUCA, but in many instances the source of and major contributor to it.[18] Globalised businesses mitigate volatility risks and uncertainty in trading environments through externalising risks and costs to society in the form of structural unemployment, variable tax discounts and, in extreme emergencies, by bail-out arrangements funded from public taxes. *Impact International* states that major future threats[19] evolve around the following events: more banking failures; currency volatilities; hostile new economic blocks advancing their self-interest; oil price volatility; sudden collapse of demand; loss of services, species depletion and biodiversity loss; skill shortages; and competition from fast-growing manufacturing nations, including African countries. In a sense we can anticipate many probable scenarios, but the uncertainty about timing and scale remains.

Organisational resilience is a required capability that assists companies to deal with the challenges associated with a VUCA world. The features of a resilient enterprise[20] include efficiency in resource and energy utilisation; active strategies to prevent resource depletion and price volatility; a diversified business portfolio across markets; positive cash-flows; and a reputable brand. A resilient business invests in the prevention of environmental damage and pollution. It also invests in rigorous employment, strategy and decision-making practices and contributes positively to the society it operates in. Two features associated with leaders in agile organisations include the ability to *anticipate and recognise* challenges and to *initiate and respond* to the change required to ensure a sustained high organisational performance.[21] The main routines and practices associated with organisational agility are summarised in Table 1.1 to integrate our understanding of how to prepare organisations be more prepared for a VUCA world.

Table 1.1: The routines of agility[22]

Strategising Dynamically	
Sense of shared purpose	The purpose or mission (outcomes other than profit or growth) and the business model (how we make money) are widely shared. Values embedded in these statements drive behaviour on a daily basis.
Change-friendly identity	There is a clear sense of "who we are" and "what inspires us". This long-term strategy explains success and encourages the organisation to change.
Robust strategic intent	The current business strategy is relevant in today's market. It clearly distinguishes the firm from other companies, but is flexible enough to change at short notice.
Perceiving Environmental Change	
Sensing	The organisation explores the future deeply, and many people within the organisation maintain continuous contact with parts of the business environment.
Communicating	Information from the environment gets to decision-makers rapidly, in an unfiltered way. Information flows easily, in both directions, between the bottom and top of the organisation.
Interpreting	Information is evaluated on the basis of the company's existing identity, intent, business model and risk tolerance.
Testing Responses	
Slack in resources	Capable resources (people, money, time, tools) are available and can be readily deployed to experiment with new ideas.
Risk management	Experiments are bounded by agreed-upon criteria for judging success and failure; the possibility of failure is accepted as a vehicle for learning.
Learning	Experience with running experiments is captured and applied with each new round, so that the company's capabilities are continuously improved.

Implementing Change	
Management and organisational autonomy	Executives delegate sufficient authority to line and business managers so that the company can execute changes with success; there is no second-guessing from headquarters, only alignment with basic strategic objectives.
Embedded change capability	The pragmatic ability to change collective habits, practices, and perspectives is embedded in line operations, not isolated in staff groups.
Performance management	Clear, unambiguous, accepted performance measures and targets are based on business model drivers with rewards that matter.

It is clear from the contextual patterns described above that we cannot continue to think about reducing uncertainty only by sound traditional decision-making and planning practices. We need to actively engage with uncertainties by using leadership agility and critical and complex thinking skills.

Practical guideline

Impact International[23] suggests the following general leadership practices to navigate successfully in a VUCA world:

- Always retain a clear vision against which judgements can be made, with agility to flex and respond appropriately to rapidly unfolding situations.
- Provide clear direction and consistent messaging against a backdrop of continually shifting priorities, supported with the use of new virtual modes of communication where necessary.
- Anticipate risks but don't invest too much time in long-term strategic plans. Don't automatically rely on past solutions and instead place increased value on new, temporary solutions, in response to such an unpredictable climate.
- Think big picture. Make decisions based as much on intuition as analysis.
- Capitalise on complexity. If your talent management strategy is working, then you should be confident that you have the right people in the right place. This will enable you to rapidly break down any challenge into bite-sized pieces and trust in the specialist expertise and judgement of those around you.
- Be curious. Uncertain times bring opportunities for bold moves. Seize the chance to innovate.
- Encourage networks rather than hierarchies – as we reach new levels of interconnection and interdependency collaboration yields more than competition.
- Leverage diversity – as our networks of stakeholders increase in complexity and size, be sure to draw on the multiple points of view and experience they offer. Doing so will help you expect the unexpected.
- Never lose focus on employee engagement. Provide strategic direction, whilst allowing people the freedom they need to innovate new processes, products and services.
- Get used to being uncomfortable. Resist the temptation to cling on to outdated, inadequate processes and behaviours. Take leaps of faith and enjoy the adventure.

Leaders should use their convening power to stimulate fresh thinking. Leaders from everywhere in the organisation should host a variety of strategic conversations to foster inclusion, multi-perspectives and innovation.

? Questions to reflect on:

How many of the above leadership practices and thinking are part of your way of leading your team, unit or organisation? What can you do to create a context conducive to just-in-time solutions based on new emerging market and industry opportunities and threats?

Application tool

Think about your own career and skill-sets to function optimally in a VUCA context. Answer the following questions to create evidence of your skills and abilities to lead positively in a VUCA world:[24]

- Give an example of when you performed well in a work environment that featured rapid change and/or ambiguity. Did you enjoy this environment? What did you learn?
- Give an example of where your ability to be decisive was put to the test when you had to convey a sense of urgency in decision-making. What was the situation, what factors did you consider when making the decision, and what was the outcome?
- How do you determine when you need to gather more information before making a decision versus making a decision based on the information you have at hand? Give recent examples of when you made a quick decision based on the information you had immediately available and a situation where you opted to collect more information before making a decision. Which decision-making style was more comfortable for you and why?
- Give an example of when you modified your personal style to achieve an important work objective. What was the situation, how did you change your approach, and what was the outcome?

To conclude this contextual overview we look at the British multi-national mining company *Vedanta* to illustrate that we still have a long way to go in order to make business a mutually beneficial and true partner of societies and Mother Earth.

Case study of Vedanta

The 2010 annual report of the British Mining MNC Vedanta states:[25]

Introduction: Vedanta Resources plc is a London-listed FTSE 100 diversified metals and mining major. The Group produces aluminium, copper, zinc, lead, iron ore and commercial energy.

Our vision: To be a world-class, diversified resources company providing superior returns to our shareholders with high-quality assets, low-cost operations, and sustainable development.

Our values:

Entrepreneurship: We foster an entrepreneurial spirit throughout our businesses and value the ability to foresee business opportunities early in the cycle and act on them swiftly. Whether it be developing organic growth projects, making strategic acquisitions or creating entrepreneurs from within, we ensure an entrepreneurial spirit at the heart of our workplace.

Growth: We continue to deliver growth and generate significant value for our shareholders. Moreover, our organic growth pipeline is strong as we seek to continue to deliver significant growth for shareholders in the future. We have pursued growth across all our businesses and into new areas, always on the basis that value must be delivered.

Excellence: Achieving excellence in all that we do is our way of life. We strive to consistently deliver projects ahead of time at industry-leading costs of construction and within budget. We are constantly focused on achieving a top decile cost of production in each of our businesses. To achieve this, we follow a culture of best practice benchmarking.

Trust: The trust that our stakeholders place in us is key to our success. We recognise that we must responsibly deliver on the promises we make to earn that trust. We constantly strive to meet stakeholder expectations of us and deliver ahead of expectations.

Sustainability: We practise sustainability within the framework of well-defined governance structures and policies and with the demonstrated commitment of our management and employees. We aim not only to minimise damage to the environment from our projects but to make a net positive impact on the environment wherever we work.

Vedanta at a Glance:[26] With an empowered talent pool of 30,000 employees globally, Vedanta places strong emphasis on partnering with all its stakeholders based on the core values of entrepreneurship, excellence, trust, sustainability and growth."

In 2014 the *Guardian* reported the following:

> **India's rejection of Vedanta's bauxite mine is a victory for tribal rights:**[27] Landmark decision backing India's 8,000-strong Dongria Kondh tribe could set a precedent for tribal people across the country.
>
> India's decision to reject a London mine's request to mine bauxite on tribal land marks a major victory for human rights in the country. For too long, tribal communities have been pushed off their land in the name of development and industrialisation, their attempts to defend their lands brushed aside or brutally suppressed. The Dongria Kondh's determination to protect the Niyamgiri hills from the mining heavyweight Vedanta Resources has paid off, despite the state government's complicity in the $2bn project.
>
> Like many tribal communities worldwide, the Dongria have a strong connection to their land. They have expert knowledge of local forests, plants and wildlife – families grow more than 100 crops and gather food from the forests including mangoes, mushrooms and honey. The 8,000-strong community has been campaigning against the mining project for almost a decade amid alleged intimidation by paramilitary police and local goons. Many locals and organisations, including activists and international groups

including Survival and Amnesty International, have worked hard to amplify the Dongria's voices. They understood this was a David and Goliath-style battle of India's tribal people fighting to protect their ways of life, and the integrity of their forests, from the wanton industrialisation that would destroy them.

The pressure on Vedanta was increased by Survival's complaint to the UK government under the Organisation for Economic Co-operation and Development guidelines for multinational companies, which in turn helped persuade many important shareholders, including the Church of England, to disinvest on ethical grounds from a company that had become notorious for the Niyamgiri project.

In 2010 the Indian government blocked Vedanta's bid to build the mine. And, finally, last April, India's Supreme Court ordered that affected communities must be consulted about the project before it could go ahead. In what was described as the country's first environmental referendum, the Dongria unanimously rejected Vedanta's proposal during 12 village consultations in August.

The central government and the Supreme Court bucked the trend of siding with industry, and defended the Dongria's right to their lands, their livelihoods and to determine their own future. And the environment ministry's decision to block Vedanta should serve as a warning to any company intent on extracting resources from tribal land without members' informed consent. Vedanta has learned this the hard way. It opened a refinery to turn Niyamgiri's bauxite into aluminium before receiving approval for the mine, and has lost millions of pounds as a result.

Some commentators are angry that such a small tribe has been able to derail a major industrial project. But the benefits of the scheme would have lined the pockets of very few, while the devastation of the Dongria and their homeland would have been irreversible. The landmark decision also flies in the face of those who believe that so-called backward or primitive tribes should be "developed" and join the mainstream. Vedanta tried repeatedly to insist that the mine would help bring "development" to the Dongria, but seemed to overlook the fact that the construction of an open-pit mine would devastate their mountain, therefore achieving little in the form of development for the tribe. The initiatives that would accompany the projects were all oriented towards permanently altering the Dongria's way of life and independence.

As the Dongria leader, Lodu Sikaka, put it: "We'll lose our self-esteem if they take away our hills and forests. Other Adivasis [India's tribal peoples] who have lost their homes are dying of desperation; they are being destroyed. Earlier they used to till their land but now they are only drinking without working. They have become kind of beggars."

The Dongria case was about much more than the community and their homeland. India has been studying the events closely as a litmus test for its democracy. It raises the following questions: when citizens reject such projects strongly, peacefully and tirelessly, should the state be allowed to bulldoze ahead with its agenda? Should the rights of the people trump the interests of industry or vice versa?

The ministry's decision to ensure that some places can – and must – be off limits to mining restores hope that India will not abandon human rights in the pursuit of foreign investment – the rights of its people will – at least sometimes – be upheld.

Questions to reflect on:

What can we learn from this case study about the role of business in society? If you were the strategy advisor for Vedanta, what would your advice to them be?

STRATEGIC THINKING DEPARTURE POINTS

Why is it that seemingly reasonable and intelligent people continue to operate in nonvirtuous ways? One of the contributing factors is the way people think and talk about the nature of individuals and organisations. "The way people talk about the world has everything to do with the way the world is ultimately understood and acted in".[28] If we continue to think about business as a cut-throat zero-sum game where dog-eat-dog is the norm, then we will have a world where people act and do in this way. However, if business were created and managed on the basis of individual trust and respect as well as collective gain based on a process led by virtuous people, a different way of doing business would emerge.[29] When we can create a more positive picture of human beings and organisation, we increase the chances of making the world a better place to live in and organisations better places to work for.[30] [31] The core departure point is that all human beings, which includes business and organisation leaders, inherently have the capacity and potential to do both good and evil. If however we continue to present organisations as characterised only by cut-throat competition, greed and selfishness, we end up feeding a corruptible monster. On the other hand, if we focus on the bright side of organisations, we "aim to increase the possibilities that organisational virtuousness will be self-fulfilling".[32] In this paradigm both business and their leaders serve as a force for good.

The way we think affects the opportunities and possibilities we can see, or not. In part, we are the result of our own thinking capacity and stance. The question we all need to think about regularly is: Do we think and reflect about how and what we think? Are we thinking good, positive things or are we overwhelmed by the continuous flow of negative data supplied by the mass media? Are we critical about what is presented as "the truth"?

In this section we will explore five interrelated thinking stances that enable strategic leaders to gift themselves with a winning starting point. They are 'Possibility thinking', 'Collaborative thinking', 'Abundance thinking', 'New Economy Values thinking' and 'Paradox thinking'.

Possibility thinking

> *"We can re-invent our work as a place of contribution rather than an arena for my success ... a contribution produces a shift away from self-concern and engages us in a relationship with others that is an arena for making a difference" – Roz and Ben Zander*[33]

Leaders of winning teams and enterprises think positively and focus on possibilities. You cannot do strategy work that focuses on changing, improving and transforming an organisation when your mind-set and attitude are negative. A hallmark of excellent leaders with a positive and empowering influence on stakeholders is that they think good things for themselves and for others. Adrian Gore, CEO of the Discovery Group, indicated at a Discovery Invest Leadership Summit that he believes that positivity and optimism are the fuel and fundamental attributes of leadership.[34] Strategy allows an organisation to be purposefully opportunistic.[35]

Ben and Rosamund Zander[36] introduced the concept of upward and downward spiral thinking. Downward spiral talk represents a way of speaking that excludes possibilities and tells us compellingly how things are going from bad to worse. We all know this type of talk and it is sometimes prevalent around smoking rooms, dinner tables, braaivleis fires, and even boardrooms. Downward spiral talk is wholly reactive to circumstance, has a victim mind-set and focuses on the abstraction of scarcity, where the limits to what is possible are emphasised. The end result of downward spiral thinking is a place of no hope, negativity and depression. It is also a place where the obstacles and problems are emphasised with a general attitude that "we" are right and "they" are wrong; or "we" cannot do anything about the current situation which "they" must fix. This is clearly not a route for strategic leaders with the intention of making a positive difference.

Finding the courage, authenticity and moral will to speak about possibilities creates an upward spiral conversation. Zander advises us that upward spiral conversations do not ignore the way things are, but thinking about possibilities empowers us to accept current challenges without being held hostage by circumstances or feeling helpless to change current realities. This is about seeing the glass as "half-full" and not "half-empty". The focus is on what we have now, whatever it may be and however little it is, that we can use to take a positive step towards developing solutions by thinking about possibilities, moving away from the bondage of problems that keep us from taking personal action. This is not about a simplistic kind of optimism, but a realistic stance on attending to real things that make up the substance in the glass. Openly attending to and appreciating what we have and acknowledging it as a gift takes us into the realm of possibility. "The capacity to be present to everything that is happening, without resistance, creates possibility".[37]

Upward- or downward-spiralling conversations have the same dynamics. Whenever there is a clear winner or loser you are in a downward spiral. Upward-spiralling conversations seek win-win solutions and are based on partnerships, mutual respect and a shared future dream, vision or intent to improve a current situation or condition.

An Afro-optimistic view of the African continent, her people and potential is part of possibility thinking. Seeing the opportunities associated with a developing continent and capitalising on them is part of a winning mind-set. The choice is clear – we can make the most of what we have or we can wait for perfect conditions that may never happen. Strategic leaders seek and seize opportunities as they emerge. Leaders with impact constantly seek ways to enlarge their personal influence domain by thinking about themselves not as victims, but victors, who are agents for change, not targets for change.

Support for this "positive possibility" thinking stance comes from Daniel Kahneman, the 2002 Nobel Prize winner in economic sciences, who indicates that optimists are more psychologically resilient, have stronger immune systems, and live longer on average than more pessimistic opposites. Optimism protects us from "loss aversion", our tendency to fear losses more than we value gains.[38] Research confirms that individuals with an optimistic and hopeful future orientation are better performers, have more perseverance and display better moods at work.[39] Kim Cameron[40] indicates that strategies that capitalise on the positive aspects of a situation or issue tend to produce life-giving, flourishing outcomes in individuals and organisations.

Questions to reflect on:

- Do you actively think about the way you think? Is it mostly upward- or downward-spiral thinking?
- Do you think of yourself as a victim or victor? What are the implications?
- What should you do more of to be experienced by others as a "possibility" thinker?

Collaborative thinking

A collaborative mind-set is another helpful thinking stance for leaders who want to work in an inclusive way to achieve results. It needs to be stressed that collaboration is not a sign of weakness nor is it a form of incompetence.

Collaboration is a powerful choice, based on the following reality check on ourselves and others: Do we all accept that none of us have THE ANSWER? Only if we do accept that we actually do not know it all – which is always the case in high human interaction-dependent situations – then we open ourselves up to the views of others. As leaders we burden ourselves with the unnecessary load of trying to be superhuman by pretending we know everything. This is a false and inauthentic starting point.

A characteristic of the work of leaders is that it always happens in the presence of other people – leadership by its nature is a team activity. We are human and no leader is perfect nor does he or she possess everything required for success. All leaders have holes, but they can become whole through their team members by capitalising on team members' strengths to augment the leader's strengths. Collaborating on skills, competences, talents and passions creates extraordinary results. The same principle is applicable to business – focus on the areas that make your business unique and find partners for the rest.

Individual collaboration manifests in different ways and is a choice between different thinking stances, as can be seen in Table 1.2.

Table 1.2: Collaborative thinking stances

Thinking stances	Self-centred: ME thinking	Collaboration: WE thinking	Dependency: I thinking
Self-concept	Expert	Collaborator	Pair of hands
Impact effect	Aggressive: ME	Assertive: Win-win	Passive-Aggressive
Relationship orientation	Parent	Adult	Child
Power/Love focus	Power without love is reckless	Power and Love	Love without power is sentimental
Attitude	Blame	100% Accountability	Complain
Role in society	Ruler	Citizen	Subject
Hierarchy focus	Boss	Community/Team	Employee

One aspect that needs to be emphasised is the interplay between power and love as a combined intent in Table 1.2. This refers to uniting power as a drive towards self-realisation, with love as an intentional disposition to help other people to develop their full potential. This enables co-existence by acknowledging and respecting others.[41] Power relations can be used in virtuous or corrupt ways, in the service of negative or positive goals, as inner and self-directed or in the service of others.[42] The positive use of power makes it possible for things to happen that would otherwise not have been feasible, by introducing new aspects relevant for creation. Positive power use also involves more listening and less force.

A collaborative mind-set fosters teamwork, zero-plus win-win outcomes and diversity – based on an acceptance of others as responsible citizens and adults who take accountability for mutually beneficial outcomes. Collaboration also requires sharing power and unconditionally embracing others as equal team members.

Linux is an example of open-source software that is developed in a collaborative way. The principles[43] that Linux follows to guide open-source development in an emergent way are: meritocratic division of labour to ensure ongoing development is done by the best willing and able human capital; conversational manners – largely virtual to create a flow and exchange of ideas; and agreed-upon standards and protocols relating to the development, testing and sequencing of product releases.

One way to increase collaboration in an organisation is group selection as a way for cooperation to take root. As tribes include members who are ready to serve one another and to sacrifice themselves for the common good, organisations can focus on selecting leaders with a preference and inclination for natural cooperation. This grows the collective and individual capacity in the organisation to perform selfless acts for the greater good. Another way to stimulate cooperation is direct reciprocity – "you scratch my back, I'll scratch yours". Simulations showed that over time direct reciprocity gives way to a more generous strategy in which players might still cooperate even if their rivals defect. This is the evolution of forgiveness where a direct reciprocity strategy allows players to overlook the occasional mistake. A variation is indirect reciprocity, where one individual decides to aid another based on the needy individual's reputation. Those who have a reputation for assisting others who fall on hard times might even find themselves on the receiving end of goodwill from strangers when their own luck takes a turn for the worse. Thus, the co-operator in this situation thinks "I'll scratch your back, and someone will scratch mine".[44]

Collaborative thinking does not however mean a new utopia. Evolutionary simulations show that cooperation is intrinsically unstable and that periods of cooperative prosperity inevitably give way to defective doom. Yet the altruistic spirit always seems to rebuild itself when our moral compasses realign.[45]

To show how a collaborative mind-set influences the way we think about managing and leading organisations, the difference between a self-centric heroic leadership approach and a collaborative leadership approach is illustrated in Table 1.3.

Table 1.3: Two ways to manage[46]

Heroic leader	Collaborative leader
There is clear separation between those who manage and those who develop products and deliver services.	The role of leaders is to help other people to do the important work of developing products and delivering services.
The "higher up" a manager is, the more important they become. The CEO is at the "top".	An organisation is an interacting network, not a vertical hierarchy. Effective leaders work throughout, they do not sit on top.
The strategy of an organisation comes down the hierarchy – clear, deliberate and bold. Strategy emanates from the chief who makes the dramatic moves. Everyone else "implements".	Strategy emerges from the network of people interacting on challenges to initiate strategic initiatives.
To manage is to make decisions and to allocate resources from the top.	Managing is about bringing out the positive energy which resides naturally in people.
The leaders get the rewards for increasing performance.	Rewards for making the organisation a better place go to all.
Leadership is bestowed on those who thrust their will upon others.	Leadership is a sacred trust earned through the respect of others.

Questions to reflect on:

- Have you made a conscious choice not to be a person who "knows it all"?
- Do you work in ways that allow others to find their voice in your presence? Examples?

Abundance thinking

How often do we think that the future will be better than we can imagine? This is the hallmark of an abundance and positive deviance thinking mind-set that does not accept scarcity as the dominant departure point. Although the threat of scarcity still dominates our worldview, scarcity as a condition in our world is often contextual and relative.[47]

Abundance thinking accepts that innovation can turn scarcity into abundance. Humanity is entering a radical transformation period where technology can raise the standards of living for all on the planet. Technology is a powerful enabler of new innovations and creates unending possibilities. According to Diamandis and Kotler[48] abundance is not, however, about providing everyone on this planet with a life of luxury: rather it is about providing all with a life of possibility. These authors identified four emerging forces – exponential technologies, the DIY innovator, the techno-philanthropist, and the rising billion – that are conspiring to solve our biggest problems. They argue that the future will be better than we think because of the following forces with abundance-raising potential:

- Technologies in computing, energy, medicine and many other areas are improving at an exponential rate and will soon enable breakthroughs that today seem impossible.
- These technologies have allowed independent DIY innovators to achieve startling advances in many areas of technology with little money or manpower. A do-it-yourself revolution is happening where DIY-ers can accomplish what was once the sole domain of large corporations and governments.

- Technology has created a generation of "techno-philanthropists", such as Bill Gates and Mark Zuckerberg, who are using their billions to try and solve the seemingly unsolvable problems of the world, especially of the developing world, such as hunger, disease and Internet ubiquity.
- The lives of the world's poorest people are being improved substantially because of technology. Examples include the "rising billion", who connect to the global economy through the Internet, microfinance and wireless communication technology.

Impactful strategic leaders accept that their job is not only to overcome major problems and challenges in the world, but also to enable the highest human potential – that is, to empower people to do innovative breakthrough work as a way of life and as a contribution to life. To live into this possibility, we need a positive deviance orientation that represents intentional behaviours and targets that depart significantly from the norms of a referent group in an honourable way.[49] The continuum of positive deviance thinking to illustrate the stretch associated with abundance gaps is reflected in Table 1.4.

Table 1.4: A continuum illustrating positive deviance[50]

	Negative Deviance	Normal	Positive Deviance
Individual:			
• **Physiological**	illness	health	vitality
• **Psychological**	illness	health	flow
Organisational:			
• **Economics**	unprofitable	profitable	generous
• **Effectiveness**	ineffective	effective	excellent
• **Efficiency**	inefficient	efficient	extraordinary
• **Quality**	error-prone	reliable	perfect
• **Ethics**	unethical	ethical	benevolent
• **Relationships**	harmful	helpful	honouring
• **Adaptation**	Threat – rigidity	coping	flourishing
	⬆		⬆
	Deficit gaps		**Abundance gaps**

The positive deviance position is clearly a high aspirational target – way beyond "normal". This is the terrain of the extraordinary, the zone of excellence based on honouring relationships and flourishing while adapting to changes. We need to remember that leadership is about learning how to shape the future and creating new realities.[51] Embracing a positive deviance stance and abundance thinking is a key departure point for leaders who want to make a positive long-term impact with and through people they encounter.

(?) Questions to reflect on:

- Do you think scarcity or abundance? What can you do to have more abundance thinking and less scarcity thinking?
- How can positive deviance thinking help you to far exceed performance expectations every time?

New economy values thinking

A VUCA world not only represents the challenges of unexpected radical and discontinuous changes, but also requires us to rethink **how** we do and fulfil our leadership tasks. Drucker[52] states:

> "Every few hundred years in Western history there occurs a sharp transformation. Within a few short decades, society – its world view, its basic values, its social and political structures, its arts, its key institutions – rearranges itself. And the people born then cannot even imagine a world in which their grandparents lived and into which their own parents were born. We are currently living through such a transformation."

One of the main shifts that affect the way we respond to external changes comes from the shift in values between the old and new economy. Christo Nel[53] has developed a view of new economy leadership practices as a response to the old economy way of doing things. He states "every facet of leadership practices and organisational life is an extension of deeper underlying values".[54] The imperatives and drivers of this shift are reflected in Table 1.5.

Table 1.5: The imperatives of a values shift[55]

Old Economy thinking	New Economy thinking
Capitalism didn't win – Communism lost first	Refining social democracy and capitalism
Market economics = Consumerism	True markets = society & community
Purpose of business is profit (Milton Friedman, Reaganism, Thatcherism)	Business is an integral part of society and must be fit and friendly to human life
Aristocracy of power	Diffusion of power and democratic values
Turf protection and control	Webs of energy and leadership
Privilege and technocratic opaqueness of information	Transparency and accessibility of information
Leadership as position & entitlement	Servant leadership and stewardship
Self-serving individualism	Sense of internal locus of control
Hero leader and hierarchic power	Diffused leadership and unleashing energy
Mechanistic – whole is the sum of the parts	Holographic – whole is in the part; part reflects the whole

Hamel[56] supports the view of redefining and re-inventing capitalism when he says that in general there is a growing societal disgruntlement with large corporations' interpretation of the implicit contract that governs their rights and obligations toward society. The current pattern of large benefits to a few executives is unsustainable in an era of stakeholder activism. The movement of business towards a more active positive partnering with societies is a growing trend. Research[57] shows that CEOs across all sectors measure their business impact by more than just profit and want their organisations to be part of shaping a better society.

The twenty-first century is the age of knowledge workers. Drucker[58] indicates that the most valuable asset of a twenty-first century institution, whether business or nonbusiness, will be its knowledge workers and their productivity. The challenge to use more than just muscle power, but also the intellect of people requires from us to re-think the assumptions we make about the abilities of people to contribute and the way we open up these spaces for them. We have to accept that all workers are knowledge workers and respect them for that.

Leading from a new economy values perspective represents a specific way of **being** a leader as well as **doing** things in a different way by serving the interest of others as a core starting point. Nel describes four waves of values that are present in varying degrees all of the time: 1st Wave – driven by coercion; 2nd Wave – driven by co-option; 3rd Wave – driven by collaboration; and 4th Wave – driven by co-creation. He acknowledges that there is no simplistic or absolute cut-off point between Old and New Economy values. "Instead it represents a spectrum of world views and values that includes everything from harsh autocracy and control to open system engagement and integration of interests".[59] Each of the waves of values form an intricate web of attitudes, relationships, beliefs and behaviours – see Table 1.6.

Table 1.6: The waves of values[60]

Leadership values	Old Economy values		New Economy values	
Primary intent	Coercion	Co-option	Collaboration	Co-creation
Secondary effect and application	Violence and demand	Money and control	Knowledge and participation	Ecology, community and imagination
	Overt or sublimated	Ownership and patronage	Information and self-insight	Environment and "7th generation"
	Leading servants	Aristocracy	Democracy	Servant leadership
Relational impact	Dependence	Co-dependence	Independence and interdependence	Integration
Power orientation	Power over	Power to	Power through	Power by, for, with
Energy manifestation	Dictate	Control	Guide	Unleash energy
Performance orientation	Demand	Exploit/entitlement	Productivity and quality	Continuous improvement
Rewards orientation	Privilege	Patronage	Performance-based	Partnerships

It is clear from the above comparison on the uses of power that coercive power "should be the refuge of last resort for the diplomatically challenged ..., not the hallmark of management's right to manage".[61] In a new economy values perspective, power is not used in a self-centric way by leaders, but to empower others to do great things. The focus is on the responsibilities of leaders rather than their power. Paradoxically (see next section) the positive use of personal and positional power in an organisational context is all about giving it away and sharing it, not with egocentric motives, not claiming special privileges, but working with and through others to make things happen that would otherwise not be possible. Power is experienced through relationships and its virtue is visible in the way leaders choose to do what they do.

Another reality is that the command-and-control approach to leadership is becoming less and less viable due to globalisation, new technologies and new ways of value creation and interaction with customers. The leader as a host and convenor of a series of conversations is using his or her collaboration and co-creation intent to move the strategic agenda of an organisation forward. Strategy emerges from a cross-organisational conversation and from leaders who take time to carefully explain the strategic agenda to stakeholders in an inclusive and participative way.

The above view of the shift in values aligns with Kanter's values-based capitalism paradigm[62] where the best companies fulfil three conditions:

- They obey the laws and regulations of the countries they operate in.
- They are guided by an enlightened self-interest to do lots of good using their core competences to develop new products and services.
- They are guided by values that stimulate them to make a positive difference in a global and local context.

Questions to reflect on:

By leading with a new economy values perspective, leaders create the conditions for sustainable high individual and organisational performance. Our strategic choices start with a personal choice about the personal leadership values and intent we embrace. When we do this we accept that the question[63] has changed from "Who am I as a future leader?" to "What type of future leader does the world need me to be?"

Also develop insights on:

- What are the implications of leading from a new economy values perspective?
- What should I personally do to lead from a new economy values perspective?

Paradox thinking

Strategic leaders with high impact and influence embrace paradox thinking as a way of dealing with complexities in a context. Paradox thinking is the ability to hold two seemingly competing ideas or "truths" in the same time and space. In this way we break the pattern of choosing between two "right" options by thinking "and" rather than "or". This is what Jim Collins[64] calls the genius of the "and". Examples of paradox thinking by leaders in high-performing organisations are reflected in Table 1.7.

Table 1.7: Paradox thinking examples[65]

Disciplined thinking and doing	*and*	Creative thinking and doing
Empirical validation	*and*	Bold strategic moves
Prudent and frugal	*and*	Big Hairy Audacious Goals (BHAGs)
Ferociously ambitious	*and*	Not egocentric
Cannot predict the future	*and*	Prepared for what they cannot predict
Zoom out – big picture	*and*	Zoom in – detail
Stability	*and*	Change
Never count on luck	*and*	Get high return on luck when luck comes

Strategic leaders also need to manage the paradox of logical thinking based on analysis **and** intuitive thinking based on synthesis and holistic reasoning. The paradoxes to embrace are shown in Table 1.8.

Table 1.8: Strategic thinking paradoxes[66]

Dimensions	Analytical reasoning perspective	Holistic reasoning perspective
Emphasis on	Logic over creativity	Intuition over logic
Dominant cognitive style	Analytical	Holistic
Thinking follows	Formal, fixed rules	Informal, variable rules
Mode of thinking	Structured	Unstructured
Direction of thinking	Vertical	Lateral
System at work	Conscious, reflective	Unconscious, reflexive
Problem-solving seen as	Analysing activities	Sense-making activities
Assumptions about reality	Objective, partially knowable	Subjective, partially creatable
Thinking hindered by	Incomplete information	Adherence to current cognitive map
Strategising speed	Slow	Fast
Strategising based on	Calculation	Judgement
Metaphor	Strategy as science	Strategy as art

Paradox thinking empowers strategic leaders with the capacity to think innovatively and inclusively about challenges and dilemmas. By upholding two competing possibilities and not choosing between them, opportunities open and enlarge. This is challenging, but possible if we want to accept complexity as an ongoing reality.

Next we explore the content and processes associated with strategy-making.

STRATEGY-MAKING

A key question to address is: What is strategy and how is it created? Mintzberg[67] reminds us of the complexities associated with strategy:

> "Strategy is not just a notion of how to deal with an enemy or a set of competitors or a market, it draws us into some of the most fundamental issues about organisations as instruments for collective perception and action."

There is general consensus that strategy is a multi-dimensional concept with the following key ingredients:[68]

> "Strategy is concerned with both the organisation and the environment; The substance of strategy is complex; Strategy affects the overall welfare of the organisation; Strategy involves issues of both content and process; Strategies are not purely deliberate; Strategies exist on different levels; and Strategy involves various thought processes."

Strategy is not an end-product in itself, but rather a construct with a clear future intent that is continuously moulded and shaped in a journey with many feedback mechanisms, e.g. customer take-up and feedback; practical application experiences; and insights of strategy collaborators.[69] Strategy formulation and execution have no end-line, but have many humble beginnings and rebuilds scattered throughout, based on the inspiration, foresight and future aspirations of people relating in a particular context. This means that strategy is a pattern of behaviour in a stream of actions that have consequences for the survival of the organisation in its competitive environment and that emerge in the day-to-day activities of the organisation[70].

Strategy has intangible features and is both a frame of mind (see Table 1.10 on strategic thinking departure points) to be developed and nurtured over time and a plan to be executed. From this perspective, strategy is much more than a document or an occasional event. It represents a way of thinking about the business, a way of looking at the world and interpreting insights and experiences to influence the view of why this organisation matters at all. Yes, there are formal strategy analysis, formulation and execution practices that make it an organisational capability, but the deeper ethos associated with strategy is a nonstop, continuous cycle. When strategy practices are mere "check-the-box" exercises to fulfil a corporate governance requirement (like King 3) and not embedded in brutally frank, transparent and courageous dialogues about the facts, they are a rain-dance into nowhere. Strategy is like an electric current – it keeps the business machine operating in a constant and fluid way. Although you cannot directly see either strategy or an electric current, you can identify its absence when the machine stops working and things start falling apart. Strategy has subtleties that are associated with the leadership and culture of an organisation. It takes time and focused effort to create a strategically focused organisation, but such an organisation can also be destroyed by leaders who do not respect the intangibles associated with strategy-making. "The process of strategy formation requires insight, creativity and synthesis, all the things that formalisation discourages".[71]

Strategy is also more than just an aspiration or a future dream. Strategy is a system of value creation with mutually reinforcing parts.[72] The idea is to create systemic growth engines (R-loops)[i] via an activity system(s) that fulfil the core strategic choices of an organisation. Porter states: "The essence of strategy therefore lies in the activities, choosing to perform activities differently or performing different activities than rivals".[73]

---

i R-loops have been covered in Ungerer, M., Ungerer, G. & Herholdt, J. 2016. *Crystallising the Strategic Business Landscape.* Bryanston: KR Publishing. pp. 23–26.

Organisational strategy is the collaborative and conscious behaviour people in organisations exhibit in an effort to ensure sustainable organisational survival. This view reflects strategy-making as a people-centric approach where organisational actors (leaders and followers) cooperate to execute strategic choices. The intended role of strategy in a firm is to create alignment on strategic efforts and focus in order to contribute to the longer-term sustainability of the organisation.

If we track organisational strategy over time, we can identify the main strategic choices that have been made to ensure a viable future. Viability is dependent on an organisation's ability to compete and assert itself in a competitive business environment and to meet multiple stakeholder expectations. The reality is that the robustness of a strategy is continuously tested in the marketplace and that different stakeholders (customers, competitors, investors, regulators, employees etc.) all expect different results and benefits from the strategic outcomes of the organisation. The evaluation of the success of an organisation is always relative to the competition within an industry. The central goal of strategy in a free-market environment should be to achieve sustainable, superior long-term returns on investment[74] and to create multiple shared values that meet the expectations of a variety of stakeholders.[75] Value creation for stakeholders is the new norm. Making a difference that matters for stakeholders is the intent. Research indicates that firms that focus on creating multiple stakeholder value, the so-called consciousness capital players,[76] deliver superior financial results while creating many other forms of wealth and wellbeing for all of their stakeholders, including society. How do they do it? It boils down to these factors:

> "these companies generate very high levels of sales because they excel at creating value for customers; they willingly operate with lower gross margins than they are capable of, yet they achieve higher net margins than their traditional counterparts. Over time, conscious businesses develop sterling reputations and grow faster. They attract more loyal customers, committed team members, higher quality suppliers and generate greater community goodwill. All of this also helps these firms earn more and receive higher valuations relative to their earnings."[77]

Drucker indicates that strategic choices should be made with a present future-time horizon mind-set. "Strategy deals with the futurity of present decisions".[78] Decisions only exist in the present and the strategic decision-maker should not focus on what the organisation should do in the future but rather on what the organisation has to do now to be ready for an uncertain future.

Differentiation is at the heart of the competitive strategy game[79] and leaders who understand this feature create and grow businesses based on sound competitive advantages (see chapter 2 for more on core competitive choices). Porter says competitive strategy is about being different, deliberately choosing a different set of activities to deliver a unique mix of values.[80] Differentiation through sound ecological and social practices embedded in the DNA of the organisation is an integral part of the strategy of the firm and the hallmark of future winners. Sustainability from a strategic perspective is more than just financial success over time, and includes ecological and social sustainability. The activities of business should create beneficial outcomes for the societies and ecologies it operates in as well as doing no harm to these bottom lines. Ray Anderson, ex-CEO of Interface, states that:

> "The economy is the wholly owned subsidiary of nature, not the other way around and ... there is no more strategic issue for a company, or any organisation, than its ultimate purpose. For those who think business exists to make a profit, I suggest they think again. Business makes a profit to exist. Surely it must exist for some higher, nobler purpose than that."[81]

The sustainability of an organisation comes not only from a competitive advantage (which can over time be eroded by competitors), but also from the ongoing capability of an organisation to create and add value to stakeholders.

> "Strategy is therefore the collective, emerging pattern – based on strategic choices – an organisation consciously exhibits and executes over time to ensure its sustainable endurance by differentiating itself in unique ways to create and add value for stakeholders. Strategy is about explaining how an organisation wants to move forward and how it wants to advance the interests of stakeholders."

Strategy-making is an organic emergent learning process of people relating to a shared future in a specific context that they have the power to influence. The dynamic nature of strategy as both a plan and an emerging pattern is illustrated in Figure 1.2.

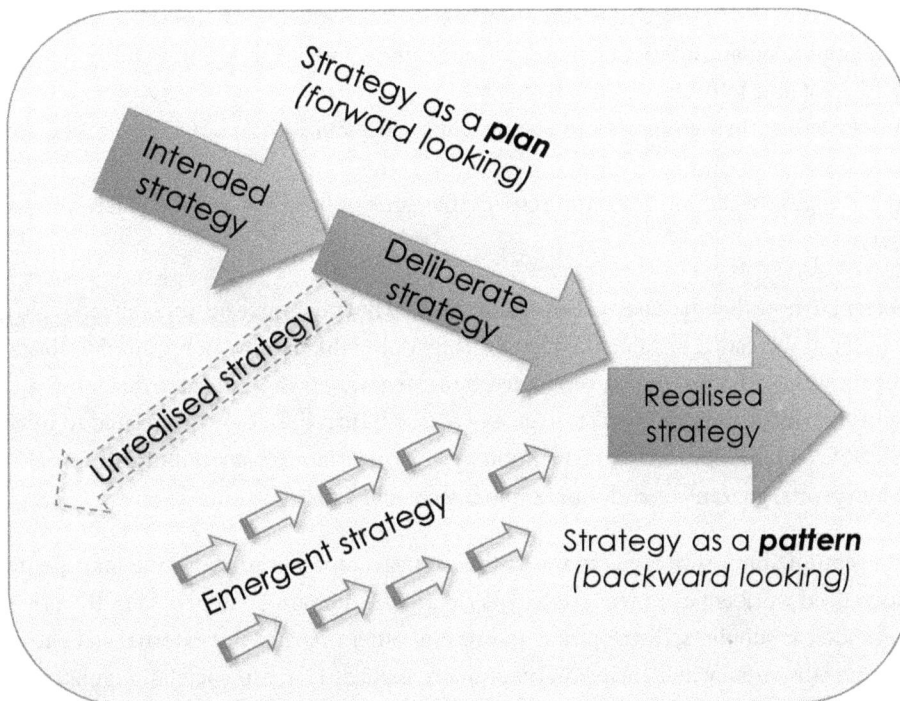

Figure 1.2: Deliberate and emergent strategies[82]

"Achieving and maintaining strategic momentum is a challenge that confronts an organisation and its leader every day of their entwined existence. It's a challenge that involves multiple choices over time – and, on occasion, one or two big choices".[83]

A great strategy reflects the following elements:[84]

- The compelling reason for the existence of the organisation is clear and is reflected in an idea and identity. The question about the difference the organisation makes in the world and why that matters is answered.
- The core strategic choices of the organisation are well understood: to do what is required today to matter tomorrow.

- The differentiating features of the strategy are well described and difficult to imitate.
- A tailored and interwoven set of activities as part of an activity system(s) for value creation is clear.
- Progress is monitored through meaningful metrics.
- A passion and a deep concern for the strategy by stakeholders to make it a lived reality.

Rumelt states: "A good strategy does more than urge us forward toward a goal or vision. A good strategy honestly acknowledges the challenges being faced and provides an approach to overcoming them. And the greater the challenge, the more a good strategy focuses and coordinates efforts to achieve a powerful competitive punch or problem-solving effect".[85]

The features associated with winning strategy players[86] are:

- They focus relentlessly on creating and maintaining a competitive advantage for today and tomorrow.
- They focus on employing an indirect tactic to outmanoeuvre and surprise competitors by applying resources where rivals are least able to defend themselves.
- They mobilise the will of their employees to win by employing action-orientated people who are impatient with the status quo.
- They stay on the edge of a caution zone and respect the game of business and the places you can play as stipulated by society.

It is however important to note that the existence of a strategy does not guarantee business success. No guarantees exist and the only way to try and create a sustainable business is by doing the hard work required to forge good strategies and flawlessly executing them.[87] This view is supported by Rosenzweig, who indicates that strategy always involves risk because we don't know for sure how our strategic choices will turn out. Risks are related to uncertain customer demands, unpredictable competition, changing technology and uncertainties surrounding internal capabilities. This makes talk about blueprints, guarantees and immutable laws a delusion.[88]

A common misconception about strategy is that it is the exclusive domain of executive management. In a VUCA world and a democratised work environment strategy is clearly the domain of all people in the organisation, as well as strategic partners such as suppliers, distributors, unions and other internal and external stakeholders. The drivers for a higher focus on transparency and inclusion on strategy matters relate to societal, regulatory, technology and economic trends.[89] Societal changes include a new generation of Facebook employees who are all connected and informed, and expect to be included in matters that influence their future. An increase in stakeholder activism is part of a societal movement world-wide to hold companies more accountable for their strategies and demand more transparency from organisations. Regulatory trends include guidelines by the Global Reporting Initiative (GRI) for integrated corporate reports that are more informative and transparent on strategy items. Technology trends that support inclusivity and openness are E-voting and Wikis as well as a continuous flow of new electronic formats and connections. Economic trends that contribute to higher demand levels for inclusion and disclosure on strategy issues are powerful stock markets and globalisation of enterprises spanning multiple economic trading areas.

This shift in the focus of strategy-making processes to being more inclusive, collaborative and co-created is well illustrated by Oxford-based Richard Whittington's view, reflected in Table 1.9.

Table 1.9: Breaking the mind-set: Strategy is only for a few, mainly inside the firm[90]

Traditional view of strategy	New view of strategy
Elitist strategy	Open strategy
Strategy as exclusion	Strategy as inclusion
Strategy as telling	Strategy as asking
Hiding strategy	Transparent strategy

Hamel indicates: "An elitist approach to strategy creation engenders little more than compliance. That which is imposed is seldom embraced. To help revolutionary strategies emerge, senior managers must supplement the hierarchy of experience with a hierarchy of imagination".[91]

This movement towards an open and inclusive view of strategy does not take any decision rights away from executives, but empowers many collaborators.

A general failure of thinking about strategy is not distinguishing planning from strategising.[92] Planning is about breaking down a process into clearly articulated steps, whilst crafting strategy is a dynamic process of connecting thought and action.[93] In this book we distinguish between the strategy activities of strategy analysis,[94] strategy formulation and strategy execution/strategy planning, the latter two of which are shaped by insights about external and internal contexts, multiple futures, strategy renewal and innovation, and entrepreneurial practices (see Figure 1.1).

Within a VUCA context and an ever-changing external environment the rhythm of strategy-making has changed. The traditional approach to strategy had the following drumbeat: Plan, plan, plan, and eventually execute. The new pattern of strategy is: Discover, do something and learn, Discover, do something and learn … This reflects a shorter gap between decision-making and execution as well as the existence of an ongoing portfolio of experiments to test potentially viable strategic options.

Another change in strategy practices is an emphasis on ensuring the execution of strategic choices that were made as part of the strategy development process. Those players who can implement their strategic choices fast have a strategic competitive advantage over their rivals. But it is not only strategy execution that matters. A delicate relationship and interrelatedness exists within the strategy process, which consists of strategy analysis, strategy formulation and strategy execution. All three of these parts are vital and require equal attention. Taking the strategy process apart and focusing only on one part is not optimal or advisable. Analysis is not strategy and strategy is not only action. Furthermore, strategies evolve over time as learning from execution brings new insights.[95] Great firms like Nike, Toyota, Amazon and Woolworths all evolved and changed over time.

Regarding the flow of the strategy process, Hamel gives us the following guideline: Traditionally it is believed that the thinkers behind strategy creation are at the top and the doers at the bottom; however, in reality the thinkers lie deep in the organisation. In order to achieve a perspective that is diversified as well as to provide unification around purpose, the strategy-making process must involve a deep diagonal slice of the organisation.[96] A top-down perspective often only achieves unity of purpose and a bottom-up process sometimes only achieves diversity of perspective, as many voices are heard and many options are explored. "Unity without diversity leads to dogma and diversity without unity results in competing strategy agendas and fragmentation of resources. Only a strategy-making process, which is both deep and wide, can achieve both diversity and unity".[97]

The main contributing features of strategy in an organisation are:[98] it sets direction; creates focus; defines an identity; sets parameters for consistency; and enables the organisation to focus its resources and exploit opportunities.

We conclude this section on strategy-making by showcasing in Table 1.10 the contrast between a pure micro-economic view and an abundance view of organisational strategy. We support both an economic and an abundance view of strategy, as it enlarges the competitive spaces and options for an organisation. We have to put an end to "either/or" thinking and embrace "and/also" thinking to reflect the contextual complexities of the world we live in – see the section on Paradox Thinking earlier in this chapter.

Table 1.10: Different strategic management departure points

Departure points	Micro-economic view of strategy	Abundance social learning view of strategy
Primary paradigm	Strategy as a plan Choice perspective Red ocean strategy	Emergent strategy Social learning perspective Blue ocean strategy
Inter-organisation views: mind-set	Scarcity: Win–lose – slicing the pie, creating a zero-sum game Independence Beating the competition	Win-win – increasing the pie, leading to a zero-plus game Interdependence Collaboration & co-opetition
Intra-organisation views: mind-sets	Political power: Centralised strategising Key actors: Top management team Decision-making primarily driven by rules and regulations Meet minimum requirements on eco-compliance Primarily about physical world and tangible assets	Distributed power – inclusive strategising Key actors: Multiple actors across hierarchical levels and boundaries Principle and values-based decision-making Strive for eco-leadership by exceeding requirements Digital and intangible assets

Case study of strategy-making in Southern Africa

Local research on the strategy-making practices in eight case study companies in Southern Africa was done from 2011 to 2013.[99] The broad purpose of the research was to develop a deeper understanding of how business strategy practices are actually being done and used in organisations in Southern Africa. Of particular interest was the underlying strategy thinking and views of strategic actors about strategy practices associated with strategic episodes. A strategic episode is a narrative description of a specific strategy activity in a context with a beginning and ending.[100] All eight company-based case studies focus on answering the following research question: What are the underlying perceived meaning and intent of strategic actors when they engage in doing strategy? The study produces both a virtuous (Figure 1.3) and a vicious (Figure 1.4) storyline about the role of strategic actors in strategising praxis.

Strategy actors are mainly executives, senior and middle managers...

Who are	Who have	Who use	Who create
• Proactive and personally involved in strategising praxis	• A visionary long-term, big-picture orientation towards strategy • Analytical thinking and sensing strategising praxis	• Aspirational strategy descriptions (vision, mission, values) to shape and direct strategising praxis	• A balanced top-down and bottom-up flow of strategic exchanges

Realising conducive strategy outcomes where:

• strategising processes are experienced as meaningful ongoing sensemaking
• strategy is evaluated as "substantial and central" to business success

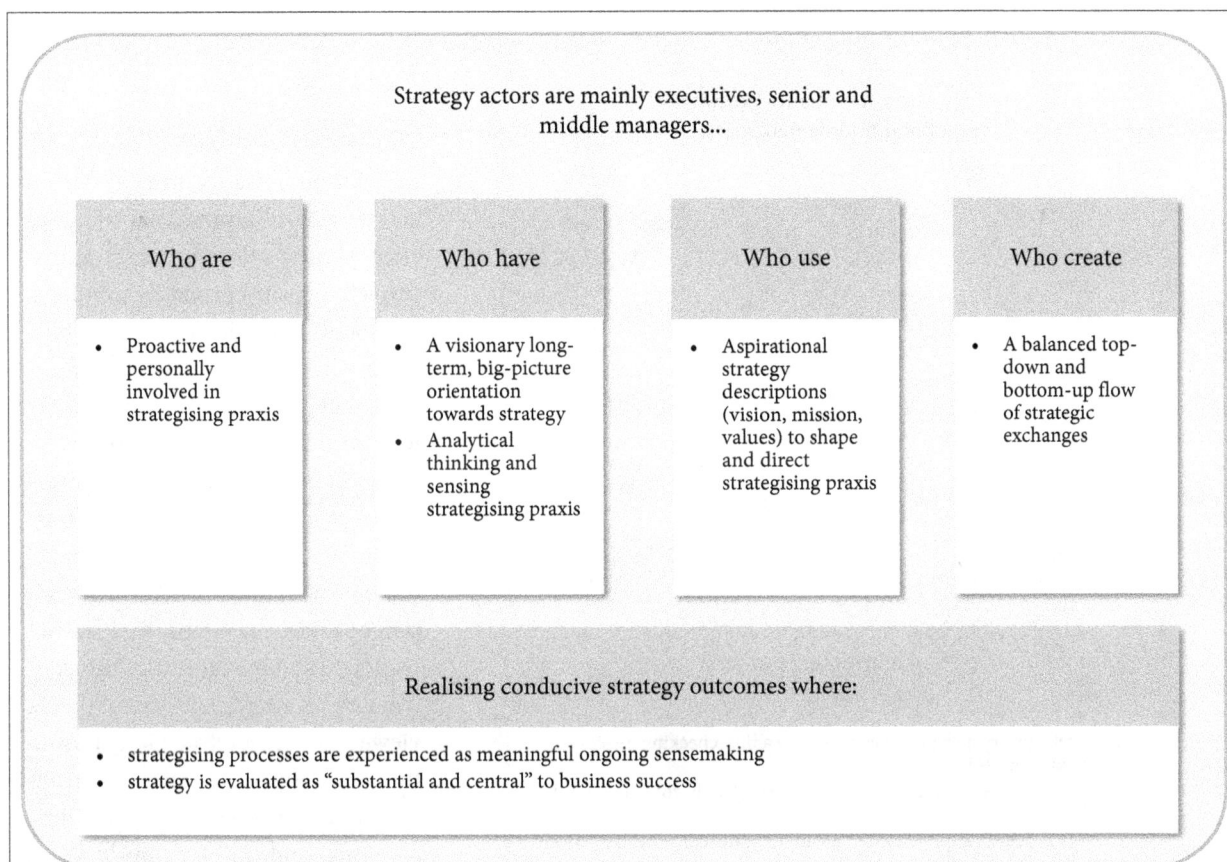

Figure 1.3: A possible virtuous story about strategic actors enabling praxis

The strategy actors selected for this study were mainly executives and senior and middle managers. These respondents indicated that strategy actors are proactively and personally involved in strategising praxis where a visionary long-term orientation is followed, were based on both analytical and intuitive thinking as core departure points for strategy. When strategic actors use aspirational descriptions and organisation structures to direct and enable strategising praxis and foster a balanced top-down and bottom-up cascading of strategic information exchanges, the cumulative re-enforcing virtuous effect of the above praxis create conducive conditions for strategising processes to be experienced as meaningful ongoing sense-making where the impact of strategy activities is described by stakeholders as substantial and central to the success of the organisation.

A vicious storyline based on the data and patterns from this study is reflected in Figure 1.4.

Strategy actors are mainly executives, senior and middle managers...

Who have	Who use	Who do
• A primarily short-term action orientation towards strategy • A strategy script where aspirational descriptions play no role	• Strategy-making activities primarily as a top-down process	• Strategy-making primarily from an analytical thinking stance with less regard for intuition and emotions

Contributing to

- corporate governance practices as mainly a box-checking, reactive and compliance-driven activity
- strategy processes experienced as restrictive, strictly governed, rigid and bureaucratic
- strategy processes experienced as an annual rain-dance with relatively little meaning and impact
- strategy impact on business is evaluated as minimal and doubtful

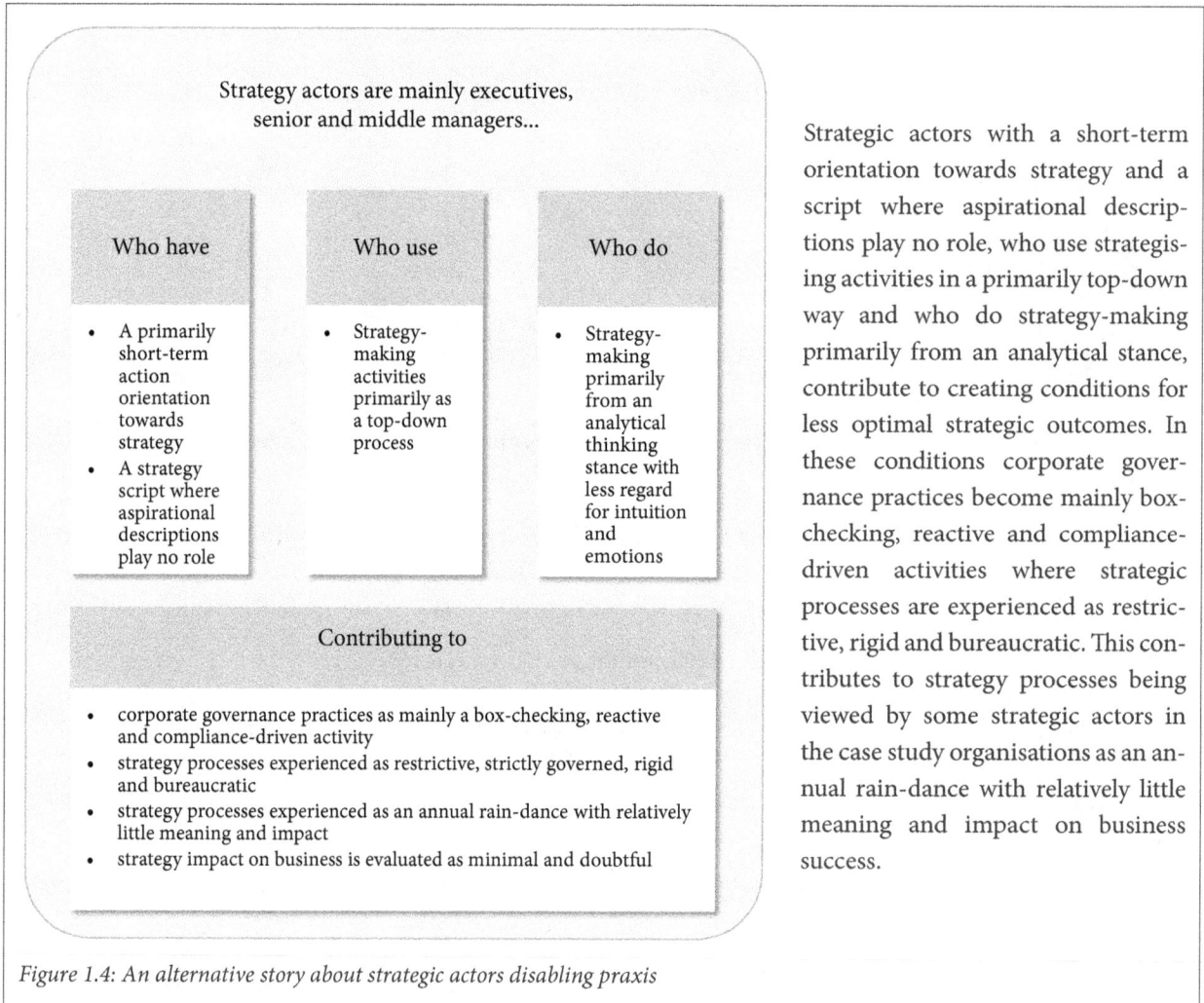

Strategic actors with a short-term orientation towards strategy and a script where aspirational descriptions play no role, who use strategising activities in a primarily top-down way and who do strategy-making primarily from an analytical stance, contribute to creating conditions for less optimal strategic outcomes. In these conditions corporate governance practices become mainly box-checking, reactive and compliance-driven activities where strategic processes are experienced as restrictive, rigid and bureaucratic. This contributes to strategy processes being viewed by some strategic actors in the case study organisations as an annual rain-dance with relatively little meaning and impact on business success.

Figure 1.4: An alternative story about strategic actors disabling praxis

STRATEGIC LEADERSHIP

We have already indicated that strategy is the contribution domain of many collaborators. So we can have a cadre of people taking responsibility for their involvement in both the creation and execution of strategy. Strategy and leadership cannot be separated and all leaders in an organisation must accept and own strategy as a core responsibility. The final accountability for the strategy of an organisation rests with board members and executive leaders. They take explicit public and legal accountability for the strategy of an organisation. Due to the complex nature of the context in which most organisations operate, it is advisable to embed the responsibility for strategy into the role description of everyone in the organisation (see chapter 5 on strategy translation). This creates the condition of strategic leadership as a shared responsibility in an organisation.

It does not matter how democratic and participative the strategy development and execution processes are, someone still needs to lead the process. These are the people we call strategic leaders. Strategy can never be based on less-than-ambitious aspirations, and to succeed with the implementation of strategy we need the commitment and support of others. This is where strategic leadership needs to balance competing demands and interests to ensure that the best strategic choices are made and executed to the benefit of stakeholders and the longer-term interest of the organisation.

We support the thinking of Mintzberg,[101] who said that it is possible to separate leading and management conceptually, but not in practice. "How would you like to be managed by someone who doesn't lead? … why would you want to be led by someone who doesn't manage?"[102] In this integrated view of leadership and management the departure point is that leadership cannot just delegate management. All managers are seen as leaders and leadership includes the practices of management.

The goal of strategic leaders in an organisation is to participate with others in the building of something that is not already there.[103] We have indicated that strategy-making is a process of continual influencing, and involves creating and shaping strategic ideals into practical executable building blocks and steps. Strategic leadership is not limited to a specific position, title or rank, but is a way of thinking and doing that advances the interests of an organisation in a positive way to the benefit of many. In this way leadership is learnt and earned, not anointed or granted.[104]

Strategic leaders make a major difference to how a firm performs, regardless of their length of time in a strategic leadership position.[105] Strategic leaders need to be seen to lead the strategy processes in an organisation in an active way and to make strategic decisions and choices based on information and sound logic (business and moral) in a timely way. The setting of a strategic agenda and ensuring progress in the execution of it are key focus areas of strategic leaders.[106] However this is not easy nor is it without challenges. Figure 1.5 reflects the broad flow of how strategic leaders shape and influence the strategy of an organisation.

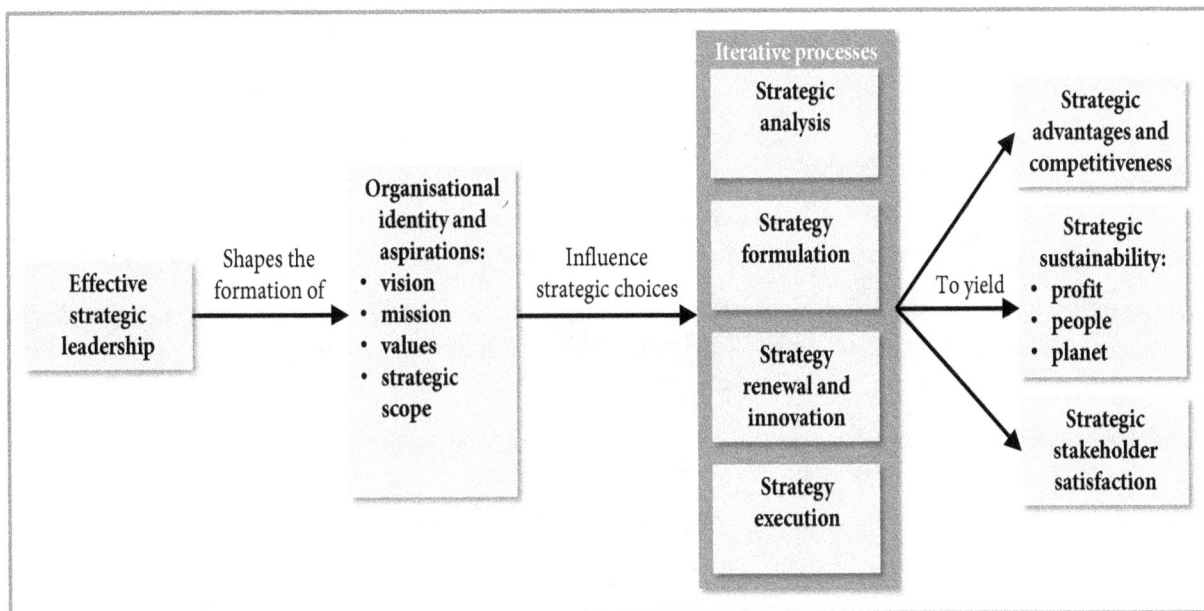

Figure 1.5: Strategic leadership and strategic management[107]

Strategic leadership[108] is the capacity to anticipate change and envision strategies, whilst maintaining flexibility and empowering others to create and sustain strategic momentum to ensure a flourishing organisation benefiting a variety of stakeholders.

So what do strategic leaders do? Mintzberg[109] helps us by identifying a variety of roles for managers and grouping them into three categories:

Interpersonal roles:
- figurehead – performing symbolic duties as a representative of the organisation
- leader – establishing the atmosphere and motivating the subordinates
- liaiser – developing and maintaining webs of contacts outside the organisation

Informational roles:
- monitor – collecting all types of information that are relevant and useful to the organisation
- disseminator – transmitting information from outside the organisation to those inside
- spokesman – transmitting information from inside the organisation to outsiders

Decisional roles:
- entrepreneur – initiating change and adapting to the environment
- disturbance handler – dealing with unexpected events
- resource allocator – deciding on the use of organisational resources
- negotiator – negotiating with individuals and dealing with other organisations

The above view was later updated by Mintzberg and is summarised in Table 1.11.

Table 1.11: The dynamic practices of managers[110]

Managerial practice	
The managerial context	This consists of both an internal and external organisational dimension.
Purpose of managing	To ensure the organisation serves its basic purpose as well as a higher purpose. This requires taking effective actions.
The person in the job	Within their own heads managers frame situations (conceive strategies, establish priorities etc.) and schedule their own time.
Framing the job	Managers frame their work by making particular decisions, focusing on particular issues, developing particular strategies to establish the context for everyone working in the unit or organisation.
Scheduling the work	Scheduling determines what is important and what needs to be done. It represents freedom to influence what gets onto the agenda.
Managerial activities take place in three forms, from the conceptual to the concrete	
Managing through information	Information dimension: Managers communicate and control. Internal communication: • Monitoring • Nerve centre for information integration

Managing through information (continued)	External communication: • Spokesperson to various publics • Nerve centre for information aggregation • Disseminating information for cross-pollination Internal controlling: • Designing strategies, structures, systems • Delegating responsibilities • Designating choices by influencing outcomes • Distributing resources • Deeming performance
Managing with people	People dimension: Managers lead inside the organisation and link to the outside. Internal leading: • Energising individuals • Developing individuals • Building teams • Strengthening culture External linking: • Networking • Representing • Convincing/Conveying • Transmitting • Buffering and gatekeeping in the flow of influence Action dimension: Managers do inside the organisation and deal outside.
Managing action directly	Internal doing: • Managing projects • Handling disturbances External dealing: • Building coalitions • Mobilising support • Negotiating

The ongoing challenge is to balance the above managerial roles to carry out a well-rounded job by swallowing the whole pill.[111] Managing multiple relationships, both lateral and hierarchical, both inside the organisation and outside its boundaries, is an integral part of the information and communication exchange role of leadership. The roles of strategic leaders go beyond merely managing an enterprise's bottom line, as can be seen from the summary perspective in Figure 1.6. Strategic leaders need to manage internal value-creation processes with and through others to create a positive societal and environmental impact that exceeds the expectations of stakeholders.

Figure 1.6: Strategic leadership roles [112]

Leadership is all about influencing for a positive impact on team-members and stakeholders. The ongoing test for a leader is whether his or her constituents and followers experience a positive contribution and influence in every situation where they interact. Do followers experience the results of decisions by the leader that are helpful to them? Leadership is therefore never only about our intent – that which we want to achieve – but always more about the impact of our interactions with others and the impact of our decisions.

Taking up a strategic leadership stance and/or role implicitly implies a shift from just thinking about a function or a part of an organisation to thinking and leading with an enterprise-wide mind-set. This transition from a specialist to a generalist is a challenge for most people. What keeps us back is what Christo Nel calls our tyranny of competency, which refers to the human tendency to hold onto ways of work that caused past success, but stand in the way of future success. Strategic leaders need to transform themselves into generalists and specialists. Research[113] indicates to make this transition successfully leaders must navigate a tricky set of changes in their leadership focus and skills. The main learnings around new skills and cultivating new mind-sets that need to be mastered by strategic leaders are reflected in Table 1.12.

Table 1.12: The seven seismic shifts for strategic leaders[114] and seven things they need to know[115]

Key shifts	Specialist to generalist	Analyst to integrator	Tactician to strategist	Bricklayer to architect	Problem-solver to agenda setter	Warrior to diplomat	Supporting cast member to lead role
Required skills and mind-set change	*Understand the mental models, tools, and terms used in key business functions and develop templates for evaluating the leaders of those functions.*	*Integrate the collective knowledge of cross-functional teams and make appropriate trade-offs to solve complex organi-sational problems.*	*Shift fluidly between the details and the larger picture, perceive important patterns in complex en-vironments, and anticipate and influence the reactions of key external players.*	*Understand how to analyse and design organisational systems so that strategy, structure, operating models, and skills bases fit together effectively and efficiently, and harness this understanding to make needed organisational changes.*	*Define the problems the organisation should focus on, and spot issues that don't fall neatly into any one function, but are still important.*	*Proactively shape the environment in which the business operates by influencing key external constituencies, including the government, NGOs, the media, and investors.*	*Exhibit the right behaviours as a role model for the organisation and learn to communicate with and inspire large groups of people both directly and, increasingly, indirectly.*
Key surprise for new CEOs	**You can't run the organisation**	**Giving orders is very costly**	**It is hard to know what is really going on**	**You are always sending a message**	**You are not the boss**	**Pleasing shareholders is not the goal**	**You are still only human**
Key challenge	*Manage your diary in such a way so as to balance the need of a variety of stakeholders for face-time with you.*	*Expand the power of those around you.*	*Have access to reliable information.*	*Be aware of the signals you are sending, dampen mis-interpretations and maximise the messages you want to send.*	*Manage upwards to get agreement from individual board members with different agendas.*	*Resist actions that are not to the benefit of the ultimate competitive position of the organisation.*	*Resist the illusion of self-importance and omnipotence.*
Warning signs	• *You are in too many meetings and in too many tactical discussions.* • *There are too many days that you feel you have lost control over your time.*	• *The bottleneck is you.* • *Employ-ees overly consult you before they act.* • *You become the endorser of everything ("Frank says. …").*	• *You keep hearing things that surprise you.* • *You learn about events after the fact.* • *Concerns and dissent reach you through the grapevine and not directly.*	• *Employees circulate stories about your behaviour that magnify or distort reality.* • *People around you act in ways that indicate they're trying to anticipate your likes and dislikes.*	• *You don't know where you stand with board members.* • *Division of roles and responsibilities between board members and management are not clear.* • *Board discussions are limited to feedback and reporting on results.*	• *Executives and board members judge actions by their effect on the share price.* • *Analysts who don't know the business push for decisions that can harm the business.* • *Management incentives are dispropor-tionately linked to the share price.*	• *You give interviews about you rather than about the organisation.* • *You have a more lavish lifestyle than other executives.* • *You have few, if any, activities connected to the organisation.*

The key decisions associated with a general management role are reflected in Table 1.13. Meeting these decision challenges and developing appropriate responses are an integral part of leading an organisation successfully.

Table 1.13: The GM's activity guidance system[116]

Key roles	Key choices	Responsibility
Originating	How can wealth be created?	To formulate and sell to key stakeholders a competitive basis for the organisation, thereby ensuring that it maintains a winning edge in the marketplace.
Designing	How should the organisation be organised?	To design the means and methods – that is, the structures, processes and a supporting culture – by which to organise and implement a winning competitive model.
Energising	How will people and systems be powered?	To ignite and fuel people's enthusiasm to drive the business system – not just within the top team but throughout the organisation.
Integrating	How should the components be optimised across various areas and levels of the business system?	To synthesise the many contributions from all parts of the organisation and to bring people and roles together in pursuit of opportunities and to overcome challenges.
Protecting	How will the assets of the organisation be maintained and renewed?	To shield the organisation – its economic and human assets – from threats, risks and disruptions emanating from external forces and from elsewhere in the firm.

(?) Questions to reflect on:

- What are the big issues on our corporate agenda?
- What opportunities and threats does the whole business face and what are the implications?
- How can I ensure the success of the entire organisation?
- Am I actively seeking to cross the edge on the seven seismic shifts for strategic leaders?
- Do I manage or do I lead?

We end this part on strategic leadership by summarising the habits of spectacularly unsuccessful executives to learn what we should not do. Learning from the mistakes of others guides us to prevent disaster proactively – see Table 1.14.

Table 1.14: Seven common characteristics associated with spectacularly unsuccessful leaders[117]

Destructive habits	Explanation	Warning signs	Rhetoric
They see themselves and their companies as dominating their environment.	Unlike successful leaders, failed leaders who never question their dominance fail to realise that they are at the mercy of changing circumstances.	A lack of respect for their customers and suppliers based on the illusion of personal pre-eminence and arrogance	*"Our products are superior, and so am I. We're untouchable. My company is successful because of my leadership and intellect – I made it happen."*

Destructive habits	Explanation	Warning signs	Rhetoric
They identify so completely with the organisation that there is no clear boundary between their personal interests and their corporation's interest.	Instead of treating organisations as enterprises that they needed to nurture, failed leaders treat them as extensions of themselves with a "private empire" mentality.	Characters who are not trustworthy stewards. Denial and defensiveness that do not create trust.	*"I am the sole proprietor. This company is my baby. Obviously, my wants and needs are in the best interest of my company and shareholders."*
They think they have all the answers.	They create an image of knowing everything, but fail to learn the implications of decisions or to listen to other viewpoints.	A leader without followers, because they do not really need other people and dissent is discouraged.	*"I am a genius. I believe in myself and you should too. Don't worry, I know all the answers. I'm not micro-managing; I'm being attentive. I don't need anyone else, certainly not a team."*
They ruthlessly eliminate anyone who isn't completely behind them.	Anyone who is not rallying behind the cause is seen as undermining the vision.	Executives depart as fast as they come on board. A revolving door at the top is a strong indication of leadership failure.	*"If you're not with me, you're against me! Get with the plan, or get out of the way. Where's your loyalty?"*
They are consummate spokespersons, obsessed with the image of the organisation.	High-profile CEOs who are constantly in the public eye settle for the appearance of accomplishing things, instead of actually achieving things. Creative accounting is used to promote the image of the organisation.	Blatant attention-seeking starting with an executive lifestyle featuring expensive tastes and places. A striking new headquarters to serve as a corporate symbol is part of this image obsession.	*"I'm the spokesperson. It's all about image. I'm a promotions and public relations genius. I love making public appearances; that's why I star in our commercials. It's my job to be socially visible; that's why I give frequent speeches and have regular media coverage."*
They underestimate obstacles.	CEOs become so hooked on their vision that they overlook the difficulties in achieving it. Even when data suggest challenges ahead, they push right ahead into the storm. This is driven by a need to be right, because admitting failure is not an option.	Excessive hype to hide problems or mask intentions that, if known, would lead people to make different decisions.	*"It's just a minor roadblock. Full steam ahead! Let's call that division a 'partner company' so we don't have to show it on our books."*
They stubbornly rely on what worked for them in the past.	The decline of the organisation is accelerated by reverting to tried-and-tested practices. Instead of considering a range of options that fit a new context, they use their own past experiences as the only decision guide.	Constantly referring to what worked in the past.	*"It has always worked this way in the past. We've done it before, and we can do it again."*

Case study from a Zen master

The following old Zen story illustrates the need and willingness of strategic leaders to be open to new ideas and new thinking; to be perpetually curious as a lifelong learner.

A powerful and self-assured man goes to a Zen master and asks to be taught about enlightenment. After sizing up the guest in an initial conversation, the Zen master invites him to have tea. The master pours. He goes on pouring even though the tea is flowing over the brim of the cup. "Stop!" the visitor calls out. "Can't you see that the cup is overflowing?" "Yes," the Zen master replies. "But a cup that is already full cannot take in anything else."[118]

Great leaders stay open to new ideas and are willing to explore new ways of leading strategy. "Success in the knowledge economy comes to those who know themselves, their strengths, their values, and how they best perform".[119] It is accepted that greatness can only be achieved from personal strengths. Knowing our personal strengths and using them as a basis for our contributions is key. At the same time we need to be aware of our weaknesses to consciously collaborate with others to use their strengths.

Practical guideline

The following questions could stimulate us to think about our leadership strengths.

Table 1.15: Reflection on personal leadership strengths[120]

Insights about personal strengths		
Reflective questions	*Content explanation*	*Comments on personal preference*
How do I learn?	Some people learn by doing. Others learn by hearing themselves talk. Some people learn by taking copious notes.	
How do I access information? Through reading or listening? Am I a reader or a listener?	Listeners get information by attentively listening to others and have a real interest and respect for the views of others. Readers like to study data and make conclusions based on material reviewed or written expert opinion.	
Do I work well with people or am I a loner?	If you do work well with people? In what relationship? Some people work best as subordinates. Some people work best as team members. Others work best alone. Some are exceptionally talented as coaches and mentors; others are simply incompetent as mentors.	

Insights about personal strengths		
Reflective questions	*Content explanation*	*Comments on personal preference*
Do I produce results as a decision-maker or as an adviser?	Some people perform best as advisers but cannot take the burden and pressure of making the decision. Other people, by contrast, need an adviser to force themselves to think; then they can make decisions and act on them with speed, self-confidence, and courage.	
Do I perform well under stress, or do I need a highly structured and predictable environment? Do I work best in a big organisation or a small one?	Few people work well in all kinds of environment.	
What are my values? Are my values and that of the organisation I work in compatible?	This is not only a question of ethics. With respect to ethics, the rules are the same for everybody – see more about the ethical lenses in the next part of this chapter. Ethics are only part of the value system of an organisation. Organisations, like people, have values. To work in an organisation whose value system is unacceptable or incompatible with one's own condemns a person to both frustration and nonperformance. To be effective in an organisation, a person's values must be compatible with the organisation's values. They do not need to be the same, but they must be close enough to coexist.	
Where do I belong?	Successful careers are not planned. They develop when people are prepared for opportunities because they know their strengths, their method of work, and their values. Knowing where one belongs can transform an ordinary person – hardworking and competent but otherwise mediocre – into an outstanding performer.	
What should my contribution be?	What does the situation require? Given my strengths, my way of performing, and my values, how can I make the greatest contribution to what needs to be done? What results have to be achieved to make a difference? Where and how can I achieve results that will make a difference within the next year and a half?	

Practical guideline

Use the competency framework in Table 1.16 to evaluate your capacity to lead strategically in an integrated way.

Table 1.16: Reflection on competencies for strategic leaders[121]

Competency framework for strategic leaders		
Competency cluster	**Competency description**	**Personal evaluation:** • **Green is well developed;** • **Yellow is partially developed;** • **Red is poorly developed.**
Personal competencies	• Manage self, internally through reflecting and strategic thinking. • Manage self, external by focusing on time, information, stress and career. • Do scheduling by applying chunking, prioritising, agenda-setting, juggling and timing.	
Interpersonal competencies	• Lead individuals by focusing on selecting, teaching/mentoring/coaching, inspiring and dealing with experts. • Lead groups through team-building, resolving conflicts/mediation, facilitating progress and running meetings. • Lead the organisation/unit by building culture. • Administer by organising, resource allocation, delegating, authorising, systematising, goal setting and performance appraising. • Link the organisation/unit by networking, representing, collaborating, promoting/lobbying, protecting/buffering.	
Informational competencies	• Communicate verbally by listening, interviewing, speaking/presenting/briefing, writing, information-gathering, information dissemination. • Communicate nonverbally by seeing and sensing. • Analyse by data processing, modelling, measuring and evaluating.	
Actionable competencies	• Design by planning, crafting and visioning. • Mobilise by fire-fighting, project management, negotiating/dealing, politicking and managing change.	

Next we explore the concept of strategic architecture as an integrating view of strategic management.

STRATEGIC ARCHITECTURE

An important part of strategy and the strategic landscape is how organisations define or "construct" their own strategic architecture. Hamel and Prahalad[122] describe a strategic architecture as the "road map of the future that identifies which core competencies to build". They introduce the concept of a strategic architecture as a broad intent of where and how an organisation wants to define itself in a strategic landscape. A strategic landscape is the broad external and internal context of an organisation. The strategic landscape of a firm can be shaped by strategic actors, but the nature of the landscape also influences the strategic options and choices of players in the landscape. Landscaping activities by strategic actors vary and can, for example, include the development of new markets and influencing legislation to ensure freedom of access to information for stakeholders.

A strategic architecture is an organisation's core logic for creating value on a sustainable basis, and therefore forms the foundation of an organisation's competitive potential.[123] It describes the context and the terrain that an organisation intentionally defines or constructs as a means to achieving a desired end. It also influences the current competitive behaviour of the enterprise and may, therefore, explain why an organisation seems not to be competitive in current terms. The departure point we take is that competitive behaviour and potential can be altered and influenced when an organisation redefines its strategic architecture. A strategic architecture view of an organisation creates a platform and enabler of strategic choices, hardwired into the organisation. It underlies the success or failure of any strategy, which as a result should be richly and concisely constructed and designed.

The strategic architecture of a firm is not equal to its business model (see chapter 3 for detail on the business model as part of strategy formulation). The strategic architecture view of a firm is a more extensive and comprehensive strategic description. One of the components of this description represents a view of the business model of a firm. A business model, therefore, is a subset of the strategic architecture.

Hamel and Prahalad[124] acknowledge that organisations should create their own environments, rather than adapting to existing ones. They found that highly successful organisations are differentiated from the rest through the fact that they creatively innovate around and leverage off their core competencies or capabilities. It seems as if such organisations are less obsessed with their competition, and are rather more concerned with reinventing themselves internally. This is in contrast to organisations that attempt to fit or adapt to their environments, often by following their competition. In this book, we accept the premise that competitiveness is internally generated and an organisation has to construct or reconstruct its fundamental underlying strategic architecture in order to be competitive.

The core elements of a view of the strategic architecture of an organisation are reflected in Figure 1.7.

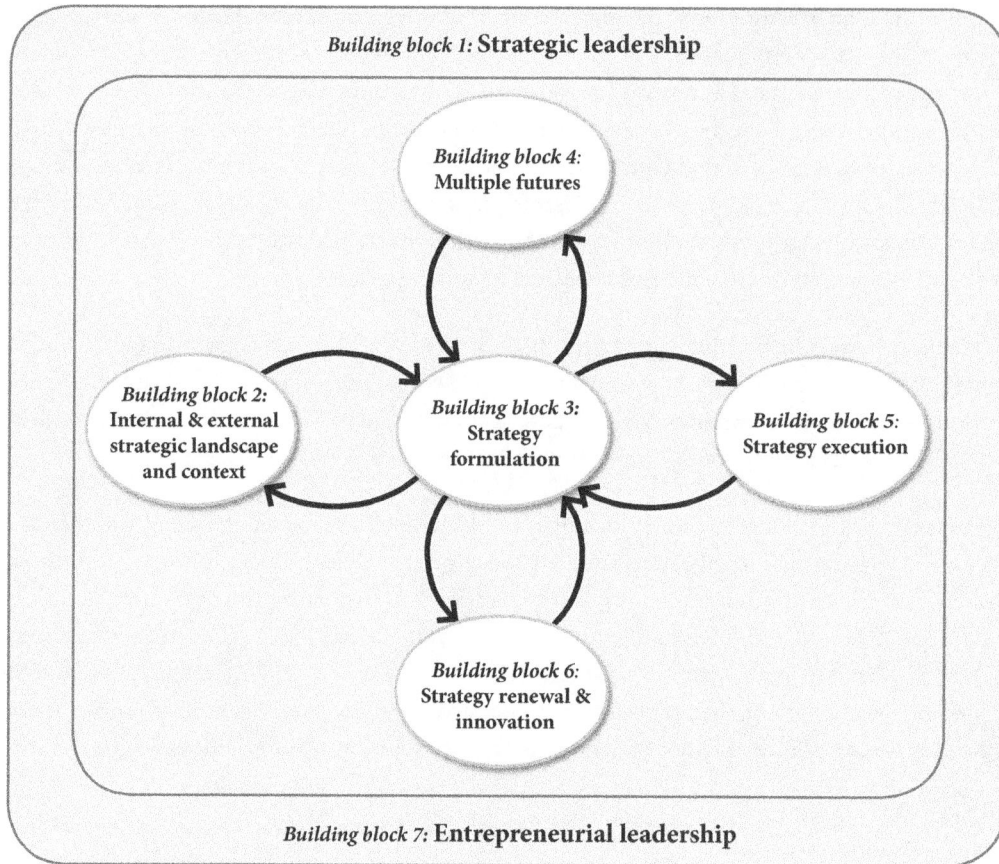

Figure 1.7: Inter-relatedness of strategic architecture building blocks

The building blocks of a strategic architecture view of an organisation can consist of the following key strategic aspects.

Building block 1: Strategic leadership as a key capacity as described in this chapter. This gives life, meaning and ongoing momentum to the strategy of an organisation.

Building block 2: The development of views on the external strategic landscape[125] and context of an organisation, which can include the following elements:

- Global and macro-trends analysis:
  - global standards applicable to the organisation's macro-external context:
    - Sustainable Development Goals (SDGs)
    - UN Global Compact
  - global risk analysis
  - analysis of national strategic priorities of a country to identify national development priorities
  - analysis of the macro-environment forces using a STEEP analysis approach
  - stakeholder analysis
  - sustainable value analysis

- Analysis of the competitive context of an organisation:
  - industry analysis
  - competitor analysis
  - cooperation with competitors analysis
- Analysis of customers of an organisation:
  - customer demands analysis
  - customer segment need gap analysis
  - customer empathy map analysis
  - customer need saturation analysis
  - customer channel phase analysis
  - customer relationship analysis
- Internal analysis practices for an organisation:
  - resource-based view of strategy:
    - core and distinctive competence analysis
    - internal value chain analysis
    - organisation culture as source for competitive advantage
  - financial analysis
  - internal risk analysis
  - governance analysis

Building block 3: Strategy formulation and development, which can include:

- a menu of strategic options and choices to consider (see chapter 2):
  - choices related to organisational identity and aspiration formulation
  - generic strategy choices – a variety of generic strategies for an organisation including high-level strategic moves and positioning options
  - grand strategy choices – 15 grand strategy options to consider as part of the strategy development process
- business model formulation and development (see chapter 3) including value creation, efficiencies and engines of growth. The creation of a clear competitive strategy formulation perspective, which reflects aspects like core competitive strategic choices, value propositions, activity systems and control points and core and distinctive competency descriptions, is a key part of this building block
- normative assessment of competitive strategies (see chapter 3).

Building block 4: The development of multiple futures perspectives for an organisation using:

- scenario planning and foresight development (see chapter 4).

Building block 5: Strategy execution with the following key contributions (see chapter 5):

- change enablement
- planning as strategic gap closing
- making strategy a reality for all through:
  - strategy translation practices
  - strategy mobilisation practices
  - strategic organisation performance monitoring

Building block 6: Strategy renewal and innovation (see chapters 6, 7 and 8). This covers the ongoing refreshment of the strategy through:

- the application of a variety of strategy innovation tools and practices like:
    - blue ocean strategy
    - sources of e-value
    - new market space creation
    - breaking through stall-points and decline
    - managing a portfolio of experiments and prototypes
- the development of inorganic growth strategies through alliances and M&As.
- the development of appropriate management practices through management innovation to ensure an alignment with a changing strategic context and management practices that support and are appropriate in a VUCA world. This is all about developing management practices that make organisations fit and friendly for human beings.

Building block 7: Entrepreneurial leadership and strategy practices (see chapter 9) to foster both entrepreneurship and intrapreneurship.

The seven building blocks of a strategic architecture of a firm are all inter-related as shown in Figure 1.7. From a systemic point of view the strategic architecture of a firm contains the key elements in a strategy system, but the system can only flourish if all the parts are connected in a virtuous way.

The virtuous cycle of strategic thinking we want to stimulate is reflected in Figure 1.8.

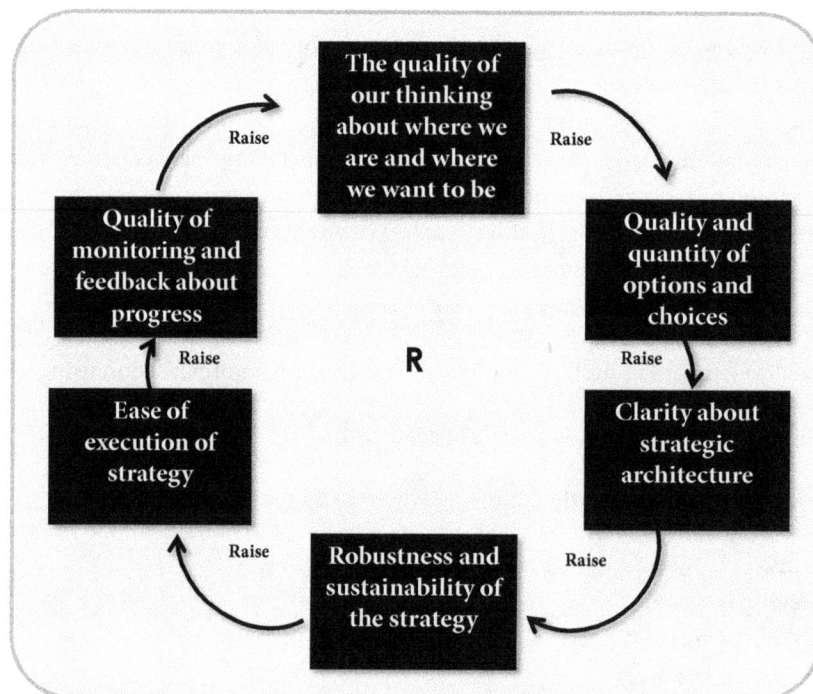

Figure 1.8: A virtuous cycle of strategic thinking

Next we turn to the last and very important part of this chapter: business ethics through the lens of virtuous leadership to create the moral boundaries for strategic leadership.

BUSINESS ETHICS THROUGH VIRTUOUS LEADERSHIP PRACTICES

> *"If you're a leader, authenticity is your most precious commodity, and you'll lose it if you attempt techniques that don't fit your strengths."* – Marcus Buckingham[126]

In this part of this chapter we introduce the concept of virtuous leadership as a springboard for ethical business practices. We argue that "ethical virtuosity is not something for the puritans",[127] but an empowering way of leading self and others in a world that is asking for moral guidance and exemplary examples. We first explore virtuous leadership[128] as a distinctive leadership practice and then use this view to explore ethical issues and approaches in strategic management.

Virtuous leadership

Our collective memory and context are filled with stories of business, political and societal leaders who conducted themselves in questionable ways through deceptive decisions and practices that raised ethical concerns. The images of leaders who misuse power and who deploy corrupt practices are too often a feature of our daily news coverage. Clearly we live in a time of moral deficit if we evaluate the track-record of many leaders in business, society and politics.

In a business context the overriding effect of upper-level leadership as a predictor of lower-level leadership practices has been confirmed by research.[129] Leaders have a substantial effect on followers, in positive and negative ways. Surveys[130] show that the behaviours of C-level executives and senior management are the most highly-rated factor connected with unethical decision-making – an example of negative outcomes associated with the practices of leaders.

The term "virtue" originates from the Greek word *arête*, which means excellence.[131] [132] A virtue is defined as "moral excellence and righteousness; goodness; and a particular efficacious, good or beneficial quality; advantage".[133] Virtue is seen as a trait of character or intellect that is morally laudable and presents an ideal to which all good living aspires.[134] Virtues (there are many) represent principles of moral character that motivate and guide behaviour towards positive ethical outcomes.[135] Virtues are accepted as dispositions that are part (or not) of an individual that can be measured and cultivated. Virtues assist us to achieve our full potential by being ethical and represent the best human being we can be.[136]

Before we define virtuous leadership we first want to argue why virtues, as a managerial concept for individuals, organisations and societies, have largely been neglected. The main reasons why virtues did not receive the required attention are:[137]

- A Western mind-set of linear progress that emphasises values such as marketisation, interpersonal competition, personal achievement and material wealth where there is little space for "old" virtues.

- In the past, virtues were frequently associated with religiosity. In a more secularised world religion has lost much of its social and cultural significance. This contributed to people ignoring virtues because they were seen as based on religious beliefs and practices.
- The growth in globalisation and widespread neo-economic liberalism has contributed to the destruction of the village as a place where transparency and moral consistency created natural limits for human communities. The village economy, with local community self-regulating virtue-based practices, has been replaced by an urban, globally connected economy where anonymity frees individuals from the village's social and moral norms. This lack of a communal ethos that fosters virtuous business practices contributes to the recent increase in corporate, societal and political scandals.

We clearly need leadership with a strong moral base. It is however important to state that a focus on virtues as a guide for leadership practices does not represent a naïve way of dealing with our moral decay trajectory, rampant personal enrichment patterns and corporate scandals. It is interesting to note that Jeff Immelt, the CEO of GE, clearly stated that he wants GE to be known as a virtuous organisation because they want to attract and motivate the most talented people. This is because virtuousness and virtuous leaders like Nelson Mandela and Mahatma Ghandi build a brand image and evoke feelings of admiration that people aspire to.[138] It is therefore clear that we are currently in need of substantially better leadership at all levels of management in all types of organisations, and virtuousness can no longer be ignored or neglected.

The construct of virtuous leadership is linked in the literature to related concepts such as moral, ethical, servant, spiritual, inclusive, authentic, transformative, transformational and responsible leadership.[139] Virtuous leadership is described as a focus **on the highest potentiality of human systems** that is **oriented toward being and doing good.**[140] A more pragmatic description states that virtuous leadership involves distinguishing right from wrong, taking steps to ensure justice and honesty, influencing and enabling the pursuit of righteous and moral goals and connecting to a higher purpose.[141]

A description of virtuous leadership that encompasses both the virtue ethics component and the behaviour aspects is as follows: Virtuous leadership represents a "leader–follower relationship wherein a leader's situational appropriate expression of virtues triggers follower perceptions of leader virtuousness, worthy of emulation".[142]

This description of virtuous leadership also emphasises the content, context and process elements of leadership.

The virtues that virtuous leaders exemplify have the following common content characteristics: they have a disposition towards "good" character traits; they are cross-cultural and reflect both Aristotelian (Western) and Confucian (Eastern) traditions; they are interrelated and manifest simultaneously where required; and they are seen as contributors to both ethical and effective leadership. The context-dependency in which virtuous leadership is embedded relates to the argument that holding and claiming a virtue consists of showing and expressing it across a broad spectrum of situations.[143] The key processes through which leader virtue influences followers are perceptually driven attribution and modelling. Attribution theory[144] states that people make judgments about the cause of a person's behaviour based on perceived behaviour consistency over time. This suggests that a leader with virtue characteristics and competencies is expected to demonstrate these consistently, although followers only have restricted opportunities to observe them. The result is that some leaders might be perceived by followers as less or more virtuous than others, based on the array of virtues the leaders exemplify.[145] By behaving in a virtuous manner, leaders are viewed by their subordinates as role models with a positive influence.[146] Followers observe and imitate the virtuous behaviour of leaders and practise these behaviours until they become habitual. Compared to the vast array of virtue possibilities, the focus of virtuous leadership is on a smaller set of behaviour-based virtues that are specifically relevant to leadership[147] (see the discussion on measurement).

Peterson and Seligman[148] developed a classification framework in which they classified 24 individual strengths linked to six broad universal virtues. These virtues transcend national and cultural boundaries. Although they do not claim universality for this framework, it represents a claim of ubiquity – the identified virtues and associated individual strengths are commonly present in all people of the world. While not everyone will be aware of these virtues or will call them by different names, they are present (e.g. *ubuntu* consists of competencies like empathy, social awareness, recognition of the wisdom of elders and valuing interpersonal relationships).[149] The six broad universal virtues consist of the following virtue strengths and competency areas:

- **Wisdom and knowledge**, which include the cognitive competencies of creativity, curiosity, open-mindedness, love of learning and perspective.
- **Humanity**, which includes the social competencies of kindness, love and social intelligence.
- **Justice**, with the associated social competencies of fairness, leadership and teamwork.
- **Courage**, which includes the personal and emotional competencies of authenticity, bravery, persistence and zest.
- **Temperance**, with personal competencies of forgiveness, modesty, prudence and self-regulation.
- The sixth and final broad universal virtue is **transcendence**, which includes the personal competencies of appreciation of beauty, gratitude, hope, humour and religiousness.

The concept competency is used in the following way: "As character traits are expressed in certain behavioural patterns they can also be called competencies.[150]

Practical guideline

Use the reflective prompts in Table 1.17 to develop a perspective on your own virtue strengths and competency areas. Also use the framework at http://www.thehappinessinstitute.com.au/freeproducts/docs/The%20VIA%20Classification%20of%20Character%20Strengths.pdf to reflect on your current strengths. You will get a list of the six universal virtues with their associated strength descriptions and you are asked to identify your personal strengths.

Table 1.17: Description of virtue strengths and competency areas[151]

Universal virtue theme	Virtue strength & competency areas	Short description	Reflective prompts[152]
Wisdom and knowledge	1. Creativity	thinking of novel and productive ways to do things	Thinking of new ways to do things is a crucial part of who you are. You are never content with doing something the conventional way if a better way is possible.
	2. Curiosity	taking an interest in all of ongoing experience	You are curious about everything. You are always asking questions, and you find all subjects and topics fascinating. You like exploration and discovery.
	3. Open-mindedness	thinking things through and examining them from all sides	Thinking things through and examining them from all sides are important aspects of who you are. You do not jump to conclusions, and you rely only on solid evidence to make your decisions. You are able to change your mind.
	4. Love of learning	mastering new skills, topics, and bodies of knowledge	You love learning new things, whether in a class or on your own. You have always loved school, reading, and museums – anywhere and everywhere there is an opportunity to learn.
	5. Perspective	being able to provide wise counsel to others	Although you may not think of yourself as wise, your friends hold this view of you. They value your perspective on matters and turn to you for advice. You have a way of looking at the world that makes sense to others and to yourself.
Humanity	6. Kindness	doing favours and good deeds for others	You are kind and generous to others, and you are never too busy to do a favour. You enjoy doing good deeds for others, even if you do not know them well.
	7. Love	valuing close relations with others	You value close relations with others, in particular those in which sharing and caring are reciprocated. The people to whom you feel most close are the same people who feel most close to you.
	8. Social intelligence	being aware of the motives and feelings of self and others	You are aware of the motives and feelings of other people. You know what to do to fit in to different social situations, and you know what to do to put others at ease.
Justice	9. Fairness	treating all people the same according to notions of fairness and justice	Treating all people fairly is one of your abiding principles. You do not let your personal feelings bias your decisions about other people. You give everyone a chance.

To expand your insight about your personal virtue strengths, also use the 18 factor behaviour-based Virtuous Leadership Questionnaire (VLQ) as reflected in Table 1.18.

Table 1.18: Virtuous Leadership Questionnaire items[153]

Leadership virtue category	Definition	Question items*
Likert-type response format (1=Never; 5=Always)		
Humanity	a character trait underlying leaders' love, care, and respect of others	17. I show concern for subordinates' needs. 7. I show concern and care for peers. 2. I express concern for the misfortunes of others.
Justice	a character trait motivating respectful recognition and protection of the rights of others to be treated fairly, in accordance with uniform and objective standards	9. I allocate valued resources in a fair manner. 1. I respect individual interests and rights when allocating responsibilities. 12. I resolve conflicts in a fair and objective fashion.
Courage	a character trait enabling leaders to do without fear what they believe is "right"	3. I act with sustained initiative, even in the face of incurring personal risk. 4. I speak up on matters of injustice and personal conviction, despite risking "backlash". 13. I initiate a long-term and worthwhile project despite risking my personal reputation. 16. I lead fundamental change though it may entail personal sacrifice and personal risk.
Temperance	a character trait helping leaders control their emotional reactions and desires for self-gratification	15. I avoid indulging my desires at the expense of others. 6. I behave unselfishly even when there are opportunities to maximise self-gain. 18. I prioritise organisational interests over self-interests. 5. I downplay personal success to avoid discomforting others who are less successful.
Prudence	a character trait enabling leaders to make "right" judgments and choose the "right" means to achieve the "right" goals	10. I exercise sound reasoning in deciding on the optimal courses of action. 14. I efficiently and effectively assess requirements demanded by any given situation. 11. I grasp the complexity of most situations when making judgments. 8. I use only the resources necessary in responding to the demands of any given situation.

Numbers indicate the sequence in which questions should be asked in a questionnaire.

After completion of the above three reflective practices (Tables 1.17, 1.18 and results from thehappinessinstitute.com), answer the following reflective questions (Table 1.19):

Table 1.19: Integration on Virtuous Leadership Reflection

Reflective questions	Responses
What are your core virtue strengths and competency areas? How can you further enhance them?	
What areas stand out as development areas that you should be sensitive to? How can you minimise the effects of these nonstrengths?	
What can you do less of to be more of a virtuous leader?	
What patterns are emerging from your evaluations of yourself? Write down your insights and reflect on this over time to deepen your understanding about your virtue strengths and development areas.	
How can you use these insights to be a more virtuous leader in your context? Virtuous practices are formed by repetitive practices.	
What new leadership practices should you engage with to build your virtuous leadership capacity?	

If we look at the description of the different virtue strength and competency areas in both Tables 1.17 and 1.18, it is clear that they represent universal and transcendent qualities that could assist leaders in their quest for a positive impact and influence. These competency areas span and infuse all other leadership competencies (such as the competency to read a balance sheet or run a meeting). These competency areas also represent the "best" virtues that humans can strive for. If we can develop a cadre and generations of leaders with these qualities, organisations, societies and the world will be a better place.[154] Capitalism with a human face will become a lived reality. The answer to "What are the right things to do?" will include a variety of perspectives representing the interest of multiple stakeholders.

Leaders who role-model virtuous behaviour contribute to improving the general ethical climate in their work environments and at the same time add to the wellbeing of employees. This goes much further than promoting ethical behaviour only through ethical codes.[155] This is all about modelling the way – showing others what to do, rather than just talking about it.

Barry Schwartz[156] states that any work that involves people is moral work. Moral work is dependent on moral wisdom and moral wisdom is based on both moral skill and moral will. Moral wisdom is seen as a key ingredient in decision-making processes, and leaders should therefore develop this skill and embrace this will. Leadership based on virtues, as described above, culminates in practical wisdom as a core part of leading successfully in a complex world.

The message associated with virtuous leadership is a message of hope – the focus is on fostering an environment which emphasises the application of best practices to assist business to be great and good, without making moral compromises. The results and impact of leaders who practise a virtuous leadership approach strikes out against all injustice. Virtuous leaders can turn organisations into engines of economic and human progress and prosperity. The ideal of a wholly just worldwide community based on virtuous leadership practices is now a real possibility.

Business ethics and strategic management

We know that leaders are always under constant scrutiny by stakeholders – the camera is always on. Leaders as representatives of the insiders in a system are under constant observation by "outsiders" of the system. This places a responsibility on leaders to be prepared to look at the "video footage" at any time and to defend the rationale for their decisions.

In general business ethics is about the application of general ethical principles and standards to the actions and decisions of organisations and the behaviour of their employees.[157] Business ethics set norms of generally expected conduct to determine what is right or wrong. In organisations the values, as reflected in the strategic descriptions, the ethical code of conduct and governance guidelines, are all guiding principle and rules that set the moral boundaries. It is expected of leaders to set the example for moral excellence and employees are guided to work within these set boundaries.

Apart from internal organisational moral boundaries and expectations, there are also a variety of international codes to which organisations can subscribe to inform their expected business practices. Examples of these global citizen initiatives[158] are:

- United Nations Global Compact: It is the world's largest corporate and sustainability initiative.
- Caux Round Table: It is an international network of principled business leaders to promote a more moral capitalism.
- Equator Principles: This is a voluntary set of social and environmental standards to identify risks in project finance.
- World Business Council on Sustainable Development: This is a CEO-led global association focusing on sustainable development.
- Global Business Oath – Young Global Leaders: The oath emerged as a response to the global financial crisis of 2008 and promotes societal and environmental sustainability.
- CERES Principles: The principles encourage investments in environmental and social sustainable projects.
- Global Sullivan Principles: It is a code of conduct on human rights and equal opportunities for companies operating in South Africa.
- Business Leaders' Initiative on Human Rights: It is a space for business representatives to share human rights best practices.
- Global Responsible Leadership Initiative: It represents a community of action and learning on responsible leadership.

Hard evidence in the form of the *Global Corruption Report* on the widespread occurrence of corruption in public institutions and businesses all over the world does not paint a positive picture.[159] This report states the likelihood that organisations in large export-orientated economies are paying bribes to win business in countries such as Argentina, Brazil, Colombia, Hungary, India, Indonesia, Mexico, Morocco, Nigeria, the Philippines, Poland, Russia, South Africa, South Korea and Thailand. Corruption occurs mostly in the case of three types of contract: public works contracts and construction; arms and defence contracts; and oil, gas and energy contracts. Corruption takes many forms, including bribes, kickbacks, price-fixing, securities fraud, regulation skirting to avoid paying minimum wages, using child labour and bypassing environmental protection regulations and laws.

A few key drivers that fuel unethical strategy practices are:[160]

- A lack of board oversight and leadership guidance that allows or creates opportunities for the feverish chase of personal gain, wealth and other self-interests by employees and leaders. An obsessive personal drive for wealth accumulation, power and status shoves ethical principles to the side to achieve self-centric goals that are not in line with generally accepted business practices.
- Extraordinary pressure on leaders and employees to achieve performance targets. This pressure might come from investment analysts, the board and senior leaders, who all push to maintain a high-growth track record for the organisation. In this chase and push to keep up the performance delivery reputation of the organisation, rules are stretched and ethical conduct is less of a priority. Linking performance bonuses to the achievement of targets further increases the pressure.
- An organisational culture that prioritises profitability and "good" performance, the bottom line, above ethical conduct and practices. A work climate that allows immoral behaviour becomes a recipe for scandal and failure. When corruption is systemically embedded in the operating practices of an organisation, it is very difficult for even honourable people not to be affected.

The case for an ethical strategy approach can be argued from both a moral and a business case perspective.[161] The moral case is based on the departure point that strategies that are in total or in some parts unethical are morally wrong and will eventually paint a bad picture of the leadership and employees of an organisation. This is why ethically principled leaders consciously choose strategic and operational actions that will pass the moral scrutiny test (see Table: 1.21) and will show no tolerance for strategies with ethically questionable or controversial elements. The business case for an ethical strategy approach is based on the premise that an ethical strategy is good business and in the best interest of stakeholders. It is also accepted that unethical strategies damage and ruin the brand or reputation of an organisation and have costly consequences in the form of fines, administrative clean-up costs, reputational damage and turnaround costs. We also know that high-potential talent is only attracted to organisations with a positive reputation and ethical track record. Creditors and investors also think twice if the reputation and ethical record of an organisation is questionable.

Organisations can implement the following practices to promote a culture of business ethics.[162]

- Describe and communicate the ethical standards of the organisation to all stakeholders.
- Continuously update the code of conduct based on feedback from stakeholders.
- Audit compliance to ethical standards and practices by internal and external agents to create feedback and improvement cycles.
- Implement whistle-blower channels independent of the organisation.
- Create a work environment where all people are treated with dignity.

Next we look deeper at five practical ways in which an organisation can choose to manage ethical practices based on modes of morality.

Practical guideline

The development road map for an organisation that wishes to develop its ethical capacity is displayed in Table 1.20. This approach is specifically designed to explain the changes in mode of managing ethics within medium to large business enterprises.[163]

Task: Use the dimensions of comparison to evaluate an organisation's current ethical practices approach and to indicate development areas for the organisation.

Table 1.20: Five approaches to managing business ethics[164]

Dimensions of comparison	Immoral mode: Unconcerned or nonissue approach	Reactive mode: Damage control approach	Compliance mode: Meeting minimum standards approach	Integrity mode: Ethical culture approach	Totally Aligned Organisation (TAO) Mode
Nature and underlying beliefs	• The business of business is business, *not* ethics.	• Need to make a token gesture in the direction of ethical standards in the form of a code of ethics.	• Organisations should be committed to apply ethical standards and monitor performance.	• The basis of ethics in an organisation is the culture.	• Seamless integration of ethics in organisation's purpose, strategy and operations.
Nature and underlying beliefs (continued)	• Ethics has no place in the conduct of business. • Companies should not be morally accountable for their actions.	• Sceptics and critics need to be silenced at least temporarily through the existence of an ethical code.	• Unethical behaviour should be prevented and punished when discovered. • It is important to have a reputation for high ethical standards.	• The behaviour associated with good ethics is based on the values of the organisation. • Applying good ethical practices represents the way we work around here.	• We interact with stakeholders in a morally responsible way and this is not negotiable. • Ethics is entrenched in organisation dialogues and decision-making.
Ethics management strategy	• There is no need to make decisions concerning business ethics – if it is legal, it is fine. • No need for specific actions on ethics management.	• Laissez-faire ethics management. • No real moral will or skill to manage ethical practices. • Ethical code is just a piece of paper. • Unethical behaviour will only be punished in extreme situations.	• Rules-based and transactional approach to ethics management to prevent and punish unethical behaviour. • A comprehensive code of ethics exists and training on it is provided to all staff. • Formal function and resources for managing ethics exist, like an ethics compliance office and a chief ethics officer.	• Values-based and transformational approach to ethics management. • Well-established ethical management function and systems. • Ethical management embedded and reinforced in culture of the organisation. • Managers have an ethics competency.	• Integrated approach to ethics management. • Everybody is responsible for ethics management and everyone is an ethics watchdog as whistle-blowers. • Peer pressure used – "that's not how we do things here". • Ethics function serves as "rudder". • Ethical heroes are celebrated and ethical stories are told.

Dimensions of comparison	Immoral mode: Unconcerned or nonissue approach	Reactive mode: Damage control approach	Compliance mode: Meeting minimum standards approach	Integrity mode: Ethical culture approach	Totally Aligned Organisation (TAO) Mode
Challenges	• Financial consequences can become unaffordable. • Some stakeholders are alienated. • Increased dissonance between personal and corporate values.	• Credibility problems with stakeholders are a real possibility. • The organisation is exposed to ethical scandals. • The organisation's reputation on ethics is below par.	• Proliferation of rules and guidelines. • Rules guide ethical actions which foster an attitude of "what is not forbidden is allowed". • The locus of moral control is the ethics system and code, not an individual's own moral compass and responsibility.	• Ongoing ethics orientation training for new employees. • Misuse of discretion granted where moral autonomy leads to moral nonconformity. • Powerful leaders undermine ethical drive.	• Relying on peer pressure and cultural norms to enforce ethical standards can result in eliminating some or many of the compliance regimes and, over time, induce moral laxness. • Lack of coordination in managing ethics.

In the next practical guideline we showcase 10 ethical compass tests which we as individual leaders can use to evaluate our own track record on past decisions.

Practical guideline

Think about ethical dilemmas you have encountered at work and in personal situations. Use the ethical compass tests in Table 1.21 to evaluate your choices.

Table 1.21: Ten tests of the ethical compass[165]

Different ethical lenses	Core question	Did your decision pass the test? Yes or No and explain
The family perspective	Am I proud to inform my family members and friends about my decision or action?	
The congruency perspective	Is this aligned and consistent with my personal values?	
The cost–benefit perspective	Are the benefits equal for all? Does a benefit for some cause harm to others?	
The dignity perspective	Are the dignity and humanity of others preserved?	
The equal treatment perspective	Are the rights of the disadvantaged given consideration?	
The front-page perspective	Would I be comfortable if this decision or action is reported on the front pages of newspapers?	

Different ethical lenses	Core question	Did your decision pass the test? Yes or No and explain
The golden rule perspective	Would I be willing to be treated in the same way?	
The personal gain test	Does personal gain cloud my judgement? Is there a conflict of interest?	
The procedural fairness perspective	Do the procedures pass the scrutiny test by those affected by the decision or action?	
The sleep perspective	Am I comfortable that I will sleep after this decision?	

To lead in a virtuous way is challenging and is not a guarantee of success or good results. However, the corporate scandals (Enron, WorldCom, Lehman Brothers, FIFA, Saambou, African Bank etc.) of recent years have shown that ignoring the role of virtues and ethical business practices is a slide to unsustainable competitive advantage, the degradation of the reputation of business in society, the destruction of profits and the tarnishing of the personal honour and reputation of individuals.[166]

We are reminded of the wisdom of Peter Drucker,[167] who said:

> "Asking "What is right for the enterprise?" does not guarantee that the right decision will be made. Even the most brilliant executive is human and thus prone to mistakes and prejudices. But failure to ask the question virtually guarantees the wrong decision."

We conclude this chapter with a case study on Howard Schulz, the legendary CEO of Starbucks, as an example of a virtuous leader who takes up his stewardship role to make both Starbucks and the world a better place. He is an exemplar of demonstrating business ethics through virtuous leadership practices.

Case study of Howard Schultz, CEO of Starbucks

Early life and career

Howard D. Schultz[168] was born in Brooklyn, New York, on 19 July 1953. He comes from a working-class family with neither of his parents completing high school. He was the first family member to graduate from Northern Michigan University. After graduating from the university with a Bachelor of Science degree in communication in 1975, Schultz found work as an appliance salesman for Hammarplast, a company that sold European coffee makers in the United States. Rising through the ranks to become director of sales, in the early 1980s Schultz noticed that he was selling more coffee makers to a small operation in Seattle, Washington, known then as the Starbucks Coffee Tea and Spice Company, than to Macy's. "Every month, every quarter, these numbers were going up, even though Starbucks just had a few stores," Schultz later remembered. "And I said, 'I gotta go up to Seattle.'"

Howard Schultz still distinctly remembers the first time he walked into the original Starbucks in 1981. At that time, Starbucks had only been around for 10 years and didn't exist outside Seattle. The company's original owners, old college buddies Jerry Baldwin and Gordon Bowker and their neighbor, Zev Siegl, had founded Starbucks in 1971. The three friends also came up with the coffee company's ubiquitous mermaid logo. "When I walked in this store for the first time – I know this sounds really hokey – I knew I was home," Schultz later remembered. "I can't explain it. But I knew I was in a special place, and the product kind of spoke to me." At that time, he added, "I had never had a good cup of coffee. I met the founders of the company, and really heard for the first time the story of great coffee … I just said … this is something I've been looking for my whole professional life." Little did Schultz know then how fortuitous his introduction to the company would truly be, or that he would play an integral part in creating the modern Starbucks.

A year after meeting Starbucks' founders, in 1982, Howard Schultz was hired as director of retail operations and marketing for the growing coffee company, which, at the time only sold coffee beans, not coffee drinks.

Schultz's enthusiasm for opening coffee bars in Starbucks stores, however, wasn't shared by the company's creators. "We said, 'Oh no, that's not for us,'" Siegl remembered. "Throughout the 70s, we served coffee in our store. We even, at one point, had a nice, big espresso machine behind the counter. But we were in the bean business." Nevertheless, Schultz was persistent until finally the owners let him establish a coffee bar in a new store that was opening in Seattle. It was an instant success, bringing in hundreds of people per day and introducing a whole new language – the language of the coffeehouse – to Seattle in 1984.

But the success of the coffee bar demonstrated to the original founders that they didn't want to go in the direction Schultz wanted to take them. They didn't want to get big. Disappointed, Schultz left Starbucks in 1985 to open a coffee bar chain of his own, Il Giornale, which quickly garnered success. Two years later, with the help of investors, Schultz purchased Starbucks, merging Il Giornale with the Seattle company. Subsequently, he became CEO and chairman of Starbucks.

In 2000, Schultz publicly announced that he was resigning as Starbucks' CEO. Eight years later, however, he returned to head the company. In a 2009 interview with CBS, Schultz said of Starbucks' mission, "We're not in the business of filling bellies; we're in the business of filling souls."

Starbucks in 2008

By the time Howard Schultz[169] stepped down as chief executive of Starbucks, in 2000, the coffee chain was one of the world's most recognisable brands and on a steady trajectory of growth. Eight years later Starbucks was suffering from a rough economy and its own strategic missteps, and Schultz felt compelled to return to the CEO seat. His previous tenure had seen promising growth, but now he faced a challenging mission: to lead a turnaround of the company he had built.

In an interview[170] Howard Schultz admitted that in 2008 he had to acknowledge to the entire company that: "… the leadership had failed the 180 000 Starbucks people and their families. And even though I wasn't the CEO, I had been around as chairman; I should have known more. I am responsible. We had to admit to ourselves and to the people of this company that we owned the mistakes that were made. Once we did, it was a powerful turning point. It's like when you have a secret and get it out: the burden is off your shoulders.

The issues of social media, digital media, and getting smart about the rules of engagement emerged as a tremendous weakness for the company. Ultimately our reputation didn't suffer, but we spent countless hours defending ourselves when in fact we have a very strong track record in environmental stewardship. We became more open and vulnerable, listened to people, and as a result started creating a new methodology, a new language, and new tools and tactics that enabled us to become best of class. We're the number-one brand on Facebook. It means that 7 million people are very interested in what we are doing and what we have to say. It has changed our go-to-market strategy – how we communicate, unveil, and innovate, and ultimately how we arrive in the marketplace. The success of the things we have done this year is directly linked to the fact that the cost of customer acquisition and communicating to the outside world is significantly lower for us than it is for people who are spending money on traditional advertising.

The challenge was how to preserve and enhance the integrity of the only assets we have as a company: our values, our culture and guiding principles, and the reservoir of trust with our people. There was unbelievable pressure from multiple constituents.

Success is not sustainable if it is defined by how big you become or by growth for growth's sake. Success is very shallow if it doesn't have emotional meaning. I think there was a herd mentality – a reason for being that somehow became linked to PE, the stock price, and a group of people who felt they were invincible. Starbucks isn't the first company that has happened to, and thankfully we caught it in time.

I think the tension is about can you be big and stay "small"? Can you maintain intimacy with your customers and your people? We understand our business very well, and we understand our customers. And to a person, we understand that we are only as good as yesterday and we have to come to work every day and try to exceed the expectations of our people and customers.

You have to have a 100% belief in your core reason for being. There was tremendous pressure in the first three or four months after my return to dramatically change the strategy and the business model of the company. The marketplace was saying, "Starbucks needs to undo all these company-owned stores and franchise the system." That would have given us a war chest of cash and significantly increased return on capital. It's a good argument economically. It's a good argument for shareholder value. But it would have fractured the culture of the company. You can't get out of this by trying to navigate with a different road map, one that isn't true to yourself. You have to be authentic, you have to be true, and you have to believe in your heart that this is going to work. Someone said to me, "You are roasting 400 million pounds of coffee a year. If you reduce the quality 5%, no one would know. That's a few hundred million dollars!" We would never do that. For example, I shut our stores for three and a half hours of retraining. People said, 'How much is that going to cost?' I had shareholders calling me and saying, 'Are you out of your mind?' I said, 'I'm doing the right thing. We are retraining our people because we have forgotten what we stand for, and that is the pursuit of an unequivocal, absolute commitment to quality.' We reinvested in our people, we reinvested in innovation, and we reinvested in the values of the company. I think the leader today has to demonstrate both transparency and vulnerability, and with that comes truthfulness and humility and obviously the ability to instil confidence in people, and not through some top-down hierarchical approach. Our differentiated model – added to the culture and values that define our company – gives us the nimbleness and flexibility to offer our products to customers through multiple channels.

Being the CEO of a public company over the past couple of years has been difficult. And lonely. The tension you describe assumes that one can't be values-driven or values-based and achieve success or the respect of the street. I don't think that is true. But the only ingredient that works in this environment is performance – so we have to perform. If we don't perform, either we have the wrong strategy or we don't deserve to be here. I think we've demonstrated that the strategy is right and the balance between profitability and having a social conscience and being a benevolent company will lead to significant long-term value for shareholders."

On the question of decisions he has made that Wall Street didn't like, he says: "Health care. Our health care costs over the past 12 months were approximately $300 million. [Starbucks offers health care benefits to any eligible employee who works at least 20 hours a week.] The thought that we would cut that benefit – I couldn't do it. Within this past year I got a call from one of our institutional shareholders. He said, 'You've never had more cover to cut health care than you do now. No one will criticize you.' And I just said, 'I could cut $300 million out of a lot of things, but do you want to kill the company, and kill the trust in what this company stands for? There is no way I will do it, and if that is what you want us to do, you should sell your stock.' What I stand for is not just to make money; it's to preserve the integrity of what we have built for 39 years – to look in the mirror and feel like I've done something that has meaning and relevancy and is something people are going to respect. You have to be willing to fight for what you believe in.

I do not believe that shareholder value is sustainable if you are not creating value for the people who are doing the work and then value for customers. Quintessentially we are a people-based company. You couldn't find another consumer brand that is as dependent on human behaviour as we are. We built Starbucks not through traditional marketing or advertising but through the experience. And that experience can come to life only if people are proud, if they respect and trust the green apron and the people they are representing. The equity of the brand is defined by the quality of the coffee but also, most importantly, by the relationship that the barista has with the customer and whether or not the customer feels valued, appreciated, and respected. That is our aspiration every day. The only way we can succeed and sustain growth and innovation is linked to the basic elements of one cup of coffee, one customer, and one barista at a time. Not innovation for innovation's sake but innovation that is relevant, usable, and, in our case, core to the culture."

On the legacy he wants to create, Schultz indicated: "Our role as leaders is to celebrate the human connection that we have been able to create as a company, and to make sure people realize the deep level of respect we have for the work they do and how they act. That is the legacy of the company. It's not to get bigger or to make more money. Here's a true example: A woman barista in Tacoma, Washington, sees a customer every day, and they become friendly as a result of her work. She begins to see that the woman looks ill. Finally she gets up the courage to say, 'You just don't look well–what's wrong?' The woman says, 'If I don't get a kidney transplant, I am going to die.' A miracle occurs: the barista is a match for the customer, and she gives her a kidney. It's incredible. I drove to Tacoma to see her, and I said, 'Who are you? I've never heard a story like this.' There are a lot of really great companies out there, and wonderful cultures, but something like this doesn't happen very often."

OUR MISSION

To inspire and nurture the human spirit – one person, one cup and one neighbourhood at a time.

OUR VALUES

With our partners, our coffee and our customers at our core, we live these values:

- Creating a culture of warmth and belonging, where everyone is welcome.
- Acting with courage, challenging the status quo and finding new ways to grow our company and each other.
- Being present, connecting with transparency, dignity and respect.
- Delivering our very best in all we do, holding ourselves accountable for results.
- We are performance driven, through the lens of humanity.

Figure 1.9: Starbucks mission and values[171]

"We have always believed building a great, enduring company requires being performance-driven through the lens of humanity. I am proud that Starbucks not only achieved another year of record financial performance in 2014, but we did so while doing more for our people and the communities we serve than at any time in our history. By staying true to our mission, values and guiding principles, I believe we've proven it is possible to build a world-class company with a conscience.

Over the next few years, our efforts will increasingly focus on three areas where we think we can have the biggest impact – building a future with farmers, pioneering green retail on a global scale, and creating pathways to opportunity for young people. With your input, we want to set ambitious goals, some of which we may not achieve. But I strongly believe that today, more than ever, companies such as Starbucks must lead, using their platforms and resources to create opportunities for their people, as well as for the communities they serve. We believe this is our role and responsibility."[172]

Environment: Pioneering sustainable solutions

As a company that relies on agricultural products, we have long been aware that the planet is our most important business partner. Our comprehensive approach to reducing our environmental impact means looking at all aspects of our business, how they intersect and how we can integrate new solutions to create meaningful and sustained change.

- **LEED® certified stores**: We are working to bring all of our stores to LEED® building standards and ensure that our approach to designing, building, and maintaining our stores is inclusive of a range of environmental goals.
- **Recycling & reducing waste**: We're working to shrink our environmental footprint and meet the expectations of our customers by increasing recycling, promoting reusable cups and reducing the waste associated with our cups and other packaging.
- **Water & energy conservation**: By conserving the energy and water we use and purchasing renewable energy credits, we're pushing ourselves to reduce the environmental footprint of our operations and help ensure access to clean water in coffee-growing communities.
- **Climate change**: Since 2004, we've been pursuing strategies to address this challenge and help farmers mitigate the impact of climate change on their farms.

Figure 1.10: Starbucks Environment focus-areas[173]

To be a partner

Being a Starbucks partner means having the opportunity to be something more than an employee. Gigantic possibilities lie ahead – to grow as a person, in your career and in your community. To live the Starbucks mission and to be a leader. It's the opportunity to become your personal best. To be connected to something bigger. To be meaningful to the world. And to be recognized for all of it. It's all here for you.

Connect to something bigger

Connecting with each other, with our customers and the communities we are a part of fosters a deep sense of purpose at Starbucks. We believe we can all become a part of something bigger and inspire positive change in the world around us. That's why we go out to do community service as a team throughout the year, partnering up with organisations to revitalize and enhance the neighborhoods we serve.

Benefits

At Starbucks, our Total Pay package is called "Your Special Blend". It's a benefits package that is tailored to the needs of our partners. And it's designed just for you.

Benefits-eligible partners (those working 20 or more hours a week) can get a wide range of perks, benefits and assistance. Your Special Blend might include bonuses, 401(k) matching and discounted stock purchase options. We offer adoption assistance and health coverage for you and your dependents, including domestic partners.

Starbucks College Achievement Plan is an opportunity for all benefits eligible U.S. partners (all brands) to complete a bachelor's degree with full tuition reimbursement for every year of college through Arizona State University's top-ranked degree programs, delivered online. In addition, to show our gratitude for our partners who are military service members and veterans, they may extend an additional SCAP benefit to their spouse or child.

Partners also appreciate our recognition programs, career sabbaticals and other time-off programs. Plus, you can take advantage of partner perks such as 30% in-store and online discounts, one free pound of coffee, box of K-Cup® Packs or tea a week.

Diversity and inclusion

At Starbucks, we strive to create a culture that values and respects diversity and inclusion. Our goal is to build a diverse workforce, increase competencies, shape a culture of inclusion and develop a diverse network of suppliers. Our welcoming work environment encourages partners to engage with one another and make Starbucks a place they look forward to working each day.

Figure 1.11: Working at Starbucks[174]

Case questions:

Based on the above information:

- What principles relevant to strategic leadership can you describe?
- What virtuous leadership practices did Howard Schultz display?
- How do you build a performance- and values-based culture?

CONCLUSIONS

From this chapter it becomes clear that strategic leadership is a multi-dimensional concept that can be viewed from various perspectives. One constant, however, is that organisations cannot excel without strategic leaders who set the expectations of and mobilise people towards a sustainable and prosperous future.

This chapter discussed strategic leadership in the context of the strategic architecture, and positioned it as the foundation for launching strategic management processes such as external and internal analysis and synthesis, strategy formulation, exploring multiple futures, strategy execution, and strategy renewal and innovation. Next this chapter discussed the VUCA environment as the new world business context, the necessity for agility to thrive in an ever-changing context, and other general leadership practices that are conducive to successfully competing in a VUCA world. From the Vedanta case study it became clear, however, that we still have a long journey to make business a truly mutually beneficial partner of societies and Mother Earth.

This chapter also discussed five inter-related thinking stances that enable strategic leaders to gift themselves a winning departure point for strategic thinking. These stances included (1) possibility thinking, (2) collaborative thinking, (3) abundance thinking, (4) new economy values thinking, and (5) paradox thinking.

Related to strategy-making, it was mentioned that (1) strategy is the collective, emerging pattern based on strategic choices an organisation consciously exhibits and executes over time to ensure its sustainability; (2) that sustainability is enhanced by differentiating the business in unique ways to create value for stakeholders; (3) that strategy is about explaining how an organisation wants to move forward and how it wants to advance the interest of stakeholders; (4) that strategy-making is an organic emergent learning process executed in a specific context in which the maker has influence; (5) that strategy-making aims to create a shared future; (6) and that strategy is dynamic and consists of both a plan and an emerging pattern. Further, a primarily micro-economic view and an abundance view of organisational strategy was discussed, together with a case that reflects both virtuous and vicious strategy cycles bases on strategic actors enabling or disabling praxis.

We continued by elaborating on key features of strategic leadership and by providing practical guidelines for reflection on personal leadership strengths and competencies. The inter-relatedness of the strategic architecture building blocks and a virtuous cycle of strategic thinking were also discussed in detail. Finally, business ethics through virtuous leadership practices were discussed in the form of (1) reflective prompts that assist in developing a perspective on one's own virtue strengths and competency areas; (2) an 18-factor behaviour-based Virtuous Leadership Questionnaire (VLQ) that expands one's insights about one's personal virtue strengths; (3) five approaches for managing business ethics which can be used to diagnose ethical praxis in an organisation; and (4) 10 ethical compass tests that can be used to evaluate past ethical decisions and to guide future ethical challenges and decisions.

In conclusion, the strategic leadership constructs and practical guidelines presented in this chapter develop our ability to step into our role as a strategic leader in an organisation. It also becomes apparent that virtuous leadership is the future and excellent businesses will embrace it, not because they are advised to live it, but because it is part of their moral fibre in any case.

Chapter 2

Strategy formulation:
Generic strategic options and choices

"A strategy delineates a territory in which a company seeks to be unique." – Michael Porter[1]

"The two most fundamental strategic choices are deciding where to play and how to win." – Roger Martin[2]

LEARNING OBJECTIVES

We indicated in chapter 1 that one of the key activities in strategy-making is the development of a heightened consciousness around the core strategic choices of an organisation. The focus of this chapter is on the broad strategic choices leaders and strategists can make as part of the strategy formulation process to position an organisation in a competitive business landscape. The main areas that we explore are:

- Choices related to the identity of the organisation. These include organisational aspirational descriptions as reflected in the vision, mission and organisational values.
- Choices related to generic high-level strategic positioning options for an organisation.
- Choices related to grand strategy options for an organisation, given the fact-based SWOT information of an organisation derived from a thorough external and internal strategy analysis.
- You will be able to use the following perspectives and tools as a basis to develop your own strategic leadership capacity.
- Develop and motivate a descriptive identity write-up for an organisation which includes a vision, mission and values statements.
- Critically examine the current identity and aspirational descriptions of an organisation to suggest improvements and changes to these statements.
- Describe and motivate appropriate high-level strategic choices for an organisation by using the following generic strategic frameworks to facilitate informed decision-making:
  - o Porter's five generic competitive strategic options
  - o Treacy and Wiersema's three value disciplines
  - o digital and physical orientation options
  - o industry-based strategy styles
  - o strategic posture options
  - o foreign market entry options
- Understand and use the relevant grand strategy alternatives for an organisation based on the following options:
  - o competence-based growth strategies
  - o external-orientated growth strategies
  - o strategic space growth strategies
  - o rationalisation strategies

INTRODUCTION

In Figure 2.1 we see that the process of strategy formulation is informed and shaped by four strategy practice domains, namely:

- Strategic leadership, which includes the thinking capacity and practices of leaders in an organisation as well as the business ethics practices using a virtuous leadership approach as described in chapter 1. Entrepreneurial thinking and practices are also part of this domain and are described in chapter 9.
- Results and conclusions from the analysis and synthesis based on an extensive external and internal review of the organisation. This aspect is not included in this book but a comprehensive guide and outline of this strategy practice domain is available in a related publication by the authors.[3]
- Perspectives based on a multiple futures review for the organisation using scenario planning as described in chapter 4.
- Insights flowing from the strategy renewal and innovation efforts of the organisation as described in chapters 6–8.

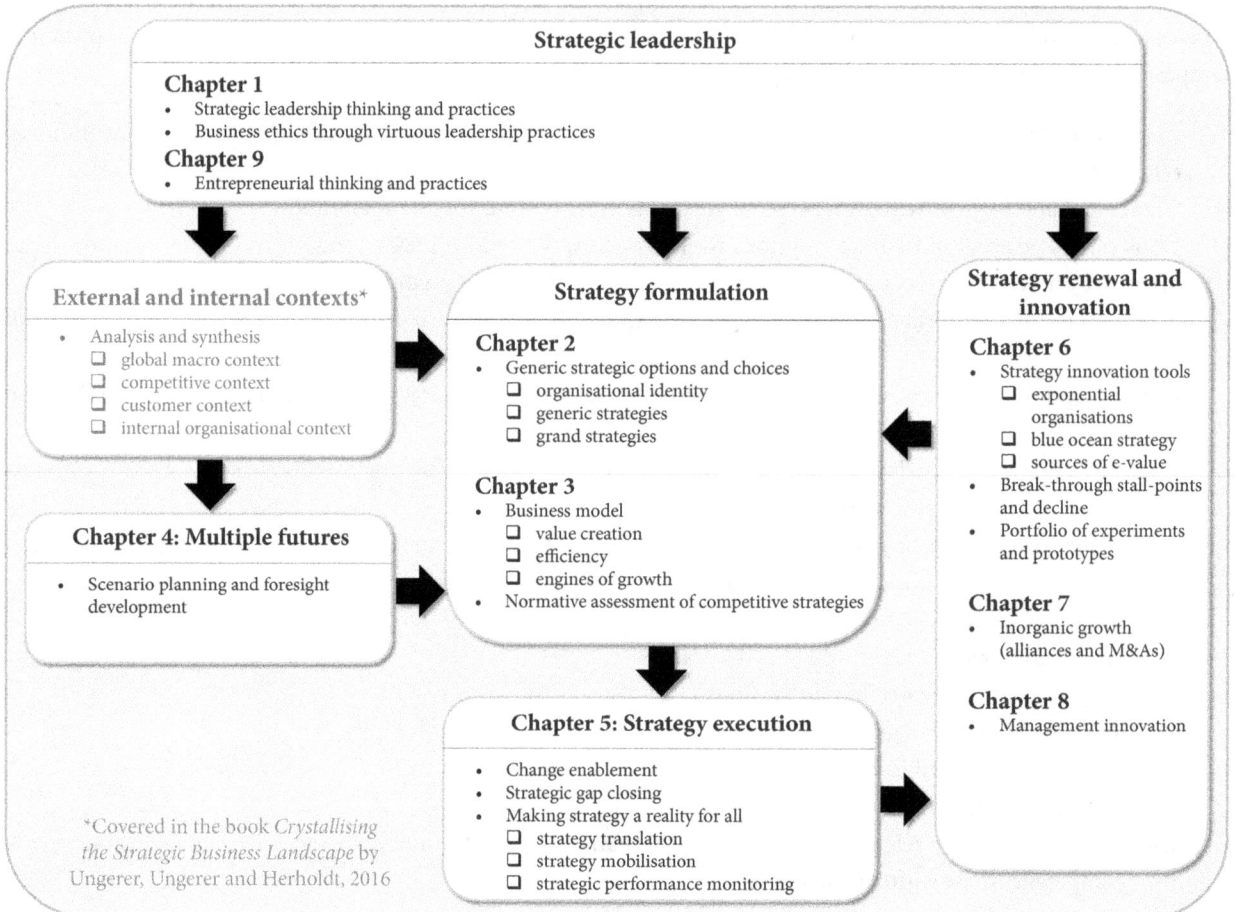

Strategic leadership

Chapter 1
- Strategic leadership thinking and practices
- Business ethics through virtuous leadership practices

Chapter 9
- Entrepreneurial thinking and practices

External and internal contexts*
- Analysis and synthesis
  - global macro context
  - competitive context
  - customer context
  - internal organisational context

Chapter 4: Multiple futures
- Scenario planning and foresight development

*Covered in the book *Crystallising the Strategic Business Landscape* by Ungerer, Ungerer and Herholdt, 2016

Strategy formulation

Chapter 2
- Generic strategic options and choices
  - organisational identity
  - generic strategies
  - grand strategies

Chapter 3
- Business model
  - value creation
  - efficiency
  - engines of growth
- Normative assessment of competitive strategies

Chapter 5: Strategy execution
- Change enablement
- Strategic gap closing
- Making strategy a reality for all
  - strategy translation
  - strategy mobilisation
  - strategic performance monitoring

Strategy renewal and innovation

Chapter 6
- Strategy innovation tools
  - exponential organisations
  - blue ocean strategy
  - sources of e-value
- Break-through stall-points and decline
- Portfolio of experiments and prototypes

Chapter 7
- Inorganic growth (alliances and M&As)

Chapter 8
- Management innovation

Figure 2.1: The strategic architecture landscape

When we start with a cycle of strategy formulation and development for an organisation, this process should be informed at least by a thorough fact-based external and internal analysis. As the strategy practices of an organisation mature over time, multiple strategy practice domains as described above will inform and form a strategy development process cycle.

We indicated in chapter 1 that strategy is the collective and emerging pattern, based on strategic choices, that an organisation consciously exhibits and executes over time to ensure its sustainable endurance by differentiating itself in unique ways to create and add value for stakeholders. Strategy is about explaining how an organisation wants to move forward and how it wants to advance the interest of stakeholders. From this description we see that central to strategy development is our ability to make sound and well-founded strategic choices. The nature and variety of strategic choices to position an organisation for differentiating and competitive benefits are described in this chapter. This should be read in conjunction with chapter 3, where the aspects related to the development of an integrated business model for the organisation based on the core strategic choices made, and the normative assessment of competitive strategies are described. The broader strategic choice domains related to strategy formulation and competitive positioning as described in this chapter and chapter 3 are reflected in Figure 2.2.

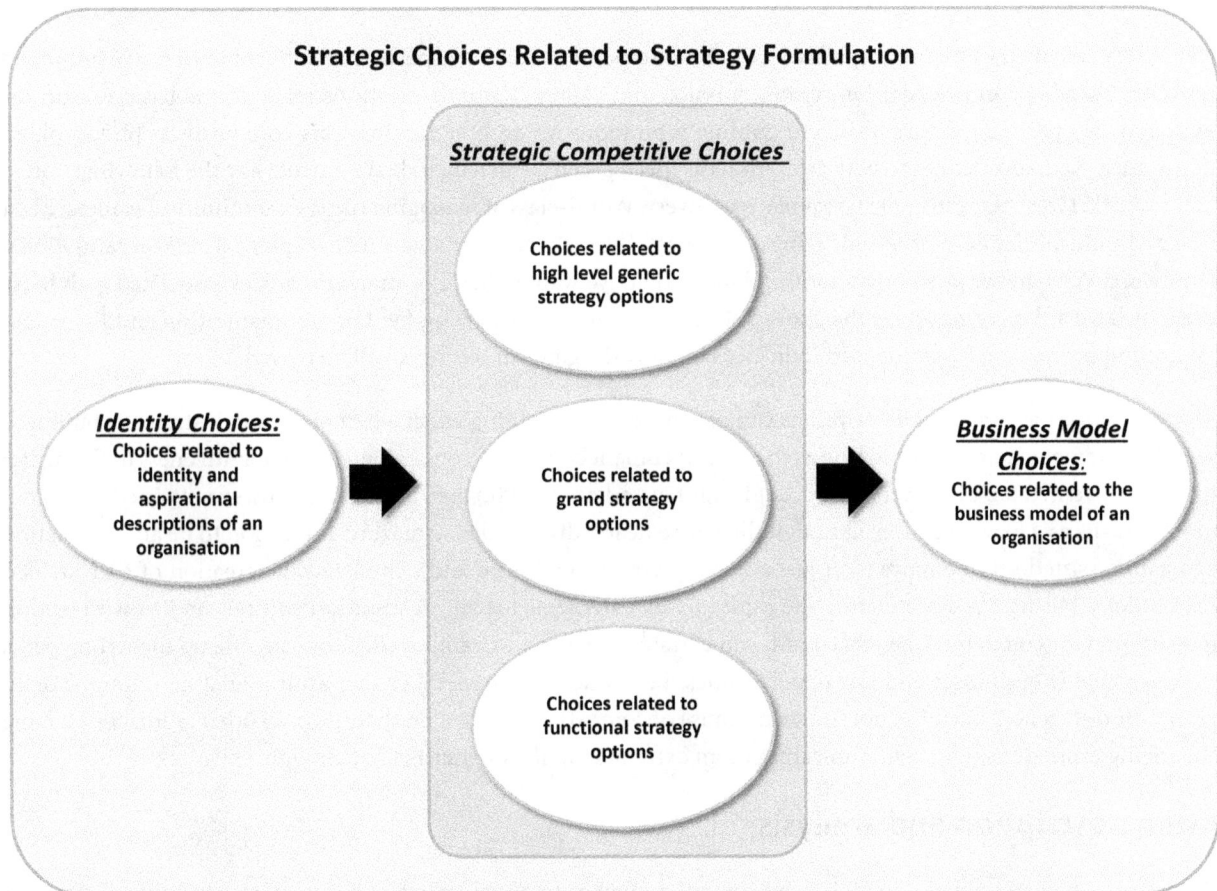

Strategic Choices Related to Strategy Formulation

Strategic Competitive Choices

Choices related to high level generic strategy options

Identity Choices:
Choices related to identity and aspirational descriptions of an organisation

Choices related to grand strategy options

Business Model Choices:
Choices related to the business model of an organisation

Choices related to functional strategy options

Figure 2.2: Strategy formulation strategic choice domains

In the next part of this chapter we discuss three different competitive strategic choice domains for an organisation. These are aspirational choices related to the identity of the organisation, the high-level strategy choices for an organisation and the evaluation of the appropriateness of a variety of grand strategy options.

STRATEGIC CHOICES RELATED TO ORGANISATION IDENTITY AND ASPIRATIONS

The concept "organisational identity" is used here as a general reference regarding how stakeholders perceive an organisation. It is about the perceptions and associations, positive and/or negative, that stakeholders have about an organisation. The identity of an organisation is formed by many inter-related factors that are influenced and created by organisational members. Some of the aspects that can shape the identity of an organisation are the leadership, the brand personality or product brands, the corporate image, the reputation, the history and track-record. Based on this identity an organisation is associated with certain attributes. Woolworths is associated with quality, Johnson & Johnson with safe products and Audi with technology. Gallup, the global research-based performance-management consulting firm, states that an organisation's identity is made up of three distinctively different, yet interrelated elements: purpose, brand and culture.[4]

From a strategic management perspective we will address the following aspects that contribute to the identity and aspiration agenda of an organisation: vision, mission and values. These descriptions relate to the basic **reason for being** and also represent future ideal and guiding aspirations for an organisation – its core business philosophies. For instance, Nedbank defines its core aspirations as "deep green", which include statements like the following: "Great place to work; Great place to bank; Great place to invest; World-class at managing risks; Community of leaders; Most respected and aspirational brand; and Living our values." The main questions we want to explore around organisational identity are: Who are we as an organisation? And who do we want to be? The strategic choices associated with these decisions have a direct impact on the chosen strategic landscape or playing field of an organisation and the values that are emphasised, representing lead indicators on how the game of business will be played.

An organisation's aspirational descriptions can also have a constraining effect when not enough stretch is built into them. For example, Xerox's positioning as the "the document company" constrained its competitiveness in the digital era. Xerox invented the PC at Xerox Parc, but it was never developed further. Serendipity however assisted 3M to not ignore post-its as a new invention, although they were nearly disregarded. Amazon's aspiration to be an information aggregator assisted it to be more than just a leading virtual bookstore and stimulated the creation of a diversified portfolio of e-businesses. Formulating the aspirational statements for an organisation will not on its own position an institution for competitive benefits, but it can certainly have a constraining effect or lead one up the wrong paths – to unprofitable businesses and lost opportunities. Let us however remember that aspirational descriptions of an organisation are a necessary, but not sufficient, cause of competitive success on their own. In other words, just having challenging aspirations (and communicating them extremely well and often) is not enough.

Vision description and analysis

Vision (from the Latin *videre* – to see) is an expression of what an organisation or group of people wants to create or achieve. It is a simple and artful expression of the broadest business aspiration of a preferred future state. A vision statement is indicative of where an organisation wants to be in the years to come. A vision therefore represents an ideal end state that serves as an attractor to stimulate innovation towards realising the vision.

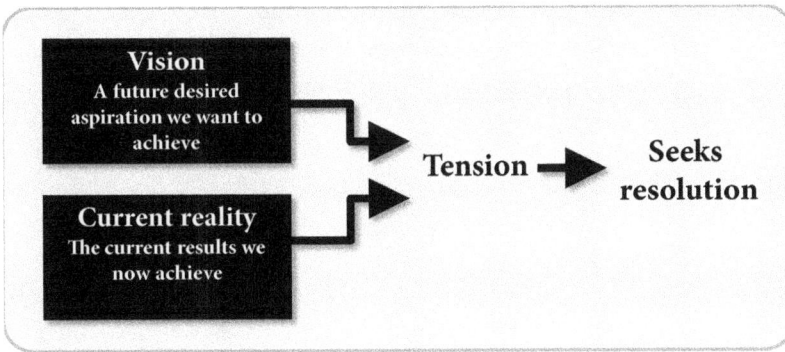

Figure 2.3: Tension between vision and current reality

A vision creates the basis for people to believe in a future because they can identify with it, and it also helps them to believe that their individual efforts make a difference in creating that better future and world. The nature of a visioning process creates the future as a neutral arena, an open space onto which people can project their future aspirations and fears. A vision clarifies the organisation's future priorities, and highlights where trade-offs might occur. The function of a well-formulated vision is to create tension between the current and future realities of an organisation. This tension seeks resolution, and the only way it can be achieved is by reaching, or trying to reach, the desired vision – to make it a reality – even if it is enduring and seemingly unachievable in the short term. This dynamic of a vision as a tension creation attract or that seeks resolution by taking actions towards achieving the vision is displayed in Figure 2.3.

Visions only have a mobilising effect towards a shared future if they are widely spread, shared and acknowledged in an organisation. The creation and spreading of a mutually created vision is the task of both leaders and strategy collaborators. Visions spread because of a reinforcing process of increasing clarity, enthusiasm and commitment. As people talk about it and integrate the vision with their capacity to own it and to make it part of their own life purpose and goals, the vision is shared and more people commit their support. As people talk, the vision becomes clearer and more granular aspects of it may emerge.

Charles Kiefer[5] states: "Despite the excitement a vision generates, the process of building shared vision is not always glamorous. Managers who are skilled in building shared visions talk about the process in ordinary terms – talking about our vision just gets woven into everyday life." If visions are co-created with and through others in a constant dialogue, the eventual spreading is done by participants. Involving key stakeholders in the development and refinement of the aspirational descriptions of an organisation is a best practice and requires innovative processes to facilitate maximum participation. Mobilising people around a compelling vision will sometimes allow it to root itself – especially when there is a charismatic leader as a sponsor. This enhances the inspirational angles of a vision. This process of "rooting" may continue and increase in value, clarity and scope, until the actual vision is more than just a single statement – it has meaning within a specific context and stakeholders interpret the strategic implications to empower themselves strategically. A key aspect about a vision is how it mobilises stakeholders' energy so they make a concerted and informed effort to make the vision a reality.

In contrast with strategic goals (see chapter 5 on strategy execution), a vision is long-lasting and does not change in the short term. Imagination, intuition and an ability to synthesise disparate information are key ingredients for the development of an impactful vision.[6] A good starting point for developing a vision is to answer the question: "What is our ultimate ambition?"[7]

Visions should however not be seen as a general panacea for all organisational dilemmas and woes. For example, a vision cannot guarantee success and is dependent on many collaborators making a meaningful contribution to shaping and executing it. To create and execute a vision, leaders as sponsors, champions and collaborator mobilisers are critical in making the vision come alive in an organisation's influence domain. It is sad to see organisations that spent a great deal of time and energy formulating elaborate visions that are displayed in boardrooms and on factory floors, but left it at that. As can be expected, very little comes from this.

Application tool

Use the requirements for a vision and the related questions and criteria as summarised in Table 2.1 to critically evaluate the vision statement of an organisation.

Table 2.1: Guidelines on development and evaluation of a vision

General requirements for a vision statement[8]

Visions must be:
- shared, and generate commitment;
- about a preferred or desired future;
- a contrast with current reality to create the desired structural tension;
- fluid and enduring;
- sustained and nurtured in a constant process as part of the strategic conversation

Visions should not be
- about vague concepts;
- solutions to current problems;
- eloquent words and statements only;
- only on boardroom walls, but must be in the hearts and minds of people

Visions can
- be unemotional;
- be emotional and inspirational;
- emerge in the course of ordinary organisational life;
- emerge from inspirational leadership;
- be detailed and granular;
- have few details, but constitute provocative and magic thoughts

Evaluation of a vision

Questions to consider:[9]
- Would it motivate you to join this organisation and continue to motivate you once you are there?
- Does it provide a beacon for guiding the kind of adaption and change required for continual growth?
- Will it challenge you?
- Can it serve as a basis for strategy that can be acted on?
- Will it serve as a framework to keep all strategic decision-making in context?

Criteria for a vision statement:[10]
- Is it directional?
- Does it give focus?
- Is it desirable?
- Is it feasible?
- Is it easy to communicate and easy to remember?

Practical guideline

An alternative way to stimulate creating inspiring and stretch visions is to ask: "What is the BIG IDEAL?" Complete the following sentence to describe the end-state and contribution of your organisation's differentiated position choice:

The world would be a better place if: ...

Ogilvy, the media and brand consultancy, indicates that their South African operation's big ideal is: "Liberating the inner greatness of companies and people". A big idea for the University of Stellenbosch Business school in 2011 was: The world would be a better place "when USB stakeholders contribute as leaders to achieve the Millennium Development Goals (MDGs)".

Tom Boardman, the legendary CEO of Nedbank, said in 2006:[11] "I truly believe that great companies achieve and maintain greatness by being vision-led and values-driven. You need a clear and compelling vision to take people along with you towards new goals and objectives. It requires passionate, committed and ethical people to move together towards a clearer vision."

Mission or purpose description and analysis

Purpose (mission) (from the Latin word *proponere* – to declare) represents the fundamental reason for a company's existence. It declares what this company is here to do, which means it spells out in which business domain a company operates and seeks success. In other words, the mission specifies the business or businesses in which the organisation wants to compete and the customers it intends to serve.[12] In this chapter "mission" and "purpose" are used as inter-related concepts. A purpose or mission is associated with a longer-term orientation and can change as the context and competitive aspirations of an organisation develop over time. The word "mission" should not be confused with the military application of it, as in "Our mission (objective) is to take this hill." Mission and purpose descriptions are longer-term strategic business domain explanations.[13]

Purpose often connects on a deeper level as a company's reason for being, and may have as much of a pulling effect as a vision, but in addition it also creates clear boundaries that spell out where the company operates. Mission or purpose statements therefore spell out what business domain an organisation operates in and seeks success in. The clearer this business domain, the more certain it is what will spell success for that organisation and the better and more focused the company will be in positioning itself in its industry and marketplace. The mission or purpose statement also gives guidance on boundaries and "what we don't do". In all cases this is extremely important in order to create focused behaviour. Strong company purposes also seem to connect strongly with that industry's reason for existence.

A well-defined mission/purpose statement gives clear guidance on the key question: "What business are we in?" Examples of this are:[14]

- Volkswagen SA is not in the motorcar business, but in the transportation business.
- BP is not in the petrol business, but in the energy business.
- Rhodes University is not in the business of education and research, but in the business of equipping people for life.
- Steinhoff International sees itself more of a supply chain than just a furniture maker and distributor.

Montblanc, part of the Richemont group, evolved carefully over time from a brand associated with writing instruments to a luxury goods brand.[15] Today they sell, beside pens, premium goods including watches, jewellery, fragrances, leather goods and eyewear.

The mission/purpose statement should also give strategic direction on the question: "What business are you not in?" Howard Schultz of Starbucks is very clear on the four things Starbucks will "never" do:[16] They will not franchise, put chemicals in their coffee beans, sell beans in plastic bins in supermarkets, and "never, never stop pursuing the perfect cup of coffee by buying the best beans and roasting them to perfection".

Application tool

Use the questions related to a mission/purpose statement and the Lift Test in Table 2.2 to develop or evaluate the robustness of an organisation's description.

Table 2.2: Guidelines on developing and evaluating a mission/purpose

Answer the following questions: • Why do we exist? Why is our existence important to others and the world in general? Why do we matter?   • What are we here to do?   • What business are we in?   • What business are we not in?   • What is our ultimate ambition?   From the answers to these questions, formulate the mission/purpose of the organisation.
The Lift Test to test the robustness of the mission/purpose description: Imagine you get into a lift with a customer. He or she asks: "What does your organisation do?"   You have until the lift reaches its destination to answer the question (in other words, no more than two minutes). Go for it!

Winning players develop a purpose for their organisation beyond the aim of "making money". They develop a purpose that sets the organisation on a route to contributing to making the world and the societies they operate in better places. Of course they are also successful in making money, but that is the result of their strategic efforts, not their direct focus. According to research by Moss Kanter, great companies work to make money, but in their choice of how to do so they consider whether they are creating enduring institutions. As a result they both invest in the future and are very aware of the needs of people and the society.[17] Google's purpose is to "Organize the world's information and make it universally accessible and useful". TED is a non-profit organisation that is devoted to "Ideas worth spreading" and does so in the form of short, powerful talks (18 minutes or less). Facebook's mission is to "to give people the power to share and make the world more open and connected". It therefore provides people with the tools to stay connected with friends and family, to discover what's going on in the world, and to share and express what matters to them. These mission statements are broad and grandiose, yet focused and compelling, serving as excellent motivators for employees to change the world.

From a stakeholder-centric view it is important to remember that stakeholders can affect an organisation's vision and mission and are also the recipients of the strategic and operational outcome achievements. Stakeholders tend to continue to support an organisation when its performance outputs meet or exceed their expectations. Research indicates that organisations that manage stakeholders well effectively outperform those that do not.[18] The major stakeholder groupings an organisation should engage with are shown in Figure 2.4.

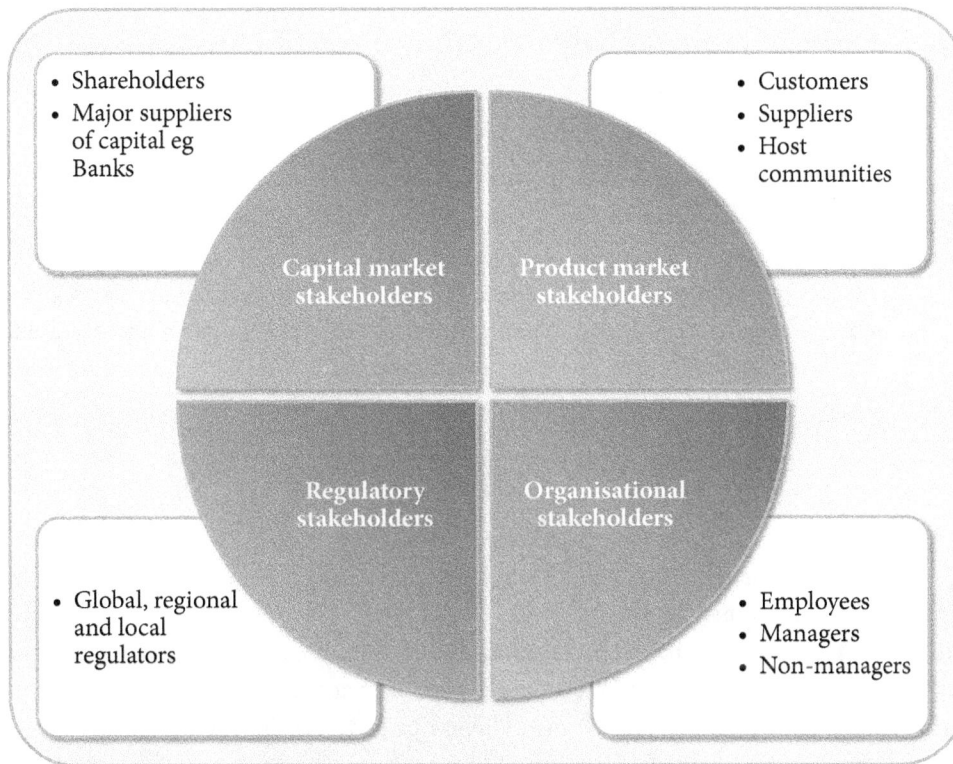

Figure 2.4: Major stakeholder groupings[19]

Organisational values description and analysis

Where much of the identity choice focuses around "what" an organisation wants to be, organisational value give us guidance on "how" these aspirational choices should be made. Organisational values describe in broad behavioural terms "how" things are done (or intended to be done) around here. More specifically, organisation values represent the beliefs, traits and behavioural norms the personnel of the organisation are expected to display in conducting business and executing strategies and operations.[20] Organisational values shape the moral landscape and boundaries of the firm and give guidance on the behavioural aspirations of an organisation. The values descriptions give direction on the "best" behavioural aspirations of how business activities and people interactions should happen.

Application tool

Use the questions that follow to develop your view on status of organisational values.

Table 2.3: Guidelines on evaluation of a values statement

It is essential to comment on how "alive" these values are.

- What processes and practices are in place in the organisation to promote and enhance the use of organisation values in the operations and strategies of the organisation?

Other questions:

- What are the gaps between intent and reality?
- How is the use of values enforced?

We need to remember: Values without actions are meaningless.

Organisation values and culture are related concepts. Malone states that a great corporate culture is a fabric of rules, experiences, myths and legends, relationships and rituals as complex as any real family – and just as difficult to describe to any outsider.[21] Organisation values form an integral part of the culture of an organisation and are a strategic choice that guides organisation stakeholders on how to execute the broader aspirations in the form of vision and mission statements.

Google's innovation focus seems to be based on the following values-related principles:[22]

- In the long run, the interests of shareholders and society at large are convergent.
  - Making the planet a "better" place serves the interests of business, and making businesses "better" serves the interests of every human being.
- A company's social legitimacy can never be taken for granted – it can and will be challenged, so live with it.
- Citizens and consumers expect companies to be not only socially accountable, but socially entrepreneurial.
- Systemic problems can't be solved by a single institution or by people sitting around conference tables.
  - Businesses are uniquely equipped to help mobilise the relevant parties and get "boots on the ground." They need to be energetic partners of public institutions and NGOs.
- "Don't be evil" (Google's famous mantra) is a *de minimis* standard.

Case study of SABMiller

The core strategic aspirational descriptions of SABMiller and an evaluation of it are reflected in Figure 2.5 as an example.

SABMiller vision, mission, values & strategic priorities (2013/2014)

	Description	Conclusions
Vision	Be the most admired company in the South African beer industry -- as an employer of choice, partner of choice and investment of choice.	The best example of its ingrained vision is SAB's acquisition of Miller in 2002. This made it the second-largest brewer in the world.
Mission	Own and nurture local and international brands which are the first choice of the consumer.	The mission is well entrenched and is very much part of the DNA of the firm. This is evident in its historic drive to enter new markets, either through acquisition or a green fields strategy, and once there to grow the brands.
Values	We are a market-facing, brand-led and self-refreshing organisation, committed to recognising, retaining and advancing our top talent. Our company personifies "South African" pride and diversity with an all-embracing culture built on great brands, great people and rock-solid values. • Our people are our enduring advantage • Accountability is clear and personal. • We work and win in teams. • We understand and respect our customers and consumers. • Our reputation is indivisible.	The values of the firm reiterate its drive to be a global leader in its industry by ensuring that its staff are working towards the common goals of the firm, in such a way that the customer is looked after and the brands of the various products are valued.
Strategic priorities	• Drive superior top-line growth through strengthening our brand portfolios and expanding the beer category. • Build a globally integrated organisation to optimise resources, win in market and reduce costs. • Actively shape our global mix to drive a superior growth profile	SABMiller's strategic priorities are highly aligned to its business strategy. It is in the words of the strategy priorities that each employee can see exactly where SABMiller intends to go and what steps are needed to get there. The vision, mission, values and the strategic priorities are all aligned with the direction SABMiller has been heading in the last 10 years and are very much part of the reason that the firm has been so successful.

Figure 2.5: SABMiller's strategic aspirational descriptions in 2013[23]

Case study of Woolworths[24]

WOOLWORTHS

Vision, mission & values

woolworths' vision is to be a leader in retail brands that appeal to people who care about quality, innovation and sustainability. The group depicts its accompanying strategy as seven strategic objectives, as shown in Figure 2.6. Of note are the realistic and achievable strategic objectives that support an ambitious and expansive vision statement. Woolworths' strategic objectives provide realistic clarity, which links to strategic and operational plans in a practical manner.

TO BE A WORLD LEADER IN RETAIL BRANDS THAT APPEAL TO PEOPLE WHO CARE ABOUT QUALITY, INNOVAITON AND SUSTAINABILITY.

Build stronger, more profitable customer relations

Be a leading fashion retailer in the southern hemisphere

Become a big foods business

Become an omni-channel business

Continue to build the business in the rest of Africa

Offer our customers simple, convenient and rewarding financial services

Embed the Good Business Journey throughout our business

Figure 2.6: WHL's vision & strategic objectives

Woolworths lists seven values that underpin its ethos and company culture, namely: quality and style, value, service, innovation, integrity, energy and sustainability. The group's values are regularly reinforced throughout the business, with measurable behavioural objectives forming part of all employees' integrated performance management plan.

The group's values are qualified by practical descriptions of how behaviours should be reinforcing their intent, as shown in Figure 2.7.

Of specific note is that several of the group's values are directly quoted in the vision statement as well, indicating a well-integrated system of vision, strategic objectives and values system to support and enable the execution thereof.

QUALITY AND STYLE	"When we deliver the best we stay focused, adopt a professional approach and demonstrate awareness of market trends."
VALUE	"When we offer value to the business, we encourage collaboration, show effective decision-making and influence others."
SERVICE	"Service means we demonstrate commitment and build effective relationships."
INTEGRITY	"When we embrace innovation, we improve processes and seek creative solutions."
INNOVATION	"When we demonstrate integrity we operate with integrity, develop ourselves and others and communicate effectively."
ENERGY	"When we act with energy, we inspire and engage, and we recognise and value others."
SUSTAINABILITY	"When we contribute to the sustainability of Woolworths, we share the vision and plan for success, support and initiate change and embrace diversity."

Figure 2.7: WHL's values

Woolworths' vision, strategy and values subscribe to best practices and are adopted at all levels of the organisation, which ensures aspirational and behavioural alignment in execution.

Conclusions on identity and aspirational descriptions

The aspirational and identity descriptions of an organisation set the boundaries of the strategic (vision and mission) and moral (values) landscape it wants to operate in. The vision and mission descriptions are central to the strategy formulation processes of an organisation (see Figures 2.1 and 2.2). The embedding of organisational values as part of the individual and team performance enhancement system of an organisation is a best practice. The revitalisation and ongoing socialising of these aspirational descriptions with newcomers, new stakeholders and new partners through various interaction mechanisms is an ongoing quest of strategic leadership.

HIGH-LEVEL GENERIC STRATEGIC CHOICES

After the aspirational descriptions of an organisation have been developed, these must be translated into holistic views of the strategic orientation of the firm before other strategy execution processes kick in (see chapter 5 on strategy execution and translation practices). This implies that the longer-term strategic goals of an organisation should be based on a set of core strategic choices about how the firm plans to best compete in a chosen marketplace.

A menu of strategic competitive choices for an organisation that strategists and leaders should ponder as part of a strategy formulation and development process is reflected in Figure 2.8. The strategic competitive choice options of an organisation can be classified into four levels: identity and aspirational strategic choices (as described above); generic strategy choices; grand strategy choices; and functional strategy choices. The details of generic and grand strategy options are described in the rest of this chapter. The aspects related to functional strategies are beyond the scope of this book, but are shown below to indicate the link to the competitive strategy choices of an organisation.

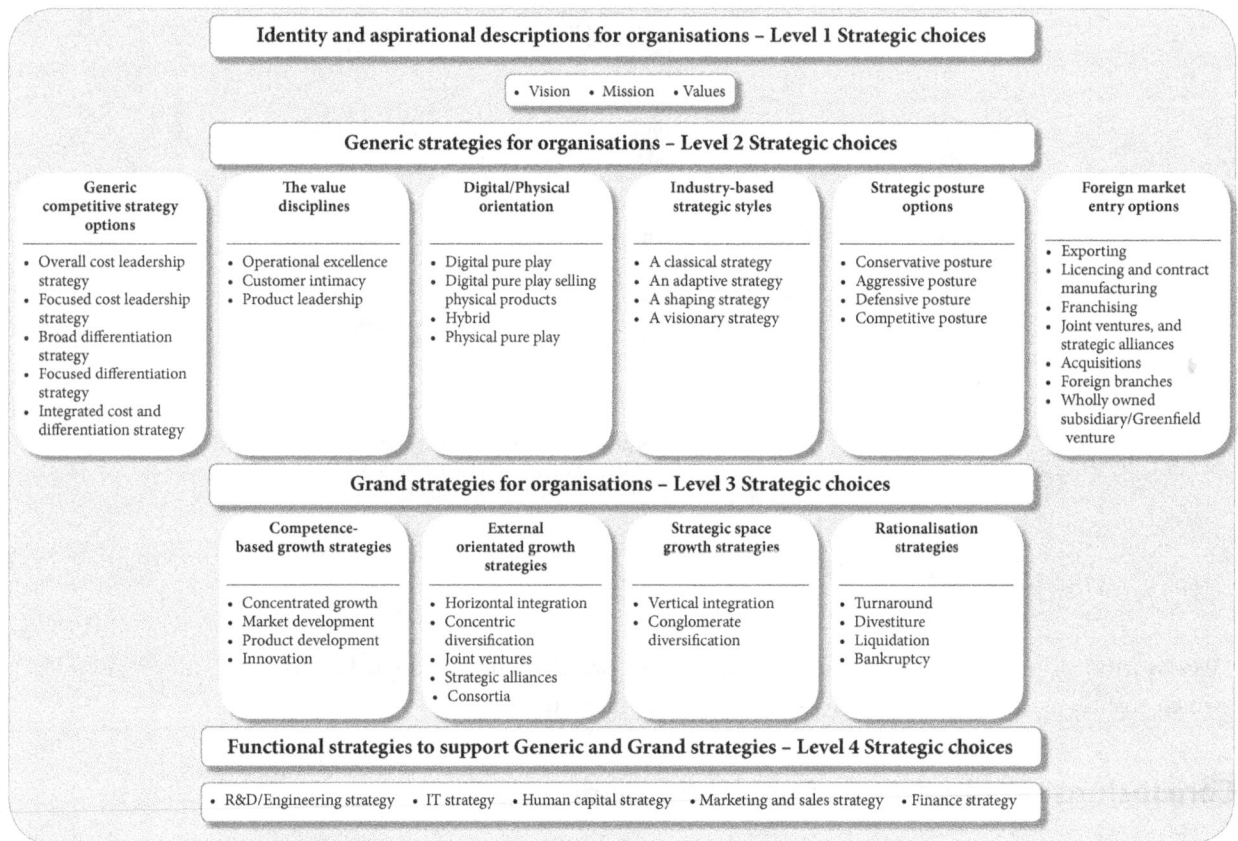

Figure 2.8: A menu of strategic competitive choices

The strategic choices described in this chapter are presented to stimulate dialogue as part of an ongoing strategy conversation to deepen our understanding of the competitiveness of an organisation's strategy. However we do not imply that the strategic options and choices described in this chapter represent all the strategic decisions related to competitive strategy positioning. It is important to remember that in chapter 3 the aspects related to the business model choices of an organisation are described as an integral part of a strategy formulation and development process (see Figure 2.1). In fact each of the strategy practice domains in Figure 2.1 represent strategic choice arenas which reinforce the importance of a higher level of awareness by internal and external stakeholders of the key decisions that influence the future competitiveness of an organisation.

In this section we introduce six different frameworks that we can use to think about the generic competitive positioning of an organisation. The following high-level generic strategic frameworks to facilitate informed decision-making, in the contextual reality of an organisation, are addressed:

- Porter's generic competitive strategic options
- Treacy and Wiersema's three value disciplines
- digital and physical orientation options
- industry-based strategic styles
- strategic posture options
- foreign market entry options

Porter's generic competitive strategic options

Competitive advantages are, according to Porter,[25] derived from the activities that are involved in creating, manufacturing, selling and supplying products and services, and winning the competitive race can only be achieved by establishing and preserving a company's distinctiveness. There are two ways in which companies can achieve this distinctiveness. The first is by performing different activities to their rivals, and the second is by performing similar activities, but performing them in different ways. Analogously, companies can either supply differentiated offerings that create unique value and enable a premium price to be charged; or they can supply similar products and services, but perform the activities more efficiently and economically than competitors, leading to a cost advantage.

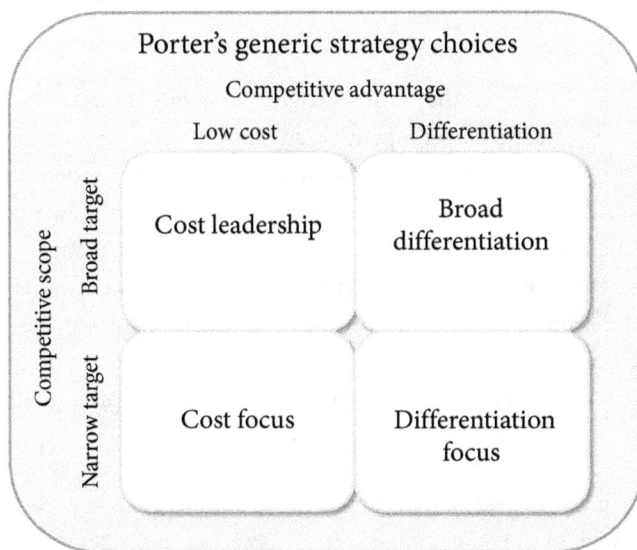

Figure 2.9: Porter's generic strategies adapted[28]

Within the strategic positioning paradigm, strategy is about the creation of a unique and valuable position, involving a different set of activities.[26] Porter[27] strongly emphasises (1) **differentiation of activities,** but also highlights that (2) **costs** can play a significant role in creating competitive advantages. Both of these strategic approaches, however, can only be realised when a company has (3) a **clear focus**. Focus describes how it aims to penetrate the market and which customers to target. These three factors led to the creation of Porter's four generic strategies, as depicted in Figure 2.9.

The **cost leadership generic strategy** refers to when a company is able to achieve lower overall costs, while offering products that appeal to a wide range of customers, mainly through underpricing competitors. This type of positioning is closely associated with economies of scale, a large market share and aggressive cost-cutting techniques. In return, low-cost strategies provide very good defences against both buyer and competitor bargaining power, as profit margins can still be maintained even in the face of strong competitive threats.[29] Examples of cost leadership companies include Wal-Mart, Shoprite, Dell Computers, AirBnB and Amazon. A **cost focus generic strategy** also achieves lower overall cost benefits and low pricing, but provides its offering to a smaller niche of customers. Examples of cost-focus companies are Capitec, Southwest Airlines, Priceline, Expedia and Agoda.[30]

A **broad differentiation generic strategy** focuses on providing a differentiated offering, while appealing to a wide array of customers. The advantage of differentiation strategies is that differentiated offerings are often perceived as exclusive, warranting a premium price, brand loyalty and customer lock-in.[31] Examples of companies that employ broad differentiation strategies are Facebook, Microsoft, Symantec Norton and Dropbox. Lastly, **differentiation focus generic strategies** provide differentiated offerings aimed at a niche customer segment that meets their tastes and requirements better than the competitors' offerings. Examples of such companies are DStv, Porche, Zynga, Prezi, 9gag and various niche online communities.[32]

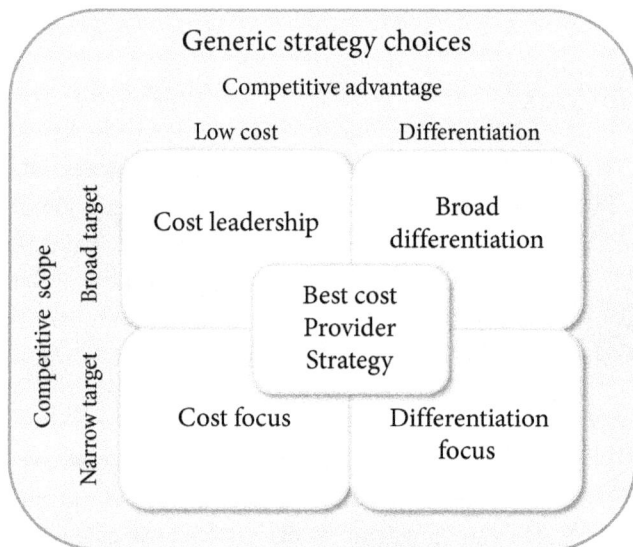

Figure 2.10: Extended generic strategies[34]

There is a fifth generic strategy type that emerged not specifically from Porter's design, but by retrospective reflection.[33] This generic strategy type is known as the **best-cost provider strategy**. Customers get more value for money by combining both good-to-excellent offering attributes with a lower cost than rivals. This creates a competitive space of lower (best) costs and prices than competitors with comparable offering features. A best-cost provider strategy simultaneously pursues both differentiation and low-cost advantages. Porter's extended generic strategies are depicted in Figure 2.10.

Each of the above generic strategies represents a particular competitive advantage with a particular competitive scope for an organisation. A competitive advantage is based on a choice between low cost or differentiation. The choice of a competitive advantage is informed by the nature and quality of internal resource strengths, capabilities and core competences, e.g. a low-cost strategy is dependent on a lean value chain and a differentiation strategy is linked to value-creating activities that customers appreciate and admire. The competitive scope consists of a broad market or narrow target market. Firms serving a broad market seek to utilise their competitive advantage on an industry-wide scale, whilst a narrow target market serves the needs of a specific group of customers. The best-cost strategy offers customers competitive prices with comparable product/service features.

In order for competitive advantages to be sustainable, explicit trade-offs in choosing how to compete are required[35] to create a tight "fit" between activities. Fit creates an interrelated web of activities (often termed an "activity system" – see chapter 3) that cannot easily be untangled, creating barriers to entry and imitation. Two types of imitator that need to be guarded against are "repositioners" and "straddlers". Repositioners copy valuable strategic positions of competitors, whereas straddlers keep their own strategic position, but copy additional activities, features or services of a superior competitor.[36]

Trade-offs protect against imitation for three reasons. Firstly, different products and services require different activities, equipment, configurations, employee behaviour, skills and management systems. It is impossible for an organisation to compete on all fronts, because competing in some areas directly prohibits the ability to compete in another area due to incompatibility. Activity incompatibility therefore prevents imitation. Secondly, even if activities are not completely incompatible, value is destroyed if activities are overdesigned or underdesigned for a specific use. Therefore, though activities may be copied, the value of the activity may be diminished for the imitator. Thirdly, trade-offs help with focusing a company to avoid internal or external confusion. Inconsistencies in a business's image and reputation create external confusion, which leads to distrust of a product or service. Internal confusion, on the other hand, may arise from a too diverse set of products and services offered, blurring organisational priorities, coordination and control. This leads to employees who are confused about company goals, which values to exhibit, or how to approach customers. These all result in suboptimal daily operations. Trade-offs therefore ensure that a company remains focused and prevents imitation.[37]

Fit also introduces the idea of designing a business holistically, whereby the system is more than its constituent parts. Three different tiers of fit exist. First-tier fit is when there is a **consistency** between activities and the overall vision, strategy and goals of the organisation. Consistency allows competitive advantages to be compounded and focuses the internal co-ordination of the business. Second-tier fit is created when activities are **reinforcing**, meaning that activities support and improve the functioning of the other activities. Lastly, third-tier fit is created when second-tier fit is **optimised**, leading to near-ideal execution of activities.[38]

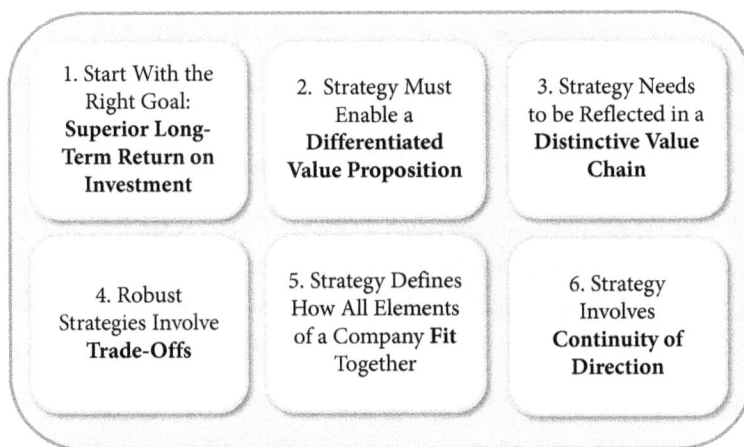

1. Start With the Right Goal: **Superior Long-Term Return on Investment**	2. Strategy Must Enable a **Differentiated Value Proposition**	3. Strategy Needs to be Reflected in a **Distinctive Value Chain**
4. Robust Strategies Involve **Trade-Offs**	5. Strategy Defines How All Elements of a Company **Fit** Together	6. Strategy Involves **Continuity of Direction**

Figure 2.11: Six principles of strategic positioning[41]

Fit prevents imitation in the following way: if an activity is linked to two others and a competitor has a 90 per cent chance to copy an activity, then the likelihood of copying that part of the system is $(0.9)^3$, equalling 72.9 per cent. With more activities entangled by a tight fit, imitation of activities becomes increasingly difficult.[39] Organisations should therefore seek to deepen their strategic positioning (rather than broadening and compromising it) by offering products and services which are aligned with their existing activity system, and which would be too expensive and difficult for competitors to supply on a standalone basis.[40] Porter summarised strategic positioning as consisting of six basic principles, as shown in Figure 2.11.

The first principle states that businesses should pursue **superior long term return on investments**. Only by being profitable can a business survive. The focus should be on economic value creation and sustained profitability of strategies. Economic value is created when customers are willing to pay a higher price for a product or service than what it costs to produce it. The second principle states that it is necessary to provide a **differentiated value** proposition. A set of benefits must be provided that differs from those provided by competitors. Businesses do not need to find the universally best way of competing and neither do they have to be all things to every customer. The business only needs to deliver unique value to a specific customer segment.

The third principle is that businesses need to develop a **distinctive value chain**. Businesses must reflect their distinctiveness by performing differentiated activities, or similar activities in different ways. Best-practices benchmarking erodes distinctiveness and makes it difficult to establish a competitive advantage. Fourthly, a robust strategy requires a business to make **trade-offs** in how it decides to compete. A company cannot be all things to all customers. Trade-offs are required and the business has to explicitly decide which products, services and activities it will perform.

The fifth principle states that a strategy must define how all elements of a company **fit** together in a mutually reinforcing way. Not only does the fit between activities increase competitive advantage, but it also makes a strategy harder to imitate. Activities that are locked in a tight, reinforcing web are much more difficult to imitate than stand-alone activities. Lastly, the sixth principle focuses on **continuity of direction** and consistency of purpose. A business needs to maintain its strategic direction, even if it means foregoing certain opportunities. Without this consistency, businesses will find it difficult to focus, develop skills, develop assets and forge long-term relationships with customers.

Research[42] shows that none of the generic competitive strategies shown in Figure 2.9 is inherently or universally superior to the others. The effectiveness of each strategy is dependent on both opportunities and threats in the external environment of the organisation and the strengths and weaknesses of the organisation based on the available resource portfolio. This implies that it is important to select a generic strategy that fits with the market opportunities and threats as well as the resource strengths and weaknesses of the organisation.

Once a generic strategic position has been chosen, it is essential that other strategic actions are aligned to this competitive choice. Porter[43] is very clear in his guidance for competitive success:

> "Broadly, the prescription is to concentrate on deepening a strategic position rather than broadening and compromising it. One approach is to look for extensions of the strategy that leverage the existing activity system by offering features or services that rivals would find impossible or costly to match on a stand-alone basis. Deepening a position involves making the company's activities more distinctive, strengthening fit, and communicating the strategy better to those customers who should value it. But many companies succumb to the temptation to chase "easy" growth by adding hot features, products, or services without screening them or adapting them to their strategy. Or they target new customers or markets in which the company has little special to offer."

Next we explore guidelines for low-cost strategies, broad differentiation strategies, and best-cost strategies.[44]

Practical guideline for creating low-cost strategies

Use the guidelines in Table 2.4 to develop insights about developing low-cost strategies.

Table 2.4: Guidelines for developing low-cost strategies

Approaches to support low-cost strategies:

• Sell standardised goods or services.
• Invest in process innovations to create lower cost of production and distribution.
• Perform value chain activities more cost-effectively than rivals:
    ○ Capture all available economies of scale.
    ○ Take full advantage of the learning/experience curve.
    ○ Operate facilities at full capacity.
    ○ Leverage sale volume to invest in R&D, advertising and to improve sales and administrative efficiencies.

- o Improve supply chain efficiencies.
- o Use digital technology to improve operating efficiencies.
- o Leverage buying power to gain concessions.
- o Use outsourcing and vertical integration to improve efficiencies.
- o Evaluate specifications for high-cost items and substitute materials and parts.
- o Use labour-saving practices.
- Eliminate or bypass cost-producing activities in overall value chain:
  - o Sell directly to end-users.
  - o Use e-solutions for processes.
  - o Shift low-value activities to suppliers.
  - o Offer frills-free products.

Required resources and capabilities:
- sustained capital investment and access to capital
- process engineering capabilities
- controlled labour practices
- products that are designed for easy manufacturing
- low-cost distribution capacity

General advice:
The target market for low-cost providers is budget-conscious customers.
Low-cost providers must still keep an acceptable level of value for customers to prevent the offerings becoming unattractive to buyers. A product offering that is too frills-free erodes the attractiveness and can turn customers off.
Keep the ratios – a low-cost strategy is sustainably profitable only when prices are cut by less than the cost advantage or the added gains in unit sales are large enough to bring in a bigger total profit despite the lower margins per unit sold.
Seek cost efficiency improvements that are difficult for competitors to imitate (see above importance of trade-offs and fit).

Examples:
Competitive scope broad: Walmart, Shoprite
Competitive scope niche: Southwest Airlines, Kulula

Practical guideline for creating differentiation strategies

Use the guidelines in Table 2.5 to develop insights about developing differentiation strategies.

Table 2.5: Guidelines for developing differentiation strategies

Approaches to support a differentiation strategy:

- Develop a deep and intimate understanding of customers' needs and behaviours.
- Invest in innovations to bring new products and services to markets that benefit both the customer and the sponsoring company.
- Sources of differentiation: a unique taste (Coke); multiple features (Microsoft Office); wide selection and one-stop shopping (Amazon); superior service (Rovos Rail); spare parts availability (Caterpillar guarantee of 48-hour worldwide spare parts availability); engineering design and performance (Mercedes, BMW); prestige and distinction (Rolex); product safety and reliability (Johnson & Johnson's baby products); quality manufacturing (Toyota, Honda); technological leadership (3M); full range of services (universal banks – Standard Bank; Barclays); top-of-the line image and reputation (Starbucks; Ralph Lauren).

- The value-adding features in an offering should be at competitive cost point to ensure customers are willing to pay the price.
- Successful differentiation enables an organisation to:
  - Ask a premium price for its product.
  - Increase unit sales due to additional customers who value differentiating features.
  - Grow loyalty to its brand due to customers' strong attachment to the differentiating features and bond with the offering.
- Use any (or a combination) of the value chain elements (supply chain, R&D, manufacturing, distribution and marketing & sales) as a source for differentiation.

Required resources and capabilities
- strong marketing capabilities
- product engineering capabilities
- creative flair
- strong R&D capacity
- corporate reputation for quality or technological leadership

General advice:

Differentiation yields a longer return and profitability if it is based on product innovation, technical superiority, product quality and reliability, comprehensive customer service, and unique competitive capabilities.

Seek differentiation features that are difficult for competitors to imitate (see above importance of trade-offs and fit).

Make both the actual and perceived value of a differentiating offering visible to customers to prevent a situation where price is the only decision factor.

Examples:

Competitive scope broad: McDonalds, Woolworths

Competitive scope niche: Apple, Moët & Chandon, W L Gore (Gore-Tex)

Practical guideline for creating best-cost strategies

Use the guidelines in Table 2.6 to develop insights about developing best-cost provider strategies.

Table 2.6: Guidelines for developing best-cost provider strategies

Approaches to support a best-cost provider strategy:
- The focus is on capturing a middle ground between pursuing a low-cost and a differentiation advantage and appealing to customers between broad and narrow markets. This represents a hybrid approach.
- It is all about a low-cost provider of an upscale product – increase attractive attributes through appealing features, good-to-excellent product performance or quality or attractive customer service and price offering at a lower level than rivals.
- The organisation should have resources and competences that create the basis for upscale features at a lower cost than competitors.

General advice:

Give customers more value for their money by incorporating in the offering attractive or upscale attributes and features at a lower price than competitors.

The target market for a best-cost provider is value-conscious buyers or value-hunting customers.

Organisations evolve to this strategic position: they seldom start here.

Examples:

Toyota's Lexus, Zara

We use the case study of Zara to illustrate the dynamics involved in a best-cost strategy option.

Case study of Zara's generic strategic choice[45]

ZARA

ZARA's competitive strategic positioning is that of a best-cost provider, as they pioneered "cheap chic".

ZARA is classified within this positioning due to:

- focus on "fast fashion" based on trends that turn over faster than seasonal wear
- unique position in owning the full value chain and therefore the ability to be priced comparatively cheaper than competing quality brands
- ability to design/produce to customers' demands
- ability to appeal to a balance of broad and niche markets, and still create their own differentiation through affordable and trendy apparel, which changes every two to four weeks

Differentiating features are:

- product quality
- fashion design – at affordable pricing
- speed of innovation/fashion trends to shelf

Zara occupies the sweet spot of combining low production cost, good quality, and fashionability while offering the customer value for money. There is a limit on the lines offered but the quick design cycle time makes up for this.

The Zara brand does not compete in the focused differentiation space but does appeal to the shopper who aspires to the nicer thing but still wants value for money at the same time.

The Zara brand's strongest rivals are from broad differentiation brands such as H&M, Nordstrom, and Ralph Lauren and Nordstrom; focused differentiation brands such as Kering, Benetton, Calvin Klein, GIII and Prada; and from the low-cost and niche market sections the Next group is growing in market share and number of stores over Europe to encroach on Zara'a space. The generic competitive choice of Zara is reflected in Figure 2.12.

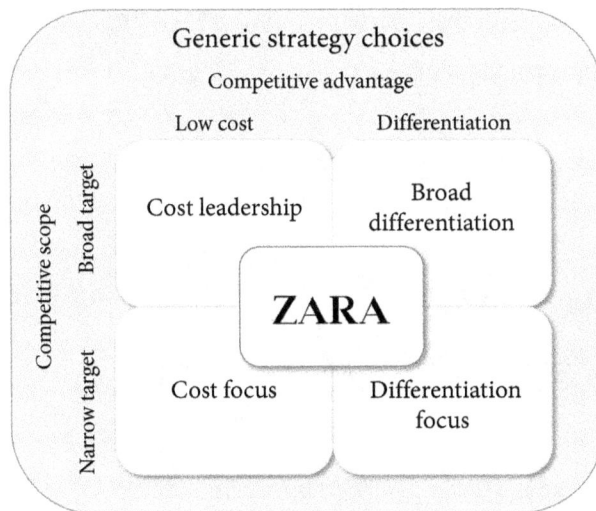

Figure 2.12: Zara's generic competitive choice

To conclude this part on generic strategic positioning choices, the different advantages and challenges associated with each of the generic strategic options are summarised in Figure 2.13.

Porter's generic strategy choices

Competitive advantage: Low cost | Differentiation

Competitive scope	Low cost	Differentiation
Broad target	Cost leadership	Broad differentiation
	Best cost provider strategy	
Narrow target	Cost focus	Differentiation focus

Market scope questions

1. Is the identified customer segment a part of a broad target market or a niche market?
2. How will the business successfully compete against a resource rich incumbent in the market space that it intends to enter?
3. Is the target market large enough to be economically viable?

Core competitive advantage choice questions

4. Does the customer primarily value price or differentiation or both?
5. How will the business ensure that it gets noticed amidst the myriad of competitors?
6. How will the business defend itself against threats from free competitors?

Key start-up question

7. What combination of market scope and core competitive advantage strategies do I have the highest chance of successfully starting up as?

*A business' generic strategy can shift over time

Porter's generic strategy choices fundamental characteristics

	Market scope choice		Core competitive advantage choice		
	Broad market	Niche market	Low cost	Differentiation	Low cost & differentiation
Orientation definition	Target the broad, total market	Target a niche customer segment within the total market	Produce offerings at a lower cost than competitors	Produce differentiated offerings that deliver unique value	Deliver more value for money
Business driver	Generalising	Specialising	Efficiency	Differentiation	Value
Distinguishing advantages	• Serves a large range of customers with similar needs • Targets largest possible market	• Better serve the niche than any other competitor • Low barriers to entry • Lower costs of e-businesses enable lower breakeven points, increasing viability of small market segments	• Can pass cost savings on to customers and under-price competition • Can earn above average profits despite the presence of strong competitive forces	• Higher profit margins • Creates barriers to competitive warfare, as customers have preferences and loyalties to particular sellers • Differentiation aids in drawing customer attention • Can defend against threats from free competitors	• Can earn above-average returns and be very powerful when executed correctly • Online customers value low costs and differentiation
Largest challenges	• Entering a broad market successfully, as every mature industry usually possesses large, powerful incumbents with enormous amounts of resources • Protecting the broad market space, as there are many adjacent competitors	• Carving out a niche where the number of customers are sufficient to economically sustain the business • Not diverging from the niche focus. Pursuing precision to prevent competitive gaps where competitors can "out-focus" the business • Establishing competitor entry barriers	• Creating and sustaining a cost advantage in an industry where economies of scale in production, distribution and other functions are not that substantial • Withstanding destructive price competition • Getting noticed amidst the myriad of other offerings • Combating competitors with free offerings	• Differentiating and sustaining differentiation in a fast paced industry where barriers to entry are low and competitive mimicking is relatively easy • Raising perceived value of offering • Not overspending and over-differentiating	• Successful execution. Simultaneously pursuing efficiency and differentiation is difficult • Escaping the "stuck-in-the-middle" syndrome, where the business isn't excelling at low costs, nor differentiation, and definitely not both

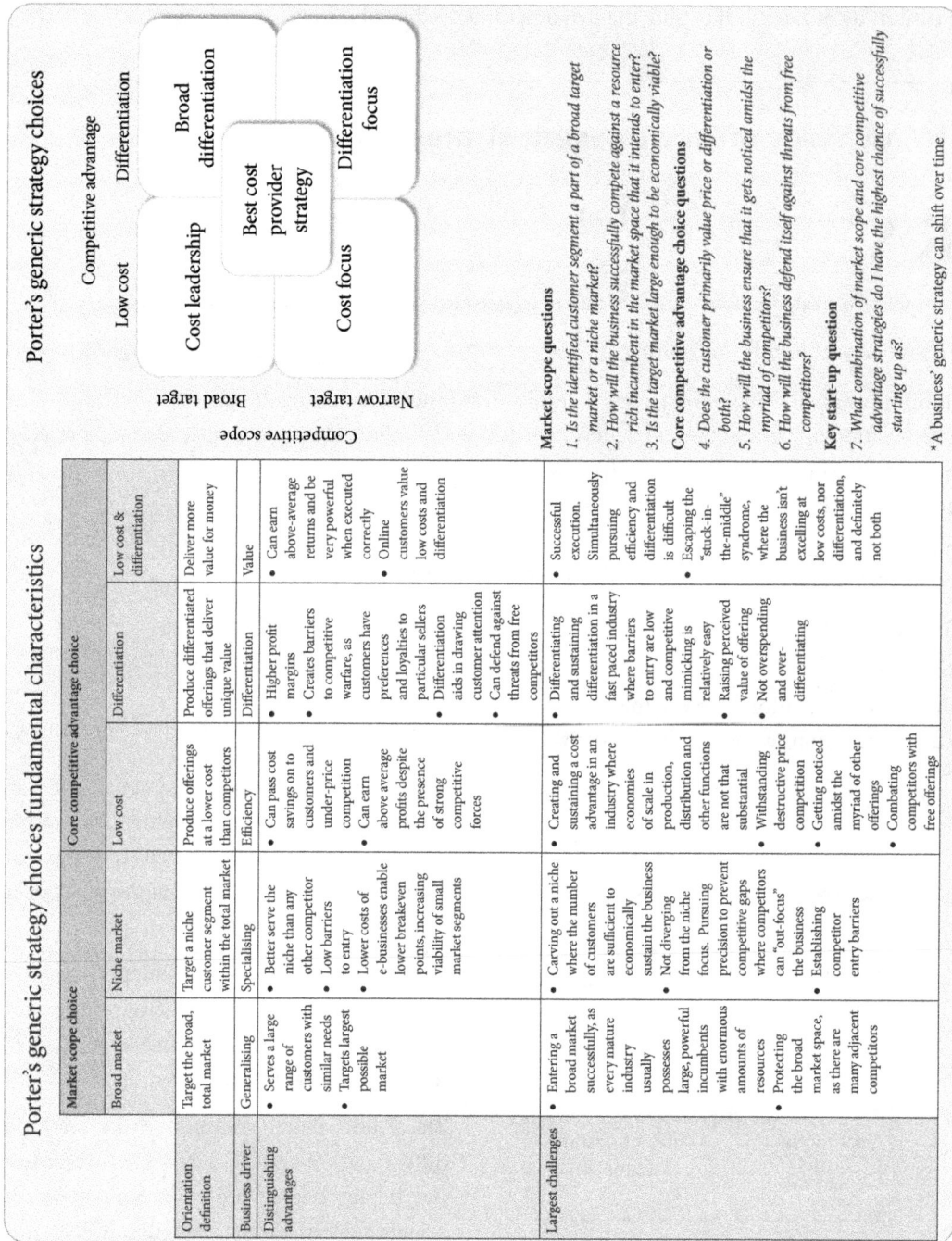

Figure 2.13: Summary of generic competitive positioning options[46]

In an organisation with distinctive different business lines with different product/service offerings aimed at different end-users and markets, it is most likely that these different businesses will have different generic strategic positions and choices. This means that in a diversified conglomerate business, different product lines and brands can have different generic strategic positions. This point is illustrated in the case study of the Shoprite group.

Case study of Shoprite Group

SHOPRITE

The Shoprite Group of Companies, Africa's largest food retailer, operates 1 751 corporate and 360 franchise outlets in 15 countries across Africa and the Indian Ocean Islands.[47] The general strategic positioning statement for the group indicates:

"The Group's primary business is food retailing to consumers of all income levels, and there are outlets from Cape Town to Accra and on some islands of the Indian Ocean. Management's goal is to provide all communities in Africa with food and household items in a first-world shopping environment, at the Group's lowest prices. At the same time the Group, inextricably linked to Africa, contributes to the nurturing of stable economies and the social upliftment of its people."

The different brands of the group each service a target market with a set of products. In Figure 2.14 some of the brands in the group are described, with an interpretation of the associated generic strategic choice.

Brand	Target Market and Competitive Advantage	Generic Strategy
SHOPRITE	Shoprite is the original business of the group and remains the flagship brand, serving the mass middle market. It's the brand with the most stores in RSA as well as the brand used to spearhead growth into Africa. The brand's core focus is to provide the masses with the lowest possible prices on a range of groceries and some durable items. Specific emphasis is placed on basic commodities, which is critical to the core target market. *LSM 4-7*	Cost Leadership
Checkers	Checkers focuses on time-pressed, higher income consumers and differentiates on its speciality ranges of meats, cheeses and wines. Its full range of groceries and household general merchandise are all promised at the consistently good value for which the Group is famous. The stores across South Africa and Namibia are located in shopping malls and other premises conveniently accessible to more affluent residential areas. *LSM 8-10*	Differentiation Focus
CheckersHyper	Checkers Hyper offers the same specialty food selections and great value as Checkers, but within large-format stores that encourage bulk rather than convenience shopping. The general merchandise ranges are far wider in Hyper stores, focusing on categories like small appliances, pet accessories, garden and pool care, outdoor gear, home improvement, homeware, baby products, toys and stationery. Checkers Hyper stores operate in South Africa only and are found in areas with high population densities. *LSM 8-10*	Broad Differentiation
Usave	Usave is a no-frills discounter focussing on lower income consumers. This smaller format, limited range store is an ideal vehicle for the Group's expansion into Africa and allows far greater penetration into underserved areas within South Africa. *LSM: 1-5*	Cost Focus
HUNGRY LION	Hungry Lion operates in seven countries and with its current growth trajectory it is rapidly extending its footprint throughout Southern Arica. Hungry Lion's goal is to provide all communities in Africa with fried chicken in a first-world Quick Service Restaurant (QSR) environment at competitive prices. Hungry Lion aims to be the leading brand in consumers' minds when considering an option for fried chicken. *LSM 4-7*	Best Cost Provider

Figure 2.14: Generic strategic position of selected brands in the Shoprite Group

Application tool

Choose and motivate a generic competitive strategic position for an organisation. Also indicate the implications for operational aspects and business model features.

Treacy and Wiersema's three value disciplines

International management consultants Michael Treacy and Fred Wiersema developed an alternative approach to generic strategy which they call value disciplines.[48] The value-discipline approach is a strategic tool that assists organisations to establish what they want their customers to value them for.

The value disciplines that an organisation can excel in are operational excellence, customer intimacy and product leadership.[49] Each area results in customers valuing the organisation in a different way. The departure point is that an organisation needs to choose one of these value disciplines to develop strategies that would deliver superior customer value and at the same time develop the other two disciplines to meet industry standards.

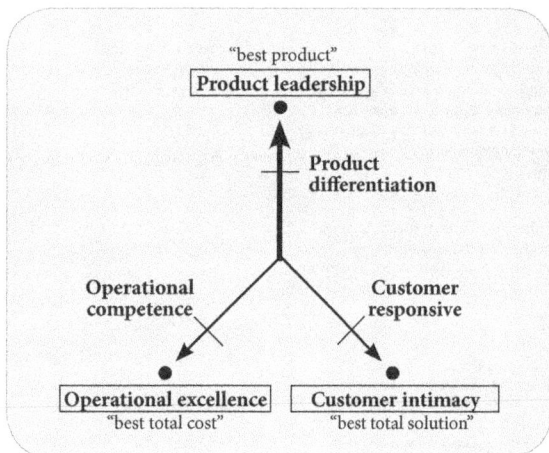

Figure 2.15: Value disciplines

When an organisation specialises in one of these disciplines, it gains competitive advantage. A focus on one of the disciplines assists an organisation to align all operational processes in support of the chosen value discipline and build a clearer understanding of what must be done to attain the desired results in the business model elements (see chapter 3 on Business models). For example, operationally excellent organisations in general have a limited range of products and configurations as this is more cost-effective to build and deliver than a vast range of products and configurations typical of a customer-intimate organisation.[50] The assumption is clear: to succeed in the marketplace, organisations must embrace a specific value discipline as part of their competitive strategy. The three value disciplines are depicted in Figure 2.15.

Operational excellence

Operational excellence represents a specific strategic orientation towards the production and delivery of products and services. An operational excellence strategy aims to accomplish cost leadership. Here the main focus centres on automating manufacturing processes and work procedures in order to streamline operations and reduce cost. The strategy lends itself to high-volume, transaction-oriented and standardised production.

The organisation that follows this strategy aims to lead its industry through price and availability by focusing on a lean and efficient operations capability. The following practices are used to foster operational excellence:[51] minimise cost by reducing overheads; eliminate intermediate production steps; reduce transaction cost; and optimise business processes. Operational excellence is characterised by offering customers competitive (low or lowest price) and hassle-free service with minimum inconvenience. A strategy of operational excellence is ideal for markets where customers value cost and availability over variety, which is often the case for mature, commoditised markets where cost leadership provides a vehicle for continued growth.

Examples of operational excellence-aligned enterprises are: BHP Billiton, Fed Ex and GE's large appliance business.

Customer intimacy

Organisations that excel at making customer intimacy their strategic focus continually shape and fit their products and services to match the needs of a specific target group. Deep customer insights are combined with operational flexibility to offer customers a quick response to a spectrum of needs raging from customised products to meeting special requests to increase customer loyalty.

Customer-intimate organisations focus on the lifetime value of customers and are prepared to invest now to create long-term customer loyalty. The focus here is not on initial cost or profit per transaction, but on creating customer satisfaction that builds loyalty to sustain lifetime relationships with a customer. Organisations with a customer intimacy orientation invest in systems that differentiate quickly and accurately the degree of service customers require and match that with the potential revenue patronage is likely to generate over time. Careful customer segmentation assists organisations to engage and service customers according to their needs, based on their flexible and responsive capacity.

Examples of customer intimacy-aligned enterprises are Virgin Atlantic, Casinos (for high rollers), the hair salon and Amazon.com.

Product leadership

Organisations that pursue the discipline of product leadership aim to deliver a constant flow of state-of-the-art products and services that delight customers. This focus on product leadership requires capabilities in the area of creativity from organisational actors to create these new offerings, to industrialise and commercialise these new ideas quickly and to continually upgrade offerings to stay in front of the competition.

Product leadership organisations invest in R&D and environmental scanning to create new offerings and foster a culture of ongoing innovation. The strength of product leaders is based on their ability to react fast to opportunities when they arise. The big aim here is to maintain the creation of a stream of new products over time to sustain product leadership, momentum and a competitive edge.

The consumer electronics, fund management, automotive and pharmaceutical industries include many companies pursuing a strategy of product leadership. Examples of product leadership-aligned enterprises are Ferrari, Pfizer, Apple and Nike.

Conclusions on the three value disciplines

The value-discipline approach is an alternative way to create a general competitive position for an organisation. It relates in some way to the generic competitive positions of Porter, where operational excellence aligns with a cost leadership strategy, and customer intimacy and product leadership support a differentiation focus strategy choice.

Application tool

Use the descriptions of the three value disciplines to choose ONE as the cornerstone for an organisation's generic competitive positioning choice. Motivate why the chosen value discipline is appropriate and how it will impact operational aspects and business model features.

Digital and physical orientation options

The next strategic choice on level 2 (see Figure 2.8) is between the different digital and physical orientations available. An organisation's digital-physical orientation refers to its relative position on the digital-physical continuum.[52] This choice is usually implicitly made based on the products that a business sells, the way that it decides to do business, or the way that it makes its offering available to customers. An explicit and conscious consideration of the different options is useful however, as the different orientations fundamentally impact the business and present different challenges and benefits.

The four broad options are shown on the digital-physical continuum in Figure 2.16:

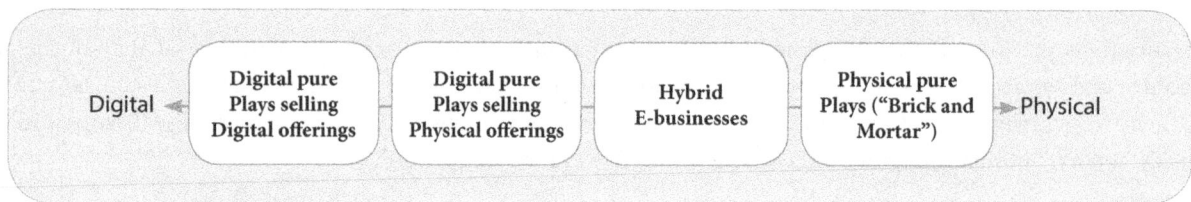

Digital ← | **Digital pure Plays selling Digital offerings** | **Digital pure Plays selling Physical offerings** | **Hybrid E-businesses** | **Physical pure Plays ("Brick and Mortar")** | → Physical

Figure 2.16: Digital-physical continuum[53]

Digital pure plays selling digital offerings largely or exclusively compete online and provide digital products or services to customers. These businesses are **entirely** digital. Examples are Facebook, YouTube, Dropbox, PayPal, WhatsApp, LinkedIn and Spotify.

Digital pure plays selling physical offerings also compete largely or exclusively online, but provide physical products or services to customers. The interactions of these businesses are strictly digital however. Digital pure plays sell physical offerings, but do not take ownership of physical products or services and do not engage in physical order fulfilment themselves. These businesses act as intermediaries that connect buyers and sellers. They generate sales through their website (for which they get commission, for instance) and make use of partnerships and extensive outsourcing to deliver the physical offerings to customers (or a similar business model). Examples of such businesses are eBay, Alibaba, Gumtree, OLX, AirBnB, Uber, Groupon and Kickstarter.

Hybrid e-businesses compete online, but partake in physical activities and order fulfilment in addition to their digital activities. Typical hybrid businesses are e-retailers such as Amazon, Takealot, Rubybox, Geekfuel and Zappos. These businesses make use of the Internet as a customer interface and sell physical products (that they own) through their website. Hybrids do not have physical stores, but require warehouses, inventory, order fulfilment systems and so forth to do business.

Lastly, **physical pure plays** are "brick-and-mortar" businesses that sell physical products and services. These businesses have physical stores and make use of traditional physical supply chains. Examples are Woolworths, Checkers, Exclusive Books and McDonald.

Yet the line that distinguishes hybrid e-businesses from physical pure plays is becoming increasingly blurred. Typical hybrid e-businesses only possess an online customer interface. The newer tech-enabled brick-and-mortar businesses, on the other hand, are providing customers a multi-channel choice of either a physical shopping experience (through their physical outlets) or a digital shopping experience (through their e-commerce websites). By their very nature, these businesses remain brick-and-mortar businesses however, as they would still be able to function via their physical channels even if the Internet did not to exist. Important in this discussion is the realisation that these orientations exist along a relative digital–physical continuum. What this continuum implies is that though a broad definition for each orientation exists, the boundaries separating them are somewhat malleable. Stated differently, businesses of the same basic digital–physical classification can be more digital or more physical relative to one another.[54]

The power of a business's digital–physical orientation lies not in the classification, but in the purposeful consideration and explicit choice of the type of offering that will be delivered to customers and how these offerings will be made available. Considering the business from this perspective could entirely reframe the business and highlight new possibilities for how the business could function. Some of the characteristics that distinguish between the orientations are outlined in Table 2.7.

Important questions to consider when choosing an orientation are:

- Which type of offering do our customers require?
- Which of these orientations is the most efficient at delivering offerings that our customers require?
- Which of these orientations will give our business the most traction?
- Given our available resources, skills and partner network, which of these orientations do we have the highest chance of successfully executing?

Finally, a business's digital–physical orientation is not necessarily a fixed choice and it is possible that a business's orientation may shift in order to meet customer demands over time.

Table 2.7: Digital–physical orientation choices fundamental characteristics[55]

	Digital pure play selling digital offerings	Digital pure play selling physical offerings	Hybrid e-business	Physical pure play
Orientation definition	Sells digital products online, usually by employing an e-commerce interface.	Sells physical products online, but interactions remain digital. Digital pure plays selling physical products do not take ownership of products and do not partake in physical order fulfilment.	Sells physical products online and partakes in physical order fulfilment.	Sells physical products offline via brick-and-mortar stores.
Ease of business development	Typically less difficult. Website development and programming can prove challenging, but automated services reduce operating complexity.	Typically less difficult. Website development and programming can prove challenging, but business difficulty is reduced by outsourcing physical functions.	Typically more difficult. Hybrids need to manage large, integrated physical value chains and these physical value-chain elements add complexity to the business.	Product, scale and formality-dependent. Informal trading on sidewalks is very easy. Building and managing an expansive network of physical stores is more difficult.
Cost of business development	Typically less expensive. Costs contingent on: • complexity of e-business website/platform developed • inherent programming capabilities of start-up team • web development tools and partnership opportunities available	Typically less expensive.[56] Unlike hybrids, physical pure plays do not require inventory, warehouses, physical order fulfilment systems or labourers.	Typically more expensive. • Hybrids require inventory, warehouses, physical order fulfilment systems and labourers. • This translates into requiring higher start-up capital and leads to higher operating costs than pure plays of similar scale.[57] • "Lean" (inexpensive) hybrids can be created; however they sacrifice many benefits (e.g. customer service) that customers may actually require.	Typically more expensive. • Physical pure plays require physical outlets, warehouses, inventory, physical order fulfilment systems and labourers. • This translates into requiring higher start-up capital and leads to higher operating costs than pure plays of similar scale.[58]

	Digital pure play selling digital offerings	Digital pure play selling physical offerings	Hybrid e-business	Physical pure play
Distinguishing advantages	<ul><li>Can capitalise on any and all of the benefits that the online medium provides:<ul><li>Can provide digital content instantly.[59]</li><li>Can allow users to experience and test trial versions before purchasing the full offering.[60]</li><li>Inherently global</li><li>Can reproduce and distribute digital products at a near zero cost. [61] [62] [63]</li></ul></li><li>Opportunity for:[64]<ul><li>Information as a source of value;</li><li>Mass customisation;</li><li>Economic principle of abundance.</li></ul></li></ul>	<ul><li>A cheaper version of hybrid e-businesses, however a lot of advantages are foregone by not taking ownership of products.[65]</li><li>Reach as widespread as partnership network.</li></ul>	<ul><li>Can provide a combination of online and offline products and services.[66] This enhances choice and convenience and can possibly provide a better overall experience.</li><li>Taking control of order fulfilment grants the opportunity to better control and affect customer interactions. In comparison to physical pure plays, hybrids can provide:[67]<ul><li>more enticing physical product presentations;</li><li>more reliable and standardised information about product characteristics and availability;</li><li>quicker and more reliable delivery;</li><li>a more favourable return policy.</li></ul></li><li>These latter three reduce uncertainty and instil greater trust.</li><li>Hybrids can also better capitalise on:<ul><li>economies of scale (through bulk purchases);</li><li>synergy effects (through bundling); and</li><li>pricing flexibility.[68]</li></ul></li></ul>	<ul><li>Physical stores:<ul><li>Provide convenience to shoppers who enjoy a physical shopping experience.</li><li>Are excellent sales channels.</li><li>Provide products instantaneously without having to wait for delivery.</li><li>Provide the opportunity for better customer service.</li></ul></li><li>Tech-enabled physical pure plays can provide a combination of online and offline products and services.[69] This enhances choice and convenience and can possibly provide a better overall experience.</li></ul>

	Digital pure play selling digital offerings	Digital pure play selling physical offerings	Hybrid e-business	Physical pure play
Typically suited to	Innovative entrepreneurs with good programming skills and deep IT knowledge.	Entrepreneurs with good programming skills and sales experience.[70]	• Incumbent retailers with a strong brand, installed customer base, established infrastructure, experience and scale in logistics.[71] • Entrepreneurs with experience in retail and logistics.	• Incumbent retailers with a strong brand, installed customer base, established infrastructure, experience and scale in logistics.[72] • Entrepreneurs with experience in retail and logistics.

Largest challenges	• Creating innovative offerings that customers will pay for.[73] [74]
	• Staying ahead of competitors in the innovation game.
	• Combating piracy. [75]
		• Building strong partnership networks and negotiating with partners.
		• Reducing buyer apprehensiveness.[76]
			• Reducing and off-loading logistical costs. Customers are not willing to pay significantly more for an online offering than an offline one,[77] and odd product geometries are difficult to assemble, pack and ship, which incurs extra costs.[78]
			• Increasing "basket" value.[79]
			• Reducing buyer apprehensiveness.[80]
				• Staying relevant in an increasingly digital world.
				  o Customers increasingly demand online sales channels and delivery, forcing offline retailers into new areas of business. This requires additional capital expenditure.
				  o Competing against digital products and services that are simply cheaper or superior online.

	Digital pure play selling digital offerings	Digital pure play selling physical offerings	Hybrid e-business	Physical pure play

Core strategies	• Seek trade-offs between the Internet and traditional approaches, where only an Internet model offers real advantages.[81] This occurs when:
	  o Customer's needs are best met online;
	  o Product or service can be best delivered through an online channel and does not require physical assets.
		• Resellers
		  o Focus on particular product categories, enabling the provision of expertise and enhanced choice to customers. Also target popular or unique brands that are in high demand.
		  o Build strong partnership networks.
		  o Cultivate secondary revenue streams.[82]
		• Other intermediaries:
		  o Identify niches in which to be a category killer.
		  o Devise ways to collaborate, co-create and capitalise on the sharing economy in the physical world.
			• Build huge scale to sufficiently "dissipate" high operating costs.[83] [84] Building a large physical value chain is enormously expensive, however.
			• Focus on niche product categories, hard-to-bring-home products and expensive products as these reduce customers' sensitivity to fulfilment costs, have higher profit margins and lower customer acquisition costs[85] as customers typically seek out these companies instead of vice versa. The paradox, however, is that it is these high basket-value items that customers are especially apprehensive of buying online.[86]
			• Eliminate physical activities to improve profit margins.[87]
				• Seek trade-offs between physical and Internet approaches, where only the physical model offers real advantages. This occurs when:
				  o The nature of the offering is inherently physical (primary sector).
				  o Customer's needs are best met via an offline, physical experience (playing Paintball vs playing Counterstrike; seeing a band live vs watching a YouTube video).
				  o Product or service can be best delivered through an offline channel.

Industry-based strategic style choices

Organisations are classified into different industries based on the nature and type of activity the business engages in to produce value for customers. Industries differ from each other on numerous dimensions, e.g. the oil industry and the Internet and software industry pose vastly different challenges and opportunities. These divergent patterns lead to the argument that organisations that operate in such dissimilar competitive environments should be planning, developing, and deploying their strategies in markedly different ways.[88]

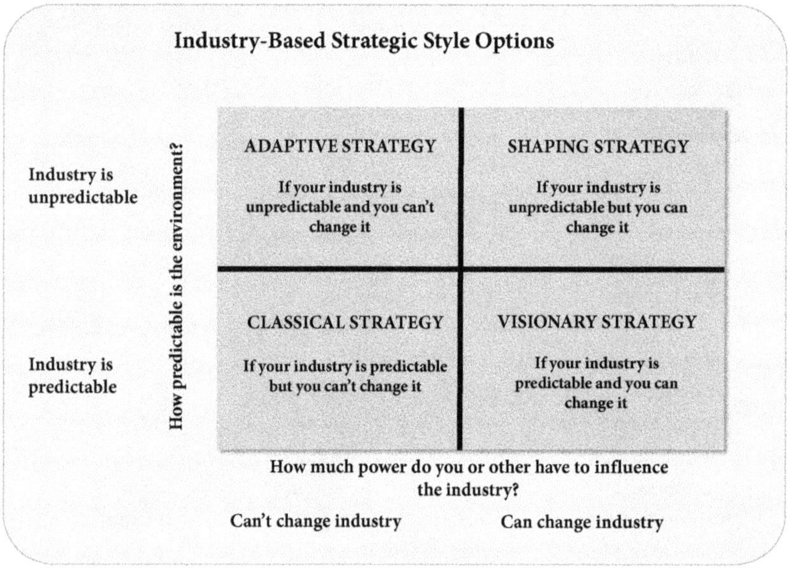

Figure 2.17: Industry-based strategic style options[91]

Reeves, Love and Tillmans[89] developed a framework that divides strategy-making into four styles according to how predictable your environment is and how much power you have to change it. "Using this framework, corporate leaders can match their strategic style to the particular conditions of their industry, business function, or geographic market".[90] The choice of the strategic style an organisation adopts starts with the assessment of the industry it operates in. In assessing an industry two primary factors can be used: **predictability** (how far into the future and how accurately can you confidently forecast demand, corporate performance, competitive dynamics, and market expectations?) and **malleability** (to what extent can you or your competitors influence those factors?). The different strategic styles based on this classification are: classical, adaptive, shaping, and visionary – see Figure 2.17.

A **classical strategy style** is appropriate when an organisation operates in an industry that is predictable but it is difficult to change the industry. Classical strategies are associated with mature industries such as the oil industry. In the classical strategy approach strategy analysts and planners invest time and effort to develop detailed perspectives on the long-term economic factors relating to demand and the technological factors relating to supply. These analyses inform future possibilities in upstream and downstream value chain activities with a 5–10-year planning horizon. This information is used in multi-year financial forecasts, which informs annual targets that are focused on improving efficiencies required to sustain the organisation's market position and performance. When extraordinary events like a war, natural disasters or external shocks occur, strategic plans are revised given a changing operating context. A classical strategic approach works for organisations in an industry where the most attractive positions and the most rewarded capabilities today will, in all likelihood, remain the same tomorrow.

An **adaptive strategy style** is required when an industry is exposed to constant changes and persistent unpredictability in the environment due to global competition, technological innovation, social feedback loops, and economic uncertainty. An adaptive strategy style entails a constant refinement of goals and tactics by shifting, acquiring or divesting resources fast on an ongoing basis. Planning cycles are shorter and may shrink to less than a year or even become continual. Plans are not detailed blueprints but contain rough hypotheses based on the best available data. Continuous feedback is important to validate assumptions. An example of this type of industry is specialty fashion retail, such as Zara who use their flexible supply approach to adapt to new fashion trends and customer taste demands. They focus continuously on changes in the fashion industry to frequently produce, roll out, and test a variety of products as quickly as they can, constantly adapting production in the light of new learning.

A **shaping strategy style** is aligned with industries where the barriers to entry are low, innovation rates are high, demand is very hard to predict, and the relative positions of competitors are in flux. A mature industry that's similarly fragmented and not dominated by a few powerful incumbents, or is stagnant and ripe for disruption, is also likely to be similarly malleable.[92] The focus here is to shape the unpredictable environment to your organisation's own advantage before someone else benefits. Like an adaptive strategy, a shaping strategy embraces short or continual planning cycles.

A **visionary strategy style** is the arena of entrepreneurs and innovators who see a future landscape and mobilise decisive actions to realise the associated opportunities. A visionary strategist considers the environment not as a given but as something that can be moulded to create a competitive advantage. Visionary strategists must have the courage to stay on track towards a vision and need to ensure that the required resources are mobilised. United Parcel Service (UPS) grasped the opportunity early to become the "the enablers of global e-commerce."[93]

Note: In their 2015 book,[94] Reeves and his colleagues from BCG added a fifth strategic style to the strategy palette which they called a **renewal strategy** approach. It is an underlying option to all four styles as described above. A renewal strategy option is appropriate in organisation turnarounds to restore the financial sustainability of a business. A summary of the five strategy styles is shown in Table 2.8.

Table 2.8: Summary of industry-based strategy styles and approaches

Key elements	Classical	Adaptive	Visionary	Shaping	Renewal
Core idea	Be big	Be fast	Be first	Be the orchestrator	Be viable
Indicators of this approach	• Low growth • High concentration • Mature industry • Stable regulation	• Volatile growth • Limited concentration • Young industry • High technological changes	• High growth potential • White spaces, no direct competition • Limited regulation	• Fragmentation • No dominant player platform • Shapeable regulation	• Low growth, decline, crisis • Restricted financing • Negative cash flows
How	Analyse, plan, execute	Vary, select, upscale	Envisage, build, and persist	Engage, orchestrate, evolve	React, economise, grow
Measure of success	• Scale • Market share	• Cycle time • New product vitality index	• First to market • New user customer satisfaction	• Ecosystem growth and profitability	• Cost savings • Cash flow
Key traps	Overapplication	Planning the un-plannable	Wrong vision	Overmanaged ecosystem	No second phase

Application tool

Use the examples and summary of industry-based strategic styles reflected in Figure 2.18 and Table 2.8 to choose and motivate an appropriate strategy option for an organisation. Also indicate the implications for operational aspects and business model features.

Examples of industry-based strategic style options

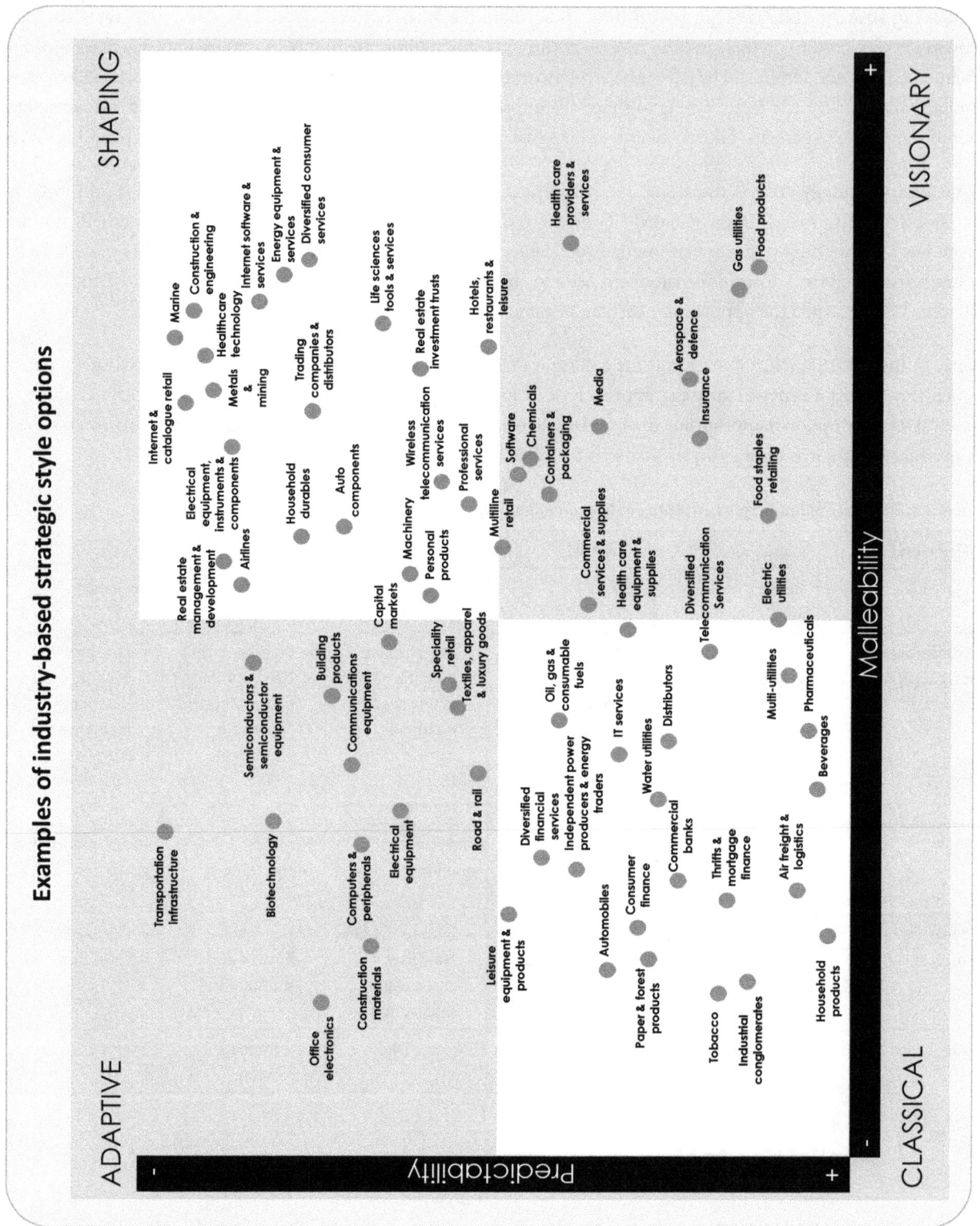

Figure 2.18: Examples of industry-based strategic style options[95]

Strategic posture options

The SPACE (Strategic Position and Action Evaluation) matrix is an approach to determine the appropriate strategic posture for an organisation.[96] The strategic posture options of an organisation are determined by the combination of two internal and two external dimensions. The internal dimensions are financial strength (FS) and competitive advantage (CA) and the external dimensions are environmental stability (ES) and industry strength/attractiveness (IS). By combining ratings on each dimension on one SPACE matrix diagram, the results guide the future strategic agenda of an organisation by indicating four strategic posture options: aggressive, competitive, conservative or defensive. These strategic posture options guide the further strategic thrust of an organisation.

The **aggressive posture** is typical of an attractive industry with stable economic conditions. Financial strength enables an organisation with this strategic posture to maintain its competitive position. An organisation in this position takes full advantage of industry growth, merger and acquisition opportunities and allocates the required resources to reap potential benefits.[97]

A **competitive posture** is associated with an attractive industry in a relatively unstable environment. This position is associated with a competitive advantage for an organisation which enables an increase in investments in marketing and sales as well as an extension of product lines. Productivity improvements and cost-cutting could also be on the agenda of organisations with this posture to improve the financial health of the organisation.[98]

A **conservative posture** is distinctive of a low-growth but stable market. Product competitiveness is the key factor to sustain financial stability. Strategic responses for organisations with this strategic posture option are product line rationalisation or new product expansions, cost-efficiency improvements, cash flow improvements or seeking more attractive markets to enter.[99]

A **defensive posture** is based on an unattractive industry where competitiveness is the critical factor. An organisation in this position usually lacks a competitive product and financial strength. Organisations in this posture could consider discontinuing marginal product lines, cost-cutting initiatives, divestments and retreat from the market.[100] A summary of the four strategic posture options for an organisation is reflected in Table 2.9.

Table 2.9: Characteristics of different strategic postures[101]

Dimensions	Aggressive	Competitive	Conservative	Defensive
Environment Industry Competitiveness Financial strength	Stable Attractive Strong High	Unstable Attractive Strong Weak	Stable Unattractive Weak High	Unstable Unattractive Weak Weak
Potential strategic responses	• Growth, including M&As • Capitalise on opportunities • Innovate to sustain competitive advantage	• Cost reduction, productivity improvement, raising more capital to use opportunities and strengthen competitiveness • Possibly merge with a less competitive rival with cash	• Cost reduction, product/service rationalisation • Invest in new search for new products, services and competitive opportunities	• Rationalisation • Divestment as appropriate

The main position on the SPACE matrix for the four strategic posture options is reflected in Figure 2.19.

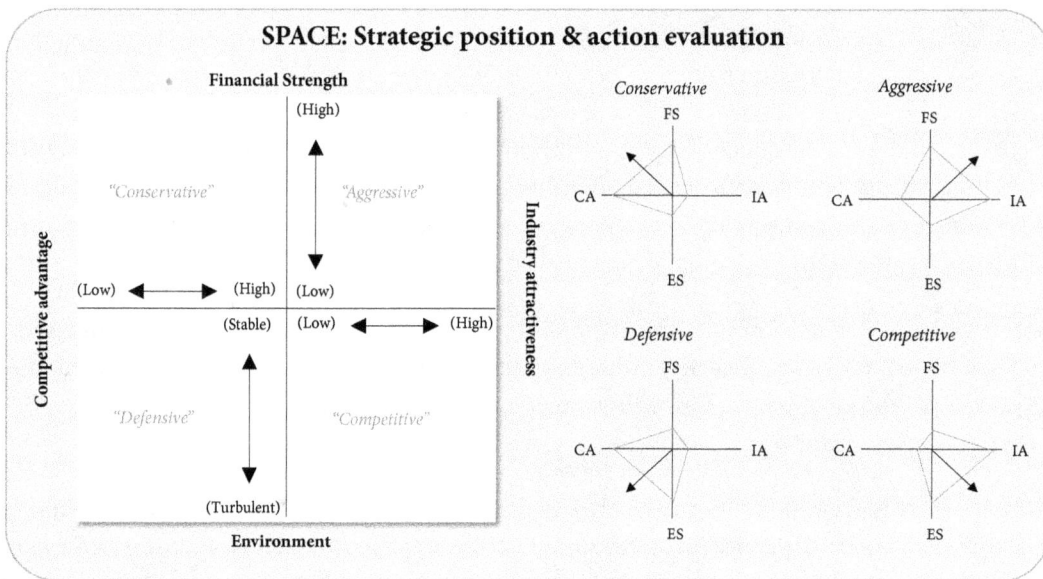

Figure 2.19: Strategic posture positions in the SPACE matrix[102]

Practical guideline

Step 1: For an organisation that you have done a strategy analysis on and that you know well, evaluate the strength of each dimension using the questions and scale in Table 2.10.

Table 2.10: Dimensions and key factors in SPACE matrix

Factors determining Competitive Advantage (CA)			
Market share	Small	-6 -5 -4 -3 -2 -1	Large
Product quality	Inferior	-6 -5 -4 -3 -2 -1	Superior
Brand and image	Low	-6 -5 -4 -3 -2 -1	High
Control over suppliers and distributors	Low	-6 -5 -4 -3 -2 -1	High
Factors determining Industry Strength/Attractiveness (IS)			
Barriers to entry	Easy	1 2 3 4 5 6	Difficult
Technological know-how	Simple	1 2 3 4 5 6	Complex
Capital intensity	High	1 2 3 4 5 6	Low
Profit potential	Low	1 2 3 4 5 6	High
Factors determining Financial Strength (FS)			
Leverage	Imbalance	1 2 3 4 5 6	Balanced
Liquidity	Imbalance	1 2 3 4 5 6	Balanced
Cash flow	Low	1 2 3 4 5 6	High
Return on assets	Low	1 2 3 4 5 6	High

Factors determining Environmental Stability (ES)			
demand variability	large	-6 -5 -4 -3 -2 -1	small
barriers to entry into market	few	-6 -5 -4 -3 -2 -1	many
price elasticity of demand	elastic	-6 -5 -4 -3 -2 -1	inelastic
price range of competing products	wide	-6 -5 -4 -3 -2 -1	narrow
Note: For simplicity only four factors per dimension are used.[103]			

Step 2: Determine the average score per factor. Table 2.11 gives an example of the application of this step in a case study organisation.

Table 2.11: Case study average score per dimension

Average score per dimension			
Competitive advantage			
market share	small	-6 -5 -4 -3 -2 **-1**	large
product quality	inferior	-6 -5 -4 -3 **-2** -1	superior
brand & image	low	-6 -5 -4 -3 **-2** -1	high
control over suppliers & distributors	low	-6 -5 -4 -3 **-2** -1	high
Average		**-1.75**	
Industry strength			
barriers to entry	easy	1 2 3 4 **5** 6	difficult
technological know-how	simple	1 **2** 3 4 5 6	complex
capital intensity	high	1 2 3 4 **5** 6	low
profit potential	low	1 2 3 **4** 5 6	high
Average		**4.00**	
Financial strength			
leverage	imbalance	1 2 3 4 **5** 6	balanced
liquidity	imbalance	1 2 3 **4** 5 6	balanced
cash flow	low	1 2 3 **4** 5 6	high
return on assets	low	1 2 3 **4** 5 6	high
Average		**4.25**	
Environmental stability			
demand variability	large	-6 -5 -4 -3 **-2** -1	small
barriers to entry into market	few	-6 -5 -4 -3 **-2** -1	many
price elasticity of demand	elastic	-6 **-5** -4 -3 -2 -1	inelastic
price range of competing products	wide	-6 -5 -4 -3 **-2** -1	narrow
Average		**-2.75**	

Step 3: Plot the values from step 2 for each dimension on the SPACE matrix on the appropriate axis and add the average score for competitive advantage (CA) and internal strength (IS) dimensions. This will be your final point on the X axis on the SPACE matrix. Also add the average scores for financial strength (FS) and environmental stability (ES) to find your final point for the Y axis. Find the intersection points for your X and Y axis points. Draw a line from the centre of the SPACE matrix to your point. This line reveals the type of strategic posture the organisation should consider with the associated strategic agenda items.

See the case study example in Table 2.12 for the application of the above steps.

Table 2.12: Case study values for X and Y axis

Values for X and Y axis				
	Internal strategic position		**External strategic position**	
	Competitive advantage		Industry strength	
X Axis	market share	-1.00	barriers to entry	5.00
	product quality	-2.00	technological know-how	5.00
	brand & image	-2.00	capital intensity	2.00
	control over suppliers & distributors	-2.00	profit potential	4.00
	average	-1.75	average	4.00
A	**Total axis X score 2.25**			
	Financial strength		Environmental stability	
Y Axis	leverage	4.00	demand variability	-2.00
	liquidity	4.00	barriers to entry into market	-2.00
	cash flow	5.00	price elasticity of demand	-5.00
	return on assets	4.00	price range of competing products	-2.00
	average	4.25	average	-2.75
	Total axis Y score 1.50			

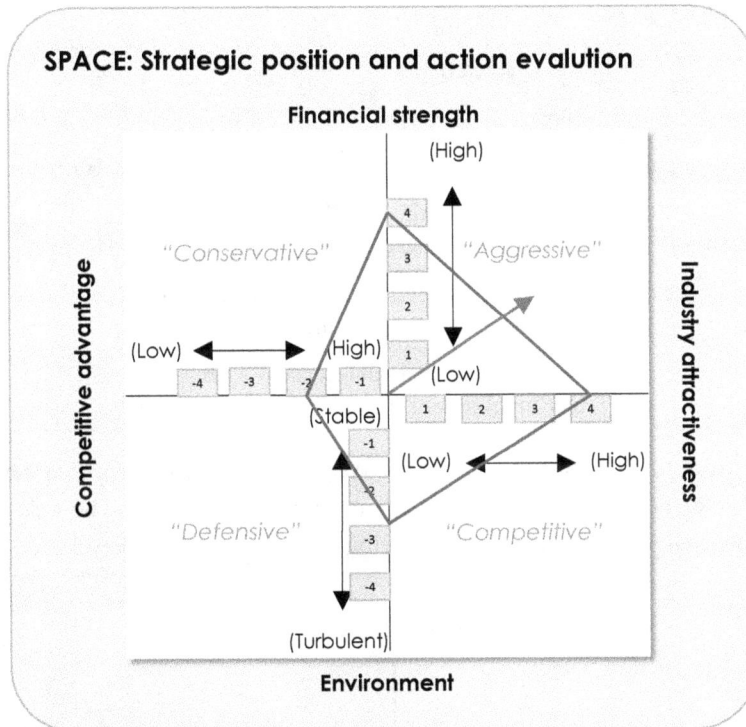

Figure 2.20: Case study strategic posture position on SPACE matrix

The SPACE matrix is a useful framework to add content to the second-level generic strategic choices of an organisation (see Figure 2.8). By evaluating an organisation's position on the SPACE matrix, possible future strategic imperatives can be established.

Foreign market entry options

The last generic strategic option combination we explore is foreign market entry alternatives. This is part of the international strategy agenda options of an organisation. In this part we discuss the following market entry modes to assist the footprint expansion strategy: exporting; licensing and contract manufacturing; franchising; joint ventures and strategic alliances; acquisitions; foreign branches; and wholly owned subsidiary/greenfields ventures.

To grow organisations continuously to increase the potential for more financial success is an ongoing challenge for business leaders. There is always a time in the development of an organisation when current local markets become saturated and the need to expand the organisation beyond the local geographical boundaries of the entity becomes a reality. Apart from choosing potential new growth markets through fact-based and data-driven information reviews, there are various options in the key questions about how this market entry should be thought about and what form it should take. The characteristics associated with these different entry modes are shown in Table 2.13.

Table 2.13: Modes of entry into foreign market and associated features[104]

Entry mode	Key characteristics
Exporting	High cost, low control
Licensing, contract manufacturing and franchising	Low cost, low risk, limited control, relatively low returns
Strategic alliances/Joint ventures	Shared cost, shared resources, shared risks, challenge of alignment of interest
Acquisitions	Relatively fast access to market, high cost, complex negotiations, challenge to merge local operations
New wholly owned subsidiary/Greenfields	Complex, high cost, time-consuming, high risk, maximum control, potential for positive returns

Prof. Jean-Louis Schaan from the Ivey Business School at Western University in Canada developed a typology for new market entrance based on how easy or difficult it is to enter a foreign market and how close or distant the culture in the host country is from that of the country of the entering organisation. This view is reflected in Figure 2.21.

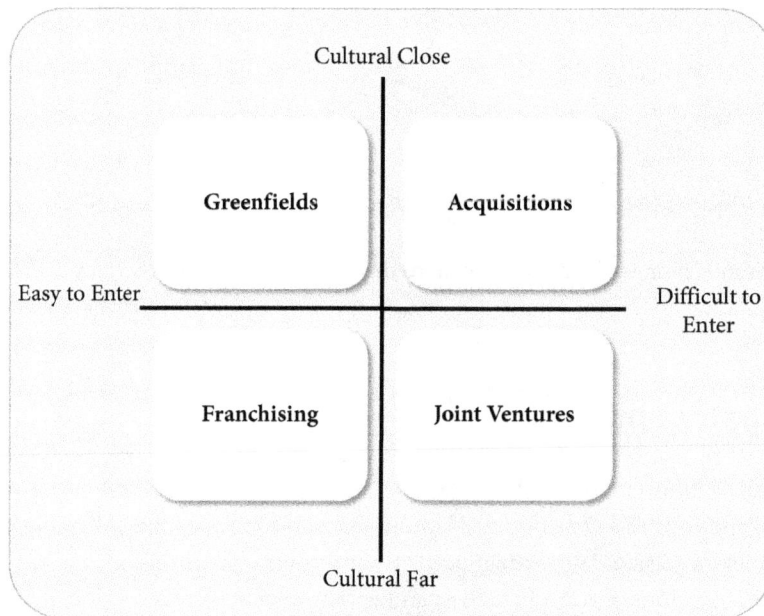

Figure 2.21: Options for foreign market entry[105]

Exporting refers to the international trade of goods and services that are shipped from an exporting company in one country to an importing company in another country.[106] The essence of this approach is to maintain a national in-country production base and to export goods to foreign markets using either company-owned or foreign-controlled forward distribution channels. The strategic sweet spot in exporting is to find markets that accept your product standards. This allows exporting of standard products into a new foreign market. Apart from marketing and distribution investments, exporting does not require additional capital and the organisation maintains control over quality. The disadvantages of exporting relate to lower control over the marketing and distribution of products in the host country and the challenges in providing customised products for each international market. Governments also make available export incentive schemes to local organisations to boost foreign currency inflows. Interesting to note is that research indicates that cost leadership strategies enhance the performance of exports from developed countries and that differentiated strategies are more successful in emerging economies.[107] Exporters usually first target markets close to their home country to learn how the process works and to prevent logistical cost being too high.

Licensing and contract manufacturing represent a formal contractual arrangement between parties where a foreign company purchases the right to manufacture and sell the local firm's products within a host country or a set of countries. **Licensing** involves the transfer of some industrial property rights from the licensor to a licensee in exchange for royalties or other income arrangements. The investment in new manufacturing and distribution capacity in foreign territories is made by the licensee. This makes licensing a very low-cost international strategy option. The risk in licensing is the ability of the licensor to gain learning experience benefits to become a competitor after the contract expires, as well as the loss of control over production, marketing and distribution of the product. Many software and pharmaceutical companies use licensing strategies. **Franchising** represents a special form of licensing. In this case the licensee allows the franchisee through a contractual arrangement to use the brand, products, operating practices and marketing strategies in a defined (foreign) market. In exchange the franchisee pays fees to the parent company based on sales volume. The franchise is operated by local investors who must comply with the franchisor polices. A franchise option is relevant when the host country is culturally far from the country of the franchisor and it is relatively easy to enter the market. McDonald's is leading the world growth through franchising.

Strategic alliances and joint ventures are formal collaborative arrangements between two or more entities with the intent to achieve mutually beneficial outcomes. These benefits can be to share risks, resources and the creation of new core competences in a host country (see chapter 7 for more detail on inorganic growth strategies). The mutual agreement on pooling of resources can include capital, production, marketing and management expertise, patents and trademarks. Trust between the partners is critical for venture success and the management of expectations needs ongoing attention. Research indicates that trust is also influenced by the different country cultures of the alliances and venture partners.[108] Incompatibility and conflict between partners are the major reasons why alliances and joint ventures fail. A joint venture is an appropriate option when the market is difficult to enter and the culture of the foreign target country is far from the entering organisations' local country culture. Research also indicates that when country risks are high, firms prefer to enter with joint ventures to manage the risks.[109]

Acquisitions refer here to buying a company in a foreign country. Cross-border acquisitions are a strategic option due to free trade that drives the continued expansion of global markets. Acquisitions are a quick way to get access to new markets. Acquisitions of assets in foreign countries can be expensive and the negotiations can be complex and time-consuming. Governing within the legal and regulatory requirements of the host country and post-acquisition culture and operating practices alignment is part of the challenge[110] (also see chapter 7 for more on M&As). Acquisitions are an option when the two country cultures are close and it is difficult to enter the market.

A **Greenfields** venture involves the creation of a new wholly owned subsidiary, and in the context of foreign market entry options, in a foreign country. The process of creating such a venture is often complex, risky and potentially costly. However, it has benefits like full control of operations and potential for above-average returns. Wholly owned subsidiaries are relevant especially when proprietary technology is involved or when specialised knowledge and customisation are required.[111] Greenfield ventures assist firms to maintain control over their proprietary systems. Greenfield ventures are appropriate when it is relatively easy to enter a foreign market and the culture is close to that of the home country.

Apart from choosing the appropriate foreign market entry option, the choice of which country to enter is a major strategic decision. Guidelines on how to make this decision include many variables. As a first-cut view, the approach of Justin Letschert, CEO of Bio-Oil – a product of Union-Swiss (Pty) Ltd in Cape Town – to identifying top potential foreign target market countries is reflected in Figures 2.22 and 2.23. Please note the figures present 2008 as a baseline. Bio-Oil is a South African product in the specialist skincare oil category. Bio-Oil has won 253 skincare awards and has become the No.1 selling scar and stretch mark product in 20 countries since its global launch in 2002.[112]

Internationalisation: Taking a local brand to the global arena

Bio-Oil Which Country to target?

GDP – Top 10	Population – Top 10	GDP/Capita – Top 10	South Africa	
1. USA	1. China	1. Qatar		
2. China	2. India	2. Luxemborg		
3. Japan	3. USA	3. Malta	GDP / Capita	81st
4. India	4. Indonesia	4. Norway		
5. Germany	5. Brazil	5. Brunei	Population	28th
6. UK	6. Pakistan	6. Singapore		
7. Russia	7. Bangladesh	7. Cyprus	Score	109
8. France	8. Russia	8. USA		
9. Brazil	9. Nigeria	9. Ireland		
10. Italy	10. Japan	10. Hong Kong		

Figure 2.22: Potential target countries based on GDP per capita[113]

Source: Justin Letschert, 2008. *Taking a local brand to the global arena: Lessons from an SA entrepreneur.* USB Leader's Angle, 27 June.

Internationalisation: Taking a local brand to the global arena

Bio-Oil *Highest combined GDP/capita and population score*

Top 20 – Scoring

1. USA	11. Netherlands
2. Japan	12. Australia
3. Germany	13. Mexico
4. UK	14. Turkey
5. France	15. Taiwan
6. Italy	16. Saudi Arabia
7. Canada	17. Brazil
8. Spain	18. Poland
9. South Korea	19. Argentina
10. Russia	20. Iran

Which country to target?

Figure 2.23: Potential target countries based on GDP/capita and population[114]

Source: Justin Letschert, 2008. *Taking a local brand to the global arena: Lessons from an SA entrepreneur.* USB Leader's Angle, 27 June.

Figures 2.22 and 2.23 show a first step in the process of doing in-depth country research to find potentially lucrative markets that are attractive. Other factors to consider in selecting target country markets are reflected in Figure 2.24. These include:

- the degree to which the "rule of law" is upheld and applied
- the effect of foreign languages on the ease of doing business
- the difference between the total population and the economically active population. "All TV viewers are not necessarily TV buyers."
- the protection of copyrights and intellectual property
- the culture and ethical practices as enablers or inhibitors of business
- the effect of different time zones (it is easier to work with countries in the same or related time zones)

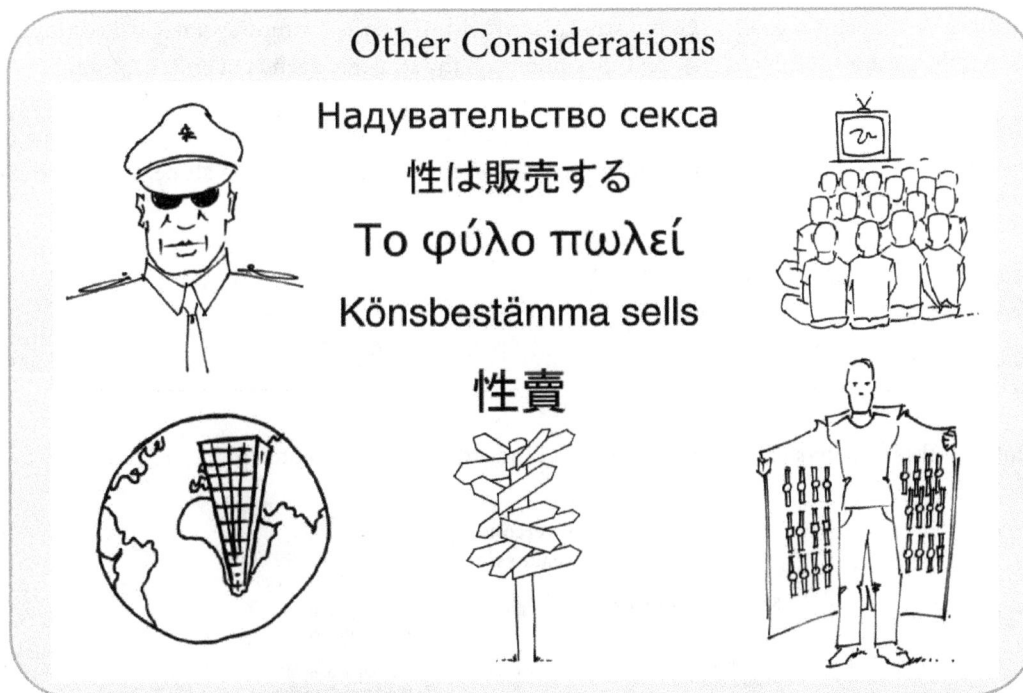

Figure 2.24: Other considerations in selecting potential target market countries[115]

Source: Justin Letschert, 2008. Taking a local brand to the global arena: Lessons from an SA entrepreneur. USB Leader's Angle, 27 June.

Application tool

Use the above information on foreign market entry options to argue the case for an organisation you are developing a strategy for. Also indicate the implications for operational aspects and business model features. Use the template in Table 2.14 to describe your choice of foreign market entry options.

Table 2.14: Foreign market entry options template

Foreign market entry choice	Rationale	Implications

GRAND STRATEGY CHOICES

Grand strategies fill the third level on the menu of strategic competitive choices for an organisation (see Figure 2.8). Grand strategies refer to 15 strategy options for the longer term and represent master strategies that organisations employ to achieve their business goals.[116] Grand strategies provide the basis for future strategic direction and action. Grand strategies, by nature, are all longer-term type options on the strategic agenda of an organisation.

Different strategies will, of course, fit different situations. In this part we describe the 15 grand strategies in four clusters to create an awareness of these different strategic choices. The different grand strategies can be clustered as follows:

- competence-based growth strategies
- external-orientated growth strategies
- strategic space growth strategies
- rationalisation strategies

The positioning of these clusters within the associated grand strategies is presented in Figure 2.25.

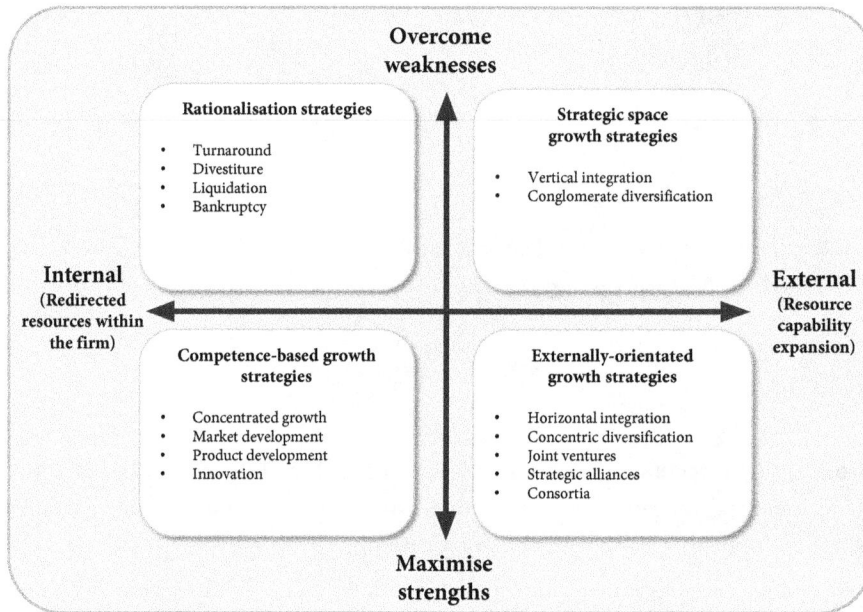

Figure 2.25: Grand strategies selection matrix[117]

Competence-based growth strategies

Competence-based growth strategies focus on maximising the internal resource strengths of an organisation through the following grand strategy options:

- concentrated growth
- market development
- product development
- innovation

Concentrated growth focuses on growing existing offerings in the existing market (a market penetration strategy). A concentrated growth strategy therefore involves capturing a greater market share of existing customers through head-to-head competition. Companies pursuing this strategy exploit their expertise in a narrowly defined competitive market and achieve superiority over competitors, who try to master a greater number of product–market combinations.

Market development focuses on growing the size of the market by extending the use of existing offerings to new customers. This involves marketing current products to related markets by adding distribution channels, expanding geographically, altering advertising promotions, or making cosmetic modifications to offerings.

Product development focuses on developing new products to serve existing customers. Product development can involve substantial modification of existing products or development of new products to be provided to current customers.

Innovation focuses on the creation of new offerings to be provided to new markets. Innovation seeks to create a new product life cycle that makes similar existing products obsolete. It is therefore sometimes referred to as disruptive innovation.[118]

External-orientated growth strategies

External-orientated growth strategies maximise the resource capability of an organisation by adding external resources through the following grand strategy options:

- horizontal integration
- concentric diversification
- joint ventures
- strategic alliances
- consortia

Horizontal integration refers to the expansion of the business by acquiring other firms at the same stage of the production-marketing chain of an industry. Such acquisitions eliminate rivals while strengthening the firm's resource position.

Concentric diversification refers to the acquisition of businesses that are related to the firm in terms of technology, products or markets. These acquisitions are done because some complementary elements exist.

Joint ventures are when two or more companies pool their resources to create and operate a new commercial organisation for the benefit of the co-owners. Joint ventures are often established because the project or function is of such a magnitude that individual companies would be incapable of successfully operating it.

Strategic alliances are similar to joint ventures, except in a strategic alliance the companies involved do not take an equity stake in one another. Often the partnership exists for a defined period or project, where after the partnership is disbanded.

Consortia are large interlocking relationships between businesses of an industry. They are designed to use industry coordination to minimise risks of competition, partly through cost sharing and increased economies of scale.

Strategic space growth strategies

Strategic space growth strategies seek to overcome resource weaknesses by adding external resource capabilities through the following grand strategy options:

- vertical integration
- conglomerate diversification

Vertical integration refers to the acquisition of firms either upstream or downstream in the industry value chain of the core business. Vertical integration can be through backward integration, where assets from an earlier stage in the value chain are acquired, or forward integration, which happens when a firm acquires assets nearer to the end-user.

Conglomerate diversification refers to acquiring businesses purely based on the fact that they are good investments. These acquisitions do not necessarily have compatibility with the core business. This forms part of the business portfolio expansion of an organisation to balance a portfolio between cyclical and counter-cyclical sales, between high-cash and longer-cash-generation businesses, or between debt-free and highly geared businesses.

Rationalisation strategies

Rationalisation strategies are internally directed with the aim of rectifying current weaknesses by following these grand strategy options:

- turnaround
- divestiture
- liquidation
- bankruptcy

Turnaround refers to restoring a firm that currently finds itself in a position of declining profits to its former glory.

As for exit strategies, divestiture refers to the sale of a firm (when part of a corporation) or a major component(s) of a firm.

Liquidation is the least attractive of all the grand strategies and refers to the sale of the firm as a whole or in part for its tangible asset value.

Finally, instead of liquidation, businesses can file for reorganisation bankruptcy. Here the business attempts to convince creditors that instead of an immediate, fractional repayment, the business can be turned around, resulting in the maximum repayment of financial obligations at some specified future time (also see chapter 7 on restructuring options).

Application tool

Given the current strategic situation of the organisation you are working on, determine which of the 15 growth strategies would be appropriate to realise your intended goal (see Figure 2.24). Motivate your choice and also indicate the implications for operational aspects and business model features. Also describe the reinforcement effects on other strategic choices on levels 1–3 (see Figure 2.8).

Table 2.15: Strategy choice template

Grand strategy choice	Rationale	Implications	Reinforcement effects

CONCLUSIONS

The process of formulating a strategy for an organisation is directly linked to the strategic choices a firm makes. Making these choices more deliberate and visible assists leaders to create a stable foundation and reference point for the development of other aspects in the strategic landscape of an organisation (see Figure 2.1). Increasing the individual and collective consciousness of an organisation's key strategic choices creates stability to facilitate change in other strategic arenas like the business model, strategy execution and strategy renewal and innovation. This is the paradox of change and stability in action.

In this chapter, three levels of strategic choice were described (see Figure 2.8):

- Level 1 strategic choices: Identity and aspirational descriptions for organisations
- Level 2 strategic choices: Generic strategies for organisations
- Level 3 strategic choices: Grand strategies for organisations

The theme of strategy development continues in the next chapter with a detailed description of perspectives associated with a business model for an organisation.

Chapter 3

Strategy formulation: Business model formulation

"A good business model remains essential to every successful organisation, whether it's a new venture or an established player ... the business model's great strength as a planning tool is that it focuses attention on how all the elements of the system fit into a working whole." – Joan Magretta[1]

LEARNING OBJECTIVES

This chapter expands on the "current business model" view discussed in Ungerer, Ungerer and Herholdt.[2] In addition to the usual business model canvas descriptions, the following will be discussed in order to guide your understanding and assist your application of business model formulation and evaluation:

- business model formulation and strategy in context
- competitive strategy
- activity systems
- revenue generation strategies
- the lean canvas
- expanded business model canvas
- customer retention
  - o control points
  - o switching costs
  - o e-loyalty drivers
- key metrics
- competitive advantage summary
- process of business modelling
- normative assessment of competitive strategies

INTRODUCTION

A business model, as its name indicates, is a model, an abstraction or a representation of the value creation and value capturing logic of the business. Business models and strategy broadly revolve around the same concepts, but exist at different levels of abstraction. Strategy can be seen as a domain, whereas a business model is a tool relevant to the domain. Strategy is a more high-level, over-arching, broad, intangible and soft concept; whereas business models are more specific and tangible, yet still conceptual. The relationships between strategy, business models and operations are depicted in Figure 3.1.

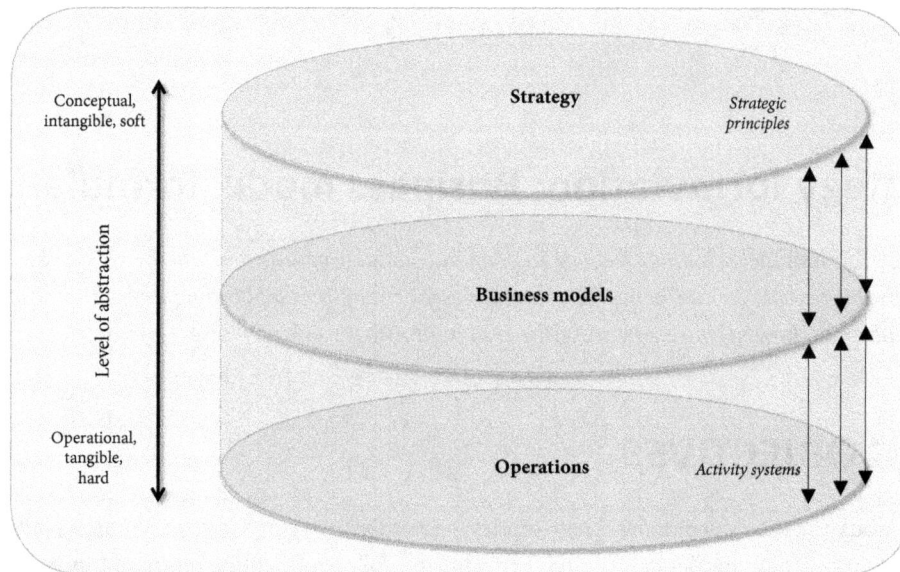

Figure 3.1: Conceptual relationships between strategy, business models, and operations

Strategy places more of an emphasis on issues regarding the core aspirational description of a business (vision, mission, values and goal-setting), the business's competitive positioning and environment, competitors and competition, value capturing, and the creation of a competitive advantage.[3] [4] [5] Business models on the other hand are chiefly concerned with customers, value creation, cooperation and partnerships, and the means by which the business sustains itself.[6] [7] Business models provide structure to (certain elements of) strategy. Business models seek to **depict** the way that value is created and delivered to customers, and how revenue is generated. A business model is therefore the business's strategy distilled into a conceptual blueprint of the value creation and capturing logic of the business.[8] [9] [10] [11]

A recurring question that often plagues inexperienced managers and entrepreneurs is whether they should use strategy or business models.[12] The answer is that it is not an "either or" case. Strategy and business models are fundamentally and bi-directionally linked. Neither strategy nor business models are a replacement for one other; both should be used and should harmoniously co-exist.[13] Strategy and business models are complements to each other and not substitutes.[14] If a strategy can hypothetically be forged separate from the business model mind-set, then that strategy can easily be translated into a business model format. Similarly, when a business model is analysed, it should be possible to deduce the strategy that created it, by looking at the consistencies between the elements.[15]

Strategy exists at a sort of "principle" level. This is also the level where ideas and hypotheses reside. Strategic consistency stems from these principles, ideas and hypotheses (see *Theory of the Business* in *Crystallising the Strategic Business Landscape*). Strategy can then be translated down into several different types of plans (just think about all the different strategic tools and frameworks that exist), with a business model being the plan that highlights the value creation and capturing logic of the organisation. These plans then eventually need to be executed, which is how the strategy tangibly and operationally plays itself out in the real world. **Where strategy is governed by principles, operations are governed by activities and activity systems.** The latter is discussed in more detail later in the chapter (see *Key Activities*).

One area of concern that still remains for many strategists regarding business models, however, is that business models have less of a focus on the competitive environment, competitors, competitive positioning, and competition. This means that it is quite possible to blissfully develop business models that do not create any competitive advantages. Given that (1) the fundamental goal of strategy is to create sustainable competitive advantages that result in supra-normal profits and shared value for all stakeholders,[16] [17] [18] and that (2) businesses without competitive advantages can't reasonably imagine succeeding against competitors who possess such advantages, this concern clearly has its merits. This is another issue that is discussed later in this chapter (see *Expanded Business Model Canvas*). However, considering the gravity of the subject and for interest's sake, some attention is briefly paid here to the competitive aspects of strategy.

Competitive strategy refers to the aspects of strategy concerned with how a business intends to compete in the market and how it intends to defend the resultant competitive position.[19] Essentially, this is largely what strategy formulation is all about. Ungerer[20] investigated which core conceptual elements or higher-level choices constitute competitive strategy, and proposed that competitive strategy primarily deals with three overarching themes: (1) environmental analysis, (2) strategic positioning, and (3) sustainable competitive advantages.

It is important to note that sustainable competitive advantages and continued competitiveness in the market are the ideal consequence of environmental analysis and strategic positioning and are not guaranteed. In a similar way, does the mere existence of a business model and a strategy not guarantee a business's success.[21] The only silver bullet that exists is doing the hard work required to formulate great strategies and flawlessly executing them. This is supported by Linder and Cantrell,[22] who state that companies succeed when "They choose an effective business model and execute it superbly. They relentlessly renew their distinctiveness as competitors threaten."

Ungerer[23] proposes that seven core conceptual elements relate to these overarching themes as shown in Figure 3.2: (1) industry selection, (2) customer segments, (3) a value proposition, (4) an activity system, (5) a core competitive advantage choice (otherwise known as Porter's generic competitive strategies), (6) strategic control points and (7) strategy evolution (renewal and growth).

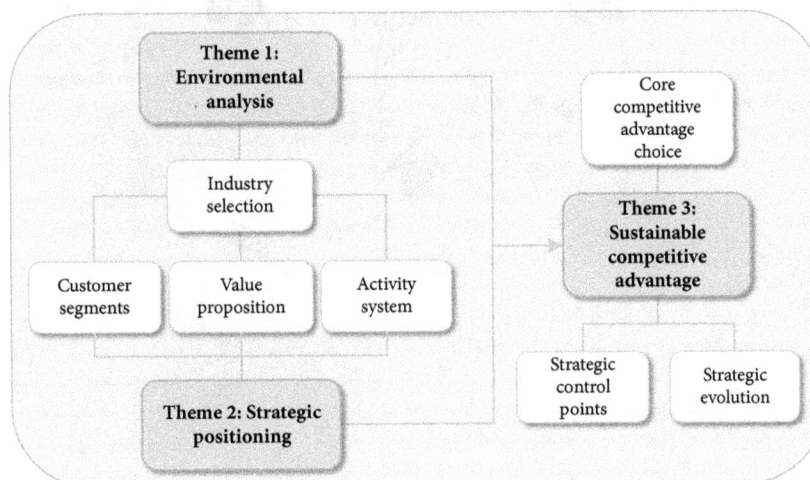

Figure 3.2: Core elements of competitive strategy[24]

The theme of environmental analysis has already been covered in chapters 2, 3, 4 and 5 of *Crystallising the Strategic Business Landscape*. Strategic positioning refers to the myriad offensive and defensive competitive moves that a business can make to position itself in the market. Markides[25] describes the core of a strategic position as the sum of answering the who–what–how questions of a business. Who should the company target as customers (customer segments)? What should be offered to them (value proposition)? And how should the strategy be executed (which activities and how should they be performed)? Strategic positioning is a far-reaching concept, but is in great part covered in chapters 2 and 3 of this book. Additional insights regarding environmental analysis, industry selection and strategic positioning can be found in Porter's 1980 book, *Competitive Strategy: Techniques for Analysing Industries and Competitors*.[26] Lastly, the sustainable competitive advantage theme highlights the need for developing competitive advantages and devising ways in which to ensure their defensibility and sustainability. There are two primary ways in which to make a business sustainable: (1) by being robust via strategic control points or (2) by being flexible via learning, adaptability and strategic evolution. The best businesses embrace this apparent paradox and employ both techniques. Control points are discussed later in this chapter, and strategic evolution has already been introduced in chapter 2 and is expanded on in chapters 6, 7 and 8.

Ungerer[27] additionally proposes that four core principles underlie competitive strategy in general, namely (1) focus, (2) differentiation, (3) robustness, and (4) adaptability. These principles are depicted in Figure 3.3.

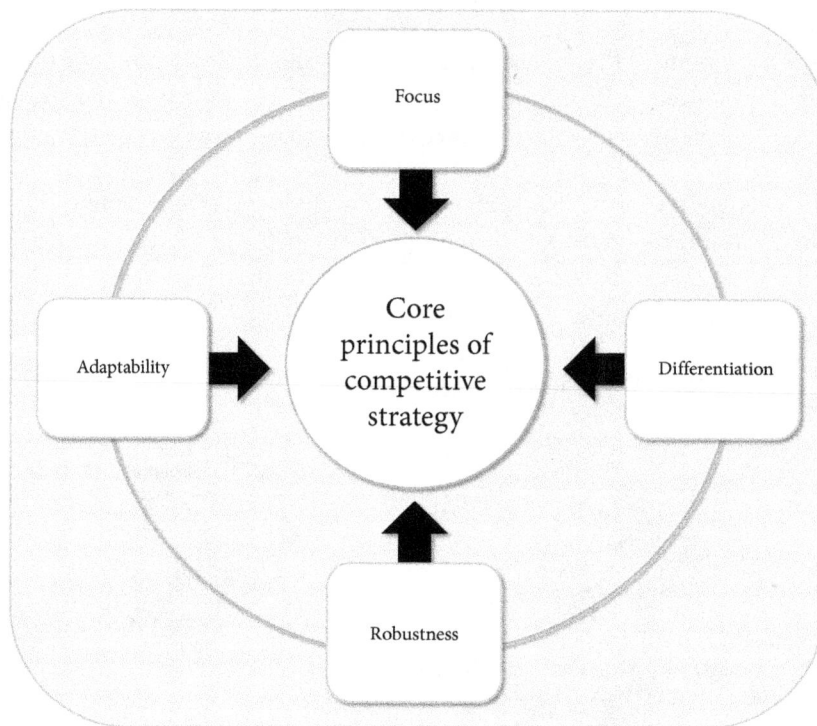

Figure 3.3: Core principles of competitive strategy[28]

Focus relates to consistency, continuity of direction and alignment that compounds the effort and advantages of the business. It also relates to clarity, fluent communication and the setting and pursuit of achievable goals.

Differentiation allows one business to be distinguished from the next and relates to novelty, uniqueness and innovation. Differentiation is the core source of competitive advantage, as even a low cost advantage can be considered a "cost differentiator".

Robustness relates to the strength or durability of a business. It deals with acquiring resources, positions and installing mechanisms that make the business, its customers and income streams defensible against competitor onslaughts.

Adaptability relates to the learning, growth, flexibility and resilience of the business. Adaptability can be described as "dynamic robustness" and it is this virtue that allows a business to shape itself to the competitive environment over time to remain relevant and competitive.[29]

If we accept that principles govern the domain of strategy, then it can be theorised that businesses that take these principles to heart, become the absolute masters of them, and are able to infuse their strategies with them will be immensely competitive and prosperous.

In the following section, the focus shifts again towards business models and business modelling.

THE BUSINESS MODEL CANVAS

Various schematics and representations of business models have emerged over the years, but the currently dominant and most widely used generic representation is that of the business model canvas, developed by Alex Osterwalder and Yves Pigneur. The business model canvas is the core business model representation used in this book and is depicted in Figure 3.4.

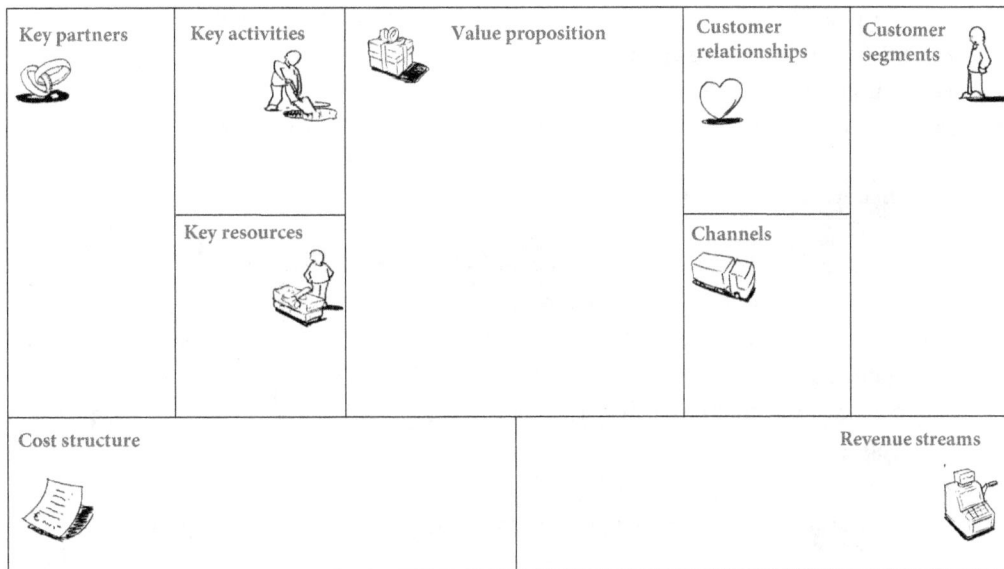

Figure 3.4: Business model canvas[30]

The business model canvas consists of nine "building blocks" that act as placeholders that need to be "filled in", "coloured in", or "populated" to explicitly articulate the business model of the business – hence the name. The canvas is constructed so that the right-hand side deals with strategy formulation (what the business will do) and the left-hand side with strategy execution (how the business will do it). Similarly, the right-hand side deals with value (delivery and extraction) and the left-hand side with efficiency (cost reductions and optimisation). As a result, the canvas can be seen as a type of value chain where the left-hand side, upper-stream efforts result in right-hand side, down-stream profits. The elements of the canvas are discussed below.[31] [32] [33]

Customer segments

Customer segments are the different groups of people or organisations that the business sells its product or service offerings to. Customer groups represent separate segments if:[34]

- Their needs require and justify a distinct offering.
- They are reached through different channels.
- They require different types of relationship.
- They have substantially different profitabilities.
- They are willing to pay for different aspects of the offer.

In chapter 4 of *Crystallising the Competitive Business Landscape* the following are discussed:

- different demographic, geographic, psychological and behavioural attributes can be used to construct a complete customer persona; and the specific, relevant customer attributes for conducting this segmentation are business- and industry-dependent
- Osterwalder and Pigneur's[35] customer segmentation taxonomy, which includes (1) a mass market model, (2) a segmented model, (3) a niche market model, (4) a multisided-platform model, and (5) a diversified model
- customer demands, customer trends and a global trend analysis
- customer need saturation scale and a customer need gap analysis
- customer empathy map for distilling customer pains and gains, and devising customer jobs-to-be-done

What needs to be defined in the customer segment element?

- the broad customer segment classification of the business (Osterwalder's taxonomy)
- the individual segments you are creating value for
- both segments of a multi-sided platform
- your most important customers
- the important characteristics that describe the segments if they do not share a collective noun or stereotype (demographic, geographic, psychological, and behavioural)
- customer pains and gains
- jobs-to-be-done, a.k.a the customer problem that needs to be solved

Value proposition

A value proposition is the bundle of benefits provided to customers. A value proposition seeks to solve customer problems or satisfy customer needs. It describes the combination of products, services and other elements that create value for a specific customer segment. Possible features that could create value for customers are (1) newness, (2) performance, (3) customisation, (4) "getting the job done", (5) design, (6) brand/status, (7) price, (8) cost reduction, (9) risk reduction, (10) accessibility or (11) convenience/usability.[36] A myriad of other possible value creation elements exist, and figuring out what these are for specific customers is crucial to crafting a sustainable business.

Additional perspectives and tools that can be used for crafting a business's value proposition are provided in chapter 6. They include:

- sources of digital disruption across supply and demand
- exponential organisations
- a source of e-value perspective that can be used to design exceptional e-business value propositions
- a perspective on techniques for creating new market space – uncontested market spaces that provide the opportunity for rapid and profitable growth
- a strategy canvas for highlighting how the business's strategy diverges from competitors'

What needs to be defined in the value proposition element?

- the products, services and resultant value that are being delivered to each customer segment
- the customer need that is satisfied
- the unique value that is delivered to each segment (unique selling proposition)
- the gain creators and pain relievers
- the minimum viable product that would satisfy customer needs (for start-ups)

Channels

Channels are the pathways that a business uses to communicate, sell and distribute its offerings to customers.[37] They involve the ways that businesses reach and connect with customers; make offerings accessible to them; and all the other interactions that occur between them. In chapter 4 of *Crystallising the Competitive Business Landscape* six generic channel phases that customers go through during their interactions with the business are mentioned, namely (1) awareness, (2) evaluation, (3) purchase, (4) delivery, (5) use and (6) after-sales support. These channel phases are generic and need to be changed to reflect the business's unique value chain and sequence of events.

What needs to be defined in the channels element?

- the unique customer channel phase value chain specific to the business
- the channels through which customer segments are made aware of offerings
- the channels that allow customers to evaluate the offering
- the channels through which offerings are sold to customers
- the channels through which offerings are delivered to customers and through which customers experience the offerings
- the channels that are used for after-sales support
- the channels that work the best
- the channels that are the most cost-efficient

Customer relationships

Customer relationships are the bonds that the business establishes with customers. Customer relationships play a crucial role in the customer experience and are key in attracting customers, retaining them and persuading them to spend more.[38] In chapter 4 of *Crystallising the Competitive Business Landscape*, six types of customer relationship were defined, namely (1) personal assistance, (2) dedicated personal assistance, (3) self-service, (4) automated service, (5) communities and (6) co-creation.[39]

What needs to be defined in the customer relationships element?

* the type of relationship established with each customer segment
* the type of relationship the different customers want the business to establish with them
* the ways in which the relationships differ
* the ways in which the relationships can be optimised for efficiency and experience

Revenue streams

Revenue streams are the business's different sources of income. A business may possess various revenue streams, and these may be unique for each type of customer segment, product or service type. Revenue streams can be broadly classified as either (1) transactional or (2) recurring.[40] **Transactional revenues** are generated from once-off customer payments. **Recurring revenues** are generated from ongoing payments to deliver a value proposition or provide after-sales customer support. Revenue streams can also be classified as being generated (1) directly or (2) indirectly.[41] **Direct revenues** are generated from actual product or service sales. **Indirect revenues** are generated indirectly from ancillary third-party sources such as advertising.

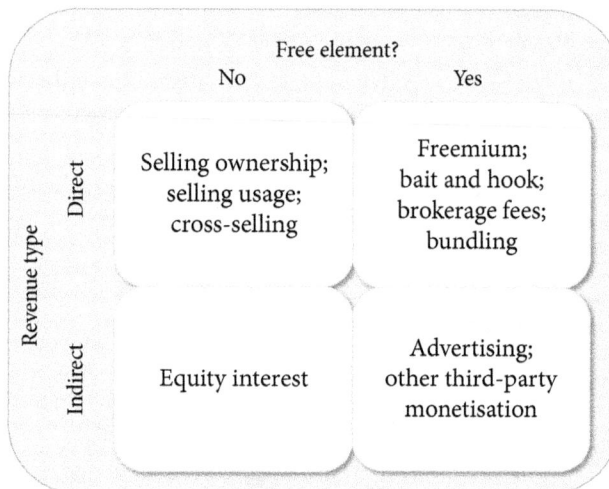

Figure 3.5: Revenue generation strategies[43]

Various types of revenue stream taxonomy exist. However, given the continued difficulty for many Internet businesses to employ suitable revenue generation strategies and the rise in popularity of free business models, Ungerer[42] provided an interesting and comprehensive revenue generation taxonomy as shown in Figure 3.5. Unique to this perspective is the distinction between strategies that contain free elements and those that don't.

Selling ownership is the selling of the ownership rights of an asset.[44] The typical example is selling physical assets, but intangible assets such as domain names can also be sold.

Selling usage is the broad practice of selling the usage of services or products, but not the ownership thereof. Several subrevenue strategies can be grouped under this strategy. **Usage fees** are generated by the classical "pay-as-you-go" model where the more a customer makes use of an offering, the more they pay. **Subscription fees** are a strategy where revenue is generated by selling continuous access to an offering,[45] such as cable television. **Lending**, **renting**, or **leasing** are when revenue is generated by temporarily granting the lessee the right to use a particular asset for a fixed period. The advantage to the lender is that recurring revenues are generated, while the lessee enjoys the usage of the product, but need not bear the full costs of ownership.[46] **Time-share** is when an offering is made available to a group of customers, all of whom have access to it for a portion of time. **Slice-share** models work in exactly the same way as time-share models, except that they are not time-bound and the different parties buy a "slice" of the total value proposition.[47] Lastly, **licensing** is when revenues are generated by giving customers permission to access and use protected intellectual property. Examples include software products where users purchase the right to use the digital software, while not actually obtaining the rights to the intellectual property.[48]

Cross-selling is the practice where a different product or service (related or unrelated) is sold to an existing customer. Ryanair, for instance, generates roughly 25 per cent of its revenue through the sale of add-on services and products, such as seat reservations, priority boarding, food and beverages, MP3 players, digital cameras, perfume and so forth on its flights.[49]

Freemium models (also known as up-selling) provide users with some basic part of the offering for free, but charges customers for access to the premium version, which includes additional content, functionalities or other benefits. Many mobile apps work on this principle. Users are allowed to test the free version, but have to pay for the full version.

Bait and hook (also known as razor-and-blade) models are when free or inexpensive initial offers lure customers into repeat business. This model is the most closely related to typical "loss leader" models. Loss leaders are products that are sold very cheaply (or provided for free), with the aim of attracting additional purchases of products with higher profit margins.[50] [51] Gillette, for instance, provides a relatively inexpensive razor that lures customers into subsequently buying blades. Cannon and HP, on the other hand, sell relatively cheap printers, but earn good margins on subsequent ink cartridge sales.[52]

Brokerage fees are earned when intermediation services are performed on behalf of two or more parties. Examples include credit card providers who earn a percentage commission each time a transaction is successfully completed, or recruitment agencies and real estate agents who earn commissions each time they successfully match a buyer and seller.[53]

Bundling is a strategy that combines offerings to obscure their individual true prices, while increasing the customer's perceived value. For bundling, an aspect of the offering is largely perceived as free, although in reality this may not be the case. Businesses may, for instance, give away a free iPad with the purchase of a new car, or mobile phone manufacturers can offer free phones, but bundle them with a service subscription.[54] The business still makes its margins on the total offering, but gains the benefit of increased customer hype.

Equity interest refers to giving customers products or services or financial aid in exchange for an equity share in the customer's business.[55] HP, for instance, has traded high-powered servers to some Silicon Valley start-ups in exchange for a share in their business. Venture capitalists and the investors from the TV show *The Dragon's Den*, also invest in businesses in exchange for equity. The transaction is direct, but revenues are generated indirectly for the investor via the customer.

Revenue can be generated through third parties in the form of **advertising, referrals and affiliate programmes**. These models all function in roughly the same way. In the classic **advertising model**, companies display banner or pop-up ads on the business's website and revenue is generated per impression or "per-click". Newer forms of advertising have also emerged based on the content of the website, such as search engine ads (Google), video ads (YouTube), audio ads (Spotify), in-game ads (Angry Birds), in-app ads (Snapchat), or native ads (Digg). For the latter, the displayed ad matches the form and function of the platform on which it appears, meaning the ad is tailored for the specific platform and audience. This makes the ad less intrusive and it is more likely that users will pay it attention. Revenue can further be generated through **affiliate programmes** where the referred party rewards the referrer. Depending on the contract, affiliates may be paid per lead generated, or paid only once a sale is generated, a form is completed, or some similar action has taken place.

Revenue can also be generated through the altruism of the community, in the form of **sponsorships and charities**, where time, money or some other type of donation is made.[56]

Additionally, Ungerer[57] provides Table 3.1 to aid businesses in broadly understanding the different revenue-generation types and to assist businesses in choosing a suitable revenue generation strategy.

Table 3.1: Revenue generation strategies fundamental characteristics[58]

Revenue strategy	• **Selling ownership**
	• **Selling usage**
	  o Usage fees
	  o Subscription fees
	  o Lending/ renting/ leasing
	  o Time/slice-share
	  o Licensing
	• **Cross-selling**
		• **Freemium**
		• **Bait & hook**
		• **Brokerage fees**
		• **Bundling**
			• **Equity Interest**	• **Advertising** (Including Affiliate Programmes & Referrals)
				• **Sponsorships & Charities**

Revenue type	Direct	Direct	Indirect	Indirect
Free element	No	Yes	No	Yes
Multisided-platform	No	Yes. Paying customers support free users.	No	Yes. The more users, the more advertisers/ partners are attracted.
Distinguishing advantages	• Generates money with each transaction • No free uses to sustain	Free offerings attract attention more easily	Profitable businesses can generate revenues disproportionate to investment	Free offerings attract attention more easily
Most suited to	• Offerings of high value that cannot economically be provided for free • Multi-staged offerings that create opportunities for cross-selling complements	• Offerings that can be versioned (basic/premium) • Durable products with consumable complements • Unique products that require effort to obtain	High value offerings or service capabilities that are not easily obtainable without significant financial investment, and whose impact could warrant an equity deal	• Offerings that cannot easily be monetised directly • User generated content/ offerings with high social value • Offerings targeting customers who can be segmented

| Largest challenges | • Creating value that customers will pay for
• Combating free competitors | • Converting free users to paying customers
• Maintaining a low cost structure to sustain free users and enable a profit | • Correctly identifying businesses through which equity interest deals will generate profits
• Convincing promising businesses to part with some of their business equity | • Generating or obtaining quality content that will attract a large number of users
• Building advertising partnerships
• Combating supplier bargaining power |

Important questions to consider when choosing a revenue generation strategy are:

1. Does the nature of the offering allow it to be charged for directly? Would customers actually pay for the offering?
2. Is it necessary to provide an aspect of the offering for free to attract attention? How will we convince users to buy the offering?
3. Via which revenue strategy would customers like to obtain the offering?
4. Which revenue strategy makes the best economic sense and which do we have the highest chance of making a success with?
5. How will the business be affected and react when facing threats from free competitors?

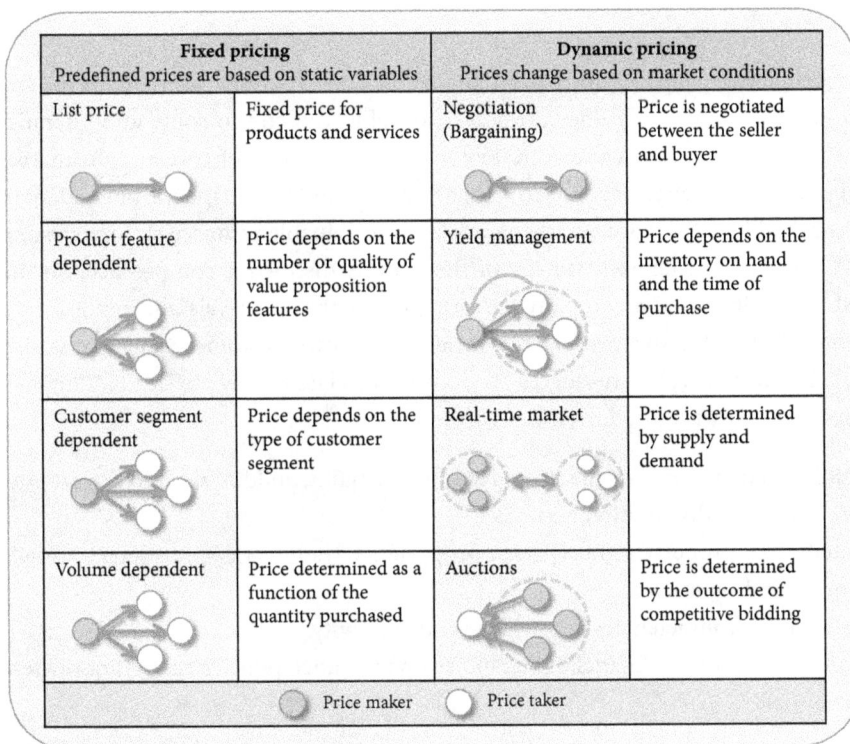

Every revenue stream also needs to be paired with at least one pricing strategy or pricing mechanism. These are the ways in which offerings are priced depending on market demand, offering features and customer segments. Different types of pricing mechanism are depicted and described in Figure 3.6.

Important questions to consider when choosing pricing mechanisms and a price point are:

1. Which pricing mechanism is the best suited to the nature of the offering and our chosen customer segments?

Fixed pricing Predefined prices are based on static variables		Dynamic pricing Prices change based on market conditions	
List price	Fixed price for products and services	Negotiation (Bargaining)	Price is negotiated between the seller and buyer
Product feature dependent	Price depends on the number or quality of value proposition features	Yield management	Price depends on the inventory on hand and the time of purchase
Customer segment dependent	Price depends on the type of customer segment	Real-time market	Price is determined by supply and demand
Volume dependent	Price determined as a function of the quantity purchased	Auctions	Price is determined by the outcome of competitive bidding
⬤ Price maker ◯ Price taker			

Figure 3.6: Pricing mechanisms[59][60]

2. How will our pricing mechanisms influence customer's perceptions of our offerings?
3. How will our pricing mechanisms influence our revenue generation ability?
4. Does our price point attract customers in sufficient numbers to be economically viable relative to our scale and costs?
5. What pricing innovations can we employ to optimise our profits?

What needs to be defined in the revenue streams element?

- the revenue stream types used for each offering and/or customer segment
- whether revenue is generated directly or indirectly
- whether revenue generation is transactional or recurring
- how the revenue strategy compensates for free elements contained in the value proposition
- the pricing mechanisms used for each revenue stream, offering and/or customer segment
- the profit margin of each offering and/or customer segment
- the contribution of each revenue stream to the overall revenues
- the actual price of offerings
- a quick break-even calculation, indicating the expected number of units sold per month and the break-even time frame

Key resources

Key resources are all the assets, competencies, people, information and other resources that are needed for the business model to function. Resources are valuable when they are scarce, durable, difficult to copy, idiosyncratic, non-tradable and non-substitutable.[61] [62] [63] Vital concepts related to key resources are those of core and distinctive competencies. A core competence is a well-performed internal activity that is central, and not peripheral or incidental, to a company's competitiveness and profitability.[64] A core competence is a more valuable resource strength than a competence, because it contributes directly to the chosen strategy of the firm. A distinctive competence, on the other hand, is a competitively valuable activity when a company performs better than its rivals and represents a competitively superior resource strength.[65] A distinctive competence creates significant customer value and is also uniquely leverageable by the business. Furthermore, key resources are commonly classified as physical, intangible, human or financial; they can be owned, leased or acquired from key partners.[66] [67]

1. **Physical resources** include tangible assets such as manufacturing equipment, land, buildings, vehicles, computers, machines, communication systems and distribution networks.
2. **Intangible resources** include intellectual property rights (patents, copyrights, trademarks, proprietary knowledge and trade secrets), brand image and reputation.
3. **Human resources** include people's skills, competencies, knowledge and creativity.
4. **Financial resources** include cash, stocks, bonds, financial guarantees or insurance policies that grant owners the rights to potential future cash flows.

Tilles[68] also notes that resources represent a business's action potential. Sufficient resources mean that the business is equipped to take action. Inversely, insufficient resources paralyse the business and prevent it from taking action.

What needs to be defined in the key resources element?

- the key resources responsible for the creation of the business's competitive advantage
- the business's most valuable assets
- the key resources necessary to communicate, create, sell, and deliver the value proposition
- the business's core and distinctive competencies

Additionally, see chapter 5 of *Crystallising the Competitive Business Landscape* for an in-depth discussion on internal resource analysis.

Key activities

Key activities are the critical activities that drive the business model. Activities are the basic building blocks of competitive advantages. All the differences between businesses in terms of costs or differentiation are derived from the hundreds of activities required to create, produce, sell and deliver products and services.[69] Costs are generated by performing activities, and cost advantages arise by performing activities more efficiently than competitors. Equally, differentiation arises from both the choice of activities and how they are performed.[70]

Activities do not function in isolation, however. Rather, underlying any good business model is a tightly integrated system of activities that supports the model's function. This web of activities is known as an **activity system**. The business's activity system represents all the key activities that the business performs to realise its strategy. Activity systems are vitally important, not only because they drive the business's competitive advantages, but also because they play a unifying role and are responsible for the sustainability of the business (see **Porter's generic competitive strategies** in chapter 2).

Activity systems propagate the idea of developing a business holistically, whereby the business system is more than the sum of its constituent parts. Activity systems bind activities together in an inter-related web and promote the ideas of fit, trade-offs and continuity of direction. This inter-related web of activities cannot easily be untangled,[71] creating competitive barriers to entry and imitation. Porter[72] therefore notes that sustainability is derived from the activity system (and the fit between components) and not the individual parts.

An example of Southwest Airline's activity system is shown in Figure 3.7.

In classifying types of activities, Osterwalder and Pigneur[74] distinguish between three broad types, namely production activities, problem-solving activities, and platform or network activities.

1. **Production activities** are prevalent in the business models of manufacturing firms and involve the design, development and delivery of products in substantial quantities and/or superior quality.
2. **Problem-solving activities** involve creativity and specialist know-how and relate to finding innovative solutions to individual customer problems.
3. **Platform or network activities** are key to businesses that have a platform or network at the centre of their value proposition and involve the development, maintenance, management and promotion of the platform or network.

Two other concepts that relate to the key activities element are the internal value chain of the business and the business's key operating procedures. The internal value chain is discussed in chapter 5 of *Crystallising the Strategic Business Landscape*, and provides insights about the internal channels and activities used to run the business. The internal value chain essentially depicts the business activities that create value for customers, and this understanding is useful in creating additional value gains or optimising efficiencies. Key operating procedures are also vital in standardising the business's operating success formula in order to deliver consistently high-quality products and services.

What needs to be defined in the key activities element?

- the key activities required to produce the value proposition
- the key activities required to establish and maintain customer relationships
- the key channel activities required
- the activity system underlying the business (linkages are important for understanding how and why the business works)
- the internal value chain of the business
- key operating procedures

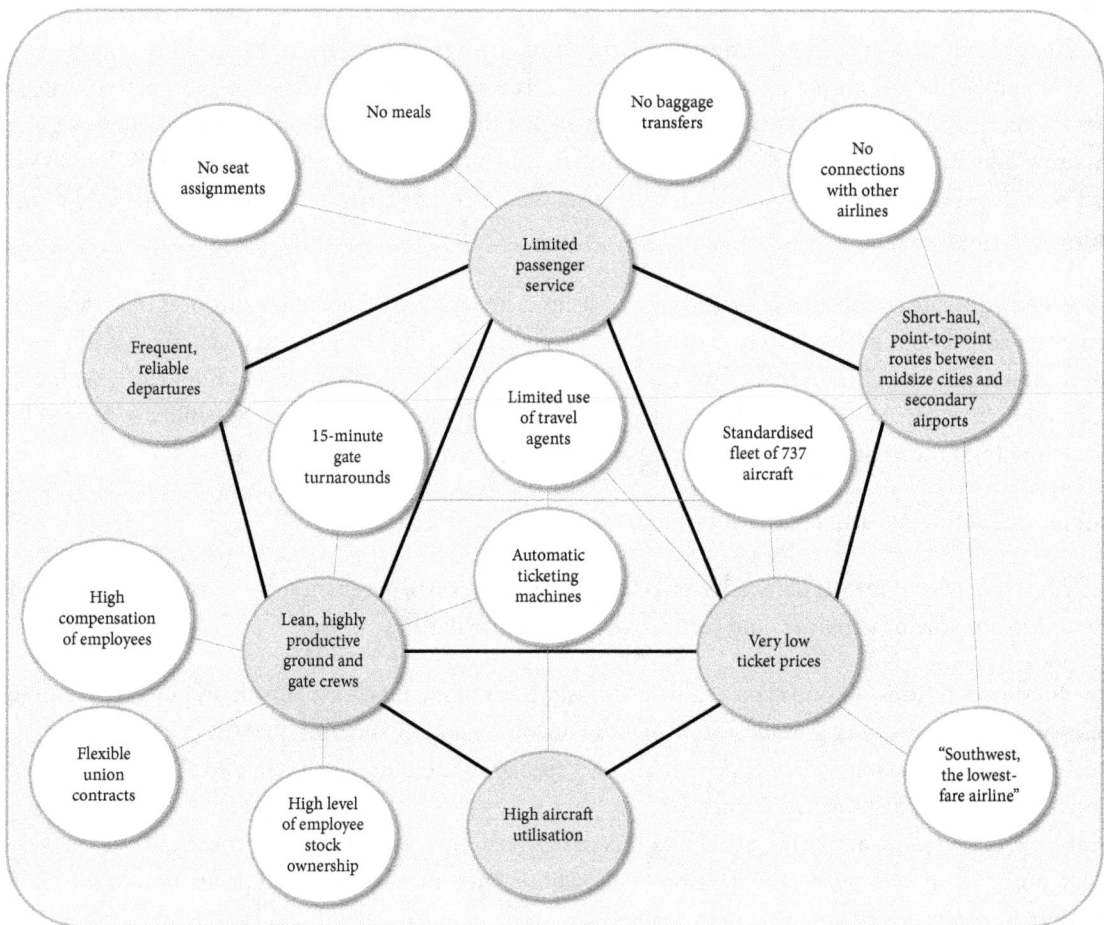

Figure 3.7: Southwest Airline's activity system[73]

🛠 **Application tool**

Develop an activity system for your business. Start by identifying higher-level themes that are crucial to the business's value creation and value capture (see the dark large circles in Figure 3.7). Identify the key activities related to each of the themes and link them together in an inter-related web.

Having constructed this perspective of the business, what insights have you gained? When growing in future, what should the business do more of to fortify its position; and which strategic choices should not be made as they could endanger the underlying value creation and capture capabilities of the business? Use Table 3.2 to capture your insights.

Table 3.2: Activity system insights analysis

Activity system theme	Rationale: How the theme and surrounding activities are currently creating/capturing value	Activities that can be added to fortify this strategic position	Strategic moves that will endanger this strategic position

Key partnerships

Key partners are all those key allies who are required in the realisation of the business model. Businesses often establish partnerships either via (1) strategic alliances between non-competitors, (2) co-opetition between competitors, (3) joint ventures to develop new businesses, or via (4) buyer-seller relationships to assure reliable supplies.[75] By making use of partnerships, businesses can (1) optimise and increase the efficiency of their business models by sharing infrastructure, resources and activities, and thereby capitalise on economies of scale, increased productivity and reduced costs; (2) reduce risk and uncertainty; and (3) acquire resources and activities that would otherwise be unfeasible or ineffective to develop or perform in-house.[76]

See chapter 7 for a deeper discussion on inorganic growth options, such as alliances and mergers and acquisitions.

What needs to be defined in the key partnerships element?

- the key partners that support the functioning of the business model
- the type of partner relationship formed
- the resources that partners provide (or a link to them in the key resources element)
- the activities that partners perform (or a link to them in the key activities element)

Cost structure

The cost structure is all the expenses of the business. Costs accrue as resources are obtained, activities are performed and partnerships are utilised. Osterwalder and Pigneur[77] differentiate between two broad cost-structure models, namely cost-driven and value-driven. Cost-driven models focus on cost minimisation. This type of business model focuses on creating lean cost structures to enable it to pitch low-price value propositions to customers. These models typically involve automation and extensive outsourcing whenever it is the cheapest option. Value-driven models, on the other hand, are less concerned with the cost implications, and instead focus on creating value for customers. These models often have a high degree of personalised service and high-quality features and functionalities.[78]

What needs to be defined in the cost structure element?

- the type of cost structure (cost-driven/value-driven)
- the fixed costs involved in the business model
- the variable costs involved in the business model
- the economies of scope that exist in the model
- the economies of scale that exist in the model
- the cost of capital
- elements of the value proposition that are given away for free (if any)
- the most important or most uncertain costs that need to be closely monitored

Practical guideline

Developing a business model from scratch is a rigorous process that often requires several hypothesis-testing iterations and inputs from various participants before the model really takes shape and becomes sensible. The canvas is intended to be used as a hands-on tool that fosters understanding, discussion, creativity and analysis of business models. Therefore, when working in a large group it is often best to print the business model canvas on a large surface and work with sticky notes to allow participants to simultaneously construct the canvas and allow for idea mobility.

It is also advised to use a combination of words, images and highlighter colours on the sticky notes to depict one's business model. Basic images are often powerful mechanisms for telling stories and conveying ideas of how the business could function. Colours, on the other hand, allow related ideas to be colour-coded, creating a flow through the business model. Depending on your business, it might even be sensible to construct separate business model canvasses for each product category or each customer segment to clearly depict how these function. Multiple business model alternatives can also be created for the same product, service or technology in order to fully explore all the business model innovation possibilities.[79 80] Also see the section *Process of Business Modelling* later in this chapter.

Finally, it is possible to hone your business model-building skills and find inspiration by mapping out every new and innovative theory of the business that you come across. By figuring out what makes the theory work, you assimilate that knowledge into your business model-building repository and can similarly apply it to your own situation.

Application tool

Use the business model canvas template in Figure 3.4 and the practical guidelines above to describe the current as-is business model of your organisation. If you are starting a new business, highlight which of the elements are the most uncertain and test those hypotheses first.

THE LEAN CANVAS

The lean canvas, developed by Ash Maurya,[81] is an adaptation of the original business model canvas. It infuses the ideas embedded in the lean start-up methodology of Eric Ries[82] and the customer development process of Steve Blank[83] into the business model canvas of Alexander Osterwalder and Yves Pigneur. The lean canvas is often preferred over the business model canvas by start-up entrepreneurs and venture capitalists as it presents a faster, looser and more "quick-and-dirty" method of business modelling.

A start-up environment is inherently fast-paced and deals with conditions of extreme uncertainty. Under the conditions of time-scarcity and uncertainty, you want to focus on the elements of the business model that are inherently the most risky.[84] From the lean start-up methodology, the biggest risk is product risk – building a product that no one wants. Start-ups should therefore have a keen focus on developing a problem-solution fit. Furthermore, when time is scarce and certainty low, it does not always make sense to sketch out the full detail of one's business model. During the early phases of business model development a lot of the "how-to's" will rapidly and unexpectedly change as new information becomes available, some doors close and other doors open. It therefore becomes cumbersome to continually update some of the elements of the business model canvas. Rather than immediately drill down into operational details, start-ups prefer to pursue clarity in the bigger picture and higher-level concept of what they are trying to achieve, as this clarity enables them to eloquently pitch their ideas to investors in simple and concise ways.

Start-ups and venture capitalists therefore prefer the lean canvas, as it adopts more of a problem-solution focus that is simpler, easier to immediately understand, and more direct and explicit in articulating what the business is trying to achieve and what the risks and advantages of the business idea are. The lean canvas is depicted in Figure 3.8.

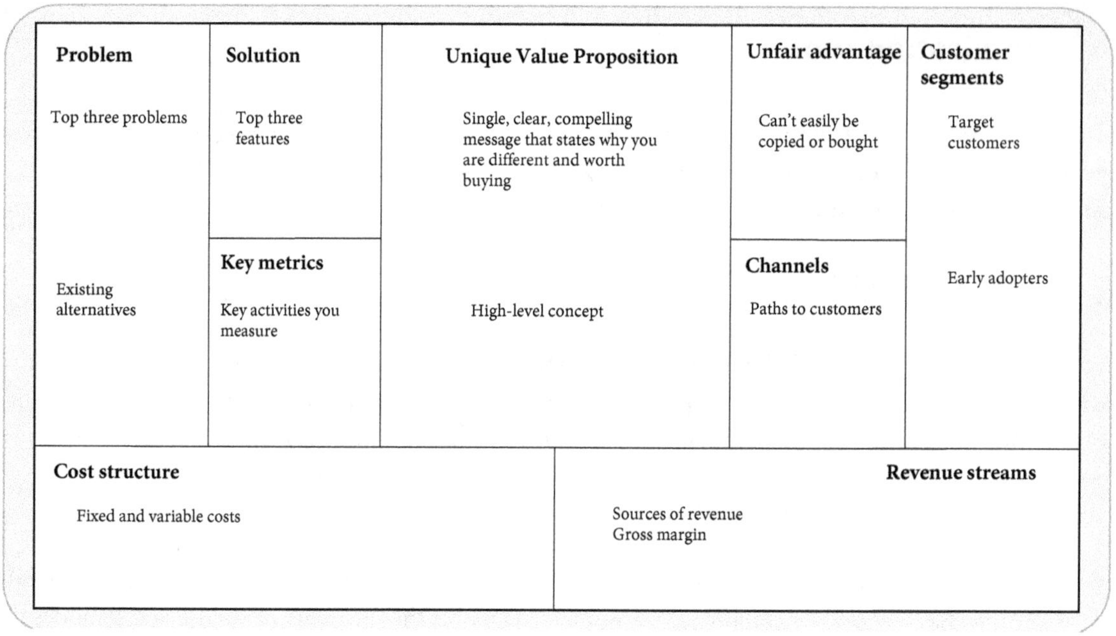

Problem	Solution	Unique Value Proposition	Unfair advantage	Customer segments
Top three problems	Top three features	Single, clear, compelling message that states why you are different and worth buying	Can't easily be copied or bought	Target customers
	Key metrics		**Channels**	Early adopters
Existing alternatives	Key activities you measure	High-level concept	Paths to customers	

Cost structure	Revenue streams
Fixed and variable costs	Sources of revenue Gross margin

Figure 3.8: The lean canvas[85]

As can be seen above, the lean canvas replaces the operations-oriented key partnerships, key activities, key resources and customer relationship elements in the business model canvas in favour of problem, solution, key metrics and unfair advantage elements. In the **problem element**, canvas users define the major problems or pain points that the business seeks to address. This element is also used to define and describe some of the existing alternatives that currently attempt to address these pains; this serves as a vital context for subsequent elements. The **solution element** is used to define the higher-level solution to the problem in a concise and powerful way, and often involves defining key features that emphasise the advantages of the new solution over the existing alternatives. The **key metrics** element is used to define the core indicators of business success. These indicators provide vital insights into the business's daily progress, overall progression towards the vision, and the long-term sustainability prospects of the business. Lastly, the **unfair advantage** element is used to define the key advantages that the business idea and start-up team have over competitors who would similarly like to provide solutions to the customer problem. This element therefore often contains features or resource descriptions that cannot easily be bought or obtained. The other elements of the lean canvas are exactly the same as in the business model canvas, except for two small changes. Firstly, the customer segment element additionally has an increased focus on defining early adopters or "perfect" customers of the business, as these customers will be the initial target of the new business. Secondly, the lean canvas advocates that businesses define a higher-level concept in the value proposition element, which refers to an **"X of Y" analogy statement** that quickly gets the business message across, e.g. "YouTube: the Flickr of video".

As a whole, the lean canvas is particularly suited for use in start-up environments, environments where uncertainty reigns, and environments where conveying the problem, solution and advantage of a new business idea in a simple and concise way is critical. The lean canvas, however, discards elements that are fundamental to the business model concept and is likely to evoke disdain from more traditional strategists and business model thinkers. We maintain that the lean canvas has its uses, but it is not suitable for existing enterprises or when deep analyses and comparisons of different businesses are necessary. For these cases the business model canvas remains superior.

In the next section, we propose an expanded business model canvas that seeks to incorporate the advantages of both the business model canvas and the lean canvas in a singular view.

EXPANDED BUSINESS MODEL CANVAS

In the introduction to this chapter it was mentioned that strategy and business models have slightly different focuses. Strategy focuses more on the creation of a sustainable competitive advantage. Business models have more of a focus on depicting customer value creation. The primary weakness of typical business model taxonomies is exactly this: they facilitate the creation of new business models, but do not necessarily emphasise competition, the creation of a competitive advantage, overall competitiveness in the market, robustness and sustainability.

Business models are exceptional tools for communication, however, as they allow enterprises to explicitly articulate their strategies and operations in succinct ways that foster understanding throughout the organisation. It would therefore be unwise to throw out the baby with the bathwater. Instead it is perhaps time to infuse business models with a more competitive flavour, thereby enhancing their relevance and potency.

In this endeavour, we combine the business model canvas and lean canvas of the preceding sections with customer retention tools[86][87] aimed at robustness and sustainability, and present you with an expanded business model canvas in Figure 3.9.

Key Partners	Key Activities	Value Proposition	Customer Relationships	Customer Segments	Customer Retention
Key partners and suppliers, and their contribution to the business	Activity system, internal value chain, operating procedures	Value promised to customers (per customer segment). Benefits provided: gain creators and pain relievers. Unique selling proposition: Compelling reason why your product/service offering is different and worth buying. Minimum viable product description (for start-ups)	Bond established with customers	Customer and user characteristics (demographic, geographic, psychological, behavioural), customer needs, pains, gains, jobs to be done	Control points, switching costs, and e-loyalty drivers
	Key Resources		Channels		
	Core & distinctive competencies, strategic assets, people		Customer touch-points; delivery, sales and communication channels		

Cost Structure	Key Metrics	Revenue Streams
Fixed and variable costs, cost drivers, cost of capital, economies of scale and scope	Core indicators of business progress and success	Income streams, pricing strategy, gross margin, rough break-even calculation

Competitive Advantage

Systemic interaction between the core competitive advantage choice, other generic strategic options and choices (Chapter 2), and all other business model components

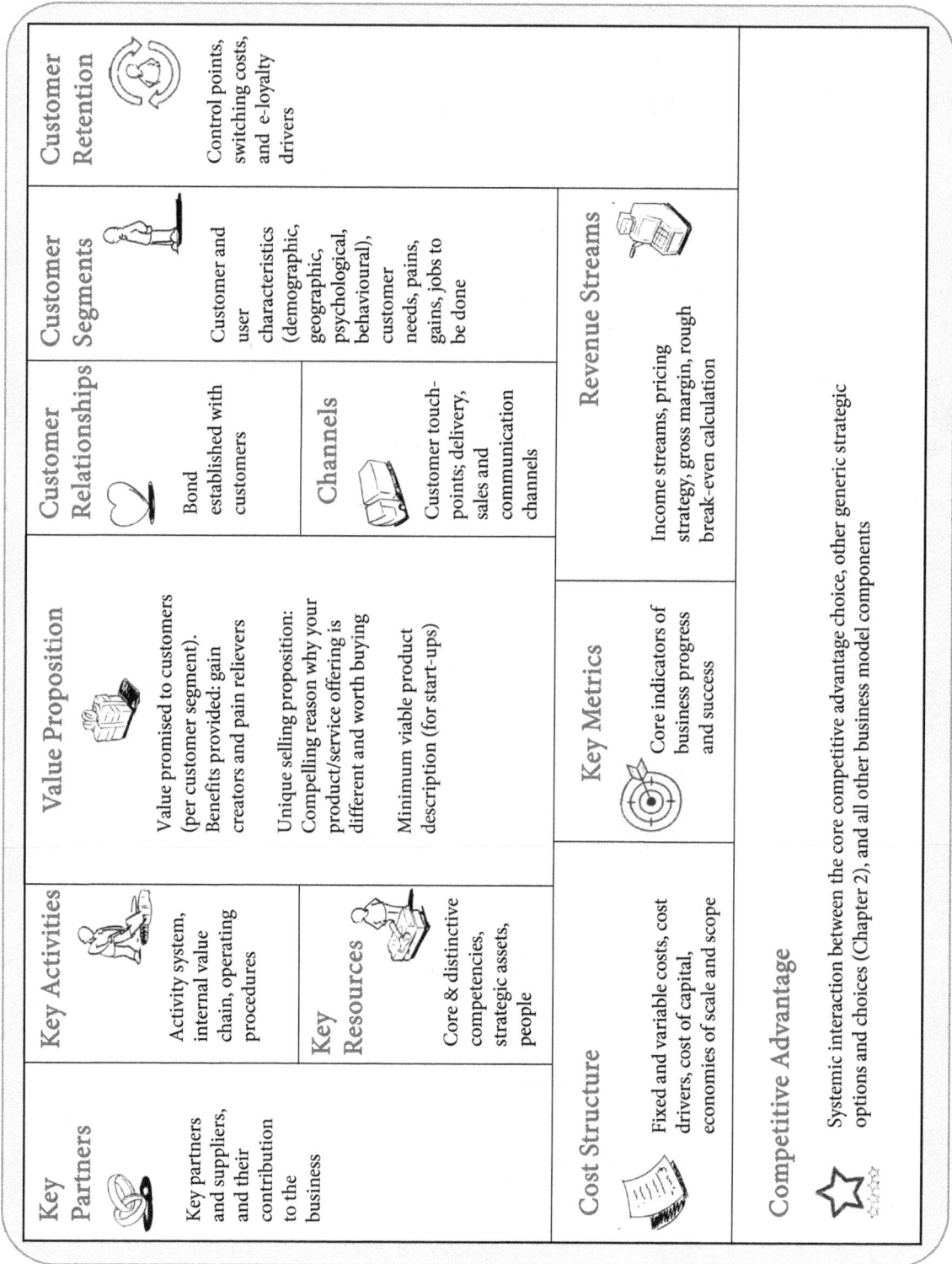

Figure 3.9: Extended business model canvas

In addition all the classic business model canvas elements, the expanded business model canvas opposite contains a new customer retention element, as well as the key metrics and unfair advantage (competitive advantage) elements of the lean canvas. Regarding the other unique elements of the lean canvas, the problem element already forms part of the customer segment element and is typically expressed in the form of a customer problem/pain or a desired gain that needs to be fulfilled. The solution element is also already contained in the business model canvas via the value proposition, channels, customer relationships and revenue stream elements – how the business will solve the customer problem, via which products and services, at what price, via which channels and by establishing which relationships.

Customer retention deals with persuading customers to return to the business for repeat purchases. It is essentially a sustainability driver. This element was added adjacent to the customer segments and revenue streams elements, as customer retention seeks to lock customers into a relationship with the business and thereby sustain its income streams. Customer retention also plays a vital role in defending the business against competitors. Customer retention therefore creates barriers to entry that locks competitors out of the market. It is an extremely important element and aspect of business that has been neglected by numerous strategy tools for far too long.

Key metrics is another vitally important element, as it measures the business's progress towards its goals. When a business's key metrics indicate that things are not going as expected, then adaptation is required. Aptly, the key metrics element was placed between the value proposition, revenues streams and cost structure elements. Financial prosperity should always be measured, as well as the business's value proposition performance in the market.

The other critical element that forces business model developers to consider the viability and competitiveness of the model is the articulation of the business's competitive advantage. Every business needs to have a competitive advantage of some sort, no matter how small, otherwise how can it reasonably expect to be successful in the market? Essentially, the whole business model and business strategy exists to create a sustainable competitive advantage (see Figure 3.2). When a strategy is distilled, it boils down to the creation of a competitive advantage. For this reason, this element was placed at the bottom of the canvas, showcasing that all the efficiency efforts realised in a lean cost structure, all the value creation efforts realised in healthy revenue streams, and all the progress on the business's key metrics need to flow down and create a sustainable competitive advantage. When this is achieved, the business becomes robust, defensible and its longevity prospects improve.

The remainder of this section discusses the three new additions (customer retention, key metrics, and competitive advantage) of the expanded business model canvas in more detail. The other nine business model canvas building-block descriptions remain intact, as previously discussed.

Customer retention

Customer retention deals with persuading customers to return to the business for repeat purchases. Customer retention has historically been a fundamental driver of business success and is important for two reasons. Firstly, from a financial perspective, the basic principle on which customer retention is based is that the costs of acquiring new customers are much higher than the costs of retaining them.[88] Businesses that are therefore able to retain customers better are thought to be much more profitable than those that have to acquire new customers every single time. Reichheld and Schefter,[89] for instance, found that a five per cent increase in customer retention leads to an increase of between 25 to 95 per cent in profitability. Other research similarly showed that loyal customers may be up to ten times as valuable as average customers over their lifetime.[90][91]

There are also those who argue that customer retention is even more critical in the digital economy than in the industrial economy, as high customer acquisition costs make many customer relationships unprofitable during the early years.[92] [93] [94] [95] [96] Only at a later stage, when the costs of serving loyal customers fall and their purchase volumes rise, do these relationships generate significant returns.[97] [98]

Secondly, from a competitive perspective, customer retention includes all the overarching actions that lock customers into a relationship with the business, prevent their defection to competitors and allow additional value to be captured. Customer retention creates barriers to entry that prevent rivals from making competitive inroads on a business's customer base. This locks competitors out of the market and protects the business's income streams. Customer retention is therefore critical to a business's long-term sustainability.[99] [100] [101]

A study by Ungerer[102] proposes that three complementary elements can assist in retaining customers: (1) strategic control points, (2) switching costs, and (3) loyalty antecedents (drivers). These are discussed below.

1.   Strategic control points

Strategic control points (henceforth referred to just as control points) are the mechanisms that businesses specifically control and leverage to prevent imitation and lock competitive advantages in for themselves.[103] Control points are sources of power and control. Slywotzky[104] mentions that "There are places on the landscape, places in the value chain, that are ten times more valuable than others in terms of profit, power and control. These special places are the control points of the business landscape."

Control points are employed to retain customers and prevent competitors from entering specific strategic spaces. Control points are customer lock-in and competitor lock-out mechanisms that assist in defending the business's income streams. The term "strategic control points" was first introduced by Slywotzky and Morrison[105], and Ungerer   et al.[106] define it as "The barricades that are erected around income streams for which the trade-offs, for competitors to enter or customers to defect, are just too high". Control points are also sometimes referred to as isolating mechanisms, which Oliver[107] describes as imitability barriers that protect a firm's competitive advantages. These competitive advantages in turn allow businesses to provide unprecedented value to customers, which makes it unnecessary for them to go anywhere else.

Control points relate to the resource-based view of the firm, which suggests that possessing resources (skills, knowledge, assets and positions) that are valuable, rare, durable, difficult to copy, idiosyncratic, nontradable and nonsubstitutable lead to differentiation and supernormal profits.[108] [109] [110] [111] [112] Control points also relate to entry barriers, which Carlton and Perloff[113] define as anything that prevents an entrepreneur from instantaneously creating a new business in a market.

Fourteen types of control point are depicted in Figure 3.10. Six of these control points are classified as being beneficial to customers and can create advantages that attract and retain customers, while eight of the control points do not provide benefits to customers.

A first mover advantage is gained when a business is first to market with a new product/service offering or proprietary product technology. Developing a first-mover advantage is contingent on the business's ability to innovate or exploit innovations of others in the market first. First-mover advantages are valuable because of the demand they invoke and the early market lead that can be built in the absence of competition. Competitors who want to compete in the first mover's domain are therefore forced to play catch-up. First-mover advantages do not last forever though, and the advantage is diminished as soon as imitation sets in. The rate of imitation, however, is subject to the complexity or novelty of the innovation. At the very least a first-mover advantage allows a business to establish a **brand advantage** and possibly **switching costs**, which can lock customers into a long-term relationship, regardless of imitators.[115]

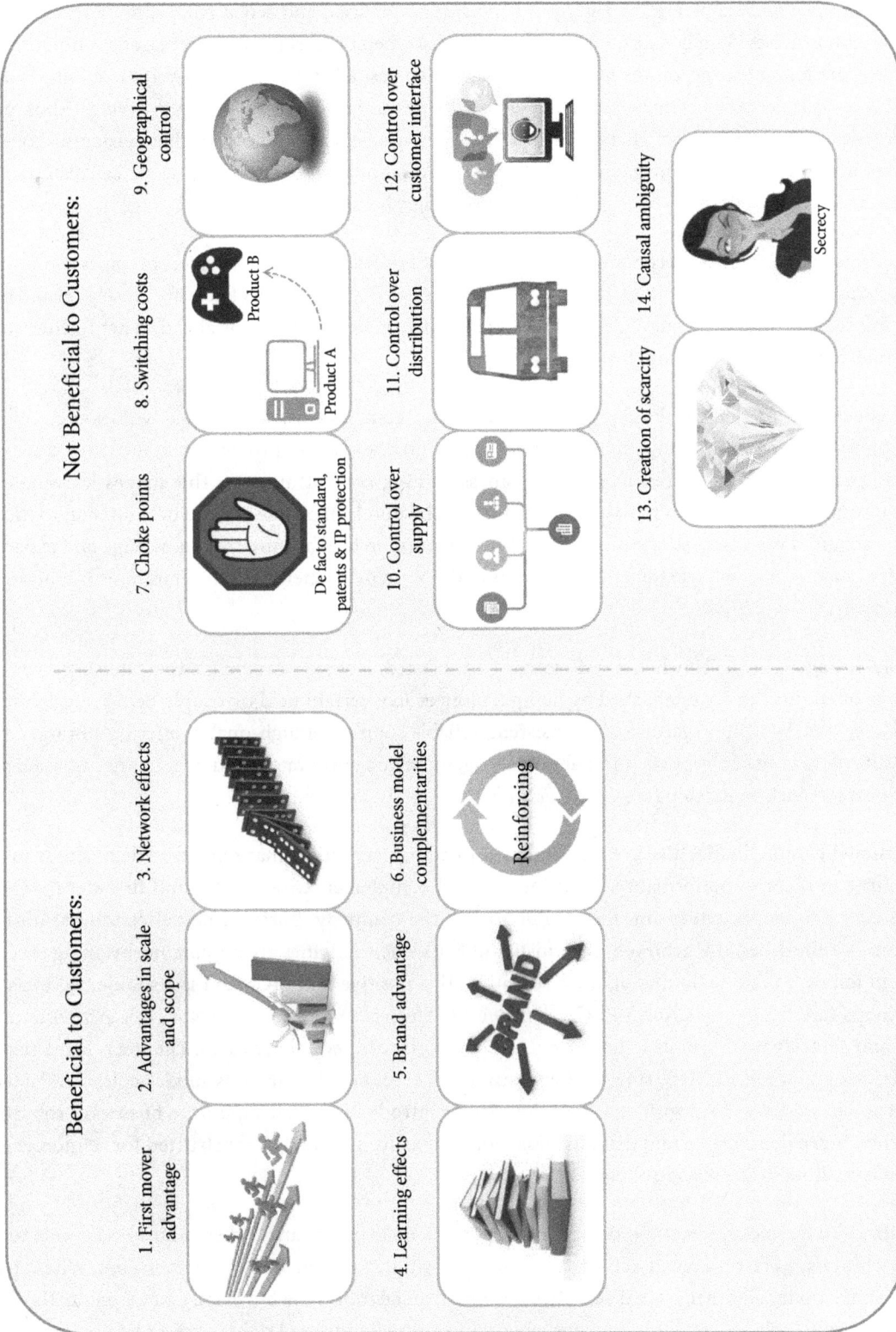

Figure 3.10: Control points[114]

Advantages in scale and scope are the supply-side economies of scale and scope enjoyed by larger or sometimes simply smarter businesses. Supply-side economies of scale exist when the cost per unit decreases as output is increased. Supply-side economies of scope, on the other hand, exist when cost advantages are enjoyed by offering a wide array of products/services that possibly make use of the same activities and resources, resulting in savings. Thus, producing product A reduces the cost of producing product B.[116] Advantages in scale and scope allow businesses to establish a price or production quantity advantage over other firms.[117] Additionally, advantages in scope can also translate into synergy effects or complementarity benefits that customers enjoy because of the extended range of choices.

Network effects are demand-side economies of scale, where a business's value proposition becomes more valuable to individual users as the total number of users in the system increases.[118] [119] Network effects are closely related to the law of increasing returns, which Arthur[120] describes as "the tendency for that which is ahead to get further ahead, and for that which loses advantage to lose further advantage".

Learning effects are the diligent development of knowledge, competencies and distinctive resources over a long period of time, which equips a company with expertise that no one else can provide. In many cases, the experience curve of employees additionally results in the business gaining cost advantages. This makes learning effects an exceptional control point, as tacit knowledge embedded in the minds of people is extremely difficult to imitate, and can only be acquired via a long, slow process.[121] [122] The other option is to acquire this knowledge and expertise from competitors, making not only customer retention, but also employee retention, of paramount importance in the digital economy.

A **brand advantage** is achieved when a well-recognised, trusted, iconic brand image is established.[123] [124] A brand advantage is often most easily established by being a pioneer in a certain field or simply being novel, but can also be earned over time by being regarded as a consistent, reliable supplier of high-quality offerings. Brand advantages are often difficult to erode (except via internal mismanagement and corporate scandal), and are sustained by brand, copyright or trademark ownership (see *Choke points*).

Business model complementarities are elements within a business model that reinforce the business model over time, resulting in superior performance.[125] Business model complementarities go beyond first-tier fit where there is a *consistency* between activities and the overall goal of the company. Business model complementarities exist when second- or third-tier fit is achieved. Second-tier fit exits when activities are *reinforcing*, meaning that activities support and improve the functioning of other activities. This positive reinforcement is also referred to as virtuous feedback loops (see *Engines of Growth* in *Crystallising the Strategic Business Landscape, Key Activities* previously discussed and Test 7 in the *Normative Assessment of Competitive Strategies* later in this chapter). Third-tier fit exists when activities are *optimised*, referring to their near ideal execution.[126] Business model complementarity is an important and powerful strategic principle (see the chapter introduction) that supports a business's robustness and sustainability. It can therefore be said that business models that are so superbly constructed for reinforcement, may themselves constitute strategic control points.

Choke points are the most powerful type of control point. Choke points arise when a business is able to position itself in such a way that no related activity can proceed without the business's intervention. When a business controls a choke point, all other related activities become dependent on the business. Choke points therefore deal with creating "monopoly" effects. This happens when a business obtains legal rights over a certain domain, or when it becomes regarded as the *de facto* standard.[127] The latter can be achieved by being the first mover or simply being superior, thereby becoming the preferred choice for most customers. Legal rights over a domain can be obtained via mechanisms such as patents, design rights, copyrights, creating and owning the standards, strategic partnership agreements, and utilising other forms of intellectual property protection.[128] [129]

Switching costs are all the costs incurred by a customer in switching to a competitor's offerings.[130] Switching costs are essentially the time, effort, financial and loss of benefit costs associated with switching to another supplier. Switching costs involve the hassle or inconvenience of switching suppliers, such as the hassle of registering, constructing a new contract, re-entering data, learning how to use a different product or service, and integrating the new system with one's own. Switching costs also include any type of expense that needs to be incurred in switching, and investments already made in complementary and durable assets that prevent customers from switching. It also includes the advantages that will be foregone once two parties have traded, in comparison to trading with other, new parties.[131]

Geographical control means gaining control over a geographic or digital location. This constitutes a control point, as it represents a space where competitors cannot follow.[132] Owned geographic locations or domain names can act as a lock-out mechanism for competitors. Walmart, for instance, put up stores in rural areas that were too small to sustain two retail chains, creating clear barriers to competition.[133] Digital spaces can similarly be controlled, for instance by creating proprietary or closed systems that only a selected few businesses have access to, or have the rights to trade on.[134]

From a value chain perspective, **control over supply** refers to controlling the supply arrangement or resources.[135] Capturing this control point can lead to significant bargaining power. This control point is related to learning effects as previously discussed, as learning effects can lead a business into becoming a specialised supplier that is exclusively capable of providing specific competencies.[136]

Control over distribution channels is controlling the physical or digital flow of offerings, by having control over the channels through which the offerings need to flow. Controlling the distribution channel can be a significant control point, as new entrants may require the use of the channel, but are not able to access it because incumbents are already fully utilising it.[137] New entrants must then persuade the distribution channels to accept their offerings, for instance by reducing their profit margins. Clearly, this acts as an entry barrier. Intuitively, the more limited or scarce the distribution channel, the fiercer the competition for the channel and the higher the entry barriers are.[138] In the worst cases, the barriers to entry are so high that companies have to create a totally new distribution channel for their offerings.

Similarly, **control over the customer interface** is controlling the customer relationship; having proprietary information about customer preferences; or controlling the customer interface or channel through which purchases are made.[139] Controlling the customer interface is a powerful control point as it affects how offerings are presented and strongly influences how much customers trust and perceive offerings.

The **creation of scarcity** also constitutes a control point. In the age-old paradigm, value is associated with scarcity. When something is scarce, profitability tends to disperse towards these points of scarcity, away from points of abundance. As such, entrepreneurs are forced to pay attention to unfulfilled customer needs and unrealised potential customer value and are forced to seek the "bottlenecks" (see *Choke points*) in the system.[140] [141] [142] However, scarcity itself can be created – for instance by differentiating;[143] intentionally making an offering exclusive; or tailoring specific offerings to customer needs.[144]

Lastly, **causal ambiguity** is the inimitability that results from difficulty in determining the source of advantage that a business enjoys. This ambiguity often results from a subtle combination of tangible and intangible assets, culture, processes and organisational attributes.[145] The agenda of causal ambiguity can be furthered by secrecy – the intentional protection of a firm's knowledge capital, management practices and strategy.

These 14 control points assist businesses in thinking about the different ways that they can capture value, create leverages and lock competitive advantages in for themselves. Slywotzky and Morrison[146] state that every good business design has at least one strategic control point, with the best business designs having two or more. These authors further state: "A business design without a strategic control point is like a ship with a hole in its hull. It will sink much sooner than it has to."

Application tool

Consider the 14 control points of Figure 3.10 and complete Table 3.3.

- Which control points have we captured to date?
- What is our rationale for believing we've captured this control point?
- What competitive advantages are we creating or sustaining through this control point?
- What potential control points can we still capture?
- What value will be realised from capturing these control points?
- What initiatives do we need to launch to capture these control points?

Table 3.3: Control point evaluation

Captured control point	Rationale	Advantage created or sustained
Potential control point	**Value that will be realised from capturing it**	**Initiative for capturing**

2. Switching costs

Switching costs are all the costs incurred by a customer in switching to a competitor's offerings.[147] Switching costs are essentially the time, effort, financial and loss of benefit costs associated with switching to another supplier. They are the exit barriers that prevent customer defection. Switching costs have been recognised as an important contributor to attaining competitive advantages[148] [149] [150] [151] [152] and are one of the control points that enjoy the most attention in literature. Kotler[153] also posits that there are fundamentally two ways in which one can create loyal customers: by increasing customer satisfaction or raising switching costs.

Switching costs deter customers from exiting the relationship with the business and therefore act as "negative" types of customer lock-in. Great care therefore needs to be taken when dealing with switching costs, as too much visibility can create negative perceptions that discourage customers from buying one's offerings in the first place. Another concern is that some switching costs are lower in e-business than they are traditionally.[154] [155] A fear therefore exists that switching costs have lost their potency. However, instead of diminishing its importance, this amplifies the importance of understanding the types of switching costs that can be used to create customer lock-in.[156]

Fifteen types of switching costs are depicted in Figure 3.11. Two of these switching costs are classified as loss of emotional benefit costs, seven are classified as loss of functional benefit costs, one as a loss of potential benefit costs, and five as non"loss of benefit" costs.

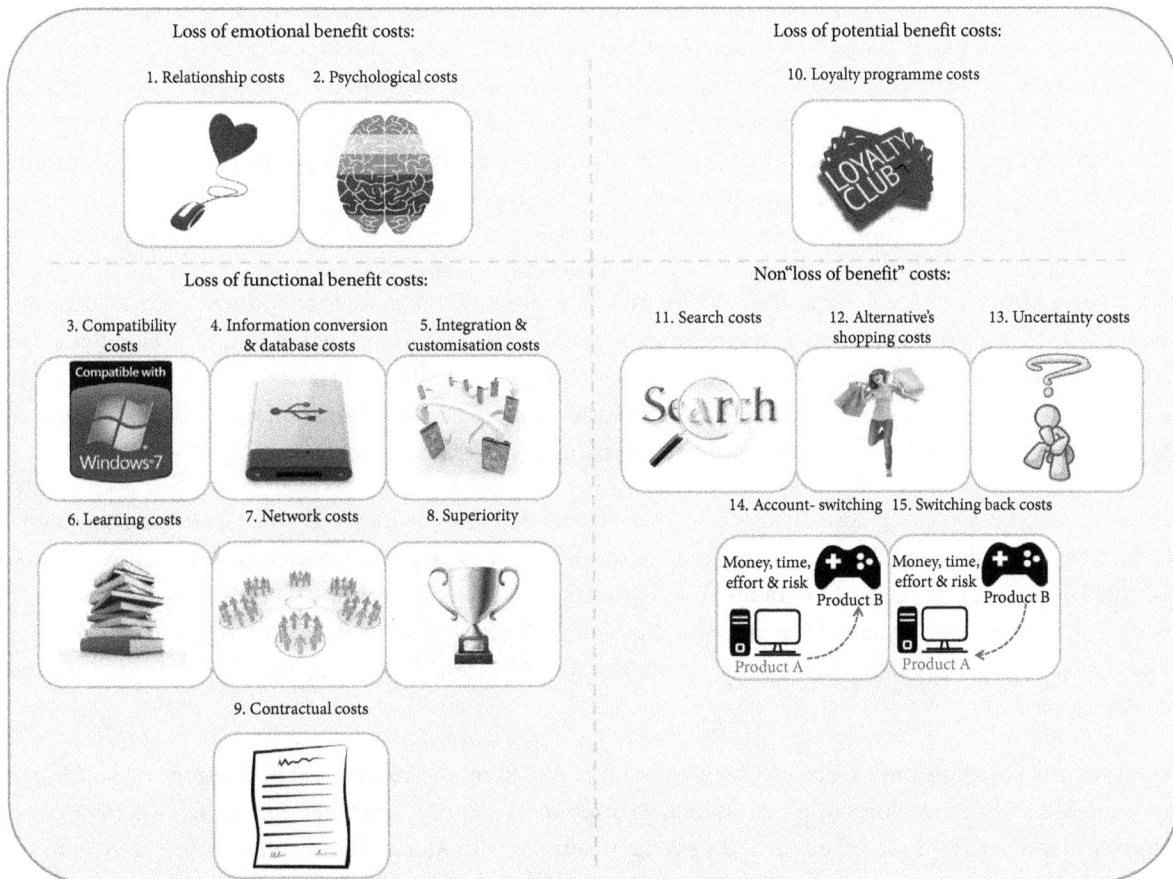

Figure 3.11: Switching costs[157]

Relationship costs are the emotional loss involved in breaking the relationship bonds with people that the customer is used to interacting with. Over time, customers develop a familiarity with suppliers. Relationship costs therefore pose strong exit barriers, as customers will not immediately experience the same level of comfort with the new supplier as the old one.[158] Deep customer relationships and customer-focused options are therefore able to create unassailable competitive advantages,[159] [160] as customers who have fostered a strong, trusting relationship with suppliers will not easily defect. An even higher level of lock-in can be achieved when customers are involved in the design, production and consumption process, also known as "prosumption". Customers who are involved in this way usually feel a sense of ownership, which further raises switching costs.[161]

Navigating strategic possibilities

Customers can also face **psychological switching costs** due to their inherent preferences. They may for instance be unwilling to give up a brand simply because they like it and feel loyal to it for noneconomic reasons.[162] Psychological switching also includes behavioural switching costs, which relate to customers' unwillingness to switch because they like their current habits and way of doing things.[163] [164] Ways in which psychological switching costs can be created are fostering strong customer relationships, creating an online community and otherwise emotionally appealing to customers.[165]

Compatibility costs arise when there is an incompatibility between some feature of the current offering and the new offering. These incompatibilities often arise because the initial offering makes use of complementary products. If a customer chooses to buy the new offering, then he or she has to buy its complementarities as well for the whole offering to function. This creates large switching costs. Furthermore, because goods and services in the networked economy typically function in systems, this makes compatibility costs more prominent than ever before.[166] Examples include hardware requiring software, videos requiring video players, and durable products requiring consumable complements (printers requiring ink cartridges etc.).[167] [168] It can therefore be said that the strategic choice of incompatibility between or among complementary products creates "proprietary" or "closed" systems.[169]

Account-switching costs involve the time, effort, risk and once-off financial expenditures such as deposits or initiation fees[170] incurred when actually moving from one supplier's account to a new account. Essentially, account-switching costs are what are commonly referred to as "switching costs". Edlin and Harris[171] call this type of switching cost "transactional switching costs"; however, this is easily confused with transaction costs, which are the costs involved with each transaction.[172] The term "account switching costs" is therefore preferred.

Apart from account-switching costs, two other types of cost that may be incurred when switching suppliers are "information conversion and database costs" and "integration and customisation costs". **Information conversion and database costs** are the cost of upgrading one's system, converting historical data into new data formats and maintaining incompatible systems.[173] In software and online services, moving data from one supplier to another may be particularly costly and the degree of data portability is therefore a big determinant of information conversion and database costs.[174]

Integration and customisation costs are the integration and customisations that will be foregone or that will once again be needed when switching to a new system or supplier. Businesses can therefore raise switching costs by convincing customers to design the business's products into their products[175] or by allowing customers to make customised changes to the business's offerings for enhanced convenience and performance. Conveniences such as default values, automatic payments, automatic subscription renewals, minimal repeated data entry and other customised settings all act as switching barriers[176] that will again need to be re-entered at the new supplier. Depending on the difficulty of changing and customising settings, significant time and effort may be required.[177] Businesses can create a similar lock-in by, for instance, giving partners access to information about their internal functions that allows partners to make more informed decisions. In this way partners may become integrated with and dependent on the business, raising switching costs.[178]

Learning costs come into play when products do not merely require customers' consumption, but also customers' active participation in their use. When switching to a new supplier, learning costs are incurred in the form of time and effort required to learn and adapt to a new product, system or interface. Sometimes learning costs pose very high switching barriers when significant learning effort is required. Industries where learning costs are particularly significant are those where products in the industry vary widely and the products are more technically complex to use.[179] Businesses can further create learning costs by training the customer's personnel to use the business's technical products[180] or, inversely, provide continued technical assistance and advice, lowering the customer's learning costs and making the value proposition more appealing.

Once a user has become a member of a community, **network costs** discourage them from leaving the network. Network costs entail the cost of forfeiting benefits that would have been gained if the customer did not leave the network.[181] Benefits that networks could provide are diverse, but often include a type of knowledge sharing, additional or special opportunities, and a sense of community and belonging. Network costs are further amplified by network effects, where more users participating in the community increases the benefit of a single user. Network costs therefore have the potential to create large switching barriers.

Superiority costs are the lock-in that can be created by simply offering superior products and services.[182] When a customer's needs are completely satisfied by a superior offering, then they will have little desire to go anywhere else. Stated differently, customers will experience a loss of benefit if they defect to an inferior offering[183].

Switching costs can also be created via **contractual costs**. Contractual costs are costs that users incur if they defect from a contract. The strength of contractual costs is that contracts can be established even in markets where switching costs are otherwise relatively low.[184] Some mobile phone carriers, for instance, partly subsidise the price of a new smartphone. In return, customers are locked into a contract that bears penalties for early termination.

Conversely, contracts can also be used to reward loyal customers. A loyalty programme at its core is nothing else than a contract between a supplier and a buyer that certain benefits will be obtained if the service or product is purchased often enough. Discounts can, for instance, be awarded when large enough purchases are made.[185] [186] **Loyalty programme costs** are therefore the potential loyalty benefits that customers forego when they switch suppliers.

Search costs are the costs that are incurred when a customer searches for new alternatives. Customers first need to find alternative suppliers, and gather enough information for them to evaluate whether switching would be beneficial. The unique characteristic of search costs is that these costs are incurred regardless of whether the customer decides to ultimately switch suppliers or not.[187]

Shopping costs are the additional costs involved in actually making purchases.[188] In the online world, shopping costs have been significantly reduced,[189] [190] but some still exist. Examples include data usage costs, credit card costs and delivery costs. Shopping costs essentially arise out of needing to "shop around" at multiple stores for multiple products. If a customer makes purchases at multiple stores, then multiple transaction costs are incurred and they will be billed for each individual delivery. Therefore if a business can provide a one-stop-shopping experience, then consumers' shopping costs will be reduced. Stated differently, an alternative's shopping costs present switching barriers to consumers who are already shopping at a business that offers a wide range of offerings.[191]

Related to search costs, **uncertainty costs** are the costs involved when customers are not able to adequately evaluate the benefits of an offering, without first using and experiencing it. Only by experiencing the offering will a customer be able to evaluate whether it suits their needs, level of expertise and whether their whole business, for instance, will be able to adapt to it. But since customers are not able to experience the offering beforehand, they remain uncertain about whether the offering will truly be beneficial. Uncertainty is a double-edged blade. It is beneficial to businesses who want to lock customers in, but a stumbling block for new customer acquisition. Advertising may provide information and claim certain benefits, but as advertisements originate from suppliers, they are often perceived as being biased. Increasingly important then, is the use of consumer ratings and reviews from experienced users to help reduce uncertainty costs.[192] Edlin and Harris[193] also note that uncertainty costs are only significant when other switching costs are high, otherwise users could test all available products and choose the one best suited to their needs. However, when other switching costs are high, uncertainty costs compound the switching cost effects. Because users are unsure about whether other suppliers' offerings are better than their current offerings, and other high switching costs prevent the customer from trying the new offerings to find out, consumers may never switch, even if they are very dissatisfied with their current supplier. Uncertainty costs are inherently linked to risk. Switching to a new supplier bears a certain amount of risk that is often perceived as higher by consumers than they actually are. Mistakes may be made in the switching process, which could cause the switching costs to outweigh the total benefit gained.[194] Also, if it is blindly decided to switch to a new system, and it does not perform as expected, then **switching back costs** (the inverse of account switching costs) will need to be incurred to revert to the old system or product.[195]

These 15 switching costs assist businesses in thinking about the different ways that they can lock customers into a relationship with the business and prevent them from defecting to competitors. It is not the aim to employ as many of these switching costs as possible, but rather to employ as many as needed to create sufficient exit barriers, while not creating overly negative customer perceptions.

Application tool

Use the 15 switching costs of Figure 3.11, complete Table 3.4 and think about the following questions:

- Which switching costs have we pursued to lock customers into business with us?
- What is our rationale for believing that we created these switching costs?
- Were these switching costs created from explicit design or are they an implicit consequence of something else?
  - This is an important question, as implicitly created switching costs often go unnoticed and may be destroyed when a new strategic direction is pursued. Taking note of these implicitly created switching costs may preserve them in future.
- Have we erected enough switching barriers? Which additional switching costs can we create? Which initiatives are needed to create these?
- Can we honestly say that our combination of switching costs will not create overly negative customer perceptions of our business?
- How could we obscure some of these switching costs?

Table 3.4: Switching cost evaluation

Switching cost	Rationale	Explicit /implicit	Initiative

3. E-loyalty drivers

Loyalty is a customer's favourable attitude to a business that results in repeat buying behaviour.[196] This definition accounts for both the attitudinal (desire to continue the relationship) and behavioural (repeat purchase behaviour) aspects required of true loyalty. False loyalty could, for instance, be displayed by customers who want to exit the relationship with a supplier, but lack suitable alternatives to switch. Similar false loyalty exists when customers are attitudinally loyal and have an intent to purchase, but the intent never turns to action.[197]

Loyalty as a customer retention technique attempts to lock customers into a continued relationship with the business from a "positive" perspective. Benefits of loyal customers for businesses include increased purchase volumes and frequency, increased positive word-of-mouth reviews about the business, increased likelihood of customers to forgive business mistakes, decreased customer sensitivity to price, and an overall increase in long-term profitability.[198] [199] [200] [201] Loyalty additionally creates synergistic advantages of brand extensions into related offerings and serves as an entry barrier that new entrants have to overcome.[202] [203] The benefits of loyalty for customers, on the other hand, include reducing their search costs for locating and evaluating offerings, and avoiding the learning process involved in switching to a new supplier.[204]

Keeping up with current times and an ever-increasingly digital world, this section focuses on the digital perspective relating to loyalty: e-loyalty. The creation of e-loyalty is perhaps an even more daunting task than creating loyalty in the physical world. Online, millions of websites and businesses are simultaneously clamouring for attention; competitors are only a few clicks away; and customers are extraordinarily empowered to compare and contrast alternative offerings with minimal effort.[205] [206] It is no wonder that there is a widely held belief that online shoppers are very fickle and that they will defect to the next exciting opportunity just as quickly as they capitalised on the current one.[207] Reichheld and Schefter's[208] research has shown, however, that this belief is ill-founded and that the Internet is actually a very "sticky" space. Most customers exhibit a clear inclination to loyalty and businesses that can correctly utilise web technologies will be able to reinforce their customer loyalty.[209] It is therefore vitally important to understand which different factors promote e-loyalty, so that these maybe incorporated to support customer retention.

Thirty-three drivers of e-loyalty are depicted in Figure 3.12. These factors are classified as relating to either (1) brand-building, (2) the value proposition, (3) trust and security, (4) customer attributes, (5) lock-in mechanisms, (6) website design, (7) order fulfilment or (8) customer service. Figure 3.12 additionally shows that loyalty does not only consist of behavioural loyalty (which can be created artificially through "negative" lock-in mechanisms), but also of attitudinal loyalty (which is dependent on specific customer attributes and can be reinforced via "positive" lock-in mechanisms). Behavioural intent therefore mediates the relationship between a customer's attitude and his or her behaviour.[210]

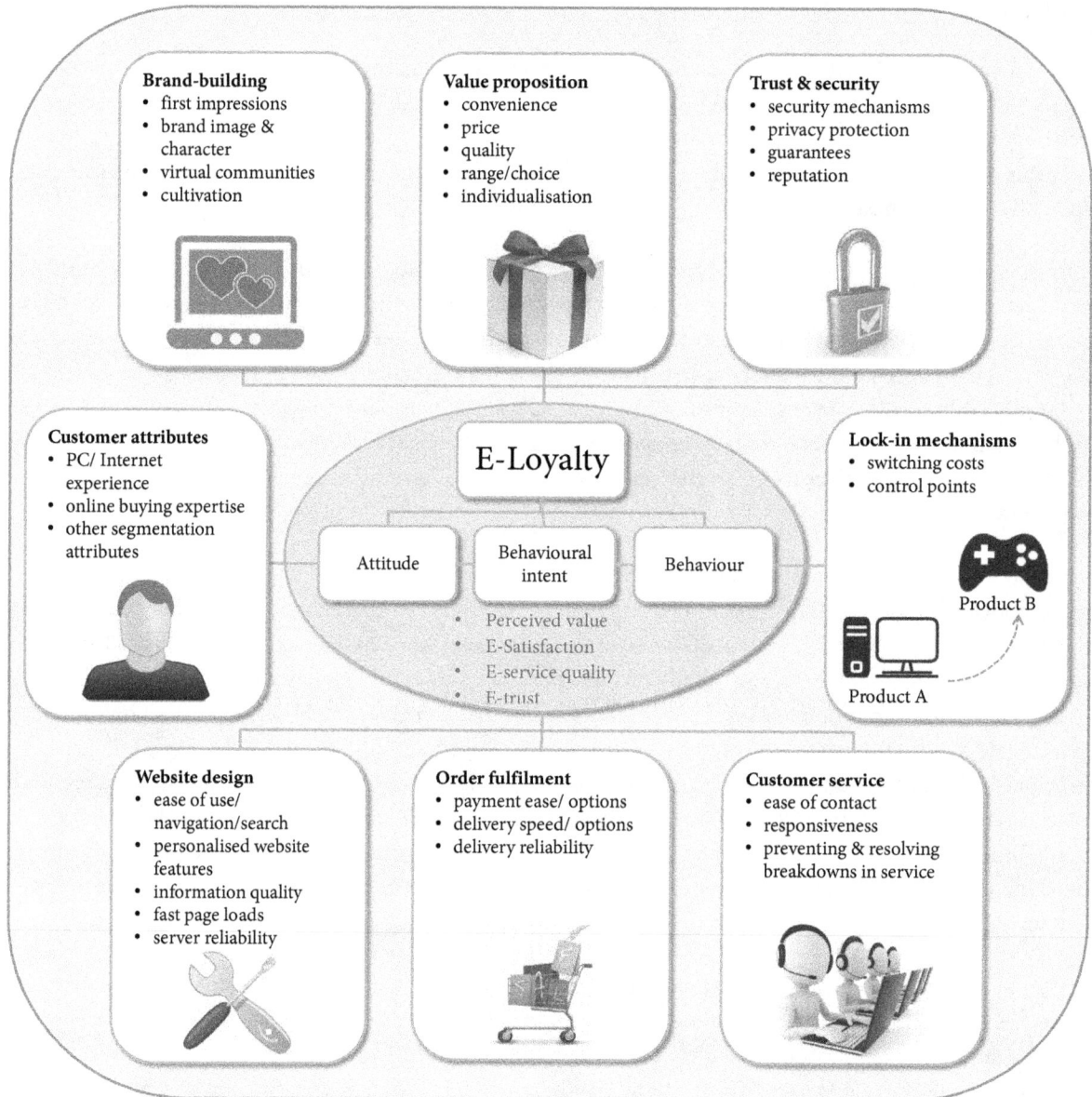

Figure 3.12: E-loyalty drivers[211]

3.1. Higher-level drivers of e-loyalty

Four commonly cited[212] higher-level factors are core to creating e-loyalty: (1) perceived value, (2) e-satisfaction, (3) e-service quality, and (4) e-trust.

Perceived value is a customer's overall assessment of the value offered by the business.[213] Perceived value is a relative and customer-specific assessment of the net utility or benefits derived from a supplier, based on the perceived rewards and sacrifices associated with the offering. Customers evaluate what is fair, right or deserved in relation to the perceived cost of the offering. These costs or sacrifices may be monetary, but may also be nonmonetary and include sacrifices such as time, effort or stress experienced. Customers therefore *perceive* a product as valuable when they evaluate their ratio of output to inputs to be aligned with that of the company's ratio, benchmarked against industry offerings.[214] Perceived value is critical to loyalty, as customers who perceive that they are not receiving the best value for money will start to consider alternatives.[215] [216]

Customer satisfaction is the extent to which customers are satisfied or pleased with the value derived from the business (based on their perceived value). Two types of customer satisfaction exist: transaction-specific satisfaction or overall satisfaction. Transaction-specific satisfaction refers to a customer's satisfaction with their most recent transactional experience with the business, whereas overall satisfaction is a customer's cumulative impression of the company.[217] [218] Overall satisfaction typically serves as a better predictor of customer loyalty, and in this book, customer satisfaction is therefore defined as a customer's overall negative or positive feeling regarding the net value derived from a supplier.[219]

Satisfaction is by far the factor that is the most discussed driver of e-loyalty and most studies find a significantly positive link between these.[220] Some authors have argued, however, that the relationship between satisfaction and e-loyalty is not linear,[221] [222] as satisfaction does not necessarily lead to loyalty, nor does loyalty necessarily point towards satisfaction. Others argue that satisfaction used to be a key metric, but that today it can only be seen as a minimum requirement to enter an industry.[223] Regardless of the perspective used, satisfying customers remain pivotal.

E-service quality is similar to customer satisfaction, but slightly different. **E-service quality** refers specifically to the extent to which e-customer service needs are fulfilled[224] – that is, the extent to which a website facilitates efficient and effective shopping, purchasing, delivery of products, and customer support services.[225] [226]

E-trust is the confidence of customers in a website's reliability and integrity.[227] It can also be the confidence that a company can be relied on to serve the best interests of customers.[228] E-trust positively and directly affects loyalty, as trust affects a customer's intent to purchase or repurchase.[229] [230] [231] Trust is essential in online business, where business is conducted at a distance and risk and uncertainties are magnified. Jack Brennan from Vanguard states that "Trust is our number one asset at Vanguard. We recognise you cannot buy trust with advertising or salesmanship; you have to earn it – by always acting in the best interests of customers. We did not design our website to sell more products and services. We designed it to educate our customers and provide better and more timely information and advice so that they can make better decisions."[232]

3.2. Brand-building

In the brand-building category, four drivers of e-loyalty are (1) first impressions, (2) brand image and character, (3) virtual communities, and (4) cultivation.

Regarding **first impressions**, Levitt[233] states that when products cannot be experienced fully before purchase, consumers are essentially asked to buy promises of satisfaction. This requires trust. Levitt[234] states that "Common sense tells us, and research confirms, that people use appearances to make judgements about realities". Users translate appearance into confidence about performance. First impressions created by a great-looking and inviting website are critical in convincing potential customers to become paying customers.[235] [236] Websites that initially disappoint will not necessarily be granted a second chance, and any chance at loyalty will similarly vanish.

Brand image and character are the overall image, personality or brand that the e-business projects to customers. Companies can employ various website designs and styles involving different text fonts, graphics, colours, logos, slogans and themes to create a unique website personality. Additionally, a domain name that is easy to remember, targeted web content, and virtual communities play a vital role in enhancing the overall brand image of a website.[237] [238] Brand-building is critical in e-business as customers are faced with an immense number of alternative choices online. The goal is therefore to create a website that appeals emotionally to customers, enhances website recognition, evokes shared associations, creates positive shopper attitudes, and builds a positive reputation to drive e-loyalty.[239]

Virtual communities are online social entities that consist of existing and potential customers that are organised and maintained by the business, and that facilitate the interaction between its various users. Users can, for instance, review and recommend products to one another, exchange opinions and information, or perform some other function. As users interact with one another and the information repository grows, the site learns more about its users while users are provided with an incentive to return, gain from and add to this information repository. Virtual communities ease decision-making for community members who draw on the knowledge of other members, facilitate word-of-mouth (see *Reputation*), give users a feeling of increased choice and control, and often also create a sense of belonging. Virtual communities can therefore increase the perceived value of a website, and act as a very good breeding ground for fostering strong customer relationships.[240]

Cultivation is the frequency of relevant information and cross-selling offers provided to customers. Cross-selling is the selling of related offerings (possibly via partners) to existing customers. Cultivation therefore aims at encouraging customers to increase their breadth and depth of purchases over time. Ways in which to cultivate customers are reaching out to them via email to alert them of promotions and new offerings, and providing them with useful information that would otherwise be difficult for them to obtain. Cultivation increases loyalty, as it reduces the likelihood of customers doing additional searches for products at other sites (reduces search costs).[241] [242] Cultivation also serves to remind customers of services that are being provided, of which customers are often oblivious under normal circumstances, and they only notice when there is a lack of service delivery. Reminding customers of these services is critical, so that occasional accidents fade in relative importance.[243]

3.3. Value proposition

In the value proposition category, five drivers of e-loyalty are (1) convenience, (2) price, (3) quality, (4) range or choice, and (5) individualisation.

Different customers have different motivations for shopping online. *Convenience* as one of them has shown to have a direct positive impact on e-satisfaction and e-loyalty.[244] [245] [246] [247] Convenience can be defined as the extent to which customers experience a website and the entire shopping experience as simple, intuitive, and user-friendly. It also includes factors that affect ease of use, saves time, makes browsing easy and minimises customer efforts.[248] Research by Reichheld and Schefter[249] found that the majority of online shoppers are not bargain hunters who want the absolute minimum **price**. Rather, the majority of customers seek convenience and use the Internet to make their lives simpler and easier. Balabanis et al.[250] similarly found that ensuring the absolute lowest price is not necessarily essential. On the other hand, because competitors are within easy reach online and price comparisons are easier to do, being within a competitive price range remains important for developing and maintaining e-loyalty.[251] [252] The same can be said of product and service **quality**, which should equally not be neglected.

Another important factor for driving e-loyalty is the **range or scope of products and services** that are offered. A wide variety of offerings gives customers a wider choice. Srinivasan et al.[253] note that traditional retailers are constrained by warehouse floor space and costs in the variety of products that they can offer, whereas e-businesses are not limited in the same way. E-businesses can make use of a wide partner network and coordinate their back-end processes to deliver customers seamless access to an entire range of products offered by their alliances. Many consumers value one-stop shopping, and in this way enhanced choice increases convenience, reduces search costs and can thus stimulate e-loyalty.[254 255 256]

Individualisation involves the tailoring of offerings and the transactional environment to an individual customer's needs and circumstances. There are three types of individualisation. Personalisation is individualisation that is initiated by the e-business and involves individualising interfaces, making recommendations based on past customer purchases and behaviour, targeting customers with specific advertisements and so forth. Customisation is individualisation initiated by customers,[257] such as changing preferences or making a special request. Prosumption (also known as co-creation) is the convergence of the production and consumption process,[258 259] where customers play an active role in designing and developing their desired offering.

All three of these types of individualisation can positively influence e-loyalty. Personalisation eases navigation, minimises customers' search time, facilitates a match between customer needs and product offerings, reduces frustration, and creates the perception of increased choice and higher product quality.[260] Customisation is highly appreciated by customers, and customers are often willing to pay premium prices for the customised products and services companies can deliver when making thoughtful use of their personal information.[261] Prosumption further fosters strong affective bonds between the customer and the brand due to the high customer interactivity required in designing a customer's ideal product.[262 263]

3.4. Trust and security

Four drivers of e-loyalty in the trust and security category are (1) security mechanisms, (2) privacy protection, (3) guarantees, and (4) reputation.

Trust and security are extremely important in e-business. It is widely believed that transactional security and overall concerns about privacy are some of the most significant issues that discourage people from shopping online.[264 265 266 267] The other fact, as shown by behavioural economics, is that people are more concerned about negative consequences than they are about equal potential benefits.[268] Customers online are therefore more concerned about perceived risks than they are about perceived gains.[269] This amplifies the importance of reducing online shopping uncertainty and risk to create e-loyalty.

Security mechanisms on the Internet are the different safeguards that ensure the security of systems, networks or data transfers. Security is concerned with protecting data from unwanted intruders. It is concerned with the confidentiality, availability and integrity of data – all the practices, processes and mechanisms that ensure that the data isn't being accessed by unauthorised individuals or parties. Examples of security mechanisms include encryptions, authentication mechanisms, firewalls, antivirus software, antispyware software and various forms of network protection.

Privacy protection is mechanisms that ensure that individuals' personal data is kept private. Privacy is concerned with the collection and use of personal data. In many cases, businesses interacting with customers will collect various types of data about the customer, which could potentially be used outside of the transaction. However, making use of a customer's data without the consent of the customer and in a way that could link the data back to the specific individual violates that person's privacy rights. An agreement needs to exist between the customer and the business about what personal data will be collected and how it will be used. Every business should therefore have a properly drafted privacy policy, as it can serve to create customer trust while providing the business legal protection.

Guarantees can also be a useful way in which customer trust can be created and buying apprehension reduced. Guarantees or warranties are formal assurance agreements that certain conditions will be fulfilled by the business. A business can, for instance, guarantee that a certain product will be the solution to a customer's problem, or a full refund will be granted. Guarantees can similarly be used to assuring a product's reliability and offer repair or replacement if it breaks.

Reputation is a vitally important driver of trust and e-loyalty. Caruana and Ewing[270] state that "many customers have difficulty remembering even prominent websites and are reluctant to pay for products from online retailers they know little about. Thus, a strong corporate reputation can be a major asset to online retailers. Conducive to reputation is the extended reach of the Internet, which amplifies the effect of word-of-mouth referrals. Not only does word-of-mouth serve as free advertising, but it also lessens the need for customer service agents, as potential customers tend to rely on existing customers for advice rather than making use of a support desk.[271] Furthermore, referred customers are also generally much more loyal than those who were enticed through promotional discounts and untargeted advertising.[272] But reputation can at the same time be a double-edged sword. As Poleretzky[273] once stated: "In the physical world, if I make a customer unhappy, they'll tell five friends, on the Internet they'll tell 5 000".

3.5. **Customer attributes**

Customer attributes that are important in driving e-loyalty are a customer's (1) PC or Internet expertise, (2) online buying experience, and (3) other relevant segmentation attributes.

Customer attributes are constants that make up a customer's profile. These characteristics cannot be altered and need to be accounted for. The first variable that influences customer purchasing apprehension, e-service quality, e-satisfaction and indirectly e-loyalty, is a user's **PC or Internet expertise.**[274] [275] The more experienced a user is with computer and Internet technologies, the more in control they feel, the more likely they are to notice potential security risks and avoid them, and the less apprehensive they are of making purchases online. This is supported by Goldstuck,[276] who found a correlation between the number of years a user has been online and his or her propensity to engage in e-commerce, bank online, launch an online business, create a personal website and so forth. On average, it takes users five years of digital participation before they feel confident enough to engage in more extensive activities. The implication of this is that when estimating the potential market size of an e-business, the Internet user-base statistics of five years previously should be used instead of current figures, as they will give a more conservative and better estimate of users actually willing to purchase.

A user's PC or Internet experience also affects how they perceive services being offered and their satisfaction with them. When users understand the technological limitations, then they are more realistic about their expectations of what a website can offer. Expertise similarly helps to correctly identify when a website or business offering is below standard. Experienced users also have a greater ability to find information than inexperienced users, and as a result have more satisfactory online experiences.[277]

Positive online buying experiences themselves are another driver of e-loyalty. When customers have experienced satisfactory past transactions, then their web apprehensiveness and perceived risk of Internet purchases decreases[278] and the likelihood of them repeating transactions increases. Businesses can therefore bolster e-loyalty and user shopping tendency by providing satisfactory online shopping experiences the first time around.

Other business-specific customer segmentation attributes can also play a role in customer attitudes and consequently affect e-loyalty (see chapter 4 in *Crystallising the Strategic Landscape* on techniques for analysing customers). Characteristics could, for instance, include psychological factors such as a customer's attitude to data privacy and security, delays and problems with purchases, website innovations or behavioural factors, such as a customer's method of access, time of access, frequency of access, depth and breadth of access, shopping behaviour, level of interactivity and so forth.[279] [280]

Interestingly enough, Zhou et al.[281] observe that demographic factors such as being male, being financially affluent, and being part of an individualistic culture increase the chances of making use of e-commerce. Zhou et al.[282] also found that psychological factors such as a keen intention and motivation to make a purchase and high perceived benefits decrease customers' risk perceptions. Companies therefore have to strive to increase their offerings' perceived value. On the other hand, customers become more apprehensive of web purchases as the cost of the purchase increases. The paradox that arises is that high-value items that are lucrative to sell online are also those products that customers feel particularly uneasy about purchasing.

3.6. Lock-in mechanisms

Lock-in mechanisms that can create behaviourally loyal customers, but not necessarily attitudinally loyal customers, include **switching costs** and **control points**. These have been discussed previously.

3.7. Website design

Website design elements that can drive loyalty include (1) ease of website use, navigation and search, (2) personalised website features, (3) information quality, (4) fast page loads, and (5) server reliability.

Factors that influence **ease of use** include **ease of navigation**, **ease of search**, ease of understanding, intuitive operations, simple website design and structure, efficient shopping and checkout processes, simple payment systems, customisable language settings and other **personalised website features** and interfaces.[283] Website design is extremely important in cultivating loyalty; Schaffer[284] found that for 30 per cent of users who do not purchase anything on a website, this is because of navigational difficulty. Information must thus be located in a logical place, in a meaningful format, whilst not being buried too deep within the website.

The personalised website features aspect, on the other hand, again highlights that websites should be designed with specific customer segments in mind. Mafé and Navarré[285] posit that the most significant factor that motivates nononline shoppers to start shopping online, is the information gained online that can assist purchasing decisions. Businesses should therefore deliver **high-quality**, relevant, possibly local or cultural-specific **content** to customers.[286] Hutt, Le Brun and Mannhardt[287] support this by stating that it is content above all that attracts consumers to a website and persuades them to return.

Lastly, technical factors such as **fast page loads**, fast response times and **server reliability** influence the customer experience and can thus also influence e-loyalty.[288] [289] Think about Zuckerberg's design philosophy when he developed Facebook: Facebook should never be offline. In the movie *The Social Network*, Zuckerberg states:

> "Let me tell you the difference between Facebook and everybody else. We don't crash ever. If the servers are down for even a day, our entire reputation is irreversibly destroyed. Users are fickle. Friendster has proved that. A few people leaving would reverberate through the entire user base. The users are interconnected. That is the whole point. College kids are online because their friends are online. And if one domino goes, the other dominoes go."

Although technical excellence in most cases is assumed as a given for any business, it remains vitally important in ensuring a satisfying customer experience.

3.8. Order fulfilment

Order fulfilment drivers of loyalty include (1) ease of payment and payment options, (2) delivery speed and delivery options, and (3) delivery reliability.

Ease of payment and payment options are critical[290] as payments need to be as convenient as possible to increase the chances of customers engaging in and executing a transaction. Customers have a myriad of choices online and making it difficult for customers to do business with you is a sure-fire way to bankruptcy.

Customers online also have a need for instant gratification. This need has blurred into the physical world and in most cases customers expect **fast delivery** of products, as well as a **range of delivery options**.[291] Door-to-door delivery has become the norm, but market leaders such as Amazon are also experimenting with other forms of delivery, such as *Amazon Locker* where Amazon ships packages to special lockers in a convenient location. Customers can then go and pick their packages up by using a unique pickup code at a time that it convenient to them. Other delivery options of Amazon include same-day delivery and *Amazon Prime Air*, their drone delivery experiment.

Delivery reliability is also crucial. When a business promises a certain delivery date, then it should make sure that it fulfils that promise. Even worse is, if customers have ordered and paid for products, but they never arrive, this creates a bad impression. Customers won't be happy at all, and the business's reputation and chance of loyalty will become zero.

3.9. Customer service

Finally, customer service-related drivers of loyalty include (1) ease of business contact, (2) business responsiveness and (3) preventing and resolving breakdowns in service.

The primary aim of customer support is to help customers with whatever problems they may have. The first step in providing quality customer support is to be **easy to contact**. Although businesses can create frequently asked questions (FAQs) sections and virtual communities to take care of a major proportion of customer enquiries, sometimes direct business contact is still necessary. E-mail contact is a popular way of dealing with many customer service issues, but a business's **responsiveness** to these emails is equally important. Sometimes customers simply can't wait. Businesses therefore need to provide an even more direct means of contact, such as providing their physical address details, toll-free telephone numbers or even have live-chat or video-calling functionalities on their websites to make customer interactions even easier.

Businesses must also exhibit proper care to **prevent and resolve breakdowns in service**. This involves paying close attention to the pre- and post-purchase customer interface activities that facilitate transactions and customer relationships; resolving disruptions in service as quickly as possible; and keeping customers informed about the status of their orders or problems. Service failures lower customers' perceptions of service quality, and in effect reduce e-loyalty and the probability of the customer making repeat purchases.[292]

It must further be mentioned that businesses would do well to regard the above 33 e-loyalty drivers as hygienes in Herzberg's[293] motivator-hygiene theory. In other words, these e-loyalty factors can be seen as the minimum entry barriers that have to be overcome in order to create a favourable environment for loyalty. The factors in isolation, or even all of them in combination, do not guarantee loyalty. They merely enhance the probability of creating loyal customers.

Application tool

Consider the 33 e-loyalty drivers of Figure 3.12 and complete Table 3.5.

- Which factors should we excel at to drive customer loyalty?
- What is our rationale for believing that we are excelling at these loyalty drivers?
- What other initiatives can we launch to further spur customer loyalty?

Table 3.5: E-loyalty driver evaluation

E-loyalty driver	Rationale	Initiative
Brand-building		
Value proposition		
Trust and security		
Customer attributes		
Website design		
Order fulfilment		
Customer service		

Practical guideline

One critique regarding the customer lock-in (specifically control points and switching costs) is that when these elements are made too visible, they can create negative perceptions that discourage customers from buying offerings in the first place. The exact opposite of the result than is desired is thus obtained. These elements therefore require subtlety in their execution, otherwise they will ward off potential customers.

Key metrics

Key metrics are the performance measures used to evaluate the business progression towards its goals. Key metrics are the indicators and analytics that allow a business to evaluate whether things are going the way they should, and they provide insights about what needs to change when things are not going as expected. In the information age (and as a part of warfare or any competitive scenario), knowledge is power. The information obtained from a business's key metrics is therefore an immense source of power. Key metrics are essential tools for navigating the competitive environment, and similar to a ship without a compass, a business without key metrics could easily get lost.

Although the specific metrics vital to each business's will undeniably vary, every business will broadly require metrics regarding each element of the business model. These include **financial metrics** (revenues and costs), **customer metrics** (segments, relationships, channels and satisfaction), **value proposition metrics** (product/service quality conformance and scale), and **infrastructure metrics** (processes and activities, resources and partners). Vitally important, however, is to also define **competitive metrics** for measuring a business's competitive standing in the market. These could include measures such as market share, market capitalisation, the business's net promoter score and other comparable benchmark metrics.

Hundreds of different types of metric exist. In the *Financial Analysis* of chapter 5 of *Crystallising the Competitive Business Landscape,* we discussed several financial ratios that could be used as financial metrics. A set of customer metrics that has gained some popularity among Internet start-ups is Dave McClure's *Start-up Metrics for Pirates: AARRR!* This acronym includes:[294]

- **Acquisition**: Monitoring the number of people that sign-up or register. This involves monitoring site traffic as well as the customer conversion rate.
- **Activation**: Monitoring the people that use your product or service. Heatmaps can provide useful insights about how people navigate and use your offering.
- **Retention**: Monitoring the number of people who return to use your offering.
- **Referrals**: Monitoring the number of people who talk about your offering and who recommend it to their friends or colleagues.
- **Revenue**: Monitoring the amount of revenue the business is generating.

While these metrics are good to begin with, they present only a tiny sliver of the possibilities. The point is that you need to find the metrics that matter to your business, and once you get thinking about it, you'll soon realise that there is a lot of information that you would like to have. Having higher-level metrics is good as a kind of dashboard, but you will need to delegate the responsibility of metric monitoring to the different departments in order to really dig into the details and uncover the faint signals in the data that will drive essential business insights.

Finally, later in this chapter we introduce a normative assessment for evaluating the competitive strategy of a business – essentially a short, higher-level list of metrics that can be useful in evaluating your strategy.

Application tool

Use Table 3.6 and devise which key metrics are essential to your business. Also indicate how these metrics are measured or how the data will be obtained (automatic online data capturing, surveys etc.); what the ideal state of the metric is (eg 100 kg/s); what the minimum threshold level is that the metric should not drop below (e.g. 30 kg/s); and what corrective actions should be taken if the threshold level is not met.

Table 3.6: Key metrics

Business model element	Key metric	How measured? Where? Who? Source of data?	Ideal state (numbers with units)	Minimum threshold level (numbers with units)	Corrective actions if threshold not met
Revenue streams					
Cost structure					
Customer segments					
Customer retention					
Customer relationships					
Channels					
Value proposition					
Key activities					
Key resources					
Key partnerships					
Market competitiveness					

Competitive advantage

The final building block in the expanded business model canvas is the competitive advantage summary. Every element defined up to this point contributes to the creation of sustainable competitive advantages for the business that need to be distilled and articulated in a succinct and coherent way in this element.

This element is vital, as it forces you to evaluate the business strategy in relation to the external competitive market, and it forces you to highlight why the business will have the upper hand over competitors or why the business is uniquely capable of entering a certain strategic space rather than competitors. Failing to articulate the business's competitive advantage points towards a business strategy that merely aims to play along, rather than playing to win. While moderate success may be achievable in this way in the short term (perhaps via luck), when competitive pressures escalate this advantage-less type of business will be the first to suffer.

For clarity's sake, it needs to be mentioned that Porter[295] notes that competing to be the best is the wrong goal. Competing to be the best pits companies against each other in a bloodthirsty and destructive zero-sum battle where competitive convergence erodes industry profitability over time. The problem with competing to be the best is that it assumes a simplified way of thinking about competition: that there is only one way to compete and there can only be one winner. This way of thinking is flawed, because if there was only one way to compete then everybody would compete in this way and there would be no need for strategy.[296] In truth, there are multiple ways to compete and be profitable in an industry.[297] A single best strategy does not exist. Just think about the variety of customers and customer needs – what might be the "best" for one customer isn't necessarily the "best" for another.[298] Therefore, instead of competing to be the best in an industry, businesses should compete to be unique;[299] and uniqueness results from performing activities that are different to those of competitors or performing similar activities differently.

A subset of differentiation advantages in the form of culture advantages was discussed in chapter 5 of *Crystallising the Competitive Business Landscape*.

What needs to be defined in the competitive advantage element?

- the business's core competitive advantage choice (Porter's generic competitive strategies)
- the business's core value discipline (Treacy & Wiersema)
- the business's digital–physical orientation
- the elements that make the business unique
- the elements that create value above the value created by competitors
- the elements that create efficiencies above the efficiencies created by competitors
- the elements that make the business robust, defensible and sustainable
- the competitive advantages of the business, derived from the systematic interaction between the core competitive advantage choice, other generic strategic options and choices (chapter 2), and all the other business model elements

Application tool

Use the guidelines above and define the competitive advantages of your business using Table 3.7. It may be helpful to define the competitive advantages on a granular level first (per product line, per product/service or per customer segment) before translating them into holistic advantages (or vice versa).

Table 3.7: Competitive advantage assessment

Competitive advantage	Rationale (compare business's performance vis-à-vis competitors)	Value of the advantage (lower costs, differentiation, sustainability)	Advantage's fit with generic strategic options and choices (chapter 2)

PROCESS OF BUSINESS MODELLING

Before we delve into the process of business model formulation, it is first necessary to highlight the larger strategic context within which business model formulation occurs. We use the basic process of the design school of strategy formulation as a point of departure. It is by no means the intent to detract from the importance of the other schools of strategy (see chapter 1 of *Crystallising the Strategic Business Landscape*); the design school just provides us with a simple way of explaining the higher-level process of strategic design. This process is shown in Figure 3.13.

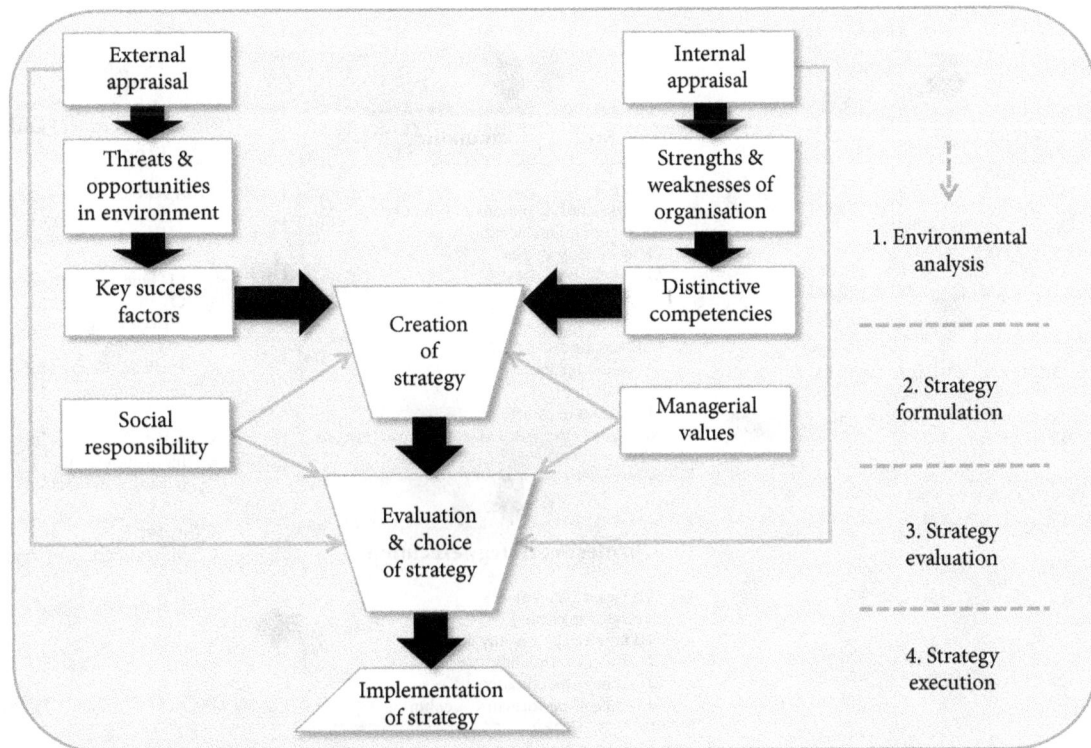

Figure 3.13: The basic steps of strategic design[300]

The design school of strategy advocates the alignment of the organisation's strategy with the configuration of its internal and external environments.[301] [302] [303] The goal of strategy from this perspective is therefore to design an organisation that achieves a fit between internal strengths and weaknesses and external threats and opportunities.[304]

Figure 3.13 shows that this type of strategic design is achieved by performing a SWOT analysis, distilling the key success factors for competing in the industry and understanding the organisation's distinctive competencies. Following this, various strategies are designed and evaluated and the most appropriate one is chosen. After this, implementation follows. This process therefore consists of four broad consecutive phases: environmental analysis, strategy formulation, strategy evaluation and strategy execution.

In chapter 1 it was also mentioned that strategy is not only the deliberate result of design, but also emerges due to the dynamic interactions that occur in the competitive environment. Implicit to this model is therefore that following execution the process is restarted, creating an iterative cycle. Depending on changes in the environment, adjustments are made to the strategy, leading to strategic renewal, growth and innovation.

In chapter 1 we proposed a model that revolves around the same principles as above: the strategic architecture landscape. This model guides the flow of this book and is shown again in Figure 3.14.

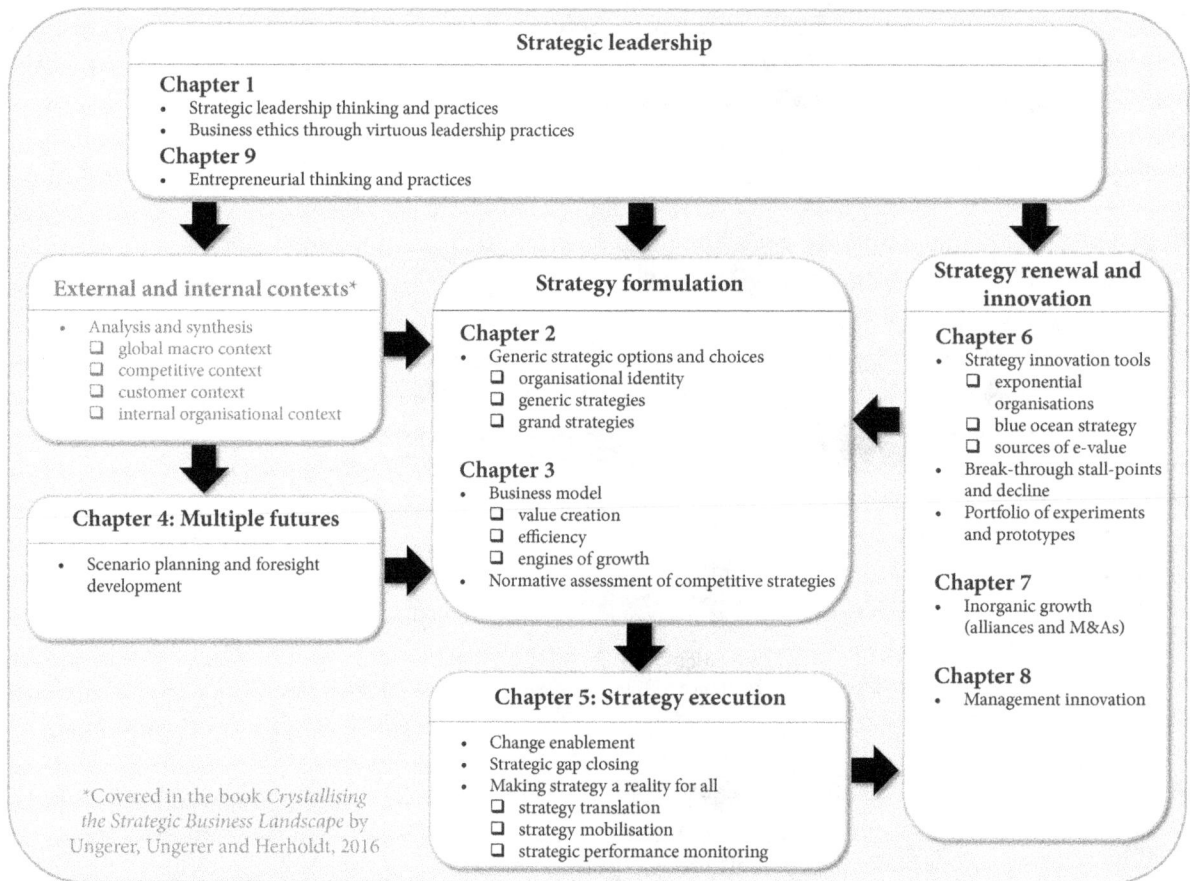

Figure 3.14: The strategic architecture landscape

Figure 3.14 shows that business modelling forms part of strategy formulation, after the higher-level strategic options and choices have been made. Rumelt[305] also eloquently states that "Strategy can neither be formulated nor adjusted to changing circumstances without a process of strategy evaluation". Strategy evaluation is therefore the last topic of this chapter.

Moving on to the detail of business model formulation, it needs to be said that the process of business modelling is not an exact science. The process will differ depending on the amount of information available, the extent to which the business idea has already been conceived, the stage of business development, the specific business context and even the preferences of the business modeller. Simply put, business modelling can occur in a variety of ad hoc ways. Some approaches lead to a favourable result more quickly, while other approaches take longer. The end result remains roughly the same, however. It really depends on the situation as to which approach is best.

In this regard, a *flexible* process that can be used for business modelling is proposed below.[306] [307] *Flexible* because deviation from the process is entirely acceptable (see *Epicentres of business models*), and this process is merely provided for modellers who have no idea where to start. In an ideal world, all the process steps would occur simultaneously – that is, the modeller would have perfect insight about all the elements of the business model at the same time, and the sequence of filling in the canvas would largely become irrelevant. Honing the ability to holistically consider the business model in its entirety is therefore of the utmost importance. In the real world, however, insights are built cumulatively as one progresses from one element to the next (revisiting and revising elements as one continues).

Before you begin constructing your business model, it is important to first equip yourself with adequate knowledge of the domain you intend to enter. Knowledge is power. You therefore need to possess adequate knowledge of the competitive environment in order to sensibly weigh the different scenarios and possibilities against each other. The environmental analysis tools provided in *Crystallising the Strategic Business Landscape* can serve as a solid foundation for accruing such knowledge. The information that you gather doesn't need to be and will never be complete or all-encompassing. However, sufficient knowledge is required to think sensibly about your business model and its competitiveness in the domain.

Secondly, you need clarity about what you are trying to achieve or why you are building the business. In other words, you need clarity about the core aspirational description of the business (vision, mission, values). As the Cheshire Cat told Alice,[308] "If you don't know where you're going, any road will get you there."

The generic business model formulation process is depicted in Figure 3.15.

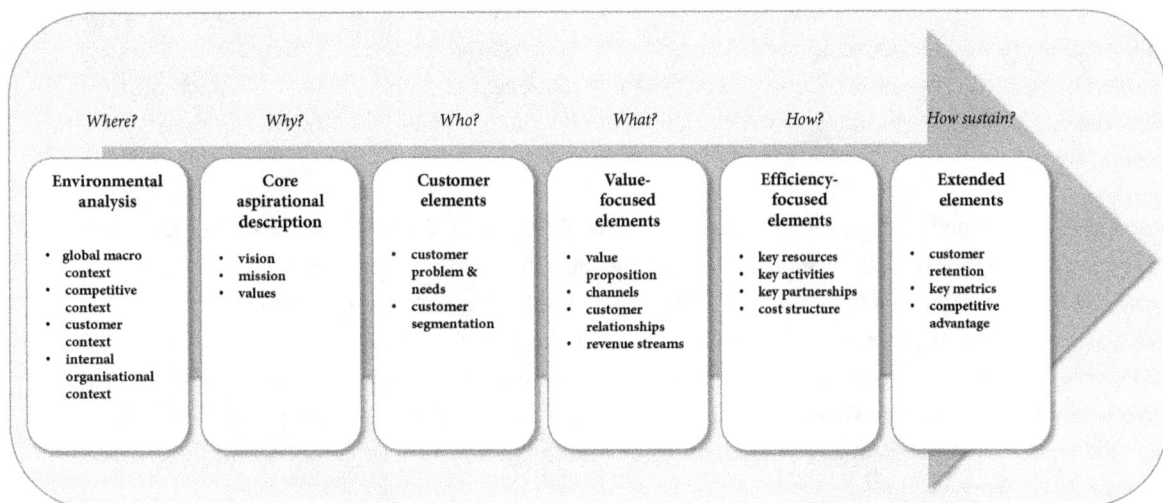

Figure 3.15: Generic process of business model formulation

The third step is to define the customer problem that your business seeks to address. Customer problems and needs are the lifeblood of a business. If the business idea does not solve a specific customer problem or cater to a specific customer need, then the business has no reason to exist.

Having such a customer problem in mind, you need to hone in on the customers of the business. Here it is important to distinguish between customers and users. Customers pay for the offerings you provide. Users do not. Sometimes they are the same people, sometimes not. It is also advisable to break broad customer segments down into smaller segments. It is impossible to build a business that serves "everyone", so focus is key. Considering the problem–customer combination, if possible focus on the customers that have the highest pain level and need your solution the most; that you can reach; on whom you can maximise your price;[309] and who represent a market size large enough to be sustainable for the business. Also, in order to initially save time, only sketch out business model canvasses for your three most promising customer segments.[310] Additional segments can be investigated later, but these three primary segments will probably account for 80 per cent of your revenue.

Next, define the value proposition and the other value-focused elements of your business. These together describe how you will solve the problem from a customer's perspective. It involves defining the products and services offered by your business, the channels through which offerings are made available, the relationships that are established with customers, and the price at which all of these are provided via the revenue strategy employed. For your value proposition it is important to be different, but make sure that the difference matters – it must be something that customers care about. Therefore articulate the benefits (gain-creators and pain-relievers) of your offering rather than articulating its features.

You can then continue to define the remaining efficiency-focused elements, which include the key resources required to execute the strategy, the key activities that will be required, key partnerships that need to be established and the cost structure of the business. Although you may have identified a great way to create customer value, the strategy still needs to be feasible. These efficiency-focused elements help you determine if that is the case.

Lastly, it is also important to define the extended business model canvas's elements, namely the business's customer retention mechanisms, key metrics and competitive advantages. These elements are crucial as they introduce a competitive flavour to business modelling. Good business models seek to lock in competitive advantages for themselves. They contain reinforcing conditions and imitability barriers that fortify the business's strategic position and enhance the business's sustainability. Good business modellers also always know in which direction they are heading and make use of a dashboard of key metrics to give them insights into navigating turbulent competitive waters.

As previously mentioned, the process described above is highly flexible and can be adapted to the organisation's specific needs and context. Osterwalder and Pigneur[311] also coined the phenomenon of "epicentres of business models", where innovation in a specific part of the business model drives the overall strategy. This means that having an epiphany about a certain aspect of the business model (for instance a novel revenue strategy) can inspire the development of a whole new business model. Business model formulation can therefore literally start in any of the canvas elements. The most important aspects to remember are that (1) all the elements of the canvas are inter-related and should be designed to reflect a tight fit; and that (2) the canvas needs to be complete, meaning that defining *all* the elements is necessary.

The different types of business model epicentre are depicted in Figure 3.16.

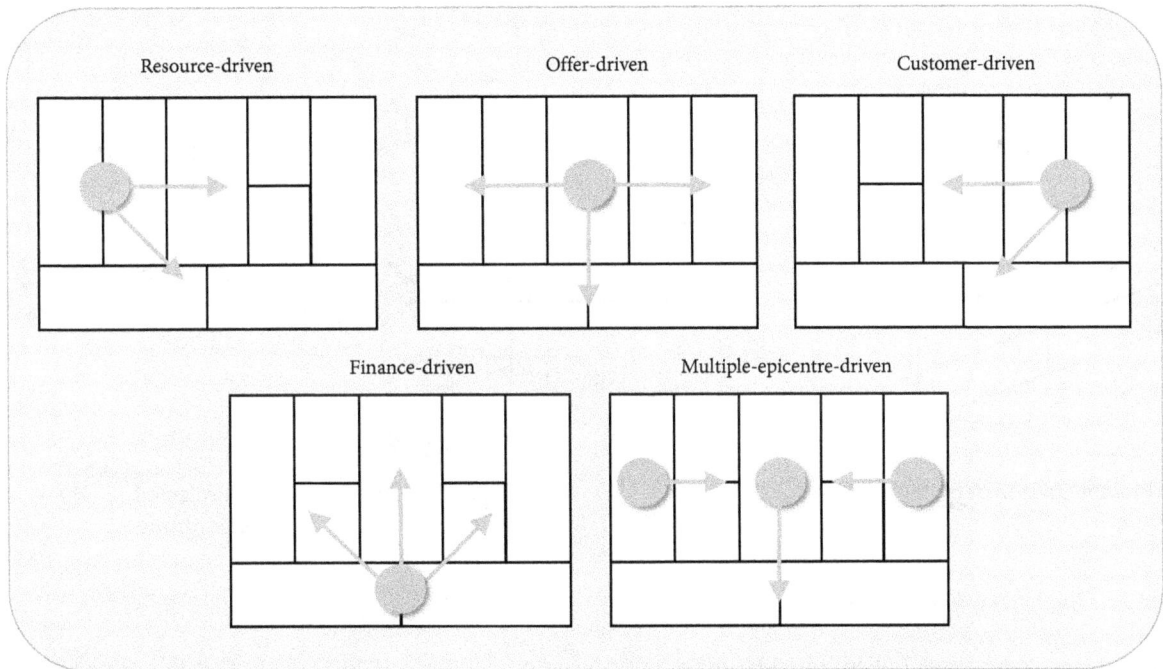

Figure 3.16: Epicentres of business models[312]

In sketching out the canvas, you may realise that many unknowns actually exist. This is normal. It is acceptable to leave sections blank to come back to later, but you should preferably sketch out your canvas in one sitting. Instead of writing down nothing, write down your hypotheses for these elements – these will need to be tested. Then, when you have documented your rough business model canvas, identify the riskiest hypotheses and start the process of systematically testing these (see chapter 7 in *Crystallising the Strategic Business Landscape*).

Business models are supposed to be living documents that grow and evolve over time. This means that when new insights become available the business model needs to be updated and adapted. We discuss scenario planning and multiple futures in the following chapter, but it is important to note that at any given time, a myriad of different strategic optionalities exist for the business. Depending on shifts in the competitive environment, it may be necessary to adopt a new business model. This process of business models evolving over time is depicted in Figure 3.17.

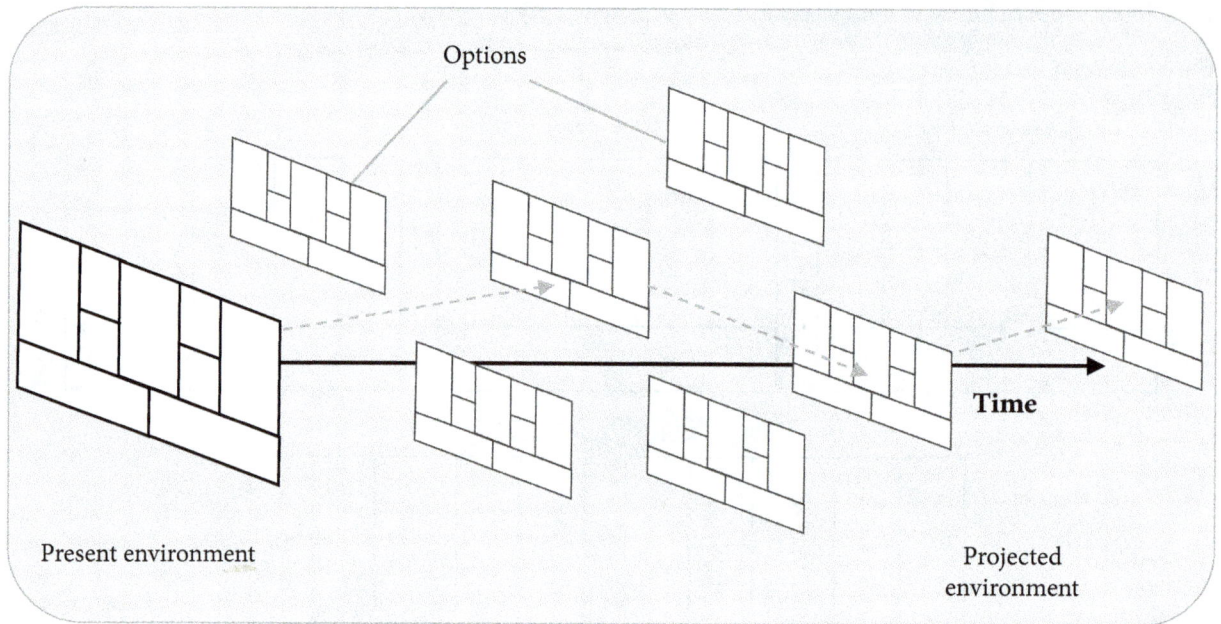

Figure 3.17: Business model evolution[313]

Finally, there are no silver bullets when it comes to business model formulation, except that the route to success involves continuous and iterative experimentation and testing, learning and improvement.

The next section discusses the last phase of the higher-level business model development process: evaluating the developed business model.

NORMATIVE ASSESSMENT OF COMPETITIVE STRATEGIES

Any strategy, once formulated, needs to be paired with a process of strategy evaluation to determine whether the strategy fulfils its creator's intent. Strategy evaluation is the appraisal of a business's strategy in order to establish its utility, truth or efficacy, and the output of a strategy evaluation process is the rejection, modification or ratification of existing strategies and plans.[314] [315] [316] Strategy evaluation isn't a once-off process, however. Concurrent assessments are needed to assure that the strategy is still fit for the ever-changing competitive environment.

In the domain of strategy evaluation, four perspectives are often employed:[317]

1. **A goal-centred approach**: assesses the degree to which predetermined strategic goals were achieved (for instance yearly balanced scorecard goals)
2. **A comparative approach**: assesses the effectiveness of the business in relation to other businesses (benchmarking)
3. **An improvement approach**: assesses how business performance has improved and the strategy has evolved over time
4. **A normative approach**: assesses the strategy in relation to characteristics of theoretically ideal, well-performing strategies

Although all three first-mentioned approaches have their uses, it is only the normative approach that looks beyond the current, obvious operating results to the conceptual aspects that underlie success or failure in the chosen domain of activity. Only the normative approach is therefore capable of evaluating the long-term merit of a strategy and uncovering its conceptual weaknesses. The normative approach is the classic approach to strategy evaluation[318] and the core focus of this section.

Advantages that the normative approach provides are:[319]

1. It can be used prospectively before action is taken and financial investments are made, whereas the other approaches can all only be used retrospectively.
2. It is conceptual and is not concerned with obtaining perfect data through rigorous performance measurements, making it less expensive and less time-consuming to perform.
3. It focuses on appraising the quality of the developed strategy and allows users to identify and possibly remedy the most obvious strategic problems in advance. This increases the strategy's robustness and instils users with greater confidence that their strategic choices will lead to successful results.[320]

A normative strategic assessment that can be used for evaluating whether a developed strategy possesses characteristics associated with high-performing, theoretically ideal strategies is shown in Figure 3.18. The assessment consists of 10 tests that are divided into four categories. Three tests relate to the logical sensibility of the strategy; two tests relate to the strategy's competitive advantage creation ability; two tests relate to the strategy's robustness; and three tests relate to the feasibility of the strategy. The 10 strategic tests are discussed below.

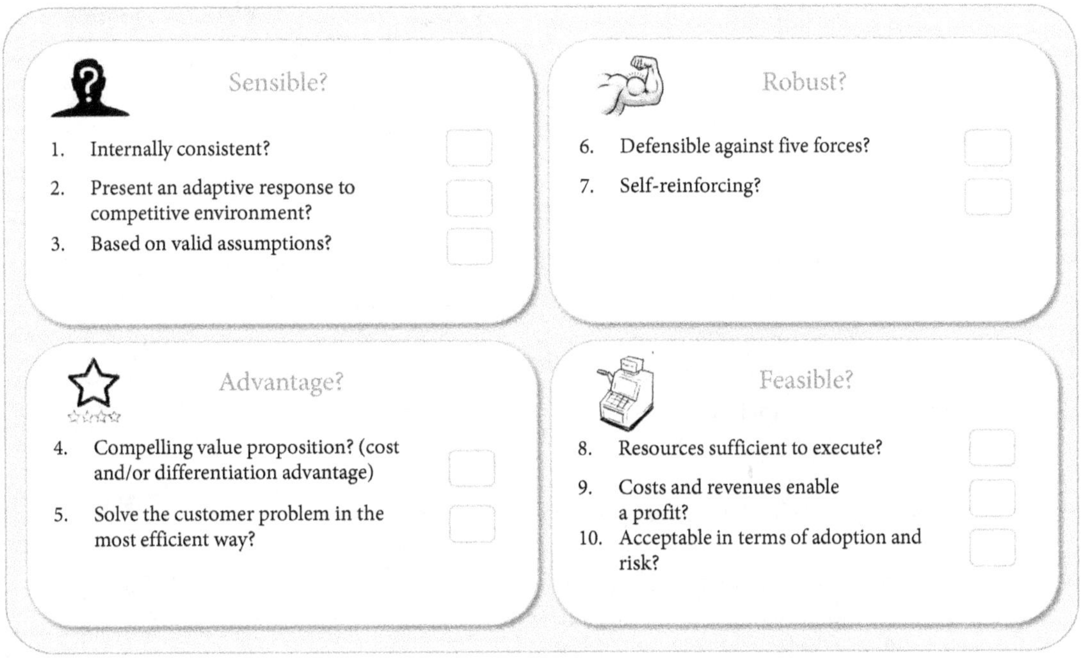

Sensible?

1. Internally consistent?
2. Present an adaptive response to competitive environment?
3. Based on valid assumptions?

Robust?

6. Defensible against five forces?
7. Self-reinforcing?

Advantage?

4. Compelling value proposition? (cost and/or differentiation advantage)
5. Solve the customer problem in the most efficient way?

Feasible?

8. Resources sufficient to execute?
9. Costs and revenues enable a profit?
10. Acceptable in terms of adoption and risk?

Figure 3.18: Strategic assessment[321]

Test 1: Internally consistent?

Theoretically ideal strategies are internally consistent.[322] [323] [324] [325] [326] [327] [328] [329] [330] Internal consistency relates to Magretta's[331] narrative test, which states that the story of the business must make sense. This means that the business must possess mutually consistent goals and policies[332] [333] that fit seamlessly together[334] to create a continuity of direction that delivers optimal results. Optimal results are possible because consistent strategies do not possess discontinuities that hinder their cumulative effectiveness.

Test 2: Present an adaptive response to the competitive environment?

Theoretically ideal strategies present an appropriate and adaptive response to the competitive environment in which they are executed.[335] [336] [337] [338] Where the previous test dealt with internal consistency, this test deals with external consistency. The developed strategy must fit its competitive environment. A harmony must exist. If the strategy does not represent an appropriate and adaptive response to its environment, then its business story is flawed[339] and more likely to result in failure. The competitive environment is also constantly changing. Presenting an adaptive response to the competitive environment is therefore not only contingent on businesses having an acute awareness of the said environment, but also on possessing the ability to learn, be flexible and adapt.

Test 3: Strategy based on valid assumptions?

Theoretically ideal strategies are grounded in reality, meaning that they are based on valid assumptions.[340] [341] [342] [343] [344] If a strategy is based on flawed assumptions then it has lost touch with reality, which can lead to its demise. When a strategy is initially formulated, all that is formulated is a set of untested hypotheses.[345] These hypotheses have to be confirmed or refuted through data gathered in the real world.[346] [347] Similar to the second test, this test also largely deals with strategic learning and adaption in a dynamic environment,[348] [349] but its interpretation can be expanded: this test is also responsible for evaluating the validity of the strategic assessment ratings of the other tests.

Test 4: Compelling value proposition (cost and/or differentiation advantage)?

Theoretically ideal strategies create advantages that result in compelling value propositions.[350] [351] [352] [353] [354] [355] [356] If a compelling value proposition is not provided, then customers have no reason to notice, l et al.one choose, the business's offerings above those of competitors. Porter[357] [358] proposes that there are two primary competitive advantages that can be pursued, namely a cost or a differentiation advantage. Given that sustainable competitive advantages that result in super-normal profits are the fundamental goal of competitive strategy,[359] [360] [361] achieving either or both of these advantages is extremely important.

Test 5: Solves the customer problem in the most efficient way?

Theoretically ideal strategies solve customer problems in the most efficient way possible.[362] [363] [364] This test goes beyond the previous, and aims at optimality. Although it is possible to develop a strategy that creates a differentiation and/ or a cost advantage, it does not necessarily mean that it is the best possible strategy or provides the best possible solution. When a strategy solves a customer problem in the most efficient way possible, it means that it gets a customer's job done and nothing else. Johnson et al.[365] describe this as the business's "precision". When a business is very precise, it is almost impossible for competitors to make inroads into its established customers. However, as soon as a strategy loses its precision and becomes slightly unfocused, it creates an opportunity for competitors to "out-focus" the initial "focuser" and better solve the customer problem.[366] [367] As this test aims at optimality, it is very difficult to pass. Its value however, is that enough brainstorming can provide an indication of where market disruption may come from, giving the business the opportunity to prepare.

Test 6: Defensible against five forces of competition?

Theoretically ideal strategies are defensible against the five forces of competition, namely customer and supplier bargaining power and the threats presented by existing rivals, new entrants and substitutes.[368] [369] Ideal strategies not only create competitive advantages, but are also able to sustain them over time and amidst fierce competitive pressures.[370] [371] [372] [373] [374] [375] [376] Mechanisms that can contribute to the robustness of the business include the control points, switching costs and loyalty drivers previously discussed.

Test 7: Self-reinforcing?

Theoretically ideal strategies are self-reinforcing,[377] [378] [379] [380] [381] meaning that they build in their strengths over time.[382] Self-reinforcement involves the creation of "virtuous cycles" or positive feedback loops that sustain the business's competitive advantages and allow it to create and capture *increased* value over time.[383] [384] Essentially, self-reinforcement is about creating synergies in the strategy that increase the entire strategy's effectiveness.[385] [386] [387] [388]

Test 8: Resources sufficient to execute?

Theoretically ideal strategies have sufficient resources at their disposal to execute.[389] [390] [391] [392] [393] [394] Resources are assets of the business, which could be financial, physical, human or intangible.[395] [396] Resources represent a business's action potential.[397] If sufficient resources are not available or acquirable, the business is paralysed. A strategy whose resource demands therefore exceed those available or acquirable is unfeasible and should be rejected.

Test 9: Costs and revenues enable a profit?

Theoretically ideal strategies deliver super-normal profits in a given industry.[398] [399] [400] [401] [402] High profitability is one of the key features of good strategies and relates to Magretta's[403] numbers tests, which state that the costs and revenues of the business must enable a profit. If the basic finance story of the business is flawed, then the business will not be able to sustain itself. Therefore strategies that do not enable a profit are unfeasible and should be rejected.

Test 10: Acceptable in terms of adoption and risk?

Theoretically ideal strategies are acceptable in terms of adoption and risk.[404] [405] [406] [407] [408] Adoption is stakeholders' willingness to embrace the strategy and value proposition. If there are some conflicting values,[409] moral dilemmas, motivational barriers, cognitive barriers, political barriers[410] or other trade-offs that stakeholders are not willing to make, then the strategy is unfeasible and should be reworked. Risk, on the other hand, can be defined as the possibility of a negative consequence occurring. All the aforementioned tests essentially build up to the ultimate evaluation of whether the sum of the strategy's risk is acceptable. The greater the number of the preceding nine tests that are failed, the higher the strategy's risk.

Practical guideline

The normative strategic assessment is intended to be used in a tick-box or simple scoring fashion to evaluate whether the conceived strategy exhibits the virtuous characteristics commonly found in "theoretically ideal" strategies. It needs to be mentioned that no strategy is "good" in any absolute sense. In every industry, there are several viable positions that a company can occupy. A single, best strategy does not exist,[411] because if it did then everybody would follow it and there would be no need for strategy.[412] Every strategy is unique may be "wrong" or "right" for the firm in question.[413]

Appraising a strategy as passing these 10 normative tests does not ensure the business's success. It only indicates that the strategy is more robust than strategies that do not pass these tests.[414] Reformulation is advised when some of these tests are failed. However, if it is not possible to reformulate the strategy in such a way that it passes all 10 tests, then it merely indicates that the strategy involves a higher degree of risk. Passing the tests and obtaining a perfect score is not the end goal. Rather, learning from the assessment and refining the business's strategy is of primary importance. If the risks are acceptable, then the strategy is "right" for the business.

Application tool

Use Table 3.8 to assess the strategy of your business.

Table 3.8: Normative strategic assessment

No.	Normative test	Rating (1 poor, 10 excellent)	Rationale for rating	Initiative for improvement
1.	Internally consistent?			
2.	Presents an adaptive response to the competitive environment?			
3.	Based on valid assumptions?			
4.	Compelling value proposition? (cost and/or differentiation advantage)			
5.	Solves the customer problem in the most efficient way?			
6.	Defensible against five forces of competition?			
7.	Self-reinforcing?			
8.	Resources sufficient to execute?			
9.	Costs and revenues enable a profit?			
10.	Acceptable in terms of adoption and risk?			

It is not advisable to average the ratings to obtain an average score for the business – God is in the details.

Case study of Uber (South Africa)[415 416 417 418 419]

Uber is an on-demand transportation service founded by Travis Kalanick and Garrett Camp in July 2010. Since its launch in San Francisco, Uber has expanded rapidly and the service is currently (April 2016) connecting drive-seekers and driver-partners in 60 countries and 404 cities worldwide. The company also boasts an impressive valuation of over $60 billion.

Uber is a multi-sided technology platform that utilises collaborative consumption to serve customers. Uber connects ad hoc drivers (some professional taxi drivers, others ordinary people) with drive-seekers who are looking for a ride. The thing that makes Uber so unique is that it doesn't employ any drivers or own any vehicles – the drivers are seen as partners and they make use of their own vehicles. For safety reasons, Uber requires police verification and a few legal documents for people to become Uber driver-partners.

On the customer side Uber is very simple to use. Customers use the Uber smartphone application and specify what type of vehicle they require (UberX – maximum four people, UberXL – maximum six people) and where they want to go to get a fare estimate. They then simply tap the application to request a driver to their current location. Alternatively, another pick-up location can be specified. A nearby idle Uber driver is then notified and has the option to accept or reject the ride. If the driver accepts, the driver's details (name, car type, Uber customer rating) are sent to the customer along with the estimated time of arrival (ETA). If he or she rejects the ride, the request is sent to another nearby Uber until a driver is found. The Uber application also allows customers to track the driver as he or she is on his or her way to the location. Similarly, the driver can track the location of the customer.

Because Uber makes use of drivers that are in close proximity to drive-seekers, waiting time for the driver to arrive is much less than ordinary taxis. Uber is also way more convenient and reliable. Where drive-seekers usually either had to look up a taxi company and call them to dispatch, or look around for an available taxi (especially problematic during peak hours), the Uber application reduces customer search costs and puts a driver at their fingertips. Uber rides are also less expensive than regular taxis.

Furthermore, Uber is a convenient and safe cashless service – once the journey is complete and the customer has been taken to their desired location, the customer is billed to their credit card. Costs are calculated as a base rate plus a driving distance rate plus a driving duration rate. Sometimes surge pricing is also applied, which incurs additional costs during peak times. No tipping is required as it is already accounted for in the Uber price. At the end of the journey, customers are requested to evaluate their experience with the driver on a five-point basis via the app. This vital information allows Uber to respond to anomalies and the cumulative rating of drivers serves to increase trust in the driver and also reduces customer apprehension about using the service.

The benefits that Uber provides to its driver-partners are that being a driver is a good way to earn additional income part-time or even full-time. Uber gives its drivers full flexibility. Uber also handles the payment of rides, which eliminates problems with change or other cash disputes. Additionally, Uber still pays drivers for being online even if they do not get ride requests. This serves as an incentive for drivers to be on the road even on days that aren't busy, which ensures that the few drive-seekers still get the quickest response to their requests on these days.

Uber has also been experimenting with new offerings, including:

- on-demand requests for boats, helicopters or motorcycle rides
- Uber services for taking kids to school and back home
- Uber services for senior citizens (cars with extra space and handles)
- UberPool, which allows users to "carpool". This entails ride-sharing with strangers who are heading to the same location and splitting the bill on arrival
- UberCargo, where logistics services can be requested on-demand for delivering goods

Uber's extended business model canvas is depicted in Figure 3.19. In this figure, drive-seekers (customers) are indicated with a star ★; Uber driver-partners are indicated with a diamond ◆; and Uber's internal operations are indicated with a circle ●.

Customer Retention

★
- Switching costs
  - ☐ Integration & customisation costs:
  - ☐ Credit card details
  - ☐ Superiority costs
  - ☐ Search costs
  - ☐ Loyalty drivers
  - ☐ Reputation
  - ☐ Preventing and resolving breakdowns in service
- Control Points
  - ☐ First mover advantage
  - ☐ Advantages in scale and scope
  - ☐ Network effects: More drivers, better experience. More customers, more drivers. Two-way referral.
  - ☐ Brand advantage
  - ☐ Business model complementarities: Driver reviews; Journey data
  - ☐ Geographical control: Major cities
  - ☐ Control over customer interface (convenience/security)

◆
- Control Points
  - First mover advantage: Job opportunity for drivers
  - Control over supply: Customers who want drives

● Control Points

Customer Segments

★
- Customers
  - Car-less individuals/ Tourists
  - Party goers
  - People who want a VIP travel experience
  - Other customers who require a quick, cost efficient cab
  - Johannesburg, Pretoria, Cape Town, Durban, Port Elizabeth

◆
- Uber driver-partners
  - Car owners who want to earn money
  - People who love to drive

Revenue Streams

★
- UberX
  - Base fare: ZAR5
  - ZAR6/km
  - ZAR0.6/min
  - Minimum fare: ZAR20
  - Cancellation fee: ZAR25
- UberXL
  - Base fare: ZAR20
  - ZAR7/km
  - ZAR0.7/min
  - Minimum fare: ZAR30
  - Cancellation fee: ZAR25
- UberBlack
  - Base fare: ZAR15
  - ZAR12/km
  - ZAR1.2/min
  - Minimum fare: ZAR50
  - Cancellation fee: ZAR45

- Transactional revenue/ direct: Pay per ride not per person
- Selling usage: The further you drive the more you pay
- Surge pricing (Supply/demand increases rates)

Customer Relationships

★
- Personal assistance: Website and social media
- Self-service FAQs
- Automated service: Review, rating & feedback system

Channels

★
- Awareness (New city launch):
  - ☐ Tech-savvy early adopters
  - ☐ Local advertising (Radio, newspapers, online, social media (Facebook, Twitter, LinkedIn, Google+)
  - ☐ Word-of-mouth Evaluation: Fare-estimates, driver reviews, word-of-mouth (baffled at great experience)
- Purchase: Billed to credit card through app
- Delivery: Local drivers
- Use: Smartphone app (iOS/Android).technology platform
- After sales support: Driver reviews, support through app

◆
- Awareness (New city launch): Cold calling professional drivers/taxis who have their own cars

Value Proposition

★
- On-demand transportation for small parties via smartphone application
  - ☐ UberX: Max 4 people
  - ☐ UberXL: Max 6 people
- Convenient: Don't have to look up Taxi companies and call to dispatch (reduced search costs). Uber puts drivers at your fingertips.
- Reliable: Don't have to rely on luck for getting a ride (location/availability, especially a problem during peak hours). Don't have to stand on street and wave arms at Taxi. A driver *will* come to your location.
- ETA and GPS tracking indicators
- Minimum waiting time: Closest idle driver-partner responds
- Ease of use: Seamless interface & navigational map
- Safe, cash-less ride: Billed directly to credit card
- Two-way referral for free rides (ZAR100 worth)
- Different car options and pricing
- Lower price than Taxi fares
- Split fees with members of your party
- Optimised shortest routes (Uber Map)

- New Product Development (Not RSA):
  - ☐ Transportation on demand: Boats, helicopters, motorcycles.
  - ☐ Uber for kids (service taking kids to school)
  - ☐ Uber for senior citizens
  - ☐ UberPool Rideshare with strangers and split bill
  - ☐ UberCargo: On demand logistics for delivering goods

◆
- Coordinates drivers to drive-seekers
- Additional source of income
- Flexible working schedules and can work part-time
- Easy payment procedure
- Drivers get paid to be online, even without ride requests

UBER

Key Metrics

★
- Number of customers, types of rides booked, frequency
- Customer satisfaction

●
- Geographical coverage
- Driver to population density (per city)
- Number & cause of technical issues

◆
- Number of driver-partners & driver ratings
- Driver-partner earnings per hour

Key Activities

- Product development & management ●
- Hiring drivers ◆
- Manager driver payouts
- Marketing & customer acquisition ★
- Customer support

Key Resources

- Technology platform ●
- Skilled drivers ◆

Key Partners

- Payment processors ●
- Map API providers
- Investors
- Drivers and their cars ◆

Cost Structure

- Technological infrastructure ●
- Salaries to permanent employees
- Launch events and marketing expenditure
- Fuel usage ◆
- Driver payouts

Competitive Advantage

☆

●
- **Core competitive advantage choice**: Best cost provider strategy (differentiation & low costs). Uber created new market space by being an intermediary technology platform that connects ad hoc drivers with drive-seekers. Capitalised on the principles of the sharing economy/collaborative consumption to differentiate itself from other means of point to point transportation – Uber is a "taxi" company without any vehicles or permanent drivers. Uber is also lower cost than available alternatives for small party transportation.
- **Value discipline**: Operational excellence. Being first to market with a product that works seamlessly. This attracts drive-seekers and driver-partners, allowing the business to scale rapidly and fortify its position.
- **Digital-physical orientation**: Digital pure play selling physical products. Digital nature allows global scale with minimal infrastructural investments, supporting the low cost position.

- **Competitive advantages**
  - First mover advantages leading to brand and geographic advantages
  - Scale advantages through network effects and being a digital platform that leverages assets (drivers and cars) it doesn't own
  - Scope advantages: Cars are maintained and updated by drivers.
  - Data superiority: GPS monitoring collects data about ride and customer reviews are used to enhance service, supporting operational excellence position.
  - Differentiation and cost advantages (value proposition – technology enabled)
    - ☐ Ease of use and convenience (seamless interface, navigation map, reduced search costs, no need to call taxi, driver drives to pickup location)
    - ☐ Payment ease (cash-less, directly billed to credit card, safe)
    - ☐ Pick-up speed (closest idle driver-partner responds)
    - ☐ Lower price (platform efficiencies)

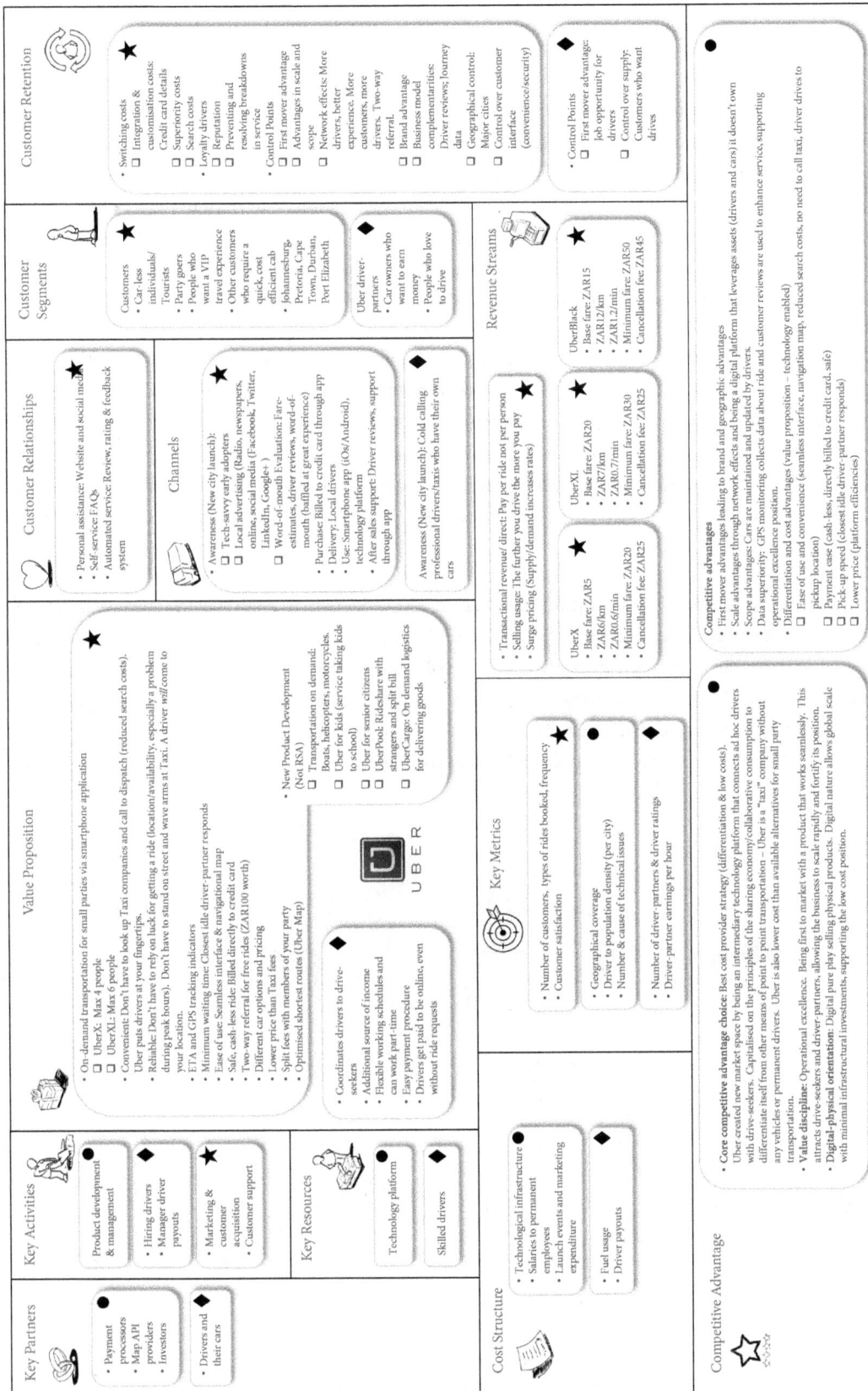

Figure 3.19: Uber's business model

CONCLUSION

This chapter expanded on the "current business model" view discussed in Ungerer, Ungerer and Herholdt.[420] First the relationships between strategy, business models and operations were discussed and the importance of strategic principles and the concept of an activity system was highlighted. The core elements of competitive strategy and its core principles (focus, differentiation, robustness, adaptability) were discussed, and it was theorised that businesses that master these principles will be immensely competitive and prosperous. It was also mentioned that a tight fit between the elements of the business's activity systems is vital as it allows competitive advantages to be compounded while creating barriers that prevent imitation, thereby adding to the sustainability of the business.

It was further mentioned that one problem with business model thinking is that business models do not emphasise competition, the creation of competitive advantages and competitiveness in the market. This is problematic, because businesses that do not create competitive advantages can't reasonably expect to outperform competitors and deliver supra-normal profits. In response to this problem an expanded business model canvas was proposed that additionally added customer retention, key metrics and competitive advantage elements. In the customer retention element, control points, switching costs and e-loyalty drivers were discussed in detail. The revenue generation section was also explained in more detail.

Furthermore, the process of business modelling was also discussed. Environmental analysis, strategy formulation, strategy evaluation, strategy execution and strategy renewal were identified as the higher-level design sequence. A flexible sequence for business model formulation itself (which involved defining the core aspirational description, customer elements, value-focused elements, efficiency-focused elements, and extended elements) was also proposed. Next a normative assessment was discussed, which can be used to evaluate whether the developed strategy possesses characteristics associated with high-performing, theoretically ideal strategies. The chapter concluded with a business model case study on Uber.

Chapter 4

Multiple futures

Scenarios are not predictions, because it is not possible to predict the future with certainty.
Scenarios represent alternative views of the future.
In scenario planning, we think about how today's decisions impact the future.
The purpose of scenarios is not to describe the future world as accurately as possible, but to
produce better decisions in terms of the future. – Peter Schwartz (Schwartz, 1996)[1]

LEARNING OBJECTIVES

At the very core of strategy work is the realisation that a company is, at any one moment in its life, faced by many possible futures – and that no one person, or group of people, can predict which one – or even which mix – will eventually materialise. That said, well-developed and thought-through scenarios focus the minds of decision makers on the most critical decisions required to "nudge" the organisation towards a more desired future, given the assumptions and information underlying the possibility spaces created by the scenarios.

After studying this chapter, you will know how to:

- Apply the various processes to develop a scenario for an organisation.
- Develop multiple perspectives on how to prepare for possible futures.
- Appreciate how scenario processes can be used to promote societal transformations (especially in the case studies about South Africa).
- Understand that a scenario is not about predicting the future.

In this section, scenarios as a strategy tool are explored. We start this chapter by going into the methodological underpinnings of the scenario approach, look at scenarios as learning tools and describe a specific scenario-building methodology by using a recent case study where scenarios were developed for the long-haul aviation industry. We do this to show leadership teams how to apply the guidelines in order to develop specific scenarios relevant to the enterprise. Scenarios constitute a way to think more comprehensively about the future – to learn from the future.

Learning from the future through scenarios casts the generic strategic options and choices (discussed in chapter 2) into a set of moulds (scenarios) that focuses the business model (discussed in chapter 3) on specific outcomes to achieve in the future. This means that the organisation is now ready for strategy execution activities (chapter 5).

THE SCENARIO APPROACH

Methodological underpinnings

Scenario-building and planning approaches are particularly useful given the uncertain nature of the multi-dimensional, multi-decade decision-making space involved in the *problematique* of dealing with multiple possible futures. Learning about possible futures, and the signposts en route to these futures, enables policy makers to manage long-term risks better and proactively seize emerging opportunities.

Adopted from military use, the first person to use it in a business setting was Futurist Herman Kahn.[2] As a planning technique, scenario-planning owes its fame to Pierre Wack and his colleagues at Royal Dutch Shell, who during the early 1970s, persuaded the board of directors to plan for the possibility of the oil price increasing – something which had never happened in the entire history of oil up till then. When the oil price skyrocketed in 1973, the board's thinking exercise allowed it to adjust to this reality sooner than competitors (who initially thought it was just a spike) and to profit from it – in the process moving from seventh place to second in size, as well as becoming the most profitable company in the industry.[3]

There are three litmus tests for the plausibility of scenarios: They must be "possible", "credible" and "relevant".[4] "Relevance" implies that a scenario should have "decision-making utility".[5] A distinction should also be drawn between scenario-building and scenario-planning, where the former can be seen as only a first step of the latter.[6] In moving from scenarios to action plans, Ringland[7] presents two helpful "tools":

- a scenario options matrix that distinguishes between the "future-robust core of strategy" (with relevance to all probable scenarios) and "focused contingent strategies" (aimed at either realising the desired future or dealing with the fall-out of feared futures); and
- a strategic positioning matrix that translates the broad strategic orientation into a planning framework. See our final case study for an example.

In addition to being plausible, scenarios must also meet the following criteria[8] [9] [10]:

- differentiation (it should not merely be minor variations of a reference case, but should present distinctly alternative futures);
- consistency (the internal logic should support the credibility of the scenario, and the narrative should be persuasive and coherent);
- challenge and creativity; and
- communication-friendliness

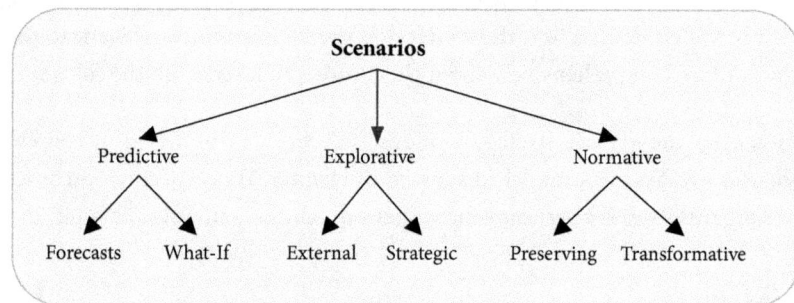

Figure 4.1: Scenario typology

Different categories of scenario can be identified. Börjeson et al.[11] summarise it as follows (see Figure 4.1):

Predictive scenarios answer the question: "What will happen?" **Exploratory scenarios** answer: "What can happen?" **Normative scenarios** answer: "How can a specific target be reached?"

Forecasts sketch out scenarios that are likely to occur emphasising those aspects of the world that are important to the forecast and **What-Ifs** set out to answer a set of questions proposed by a particular group of people.

External scenarios focus on the likely impact of external factors on the future and **Strategic scenarios** examine how we can influence the future by our own actions.

Preserving scenarios investigate how we can achieve a goal or goals by adjusting our current situation and **Transformative scenarios** ask how we can achieve our goals while the underlying systems are changing.

Within these categories, there are a whole host of **techniques** and every scenario practitioner has his or her own preferences. Techniques can be clustered, however, and Börgeson et al.[12] have a useful classification:

- Generating techniques generate and collect ideas, knowledge and views regarding some part of the future, using common data-gathering techniques such as workshops and surveys.
- Integrating techniques integrate parts into wholes using models based on quantitative assessments of probability or relationship, such as time series analysis and systems models.
- Consistency techniques ensure consistency among different forecasts such as morphological analysis and cross-impact analysis.

All these techniques aim at producing data that will be useful to understanding elements of the strategic landscape faced by the firm. For (much) more information about analysing and crystallising the strategic landscape, see Ungerer et al.[13]

... but do they work?

It is easy to write about scenarios creating the veneer of utility and scientific soundness, but do they work? According to recent research, the scenario methodology has effects in the workplace. Here are some:

- According to Philip Meissner and Torsten Wulf, it reduces the framing bias and improves perceived decision quality.[14]
- Ronald Bradfield found that it reduces the confirmation bias.[15]
- According to Paul Schoemaker, it reduces the over-confidence bias by challenging prevailing mindsets.[16]
- Chermack and Nimon found that it influences a broad range of mental models held by decision-makers.[17]
- Celeste Varum and Carla Melo state that it significantly enhances the ability to deal with uncertainty and the usefulness of the overall decision-making process.[18] They also found that the main benefits of using scenarios are improvement of the decision making process and the identification of new issues and problems which may arise in the future.

Maybe the best way to test the effectiveness of the scenario method is to look at old scenarios and to gauge how effective they were in helping participants envision something like the future we are currently experiencing. Firstly, we will look at one such case study that was done for the Office of the President of South Africa in 2008. We only provide an abridged version of the scenarios – please read the complete version at www.thepresidency.gov.za/docs/pcsa/planning/**scenario**/welcome.pdf

Case study: Recent scenarios for South Africa

The effects of good government on living in South Africa (till 2025)

A report released in September 2008 by the Office of the Presidency reflected on the impact of public policies. *South Africa scenarios 2025: The future we chose?*[19] looked back at three paths that the country may have traversed by 2025. The research presented, the scenarios envisaged, and the question-mark in the title were all meant to provoke discussion and debate.

The task team said:

Scenarios are not predictions, nor roadmaps; they are constructed stories about a particular point in the future and some informed speculation about the crosscutting paths that might get us there. The power of scenarios lies in provoking a sense of what might be possible and in combining probabilities in ways we might not have thought of previously … They often allow the detection of faint signals that may disrupt even the most thorough planning cycles. They are designed to help identify pitfalls and options, and factors in the future we may choose to adopt or avoid.[20]

Methodology

Concerning methodology, the task team wrote:

> "The research for this scenario exercise started with a concerted attempt to understand a wide range of forces at work in the world and in South Africa in 2008. This involved 65 interviews with well-placed South Africans, as well as a series of working sessions with a core group of about 40 people, drawn from academia, business, unions, political parties, and think tanks. As a result, we were able to identify 24 variables, or factors that are key shapers of our reality and which we need to understand in order to construct views of the future."[21]

Practical guideline: Using key driving forces (KDFS)

Key trends for each variable were identified. From these 24 variables, seven Key Driving Forces (KDFs) were identified. These KDFs are aggregations of trends that are likely to be the most fundamental shapers of our world and our country to 2025, and that are most likely to create the context that the seventh democratically elected government and society at large will face in the middle of the 2020s. The KDFs form the bedrock of the scenario storylines. While some KDFs identify factors that can be influenced through the agency of government, great attention is paid to those variables with the highest levels of uncertainty and impact. As such, what these storylines depict are just three of the possible combinations of the various KDFs. There are many more combinations that can be devised, but these stories have been constructed to provide the most plausible but challenging narratives of what hurdles the country might have to jump in the build-up to 2025.

These scenarios are not "worst-case" scenarios – a technique often used to contemplate unlikely, but not impossible, turns of events in the future. Worst-case scenarios can be very useful, and in debating the storylines, some important "outriders" can be explored in more detail, and some such storylines can, indeed, be generated. The scenarios presented here only occasionally hint at such "Black Swan" events. A deliberate effort has also been made to avoid positing a "best-case" scenario. Similarly, "outriders" of outcomes better than the most optimistic of the three storylines can be generated through debate. These scenarios are therefore neither "worst-case" nor "best-case" scenarios, and try to avoid the simple polarities of "high road" or "low road" scenario-making. Instead they steer towards various plausible combinations of events from clear antecedents in 2008. Every element that emerges fully formed in later years – in these scenarios – has its roots in some current reality. We could do worse than any of the "worst-case" elements that might form part of a particular scenario. We may do considerably better than any of the most optimistic elements described in any of the three scenarios.

Having "seen", at least in our mind's eye, some worked-out glimpses of the future, we might be moved to try to anticipate some outcomes and secure others. Indeed, these scenarios are meant to provoke introspection about long-term planning, about how policy is translated into action in order to help avoid calamity and to embrace opportunities more fully.

Practical guideline: Clarify assumptions

Assumptions about KDFs most likely to shape South Africa to 2025

KDF 1. Shifts in global economic power: The rapid industrialisation and growth of China and India, and their burgeoning demand for resources and markets, is changing the world in profound ways. By 2025, given current trends, China's GDP is expected to be about the same as the United States of America's (the United States of America's GDP is currently more than double the GDP of China and India combined), reflecting three decades of Chinese growth at more than double the rate of the United States of America and the EU.

Will the growth of Brazil, Russia, India and China and the oil bounty of many Middle Eastern countries do more for the economic growth of Africa in the next 20 years than 60 years of Western investment and aid have achieved? While this appears likely to be the case, there are significant dangers too: China and Russia may be as cavalier in their disregard for democracy and human rights as the United States of America and ex-colonial powers have been in the past.

Trade as a percentage of global GDP is shifting upwards at an accelerated rate. By 2025, trade in goods and services will account for more than half of global GDP. The ability to trade with others is becoming more important to any country's ability to grow than ever before. Africa's economic clout also grows significantly by 2025; the key question is how much of this is driven by South Africa, or how much others take the lead over time as other continental powers grow faster, or are led better, than South Africa.

KDF 2. Shifts in global political power: While shifts in international power relationships partly reflect shifting economic power, they do not do so in mechanical ways. The United States of America's military budget is still larger than those of the next 15 largest economies, including China, combined. By 2025, the United States of America has still by far the most formidable armed force in the world, although on a much smaller scale than in 2008. Despite this, a multi-lateral approach to global problems is likely to have taken root, with an expansion of early intervention mechanisms, the rapid deployment of peace keepers, and more united action by formations such as the UN, the G5, G8, G13 and G20.

Current trends suggest far fewer armed conflicts than ever before in human history over the next decade or so. But it is also possible that conflicts over resources disturb this trend: are there sudden resource tipping points that would propel otherwise peaceful nations into war? And how much more powerful will Africa, or key African states or blocs, become as world players, and what will shape this?

South Africa's leading role in reshaping elements of international discourse over the past 15 years, and in re-imagining Africa, may be challenged by other fast-growing power blocs in East and West Africa, and by South Africa pursuing more narrow national and regional interests in the future.

KDF 3. Resource constraints: The world is already caught in an energy gap between the age of fossil fuels, particularly oil, and the slow development of the coming age of alternative fuel sources. By 2025, nuclear, hydrogen, sun and wind will be the predominant emerging energy sources. But, on current trends, the transition may not be well managed. Higher costs of food production may become ever more entrenched, and international tourism and mobility are likely to be negatively affected. The growing shortage and deterioration in quality of other critical resources, particularly soil, air and water, are also highly likely to become key global issues.

Locally, three additional KDFs mirror these global drivers.

KDF 4. South Africa's economic growth: An elemental shaper of the future of South Africa is our economic performance. How fast does the economy grow and along what paths? How competitive and productive does it become? The way in which the fruits of this growth are shared is as important as growth itself: is the economy ever able to create decent and sustainable jobs at a rate greater than the growth of the labour force?

Faced with persistent long-term structural unemployment, what measures will the new government adopt? How responsive will the private sector be to national imperatives? Will the rapid decline in South Africa's manufacturing, mining and agricultural sectors in relation to their relative contribution to GDP be arrested and reversed – and how? As critical as these internal factors are, South Africa's relationship with Africa will be as important. Can our economy become more integrated into Africa?

KDF 5. Governance: How able, competent, efficient, honest and legitimate is government going to be in 2025, and in the years leading to 2025? Will it be able to promote national competitiveness and drive the economy forward, or will it inhibit innovation, productivity and social inclusion? How well will it deal with the key issues of health, education, crime and corruption over time?

Related to this are matters pertaining to electoral politics and dynamics within the largest political alliances: the tone of political discourse, the conduct of the leadership and centripetal and centrifugal trends tugging at the ruling party. Ultimately, will leadership engender a greater sense of purpose and unity?

KDF 6. Social fabric: The state has the resources to fashion at least a basic sense of nationhood, and a sense of human solidarity that cuts across class, gender, race and ethnic divisions. It can do this, among other ways, by providing citizens, especially the youth, with the skills to operate in a twenty-first century economy, increasing citizens' average levels of wellness, and creating a sense of security and belonging. Government can also help invoke a sense of pride and aspiration by articulating an engaging national narrative and by standing for the highest good. But there are limits in this regard. Many of the dynamics that impact on social cohesion depend on value systems within society.

Their forging is the domain of educational, religious, community and other sectors, including the nation's arts and cultural productions. How will government interact with these socialising forces for maximum national benefit?

Note: **Technology and the road to tomorrow**

A key crosscutting driver is technology. By 2025, billions of people will have access to always-on, high-bandwidth communication devices, which will allow users to network and connect in dynamic new ways. This is already rapidly changing the way people work, where they work, how much they travel to and from work (and on work-related trips), how they make and market their goods and even how they form and foster relationships. Technology is also likely to fuel democracy and openness, increase human lifespan and allow for both greater productivity and more leisure time.

Although access to technology is likely to continue to be uneven, a key trend already evident is that the poor everywhere are embracing technology as fast as they can afford to, exploiting it as a key avenue out of disconnectedness and penury. South Africa also stands to benefit if fuel-cell technology becomes an important source of energy, or if, as the oil age gives way to the hydrogen age, South Africa's Pebble Bed nuclear technology is more widely applied.

Summary

The story of 2025 – of what South Africa faces then, and the routes we took to get there – will be told mostly in reference to these KDFs.

- How did we respond to environmental degradation and the challenges of energy sources?
- How did we negotiate our way between the competing demands for our resources and access to markets?
- How did we educate people and grow the economy?
- How did we improve the quality of people's health?
- How did we measure and improve governance, using the metrics of legitimacy, participation and efficiency?

These are some of the questions that will need to be addressed, and that will no doubt be answered in the great Thirty-year Review that will be published as the nation prepares to celebrate 30 years of democracy in 2024. Will it be a review of celebration? Will we rue opportunities lost, or revel in having seized them? Will we be living longer, better, and in greater harmony with others? Will government be doing more with less, staffed by the brightest and the best? Or will we be stuck in a culture of sluggishness and mediocrity? The answers to these questions will describe the paths we travel to the seventh democratic election in 2024, and to the South Africa and the world we live in by 2025.

The scenarios outlined in these pages reveal the broad contours of three of these possible paths. These three stories have been chosen to characterise three specific balances between the main KDFs focused on, and a variety of other factors that will shape the reality that all South Africans will face. Critically, they have been woven together taking into account the degree of plausibility of the various combinations. But they are not exhaustive by any means.

We hope that they begin a dialogue about the future we choose.

SCENARIO 1: Not yet Uhuru:

A government strongly committed to accelerating economic growth struggles in the face of deteriorating global conditions and severe ecological challenges …

Synopsis

Me first, you later. While government strove to deliver on its commitment to the poor, ideological divisions and a "me-first" spirit of rank materialism within the political leadership compromised its good intentions.

The have-lots vs the have-nothings. The poor made up a slightly smaller demographic in 2025, but their disenchantment with the system soared to volatile new levels, as the gap between the "have-lots" and the "have-nothings" grew wider than ever. This acute sense of relative deprivation, in the context of a world obsessed by brands and "getting and spending", made South Africa more combustible than ever.

Black power, white money. Senior management in government was almost exclusively black in 2025, but the nation's wealth still lay overwhelmingly in white hands. The economy remained divided along racial lines, with white management occupying more than 60 per cent of the boardroom seats of power.

The earth lies screaming. For the first time in history, as the natural environment buckled under the strain of more than 200 years of rampant industrialisation, the doomsday nightmare of an environmental cataclysm appeared to be on the verge of coming true.

SCENARIO 2: Nkalakatha:

Determined to play a more central role in the economy, government prioritises poverty reduction and skills enhancement by articulating a national vision and fostering partnerships …

Synopsis

The dreamers become the do-ers. Narrowing the gap between vision and delivery, government set the pace for a new era of action and application. Gradually, the notion of the developmental state edged towards everyday reality.

One nation, one destiny. While there were significant trade-offs to be made in the pursuit of a better life for all, government succeeded in reducing the once-widespread sense of social alienation, by clearly articulating its vision and placing a deep emphasis on participation and a common national destiny.

The environment matters too. Although growth and redistribution remained on top of the national agenda, government began to take a more proactive stance on matters of environmental change and sustainability, with mixed results.

Time to bite the bullet. In the aftershock of a global economic collapse, government cut spending and introduced tough austerity measures. But the nation bit the bullet and worked together to weather the crisis.

SCENARIO 3: Muvhango:

Despite an initial resurgence of the economy, and positive world conditions, the government battles to govern well …

Synopsis

Bang goes the boom: In the slipstream of the 2009 elections and a successful 2010 World Cup, the economy boomed, and the growth rate breached 5.5 per cent. But the euphoria was short-lived, as poor planning and coordination, exacerbated by political in-fighting, started taking their toll on the economy.

Politician vs politician: Service delivery suffered, and corruption increased, as animosity among politicians reached startling new levels. Efficiency levels declined, as measured by unqualified audits, proportion of budgets spent and citizen satisfaction surveys.

The champ slips up: The economy, after a few good years, was on the skids. Foreign multi-nationals and private equity funds began cherry-picking key South African assets. South Africa's proportion of continental GDP declined to such an extent that by 2025 the country had lost its unrivalled pre-eminence on the continent.

The brink of a new era: Standing at the edge of a cliff, a new ANC went back to the nation, humbly, and demonstrated signs of a revival of idealism.

Acknowledgements: These scenarios were prepared by the Policy Co-ordination and Advisory Services (PCAS) in the Presidency. The project worked with a core team made up of officials from various departments and outside experts drawn from the private sector, civil society and community groups. The project also benefited from a wide range of interviews with leaders from government, the private sector, civil society and research institutions. The *Deutsche Gesellschaft für Technische Zusammenarbeit* (GTZ) funded the project through the Economic and Development Policy Advisory Programme (EDAP).

Case study: A time traveller's guide to our next 10 years

Contrast the above set of scenarios with those produced by Frans Cronje[22] of the Institute of Race Relations in April 2014, shown in Figure 4.2.

These descriptions were taken from summaries provided by the Institute of Race Relations[23] and the 702 radio station[24]. Cronje's book provides ample details about assumptions and KDFs, and fleshes out each scenario considerably.

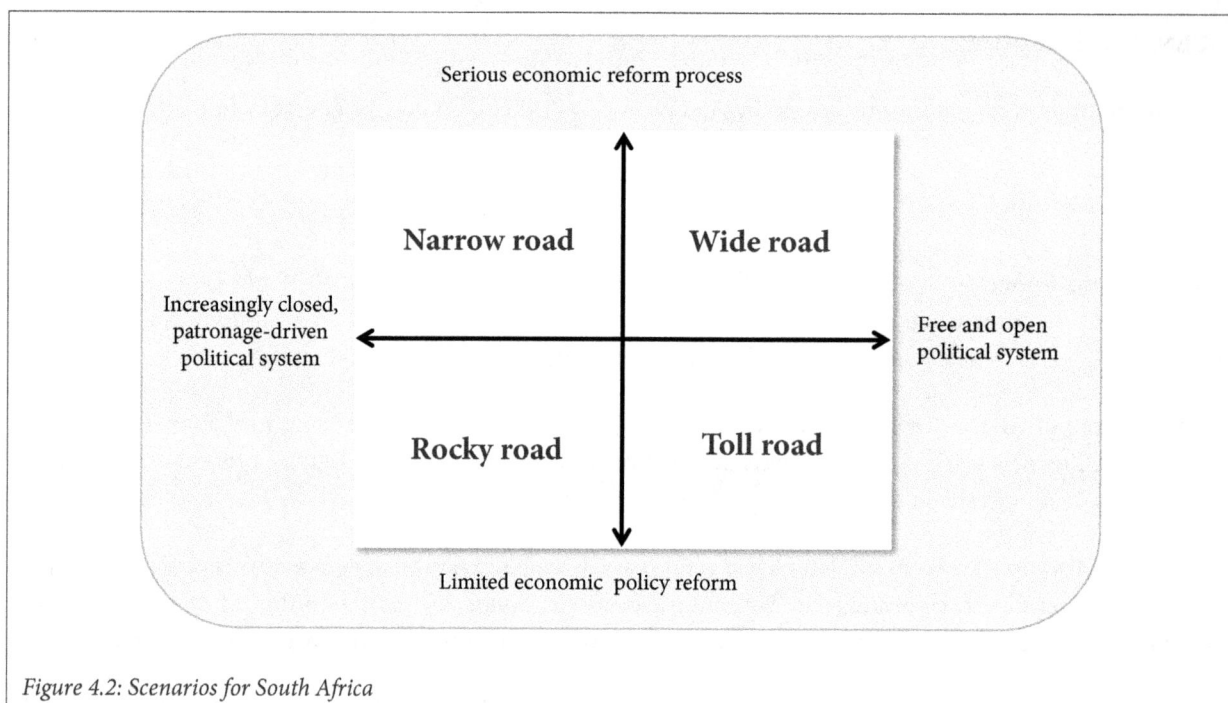

Figure 4.2: Scenarios for South Africa

Scenario 1: The wide road:

The top three **road signs** we look for in this scenario are:

- Firstly, that the ANC increasingly comes to realise that it is in trouble.
- Secondly, a leadership shift in the party that squeezes out those individuals who are likely to resist pro-growth reform.
- Thirdly, that the new leadership seeks to convince South Africans of the need to support reforms at the same time as moving on labour market deregulation.

The ANC realises it needs to reform. It is starting to understand that the only hope of long-term survival is to secure the economic performance needed to create the jobs it needs to meet the expectations of its supporters. Labour market regulation has long been a policy holy cow, but the party moves towards **deregulation**, which, in turn, opens the way to other reforms. See these three indicators materialise and you can start to assume that an **economic recovery is plausible** securing South Africa's future as a free and open society.

In the wide road scenario the ANC win that 2024 election with a comfortable majority, having been forced into a series of major policy reforms by the dire economic environment it confronted in the aftermath of the 2014 election. Following a series of leadership changes the ANC sought, and won, a popular mandate for real economic reform and by 2024 the economy was growing by 5 per cent and the unemployment rate had fallen from 25 per cent to 15 per cent. South Africa remained a free and open society and was well positioned as the gateway to a booming Africa and a top global emerging market.

Scenario 2: The narrow road:

South Africa becomes a high-growth, high-performance economy in an increasingly closed political and social system.

Here we are looking for the following **road-signs**.

- First, we again see more and more ANC leaders admit they are in trouble.
- Second, they undermine any mechanisms (trade unions, civil society activism, parliamentary opposition, a critical media) in order to be able to act with impunity.
- Third, the ANC moves on labour market deregulation for the same reasons as set out in Scenario 1.

After the 2014 election the ANC realises the trouble it is in. It recognises that to stay in power it has to drive investment and the economy in order to meet the expectations of its supporters. It needs radical reforms. Following China's lead, the ruling party becomes über-pragmatic ("It doesn't matter if the cat is black or white as long as it catches the mouse"). Gambling that it would never get a popular mandate for reform, the party sought to undermine democratic safeguards, forcing through a series of conservative, Thatcherite reforms in a desperate bid for economic recovery and therefore political survival. It undermined trade unions and forced the dramatic deregulation of labour markets while abandoning BEE and affirmative action policy – all in the single-minded pursuit of investment-led growth.

It faces a lot of opposition and, in order to push through sweeping economic reforms, it starts to erode the capacity of its opponents to fight it in the courts. We are left with an increasingly closed political system which is applied to create the most business- and investor-friendly scenario you can imagine.

Ten years later South Africa was growing sustainably at 5 per cent of GDP and unemployment had again fallen to 15 per cent. Economic recovery saw waning ANC political support recover, driven by South Africans who were only too happy to trade a degree of liberty for personal economic progress.

Scenario 3: The rocky road

The top three **road signs** here are as follows:

- First, the party leadership is in denial about the state of the South African economy.
- Second, a united leftist leadership centred around the South African Communist Party is able to entrench itself as the engine of ideas of the ANC and then to set about the destruction of democratic institutions.
- Third, there are no moves towards securing a better investment space but rather the opposite, as business regulation is tightened, racial policy is more strictly enforced, and property rights eroded.

After the 2014 election the ANC denies it has a problem. It blames everyone except itself. It sheds its reformist leaders. It intervenes in the economy in an increasingly draconian fashion. It realises it can't deliver on its supporters' expectations and, as a result, tears down democratic institutions in order to rule with impunity. South Africa becomes a lot poorer.

In the rocky road scenario a violent and corrupt black-nationalist regime bludgeoned its way to a narrow 2024 electoral majority. The ANC has fallen in with the EFF and the radical left. Property rights and the rule of law have been abandoned. The economy ended the decade in recession as unemployment rates hit record highs. Populist demands for increased state intervention amidst the economic demise were cleverly exploited by the government to destroy democratic safeguards. South Africans were shocked and dismayed at the speed with which the economic catastrophe overtook them – but powerless to fight back.

Scenario 4: The toll road

The **road signs** here are:

- First, that the party remains in denial about its failing political fortunes.
- Second, it becomes increasingly internally divided as factions turn on each other.
- Third, the broader opposition uses unfettered access to democratic institutions (parliament, the courts, the media etc.) to offer clear policy alternatives sufficient to capture the confidence of increasingly disappointed voters seeing the ANC majority slip to below 50 per cent in 2024.

This is again a scenario in which the ANC remains in denial about the trouble it is in. This time, however, it remains divided against itself. No clear leadership or policy direction emerges, with the one benefit that democratic institutions remain intact as the ANC's popularity falls all the way into a 2024 electoral defeat.

In the toll road scenario a new black-led DA has won the 2024 election with a small majority. The decade to 2024 saw the ANC simply unable to meet the expectations of its supporters. Negative political momentum growing out of weak economic performance, unchecked corruption, and extraordinary incompetence overwhelmed the ANC's ability to maintain political control of South Africa. The economy has spent 10 years in the economic doldrums with growth averaging less than 3 per cent of GDP as unemployment rates hovered at around 25 per cent.

Now an untested DA government has five years to prove it has the policy mix to reverse South Africa's failing fortunes before the political pendulum starts swinging again in 2029.

Application tool: Reading scenarios

When developing scenarios of the future, it is useful to apply two different lenses.

- An objective lens describes the probability space in which the future will unfold and makes the range of imagined outcomes plausible and likely. This means that you have to understand the essential forces which will co-create the future. This engages the "mind".
- A subjective lens projects the hopes and fears – conscious or unconscious – of the intended readers onto the future. The subjective lens focuses on what is most meaningful and would be preferable, thereby engaging the emotions and the "heart".

Neither lens is sufficient without the other. Using only one of these lenses, the future becomes either a dry intellectual exercise devoid of meaning, or a playful fantasy devoid of importance. Applying these two lenses jointly however, people can identify meaningful images of the future that exercise a surprising attraction and that illuminate strategic insights and invite concerted action.

"Read" the above two scenarios by answering the following questions:

Application tool: Reading scenarios

Scenario set	Overall, how well does it work for you (or not)? Why?	Is it plausible and likely (or implausible and unlikely)? Why?	Does it describe the hopes and fears of likely readers (or not)? Why?	What could the scenario writers do to improve it?
The effects of good government on living in South Africa (till 2025)				
A time-traveller's guide to our next 10 years (till 2024)				

How would you describe the essential differences between these two sets of scenario?

In your opinion, what difference did the mental models of the writer(s) make?

What difference did the intended audience(s) make?

Now find the current scenarios for your firm (or one of your choice) and apply the above matrix and questions to it.

Summary so far:

By now it should be clear that scenarios work because they engage the hearts and minds of the intended readership.

Scenarios are not predictions about the future, but they open up plausible possible futures to help decision-makers navigate towards it. In order to develop scenarios a whole host of tools and techniques are available and scenario writers mix and match to use their skills and the challenge of "seeing" possibilities.

In essence, scenarios are learning tools.

SCENARIOS AS LEARNING TOOLS TO VISIT THE FUTURE IN ADVANCE

Now that you have had a look at two scenarios about South Africa's possible futures, you will notice that no one scenario is perfectly applicable to today, but many supply bits of clarity and provide a text for our current experience. In short, scenarios help us, not to foresee the future, but to learn about it in advance; to rehearse the future before it arrives.

This means that we are better prepared for the actualities if, and when, they arrive.

What is scenario learning?

As we have seen scenarios are not forecasts of the future, nor are they attempts to predict the unpredictable. They represent a willingness to **learn** in a nonthreatening way from the identified possible futures. They enable leadership teams to rehearse different futures. This sensitises role players about how the future may be quite different from the present, known circumstances.

So, scenarios enable management teams to visit the future in advance to develop a richer understanding of what a successful business concept should look like to meet the challenges and opportunities locked up in the future. They constitute a **visual interactive dialogue** process to develop innovative foresight. Peter Schwartz[25] defines scenarios as a "tool for ordering one's perceptions about alternative environments in which one's decisions might be played out".

The problem with the future is not that it is unknowable; the problem with the future is that it is different.[26] One of the end products of scenarios is qualitative descriptions (in detail or in summary format) of possible futures. Each of these possible futures represents a definite outcome, given the chosen critical forces (or KDFs) that will influence the future. Credible and relevant hypotheses form the basis of the content and are verified as part of the scenario-building process by plausible evidence, confirming the possibility that the projected descriptions could take place.

Another outcome is identified opportunities based on the various futures described. This ensures that we are more proactive than reactive, that we identify what needs to be changed to benefit from anticipated changes and thereby influence and capitalise on the future we want and envisage.

The scenario process does not consist of single-dimension or one-shot predictions. It is also not another version of industry analysis.[27] It is a deep search for insights on how the future could change and what possibilities these hold for the organisation. It directs the dialogue to the point where answers are developed about the decisions and actions needed to be taken today to be able to succeed tomorrow.[28]

Building scenarios and recording these as learning aids with teams who want to think about the future can be compared to the use of flight simulators to train pilots. Scenarios are flight simulators to future destinations. Visiting these destinations in advance gives decision-makers the chance to get acquainted with the new territory and its associated landscape.

The fuel for scenario development and learning is imagination

The scenario approach requires an entrepreneurial spirit, and a mind and attitude that are prepared to search for gaps, spaces and chances to create and craft new possibilities. Gary Hamel[29] confirms this stance when he says "the goal is not to speculate on what might happen, but to imagine what you can actually make happen".

Imagination capacity is a key component of successful scenario development. What is needed here is the **capacity to reconstruct reality in a new combination or configuration that gives modern and fresh meaning** to known constructs. It is the ability to escape the restrictions of current thinking paradigms and to come up with creative insights. Our ability to learn is constrained only by our understanding of information in the scenario and our own imagination. Getting rid of our own preconceived ideas and our own prejudices might well be the biggest challenge to engaging constructively in a scenario development and learning process.

Practical guideline: Spotting discontinuities

Scenarios are not only about the future, they are also about the here and now. A here-and-now focus forces one to look closer for present-day discontinuities. **What is already changing now? Where is the rate of change changing?** This is an indication of possible discontinuities that can be exploited, because the fast-changing variables will eventually influence the slower-changing variables. To be first and fast with a new business concept might represent potential for competitive differentiation. Leading edge benefits need to be balanced with the pain associated with bleeding edge, however. Scenarios provide a tool where the upsides and downsides of new ideas and competitive positions can be worked with. **The slow will follow the fast ... eventually**.

The ability, openness and courage to identify opportunities based on the scenario information are the challenge leadership teams face when engaging in a scenario process.

Application tool: Purpose and goals associated with scenarios as a learning and discovery tool

As already indicated, the focus is not only on the development of possible future scenarios, but also on the creation of a **deeper understanding of the implications** of these unfolding futures for the present situation. This creates **creative tension**, which energises the team to initiate new and different strategic actions. Given this active learning approach to scenarios, what are the goals?

Application tool

Use a recent scenario exercise in your enterprise (or one you are familiar with) and decide how well it met (or not) the goals of a scenario learning process. What could the team have done to have learnt more?

Goals of a scenario learning process

These include the following:

- Enhance and enrich the team's understanding of the combined effect of forces and trends that will impact their future.
- Stimulate new, fresh and insightful dialogue about the future, based on the possibility spaces identified in the different scenarios.
- Create a new and expanded basis for decision-making.
- Add new perspectives, ideas and voices in the dialogue about the future competitive positioning of the organisation.
- Rehearse the future in advance – learn from it before its actual occurrence.

- This enables strategic agility: when the specific scenario starts to unfold, the organisation is ready and equipped to deal with the new circumstances.
- Apply the information and wisdom from the multiple scenarios to present-day decisions.
- Increase the capacity of a system to respond more appropriately to future events through foresight.

Application tool

Use the scenario(s) you used in the above application exercise and determine how many of the possible benefits were derived from the exercise, in your opinion. What could the scenario builders have done to benefit more?

Benefits of multiple scenarios

- The idea of multiple scenarios rests on the departure point that straight-line learning and planning is a recipe for failure. In this context straight-line thinking represents many arrows aiming at one single end state. The future is too uncertain, too complex and too unpredictable to be fitted into only one possibility. Taking multiple options and positions increases your chance and opportunity to take advantage of possible futures as events unfold over time. This will prevent a situation where straight-line thinking and a single position become a straitjacket and a dead end.
- Multiple future scenario positions enable an organisation to recognise the lead indicators of an unfolding scenario well in advance. This time advantage creates the space for creative thinking and restrategising to initiate first-mover breakthroughs.
- Scenarios extend and enrich our competence to think about the future in a more diverse way. In doing this we enlarge the range of possibilities and alternatives to consider.

Application tool

Using the same scenario(s) as above, determine – in your own opinion – which of the disadvantages of the scenario approach applied. Why do you think this?

Disadvantages of the scenario approach

Mietzner and Reger[30] mention a few disadvantages:

- The practice of scenario planning is very time-consuming. It is not something that can be condensed into a half-day or one-day activity. Elements of the process – like a data-gathering exercise during a conference, or explaining the detail of scenarios after they are completed – can be squeezed into such a timeframe, but the whole process takes much more time.
- The qualitative aspects of the scenario process need careful selection of suitable participants/experts, and finding them – and finding their time – is often difficult.
- The team drafting the scenarios should have a deep understanding and knowledge of the field under investigation. Data and information from different sources have to be collected and interpreted, which makes scenario building even more time-consuming.

- There is always the temptation to focus on black and white scenarios or the most likely scenario (wishful thinking) during the scenario-building process. We have to resist the temptation to work out one scenario beautifully and to neglect others.

GUIDELINES ON HOW TO MOBILISE TEAMS FOR A SCENARIO DEVELOPMENT DIALOGUE

The following section covers the steps leadership teams can follow to develop scenarios in detail. The process described in this chapter to develop scenarios is classified as a future-forward, outside-in approach. This means that team members use their knowledge about the present and emerging future to build the scenarios. In this process, they also analyse the environment to identify driving forces that can influence the future of the organisation. This approach is simple, visual, focused and interactive. This creates energy and speed. In this approach, scenarios are context- and company-specific. The implication is that examples of other companies' scenario outputs are not useful inputs. Every organisation should increase its own strategising ability by developing enterprise-specific scenarios. In working with teams as both generators of ideas and being responsible for ensuring that something happens with the output, the following systemic assumptions are relevant:

- All the required knowledge to think about the situation is already in the system through collective intelligence. The system wants to move to a new level of understanding and will make sense of new information in its own unique way. This will enable the system to develop its own answers for its specific situation.
- Participation is by choice and everybody who attends is self-motivated to contribute. The more diverse the genetics of the team, the better.
- The main contribution of the consultant is to create a common workspace for the team members to mobilise their energy, based on the conceptual frameworks introduced to them.
- Identity, information and relationships are the core and basic building blocks for self-organising. If these variables are leveraged, the team will have the necessary capacity for sense-making and high performance. See chapter 7 for more on self-organising as a strategic conversation principle.

Practical guideline: Initial preparation activities for the participating team

An information pack containing some background information is helpful to stimulate the thinking of members participating in the scenario development process. Some information can be supplied and other information can be gathered by the team as preparation prior to the engagement. Data on scenarios as a learning tool, data related to world trends in the industry, technology, demographic, socio-economic and political trends are helpful. Market trends and consumer trends and needs are all valuable information to enrich the variety of perspectives. See the following case study for examples.

There is not only one reality. We all create our own interpretations. This variety is essential for the emergence of insight.

However, what is most valuable is the participant's openness and willingness to fully engage in the process, allowing the process to disturb him or her in order to enrich the dialogue with their new-found insights. Thinking carefully about the composition of the team is a critical success factor. All the members of the senior decision-making team should participate because this is an integral part of strategy development. Usually senior teams are lacking in diversity. To add spice and richness to the dialogue, the team should be supplemented with diverse voices, views and backgrounds from the wider organisation.

The following questions stimulate the team's thinking about the work they will do at the scenario development retreat and help them to prepare.

Given the information in the data pack, prepare your own answers to the following:

- Identify the major trends in the documentation (as well as other trends that you have knowledge of) that impact directly on your line of business.
- Which of these trends do you have control over and which not?

THE PROCESS OF SCENARIO DEVELOPMENT: STEPS AND CONTENT

To develop the steps and content overview, we will follow the steps and content highlights from our final case study:

Case study: 2050 scenarios for Long-Haul Tourism in the evolving global climate change regime[31]

The **Abstract** for the complete case reads:

Tourism and its "midwife", aviation, are transnational sectors exposed to global uncertainties. This scenario-building exercise considers a specific subset of these uncertainties, namely the impact of the evolving global climate change regime on long-haul tourism (LHT), with a 2050 horizon. The basic *problematique* is that unconstrained growth in aviation emissions will not be compatible with 2050 climate stabilisation goals, and that the stringency and timing of public policy interventions could have far-reaching impacts – either on the market for future growth of LHT, or the natural ecosystem on which tourism depends. Following an intuitive-logic approach to scenario-building, three meta-level scenarios that can be regarded as "possible" futures for the evolution of LHT are described. Two of these, *i.e.*, the "grim reaper" and the "fallen angel" scenarios, are undesirable. The "green lantern" scenario represents the desired future. Long-haul tourist destinations should heed the early warning signals identified in the scenario narratives, and contribute towards realising the desired future. They should further guard against being passive victims if the feared scenarios materialise, by adapting, repositioning early upon reading the signposts, hedging against risks, and seizing new opportunities.

In what follows, we are not going to reproduce the complete case study here, but enough to demonstrate the methodology and its outcomes. The authors used the following eight-step "frame":

Table 4.1: The eight-step scenario-building approach

Steps	Description	Activity
1	Demarcate the context of the scenario exercise, including the unit of analysis, level of analysis, time horizon and key concepts.	1
2	Describe the *problematique*, and brainstorm critical aspects or external drivers of change at the meta-level and in the contextual and transactional environments that could affect the prospects for LHT over the next four decades. These may include "predetermined" trends or phenomena "already in the pipeline", but the focus is on "uncontrollable" uncertainties in the contextual environment, with "high potential impacts".	2
3	Based on the environmental analysis, cluster the first-cut list of drivers and/or uncertainties, identifying a limited number of overriding driving forces "that set the pattern of events and determine outcomes".	3
4	Assess the overriding drivers in terms of their degree of uncertainty, potential impact and controllability, using a two-dimensional ranking space technique as well as an inter-relationship diagram.	
5	On this basis, identify and describe the two "root cause" driving forces, and construct a two-dimensional matrix-type scenario gameboard, which will form the basis of the scenario logics.	
6	Identify the conceivable scenarios in the possibility space, and do a first-cut assessment of their plausibility and differentiation. Within this "possibility space", now eliminate "combinations that are not credible", while maintaining "a reasonable range of uncertainty".	4
7	Develop the scenario narratives or "rehearsals of the future" by fleshing out the scenario logics. In the process, continuously assess the plausibility, internal consistency and relevance of each narrative, refining the storylines as required. To enhance decision-making utility, identify signposts (also referred to as "lead indicators" or "turning points") for the alternative scenarios, and explicitly state any assumptions that underpin the scenario narratives. The narrative should also include indications of strategic imperatives, be they opportunities or risks, from the perspective of the unit of analysis. To challenge the limits of the mental models that underpin these narratives, identify any "wild cards" that may quite significantly disrupt a given scenario.	
8	Finally, in moving from scenario-building to integrated scenario-planning, or from "visualisation to realisation", articulate the most desired future and ways of achieving this future, both at a strategic level and by identifying critical actions that could assist to realise it. Use Ringland's[32] scenario options and scenario-positioning matrices to translate scenarios into a broad strategic orientation, positioning and planning framework for action.	5

Note: *In the case study you will notice that some steps form part of the same scenario-building activity.*

Activity 1: Demarcate the concept

The aim of Activity 1 is to decide upfront what you plan to investigate. Do this to overcome the dangers associated with "analysis paralysis" – by deciding on what you plan to investigate and (maybe more important) what you are NOT going to investigate.

A1.1. The unit of analysis and focus

Many mega-trends and risks may of course affect the unit of analysis, i.e. LHT, over the next four decades. These include geopolitical risks; systemic financial risks; the economic prospects of tourism source markets; ageing populations who shape demand patterns; tourism logistics and supply chain disruptions, such as terrorism, natural disasters and pandemics; the disruption of technology-enabled tourism marketing; consumer demands shaped by greater customisation and disintermediation; natural resource, environmental and ecosystem degradation; and skills and talent mobility.[33]

However, given the urgency of the climate change challenge indicated by science,[34] coupled with the prominence that the decarbonisation of aviation and tourism is receiving in public discourse[35] as well as in academic literature,[36] the primary focus here is narrower. It also addresses a gap identified in a 2010 literature review by Dubois and colleagues,[37] namely that there are "very few long-term scenarios that focus on both climate change and tourism and, of the studies that do so, none consider avoiding dangerous climate change objectives" (i.e. **the 2°C rise in global temperature** normative assumption).

A1.2. The level of analysis

The level of analysis is firstly international, which is why the starting point for the environmental scan is an exposition of alternative political, economic, social, technological and environmental (PESTE) futures at the meta-level. Consistent with scenario-building in a transnational industry landscape, the level of analysis is secondly also sectoral, which is why the PESTE analysis is expanded to a high-level overview of market, industry and consumer driving forces. Even though the level of analysis is global, the strategic implications of the scenarios have decision-making utility at national-destination levels.

By way of motivation: (i) The aviation industry is an archetypal transnational industry.[38] (ii) Tourist destinations that depend on airlift from a portfolio of worldwide tourism source markets are exposed to global aviation trends and multi-lateral climate policies. (iii) Future technology research and development (R&D), investment and public policy to accelerate air transport decarbonisation will predominantly be at the level of global supply chains. (iv) The future of the climate change regime will be decided globally, be that through a multi-laterally negotiated climate deal or due to the disintegration of negotiations at that level.

A1.3. The time horizon

The 2050 time horizon is consistent with studies that have considered tourism mobility in the context of long-term environmental challenges. The year 2050 is an important reference point in international climate change negotiations and represents a milestone for the stabilisation of greenhouse gases (GHGs) in the atmosphere. In addition, the technology life cycle in aviation involves long lead times – often in the range of ten to 20 years for new technology R&D and commercial deployment, with aircraft stock having residual lifespans of three to four decades and even longer for other physical infrastructure such as airports. Furthermore, the decarbonisation trajectory for aviation up to 2030 is relatively certain compared to that after 2030. Many of the technological, infrastructural and operational efficiency improvements that will reach maturity by 2030 are already in the pipeline. The major uncertainty in terms of the decoupling of aviation growth from emissions growth relates to the period 2030 to 2050.

A1.4. Definitions and concepts

"Tourism" is defined as "the movement of people to places outside their usual place of residence" for personal, business or leisure purposes, but not for employment, including at least an overnight stay.[39] References to "long-haul tourism" are understood to include (i) journeys over 1 500 km, (ii) journeys with a flying time of over two hours, or (iii) journeys over shorter distances or time spans, but where airlift cannot be easily substituted due to extreme geographies or other barriers. Based on the high correlation between international **revenue passenger kilometres** (RPKs) and tourist arrivals, RPKs are used as a proxy for tourist arrivals.

Decarbonisation of aviation could involve absolute emissions reductions or relative deviations from the baseline. Climate change mitigation policies could include command-and-control type limits on emissions (i.e. directive-based), market-based incentives (e.g. emissions trading/off-setting or carbon taxes), or consumer behavioural change achieved through information-based approaches.

Authors[40] elaborate on the typology of the range of available environmental public policy tools. These policies could be adopted globally, regionally or nationally.

Activity 2: Environmental scan

This activity covers the scanning of the environment for trends within the demarcated area (Activity 1). The rule is to gather enough information to help you and your client understand the forces at work in the business environment, not to drown them in data. The only way to guarantee this is to draw **conclusions** yourself – not to leave it to the client system.

A2.1. The meta-level contextual environment

This section is based mainly on NDT,[41] Hichert,[42] Lipman,[43] Saunders[44] and WEF (World Economic Forum).[45] Some drivers and uncertainties are meta-level trends, while other macro-level trends are at the sectoral level, closer to the unit of analysis (see Figure 4.3).

The use of expert opinion – both from within the client system and outside it – is crucial. Figure 4.3 shows the outcomes of this exercise in terms of its impact on long-haul tourism, after the authors categorised all the data gathered under useful headings. The text following the graphic highlights the **conclusions** the authors arrived at.

Based on internal and external expert opinions, probabilities were assigned to each of these alternatives (indicated between brackets in Figure 4.3).

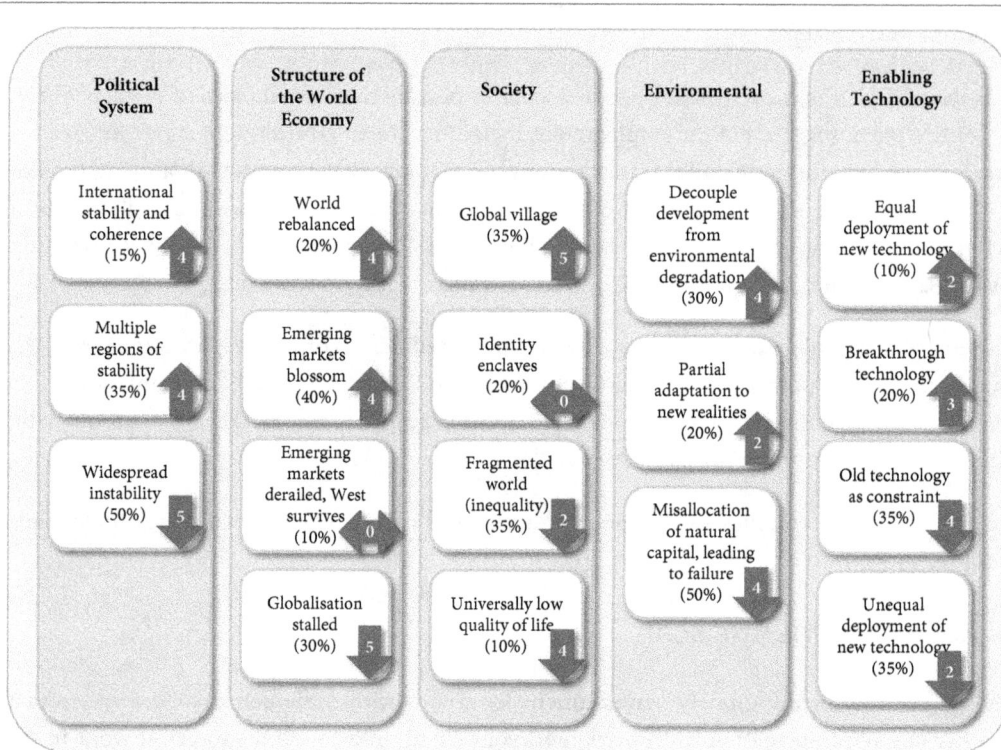

(%) = estimated probability; Arrows: Direction of impact (↑ = positive; ↓ negative; ↔ = neutral) and strength of impact. (1 = weak; 5 = strong) on long-haul tourism (unit of analysis) by 2050.

Figure 4.3: The meta-level context

Systemic political stability, be it the result of either multiple regions of stability or improved international coherence, is assigned a 50 per cent probability, as are the prospects for widespread global instability by 2050.

Based on McKinsey's Global Economic Scenarios, four alternatives for the evolution of the structure of the world economy over the next few decades can be identified.[46] Only a 30 per cent probability is assigned to the "rollback of globalisation", or deglobalisation, which will in turn reduce social surpluses. Such a future will be characterised by multiple economic crises and the economic collapse of the developed world, which will in turn pull down the emerging economies and global growth in its slipstream. There is only a slim chance that emerging markets' strong growth drive will derail if the West survives, whereas a future with blossoming emerging economies is assigned the highest overall probability. The latter could either form part of a rebalanced world economic order or, despite a slowdown in the developed world, could realise if the emerging economies manage to insulate themselves against economic slowdown in the traditional developed-country markets by developing "South-South trade" routes and succeeding in suppressing bubbles in their economies through capital controls, fiscal policy and financial regulation.

In terms of social forces, four possible alternative futures were identified: a fragmented world with high levels of inequality (35 per cent); universal low quality of life (10 per cent); symbiosis in a global village characterised by less conflict and improved international harmony (35 per cent); or the emergence of identity enclaves, in which discrete groups define social structures (20 per cent). Many of these alternative futures for social organisation will be affected by the alternative economic and political outlooks referred to above.

A rather pessimistic view prevailed in respect of environmental sustainability, with a 50:30:20 split between continued misallocation of natural capital, successful decoupling of development from environmental degradation, and the manageability of adaptation to unavoidable environmental change. The direction of change is intricately linked to economic growth and prosperity, and the water–energy–food–climate nexus.

Finally, in terms of the use and availability of enabling technologies, a 35 per cent probability was assigned to old technology acting as a constraint on growth, development and environmental decoupling. A similar probability was assigned to the unequal deployment of technology, meaning that skewed development will continue perpetually, and only a 20 per cent chance was foreseen that breakthrough technology would disrupt current perceptions of the future world order.

These meta-level trends, expressed as alternative futures, are important dimensions against which to assess the robustness of the assumptions underpinning the scenario narratives. They are also useful in identifying "wild cards" that could disrupt the storylines, an aspect that is touched on later in the case. Furthermore, they may compound the impacts of the drivers and uncertainties at a sectoral level.

A2.2. The contextual and transactional environments (sectoral level)

Moving from the meta-level to a sectoral level, Figure 4.4 summarises the major trends and uncertainties in the contextual and transactional environments, many of which are extensions of the meta-level trends and uncertainties identified in Section 2.1.

These possible alternatives in the macro-sectoral environment, as well as the different possible market, industry and consumer forces in the transactional environment, create the context for the identification of key change drivers and uncertainties, which are the focus of the next step.

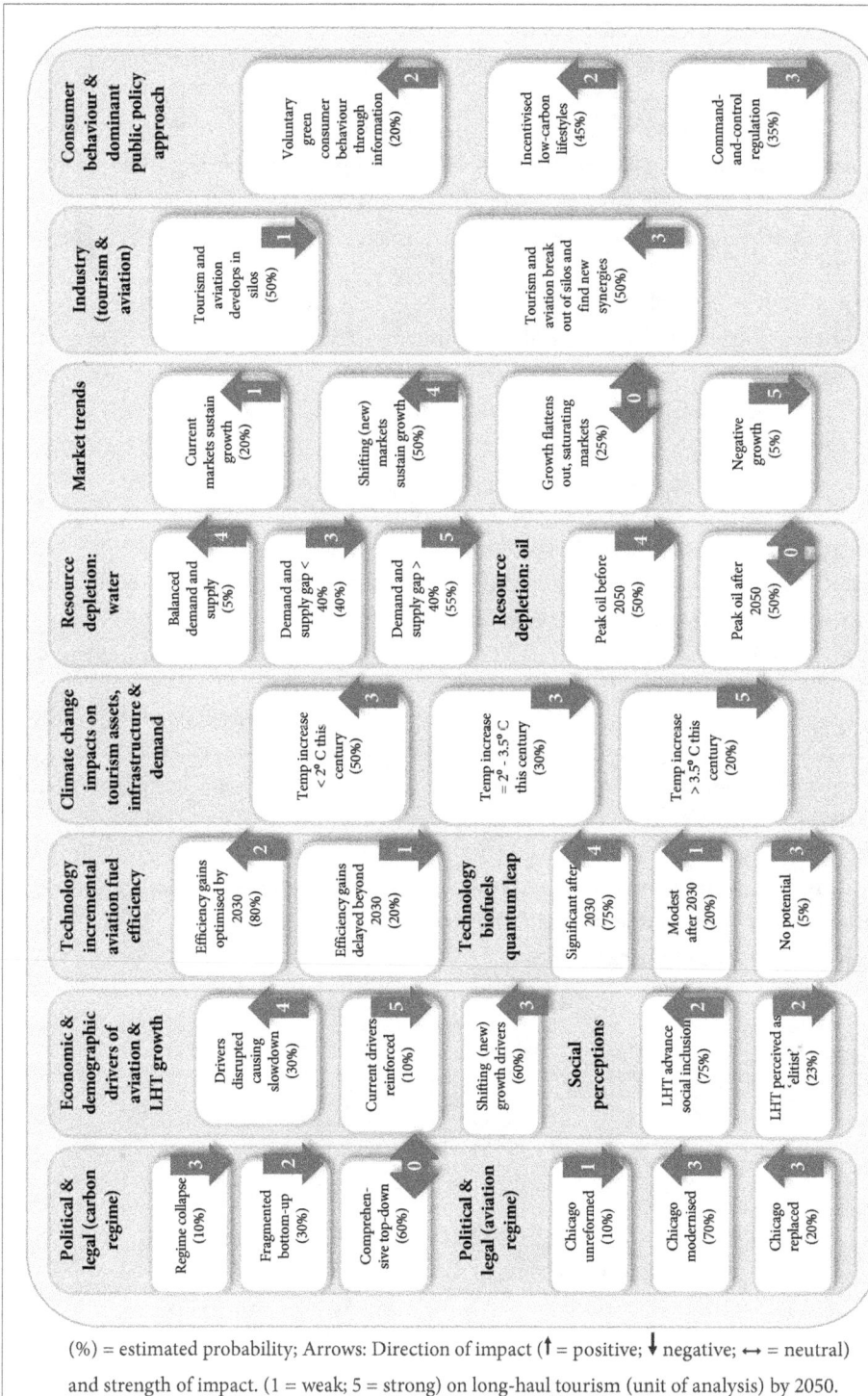

Consumer behaviour & dominant public policy approach
- Voluntary green consumer behaviour through information (20%) [2]
- Incentivised low-carbon lifestyles (45%) [2]
- Command-and-control regulation (35%) [3]

Industry (tourism & aviation)
- Tourism and aviation develops in silos (50%) [1]
- Tourism and aviation break out of silos and find new synergies (50%) [3]

Market trends
- Current markets sustain growth (20%) [1]
- Shifting (new) markets sustain growth (50%) [4]
- Growth flattens out, saturating markets (25%) [0]
- Negative growth (5%) [5]

Resource depletion: water
- Balanced demand and supply (5%) [4]
- Demand and supply gap < 40% (40%) [3]
- Demand and supply gap > 40% (55%) [5]

Resource depletion: oil
- Peak oil before 2050 (50%) [4]
- Peak oil after 2050 (50%) [0]

Climate change impacts on tourism assets, infrastructure & demand
- Temp increase < 2° C this century (50%) [3]
- Temp increase = 2° - 3.5° C this century (30%) [3]
- Temp increase > 3.5° C this century (20%) [5]

Technology incremental aviation fuel efficiency
- Efficiency gains optimised by 2030 (80%) [2]
- Efficiency gains delayed beyond 2030 (20%) [1]

Technology biofuels quantum leap
- Significant after 2030 (75%) [4]
- Modest after 2030 (20%) [1]
- No potential (5%) [3]

Economic & demographic drivers of aviation & LHT growth
- Drivers disrupted causing slowdown (30%) [4]
- Current drivers reinforced (10%) [5]
- Shifting (new) growth drivers (60%) [3]

Social perceptions
- LHT advance social inclusion (75%) [2]
- LHT perceived as 'elitist' (23%) [2]

Political & legal (carbon regime)
- Regime collapse (10%) [3]
- Fragmented bottom-up (30%) [2]
- Comprehensive top-down (60%) [0]

Political & legal (aviation regime)
- Chicago unreformed (10%) [1]
- Chicago modernised (70%) [3]
- Chicago replaced (20%) [3]

(%) = estimated probability; Arrows: Direction of impact (↑ = positive; ↓ negative; ↔ = neutral) and strength of impact. (1 = weak; 5 = strong) on long-haul tourism (unit of analysis) by 2050.

Figure 4.4: The contextual and transactional environments

A2.2.1 The contextual environment

Political and legal influences

Uncertainty about political stability, as observed in the meta-level macro-environment, is perpetuated in global climate change and aero-political negotiations. As it stands, the prospects for multi-lateralism prevailing, as opposed to disintegration into a fragmented climate regime or complete regime collapse, are uncertain. Despite commitments to conclude negotiations on a post-2020 climate regime under the United Nations Framework Convention on Climate Change (UNFCCC) by 2015,[47] or to make progress in negotiations on a **market-based mechanism** (MBM) for aviation emissions under International Civil Aviation Organization (ICAO) by 2013,[48] the future-regime architecture remains uncertain. Should multilateralism prevail, this could lead to a multi-lateral agreement imposing top-down and legally-binding carbon constraints in the next two decades, or, alternatively, a bottom-up pledge-and-review type regime. However, as 2050 approaches and the impacts of climate change become more evident, the probability of a multi-laterally agreed, top-down burden-sharing regime for climate change mitigation (i.e. strict limits), including for aviation emissions, becomes greater.

A global price on carbon linked to the capping of allowable emissions would in all likelihood then become a reality, or, if not, at least an alternative-regime architecture that imposes carbon budgets/constraints. In the absence of a global solution, countries and regions can be expected to resort to unilateral action (which, in turn, may trigger retaliatory trade wars and aviation/tourism supply chain disruptions), or carbon constraints could be introduced through the global trade regime (such as border tax adjustments).

In addition, it is also unclear what the future for the regulatory regime for aviation will hold. Negotiations on a global MBM for aviation emissions under the ICAO have been at an impasse for nearly 15 years, and because aviation has been treated as a special case in the UN system, international aviation emissions have for all intents and purposes been excluded from UNFCCC negotiations (see Article 2.2 of the Kyoto Protocol).[49]

Currently, the aviation industry is regulated by the Chicago Convention, which was adopted in 1944, before the era of modern commercial aviation and the globalisation of trade. It has been argued that this regime inhibits industry growth, competition and liberalisation of the skies. The probability of this regime being replaced by a new treaty is regarded as small, and given the transnational nature of this industry, continuation of the status quo is also unlikely. Some modernisation of the Chicago regime by tying in air transport services with the world trade regime is a possibility.[50]

Economic and demographic influences

Based on current economic and population trends, including the shifting balance of economic and political power "from North to South and West to East", new patterns of global GDP growth – and with that, aviation and tourism growth – are emerging. Tourism growth is driven, inter alia, by the rapid expansion of the world's middle class, the spread of global trade, the revolution in information and communication technologies, the increasing prominence of tourism in national development plans, and a real decline in the cost of air travel. In their 2030 tourism demand modelling, the UNWTO[51] attaches the greatest weighting to (i) GDP growth, (ii) the real cost of air travel (which is in turn linked to load factors, fuel prices and fuel-efficiency gains, and global networks that render destinations more accessible), and (iii) maturing GDP elasticity of tourism demand.

Over the past four decades, air traffic growth in turn was strongly negatively correlated with the real cost of air travel, where the latter has seen a decline of approximately 60 per cent since 1970. Over the same period, RPK growth has tracked world trade growth and GDP growth, but it has proved to be more sensitive to world trade than GDP growth. Other drivers of aviation growth include growth in foreign direct investment (FDI) flows; the gradual deregulation of the skies, allowing for greater competition; the spread of airline alliance strategies and hub-and-spoke configurations, and the burgeoning middle class in the emerging markets. Another significant trend fuelling air travel and competition has been the rise of new-model low-cost carriers.[52]

The single biggest driver of future growth will likely be the rapid income growth in emerging economies. While the traditional tourism source markets remain flat following the 2008/9 economic downturn and the prevailing Eurozone crisis, emerging market outbound travel is growing by just under 10 per cent per annum. These countries will bring some "2 billion new middle class consumers [into the potential market] by 2030".[53] By 2030, the size of the global middle class is likely to grow to 4.9 billion, of whom between 3.2 and 3.9 billion will be located in emerging economies.

Coupled with increased connectivity between major cities, urbanisation in emerging markets is a strong lead indicator of future aviation and LHT growth. IATA[54] highlights that 20 per cent of global air travel is currently generated by 26 mega-cities (>10 million population) and 40 per cent by 62 metropoles (>5 million population).

Social influences

Future public perceptions about LHT and aviation are important. LHT may be regarded as a "force for good" that leads to social inclusion and a transfer of resources from the "haves" to the "have-nots". Because of its direct impact on GDP and job creation (in particular for young people and women) as well as other indirect and induced impacts in the broader economy, LHT is well positioned as a vehicle for social inclusion. Of the approximate 260 million total jobs sustained by travel and tourism in 2011, 100 million were direct, meaning there is a multiplier of 1.6 in employment creation potential into the broader economy. In 2011, the direct, indirect and induced contribution of tourism to global GDP was some 9 per cent.[55]

That said, one of the future risks is that tourism as a leisure activity may be seen by local populations as an elitist activity, especially if it is not practised in an ethically, culturally sensitive and preserving, and environmentally responsible fashion. This could introduce a future that can be described as one for the "happy few", where locals despise tourists, and those with money have limited time for holidays and pay high prices for their holidays, and those with plenty of free time for cheap vacations at home or visiting friends and relatives do not travel internationally and view LHT with much suspicion, thereby reinforcing "social polarisation".

Technological influences

The starting point is to consider historical fuel-efficiency improvements in the aviation industry. Dray, Evans and Schäfer[56] stress that "[s]ince 1970, new aircraft have become more fuel-efficient at the rate of 1 per cent – 1.5 per cent per year on average. The typical lifetime of an aircraft in the global fleet is around 30 years, so aircraft nearing the end of their lives can use 30 per cent or more extra fuel than corresponding new models". If these numbers are extrapolated into the future, the fleet in 2020, of which 42 per cent are expected to be new aircraft, will on average be 25 to 30 per cent more fuel-efficient than current stock. Considering that fuel makes up at least 30 per cent of airline operating costs, there is a strong bottom-line incentive to reduce emissions through efficiency improvements.

IATA has committed the airline industry to a peak-plateau-and-decline emissions trajectory, reducing its net carbon footprint to 50 per cent below what it was in 2005 by 2050.

What should be stressed is that after 2030, the mitigation potential of the first three pillars (i.e. the medium-term decarbonisation options excluding long-term step changes), will nearly have reached its full potential.[57] Beyond 2030, the aviation industry enters a period of great uncertainty in respect of ways and means to achieve climate mitigation targets. By all indications, save for radical technological breakthroughs, only the gradual replacement of kerosene jet fuel with lower-carbon second-generation biofuels is on the horizon as a radical post-2030 technological solution – but even this option is clouded by uncertainty about feedstock production, its financial viability (given the prevailing subsidisation of kerosene jet fuels), and environmental sustainability considerations, such as lifecycle emissions and the impact of land-use change on emissions.[58] The "sustainable aviation biofuel mitigation wedge" lends itself to incremental drop-in over the next two decades, but, realistically, given the likely long lead times to develop the supply chain (involving feedstock production, production plants and refineries, blending facilities and new global distribution systems), a meaningful contribution will materialise only after 2030, which is when steep, absolute emissions reductions over a two-decade trajectory are required to meet industry's targets. WEF has estimated that, by 2050, 13.6 million barrels of low-carbon jet fuel would be required per day to meet these targets.

IATA[59] estimates that the drop-in of six per cent sustainable biofuels in the global aviation fuel mix could reduce emissions by 5 per cent by 2020. This will however be a modest contribution compared to what is required after 2030. ATAG's[60] indicative share of drop-in biofuels in the total jet fuel mix is 1 per cent in 2015, 15 per cent in 2020, 30 per cent in 2030, and 50 per cent in 2040. However, due to the uncertainty about feedstock availability (which links to sustainability considerations, and physical land and water availability), other analysts suggest more conservative assumptions. To deliver the volumes required by 2050, a number of barriers have to be addressed. These are (i) technical viability, safety, practicality and certification; (ii) the financial case for investment; (iii) environmental sustainability; (iv) scalability of feedstock production, processing and distribution, and (v) competition from the automotive sector.

Depending on the scale achievable for biofuels drop-in, the creation of a global MBM that allows for off-setting of aviation emissions against cheaper emission reductions in other economic sectors are therefore indicated. Simultaneously, an MBM that puts a price on carbon could also provide a critical price incentive for investment in the development of a second-generation biofuels industry.[61] However, due to the complex aero-political and climate change negotiating dynamics referred to earlier, creating such an MBM is clouded by significant political uncertainty.

Environmental influences

By mid-century, a business-as-usual (BAU) scenario would result in (aviation and) tourism emissions exceeding the emissions budget for the entire global economy. Although aviation is responsible for only 2 per cent of global carbon emissions, it is emitted by an even smaller percentage of the world population who travel. On a per-capita basis, "a single long-haul journey may exceed what can be considered sustainable per capita per year emissions" for any individual.[62] The increase in the carbon footprint of aviation will also be driven by changing consumer behaviour, specifically the twin trends of travelling over longer distances and for shorter stays.

Global absolute emissions need to peak and start declining in absolute terms within this decade if there is to be a (50/50) chance of avoiding a temperature increase of more than 2° C during this century[63] – a level which will already have far-reaching consequences, but is regarded as more manageable. Should the average global temperature increase breach certain temperature increase thresholds, the Intergovernmental Panel on Climate Change (IPCC) suggests that various tipping points will be reached, causing irreversible damage to ecosystems, human livelihoods and, by implication, tourism assets.

Resource depletion

Related to environmental concerns are resource constraints – more specifically, the prospects for so-called "peak oil" before mid-century as well as the threatening gap between water supply and demand. **Peak oil is the point in time when the maximum rate of crude oil** extraction is reached, after which the rate of extraction is expected to begin to decline … forever.

The WEF's 2012 environmental scan for global risks identifies water, which is located in the "water–energy–food–climate" security nexus, as a potential resource constraint with far-reaching consequences for many economic sectors. These sectors include tourist destinations that compete with other economic sectors for water resources, for example freshwater-based tourism activities, golf tourism, agri-tourism and eco-tourism.[64]

Essentially, there are four critical issues in respect of oil, namely price, supply, availability and substitution capacity. The timing of "peak oil" (i.e. the point at which half of all usable reserves are extracted) is central to any scenario. In the case of aviation, with its unique safety requirements, only second-generation drop-in biofuels offer a realistic low-carbon alternative, assuming sustainability and scalability (as discussed above). Should oil production peak before 2050, more erratic supply, energy inflation and volatile fuel prices could affect consumer demand and aviation growth, and passenger modal shifts could become the order of the day. By all indications, global oil demand will increase towards 2050, but there will also be new sources of energy that will slow demand growth compared to BAU. What is not certain is whether new technologies and high oil prices "will bring vast quantities of new oil to market", or whether the world faces an oil crunch over the next four decades that will "cripple global economic growth".[65]

A2.2.2. Market, industry and consumer trends in the transactional environment

Market overview

Long-haul tourism is expected to grow from 982 million in 2011 to 1.36 billion by 2020, and to between 1.7 and 1.9 billion by 2030, assuming 3.5 per cent compound annual growth.[66] Tracking the global shift of economic power towards emerging economies, much of the new outbound tourism growth will be from Asia, with China and India leading the way, but with other emerging markets in Latin America and the continent of Africa not lagging far behind.

Industry overview

In the case of tourism, the value chain is deeply fragmented, linkages between subsectors are poorly developed, and 80 per cent of industry players are small, medium- and micro-sized enterprises (SMMEs). The aviation supply chain consists of various public and private role players in the vertical supply chain that often have conflicting interests; for example, the oil companies have different interests to airlines in respect of R&D for second-generation biofuels.[67] Likewise, striking a balance between public and private investment in more climate-friendly technology and infrastructure is a complicated task. The lack of agreement on burden-sharing for decarbonisation between airframe manufacturers, engine manufacturers, airport and air traffic navigation authorities and airlines, points to a massive market failure. Even though many carbon abatement options entail zero or negative net cost over the medium term, upfront capital and the distribution of investment burdens through the value chain present a major challenge.

Turning to the interconnectedness of aviation and tourism: Clearly, failure in one cluster has a massive impact on the system as a whole. For example, aviation and tourism are:[68]

- equally affected by archaic global legal frameworks that govern the airspace and ownership of airlines, and that limit competition in the skies as well as capital mobility;
- equally vulnerable to terrorist attacks in tourist destinations, cyber-terrorism (for example the threat of sabotage of air traffic navigation systems), geo-political tensions in key hot spots, pandemics such as the H1N1 influenza, natural disasters (for example the 2010 Icelandic volcanic eruption), and extreme weather conditions; and
- equally exposed to global exchange rate volatility, rising oil prices, new security concerns, nontariff trade barriers (for example visa requirements, discriminatory travel taxes and travel advisories) and external economic shocks.

Governments are increasingly recognising the integrated nature of the aviation and tourism value chains, despite the fact that they are more often than not regulated by different government line functions, with planning often occurring in silos.

The consumer landscape

Changes in the consumer landscape (e.g. the rise of green or bounded consumerism) can be voluntary, incentivised or mandatory. Voluntary behavioural change (e.g. voluntary emissions off-setting for flights, passenger modal shifts from air transport to high-speed, mass-transit land transport, vacationing closer to home, and substitution of business travel with video-conferencing and other modern ICTs) is generally associated with higher awareness levels, moral persuasion, austerity measures and other industry and government-driven information-based approaches. Incentive-based behavioural change can be expected to be motivated by the pricing of carbon.

Finally, command-and-control-type public policy interventions, such as the introduction of personal carbon quotas, capped airline emissions or strict limits on airport infrastructure expansion, could all reduce travel propensity.

British Airways Chief Executive Officer (CEO) Keith Williams recently observed:[69] "Now consumers live in a world where they are being educated about how their actions can affect the world's fragile ecosystems and the global climate; we have seen a significant shift in the demand for ethical travel and green holidays."

As it stands, however, the uptake of voluntary off-setting of aviation emissions is at an introductory stage, and although it is growing, it is from low baselines.

The same applies to the substitution of business travel. Partly in response to the global financial crisis of 2008/9 and associated industry austerity and productivity enhancement measures, as well as technological advances, the uptake of videoconferencing and other virtual meeting ICTs is on the rise.[70] However, whether this rapid growth will be sustained is uncertain. A recent study by Oxford Economics points to only limited substitutability – more specifically, that the return on investment in business travel is 1:12,5 (travel investment to revenue), and that face-to-face meetings with new and existing customers are respectively 85 per cent and 63 per cent more effective than virtual meetings.[71]

On the regulatory front, there are early indications that demand-side management in respect of LHT could become a reality in the future. The UK Climate Change Committee[72] and others all observe that active government intervention may be required in the medium term to encourage substitution of business tourism with ICT as well as passenger modal shifts away from air transport, to suppress growth in airport infrastructure, and to disincentivise long-haul leisure travel by charging consumers for flight emissions. Looking to 2050, some analysts even foresee scenarios in which hard carbon constraints, such as personal carbon budgets or quotas, could be introduced. However, there are also those who believe that the shift will be in an opposite direction, at least in the next few decades, and that radical increases in demand due to the emergence of unbridled "Low Cost Low Fare Model" air transport are on the cards.[73] The latter would be characterised by lower-cost air travel due to the deregulation of the airspace, as well as increased competition, higher capacities and the spread of hub-and-spoke network models.

A2.3. Summary of the *problematique*

Many tourist destinations are heavily dependent on air transport for market access. Over long distances, passenger modal shifts to high-speed rail or water transport are simply not practical. Globally, on average, five out of every ten international tourists use air transport to reach destinations. Air transport, in turn, is (currently) entirely dependent on fossil-intensive kerosene jet fuels.

Tourism is an important contributor to global economic growth, job creation and social inclusion. At the same time, however, there is a negative side to the "balance sheet": The travel and tourism sector is responsible for 5 per cent of global carbon emissions, with the air transport sub-cluster responsible for 2 per cent (of which 38 per cent from domestic travel and 62 per cent from international travel). Eighty per cent of air transport emissions can be attributed to passenger journeys over 1 500 kilometres, a distance over which air transport is not realistically substitutable. Air transport's CO_2 emissions under BAU are expected to increase more than threefold to 1 631 million tons of carbon dioxide (MtCO2) by 2035, and fourfold to some 2 000 MtCO2 by 2050, taking aviation's share to 53 per cent of total travel and tourism emissions and 3 per cent of global carbon emissions by 2035.[74]

Air traffic growth without carbon abatement may soon bring its carbon footprint in conflict with global climate policy, and particularly in conflict with an emissions trajectory that will limit the global temperature increase to below **2°C above pre-industrial l**evels during this century. Simultaneously, the tourism sector is extremely vulnerable to global warming, and has a strong interest in avoiding dangerous climate change (i.e. ecosystem tipping points associated with a temperature increase of more than **2°C**).[75]

Due to fuel efficiency gains of 1.5 per cent/annum, air transport emissions currently increase at a slower rate (i.e. at a 3 per cent compound annual growth rate, or CAGR) than air traffic (i.e. 4.5 per cent CAGR). Regardless, given industry's targets for 2050, this leaves a mitigation gap of more than double today's total aviation emissions, or nearly 1 700 $MtCO_2$ per annum in 2050.[76]

Against this backdrop, it is clear that carbon constraints (e.g. caps, other limitations and/or carbon pricing) imposed by a future climate change regime could have profound impacts on LHT markets, whereas the absence of constraints (read: unbridled emissions growth) will affect tourism ecosystem assets and long term sustainability.

At the one extreme, the current failure of governance could persist, and the failure of markets to internalise the cost of environmental externalities could continue. At the other, the policy environment could become more stringent through a combination of climate change response policies, thereby increasing the real cost of air travel in a very price-sensitive tourism and aviation industry.

Activity 3. The key uncertainties, overriding drivers of change and the scenario gameboard

(See Steps 3–5 of Table 4.1)

Based on the foregoing analysis, key uncertainties and drivers of change that could affect LHT in general, and particularly LHT in a carbon-constrained world, were identified. These drivers and uncertainties can be clustered into seven overriding drivers, as summarised in Table 4.2 (which should be read with Figures 4.8 to 4.10).

Table 4.2: Narrative description of the overriding drivers

Overriding driver	Description
1. Climate change impacts on tourism destinations	Because tourism and aviation represent only 5 per cent of global emissions, and meeting "required by science" (RBS) mitigation targets for 2050 thus depends on many other economic sectors, this driving force is in the high-uncertainty, low-control quadrant. However, should the average global temperature increase move into dangerous territory by triggering critical ecosystem tipping points, the potential impacts on the tourism economy will likely enter the "high-impact" zone during the second half of the century, but not within the 2050 time horizon.
2. Carbon constraints	This is by-and-large a political driver. A key uncertainty is whether multi-lateral negotiations will introduce carbon constraints. As will become evident in the scenario analysis, the timing of a political decision on carbon limits/carbon pricing could be a game changer in terms of decarbonisation – regardless of whether this involves a price instrument like carbon taxes or a quantity instrument like emissions trading (e.g. cap-and-trade, baseline-and-credit or offsetting).
3. Medium-term carbon abatement levers (pre-2030)	These levers of change have low uncertainty, because many are already in the pipeline. These interventions may actually lead to further declines in the real cost of air travel. Even so, the impact on LHT would only be moderate to low, given that LHT growth also depends on a range of other variables. The tourism sector may be able to exert moderate influence towards implementing some of these measures – overall, though, control is low.
4. Long-term decarbonisation (post-2030)	This is primarily a technological and behavioural driver. Decarbonisation through radically new (unknown) technologies, the drop-in of sustainable biofuels as jet fuel and/or the offsetting of unavoidable emissions through an MBM falls outside the tourism sector's direct sphere of influence, and is highly uncertain for a number of reasons, including the political uncertainty about the nature and time frames for the introduction of carbon constraints (e.g. MBMs that act as price incentives), and the question marks over the scalability and costs of biofuels. The alternative to industry meeting RBS mitigation targets through technology deployment would be for governments to introduce physical constraints on the expansion of airport infrastructure, induce behavioural change among consumers, invest in infrastructure for passenger modal shifts, and incentivise information communication technology (ICT) alternatives to business travel. All these interventions fall within the high-uncertainty and no-control quadrants, and could impact on LHT through intermediary variables, such as aviation growth and the real cost of air travel.

Overriding driver	Description
5. Real cost of air travel	Uncertainties relate to carbon pricing, other taxes and levies, oil prices and peak oil, scale economies and load factors, fuel-efficiency improvements (driven mainly by the medium-term carbon abatement levers outlined above) and the liberalisation (versus tighter regulation) of the airspace to allow for greater competition and growth of new business model, low-cost airlines. In terms of LHT demand as well as aviation growth, this is a high-impact, moderate-control driving force that also stands in direct relation to carbon constraints (read: carbon pricing) and the marginal cost of medium-term and long-term carbon abatement.
6. Aviation growth	Aviation growth, or slowdown, will have a direct impact on LHT. By and large, because of institutional and regulatory silos that fragment the aviation–tourism value chain, aviation growth is a driving force outside the tourism sector's sphere of direct influence. Aviation growth is exposed to a range of factors with various degrees of uncertainty attached to them, particularly the real cost of air travel (including oil prices), globalisation and the counter-trend of fragmentation, which could in turn have a negative impact on trade flows and business travel, the state and balance of forces in the global economy (e.g. emerging-market growth versus stagnation, the timing of global peak middle class, world trade and GDP), future consumer preferences (e.g. green consumerism), investment in airlift infrastructure versus mass-transit systems, and airline and airspace liberalisation. On balance, this driving force falls in the moderate-uncertainty zone.
7 Demand side of long-haul tourism	Demand is highly correlated with aviation growth and trade volumes, and will have a definite impact on LHT. Although a range of driving forces within the organisational environment come into play, and are thus within the control of the tourism sector, tourism demand strongly depends on external variables very similar to those that drive aviation growth and the real cost of travel. This is thus a driving force of moderate uncertainty.

The seven overriding drivers were plotted on a control/certainty matrix (see Figure 4.5), impact/certainty matrix (see Figure 4.6) and a relationship strength map (see Figure 4.7). Based on all these analyses, two principal driving forces were selected for the scenario logics, namely (i) carbon constraints, and (ii) the long-term decarbonisation of aviation. These forces constitute the axes on the scenario gameboard (see Figure 4.8). (In an earlier iteration of the scenario gameboard, the vertical axis was assessed by its financial impact, namely a "high and global" versus a "low and ad hoc" price on carbon, rather than by the stringency of the climate change regime. It was initially argued that it is the price on carbon that will ultimately affect the real cost of air travel, aviation growth, incentives for decarbonisation, and LHT's carbon footprint.

However, we decided that the two axes of Figure 4.8 should be more independent of one another. A high carbon price (vertical axis) would lead to greater decarbonisation (horizontal axis), while the converse is also true. Therefore, any scenarios in the "high carbon price/low decarbonisation" and "low carbon price/high decarbonisation" quadrants would *a priori* not be that plausible. In the final analysis, it was thus decided to work with two more independent axes and, given the political uncertainties alluded to in earlier sections, without defining the "carbon constraints" axis in terms of regime architecture and without assuming carbon pricing.

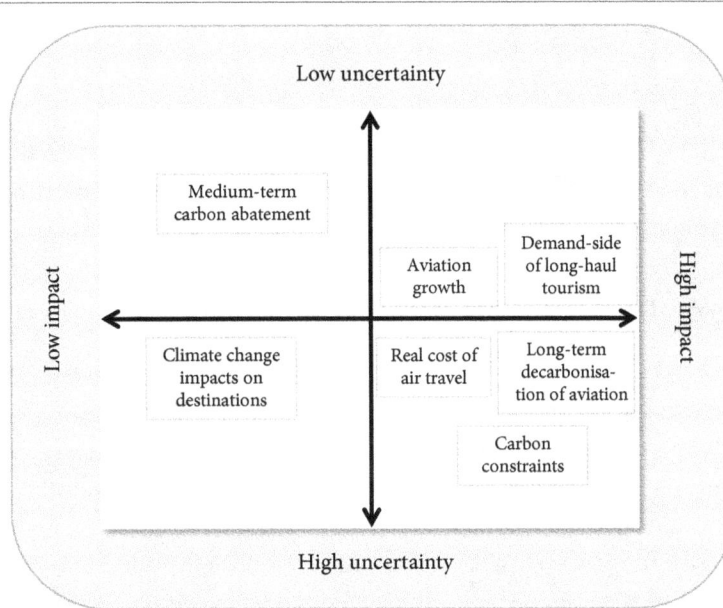

Figure 4.5: Overriding driving forces relative to "certainty" and "impact"

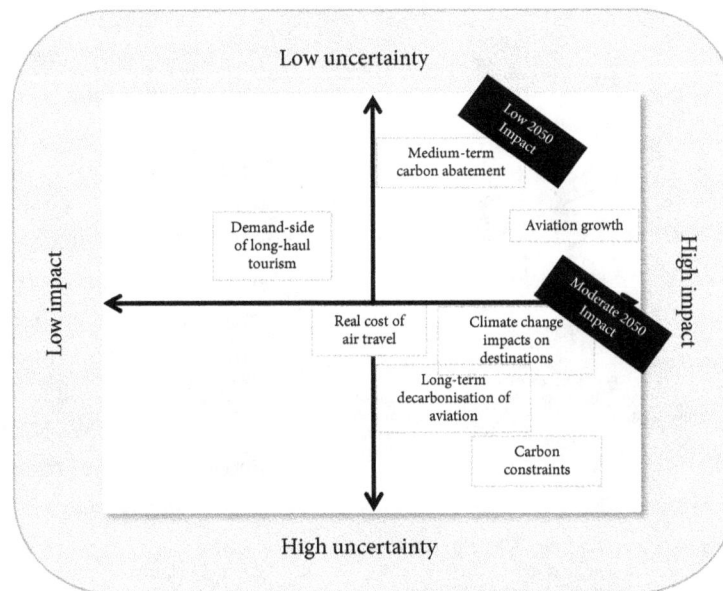

Figure 4.6: Overriding driving forces relative to "certainty" and "control"

Vertical axis: Carbon constraints [political driver]

The "carbon constraints" driving force is primarily a political driver and is assessed by its stringency, namely strict limits or a lax regime – but without being specific about the architecture of the regime (e.g. top-down versus bottom-up, or carbon pricing through emissions trading versus a carbon tax). The plausible zone on the vertical axis of the scenario gameboard (Figure 4.8) excludes the "no constraints" extreme. Besides the nature of the regime, the timing of a political decision is also a critical variable (see scenario narratives).

Horizontal axis: Long-term decarbonisation of aviation [technological and behavioural driver]

The horizontal axis ("long-term decarbonisation" of aviation) runs from (i) carbon-neutral aviation (meaning zero net emissions by 2050) through (ii) IATA's decoupling target (i.e. 50 per cent below 2005 by 2050), (iii) IATA's targeted 2020 Compressed Natural Gas (CNG) or emissions plateau trajectory extended to 2050, (iv) a mere extension of the current base-case trajectory to 2050 (this means the trajectory that optimises operational, infrastructural/ATM (air traffic management) and incremental technology-efficiency improvements by 2030, but does not extend the compounding effect of the 1.5%/annum fuel-efficiency gains beyond 2030), to (v) a "frozen technology" trajectory, in which emissions intensity remains unchanged up to 2050 (air traffic grows at 4.5 per cent and emissions at 3 per cent per annum up to 2050).

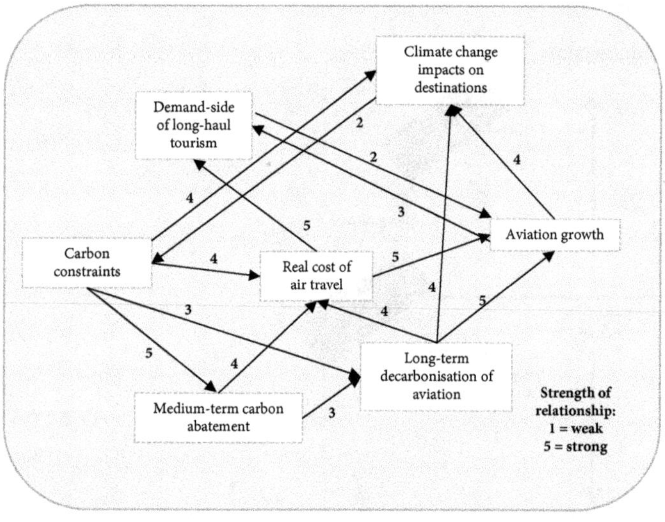

Figure 4.7: Relationships between overriding drivers of change

Underpinning these "states of being" along the horizontal axis are a range of possible technological and behavioural drivers. The plausible zone on the scenario gameboard (Figure 4.8) excludes (i) carbon-neutral aviation, which cannot credibly be regarded as realisable by 2050, as well as (ii) the frozen technology extreme (given current developments already in the pipeline). Some regression from the "current trajectory" base case is not to be excluded, as indicated by the positioning of the line for the plausible zone in the space between "frozen technology" and "current trajectory" in Figure 4.8.

Based on these parameters, the gameboard in Figure 4.8 indicates the "plausible extremes of the uncertainties". This frames the parameters for the scenario storylines, which are described next.

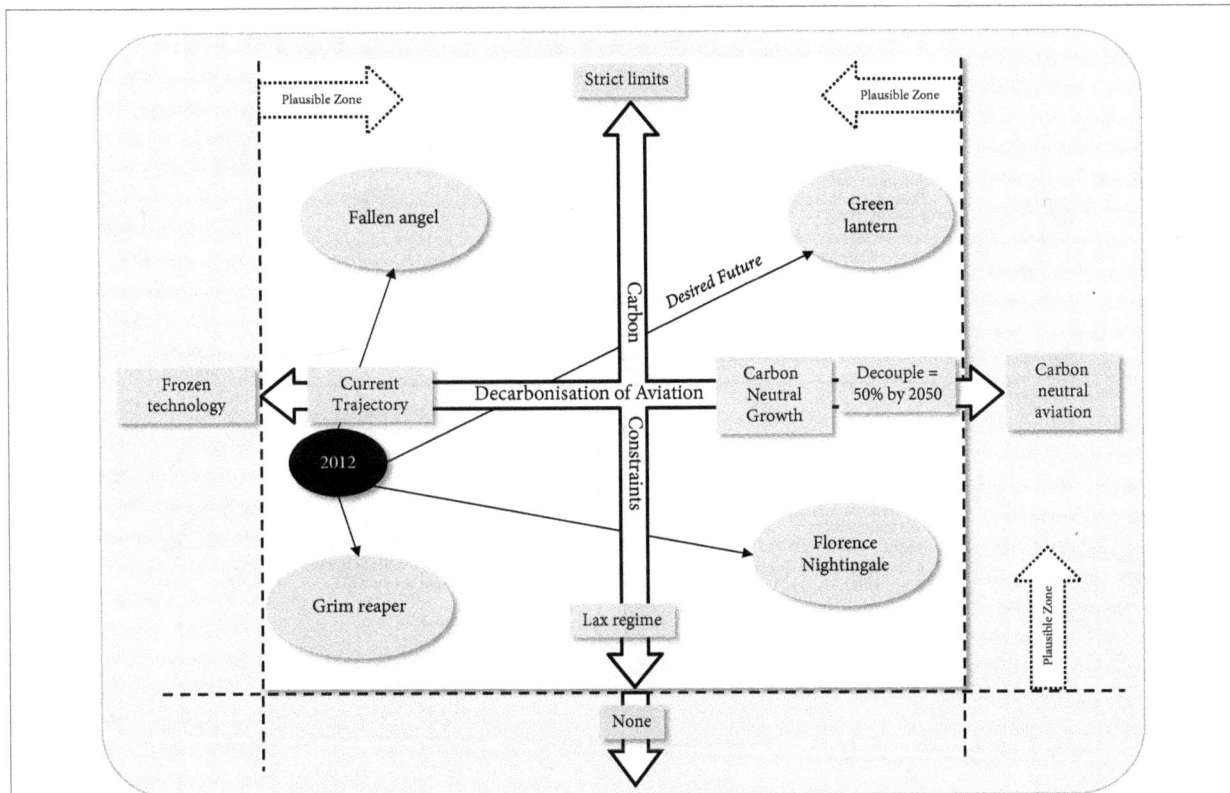

Figure 4.8: 2050 scenarios for long-haul tourism in an evolving climate change regime

Activity 4: 2050 scenarios for long-haul tourism

(See Steps 6 and 7 in Table 4.1)

A4.1. Introduction

In the initial possibility space, there are four scenarios for LHT in 2050: a "green lantern" scenario, which is most desired, and three feared scenarios, namely "fallen angel", "Florence Nightingale" and "grim reaper". However, in the final possibility space (see Figures 4.9 and 4.10), the Florence Nightingale scenario is eliminated because of plausibility concerns (see 4.2.4).

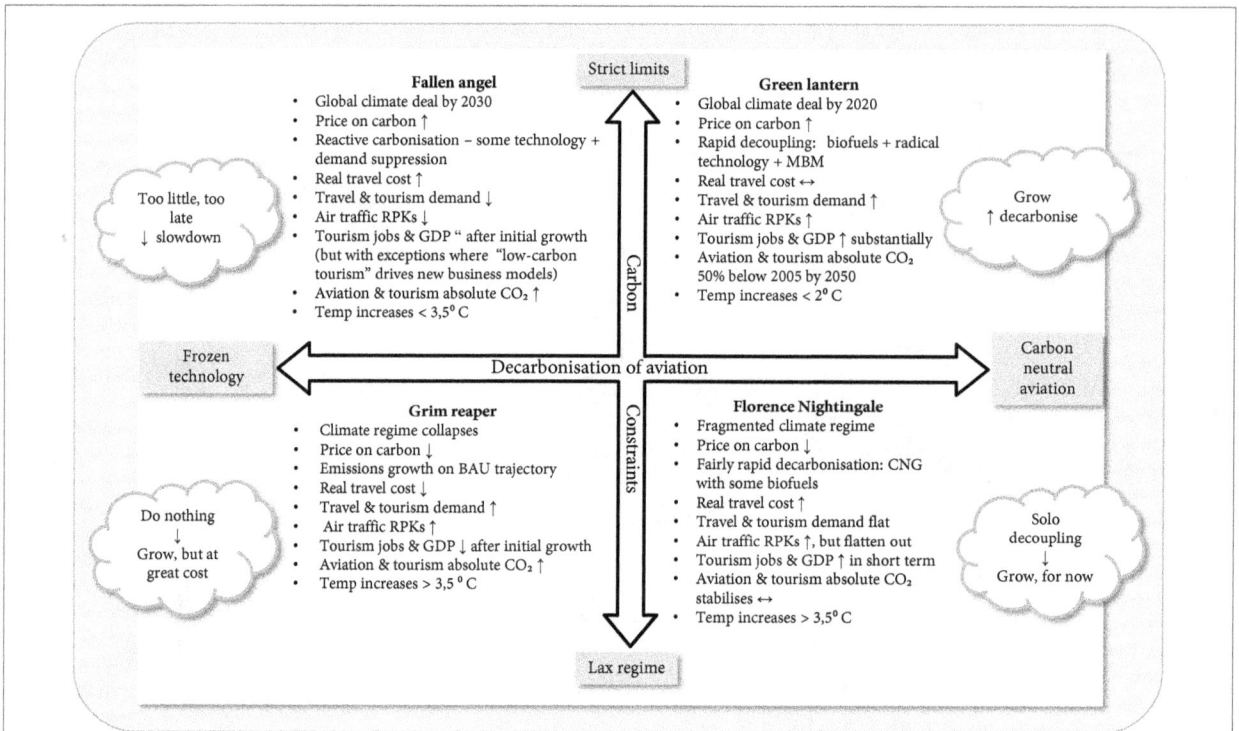

Figure 4.9: Four scenario narratives

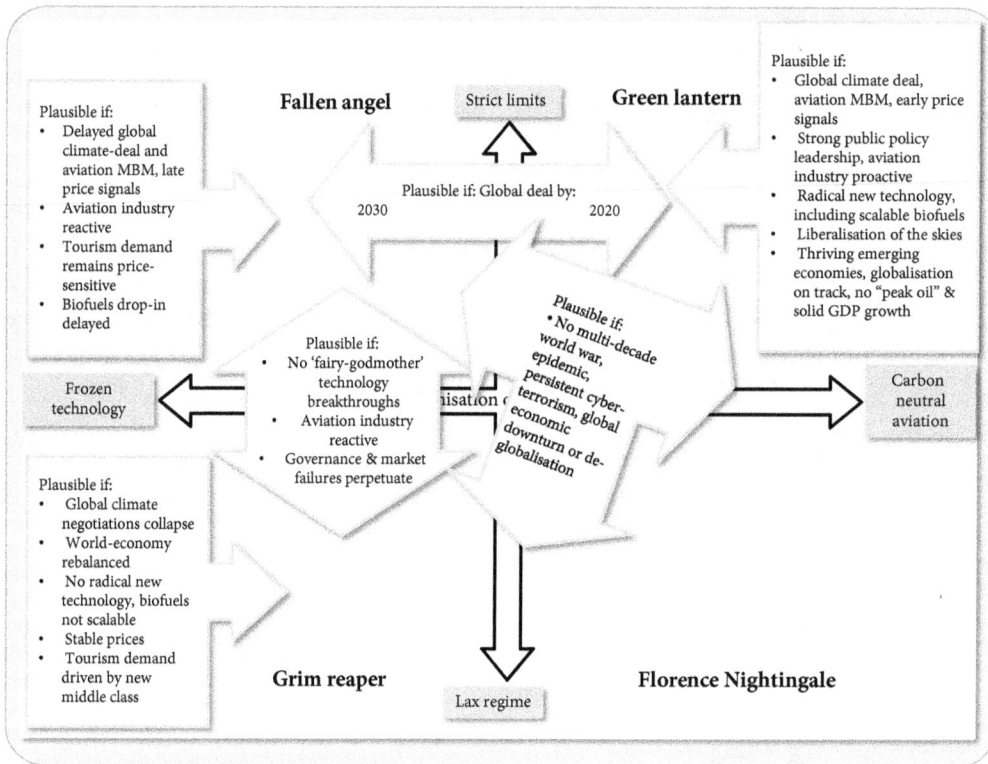

Figure 4.10: Plausible scenarios

Of course, the road to 2050 starts in 2012. Therefore, the first question is: Where are we today?

The story of the status quo: Where are we in 2012?

After a solid recovery in international tourist arrivals following the global economic downturn of 2008/9, the world is holding its breath for a historic year: for the first time ever, one billion international tourist arrivals are expected in 2012. For an industry that had only 25 million international arrivals in 1950, this represents remarkable growth and it is predicted that the best is yet to come.

But this is not the full story. In 2012, there are also various uncertainties on the horizon. For starters, there is the uncertainty about the outcome of UNFCCC negotiations on a global and comprehensive post-2020 climate change regime, and ICAO negotiations on a global sectoral MBM for controlling international aviation emissions. If negotiations in these two forums succeed, a global and progressive price on carbon combined with absolute limits on emissions may be knocking on the door of the future. This will surely affect growth in LHT, depending on what happens with the decarbonisation of aviation over the next four decades. By 2050, carbon pricing can double fossil fuel prices. If negotiations fail, who knows what may happen? A fragmented regime may see further unilateral imposition of carbon constraints by major blocs such as the EU, which, in 2012, for the first time included international aviation in its own Emission Trading System (ETS), or a very weak and fragmented climate regime that disregards RBS may prevail for the next few decades. In the long run, this would of course hold dire consequences for LHT destinations, especially if the average temperature increase exceeds **2°C during this century**.

Fortunately, in 2012, the aviation industry is responding proactively to the prospects of a carbon-constrained world. But, of course, these are good intentions that must still be turned into actions. Even achieving what is labelled the "current trajectory" will surely not be plain sailing. Depending on the nature of the evolving climate change regime and the decarbonisation of aviation, combined with many other major uncertainties, the future of LHT up to 2050 is hanging in mid-air.

A4.2. 2050 futures: The scenario storylines

Given the uncertainties moving forward from the status quo in 2012, it is possible to imagine more than one narrative for the future. These possible futures (depicted in Figure 4.8 and summarised in Figure 4.9) are described next. The approach is to take a retrospective look, from 2050 backwards.

A4.2.1. The "green lantern" scenario

The green lantern: where are we in 2050?

The meaningful decoupling of aviation and LHT growth from carbon emissions exemplifies the global paradigm shift towards a green economy over the past four decades. In response to early warning signals in the 2010s that a future climate change regime will put a binding cap and an escalating price on aviation emissions, the rapidly growing aviation and tourism sectors proactively repositioned to become green lanterns of prosperity. These sectors contribute their fair share to ongoing efforts to limit the temperature increase to below **2°C above pre-industrial levels,** while growth in tourism demand and its associated developmental benefits continue to outstrip all expectations. Globalisation and rapid economic growth in what was formerly known as emerging economies are driving LHT and aviation growth. Although air travel as such is not yet carbon-neutral, the industry's four-decade-old commitment to reducing emissions to 50 per cent below 2005 levels by 2050 became a reality. All indications are that the world will be spared the worst impacts of climate change over the remainder of this century.

How did we get here?

2012 to 2020

After receiving an unambiguous negotiating mandate at the ICAO General Assembly in 2013, the architecture of an open cap-and-trade ETS for international aviation emissions was finally agreed in 2016. This coincided with the conclusion of UNFCCC negotiations, which was only possible because all major economies felt comfortable that they would not be competitively disadvantaged or unfairly treated by a global top-down burden-sharing climate change regime coming into effect in 2020.

Because of the long-term and legally binding nature of these global regimes, which combine command-and-control-type emissions limits with market-based price incentives, the aviation industry and governments started to invest in meaningful public-private partnerships (PPPs) towards decarbonising air transport long before 2020. "Low-carbon" became the new buzzword for competitiveness.

2020 to 2030

By 2030, the carbon abatement potential of operational, infrastructural and ATM as well as incremental technology-efficiency improvements foreseen in 2012 (as per IATA's four-pillar strategy) had been fully realised. It was a demonstration of unprecedented political will combined with cooperation across the entire aviation value chain. The modernisation of the eight-decades-old Chicago Convention (by closing the gap with the global trade regime, which is more appropriate for the age of globalisation) surely also played a part. Although the efficiency improvements extended linearly into the future, this alone was not enough to meet industry's CNG goal for the next decade, and the post-2020 sectoral cap-and-trade ETS became the vehicle to offset those aviation emissions exceeding a CNG plateau trajectory against other economic sectors.

The post-2020 ETS also created a long-term price incentive for R&D spending and investment in the required commercial-scale production to bring radical new technologies, including second-generation drop-in biofuels, to market after 2030. Price parity with dirty kerosene jet fuel was reached by 2025.

2030 to 2050

The big winners in the low-carbon aviation and biofuels race since 2030 have clearly been Africa, Brazil, India and China. As China rolled out its new generation of aerodynamic aircraft, Africa succeeded in allocating sufficient land for biofuel feedstock production. The massive investment in second-generation biofuels production created many new job and income opportunities in African countries, where feedstock comprises vegetation such as jatropha, which is today grown on degraded wastelands, and algae, which are produced in polluted and coastal waters. Because of early collaborative R&D investment with multinational oil companies, and support by regional development banks and visionary governments for the piloting of biofuel production and refinery facilities, Africa today owns many of the intellectual property rights in this competitive market space, and is also a market leader in converting urban waste into biofuels. In addition, now that intra-African tourism has taken off and is heavily supported by a new middle class and the growth of lower-cost airlines, it is also a major consumer of home-grown low-carbon jet fuels.

The volume of second-generation biofuels that would have been required to meet industry's 2050 targets on its own would have been seven times the total volume of first-generation biofuels in the market in 2010. If all these biofuels had to be sourced from jatropha, a land area of one million km^2 would have been needed. Even though biofuels did not materialise at the scale required to meet industry's 2050 targets on its own, mainly due to limits to feedstock production, other radical new technologies, including blended-wing/body design, on-board fuel cell systems and previously inconceivable engine architecture became commercially viable by 2045, and managed to close the gap between RBS and actual emissions by 2050. (Radical aeronautical technology did not change the landscape significantly by 2030. The production of a new model/engine involves long lead times. Moreover, even if some breakthrough "fell from the sky", it would also have required a long lead time to scale commercial uptake before it could make a serious dent in overall industry performance.) As a result, air transport became less reliant on more expensive emissions trading to offset emissions, thereby keeping the real cost of air travel stable.

Coupled with the rapid growth in tourism demand spurred by economic growth from China, India, Brazil and Africa, the last two decades have witnessed sustained growth in LHT and air traffic RPKs, thereby creating many new tourism-related job opportunities and increasing the tourism sector's contribution to global GDP.

What have been the turning points and signposts over the last four decades? What is assumed in this scenario? And which "wild cards" could have disrupted this storyline?

The four-decade low-carbon revolution required visionary political and industry leaders, who stood ready to take the tough policy and investment decisions needed. Very little would have moved forward had the major forces not buried the hatchet in climate change negotiations – this was the first major signpost. The second signpost was the agreement on a long-term policy signal (i.e. cap-and-trade regime) under ICAO, which also provided the critical price incentive beyond 2020.

Only once it became clear that "perverse subsidies, such as the non-taxation of kerosene"[77] would make way for a progressive price on carbon, the different interests in the vertical aviation industry supply chain (including airframe and engine manufactures, fuel producers and distributors, airlines, airports and air transport navigation authorities) cooperated at a higher level.

The aviation industry, working proactively on its own, would not have been enough – it needed its public-sector partners to resolve outstanding operational and infrastructural inefficiencies caused by decade-old conceptions of national sovereignty, allocate sufficient land and water for biofuel feedstock production, form R&D partnerships, set global standards in ICAO, and establish creative new funding mechanisms for technology deployment to de-risk private-sector investment. All of this led to the third and most significant signpost, which was when aviation carbon emissions started to decline in absolute terms after 2030, with LHT (assessed by RPKs) growing unhindered. However, this in itself would not have been enough to close the gap. Without radical new technology breakthroughs and commercialisation by 2045, this scenario would not have materialised.

Finally, the liberalisation of the airline industry and increased competition in the skies, stable oil prices and a delay in peak oil, sustainable economic growth in Africa and the former emerging economies, linked to urbanisation and the growth of mega-cities, as well as the continued globalisation of trade, were all indispensable for the exponential growth in LHT demand and airlift.

Ultimately, multilateralism and global political stability had to prevail, and globalisation had to stay on track, with emerging economies providing the necessary new impetus to the global economy. A multi-decade economic depression or deglobalisation mega-trend, which slowed down global trade and depressed household disposable income, would have been major "spoilers" in the successful development of this story.

What were the implications for LHT destinations? Any risks and opportunities? And, at a strategic level, how did tourist destinations respond?

Due to the decoupling of LHT growth from emissions growth, destinations were able to continue reaping significant social and economic benefits, but in an environmentally responsible way. This is what the new generation of green travel consumers expect. Most destinations continue to balance domestic, regional (i.e. land arrival) and long-haul air arrival markets, as well as leisure and business tourism, mainly to hedge against unforeseen external economic and security shocks and other potential supply chain disruptions. Some destinations continue to exploit low-volume, high-value markets, while many others focus on mass-based tourism – unaffected by carbon constraints. That said, there is disproportionate growth in "proximity tourism" (domestic and regional), though not to the same extent as in the "fallen angel" scenario.

Due to a collective and ambitious global climate change effort, including all countries and economic sectors, global emissions peaked and started to decline early enough to avoid a temperature increase of more than 2°C. Other than for the most vulnerable small-island tourist destinations and least developed countries with low adaptive capacities, dealing with the unavoidable impacts of climate change on ecosystem assets and other tourism infrastructure remains manageable.

A4.2.2. The "fallen angel" scenario

The fallen angel: where are we in 2050?

In 2050, the tourism sector is often compared to a "fallen angel": due to its historical contribution to GDP and employment, it had so much potential, but today it is shackled to the ground by carbon constraints. Air transport's carbon footprint became the Achilles heel of LHT. Due to the aviation sector's failure to deviate much below its 2010 "current trajectory" for decarbonisation, and in the face of the escalating price on carbon following a (delayed) global climate deal in 2025, LHT is disincentivised through a combination of various public policy tools. By 2040 passenger growth stalled, and by 2050 growth had moved into negative territory. The impact on global employment and GDP is negative, with the exception of a number of destinations that switched to local and regional tourism (so-called low-carbon proximity tourism) early on. Unfortunately, the global aviation industry's response over the past four decades can only be described as "too little too late", and LHT is paying the price.

How did we get here?

2012 to 2030

Unfortunately, in the 2010s, rather than agreeing on a global sectoral ETS that provided a price incentive for R&D investment in radical technology solutions and the building of a sustainable biofuels value chain, the aviation sector adopted a wait-and-see approach.

After a ten-year delay to conclude negotiations on a post-Kyoto climate regime, the major forces resolved their outstanding differences by 2025, and agreed on a binding, top-down climate change regime with an absolute cap on global emissions to come into effect by 2030. As in the "green lantern" scenario, this regime includes flexible mechanisms that allow for ET within and between economic sectors, with a progressive, global price on carbon. But because of the lost decade, the binding RBS emissions reduction targets were extremely steep.

The aviation sector did achieve some deviation from the BAU baseline between 2012 and 2030, but the industry goal of CNG after 2020 did not materialise until 2030. Ironically, many carbon abatement opportunities with net negative costs, in other words those that would have led to cost savings, were forfeited. It was a classic case of market failure combined with (national and multilateral) governance failure. For example, there were unnecessary delays and a lack of political will in the United States of America and the EU in implementing the Single European Sky ATM Research (SESAR) and the Next Generation Air Transportation System (NextGen) (which would have led to major operational and ATM-related fuel efficiency gains); agreement in the ICAO on CO_2 standards for new aircraft stalled; governments waited until 2025 to agree on interoperability standards for ATM and airport infrastructure; and so on. In addition, conflicts of interest in the vertical aviation supply chain persisted: oil companies were basically holding airlines hostage by not investing in low-carbon biofuel development. Overall, the industry just never got its act together, and due to a lack of leadership and vision, the message that "co-opetition" was in everyone's best interest simply never hit home.

2030 to 2050

As emissions peaked at such a late stage and such a high level, the IATA goal to reduce absolute emissions to 50% below 2005 levels by 2050, without slowing down growth in air traffic and international tourism, became an impossible dream. Even over the two decades since 2030, industry aspirations of rapid decoupling got stuck in the mud too often. As a result of a lack of early investment in low-carbon R&D and the allocation of land for second-generation biofuel feedstock production by governments, the balance of mitigation efforts shifted from the technology-driven and fuel-switching options foreseen in the 2010s, to suppressing LHT demand through economic measures, i.e. changing behaviour through punitive carbon pricing and individual carbon budgets. Between 2030 and 2040, as conditions to bring in tourists got more costly, some governments that relied heavily on LHT were inclined to "subsidise" some aspects of travel in one form or another; however, this turned out to be unsustainable in the long run.

The price on carbon, which took effect in 2030, came too late to act as an incentive for proactive investment in R&D for second-generation biofuels and other radical technologies. Before 2030, the financial and technological risks of biofuels investment were just too high for private investors. Governments also never came to the party with fiscal incentives that would de-risk private-sector initiatives. In fact, as early as 2015, it became clear that the more proactive automotive industry was going to win the race for access to the limited volume of feedstock available for the production of low-carbon biofuels.

By 2035, the price of carbon was so steep that it became a moderate disincentive for leisure and business travel. Because of narrow industry profit margins, these costs were passed on to airfares and the cost of cargo. By 2040, the real cost of air travel, which now fully internalised the cost of externalities, became a serious disincentive for leisure tourism. Business travel also slowed down as carbon constraints on global trade started to weigh in, and governments invested heavily in public awareness campaigns aimed at moral persuasion, encouraging people to travel less and closer to home, and businesses to replace travel with ICT solutions as their contribution to slowing down climate change. At least, that was until 2040. By then, the gap between BAU and RBS emissions trajectories forced governments to legislate for low-carbon lifestyles, and individuals had to start living within personal carbon budgets, purchase carbon allowances from other households, or face stiff penalties.

By 2050, overseas tourism becomes an exception, but is still possible and for individuals with energy-intensive life-styles, marginal costs for more tourism are high; and for the wealthier, options to buy permits may be limited. After 2040, many governments also limited the construction of new airport infrastructure, and some were forced to act against airports that failed to meet the strict and mandatory operational and ATM efficiency standards adopted under the ICAO.

Tourist mindsets also changed and "going local" became the new buzzword. Netflix's virtual tourism experiences have become very popular. Today, many holidaymakers choose to deal with their "carbon guilt" by vacationing closer to home. Tourists started switching to lower-carbon mass-transit systems for holidays under 1 500 kilometres for the best part of the last two decades. It was no longer fashionable to boast about "our overseas holidays", and the "why" and "how" of travel has taken centre stage over coffee-table discussions. The hotel and restaurant industries follow a similar pattern: concerns about so-called "carbon food miles" drove initiatives like "hyper-local sourcing", and the green cost-saving imperative led to the introduction of "metered" energy and water consumption for hotel guests.

Linked to emerging trends of deglobalisation, especially as the growth in emerging economies flattened out by 2035 and traditional developed-country markets entered their second decade of float economic growth, a slowdown in global trade also weighed in on LHT growth. The negative impact on business tourism was compounded by the rapid advances in three-dimensional (3D) visualisation and other new-generation communication technologies. Videoconferencing increasingly replaced what used to be a lucrative business tourism subsector.

What have been the turning points and signposts over the last four decades? What is assumed in this scenario? And which "wild cards" could have disrupted this storyline?

A key turning point was when climate change negotiations collapsed in 2015, and remained deadlocked for a decade. Missing the aviation industry's post-2020 CNG goal was then a given, as industry moved into reactive mode and ICAO negotiations on an MBM disintegrated. Role players in the value chain simply assumed that there would be no price incentive to invest in R&D for radical new technologies and biofuels that would make a difference after 2030. The next signpost was when climate negotiations picked up new political momentum by 2020. Immediately, it became clear that the aviation industry, with its long R&D lead times, was caught unprepared. When air traffic growth (as reflected by RPKs) – a lead indicator of LHT – dropped to below 2 per cent per annum by 2040 as the price on carbon and real travel costs escalated, the overall decline in the prospects for LHT became an established mega-trend.

Of course, things could have been different had a "wild card" exogenous to the aviation and tourism sectors, such as a technology fix for carbon sequestration or "fairy godmother"-type solar or hydrogen-fuelled planes, entered the scene, or had a multi-decade world war, epidemic, global economic downturn or deglobalisation decimated the carbon emissions of other major emitting sectors in general, and air traffic volumes in particular, thereby reducing the pressure on air transport to deal with its carbon footprint, and dramatically increasing the opportunity cost of leisure and business travel. For a few dreamers, teleportation of tourists between continents never materialised beyond science fiction movies. The timing of peak oil is a wild card in this scenario.

What were the implications for LHT destinations? Any risks and opportunities? And, at a strategic level, how did tourist destinations respond?

The nature of tourism had to change. At a macro-level, many destinations delinked tourism from aviation, and started reducing absolute aviation emissions – not through technology-driven decarbonisation, but through demand management, i.e. by suppressing LHT/passenger growth. In the face of carbon taxes and due to the high price elasticity of demand, LHT entered its darkest decades in history. Though LHT previously represented lower volumes compared to domestic and regional land arrivals, it had disproportionately high value in terms of tourism receipts (i.e. spending).

Consequently, job losses and GDP impacts were disproportionate to the loss in volume over the last few decades. Most destinations experienced negative tourism GDP and job impacts. Some destinations, however, had the foresight to reposition early. They decreased LHT's share in their portfolios and, by 2020, in anticipation of unavoidable carbon constraints, shifted their focus to domestic, regional and short-haul tourism. They invested heavily in mass-transit systems rather than new airports and government-subsidised airlines. These early movers also refocused their market segmentation and value propositions from mass-based low-cost markets to premium markets that deliver higher-yield tourists, which also happen to be less price-sensitive. They also only target and attract "visitors who have an affinity with its environmental outlook and [low-carbon] way of life".[78] For them, so-called "slow" (by train, boat or bicycle) and "low-carbon" tourism became a tagline that created competitive "green" advantage in marketing and destination branding. By recognising that LHT is not an unambiguous "good", and that it has environmental limits, these destinations proved that alternative modes of tourism and, by implication, less LHT could still provide equal wellbeing to their populations.

Due to the lost decade, and even though the worst impacts of climate change have been avoided, many tourist destinations still have to invest heavily in measures to adapt to unavoidable climate change, especially in low-lying coastal areas, small-island states and water-stressed regions. A temperature increase of more than **3.5°C is not on the horizon during this century,** but the dream of avoiding a temperature increase of more than **2°C is lost.** Nevertheless, tourist destinations that depend heavily on the natural environment and climate itself have started to experience demand impacts, for example because of the decline in snow-based tourism activities and the spread of vector-borne diseases to former tourist hotspots.

A4.2.3. The "grim reaper" scenario

The grim reaper: where are we in 2050?

Like the grim reaper, aviation and LHT have been raiding the global commons without an environmental conscience ever since global climate change negotiations collapsed in the late 2010s. There is no global limit/price on carbon that internalises the cost of negative externalities, and the real cost of air travel keeps falling on the back of new economies of scale, higher load factors, technology-driven fuel-efficiency improvements and stable oil prices. Both air traffic and emissions grew nearly unabated for four decades. This was fuelled by an expanding global middle class in the former emerging economies and Africa, persistent GDP growth in the traditional developed countries, rapid urbanisation and growth in mega-cities in Asia, booming business travel associated with the ongoing globalisation of trade, and mass-based leisure tourism supported by expansive low-cost airline networks and a consumer mindset focused on hedonistic experiences. The atmosphere is on track to warm by more than 3.5°C during this century. Climate change has already breached critical ecosystem tipping points, with devastating social and economic impacts on many tourist destinations.

How did we get here?

2012 to 2030

Due to a continued deadlock between the major economies, climate change negotiations under the UNFCCC first derailed in 2015. There were various failed attempts to restart the process and seek new mandates, but member parties increasingly lost confidence in multilateral governance and the United Nations system. Eventually, following a UNFCCC Conference of the Parties (COP) 27 decision to that effect in Houston, Texas, in 2021, the UN Secretary-General had no choice but to dissolve the UNFCCC. This also meant that negotiations on an MBM for controlling and pricing international aviation emissions under ICAO came to an end. Anyhow, as an institution, ICAO had much more important challenges to deal with, including managing the security (e.g. cyber-terrorism) and navigation aspects associated with the rapid growth in air traffic worldwide. The collapse of negotiations on MBMs came as no surprise either: the narrow sectoral interest of a significant number of its member parties, defending the interests of national airline carriers, has for decades been to oppose any attempts to internalise the cost of environmental externalities – and quite understandably so, because, as early as 2010, the global airline industry operated on an average profit margin of less than 1 per cent, not even covering the cost of capital.

Today, many play the blame game in seeking scapegoats for the historic market failures and the collapse of multi-lateral governance in the 2010s. What is clear is that very few players are blameless, including consumers who just never committed to paying a premium for a low-carbon lifestyle. Ironically, the airlines and aircraft manufacturers carry the least blame – they at least invested in incremental technological, operational and infrastructural efficiency improvements up to 2030, motivated not by climate change considerations, but by the fact that fuel costs constituted more than 30 per cent of their operating costs during those two decades. However, airlines' efforts were not enough. What was lacking was the political will on the part of governments to agree on an RBS top-down climate regime, to optimise flight routes and ensure interoperability of ATM systems, to derisk investment in developing second-generation biofuel supply chains through creative incentive mechanisms, and to introduce fuel-blending mandates that would have forced the most guilty parties, namely the multi-national producers and distributors of kerosene jet fuel, to take the low-carbon challenge seriously. In the 2010s, while airlines were struggling just to break even, these oil companies made a massive 10 per cent net profit on a jet fuel supply of nearly $200 billion per annum.

2030 to 2050

In the meantime, growth in LHT (assessed by aviation RPKs) continued at a CAGR of more than 4.5 per cent per year, driven mainly by the new markets from China, India and Brazil, but also elsewhere. As air transport demand boomed in the absence of accelerated decarbonisation, IATA's post-2020 targets dissipated. Even with fleet renewal and efficiency gains at a normal pace up to 2030, absolute emissions reductions never materialised. There were no meaningful public-sector investments in, or incentives for, accelerated operational, infrastructural or technology-efficiency improvements up to 2030, or for switching to second-generation biofuels after 2030.

By 2032, as the impacts of climate change became more visible and unavoidable, a new round of climate change negotiations was launched. World leaders, increasingly concerned about climate refugees fleeing low-lying coastal areas and small islands, and the implications this had for achieving the Millennium Development Goals, convened in Brazil for the so-called Rio + 40 Earth Summit. The negotiations that followed eventually reintroduced, after a three-decade vacuum, a Kyoto Protocol-like top-down compliance regime, also for dealing with aviation emissions, but it was too late. The world was already committed to a temperature increase of **3.5°C at best.**

What have been the turning points and signposts over the last four decades? What is assumed in this scenario? And which "wild cards" could have disrupted this storyline?

When climate change negotiations stalled in the late 2010s, it was clear that the writing was on the wall for a regime that would accelerate the decarbonisation of air travel. Linked with a rebalanced global economy that showed strong growth for three of the last four decades, this created an inescapable new reality – and a daunting one at that. Had there been more visionary political and industry leaders in the 2010s and 2020s, had peak oil realised, or had new sources of oil not been discovered off the coast of Africa as output from the Middle East increased, maybe the cost of air travel would have stopped declining in real terms earlier on. A number of other wild cards similar to those that apply to the "fallen angel" scenario could have disrupted this turn of events, but alas, the world failed to decouple development from resource depletion.

What were the implications for LHT destinations? Any risks and opportunities? And, at a strategic level, how did tourist destinations respond?

For LHT destinations, this is what Strong[79] refers to as "Armageddon"– an overlap of the impending climate, energy, water, food and population crises. Even though LHT continued to grow unabated, with positive impacts on GDP and jobs until about 2040, destinations are today struggling to deal with physical damage costs associated with climate change, as well as related socio-economic pressures. Today, ecosystem collapse, unprecedented water scarcity, and community/interstate conflicts over water resources in many destinations have a negative impact on tourism demand as well as comparative advantage between destinations – destroying jobs, GDP and foreign exchange earnings in its wake.

As climate tipping points are breached and impacts become irreversible, tourism assets are depleted, due inter alia to extreme weather events, water stress, sea-level rise and coastal erosion, ecosystem and biodiversity loss, and unpredictable weather patterns. The nature of the tourism supply side (i.e. nature-based product offerings) and concomitant demand patterns, including tourists' destination selection and seasonality of demand, are all in flux, and will increasingly be so over the next five decades. That said, a limited number of destinations were able to reposition proactively, diversifying their product offerings to rely less on nature-based, climate-sensitive tourism and more on shopping, the meetings, incentives, conferencing and exhibitions industry, and other niche offerings.

A4.2.4. The "Florence Nightingale" scenario

Florence Nightingale: where are we in 2050?

Despite the collapse in multi-lateral climate change negotiations during the 2010s, the aviation industry made significant gains with voluntary decarbonisation. However, rather than multilaterally agreed carbon limits/pricing, a multi-decade oil price spike caused by ongoing geopolitical conflicts drove industry investment towards a low-carbon revolution. Due to significant efficiency improvements, real travel costs remained stable, and air traffic and LHT growth continued unabated, especially as emerging economies became the drivers of global trade and prosperity. Well, at least initially. By 2030, higher oil prices (which, by then, constituted 40 per cent of airline operating costs) and the financial burden of reducing its carbon footprint weighed on the real cost of air travel and, ultimately, LHT demand. As most other economic sectors were not similarly exposed to higher oil prices, and did not face similarly constraining climate policies, aviation and LHT carried the "lantern" largely on their own, much like the good-natured Florence Nightingale. Consequently, the world is committed to a global temperature increase of more than **3.5°C during this century.** This is bound to wreak havoc with climate-sensitive tourism destinations over the remainder of the century, with early effects evident in the decades running up to 2050, including sea-level rise, species loss, the spread of vector-borne diseases and land degradation.

A reality check: is this scenario plausible?

On balance, this scenario is internally inconsistent in three respects: firstly, given the transnational nature of the industry, it is unlikely that aviation decarbonisation beyond the current trajectory will realise without the price incentive created through a global deal on climate change. Although many of the available carbon abatement options for the two decades after 2010 are affordable (i.e. with net negative cost) without a price on carbon, beyond 2030, the real game-changing carbon abatement opportunities will need the "push" of a progressive carbon price. In addition, without a global ETS that allows for offsetting against cheaper carbon abatement opportunities in other economic sectors, the marginal cost of aviation decarbonisation will simply be too high. Without a public policy intervention, all the root causes of the prevailing global market failure will thus remain in place. Furthermore, in the absence of a global climate deal, it will likely be an insurmountable political task to convince a sector with a relatively small, albeit growing, carbon footprint and exceptionally narrow profit margins to "go it alone" by carrying such a heavy mitigation burden – especially if the worst climate change impacts on tourist destinations during the remainder of the twenty-first century will not be avoided due to the unchanged behaviour of the other 98 per cent of emitters.

Secondly, in the absence of a global climate deal, this scenario is only plausible if decarbonisation in air travel is "pushed" due to a multi-decade oil price spike, which provides a price incentive for the development of low-carbon biofuels. However, such an oil price spike will also affect other energy-intensive economic sectors, in particular land transport. That would only serve to intensify the competition for biofuels with the automotive sector, which would in turn trigger an increase in the real cost of air travel and, due to the price elasticity of demand, would lead to a change in long-haul travel behaviour. Finally, the kind of geopolitical conflict that would trigger the type of long-term oil price spike implied is also likely to disrupt aviation and LHT supply chains through other mediating driving forces, thereby compounding the internal inconsistency of this scenario.

A4.3 Summary of strategic choices

There are three plausible (though not equally desirable) meta-level strategic choices, namely:

(i) to decarbonise and grow (green lantern); (ii) to do nothing, grow in the short term, but eventually face Armageddon (grim reaper); or (iii) to do too little too late and slow down (Fallen Angel) (see Figure 4.9).

All of these scenarios are only plausible under certain conditions and assumptions (see Figure 4.10). Moving from "visualisation to realisation" of the desired "green lantern" scenario will require leadership from visionary decision-makers in government and industry, and behavioural change on the part of tourists. At the same time, tourist destinations need to hedge against the feared scenarios.

Activity 5. Strategic choices: From visualisation to realisation

(See Step 8 in Table 4.1)

Activity 5 is the "payoff" of the exercise. At this stage the client system has to make some decisions about the strategic options it chooses. The real danger at this stage is to choose the "best" scenario developed, but this is rarely possible – and often not desirable in the shorter term. You have to develop it with the clients, or at least spell out what these shorter-term options are.

A5.1 Introduction

However intuitively obvious the choice of the "green lantern" scenario may sound, the tourism sector will be but one player in the low-carbon revolution. The challenge for tourist destinations will be to develop robust, future-oriented strategies that allow for reflexivity, risk management and adjustment as the narrative of tomorrow unfolds. There are a number of broad strategic choices and concomitant planning actions that could assist LHT destinations to navigate their way into the uncertain future. Essentially, what is required is a package of measures or "carbon-smart" tourism market restructuring approaches tailored to each destination's unique characteristics and exposure to the various macro-level driving forces, not least their distance from the tourism source markets of the future and their exposure to climate risks. This broad strategic orientation and the planning framework for actions can be presented as matrices (see Tables 4.3 and 4.4). Understanding that they cannot control the contextual environment, but can at best influence the transactional environment, these strategies should focus on what is achievable (see Table 4.3).

The indicated strategic orientation requires LHT destinations to adapt to climate change, hedge against uncertainty and market risks, decarbonise underlying activities, and then, depending on the signposts or indicators for emerging scenarios, seize new opportunities and deploy contingent strategies.

Table 4.3: *From visualisation to future-robust strategies: The scenario options matrix*

Strategic thrust	Actions	Green Lantern	Fallen Angel	Grim Reaper
Future-robust core of strategy (all three scenarios)				
Adapt to climate change	Readiness: Develop tourism vulnerability assessment tools to understand and mitigate climate change risks*	++	++	++
	Resilience: Adapt to unavoidable climate change and develop capacity to absorb climate impacts*	+	++	++
	Resistance: Develop climate-resistant physical infrastructure**	+	++	++
Hedge against uncertainty and risk	Demand-side: Follow portfolio approach to market segmentation (balanced portfolio of long-haul, regional and local tourism source markets, as well as business and leisure markets)*	++	+	O
	Supply-side: Diversify tourism offerings beyond nature-based and climate exposed sectors*	+	++	++
Decarbonise underlying activities	Government regulation and incentives for low-carbon transformation of tourism supply chain (e.g. land transport, accommodation); promote green consumerism through awareness campaigns*	++	++	- -
	Low-carbon transformation of aviation supply chain (operational, infrastructural and technological efficiency improvements, as well as carbon off-setting/price incentives)**	++	++	-
	New investment in regional, land-based mass-transit systems (e.g. high-speed rail connectivity)**	++	++	O
Partly robust strategy (Fallen Angel and Green Lantern)				
Seize opportunities	Seize opportunities presented by low-carbon forms of tourism and green consumer sentiment (passenger modal shifts over short- to medium-haul, localised tourism, carbon-neutral accommodation and car rental, "green" branding/marketing)*	++	++	-
Focused contingent strategies (Fallen Angel)				
Decouple tourism from air transport	Switch to lower-volume, higher-value source markets*	-	++	- -
	Develop land arrivals and local tourism as mainstays of sustainability*	O	++	- -
Focused contingent strategies (Grim Reaper and Fallen Angel)				
Decouple tourism from nature	Supply-side: Replace nature-based tourist activities with new offerings*	-	+	++
Economic diversification	Diversify economy away from reliance on tourism receipts for GDP and jobs**	- -	+	++

Legend: *: Organisational environment; **: Transactional environment; ++: Very promising in this scenario; +: Suitable for this scenario; O: Neutral in this scenario; -: Not possible in this scenario; - - : Causes problems in this scenario

Table 4.4: *From visualisation to future-robust strategies: Strategic positioning and planning matrix*

	Planning-oriented strategies	Reactive/preventative strategies			Proactive strategies
	React to recognisable trends	Manage future risks	Stay flexible and hedge	Exploit future opportunities	Develop and reach own visions
Focused contingency planning (based on reference scenario)		Decouple tourism from nature (Grim Reaper).		Predominantly land arrivals and local tourism (Fallen Angel)	
		Diversify economy away from tourism (Grim Reaper).		Lower-volume, higher-value source markets (Fallen Angel)	
Robust planning (based on several scenarios; at least desired "green lantern" scenario)	Deploy tourism vulnerability assessment tools.	Build resilience capacity to deal with climate impacts.	Portfolio approach to market segmentation	Seize opportunities of low-carbon forms of tourism and green consumer sentiment.	Create low-carbon competitive advantages by transforming tourism supply chain and consumer behaviour.
	Adapt to unavoidable climate change impacts.	Climate-resilient infrastructure	Diversify tourism offerings beyond nature-based and climate exposed sectors.		Accelerate decarbonisation of air transport.
					Invest in regional, land-based mass-transit systems.

A5.2 Adaptation

Regardless of the scenario that unfolds, destinations will have to adapt to unavoidable climate change. Destinations will be differentially exposed, sensitive, and adaptable to threats, and the need to adapt will depend on local circumstances, the capabilities (i.e. available resources) to adapt, the global warming range (i.**e. 2°C, <3.5°C, or >3.5°C**) and ecosystem tipping points breached.

To understand the extent of the problem, locally scaled tourism vulnerability assessment tools need to be developed. Vulnerability assessments and adaptation can enhance destinations' resilience, resistance and readiness. Resilience is the ability to absorb changes in climatic conditions, whereas resistance reduces the scale of the impacts that will affect tourism. Readiness is the destination's ability to mitigate risks and capitalise on new opportunities.[80]

Therefore, adaptation priorities on the tourism side include improving the capacity for coping with the short-term impacts of climate variability, focusing especially on the most threatened ecosystems and conservation areas, marine resources and other ecosystem goods and services that support livelihoods and maintain our environmental health and integrity; improving conservation planning (for example wetland restoration or corridor development that allows for species migration in conservation areas); climate-resistant and resilient infrastructure development; enhancing natural and physical protection of coastlines and beaches; operational interventions, such as producing snow or improving irrigation techniques; and the combating of health threats (for example malaria).

A5.3 Market development

In terms of market development, LHT destinations will be well advised to follow a risk management approach on the demand and supply sides. On the demand side, it will be best practice to develop short-haul, regional and domestic/local tourism as key market segments in a balanced portfolio, thereby hedging against the imposition of carbon constraints that could in future reduce LHT propensity. Likewise, a balance between leisure and business tourism is indicated.

Destinations should also leverage the emerging green consumer sentiment by integrating low-carbon destination and transport labelling with destination marketing and branding strategies and by mainstreaming sustainability strategies into their business models. Tourists, in turn, need to apply bottom-up pressure for change; vote with their feet by creating markets for sustainable and low-carbon tourism offerings; and reward the early movers on the industry side with increased market share.

On the supply side, diversifying product offerings to reduce dependence on climate-sensitive and nature-based tourism offerings would be a good precautionary step.

A5.4 Internal decarbonisation

The tourism sector also needs to decarbonise its own internal value chain, including accommodation and land transport, not least through energy-efficiency retrofitting and the roll-out of renewable energies; promoting passenger modal shifts where mass-transit systems are practical; greening supply chains; and educating consumers and employees. Not only might this stimulate new demand in the green consumer market segment, but it could also entail significant operating cost reductions.

Governments have a key role to play and could integrate low-carbon considerations with tourism master plans, destination marketing budgets and consumer awareness campaigns, as well as deploying regulatory approaches such as the introduction of benchmarks for low-carbon tourism, green building codes, and labelling or certification rules.

A5.5 Low-carbon air transport

In addition, in the transactional environment, tourism government line functions and industry should add their weight to efforts to agree on a global regime for managing aviation emissions under ICAO sooner rather than later. In all the scenario storylines, the timing of carbon limits/carbon pricing is a game-changer. The objective would be twofold: to avoid the worst climate change impacts, and to create the required market certainty and long-term policy signals to accelerate decarbonisation of the aviation value chain.

In addition to the focus on air transport, there will be a need to work with other government line functions to modernise and optimise air space organisation, create incentive frameworks for energy-efficiency and renewable-energy roll-out, decarbonise national electricity grids, and invest in more environmentally friendly urban planning, accessible public transport, and integrated, multi-modal transport networks as part of a broader shift to "green cities" and low-carbon tourist destinations.

A5.6 Contingency plans

Should RBS levels of decarbonisation not materialise, stakeholders in LHT will have to envision tourism futures that are less dependent on air travel. Should a price on carbon become unavoidable as global efforts to address climate change intensify, the profitability of energy-intense forms of tourism (long-haul, air transport-based, luxurious cruises) will decline and the profitability of low-carbon forms of tourism (rail- or coach-based, short- to medium-haul, longer stays, domestic, low-carbon accommodation) will improve. This will require (i) a shift in marketing budgets to domestic and short-haul land arrival markets, (ii) investment in massively upscaled mass-transit systems, such as high-speed rail, to extend regional connectivity, and (iii) the development of appropriate product offerings that at least attract long-haul, lower-volume, higher-value markets and, in some instances, that depend less on nature itself.

Clearly, LHT is not an unambiguous "good", and, in some destinations, different manifestations of "low-carbon tourism" hold the potential to contribute equally to societal well-being (i.e. GDP, employment and environmental sustainability). However, for small islands and other remote destinations that rely disproportionately on air arrivals, failure to decarbonise aviation is a daunting prospect, and with limited opportunities for economic diversification away from tourism, the future will be bleak and the options limited should the "green lantern" scenario not materialise: they will either literally sink due to sea-level rise ("grim reaper" scenario), or they will sink in economic terms ("fallen angel").

Conclusion to the case study

The story of LHT over the next four decades hinges on the nature of the future climate change regime and the positioning of aviation within it. For both variables, the turning points are political, and for the decarbonisation of aviation, much depends on technological change, coupled with behavioural change. Turning points are political, in that global climate change negotiations and regime formation may or may not trigger a price or other limits on carbon, which in turn has various potential cross-impacts, including on R&D for low-carbon jet fuels (by providing a price incentive), reducing absolute emissions through offsetting (with an MBM being the intermediate variable) and consumer behavioural change (because the real cost of air travel internalises negative externalities). Technological change will entail that which is known but uncertain, namely the scalability of second-generation biofuels, but also an unknown "space", namely radical technology breakthroughs that are still inconceivable today.

Regardless of which one of the three scenarios materialises, the consequences and flagposts are clearly defined. Long-haul tourist destinations should heed the early warning signals identified in the various scenario narratives. Above all, in their respective spheres of influence, they should become passionate advocates for the desired future, i.e. the "green lantern" scenario. They should also guard against being passive victims if the feared scenarios materialise, by adapting, repositioning early upon reading the signposts, hedging against risks, and seizing new opportunities.

Finally, much can be learnt by building scenarios. The intuitive-logic scenario process had great value; it stretched the imagination, challenged orthodoxies, unleashed creativity, and concentrated the mind to consider future-robust as well as contingent strategies. As a sense-making exercise, the scenario-building process created a better understanding of the status quo, and the risks associated with "doing nothing". As an exercise in long-term strategic direction setting, it brought to the fore high-level strategic choices in both the organisational and transactional environments that could be exercised or influenced by long-haul tourism destinations and governments. Five broad areas for action were identified, namely: adaptation, market development, decarbonisation of the tourism value chain, transitioning to low-carbon air transport, and developing contingency plans.

Although many things are uncertain, one certainty is that the various scenario storylines will likely all turn out to be wrong. We can be sure that there will be "black swans", wild cards, "fairy godmother" technologies and other "unknowables" that are inconceivable and unimaginable today. Maybe carbon-neutral aviation becomes a reality, or the world as we know it experiences an unimaginable political or economic disruption that freezes tourism growth for decades. In that case, we will be back in a stretch zone where we depend on human intuitive logic to imagine and learn from the future. However, at least for now, we have some pointers to guide us towards a desired future.

This concludes our case study and this chapter, but here are some final thoughts:

FINAL THOUGHTS ON SCENARIO DEVELOPMENT AND THE LEARNING PROCESS

The process is time-intensive and the leadership team must commit to this involvement.

- Learning is a team activity and all role players should be involved in all the stages, otherwise the return on this effort will not be optimal.
- Focus and schedule more time for the dissection and implications of the scenarios than the building or developing of them. The purpose is to use the scenario information as impetus for our strategy. The scenario information is a means to an end and not an end in itself.
- Very often teams do not utilise the full potential and richness of scenario information. Operational and time pressures are the main reasons for this. The fact is that the system seduces the role players into an operational mindset. Another reason is the leadership team's impatience and unwillingness to "swim" in the scenario information. This might be an unconscious way to avoid confronting the future head on. By working in and with the information, it becomes part of the team's thinking and the possibility that concrete actions will flow from it is multiplied.
- Consciously connect the scenario information with the present. This is important for relevance, proactive strategy development and making the future alive in the "here and now".
- The scenario development process described here is not centred around a content expert consultant. The tacit knowledge of the leadership and other insiders is the primary resource. The process should not be positioned as a staff exercise performed in an "ivory tower" setting. All involved in the process are at the same time experts and learners. The more diverse the participating group, the better. Optimum group size for this type of process is between 10 and 15. Outputs should be visible on a shared working space for the team to facilitate team dialogue and deeper understanding.

- The scenario output should not be forced on other teams in the organisation as a one-way communication process. The scenario information output should be part of input to the strategy development of these teams. These teams must rework at least the implications of the multiple scenarios for their own environment to ensure relevance, commitment and acceptance.
- The result of the process should be, at least on a concept level, new ideas on how to be more competitive in the future. Some of the end results are early warning signs or lead indicators for critical variables in each scenario. This also enables management teams to develop different time-scaled strategies for the short, medium and longer terms.

Action after understanding is essential to make the strategies relevant. Scenario information should be reworked to describe the implications of the different scenarios for our current strategies. This then becomes an input for subsequent discussions about future strategic positioning.

CONCLUSIONS

Scenario learning is becoming part of the strategy practice of many leading international companies like Shell, Xerox, AT&T, Motorola, and South African-based companies like Anglo American, Sasol, Absa and Eskom. All these companies share the realisation that the most basic strategic challenge in this millennium is how to prepare business teams for the anticipated changes in their markets and business models, and how to leverage these changes as opportunities for competitive strategies.

The value of scenario-based learning is that it:

- informs strategic decision making by creating diverse connections.
- challenges current assumptions and mental models.
- disturbs decision-makers to proactively act on changing patterns.
- produces lead indicators that allow decision-makers to monitor how the future is evolving.
- empowers decision-makers to ask new questions.

The process follows a sequence of anticipation – where the different potential futures are developed and described – and an insight phase – where strategies associated with each scenario are crafted to stimulate a core approach to these potentially impactful and diverse futures.

The future starts today; be there now.

Chapter 5

Strategy execution and change management

"In the business world, the rear-view mirror is always clearer than the windshield." – Warren Buffett[1]

INTRODUCTION

So far, chapters 2, 3 and 4 guided you through the process of opening up a "strategic choice space" or "arena", giving you as wide as possible a range of choices. Figure 5.1 serves as a reminder of the strategic journey you have been on.

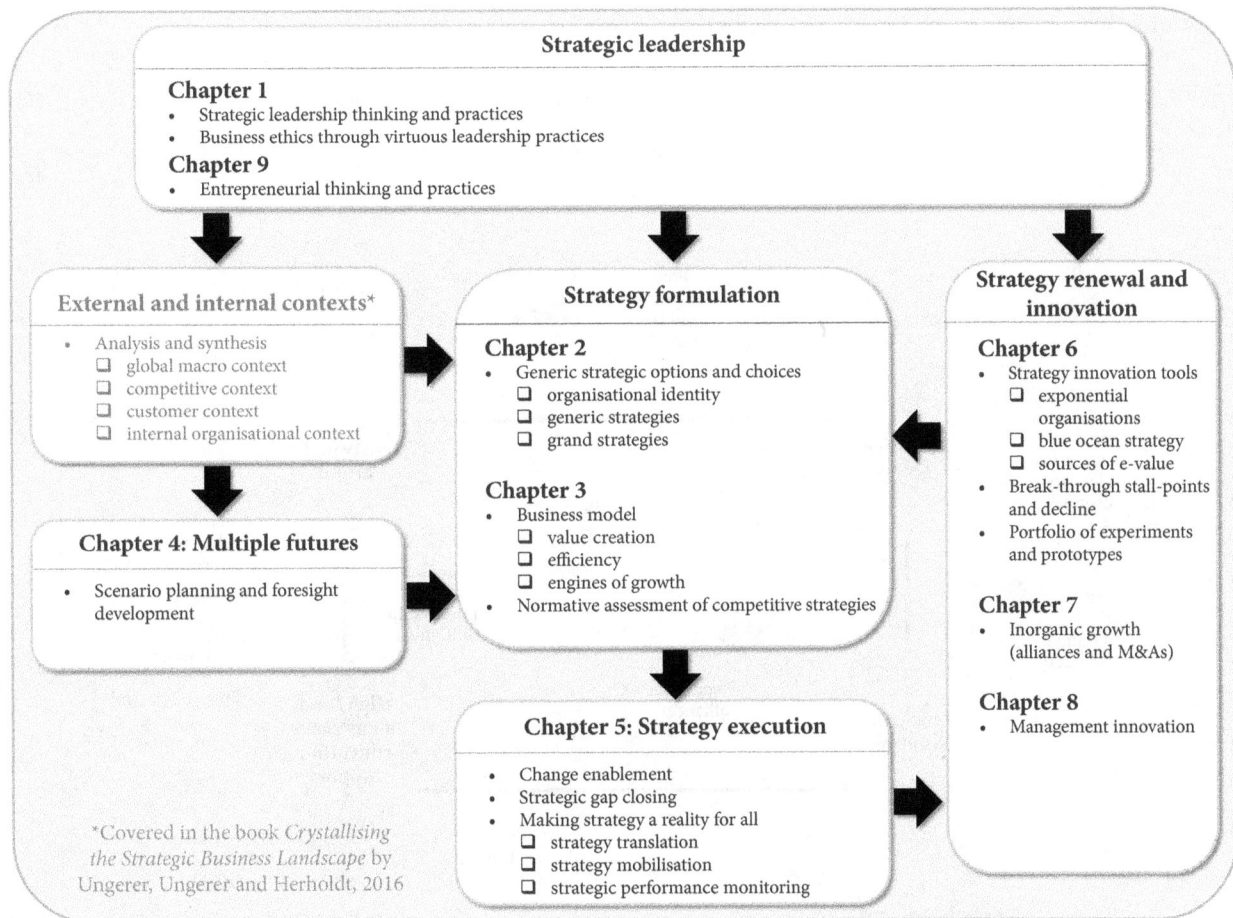

Figure 5.1 *The strategic architecture landscape*

During this process the strategy team developed an appetite for certain choices above others and through the give and take of discussions (formal, but often informal) the team arrived at a set of possible strategic choices.

Reticulating them through the enterprise's business model (and changes to the model) and activity systems firmed up the choices – even to the point of discarding certain early favourites and adding others (maybe less exciting, shiny-

and-new, but more sensible). In particular, considering how to capture value[2] (including the use of control points), finally firmed up the choices for the next strategic period.

Taking these provisional choices through a scenario process further crystallises the impact that they are likely to have on the possible futures of the enterprise, clarifying why a certain set of organisational actions will steer the firm in a more desired direction.

Deciding on the final set of strategic goals to be achieved during a certain performance period (i.e. by an agreed-upon end date) is, for many, actual strategy-making. Many – maybe more practical types – will suddenly become interested when this stage is reached, but it is important to understand that these strategic goals are not arrived at arbitrarily (… because the boss says so …), but that they are the outcome of a long and deliberate process of "decisioning". At this late stage there is little room left for "influencing" decisions, or even for "negotiating" outcomes. Paradoxically, the innovation space is now in the "how" we execute the strategic goals.

Figure 5.2 is an example of such a set of actions for a strategy team in the low-cost banking system of a South African bank.

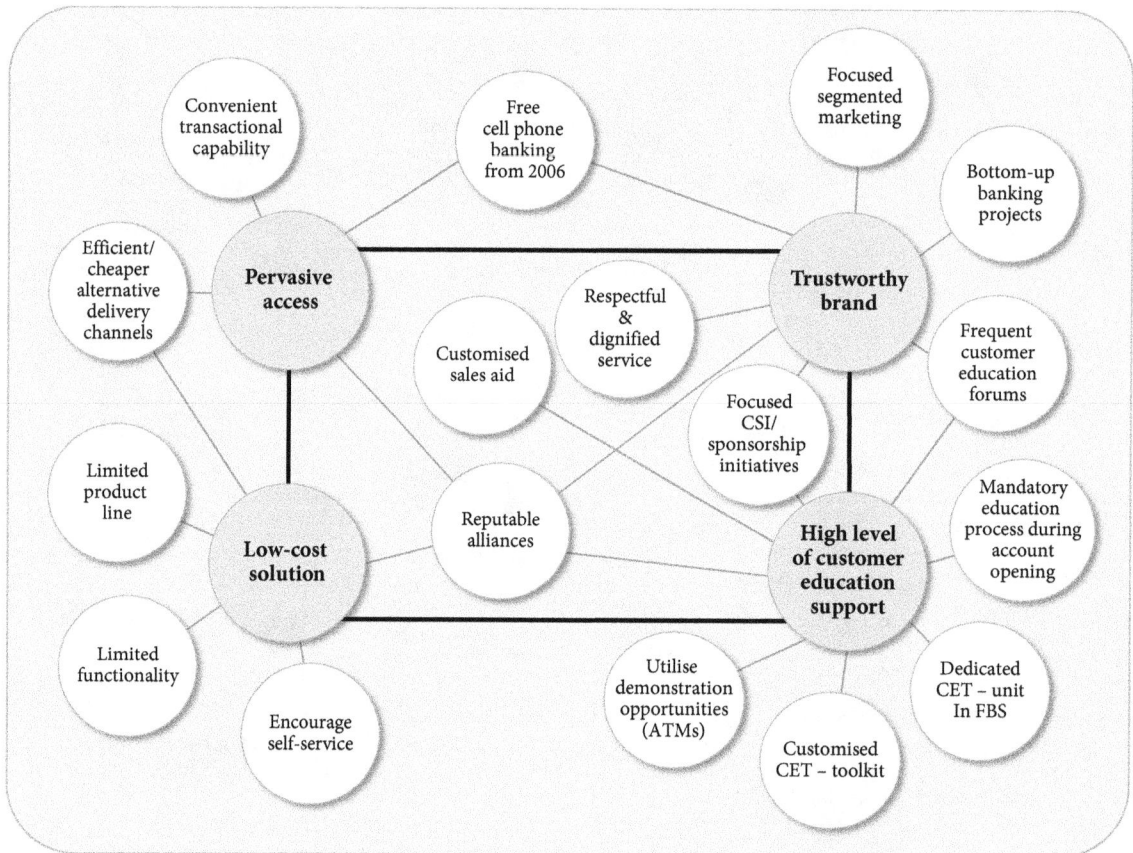

Figure 5.2: An activity system view indicating strategic focus areas

As we saw in chapter 2, these strategic goals and activities are not visions, but short- to medium-term projects/initiatives to achieve measureable outcomes. As they are achieved they suggest other project-like, shorter-term activities and actions en route to achieving the vision.

Strategy execution is the strategic activity required to make these strategic goals part of the performance contract of every relevant employee, translated into the business language of their organisational level and function. Of course, these new or revised goals always imply changes to the way things are currently done and therefore people have to be empowered to deal with change.

There is always a gap between where we are and what we are aiming for. Strategy execution is about gap-closing actions. The strategy map and balanced scorecard are useful technologies to explain the transition from strategy to individual objectives. This creates a "line of sight" explaining the impact of a particular job on the strategy of the firm.

But strategy is not only a rational, intellectual exercise. Change enablement/management highlights activities and principles aimed at touching on the more emotional – and often illogical and counter-intuitive – side of change and resistance to change. The well-known impact of culture and the resistance caused by the very tools we use during change management are also discussed in this chapter.

This chapter deals with:

- strategic planning as strategic gap-closing activities
- making strategy a reality for all:
    - o strategy translation using the strategy map and balanced scorecard
    - o strategy mobilisation by translating business goals into individual performance objectives
    - o change enablement/management principles and activities
- enterprise strategic performance monitoring mechanisms

STRATEGY EXECUTION PRINCIPLES

Whether you come up with a brilliant strategy, a killer app, an astounding new product idea, plans for a slick new merger, or whatever strategy – it comes to nothing if you cannot implement it. There are many guides to developing strategy, but few to help with implementation. Small wonder that many companies – large, medium and small – struggle with implementation.

In a recent survey[3] of nearly 8 000 managers in more than 250 companies over a period of five years, the authors found that somewhere between two-thirds to three-quarters of organisations struggle with strategy execution. In 2004 Marakon Associates and the Economist Intelligence Unit surveyed senior executives from 197 companies worldwide with sales exceeding $500 million. In the opinion of the executives surveyed, their companies only realise around 60 per cent of the potential value contained in their strategies.[4] Competent execution can realise the missing 40 per cent, or at least a greater part of it.

Kaplan and Norton (2008)[5] – of whom much more later – show that companies that effectively execute their strategy evidence an impressive 50–150 per cent increase in value. Those that don't continue to battle the odds against success.

Strategy execution principles linked to systems thinking

- Strategy execution is a systemic process of interconnected activities.
- Strategy development and positioning are primarily based on reinforcing processes in the form of growth engines aimed at producing cumulative, quantum leaps.
- Nothing grows forever – eventually growth engines reach their limits. The best time to start planning for this is when the growth-loops are still working well. This thinking approach creates the time space to reconfigure the growth variables to counter these balancing forces.
- Strategy planning and implementation require a different mindset from strategy development. Strategy development is primarily concerned with creating growth engines (R-loops). Strategy planning is more about initiating gap-closing activities (B-loops), closing the gap between where we want to be and where we presently are (see Figure 5.3).

Application tool

Use the latest strategy documentation of your organisation (or one you are familiar with). In your opinion, how well does it apply the strategy execution principles listed above?

Principle	Application (1=poor; 10=excellent)	What (in your opinion) can be done to improve this?
A company-wide systemic process of interconnected activities		
Primarily based on reinforcing processes in the form of growth engines aimed at producing cumulative, quantum leaps		
Start planning to counter B-loops (limiting forces) when the growth-loops are still working well. Reconfigure the growth variables to counter these balancing forces.		
Strategy development is primarily concerned with creating growth engines (R-loops). Strategy planning is more about initiating gap-closing activities (B-loops),[6] closing the gap between where we want to be and where we are presently.		

Strategy execution as gap-closing activities

Strategy execution is about gap-closing activities that will realise the desired future state sooner and faster.

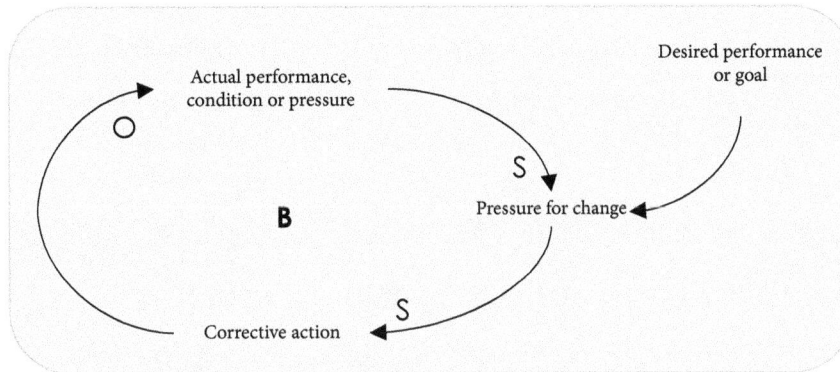

Figure 5.3: Strategy execution as gap-closing activities

The bigger the deviation from the expected or planned standard, the greater the pressure to do something about it. The pressure is normally released through new corrective actions aimed at closing the gap between the current position and the desired state. From another perspective, it can also be said that a characteristic of a balancing process is that it has a goal (implicit or explicit). This goal creates a condition or pressure that drives a corrective action(s) aimed at correcting or adjusting the performance or relieving the pressure situation.

In natural systems this action persists until the gap is closed. In business however, we can choose to persist or not. This choice to initiate **gap-closing activities,** or not, is at the heart of strategy planning. The essence of a successful **execution and implementation mindset** is to relentlessly focus on initiatives that will bring our current reality closer to the desired future state, sooner and faster.

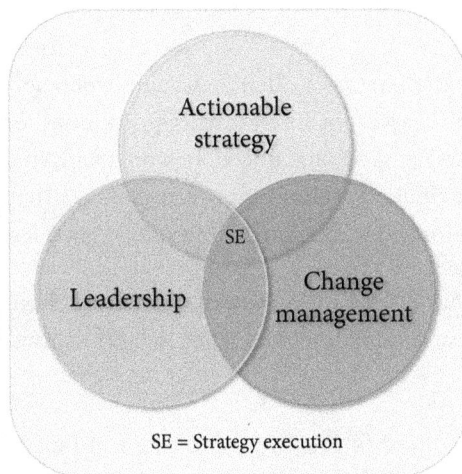

Figure 5.4: Strategy execution mindset

Figure 5.4 illustrates the strategy execution and implementation mindset.

The strategy execution mindset enables all role-players to understand that execution requires an actionable strategy – one that does not rely on catchphrases and "marketing talk", but that highlights the strategic goals to be achieved **and the effort required** to achieve them.

Strategy execution is largely about people – those necessary to implement the changes required by the new strategy. Change management is essential to empower them to act. This is discussed in more detail later in the chapter.

The process of execution and implementation cannot be delegated away – the CEO, executives and strategy team remain responsible for seeing that the strategy they developed is implemented. Any strategy is the promise made to shareholders (and other stakeholders) about what the organisation will achieve at some well-defined point in the future – usually a financial or calendar year-end. Delivering on this promise is the biggest job of the board, the CEO and the senior team.

How do executives think they perform against these expectations? Research[7] published by PwC in 2014 gives an indication (see Figure 5.5):

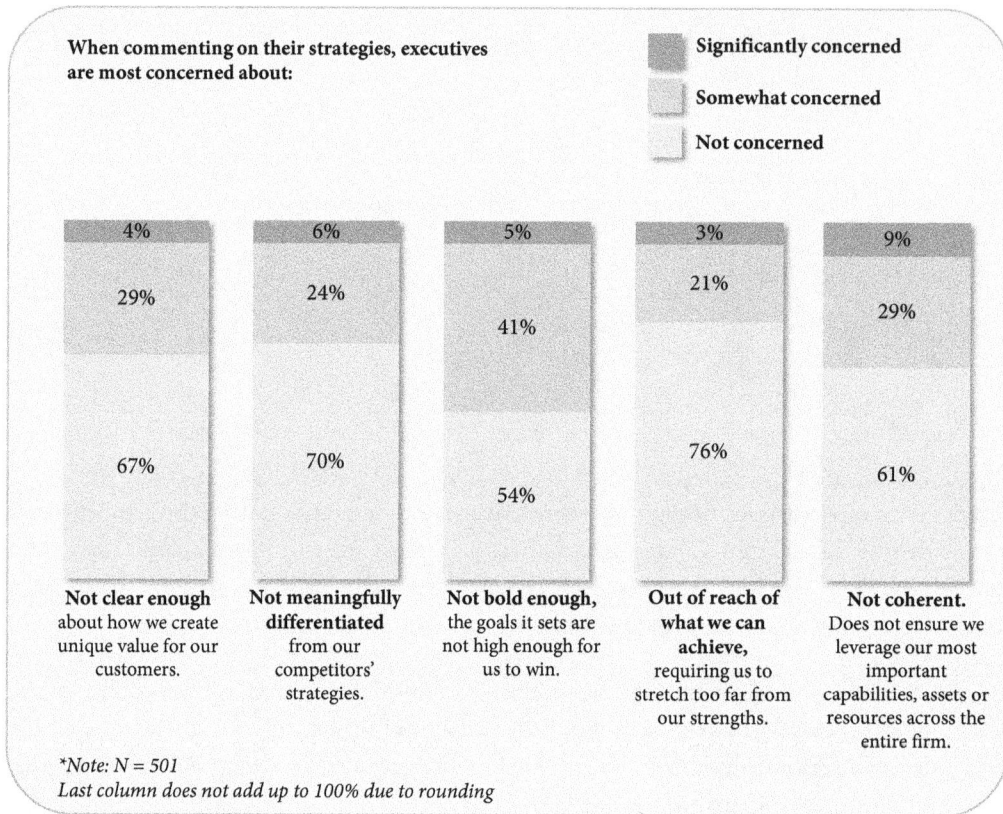

			Significantly concerned
			Somewhat concerned
			Not concerned

When commenting on their strategies, executives are most concerned about:

Not clear enough about how we create unique value for our customers.	Not meaningfully differentiated from our competitors' strategies.	Not bold enough, the goals it sets are not high enough for us to win.	Out of reach of what we can achieve, requiring us to stretch too far from our strengths.	Not coherent. Does not ensure we leverage our most important capabilities, assets or resources across the entire firm.
4%	6%	5%	3%	9%
29%	24%	41%	21%	29%
67%	70%	54%	76%	61%

*Note: N = 501
Last column does not add up to 100% due to rounding*

Figure 5.5: Why strategies are difficult to execute

It's not that companies aren't trying to execute their strategies. It's that the strategies often aren't implementable or designed to win. Leaders frequently focus too much on screening the market for interesting opportunities, or activities that will merely bring them up to par with competitor products and services, and not enough on identifying the strategic opportunities their company – as an integrated whole – is uniquely well positioned to pursue. They therefore fail to provide people and functions in the organisation with reasons to work together to exploit synergies.

Of course, this has an effect on how companies execute these strategies. Executives are even more concerned about their company's ability to implement its strategy. Alignment, focus and conflicting priorities seem to be the things that concern many executives.

Strategy planning always occurs against the backdrop of a preferred or desired future. In practice there are many obstacles that stand in the way of moving constructively to a planning phase. These barriers prevent excellent plans from being executed. Considering some of these factors will help avoid these common patterns (see Figure 5.6).

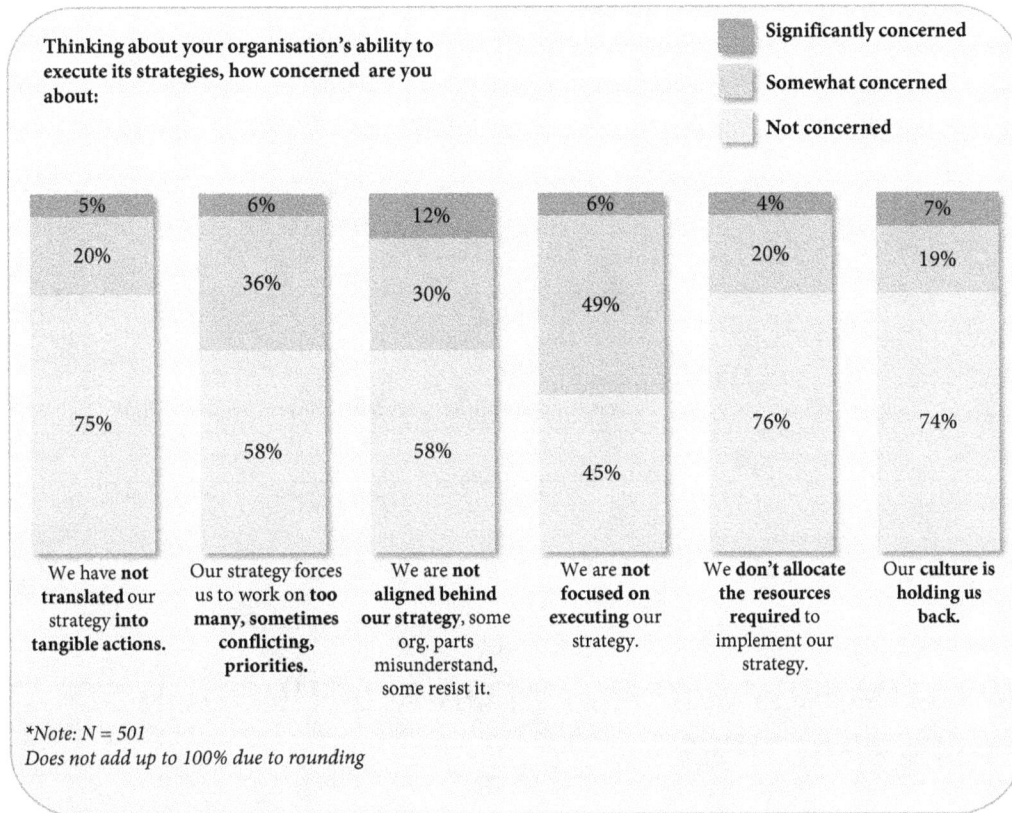

Figure 5.6: Execution obstacles

Obstacles to implementing our best thinking

Here are some of the more common obstacles:

- The desired direction is unclear and lacks an actionable proposition(s) – therefore the required effort is unclear. This means that there is not enough of a gap between "current" and "desirable" for the natural, automatic B-loop "pressure for change" to occur.
- Mobilising resources takes time, energy, commitment, courage and leadership, because you normally have to re-allocate them from somewhere else in the firm.
- Strategies are seen as fixed, not open to creative adaptation, and are closed to feedback from reality.
- The requirements for success (like the subject knowledge required and interdependencies between key strategic variables and role-players) are underestimated. Intellectual talk is seen as more valuable than actual doing.
- There is a desire to plan everything in detail before we move – instead of learning and adapting as we go.
- Strategy is only a reality for a selected few. It might be in the heads of a few, but not in the toes of many.
- There is a desire to implement it all at once. Prototyping, phased rollouts, version releases, etc. would be a better strategy.
- People are afraid to take risks and make mistakes. They do not understand that this is how we learn (especially if we are developing competencies that are new – and therefore difficult to replicate). Learning costs time and money.

- There is destructive internal competition. Energy is focused on internal silos instead of externally – towards competitors.
- There is a belief that upgrading to or acquiring new technology is a strategy – this is untrue. Its application is a strategy, not its acquisition.

Application tool

Which of the above obstacles and those in Figure 5.6 apply to your organisation (or one you are familiar with)? What (in your opinion) can be done about it?

Obstacle	What (in your opinion) can be done to improve this?

MAKING STRATEGY A REALITY FOR ALL THROUGH STRATEGY EXECUTION PRACTICES

"The team that executes first, wins." – Paul Roberts[8]

In the fast-moving world of today, implementation has become more important than ever before because:

- Competitors have an increasing ability to catch up with our current best innovations.
- The life span of new ideas is getting shorter.
- Information is easily and freely available and accessible.
- Talk is cheap. Customers and shareholders no longer judge management by their promises, but on what they actually delivered.
- It is more important to be fast and part of the action than to be perfect, an also-ran or to miss the opportunity entirely.

Figure 5.7 gives a birds-eye view of the whole process of strategy-making and execution.

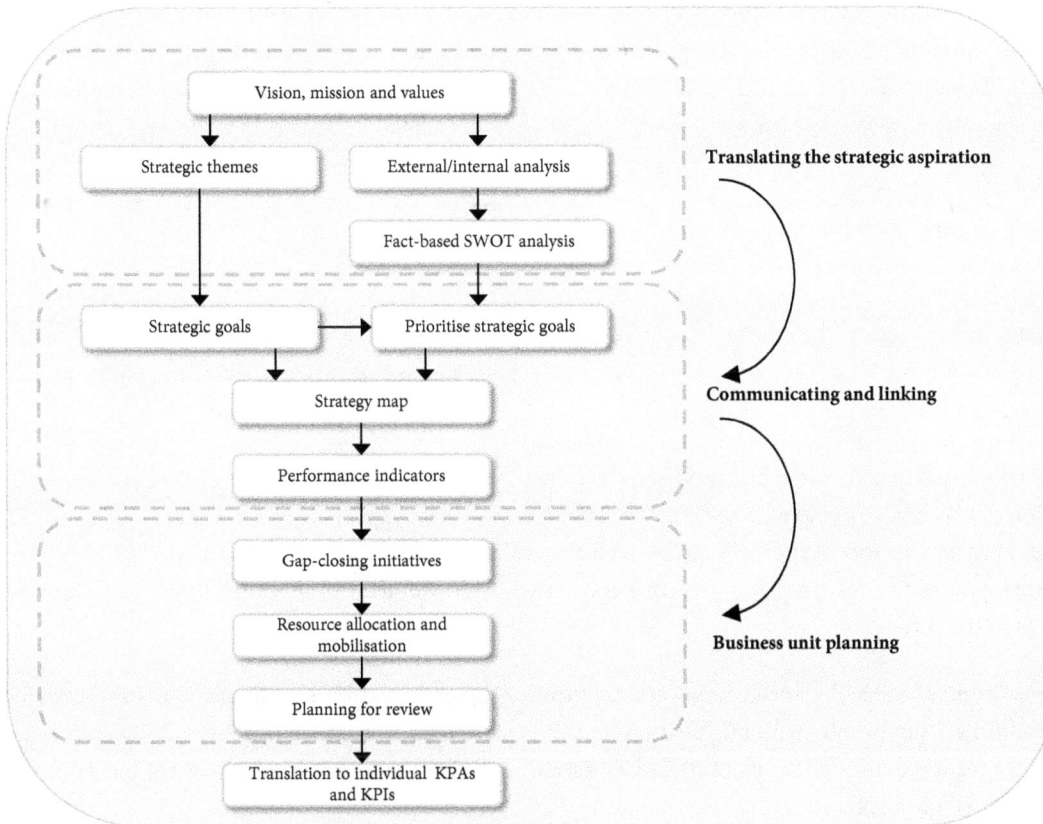

Figure 5.7: Birds-eye view of the strategy-making and execution process[9]

Figure 5.7 might lead you to think of strategy as a linear process. In practice it is circular, as shown in Figure 5.1. As you can see strategy formulation, strategy execution and strategy renewal form a loop, where the strategy is continuously reformulated on the basis of learning during execution and other innovations – causing constant renewal.

This means that everyone in the organisation, in principle, can contribute to making and remaking strategy at any time. Of course there are time-frames and due dates, but they often serve as convenient milestones rather than a cumbersome restarting of the strategy engine. In this way strategy and execution actions serve as a fly-wheel, constantly driving the enterprise forward; it learns as it goes, tinkering with the strategy continually to make it better and more responsive to changes in its strategic landscape.

> **Continuous feedback makes strategy execution an emerging process based on local knowledge.**

In our experience it is useful for the **first step** in execution planning to be the development of a strategy map.

Step 1: The strategy map

The strategic planning cycle starts with the development of a strategy map based on strategic goals derived from the strategy formulation activities. A strategy map is a one-page integrated summary of the strategic goals of the firm (see Figures 5.10, 5.11, 5.19, for instance).

The **strategy map** is a mechanism to focus the entire business on the strategy to ensure coherent thinking and action. The map allows for the strategy to be simplified and translated into a visible and descriptive framework without ignoring its full complexity. The strategy map tells the complex story of the strategy of a business in a concise, focused and visual way on one page. The strategy map template, when populated fully, provides the ideal platform for:

- strategy clarification
- strategic alignment and translation
- strategy execution

The core content structure of the strategy map is based on the work of R.S. Kaplan and D.P. Norton.[10] To have a more balanced view on any business, they advocate the use of the following perspectives to describe more comprehensively the issues facing a business:

- financial perspective: the financial results we are aiming for
- customer/stakeholder perspective: what customers/stakeholders expect
- internal process perspective: processes we need to excel at
- resource perspective/learning and growth perspective: what we need to invest in today to ensure sustainable success in the future

The four perspectives of the balanced scorecard capture a simple, yet extremely elegant and sound, virtuous cycle or engine of growth applicable to all business organisations. Delighting customers generates revenue, which funds investments in resources needed to create effective internal processes that enable the delivery of the value proposition to the customer (Figure 5.8).

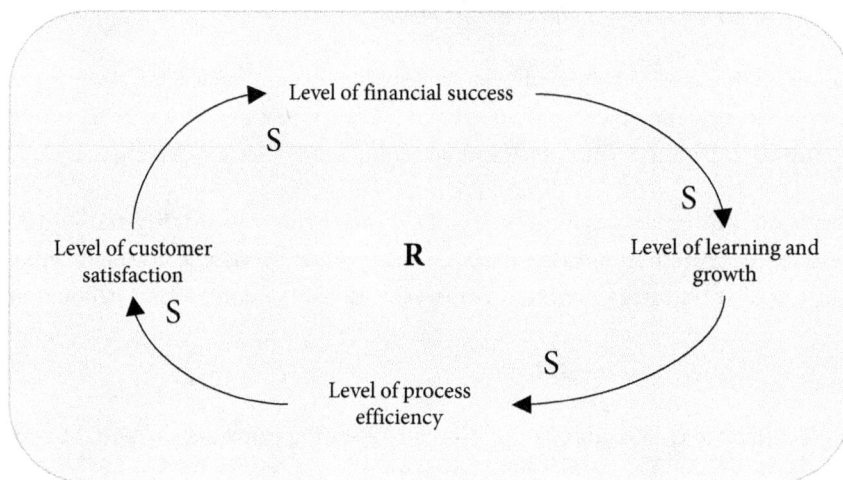

Figure 5.8: Virtuous "balanced scorecard" loop

Reading the loop: The more learning and growth, the more process efficiency, the more customer satisfaction, the more financial success, the more learning and growth you can afford, the more/better process efficiency … and so on – a growth engine.

The strategy map is in essence a visual translation of the key strategic elements of the organisation's strategy. It is a framework by which we ensure linkage between all aspects necessary to achieve the envisaged business vision.

In the strategy map the principles of a **balanced approach** are retained in the following ways:

- It links both lag elements (the strategic results we aim for) and lead elements (the strategic drivers of our strategy) in one comprehensive framework.
- The causal relationships between key strategic variables in each of the four perspectives of the balanced scorecard and between the different perspectives are shown (see Figure 5.19, for example). In this way attention is focused on the interrelationships between the different components. Thinking through the causal relationships enhances the robustness of the strategy.
- The strategic initiatives that flow from the strategic goals are oriented to the short and longer term to allow for immediate actions and initiatives that will take more time to execute.
- The financial and customer components of the map can be viewed as more externally orientated, while the internal and resource perspectives reflect a more internal orientation – again a balance.

To build the strategy map, the following **assumptions** are made:

- The team participating in the strategy process knows the business.
- The team is able and willing to make the right choices for the business to excel – there are few destructive politics and little jockeying for positions.
- The strategy map is not fixed, but fluid and open to change because of the many feedback loops that inform it constantly. These loops arise from both the internal and external organisational environments. A strategy map's lifetime is about three years. It should be reviewed and renewed in cycles of three years.

The approach to strategy planning and implementation making use of a strategy map reflects the complexity of the business in an elementary way without losing any of the strategic building blocks. The variable elements in the map are formulated as strategic goals with supporting success indicators. A **strategic goal** is an open-ended, high-level qualitative statement of "what" you intend to achieve – it is about an improved future position. The arrows indicate cause-and-effect relationships between variables.

Before we start populating the perspectives of the strategy map, let us look at an example of a completed strategy map (see Figures 5.9 and 5.10), for a technical specialist unit in Synfuels – a division of Sasol.[11]

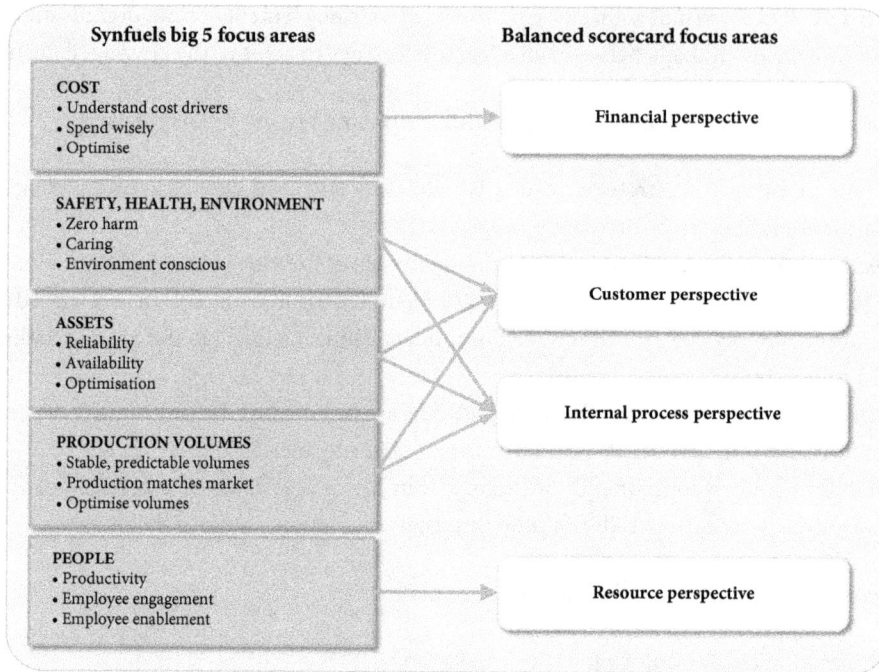

Figure 5.9: Merging the balanced scorecard with Synfuels' strategic goals[12]

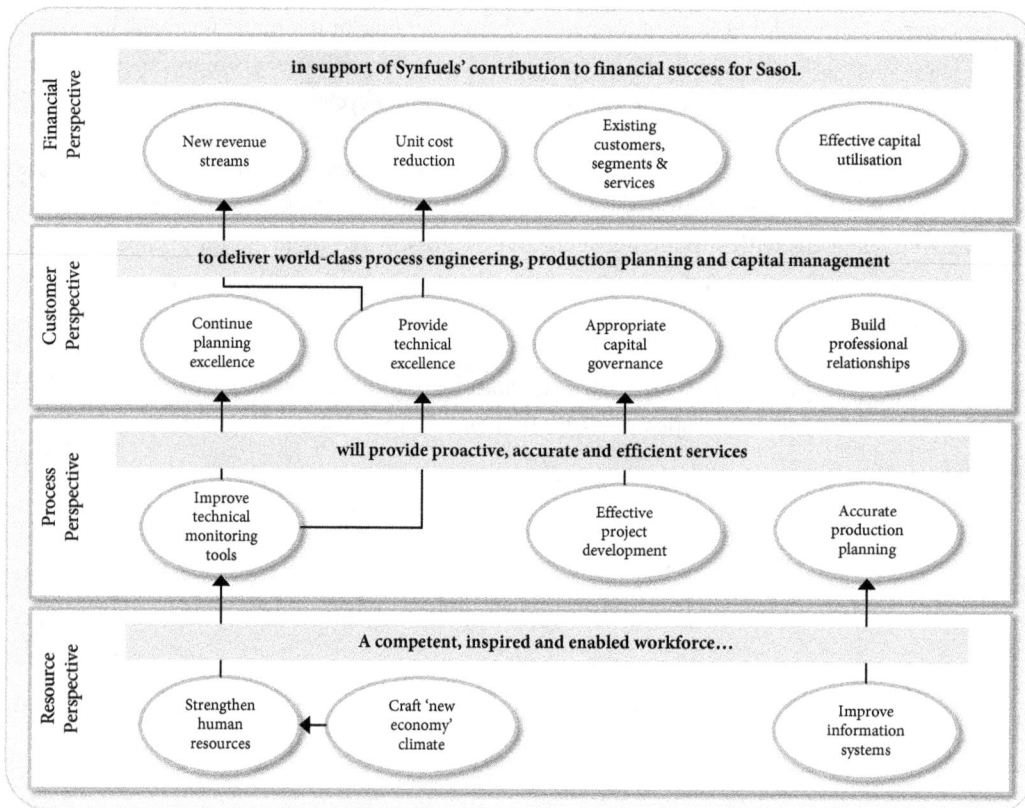

Figure 5.10: Strategy map reflecting strategic goals

The strategy map is not only for enterprises that do business for profit, but also for not-for-profit concerns. Figure 5.11 is an example of such a map.

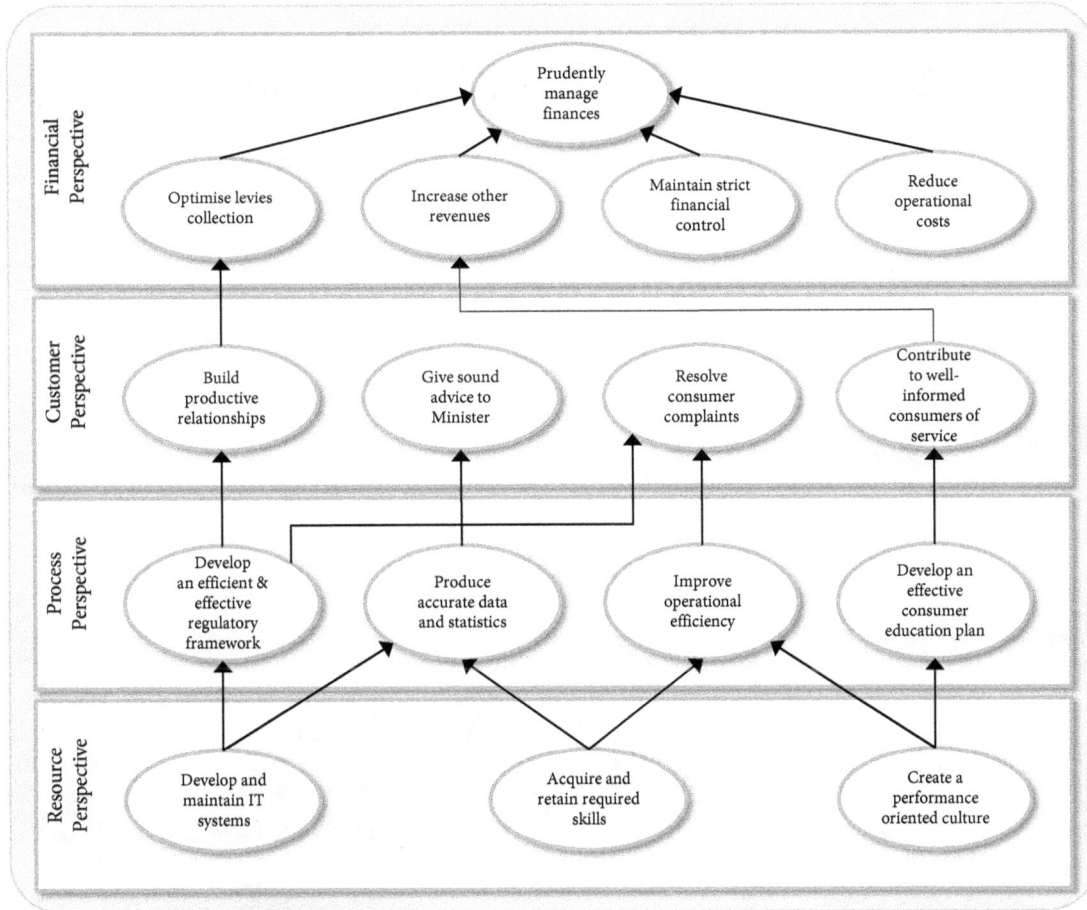

Figure 5.11: Strategy map for a state-owned enterprise

Populating each of the perspectives of the strategy map

Financial/business perspective

Key question: To succeed financially, how should we appear to our shareholders?

The financial perspective is primarily about the measurement of financial results. A key thought to consider is: "What will indicate progress to shareholders and how will we measure this?" The idea is to generate measurements on every goal that will effectively measure movement (progress, stalls or regression) in respect of that goal.

Basic variables here should support typical themes like profitability, revenue growth and productivity improvement, which are caused by a change in the relationship between revenue, risk and productivity/cost/asset utilisation. The key activity for a leadership team is to develop the financial perspective relevant to its business, taking into account the causal relationship between the strategic variables – what causes what?

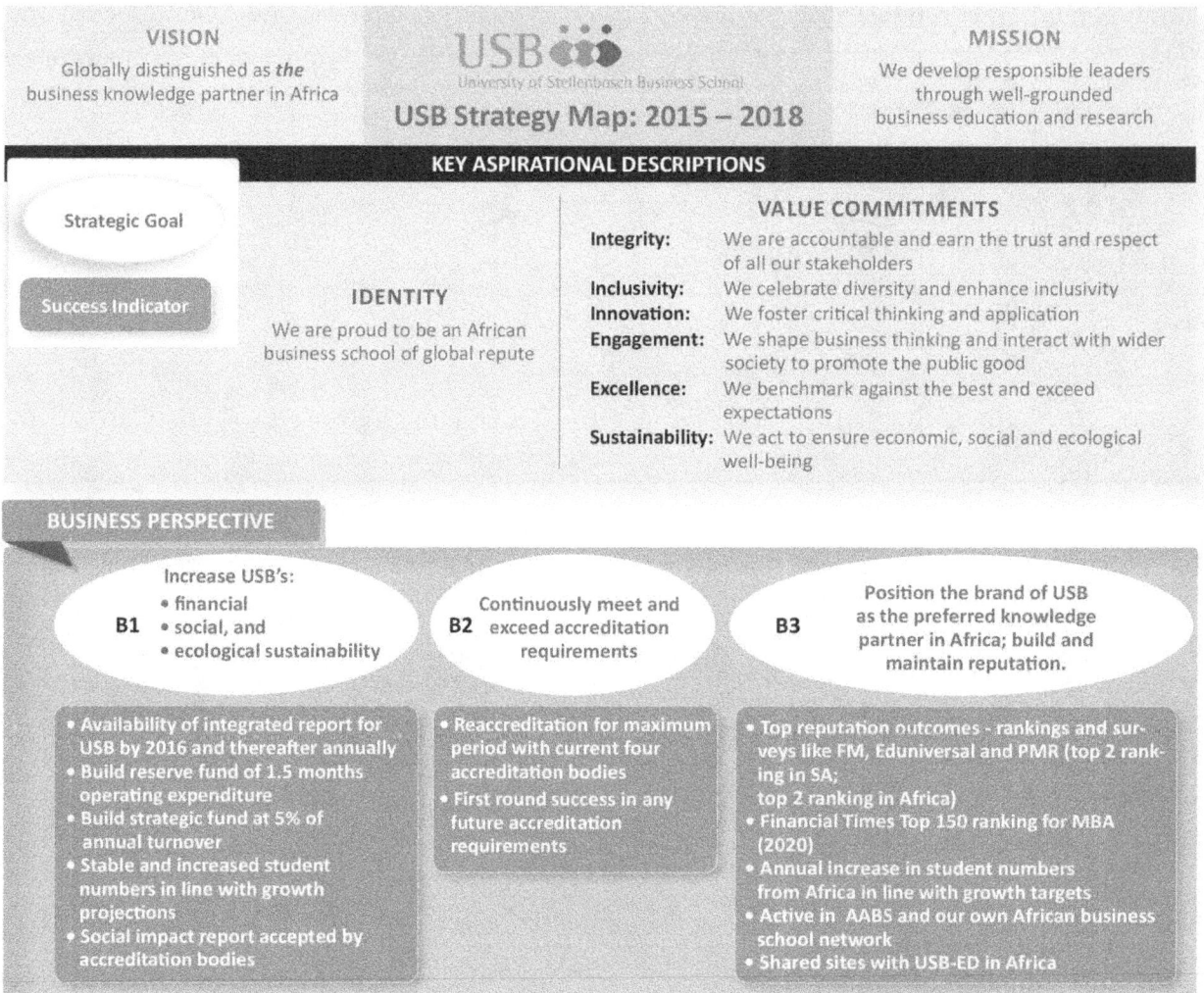

VISION
Globally distinguished as *the* business knowledge partner in Africa

USB
University of Stellenbosch Business School
USB Strategy Map: 2015 – 2018

MISSION
We develop responsible leaders through well-grounded business education and research

KEY ASPIRATIONAL DESCRIPTIONS

Strategic Goal

Success Indicator

IDENTITY
We are proud to be an African business school of global repute

VALUE COMMITMENTS

Integrity: We are accountable and earn the trust and respect of all our stakeholders
Inclusivity: We celebrate diversity and enhance inclusivity
Innovation: We foster critical thinking and application
Engagement: We shape business thinking and interact with wider society to promote the public good
Excellence: We benchmark against the best and exceed expectations
Sustainability: We act to ensure economic, social and ecological well-being

BUSINESS PERSPECTIVE

B1 Increase USB's:
- financial
- social, and
- ecological sustainability

B2 Continuously meet and exceed accreditation requirements

B3 Position the brand of USB as the preferred knowledge partner in Africa; build and maintain reputation.

- Availability of integrated report for USB by 2016 and thereafter annually
- Build reserve fund of 1.5 months operating expenditure
- Build strategic fund at 5% of annual turnover
- Stable and increased student numbers in line with growth projections
- Social impact report accepted by accreditation bodies

- Reaccreditation for maximum period with current four accreditation bodies
- First round success in any future accreditation requirements

- Top reputation outcomes - rankings and surveys like FM, Eduniversal and PMR (top 2 ranking in SA; top 2 ranking in Africa)
- Financial Times Top 150 ranking for MBA (2020)
- Annual increase in student numbers from Africa in line with growth targets
- Active in AABS and our own African business school network
- Shared sites with USB-ED in Africa

Figure 5.12: Strategy map: Financial perspective

Customer/stakeholder perspective

Key question: To achieve our vision/purpose and to succeed financially, how should we appear to our customers/ stakeholders?

The customer perspective is primarily about the value proposition. The key activity for a leadership team is to develop the core goals related to the elements of the value proposition. Basic themes within which to develop goals are service/product attributes, pricing, customer relations and delivery channels; but, in the final analysis, they have to fit your customer requirements as in Figure 5.13.

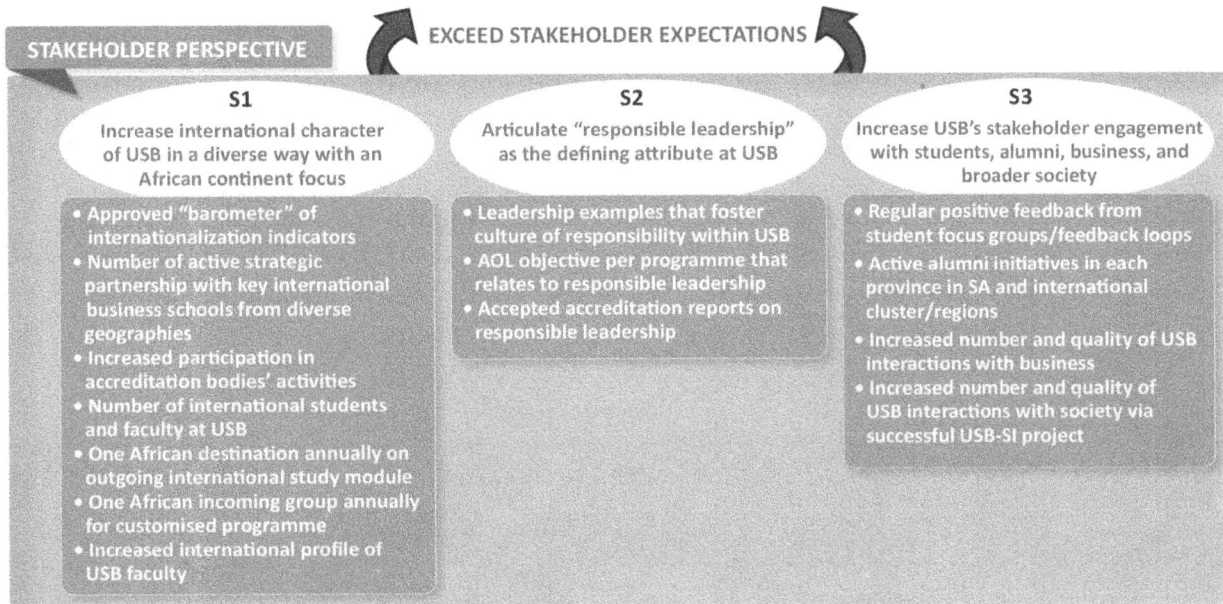

Figure 5.13: Strategy map – customer/stakeholder perspective[14]

For each identified variable, develop key success indicators (KSIs) that will add meaning to the strategic goal. These indicators will confirm that there is progress on the achievement of strategic goals. KSIs should be output-orientated, descriptive in nature, not initiatives and not a sequential description of process steps. An example of potential elements in this perspective is shown in Figure 5.14.

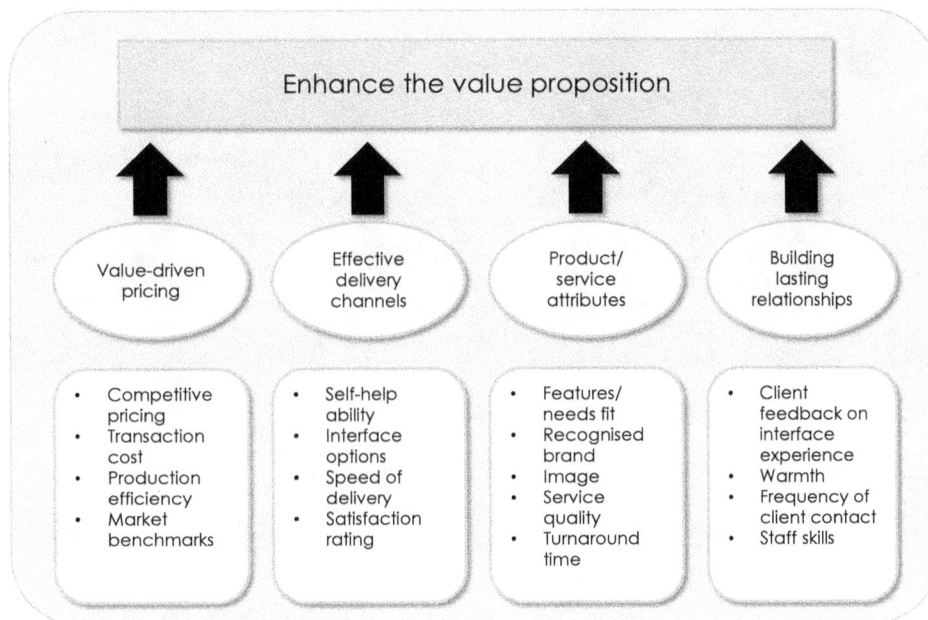

Figure 5.14: Examples of Key Success Indicators (KSIs)

Internal processes perspective

Key question: *To satisfy our customers and shareholders, what internal processes should we excel at?*

The basic premise is that internal processes should support the achievement of strategy. In this perspective the leadership team needs to think of the total value chain in a client-to-client process, from engagement, to transacting, to fulfilling service needs. Business teams should start by identifying core processes that influence customers directly. Thereafter, identify the secondary processes for the business. Sort the processes to get to a prioritised higher level of process in the value chain. The strategic activities are most productively grouped in a set of three to six processes. For each identified key process, develop KSIs for improved efficiency.

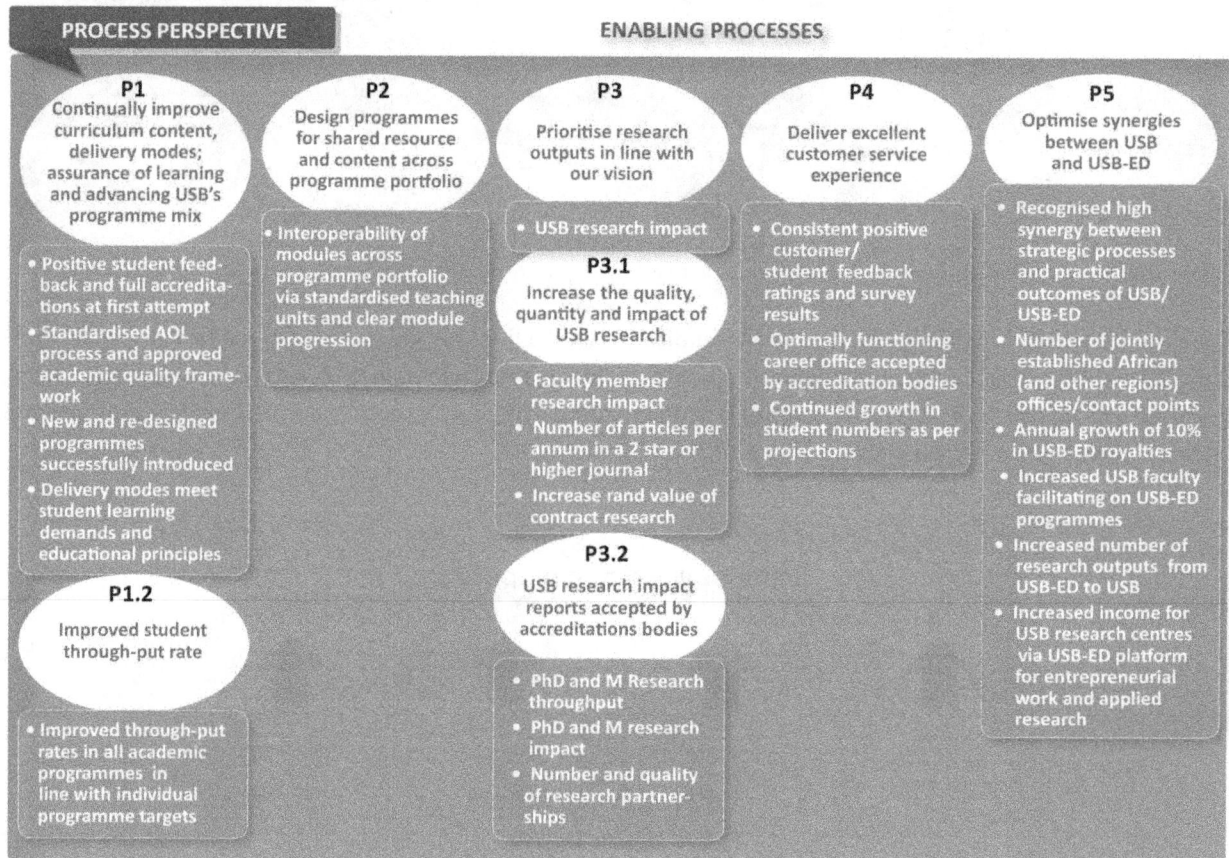

Figure 5.15: Strategy map – internal process perspective[15]

There are also other formats. Figure 5.16 is an example (with possible KSIs):

Innovation process	Customer management process	Operating process	Regulatory and social
• Product development time • Product management efficiency • Speed to market • Availability of alliance network	• Level of sales • Problem-solving and solution supply • Customer service levels • Relationship management	• Supply-chain management • Quality improvement • Operational efficiency • Risk management • Systems development	• Social responsibility • Environmental friendliness • Safety management • Health management

Figure 5.16: Example of possible metrics for the internal process perspective

Resource perspective

Key question: To achieve our purpose, how will we sustain our ability to change and improve?

The fourth perspective identifies the root (or lead) strategic variables the business needs to support and invest in for sustained long-term growth and improvement. Included here is the specific support required for processes identified in the internal business process perspective. Organisational learning and growth come from four principal sources:

* human capital (skills/training)
* technology (systems and information)
* infrastructure (physical assets)
* climate for action (creating the desired culture)[16]

These themes provide guidelines for a leadership team to develop the relevant strategic goals and supporting KSIs. See Figure 5.17.

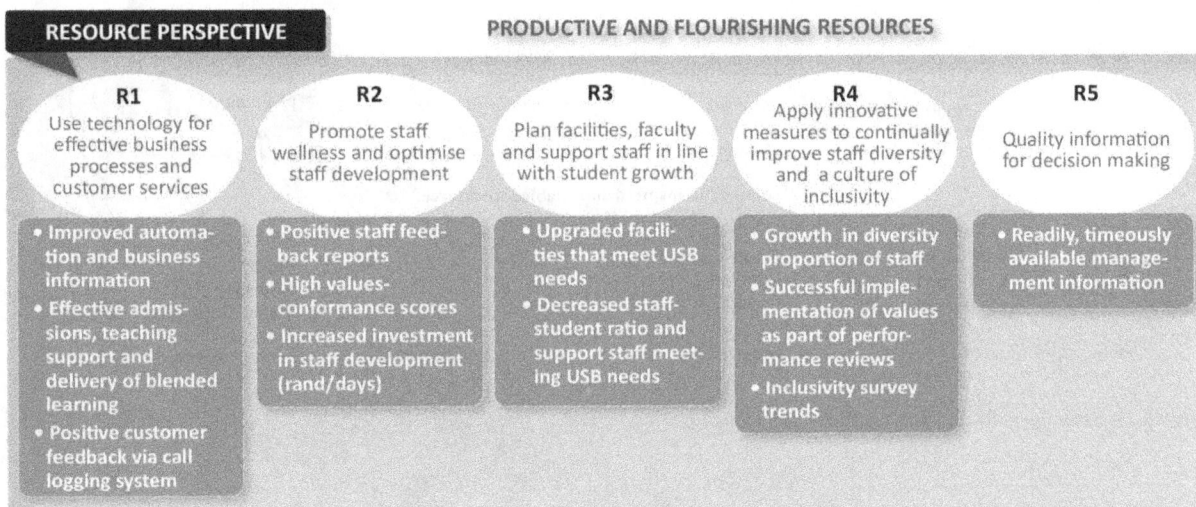

Figure 5.17: Strategy map – resources perspective[17]

Notes for developing a strategy map

Related to the *content* of the map

The map consists of three elements:

- *Goals* are statements about "What needs to be aimed for on a strategic level?" These are shown in circles in Figure 5.18. Strategic goals are oriented towards the longer term. They are not short-term objectives or how-to-action-oriented.
- *Arrows* show the cause–effect relationships between strategic goals within a perspective and between perspectives. The logic in the map allows for specific strategic goals (with their sets of indicators) to be arranged in cause–effect relationships, showing which other strategic goals they drive, as shown in Figure 5.18.
- *KSIs* are helpful to guide our efforts. They indicate whether we are on the path to achieving success for a specific strategic goal. These are shown in Figure 5.19.

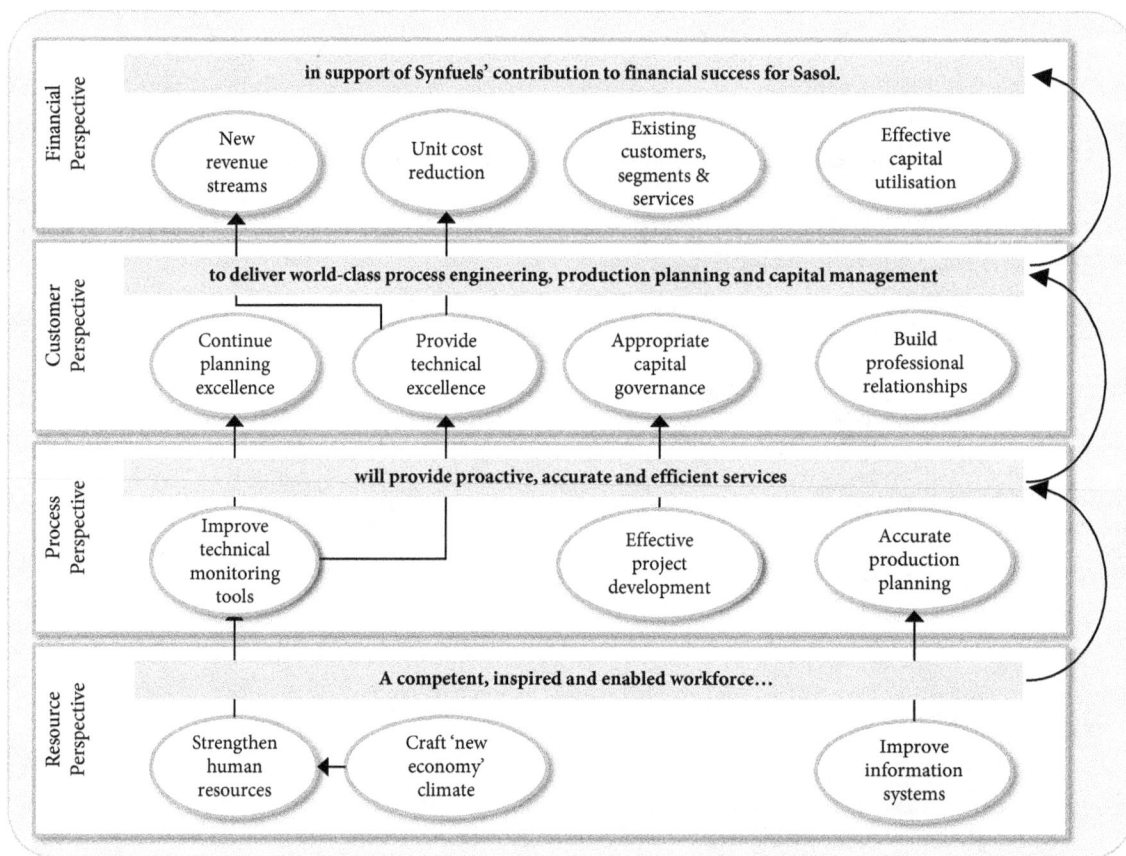

Figure 5.18: Strategy map showing goals and relationships[18]

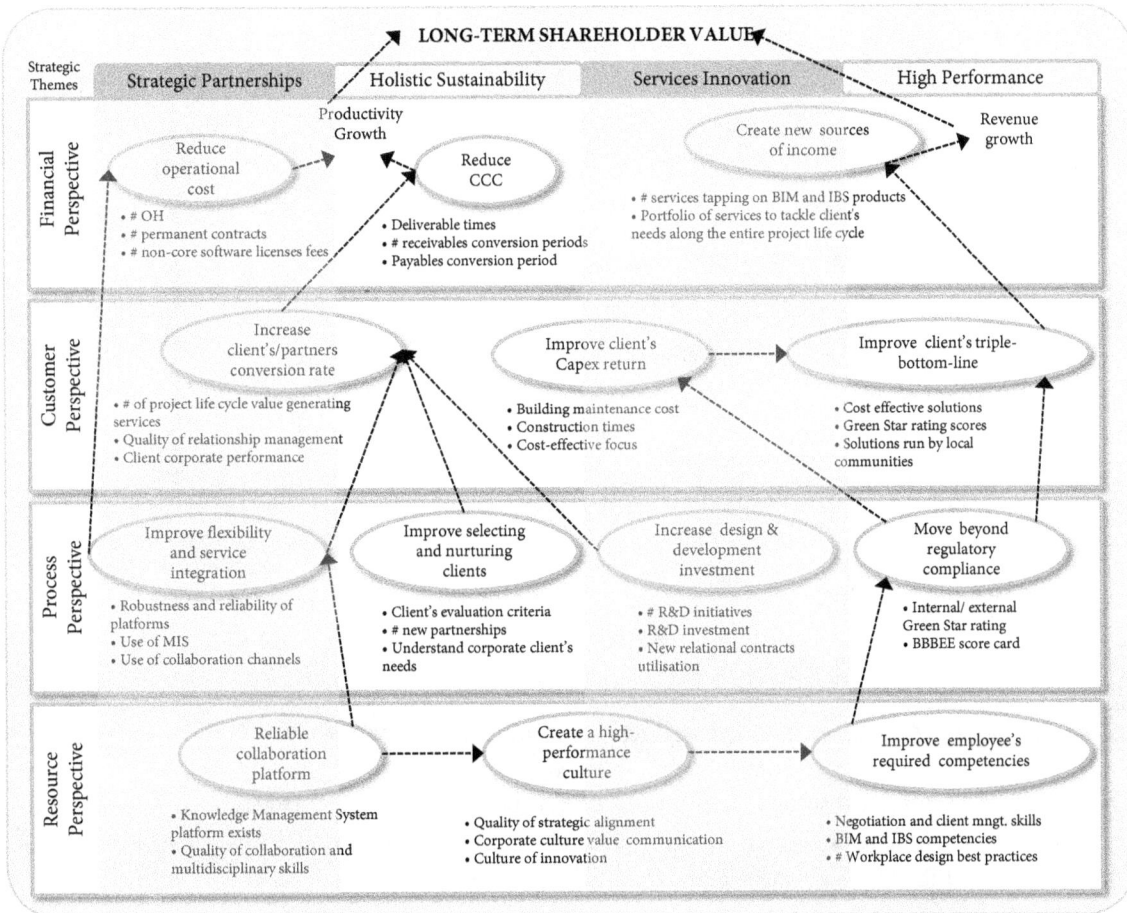

Figure 5.19: Strategy map showing KSIs[19]

Notes for developing a strategy map content (continued)

- The end product should reflect the systemic relationship between the strategic variables. In general, one can say that the bottom perspectives precede the top perspectives in time – see Figure 5.20. This reflects a lead–lag relationship between each of the perspectives, i.e. internal processes cause the customer perspective. There is however also a lead–lag relationship between variables in each perspective (see also Figure 5.18).
- This is not a theoretical exercise, but describes in a practical and more detailed way what will contribute significantly to achieving the vision and strategic themes (see especially Figure 5.19).
- The goals in the strategy map should reflect strategic elements that are within the control of the leadership team. This will prevent unrealistic nonsustainable goals that sound good but are not practicable.
- Ensure that these arrows represent cause–effect relationships, not sequential process steps. It is **not** "this *then* that" thinking, but an increase/decrease in **this causes** an increase/decrease in **that**. See Figure 5.20.
- The focus is always on a strategic level and care should be taken not to get bogged down in operational detail. The acid test is whether the issue has a direct impact on the longer-term future. Operational improvements are addressed as part of the process of developing initiatives later in this chapter.

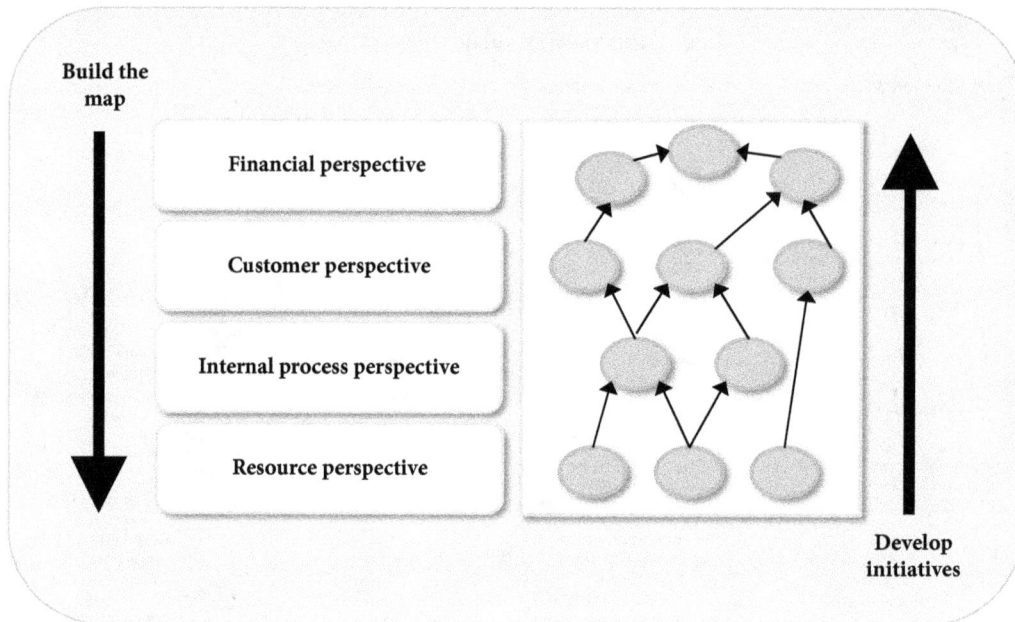

Figure 5.20: Process of creating the strategy map

Notes related to the process of creating a strategy map

- The process of creating the strategy map is just as important as the content. This is a participative process in order to create alignment and shared meaning on what needs to be focused on strategically. Participants must own the data and the logic of what the preconditions or drivers (lead elements) are for creating the expected strategic results (lag elements).
- Create a shared working space where all team members can see the unfolding of their best thinking. A sheet of brown paper divided into the four perspectives is useful. The map creates a shared working and thinking space for team members and should be in a large enough format to make it a visible reference tool for all.
- Start building the map from the financial perspective, which represents the lag factors (or results the leadership team is aiming for).
  - Build each perspective separately from financial to customer to internal processes to resource perspective. Each perspective should be built independently and linked later (with arrows) to show interdependencies. Arrows are used to indicate the cause–effect relationship between variables. The basic idea is that the arrows should move from bottom to top to highlight the lead–lag/driver relationships.
  - Post-it notes are useful in this process. Generate ideas on Post-it notes first and then group and regroup until you are satisfied with the concept and formulation of your strategic goals and KSIs.
  - Only draw the cause and effect relationships once the strategic goals and success factors have been clarified.
  - Don't overcrowd the map with too many arrows. Only indicate the primary relationships. (We accept that eventually everything is linked to everything else, but the intention is not to show that.)
  - The process of developing a map should be an interactive team activity. This is done to create alignment and a "rich" understanding and insight. The temptation is always there to give this demanding task to the "brightest" team members. The power of collective wisdom, shared meaning and discovery is lost if teams allow this.

○ Once the strategy map (goals and success indicators) has been completed, the shorter-term strategic initiatives can be formulated. It is important to realise that strategic initiatives are built from bottom to top. For detail see **Step 3** later in this chapter.

○ Experiential learning exercises to demonstrate the systemic principles of lead–lag and cause and effect greatly enhance participants' capacity to think in this paradigm. Preparing participants for the journey they are about to undertake is as important as the journey itself.

Step 2: Prioritisation of strategic goals and strategic measures

Strategy is all about choices. We now need to identify those goals which need attention during the next planning cycle (usually 12–18 months) – the 20 per cent that will cause an 80 per cent result. It is not possible to focus simultaneously on all the strategic goals defined in each perspective of the strategy map. Strategic focus is the name of the game during this phase. As there is progress over a period of time, the focus can change. It is however necessary to focus attention and energy on those higher-leverage or lead goals that will enhance the execution of the strategy in significant ways. These goals present those priority focuses that will **START** the realisation of the strategy. Use the following criteria to choose between the different goals:

- impact on business results
- driver logic (what causes what)
- critical to realising strategic architecture/business model

The leadership team should choose two to three goals in each of the perspectives except the financial, because the financial perspective is a lag in totality. Any acceptable, visibly democratic process can be used to reach consensus.

How many goals? The practical concept of seven plus or minus two applies. Individuals in strategy teams can only concentrate comfortably on an average of six to nine concepts at a time. The number of goals should therefore be kept in this range. Highlight these goals on the strategy map. Figure 5.21 gives an example of such a "critical path" or "strategic skeleton" in the strategy map.

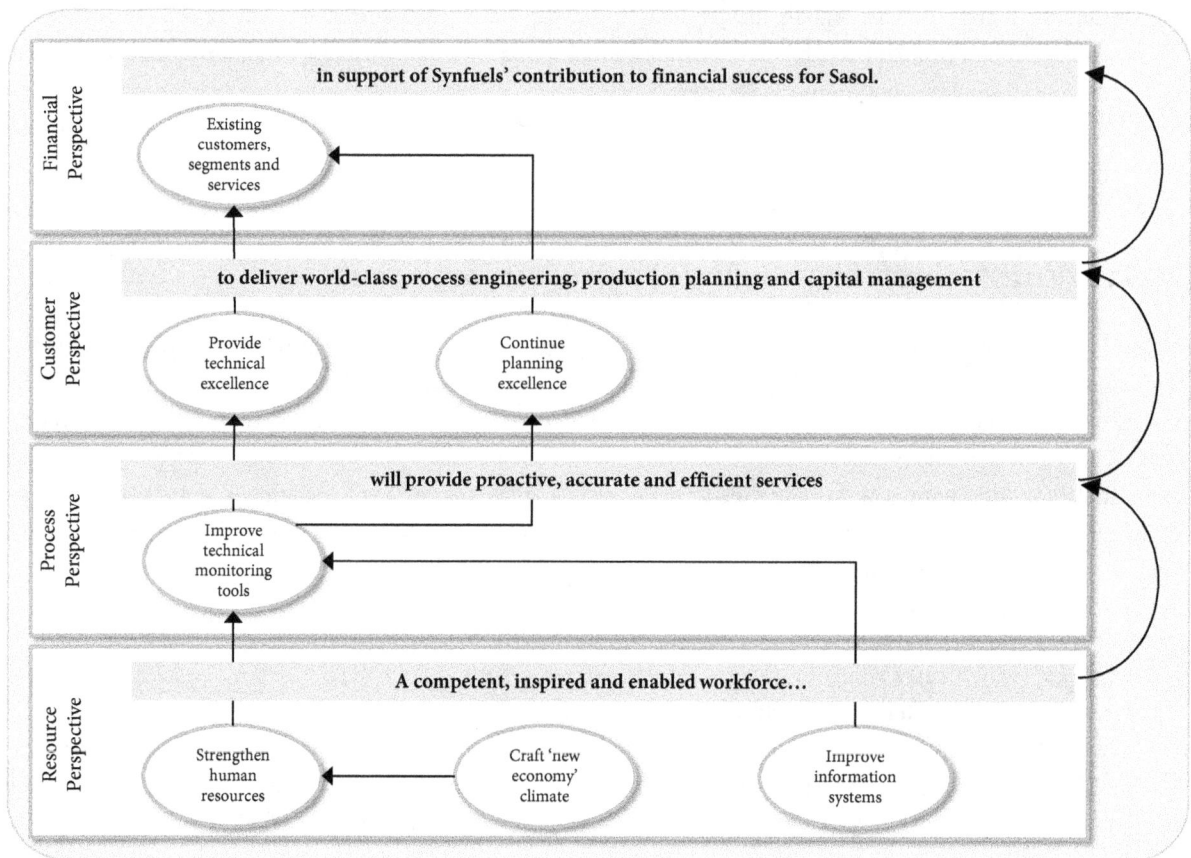

Figure 5.21: Strategic "skeleton" in the strategy map

Notes for developing strategic measurements

Timely information can prevent disaster, but news that is late is worse than bad news. The point is that we need measures on a strategic level to inform us whether we are on track toward implementing our strategy (or not). This is much like developing a strategic "dashboard" of important indicators of success. It is also important that we develop a comprehensive dashboard covering lead and lag elements in our strategy map, enabling us to get early warning signals if things do not go as planned.

Strategic measures should therefore give an indication of progress towards the realisation of chosen strategic focuses for the next planning cycle. These measures are developed around the chosen strategic goals in the strategy map.

Strategic measures should:

- be unambiguous.
- be comprehensive in covering the domain of the strategic goal and consistent with the logic in the strategy map.
- be descriptive and indicative of the trend as it develops over time (behaviour-over-time graph).
- make use of a few meaningful measures rather than many. In this case less is more.
- include a desired performance level/target.

- recommend the frequency of measurement.

Key questions:

- What will be the one measure, existing or new, that will give the best indication of performance around this goal?
- What efforts are necessary to create and operationalise the measures? (How will these measures be embedded in our organisational processes?)
- The success indicators related to each strategic goal should give important clues to the type of measurement required.

Table 5.1 is an example of completed strategic measures.

Table 5.1: Strategic measures[20]

Theme	Strategic Goals	Measures
Financial Perspective		
Efficiency and effectiveness of management of the Authority	Optimise levies collection and related income	1. % of growth per year 2. Amount of unpaid levy 3. Amount of bad debt 4. Number of entities owing levies 5. Average amount owed per institution
	Increase other income	1. % of growth per period 2. Increase in number of sources
	Maintain strict financial control	1. % and amount of deficit/surplus 2. Variance between budgeted and actual 3. Amount of unplanned expenditure
	Reduce operational cost	1. Increase/decrease in overall expenditure 2. Overall cost against actual performance/ results
Customer Perspective		
Key stakeholders relationship	Build a productive relationship with key stakeholders	1. Attendance to meetings and other forms of engagement 2. Value of feedback/correspondence received from stakeholders 3. Results of stakeholders' survey
	Give sound advice to the minister	1. Number of pre-emptive initiatives 2. Promptness on attending to follow-up minister requests
	Amicably resolve all consumer complaints	1. Number of unresolved complaints 2. Results of consumers' surveys
Consumer literacy	Improve the financial literacy level of consumers	1. Consumer survey results 2. Number of related complaints submitted
Internal Perspective		
Effectiveness of the regulatory framework	To develop an efficient and effective regulatory framework	1. Number of issues raised not covered by the framework. 2. Number of requested intervention in reviewing the framework

Theme	Strategic Goals	Measures
Availability of regulatory data and stats	Ensure availability of accurate data and statistics	1. Sources of accurate data and stats 2. Turnaround time in addressing related requests 3. Resources utilised per related request
Operational efficiency	Improve operational efficiency	1. % of improvement in efficiency on processes 2. Turnaround time of major processes 3. Accuracy of end results (number of process instances repeated) 4. Ratio of performance to resources utilisation
Consumer literacy	Develop and execute effective consumer education plan	1. Existence of an effective plan 2. Number of initiatives successfully carried out as per plan 3. Results of impact assessment on literacy level of consumers
Resources Perspective		
Availability of appropriate Information Systems (ISs)	Develop and maintain required ISs	1. % improvement in efficiency caused by ISs. 2. Number and nature of required but unavailable ISs 3. Cost benefit analysis results on deployed ISs
Required talent and skills	Acquire and retain required skills	1. Staff turnover 2. Average number of vacant key positions 3. Staff survey results 4. Number of resignations from key positions per given period 5. Number of eligible applications received per key position
Performance culture	Create a performance oriented culture	1. Employee performance oriented index results 2. Number and nature of performance related complaints from managers and other employees 3. Overall organisational performance per given period 4. Number of performers below expected level per given period

Template for developing strategic measurements

Measurement is a continuous learning process – the results of the measurement create feedback that creates the base for new actions and initiatives and even new measures where necessary.

The process for determining strategic measures can be extended to set targets; see Table 5.2.

NOTE: *The key question is: What performance levels/targets can be set to bring about radical improvements?*

Table 5.2: Extending strategic measures into target-setting[21]

CORPORATE SCORECARD			
Theme	**Strategic Goals**	**Indicators**	**Target for year xyz**
Financial Perspective			
Efficiency and effectiveness of management of the Authority **(Weight: 25%)**	Optimise levies collection and related income	1. % of growth per year 2. Amount of unpaid/ outstanding levy 3. Amount of bad debt 4. Number of entities owing levies 5. Average amount owed per institution	1. 5% overall 2. To be reduced by 60% 3. Reduced by at least 30% 4. Reduced to less than 2% of all registered entities 5. To be reduced at least by 50% of the previous year
	Increase other income	1. % of growth per year 2. Increase in number of sources	1. Increase by at least 5% 2. Have at least two more sources
	Maintain strict financial control	1. % and amount of deficit/surplus 2. Variance between budgeted and actual 3. Amount of unplanned expenditure	1. Overall to be with ±5% of the budget 2. Variance to be within 5% 3. Less than 2.5% of unplanned expenditure
	Reduce operational cost	1. Increase/decrease in overall expenditure 2. Overall cost against actual performance/ results	1. Decrease expenditure by at least 2% 2. Maintain same proportion between performance and cost incurred
Customer Perspective			
Key stakeholders relationship **(Weight: 15%)**	Build a productive relationship with key stakeholders	1. Attendance to meetings and other forms of engagement 2. Value of feedback/ correspondence received from stakeholders 3. Results of stakeholders survey	1. Increase attendance by 15% overall 2. Increase response by 15% 3. Increase stakeholder satisfaction index by 5%
	Give sound advice to minister	1. Number of pre-emptive initiatives 2. Attending to follow-up minister requests	1. At least one pre-emptive initiative every quarter 2. Reduce response time by 10%
	Amicably resolve all consumer complaints	1. Number of unresolved complaints 2. Results of consumer surveys	1. Resolve all (solvable) complaints by the end of the year 2. Increase consumer satisfaction index by 5%

Theme	Strategic Goals	Indicators	Target for year xyz
Consumer literacy	Improve the financial literacy level of consumers	1. Consumer survey results 2. Number of nonNAMFISA related complaints submitted	1. Increase consumer literacy index by least 5% 2. Reduce irrelevant complaints by 20%
Internal Perspective			
Effectiveness of the regulatory framework **(Weight: 15%)**	To develop an efficient and effective regulatory framework	1. Number of issues raised not covered by the framework. 2. Number of requested intervention in reviewing the framework	1. Reduce such issue by 50% 2. Reduce such interventions by 50%
Availability of regulatory data and stats	Ensure availability of accurate data and statistics	1. Sources of accurate data and stats 2. Turnaround time in addressing related requests 3. Resources utilised per related request	1. Increase data source by at least two units 2. Reduce turnaround time by 25% 3. Reduce resource utilisation per request by 20%
Operational efficiency	Improve operational efficiency	1. % of improvement in efficiency on processes 2. Turnaround time of major processes 3. Accuracy of end results (number of process instances repeated) 4. Ratio of performance to resources utilisation	1. Improve operations efficiency by 20% 2. Reduce overall turnaround time by 10% 3. Reduce repetition of processes by 75% 4. Maintain same ratio between actual performance and resources utilised
Consumer literacy	Develop and execute effective consumer education plan	1. Existence of an effective plan 2. Number of initiatives successfully carried out as per plan 3. Results of impact assessment on literacy level of consumers	1. Draft and approve the plan during the year 2. Execute 90% of planned activities 3. Increase literacy level of consumers by 15%
Resources Perspective			
Availability of appropriate Information Systems (ISs) **(Weight: 15%)**	Develop and maintain required ISs	1. % improvement in efficiency caused by ISs. 2. Number and nature of required but unavailable ISs 3. Cost benefit analysis results on deployed ISs	1. Improve efficiency by 20% using IS 2. Deploy 100% of required and budgeted systems during the years 3. Achieve overall positive benefit against cost of ISs

Theme	Strategic Goals	Indicators	Target for year xyz
Required talent and skills	Acquire and retain required skills	1. Staff turnover 2. Average number of vacant key positions 3. Staff survey results 4. Number of resignations from key positions per given period 5. Number of eligible applications received per key position	1. Reduce turnover by 10% 2. Reduce average vacant position by 50% 3. Increase staff satisfaction index by 20% 4. Reduce number of such resignations by 50% 5. Increase eligible response by 25%
Performance culture	Create a performance oriented culture	1. Employee performance oriented index results 2. Number and nature of performance related complaints from employees 3. Overall organisational performance per given period 4. Number of performers below expected level per given period	1. Increase employee performance oriented index by 20% 2. Decrease such complaints by 75% 3. Increase overall organisation performance by 10% 4. Reduce number of performers below target by 75%

The complexity of the goal should warrant the complexity of the measurement.

Step 3: Developing gap-closing strategic initiatives

The following basic assumption drives this part of the process: The team developing the strategy is in control and able to implement or effect the implementation of the strategic initiatives. A strategic initiative is shorter-term actionable and executable activities aimed at improving the performance of a particular strategic goal. Although shorter-term, strategic initiatives are not day-to-day operational work. In essence these are gap-closing, balancing activities aimed at rectifying nonoptimal or malfunctioning situations.

Initiatives are primarily developed for the prioritised strategic goals, identified during the goal prioritisation process in Step 1. This ensures that the available resources and energy are deployed in the priority areas in the business and not spread too thinly for any major impact.

Speed of execution is always of the essence because it is a possible competitive advantage.

Identify the critical strategic initiatives or projects per goal that will contribute to the achievement of the goal.

Initiatives should be:

- things we can influence **now**
- actions with a high impact (20/80 principle)
- executable in a relatively short timeframe (rarely more than a year)

Start the initiative development process from the bottom of the map. This will ensure that the lead factors are put in place first, to enable subsequent lags.

Template for strategic initiatives

The whole team generates ideas on Post-it notes around essential initiatives to improve the identified goals. Subteams are then given the task of finalising the initiatives per goal based on the inputs received. During this phase the options and choices relevant to specific strategic goals (see Figure 5.2) should also be considered.

The allocation of responsibilities, due dates and measures will ensure that there is no uncertainty about **who should do what** after the planning session is completed. Measurements on this level are standards that will indicate progress with the execution of the strategic initiatives. Due dates are the expected completion dates.

Strategic goal	Strategic initiatives	Responsibility	Due dates	Measurement

NOTE: The strategic initiatives are all related to the prioritised strategic goals. This implies that "business as usual" activities should not be included as initiatives. These (obvious) run-of-the-mill routines will in any case happen and should not clutter the strategic focuses.

> **Effective initiatives are actions that make a difference, actions that create synergy in an organisation and do not work against each other.**

Common traps associated with strategic initiatives development

The trap of "I know" but "I don't do"

The development of initiatives represents those things the leadership team collectively know they should do to bring about change. Due to perfectly normal unconscious and irrational group patterns, it often happen that leadership teams avoid or delay the initiation of change that will cause significant improvements. This is a stall position and can be overcome by being aware of this tendency and by consistently checking with team members whether the proposed action really represents the team's best thinking.

The trap of old paradigms

Another thinking trap in developing initiatives is that it is based on our old paradigms, the way we used to do it, and/or individual personal hobbyhorses and preferences. The challenge is to think fundamentally differently about initiatives that will create a sustainable competitive advantage for the business. It is often more difficult to get rid of old ideas and practices than to get new ones in.

The trap of too little stretch and innovation

After identifying initiatives, evaluate them critically for stretch, innovation and potential for competitive advantage. Only include initiatives the leadership team is serious about and those that will make a difference to customers, other employees and shareholders or that will enhance internal processes. These initiatives are not for show, but for doing.

The trap of agenda confusion

The strategic initiatives described above refer to important strategic high-value issues and can be described as key items on the strategic agenda of the organisation. These might include new strategies to capture high-financial-value opportunities, strategies to prevent value destruction, strategies that contribute to the establishment of new capabilities or strategies that will change the performance pattern on a strategic goal in a significant way. So in general, strategic initiatives are high-value ticket items of a strategic nature which, if successfully executed, will change current performance trends.

The issue around agenda management is as follows: What about the ongoing business-as-usual issues that by nature have a more incremental improvement pattern? There is a need in teams to have sight of their more operational improvement initiatives. It is therefore useful to distinguish between a **strategic agenda** (as described in this chapter) and a **performance improvement agenda** that captures the ongoing effectiveness and efficiency initiatives in the organisation. This distinction facilitates focus and ensures that the strategic agenda is not cluttered with operational enhancement initiatives. It also ensures line of sight for the leadership team on continuous improvement efforts aimed at the strategic goals as defined in the strategy map of the organisation.

Step 4: Resource allocation and mobilisation

With the strategic initiatives completed, the classical management mistake is to think things will happen naturally "because leadership said so". In reality things happen because there is an understanding of why things need to change and what leadership is aiming for. A commitment to change is shown in the allocation of resources (like time, money, people, enthusiasm) to particular strategic initiatives. The budget process should be linked to this phase because the financial implications of strategic initiatives will become visible as the content is executed.

ROI criteria should be applied in all resource allocation decisions. The principle of an internal free market for resources should apply. This implies that a resource is deployed where the best return for that resource is expected. In the case of talent, these resources are allocated not on the basis of where the individuals report but based on their skills and the expected returns for the total business. Capital is allocated on the principle of highest expected returns for the enterprise for the risk involved in a venture/initiative.

One of the best ways to allocate and manage resources is to work in project mode, especially useful in implementing strategic initiatives. This ensures that identified strategic initiatives are planned and executed in an orderly fashion and within a specific time-frame. The following guidelines are useful in the mobilisation of project teams:

- **Find leaders and team members with a reason to believe. Broadcast to the organisation:** "Who wants to be part of this initiative and why?" By matching individual and organisational needs leadership can ensure motivation and increase the possibility of success.

- **Use strategic initiatives as developmental opportunities.** Talent is attracted to places where growth, excitement and challenge are part of the game. Tell people about the range of project challenges and personal development they can expect to encounter as part of the strategic initiatives execution. These opportunities can be used as developmental exposure for talent in the business. Use mentoring principles to pair novice project managers with a project veteran to enhance knowledge transfer and learning.
- **Manage the momentum and enthusiasm.** Life as a project manager revolves around managing unexpected occurrences and making trade-offs. Organise a weekly schedule of updates, discussions and decisions. This weekly rhythm helps to put a premium on fast information and decisive action. We also suggest that all projects are reviewed every 13 weeks (or annual quarter) to check on progress and to decide if continued investment is still necessary.

Step 5: Planning for review

Strategy development and strategy planning should not be seen as a once-off, annual ritual. Strategy needs to be alive, lived and "in our toes". Actions should reflect the intention and priority of strategy and strategic focuses.

It is therefore important to identify practices related to current management processes that need to be changed to reflect the new focuses. This means that leadership needs to think carefully about the types of meeting they have, the items on the agenda and ways of communicating strategic focuses continually and consistently.

The new strategic messages should be packaged and presented in new and innovative ways. Organising the weekly management meeting around the four perspectives of the strategy map is one way of ensuring a continued and balanced focus. Each week of the month a different perspective is discussed in terms of:

- measurement feedback
- initiative progress related to a particular perspective
- market trends

Part of the process of making strategy alive is to develop visual communication materials. These materials should reflect essential parts of the strategy and focuses. The strategy map should also be displayed in areas that are frequently visited by staff, e.g. meeting rooms. Opportunities to report on progress and improvements should be part of the layout. Putting strategy in the communal domain is part of making strategy everyone's business. Providing truthful feedback is part of the continuous learning curve.

Opportunities to reflect should be part of these new work practices. Leadership teams need to reflect more on why things are working than the way they are working. Teams need to move beyond the point of just finding a scapegoat when things do not work out as planned or just accepting excellent performance as a given. When things don't work out as planned, blaming will not solve the problem, nor will endless analyses. Reflective conversation to develop an institutional memory to prevent the business and leadership team from making the same mistakes over and over again in future is essential. On an individual level and collectively in teams, learning through feedback should be part of the new working practice culture. This is a normal part of the execution cycle, especially as part of the change management effort – to be discussed later in this chapter.

Step 6: Translating strategy into operational levels

The next step in the strategy planning and implementation process is to make the information generated in the previous steps accessible to other role players in the strategy execution value chain – all other people in the organisation who can influence the strategy outcomes. Strategy is only meaningful once it has been "localised". This means that it has to be cascaded in such a manner that the local teams feel that they at least participated in sense-making for their local domain challenges.

The outputs of the strategic planning process serve as inputs for other organisational levels to systematically translate them into necessary actions. In this way the strategic outputs of a higher level are used as inputs for the next level.

The strategy map and strategy plans of the total business as developed by the leadership team are used as an input to develop appropriate operational plans on the next levels of organisational accountability. The operational plans of functional or departmental teams are used as input for operational teams. The outputs of operational teams are inputs for individual employees' Key Performance Areas (KPAs) or individual strategic objectives.

In this way the strategy of the business is distributed to all constituencies in an appropriate, interpreted format without ignoring the key strategic focuses relevant for the different operational areas. The number of repetitions of the translation process depends on how many levels of accountability the business has structured for (see Figure 5.22).

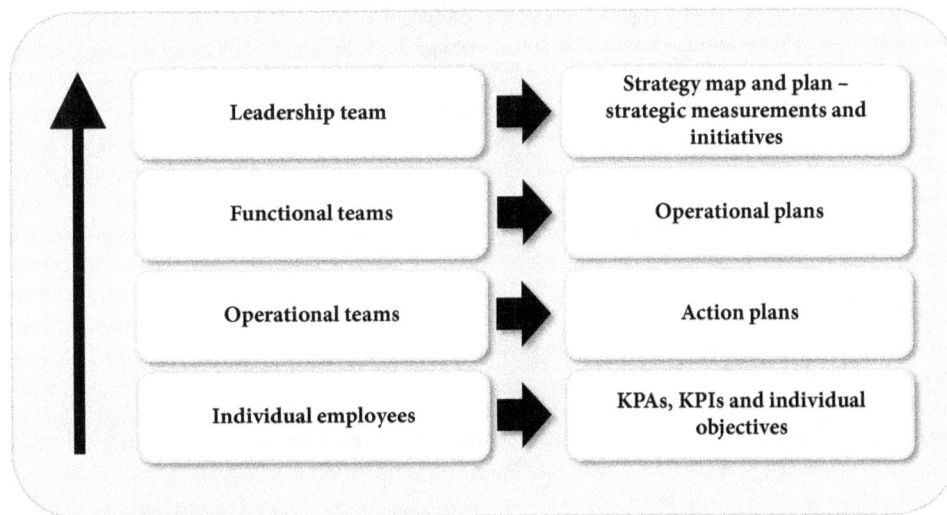

Figure 5.22: Hierarchy of plans

Template for strategy translation to operational levels

Figure 5.23 shows the tool that is used to translate the strategy into the rest of the organisation. The process starts by identifying the teams that report to the senior leadership team members. A strategy interpretation and translation meeting is arranged for each of these teams. The strategy map, strategic measurements and strategic initiatives for priority strategic goals as developed by the leadership team, are shared as an input. The functional or operational team uses the template (Figure 5.23) to develop their response on each of the strategic goals. In other words, a template is completed for each strategic goal that the functional or operational area will make a contribution to. **The**

strategic goals, strategic measurements and strategic initiatives are used as standard inputs for each team on the next levels of organisational accountability. This ensures that strategic effort flows towards the execution of the identified priority strategic goals.

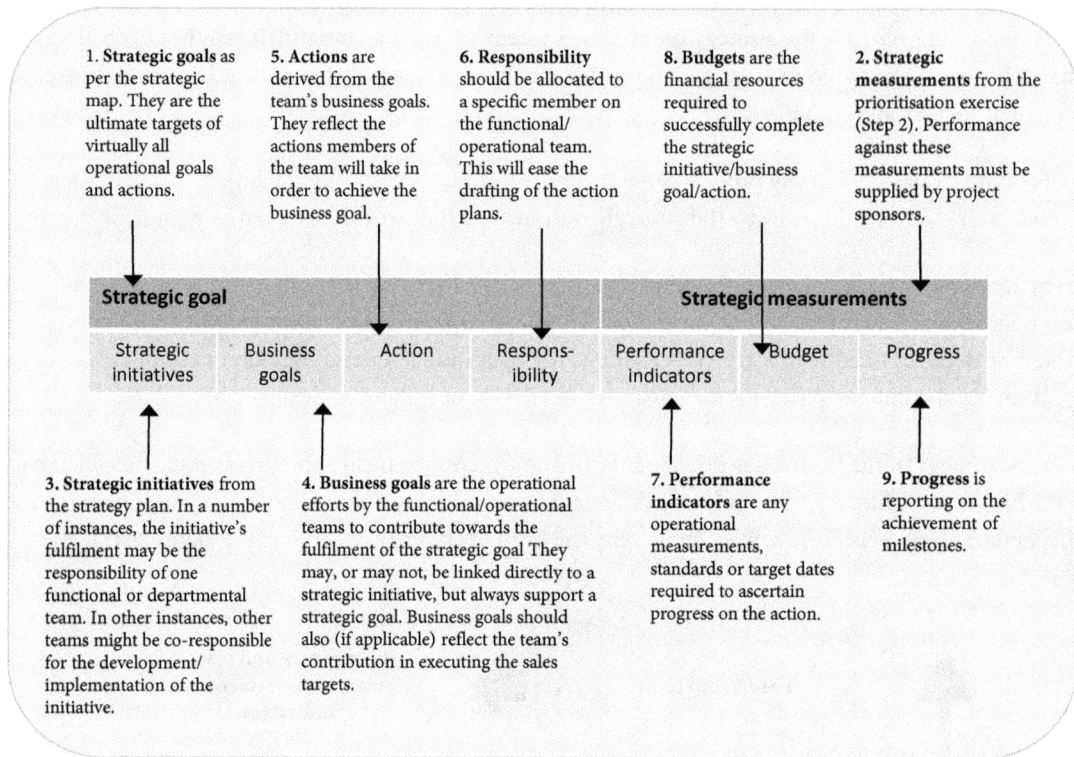

Figure 5.23: Operational planning template for strategy interpretation and translation

The template consists of the following elements:

- Strategic goal: This is the priority strategic goal as identified by the leadership of the business and is indicated on the strategy map.

- Strategic measurements: These are the measurements that will give an indication of change related to the priority strategic goals.

- Strategic initiatives: They are linked to a priority strategic goal and represent the leadership's best thinking on what should be done to make progress towards achieving the specific strategic goal. The functional and operational teams interpret the relevance of this initiative to their area of responsibility and develop their response by formulating a business goal(s).

- Business goals: This is the response of functional and operational teams to how they will contribute to the achievement of a strategic initiative. If a strategic initiative is not directly applicable to a team, but the team identifies contribution areas to support the related strategic goal, it should be documented as part of the business goal. The latter then reflects the team's own effort to bring about progress on the strategic goal.

- Actions: These are the actions the operational or functional teams will take to achieve the related business goal(s).

- Responsibility: This ensures that team members have clarity on their expected contributions as individuals or as members of a task team.
- Performance indicators: These are the qualitative or quantitative measures the team develops to track their progress against the planned actions.
- Budget: This reflects the financial requirements to execute the goal successfully.
- Progress: This space is an ongoing record of comments and feedback on progress as time elapses. This should give an indication on the progress towards goal achievement.

Table 5.3 is an extract of such an exercise for a single strategic goal, in this case, Financial Performance. This extract is for display purposes only.[22]

Table 5.3: Operational planning exercise (extract)

Strategic Objective	Specific Objective	KP Question	KPI	Collection method	Target	FQ	Dysfunctional behaviour	Audience
Productivity Growth	Increase Cash Flow Margin Ratio	What's our ability to translate sales into cash?	Operating CF ÷ Net Sales	Cash and Income Statements	+20%	Annual	Avoidance of difficult sales	Directors
Financial Performance / Reduce cash conversion cycles	Improve deliverable times	How well are we achieving our planned milestones?	Milestone or task completion vs. plan	Report from TL	1 St. Dev 85%	Quarterly	Reduce in documentation quality	Mid Level/ Directors
	Reduce receivables conversion periods	How much could we improve our collect payments cycle?	Days receivable collection	Balance Sheet	- 25%	Quarterly	Harsh customer relations	Directors
	Increase payables conversion period	How well can we negotiate our payment obligations?	Days payables conversion rate	Balance Sheet	+15%	Quarterly	Harsh supplier relations	Directors

Strategy translation: Contracting for individual performance

The last step in the process of strategy planning and implementation is to integrate the strategic responsibilities of individuals with the performance management contracts of the respective employees. This is the point where actions related to strategy are integrated with daily operational work. The building blocks of the process are the following:

- *Key Performance Areas (KPAs):*
  - KPAs are generic categories of value-adding behaviour that are essential to effective performance in a particular role.

- o KPAs are not necessarily derived from or directly linked to the strategic or business goals of the business.
- o KPAs will cover approximately 80–85 per cent of an employee's activities.
- o A maximum of eight KPAs should be assigned to a particular employee (preferably four to six).
- o These KPAs could include one compulsory KPA, namely self-development to foster a culture of continuous learning.
- o KPAs are weighted to reflect the priorities in an individual's role. These weights will change as the priorities of the individual change.
- o Examples of generic KPAs are contribution to income generation; cost/operational budget management; human capital management; and external networking.

- **Key Performance Indicators (KPIs):**
  - o KPIs are measures that indicate to what degree expected performance on the respective KPAs was achieved.
  - o Examples of generic KPIs are ROI, ROE, market share, resource utilisation and leveraging, competence building and retention, morale and climate and positioning of business.

- **Personal objectives**
  - o Personal objectives are the specific output-related actions/projects related to the strategy planning and implementation process and the operationalisation thereof, as required from each individual.
  - o Personal objectives are derived from and are directly linked to the strategic and/or business goals and/or actions of the business as determined during the strategy planning and implementation process.

Table 5.4 is an example of performance contracting for a single strategic goal – in this case, High Performance (extract for display purposes).[23]

Table 5.4: Contracting for performance (extract)

Financial Performance	Strategic objective	Strategic goal	Initiatives	Owner	Due	Milestones	Budget	Test criteria				
								Strategic importance	Profit Potential	Resource requirement	Do-ability	Urgency
Client Satisfaction	Increase client's/ partner's conversion rate	Improve win-win orientated relationship manage-ment	Short presentation for Staff, TL and Directors, in order to expose them to "principled negotiation" and "nonadversarial bargaining". Find supporters and develop monthly workshops.	Another	30/08/12. Weekly update	• Preso attendees • # of registered people for workshops	Regular staff time	H	H	M	H	M

Internal Processes	Innovation	Make use of new relational contracts (IPD) and improve knowledge about it	Put together a presentation with the key findings of your dissertation. Form a group with key interested TL and Directors and search for legal counsel. Present to tentative clients and seek for a pilot project.	Another	15/03/13 Weekly update	• Successful thesis hand over • Finding of legal advisor	Regular staff time	H	H	H	M	L
Learning & development	Culture of high performance	Improve strategy communication and strategic alignment	Prepare a short seminar in order to share, explain and motivate staff members about the use of the BSC. Identify key interested members and develop an implementation team.	Another	30/07/12 Weekly update	• Seminar attendees • # of key interested team members • # of new BSC projects	Regular staff time	H	H	M	H	H

In general ...

- Translation and contracting for individual performance is the final step in the strategy planning and implementation process. This ensures that the key strategic goals of the business are hardwired into the plans of the business on different levels and that the final vital link to individual contributions is clear and formalised. The KPAs, KPIs and personal objectives form the core of a performance management system.
- This final step should always be done with the "big picture" of the context, the strategy map and vision of the business in mind. Individuals should not be allowed to establish their individual contract with **only** their own preferences, paradigms and interests in mind. The question is always: "What is in the best interest of the business in total, given the vision and intent from the strategy map?" This does not mean that there is no room for individual creativity and innovation. These local perspectives are, however, always within the overall strategic intent of the business. Strategy should not be undone at the bottom.
- The outcome of the strategy planning process is strategic alignment. Strategic alignment is a very fragile concept. Therefore leadership needs to reconfirm the strategic priorities of the business continuously to ensure concerted and focused strategic effort.

Practices to increase the speed of strategy implementation

An improvement in the speed of implementation is the result of a process and not an end in itself. This means that specific enabling conditions and support processes will enhance the speed and depth of strategy implementation. Here are some ideas to consider:

- A compelling set of **goals or a vision** is necessary to create constructive tension between the current and future desired strategic position. This creates the capacity in organisations to channel energy towards the realisation of the vision and/or goals. It also directs energy away from power plays and organisational politics towards the vision and strategic goals – away from the narrow needs of individual role players. The process of creating a vision (see chapter 1) and the development of a **strategy map** as described in this chapter unleash positive organisational energy that enhances the probability of faster and more successful implementation.
- The richer the **diversity** of the team that participates in the strategy development and planning process, the more they will be able to proactively identify potential obstacles in the way of implementing the team's ideas. Diverse teams have the ability to challenge assumptions and mental models more easily and to develop solutions that are acceptable and will make sense to a wide variety of stakeholder groupings. This decreases resistance to change and enhances the speed of implementation. Diversity here refers primarily to a diversity of hierarchical organisational levels.
- Frequent and open **feedback** from participants in the strategy implementation process to the leadership team creates a mutual platform for **information sharing**. Eyeball sessions are extremely helpful in clarifying concerns, creating new perspectives and adjusting the plan based on feedback. This interactive strategic conversation enables smooth and fast implementation.
- **Closeness in space** and proximity are beneficial for co-operation and team work. When everyone who interacts on the execution of common goals can connect to everyone else frequently, it builds the implementation capacity positively. This is however not always possible, even though modern communication technology has reduced the problems associated with space and time. A way of mobilising a total organisation towards goal achievement is Large Group Interactive Events (LGIE). A LGIE is a process where all the role players affected by a specific issue – in this case the strategy of the business – get together in the same place and time to co-create shared meaning on the strategy. In this way up to 1 000 people can be mobilised at once.
- **Strategy on one page.** The assumption with the development of a strategy map and balanced scorecard is that it is possible to translate the complexities associated with a strategy. To assist with this conversion process it is helpful to summarise the strategy of the firm on one page. The ability of firms to create simplified representations of their strategy, preferably on a single page, has become the hallmark of informed communication, mass strategy participation and strategy execution (see Figure. 5.24 for a framework to develop a one-page view of the strategy of the organisation).

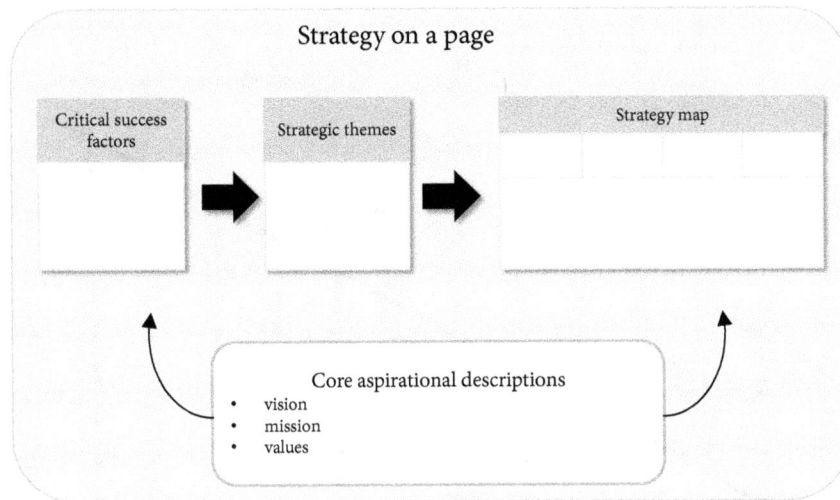

Figure 5.24: Framework for strategy on one page

- **Positive deviance** represents a general optimistic view of the world and a belief in our ability as individuals to make small but potentially impactful contributions. This represents a perspective where we prefer to see the glass as "half-full rather than half-empty". Strategy execution is all about making progress with the practical implementation of our strategy. The mindset with which we engage on this journey is crucial for its success. The field of positive psychology has shown hard evidence that a positive mindset is something that we all can learn to adopt. The effect of this positive stance has far-reaching implications for our ability to cause and contribute to significant progress and movement in the strategic landscape. The following strategy execution routine leverages this standpoint:
- At strategy execution progress reviews, ask participants to talk and share their best experiences with successful implementation of the strategy. This represents "moments of personal greatness" for the participants and emphasises the celebration of successes, rather than spending hours talking about things we do not have like resources, support and systems.
- The next routine is to follow up on these successes by asking team members to talk about and plan how team members can leverage the collective genius and strengths of the team to make strategic success an ongoing reality.
- **Strategy execution cycles** have become shorter and shorter due to the need of leaders to adapt and review strategic progress on a more regular basis. The longer-term planning cycle is still three to five years, but within this planning horizon the best practice is to reflect on progress every 90 to 100 days. In this way the review cycles are shortened to accommodate emerging developments in the strategic landscape of the firm (see Figure 5.25 for a visual representation).

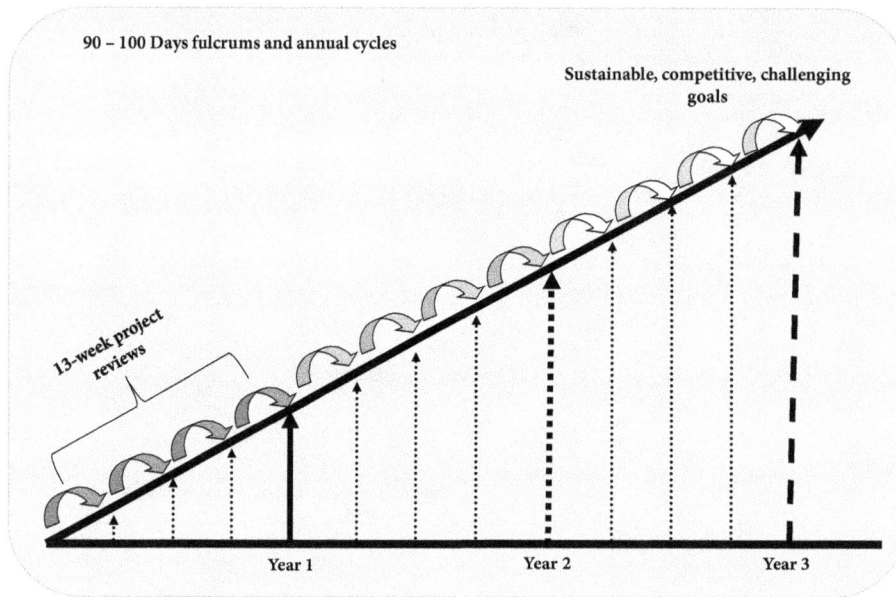

Figure 5.25: Shorter strategy execution review cycles

- **Strategy execution is informed as much by a top-down approach as by a bottom-up approach.** We have stated that strategy execution is informed by the strategic architecture of the firm. This in a way can be seen as a top-down view of the firm. Paradoxically, a bottom-up emergent view of the strategy execution progress is just as important. This is achieved by lowering the centre of gravity of the strategic dialogue process to facilitate reviews from "the ground" (see Figure 5.26).

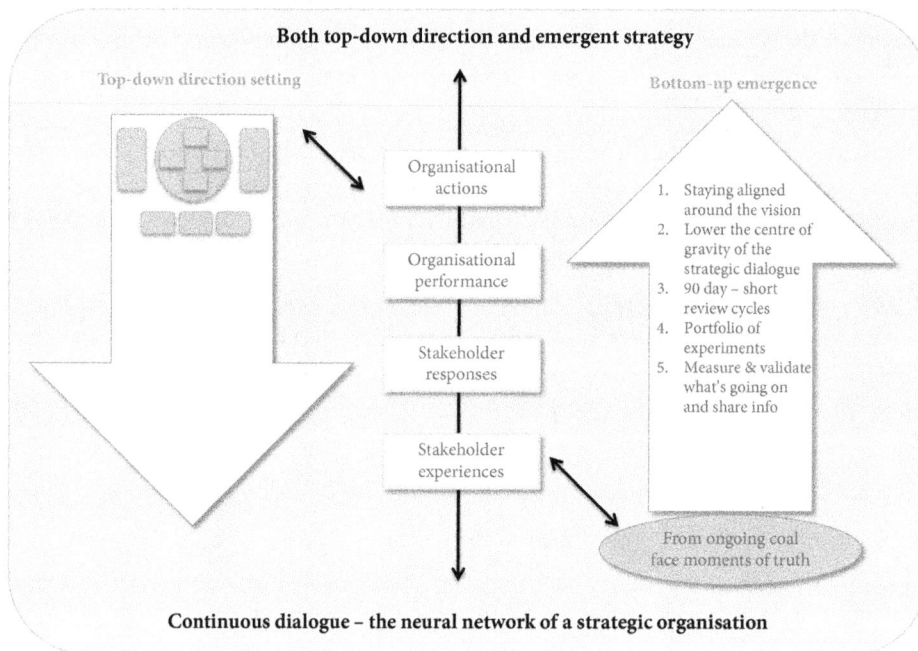

Figure 5.26: Strategy execution informed by both top-down and bottom-up perspectives

The paradox of implementation

This chapter put forward the argument of implementation of strategic choices as a competitive advantage for companies. Although implementation is of the utmost importance, it is necessary to warn against a blind orientation. Implementation of strategic plans can never be done in a vacuum. Feedback from the competitive landscape and from the internal implementation teams should always be part of the process. This implies that we should not be rigid about the implementation of strategic plans. They have to be informed and reshaped continuously as new information is fed back from the external and internal landscapes – an openness to market changes and conditions that can influence the appropriateness of plans. What we clearly cannot advocate is the mindless implementation of plans and strategies that seemed like a very good or even excellent idea at a specific point in time.

The excellent implementation of wrong ideas will create organisational death sooner and more efficiently. This is the phenomenon of a vicious reinforcing loop in action.

The dynamic world of today requires leaders to execute their plans and ideas skilfully, without losing sight of a changing world and markets. The paradox is clear: the more we focus on strategy implementation, the more we should open ourselves (and our organisations) to feedback on a continuous basis.

Summary of strategy execution and implementation

The challenge we all face in our personal and business lives is to move away from good intentions to real action and the implementation of our best ideas. It is good to have a business strategy, but it is much better for the business to empower all employees to actively contribute to the execution of the strategy. In this way the organisation becomes focused on its strategy.

Change management (or change enablement) is the name we give to the many organisational activities aimed at empowering all employees to contribute their best to making the strategy a reality.

CHANGE MANAGEMENT/CHANGE ENABLEMENT

In this section of the chapter we cover the important organisational work required to enable people to change. If we fail at this, all the work we have done up to now is for naught.

And many companies do fail at this. Mike Hammer – the father of organisational re-engineering – estimated[24] that somewhere between 50 per cent and 70 per cent of change efforts fail. People resist change actively – by doing what they know they should not – and passively – by not doing what they know they should.

Why?

Because too many leaders – under the influence of simplistic marketing and public relations thinking frames – view change management as merely sugar-coating the unpalatable. Traditional "sticks" and "carrots" get most attention and become the all-important "wrapping" that must conceal the banal truth that this is just another change for the sake of it, rather than a carefully thought-through response to the current organisational reality.

When leaders say: "we need to stir things up around here" they are usually concocting a smokescreen for some political reshuffling of deckchairs on the Titanic, or they are spinelessly bowing to some arbitrary demand from shareholders. Blaming impersonal "market forces" for change has never convinced other employees of the benefits of changing perfectly adequate working practices.

The following change management practices reinforce the top-down idea that a chosen senior few have decided and the rest of us must just execute slavishly:

Project plans

A proper project plan is a prerequisite for the project team, who have to manage the change, but means little (if anything) to the people in the client system who have to implement the change. At best, the project plan is an instrument to remind them **when** they are going to be in trouble about **what**.

New/updated policies

Managers who have to ensure that behaviour conforms to a predictable (i.e. minimum) standard require policies, but they mean little to people who have to do the work. Everyone knows that to do your job well, you have to ignore obstructive policies; in other words, you have to find creative shortcuts and better ways of doing things. Policies are merely there to give your manager an excuse to discipline you if he or she doesn't like you anymore.

Newsletters

Well-designed newsletters are a useful repository for the decisions the project team and management have taken. They also serve the purpose of allowing the project team and management to say: "But we told you so".

People who have to do the (extra) work caused by the project know that if they read all the newsletters they will end up reading the whole day and get fired for not doing their job. However, newsletters often have interesting information like which jobs will be lost because of the project and which undeserving person will be promoted as a result of it.

Surveys

Well-designed surveys give programme management insight into how well people are tolerating the change. It also sets up a scoreboard allowing departments (and project teams) to compete with one another.

People being surveyed know that they can tick any box, because there is no feedback or action regardless of the outcome. So they usually tick somewhere in the middle and no one has to do anything. Sometimes, however, surveys come in handy to show general displeasure – for instance, after annual increases.

Road shows

Road shows help the project team and management to handle of the burden of communicating in only a few sessions. The project team and management can now truthfully say: "But we told you so".

Managers also get a chance to practise their presentation skills.

People who have to do the (extra) work caused by the project know that the road show helps project and organisational management feel they have **really** communicated (fancy slides and all).

But being told what to do **very clearly** unfortunately does not motivate other staff members; it merely reinforces the top-down nature of the exercise.

There is usually a coffee break, however, where the braver staff members can voice their concerns about the project. Unfortunately the manager cannot deal with these because he or she is on their way to the next road show session.

The change enablement plan

By combining all the change management activities discussed so far (and some extra ones the consulting house picked up in another country – therefore a **world** best-practice), the project and management team use them all, rather than just one or two.

People who have to do the (extra) work caused by the project cannot ignore or hide from the change management activities. At a maximum, people feel that the organisation provides them with a clear outline of the proposed changes and that the road show presenter is serious about it (for now, because next year the same job title will be just as serious about a new set of instructions for the troops).

Application tool

You will have noticed that these tools are not judged as very useful. You might disagree.

How often do we use this?	What is good about it?	What are its limitations?
Project plans		
New/updated policies		
Newsletters		
Surveys		
Road shows		
Change enablement plan (sometimes as part of the project plan)		

What other instruments/processes do you use?

Description of tool	What is good about it?	What are its limitations?

If the above change interventions are our standard response to planned changes, it is no wonder that so many change efforts fail. Donald Sull, Rebecca Homkes and Charles Sull (2015) report[25] on over 40 change programmes accompanying new strategies over a period of nine years, as well as a survey of around 8 000 managers in over 250 companies. In their article they explode the following myths:

Myth 1: *Alignment equals execution*: Most companies followed the alignment processes described earlier in this chapter and almost all the managers surveyed had a clear and specific list of activities they were responsible for – in their silo. They trusted themselves, their immediate managers and their manager's manager to deliver on promises, but they did not trust their peers (or their manager's peers) to deliver. What was lacking was alignment between organisational units, strategic business units (SBUs) and other organisational silos. In other words, the most senior leaders – and in particular the most senior leader, the CEO – neglected the work of co-ordinating the efforts of the most senior team, leaving power barons in charge of their fiefdoms where they could vie for the top job by stabbing each other in the back. Or, if not actively undermining the efforts of other silos, at least not actively supporting them. To remedy this, the most senior executives have to establish and actively manage coordination across departments and create proper tracking mechanisms of performance commitments (promises) to turn the new strategy into a reality. The CEO should keep track of conflicts and problems between SBUs and solve them. This task cannot be delegated to a project office.

In summary, we do well at cascading performance goals **down** the organisation, but fail to do the same **across**.

Myth 2: *Execution means sticking to the plan*: Most plans don't survive contact with reality. The planned actions are already somewhat out of date when they are typed and formalised. Therefore plans must be updated regularly to take account of changed circumstances. And, of course, the updates should be coordinated across organisational units to combat the perceptions that people are not delivering on their promises. Co-ordination is especially important if it happens with units outside organisational boundaries – with stakeholders such as suppliers, shareholders and the communities we serve. Everyone needs to be aware of changes to the plan and performance contracts have to be updated and renegotiated as required.

This issue was also discussed earlier under "the paradox of implementation" – the more we focus on implementation, the more we should open ourselves (and our organisations) to feedback on a continuous basis. And we should especially be on the lookout for feedback that points to the fact that our plan was not absolutely the best one we could possibly make. Every plan can be improved over time.

Changes to the plan invariably imply changes to resource allocations, and most companies don't do this well – especially when it comes to shifting people to where they are most required, the survey found.

Figures 5.27 and 5.28 throw some light on this organisational dilemma.

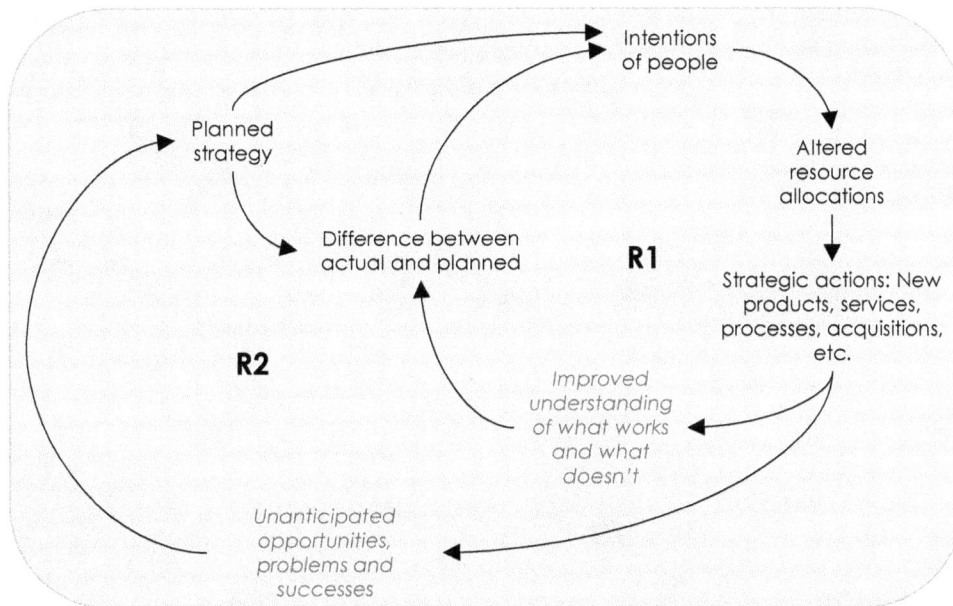

*Figure 5.27: Executing the plan (R1) **and** changing it for the unanticipated and unforeseen (R2)*

Of course, it is no secret that we have to do everything in our power to execute the strategy – or the promise we made to our stakeholders. But changing circumstances often require changes to plans in order to still keep this promise. A word of warning though – beware of people who change plans because they can see they will miss contacted targets and then blame the very changes they instituted for their underperformance!

Figure 5.28 explains how executives ensure that planned changes happen.

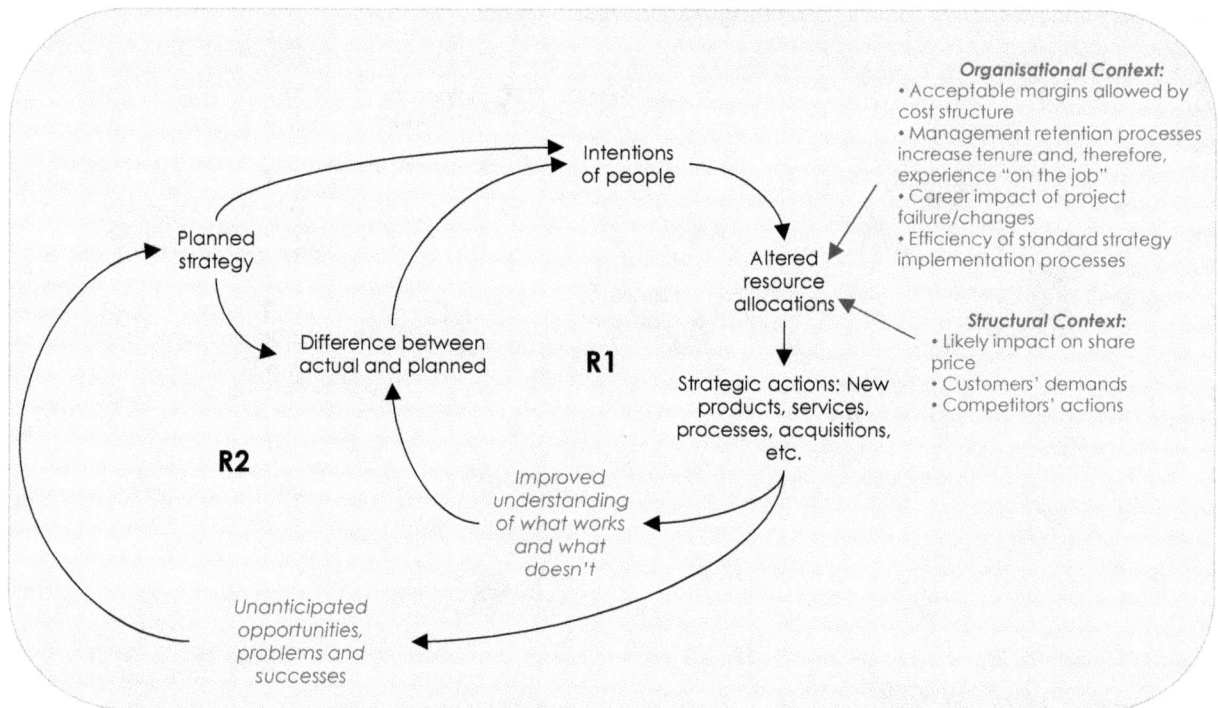

Figure 5.28: How to "leverage" strategy (A short course for executives)

Figure 5.28 shows that altered resource allocations are the most important leverages that executives must use to ensure strategy execution. This makes it all the more shocking that in the survey 9 out of 10 managers believed that some of their organisation's major strategies would fail due to lack of resources. Resource allocation is a senior leadership responsibility and, with interunit coordination, their major contribution to the success of strategy execution.

Myth 3: *Communication equals understanding*: Many executives believe that relentless communication is their key contribution to execution success, as they rush from one road show to another. The survey, however, could not find anyone who could list more than two out of five of the current corporate strategic objectives. One of the reasons is that strategy communication sessions are often cluttered with other information (the culture-study outcomes, new procedures and other changes unrelated to strategy). Another problem is delivering a consistent message to all stakeholders and not confusing strategic information with marketing "spin". Using the strategy map, referring to it frequently and keeping it updated to reflect changes are easy ways of helping everyone to understand the strategy and its context.

Myth 4: *Execution should be driven from the top*: We have referred to the crucial role of the CEO and other senior leaders, but this does not imply that change happens from the top down. Larry Bossidy, when he was CEO of AlliedSignal, got far more involved than most CEOs – personally doing performance reviews with managers several levels down, etc. – and the effect showed in their results, as he describes in his book *Execution*.[26] But when he left "the discipline of execution … unravelled". Concentrating power at the top may work in the (very) short term, but it is seldom a sustainable way to performance. In a complex – even international – organisation, decisions have to be made by virtually everyone. Decisions like "shall we exploit this opportunity now or wait until we have coordinated with our counterparts in other departments?" can only be made where and when they occur and by the team that is there. No doubt the organisation has many leaders, formal and informal, and, in fact, everyone is a leader at some stage. Sull, Homkes and Sull put it best when they say:

> "In large, complex organisations, execution lives and dies with a group we call "distributed leaders," which includes not only middle managers who run critical businesses and functions but also technical and domain experts who occupy key spots in the informal networks that get things done. The vast majority of these leaders try to do the right thing. Eight out of 10 in our sample say they are committed to doing their best to execute the strategy, even when they would like more clarity on what the strategy is."[27]

Strategy should therefore be driven from the middle, but guided from the top. Senior executives should know who the informal and formal leaders are whom people naturally follow. These influencers should receive special attention and their support enlisted to make change efforts succeed. Not everyone wants to be, or needs to be, a manager. Often the very fact that they are not enslaved by their fringe benefits and weighed down by their bonuses makes people more credible. These "champions" of change need to understand the strategic context and the strategic goals of the organisation. Their support is crucial for the successful execution of strategy, therefore a simple road show will not do. When we survey these middle management and informal leaders we found that their efforts are often hampered by the C-suite who, according to more than a third of distributed leaders, participate in "factions within the C-suite and that executives there focus on their own agendas rather than on what is best for the company".[28] What is crucial for senior executives in these cases – as in most – is not what they say, but what they do.

Myth 5: A performance culture drives execution: Most of the organisations surveyed had a fair to very robust performance culture. What is less useful is if **only past performance** is recognised, as it is in the annual salary review. Failure to recognise behaviours that **cause** good performance (like agility, the ability to experiment despite the possibility of failure, the ability to change plans to capitalise on unexpected opportunities, teamwork, ambition, etc.) need to be rewarded as well. These aspects are seldom highlighted in the company values list or the performance appraisal. Too often performance is measured by what can be counted – usually monetary outcomes – and aspects more difficult to measure are overlooked.

Seasoned change managers will always mention culture as one of the intractable problems associated with resistance to change, and we look in more detail at this aspect in the next section.

Application tool

Which of the above myths are still unexplored in your organisation?

Myth	How do I recognise it?	What can I do to change it?
Alignment equals execution.		
Execution means sticking to the plan.		
Communication equals understanding.		
Execution should be driven from the top.		
A performance culture drives execution.		

Understanding the paradoxes of culture

More often than not, executive plans crash into culture, invariably coming second. Culture always wins in the end. Executives come and go, even owners come and go, but culture stays.

The answer to why culture is so overpowering is that it consists of a series of interlocking paradoxes. Remember, a paradox consists of opposing terms; both are true, neither is wrong, therefore they are both right! It is, however natural that every one of us, every organisation, region, ethnic group and even country, prefers one side of the paradox to the other.

There are many ways to explain this (and many models), but we prefer the work done by Fons Trompenaars and Charles Hampden-Turner[29] (see Figure 5.29) who developed a framework for cross-cultural communication applied to general business and management. This involved a large-scale survey of 8 841 managers and other employees from 43 countries.

Dimensions of culture	AND other dimensions of culture	Essential question
Universalism (we value consistency)	Particularism (we value flexibility)	What is more important — rules or relationships?
Individualism (we value individual creativity)	Communitarianism (we value teamwork)	Do we function best as individuals, or as a group?
Specific (we value analysis, low attention to context)	Diffuse (we value synthesis, high attention to context)	Involvement, commitment, context. How separate do we keep our private and working lives (and others like religious, political, etc.)?
Neutral (we value control)	Affective (we value passion)	Do we display our emotions?
Achievement (we are egalitarian, doing-oriented)	Ascription (we are hierarchical, being-oriented)	Do we have to prove ourselves to get status, or is it given to us (birth, position, etc.)?
Synchronous time (we value the synchronic)	Sequential time (we value the sequential)	Do we do things one at a time or several things at once?
Internal (we value push — an internal locus of control))	External (we value pull — an external locus of control)	Strategy and Planning — Do we control our environment or are we controlled by it?

Figure 5.29 The paradoxes of culture (... both/and ...)

Every social system (person, group, region, country, etc.) can place them/itself on a continuum of, for instance, universalism and particularism. No culture is ever in the middle; it will always choose one side or the other. A short description of each of the dimensions follows in Table 5.5.

Table 5.5: Short overview of (some) important dimensions of culture

Dimension	Description	Favourite Strategies (How it shows up in the workplace)
Universalism Typical universalist cultures include the U.S., Canada, the U.K, the Netherlands, Germany, Scandinavia, New Zealand, Australia, and Switzerland.	Laws, rules, values, and obligations are important. Deal fairly with people based on these rules, but rules come before relationships.	Help people understand how their work ties into their values and beliefs. Provide clear instructions, processes, and procedures. Keep promises and be consistent. Give people time to make decisions. Use an objective process to make decisions yourself, and explain your decisions if others are involved.
Particularism Typical particularistic cultures include Russia, Latin-America, and China.	Each circumstance, and each relationship, dictates the rules that we live by. Our response to a situation may change, based on what's happening in the moment, and who's involved.	Give people autonomy to make their own decisions. Respect others' needs when you make decisions. Be flexible in how you make decisions. Take time to build relationships and get to know people so that you can better understand their needs. Highlight important rules and policies that need to be followed.
Individualism Typical individualist cultures include the U.S., Canada, the U.K, Scandinavia, New Zealand, Australia, and Switzerland.	We believe in personal freedom and achievement. You make your own decisions, and you must take care of yourself.	Praise and reward individual performance. Give people autonomy to make their own decisions and to use their initiative. Link people's needs with those of the team or enterprise. Allow creativity and learning from mistakes.
Communitarianism Typical communitarian cultures include countries in Latin-America, Africa, and Japan.	The group is more important than the individual because it provides help and safety, in exchange for loyalty. The group always comes before the individual.	Praise and reward group performance. Don't praise individuals publically. Allow people to involve others in decision making. Avoid showing favouritism.
Specific Typical specific cultures include the U.S., the U.K., Switzerland, Germany, Scandinavia, and the Netherlands.	We keep work and personal lives separate and believe that relationships don't have much of an impact on work objectives. Good relationships are important, but people can work together without it.	Be direct and to the point. Focus on people's objectives before you focus on strengthening relationships. Provide clear instructions, processes, and procedures. Allow people to keep their work and home lives separate.
Diffuse Typical diffuse cultures include Argentina, Spain, Russia, India, and China.	There is an overlap between work and personal life. Good relationships are vital to meeting business objectives, and relationships with others are the same, whether at work or meeting socially. We spend time outside work hours with colleagues and clients.	Focus on building a good relationship before you focus on business objectives. Find out as much as you can about the people that you work with and the clients that you do business with. Be prepared to discuss business on social occasions, and to have personal discussions at work. Try to avoid turning down invitations to social functions.

Dimension	Description	Favourite Strategies (How it shows up in the workplace)
Neutral Typical neutral cultures include the U.K., Sweden, the Netherlands, Finland, and Germany.	We make a great effort to control our emotions. Reason influences our actions far more than our feelings. We don't reveal what we're thinking or how we're feeling.	Manage your emotions effectively. Watch that your body language doesn't convey negative emotions. "Stick to the point" in meetings and interactions. Watch people's reactions carefully, as they may be reluctant to show their true emotions.
Emotional Typical emotional cultures include Italy, France, Spain, and countries in Latin-America.	We want to find ways to express our emotions, even spontaneously, at work. In our culture, it's welcome and accepted to show emotion.	Open up to people to build trust and rapport . Use emotion to communicate your objectives. Learn to manage conflict effectively, before it becomes personal. Use positive body language and have a positive attitude .
Achievement Typical achievement cultures include the U.S., Canada, Australia, and Scandinavia.	We believe that you are what you do, and we base your worth accordingly. Our culture values performance, no matter who you are.	Reward and recognise good performance appropriately. Use titles only when relevant. Be a good role model.
Ascription Typical ascription cultures include France, Italy, Japan, and Saudi Arabia.	We believe that you should be valued for who you are. Power, title, and position matter in our culture, and these roles define behaviour.	Use titles, especially when these clarify people's status in an organisation. Show respect to people in authority, especially when challenging decisions and don't "show up" people in authority. Don't let your authority prevent you from performing well in your role.
Sequential Time Typical sequential-time cultures include Germany, the U.K., and the U.S.	We like events to happen in order. We value punctuality, planning (and sticking to our plans), and staying on schedule. We say "Time is money," and we don't appreciate it when our schedule is thrown off.	Focus on one activity or project at a time. Be punctual. Set clear deadlines. Keep to deadlines.
Synchronous Time Typical synchronous-time cultures include Japan, Argentina, and Mexico.	We see the past, present, and future as interwoven periods. We often work on several projects at once, and view plans and commitments as flexible.	Be flexible in how you approach work. Allow people to be flexible on tasks and projects, where possible. Highlight the importance of punctuality and deadlines only if these are key to meeting objectives.
Internal Direction (an internal locus of control) Typical internal-direction cultures include Israel, the U.S., Australia, New Zealand, and the U.K.	We believe that we can control our environment to achieve goals. This includes how we work with teams and within organisations.	Allow people to develop their skills and take control of their learning. Set clear objectives that people agree with. Be open about conflict and disagreement, and allow people to engage in constructive conflict.

Dimension	Description	Favourite Strategies (How it shows up in the workplace)
Outer Direction (an external locus of control) Typical outer-direction cultures include China, Russia, Saudi Arabia and Africa.	We believe our environment, controls us; we must work with our environment to achieve goals. At work or in relationships, we focus our actions on others, and we avoid conflict where possible. We often need reassurance that we're doing a good job.	Provide people with the right resources to do their jobs effectively. Give people direction and regular feedback, and show how their actions are affecting their environment. Reassure people that they're doing a good job. Manage conflict quickly and quietly. Do whatever you can to boost people's confidence. Balance negative and positive feedback. Encourage people to take responsibility for their work.

This is quite detailed, but useful when working with someone (or some group) that has a different profile from our own preferences.

By now you realise that the model could also (maybe more correctly) be drawn as shown in Figure 5.30.

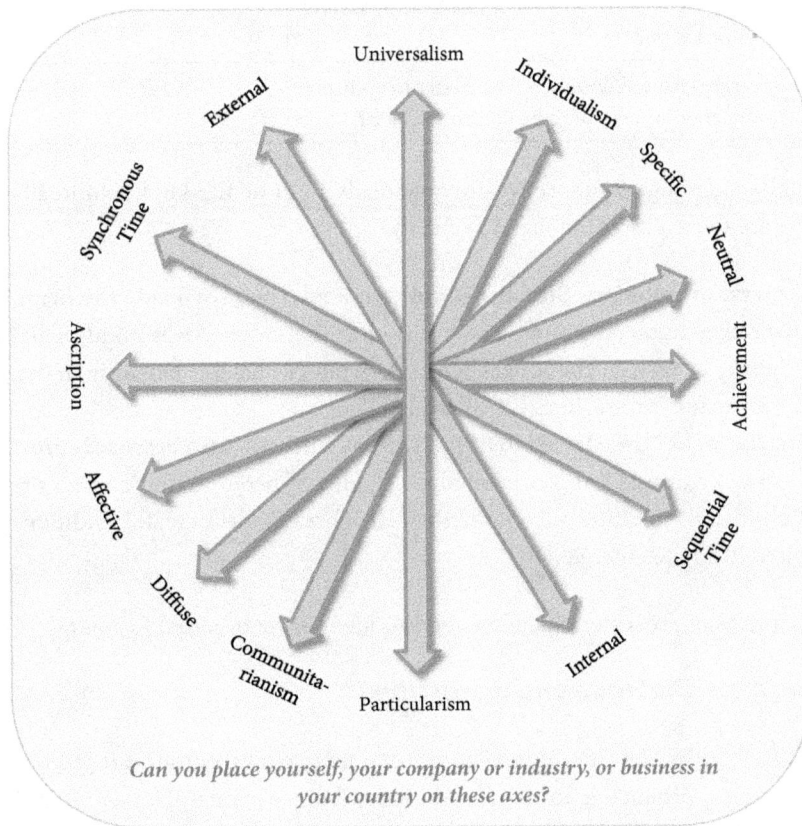

Can you place yourself, your company or industry, or business in your country on these axes?

Figure 5.30: *The paradoxes of culture*

Application tool

What is your own profile? What is your preferred work culture?

Table 5.6: Analysing my preferred work culture

Culture dimension	Key question	What do I prefer? What are the consequences?
Universalism vs Particularism	What is more important for me – rules or relationships?	
Individualism vs Communitarianism	Do I function best on my own, or in a group?	
Specific vs Diffuse	How separate do I prefer to keep my private and working lives (and others like religious, political, etc.)?	
Neutral vs Affective	Do I prefer to display my emotions?	
Achievement vs Ascription	Do I prefer to prove myself to get status, or for it to be given (birth, position, etc.)?	
Sequential Time vs Synchronous Time	Do I prefer to do things one at a time or several things at once?	
Internal vs External locus of control	Strategy and Planning – Do I prefer to control my environment or to be controlled by it?	

With this enhanced understanding of culture we are now ready to untie the knot behind all change management efforts. In essence there are two cultures that need to change:

1. **Breaking the "leadership" mindset: Strategy is only for a few, mainly inside the firm:** From everything we have learnt about strategy implementation so far, it is clear that a top-down mindset and top-down activities are destined for failure, at least in the longer term. So strategy-making has to be more open, inclusive and transparent to be successful. We are, in effect, all leaders.[30]
2. **Strategy execution has to be "translated" to fit the various cultures (also personal cultures) that will execute it:** It is clear that strategy translation processes allow groups of people – some writers refer to "tribes"[31] – to mobilise around an idea of the future – a hope they all share. Leaders create conditions for such an idea or "picture" of a desired future to emerge.

Following are some examples of processes that allow such an idea (or set of ideas) to emerge.

Dialogue and discussion

In the new knowledge economy, conversations are the most important and productive form of work. Knowledge workers discover what they know (and what their colleagues know) through conversation. Conversations (not rank, title, power or position) determine who is "in the loop" and these loops create the shape of the organisation and the products and services it produces. Conversation increases organisational intelligence.

Through conversation knowledge workers discover who their customers are and establish relationships with them. Conversations help us learn what really turns customers on, what is important to them and how they experience doing business with our company.

Conversations also enable us to change and renew our organisation. Companies that practise the art of dialogue are more likely to pick up subtle changes in consumer patterns, more likely to spread this insight rapidly through the organisation and by this fast response, better able to shape the environment in which slower competitors have to play "catch-up" rather than compete.

The LGIE is one such technology where large groups (only limited by the size of the venue – in other words 500 to 1 000 people at a time) can come together to discuss the strategy and how it could be executed.[32]

Face-to-face contact is still the best, but in the modern world discussions occur by using social networks, news and bookmarking, blogs and microblogging, video and photo-sharing, message boards, wikis, virtual reality and social gaming techniques, podcasts and real simple syndication (RSS).

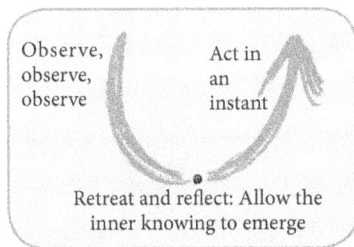

Observe, observe, observe

Act in an instant

Retreat and reflect: Allow the inner knowing to emerge

Initiating change – leveraging your own self

U-procedure and theory U is a change management method to change unproductive patterns of behaviour. It was developed by Friedrich (Fritz) Glasl and Dirk Lemson of the NPI (Netherlands Pedagogical Institute) in 1968[33] and presented systematically from the 1980s. It has been used in organisation development and social development since that time.[34] Following Glasl's special interest in conflict issues, the method has also been explicitly developed to handle the consciousness and process issues associated with relational dynamics and conflict resolution.[35]

Since the early 2000s it has been elaborated as theory U (also called "U" methodology) by C. Otto Scharmer, incorporating also his theories of *presencing* which draw on collaboration between Scharmer and his colleagues Peter Senge, Joseph Jaworski and Betty Sue Flowers.[36]

Otto Scharmer describes the U process as follows:

> "When leaders develop the capacity to come near to that source, they experience the future as if it were "wanting to be born" – an experience called "presencing." That experience often carries with it ideas for meeting challenges and for bringing into being an otherwise impossible future. Theory U shows how that capacity for presencing can be developed. Presencing is a journey: As the diagram illustrates, we move down one side of the U (connecting us to the world that is outside of our institutional bubble) to the bottom of the U (connecting us to the world that emerges from within) and up the other side of the U (bringing forth the new into the world). On that journey, at the bottom of the U, lies an inner gate that requires us to drop everything that isn't essential. This process of letting-go (of our old e.g.o and self) and letting-come (our highest future possibility: our Self) establishes a subtle connection to a deeper source of knowing. The essence of presencing is that these two selves – our current self and our best future Self – meet at the bottom of the U and begin to listen and resonate with each other. Once a group crosses this threshold, nothing remains the same. Individual members and the group as a whole begin to operate with a heightened level of energy and sense of future possibility. Often they then begin to function as an intentional vehicle for an emerging future."[37]

All the techniques discussed so far in this chapter can fit into a scheme demonstrating the general trend in change enablement techniques (Figure 5.31):

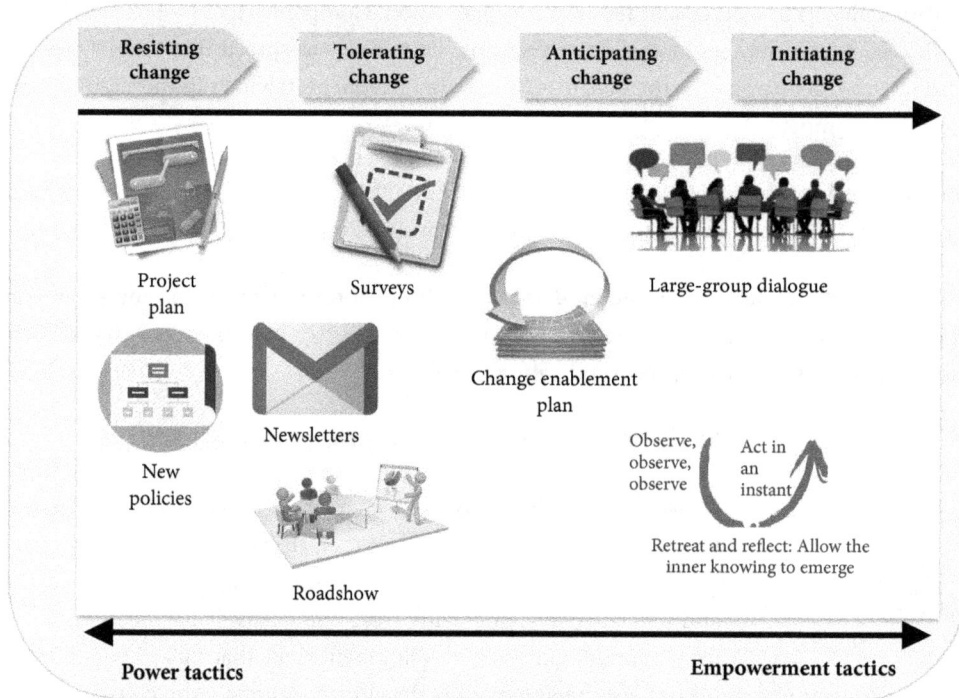

Figure 5.31: Change enablement interventions as power tactics versus empowerment

The interventions represented above are mere examples to illustrate the following principles:

1. Some change management tactics are designed to – and rely on – the power principle: "I am the boss, and you will do it because I say so". Sociopaths – who only understand the world in terms of power relationships (grovel in front of those who have power over you and lord it over those you have power over) – might be comfortable here, but the rest of us resent it and resist it where we can. If the techniques are less blatant (read sugar-coated) it helps us to at least tolerate change.

2. As you move to the right of the graphic, leaders give other employees increasingly more power over their working lives, i.e. empowerment. This helps us to anticipate change, and in those cases where the organisation spends time and money – these development programmes often take three or more years to complete – to really empower us, we initiate change ourselves . When we have found our own "voice", understand what we have to do and see the gap between where we are and where we want to be, we automatically introduce gap-closing initiatives. In these cases executives merely shift resources to initiatives with a better chance for greater bottom-line impact over the required term.

The last remaining question, then, is: What interventions work best? How do I best lead change?

Many of you will be familiar with the work of John Kotter,[38] an influential writer on change leadership. His research, first published in 1995, found that only 30 per cent of change programmes are successful. His famous eight-step process was supposed to remedy that and it became one of the most widely used strategies for change leaders.

When McKinsey & Company asked a similar set of questions in 2009, they discovered that the success rate of change programmes – many using Kotter's eight steps – was still 30 per cent! As Scott Keller and Carolyn Aiken[39] were assessing these results, it dawned on them that change programmes assume that people are rational and that they will respond rationally to change interventions. Change leaders with this assumption would typically apply their own "common sense" intuition and misdirect time and energy, create messages that miss the mark, and experience frustrating unintended consequences. If economics could be transformed by understanding the unconscious and irrational biases of people, Keller and Aiken argued, maybe change enablement could be too!

Here follows a short summary of their – often counter-intuitive – suggestions:

Helping people to create a compelling story

Suggestion 1: **What motivates you doesn't motivate (most of) your employees.** Two types of story are mainly told during change interventions: The first is the "good to great" story along the lines of "Our historical advantage has been eroded by intense competition and changing customer needs; if we change, we can regain our leadership position, becoming the undisputed industry leader and leaving the competition in the dust." The second is the turnaround story along the lines of "We're performing below industry standard and must change dramatically to survive; incremental change is not sufficient – investors will not continue to put money into an underperforming company. We are capable of far more based on our assets, market position, size, skills and loyal staff. We must become a top-quartile performer in our industry." These stories make an MBA business case, but life is not a business case.

There are at least five sources of meaning for humans at work: impact on society, the customer, the company/ shareholder, the working team, and "me" personally. Explaining your business case touches none of these. You only end up shouting ever louder, like some deranged tent-preacher of old, with just as much success – about 30 per cent! The key to a good story, Keller and Aiken claim, is to tell one story that impacts all five of these sources at once. Better still:

Suggestion 2: **You're better off letting them write their own story.** Research indicates that when employees choose for themselves (versus "being told"), they are more committed to the outcome by a factor of almost five to one.[40] Time communicating the message should be dramatically rebalanced towards listening versus telling. Once people are clear about what is expected of them, allow them to come up with those implementation actions they will find useful, practical and doable. Allow them to come up with their own visions for their business units – provided they support the enterprise vision. Allow them to "own" the case for change.

Suggestion 3: **It takes both "+" and "–" to create real energy.** Deficit-based approaches ("solve the problem") to change can create unproductive fatigue and resistance. Constructionist-based approaches ("capture the opportunity") generate more excitement and enthusiasm, but lead to risk-averse, safe solutions. By pursuing both approaches simultaneously, managers can neutralise these downsides and maximise impact in mobilising the organisation. When using the LGIE for strategy discussions, it is normal to spend one-third of the time discussing what is wrong with the current situation to build dissatisfaction (nobody moves from a position if they are satisfied with it); another third is spent on visioning and a possible positive future; and the last third on steps to attain the vision.

Role modelling

Suggestion 4: **Leaders believe they already "are the change."** Most executives have the will and skill to role model, but don't actually know "what" they should change due to their self-serving biases (if they didn't think what they were doing was right, they wouldn't be doing it). This means that even when they change their behaviour it is often superficial, part of an act, convincing no-one. This means that they do not realise that it was their old behaviour patterns that caused the poor/under-performance everyone is now so dissatisfied with. They have to be the change, because their previous behaviour was, to a large extent, the reason why change is now required. Smart use of concrete 360-degree behavioural feedback can break through this barrier.

Leadership development programmes (like the U-process discussed above) are useful tools to ensure real, fundamental changes in executive behaviour, creating more appropriate models for other staff members to emulate.

Suggestion 5: **Influence leaders aren't *that* influential.** It is not enough to invest in a few rather than in many as a way of catalysing desired changes, no matter how appealing the idea is. New research shows social "contagions" depend less on the persuasiveness of "early adopters" and more on how receptive the "society" is to the idea.[41] While influence leaders are important, don't over-invest in them – your effort should also be spent enlisting a new tribe. Sponsors of the change should stay with the project at least until critical mass is obtained – enough people support the change so that it becomes self-sustaining, part of the organisational culture.

Reinforcing mechanisms

Suggestion 6: **Money is the most expensive way to motivate people.** A change programme's objectives should be linked to employee compensation to avoid sending mixed messages, but it does not motivate people. In fact, we have been aware that the following common change tactics have a **negative** impact on motivation/engagement since the 1970s and early 1980s!

- manipulating rewards[42]
- close supervision[43]
- threat of performance appraisal[44]
- deadlines[45]
- competition[46]

It might create **movement** – and a lot of marketing/PR/communication smoke and mirrors – but **no motivation,** no sustained, internal drive. There is a better, and less costly, way. Small, unexpected, inexpensive, **symbolic** rewards have disproportionate effects on employees' motivation during change programmes. Like the CEO of a bank that sent handwritten thank-you notes to everyone who had been with a change programme for six months or more. The reason these small, unexpected rewards have such impact is because employees perceive them as a "social exchange" with the company versus a "market exchange." A social exchange happens when you thank your mother-in-law sincerely for a meal she prepared, whereas a market exchange would occur if you insist on paying for the ingredients and her time (what a truly horrible idea!).

When it comes to change, social norms are not only cheaper than market norms, but often more effective as well. By way of example, consider the American Association of Retired Persons (AARP) which asked some lawyers if they would offer less expensive services to needy retirees, at something like $30 an hour. The lawyers said no. Then the programme manager from AARP had the idea to ask the lawyers if they would offer free services for needy retirees. Overwhelmingly lawyers said yes![47]

Suggestion 7: **A fair process is as important as a fair outcome.** Employees will go against their own self-interest if the situation violates notions they have about fairness and justice. "Ultimatum games" offer a compelling example of the irrational forces at play here. Give a stranger $10. Tell them they must split the money with another stranger in any way they wish. If the person accepts the offer, the money is split. If they reject the offer, no one gets any money. Studies show that if the offer is a $7.50/$2.50 split, more than 95 per cent will reject it, preferring to go home with nothing rather than to see someone "unfairly" receive three times as much as they do.[48] This experiment delivers the same result if the amount to be split is as much as two weeks' wages![49]

A key aspect of a fair process is that it responds to a basic human need. This need relates to our expectation to be valued as a human being, to be respected by others, to be taken seriously and to understand the rationale behind specific decisions. "People are sensitive to the signals conveyed through a company's decision-making processes. Such processes can reveal a company's willingness to trust people and seek their ideas – or they can signal the opposite."[50] The key ingredients of a fair process are: engagement, explanation and expectation clarity. "Fair process builds trust and commitment, trust and commitment produce voluntary cooperation, and voluntary cooperation drives performance, leading people to go beyond the call of duty by sharing their knowledge and applying their creativity."[51]

Careful attention should be paid to achieve a fair process and fair outcomes in making changes to company structures, processes, systems and incentives. In this sense, money is important, but only because it conforms to the subjective value-judgements underlying fairness and justice.

Capability-building

Suggestion 8: **Employees are what they think.** Behaviours drive performance. Mindsets (the thoughts, feelings and beliefs held by employees) drive behaviours. Capability-building should focus on technical skills as well as shifting underlying mindsets that enable the technical skills to be used to their fullest. So it's about the hard stuff **and** the soft stuff.

The root causes of performance are mostly found in the irrational beliefs people hold – their values, their worldviews, the stereotypes they cling to, etc. Search here for the reasons why so many mergers and take-overs go wrong, or at least don't deliver the expected results. A systems thinking approach is invaluable to understanding the logic in this illogic! It can also explain why these irrational ideas persist and continue to drive behaviour, outlasting any and every set of change management interventions. In chapter 1 of the companion book to this one[52] we refer to the work of Daniel Kahneman – specifically system 1 and system 2.

Suggestion 9: **Good intentions aren't enough.** Even with good intentions, it is unlikely employees will apply new skills and mindsets unless the barriers to practice are lowered. Too many leaders, once they have preached the new gospel, don't want to know that it is difficult to implement. Like Stalin, all they want to know is that the new five-year plan is being implemented and that it is working brilliantly – no matter the negative impact on human lives and the destruction of value it causes. It is estimated that, although the first five-year plan turned the Soviet Union into an industrialised country, it was also the primary cause of the famine of 1932, when grain production was 32 per cent below average, which resulted in at least 20 million deaths (the lower estimate!).[53]

A better approach is to use a step-wise programme – simple, basic new skills and mindsets are developed and practised in the field for a couple of months, before more advanced modules (with practical application in between), ending off with a master class, aimed at ironing out difficulties and adjusting unrealistic plans.

These principles can be implemented regardless of the techniques you choose to enable people to implement proposed changes.

Application tool

Use the following grid to evaluate the last change programme you managed (or were associated with) and evaluate it:

Questions to be answered when managing change	Did you answer it adequately? (Yes/No)	What could you have done better?
Goals of change What are the goals of our change? What are the desired behaviours of each group of stakeholders in order to achieve these goals? What do we want them to feel, think, and as a result of that, do, when we communicate with them?		
Risks associated with proposed change What are the external pressures on our organisation? What potential risk events could occur that have a likelihood and consequence which is unacceptable? What positive risk events can we make more likely to improve the environment in which your organisation operates?		
Expected leadership behaviours What leadership behaviours are required? What behaviours do we currently exhibit? What changes to attitude and skill do we need to be successful leaders of the change? Who will not make it as a leader of the change? Can they be effectively bypassed or educated to change, or will they need to go? How do we measure whether leaders are displaying the necessary behaviours?		
Mindset management What is the existing mindset of groups of stakeholders and individuals? Who can be used to support the change? Who needs to be provided an environment which they find motivating to accept and support the change? What elements are needed to create that environment?		
New capabilities What capabilities do our people need? What is the best way of ensuring they learn the new skills required and have the opportunity to transfer that back to the workplace?		
Reinforcing/support What supporting structures do they need in terms of processes and procedures? What will be adequate as reward and/or recognition to make their attitude a positive one?		

ENTERPRISE STRATEGIC PERFORMANCE MONITORING MECHANISMS

Strategic rhythm is an important part of strategy execution success. People in an organisation need to know what is happening when and who is doing what with regards to an ongoing strategy development and execution process. A core departure point is that the annual and rolling budgeting process must be closely aligned and integrated with the annual and multi-term strategy planning practice of an organisation.

To ensure tight alignment between the strategy intent and the budget requires integration on the following key events and plans:

- the creation of an integrated medium-term plan (MTP) with a three-year planning horizon;
- the creation of an integrated short-term plan (STP) with a one-year planning horizon; and
- the monitoring of annual organisation and business unit performance through quarterly performance dialogues (QPDs) focusing on three-monthly progress reviews

An integrated planning approach aims to ensure that business planning across the organisation is goal-driven, fact-based, issues-oriented, value-maximising, consequential and continuous. An integrated strategy and budget planning process reflects the key component parts, as in Figure 5.32.

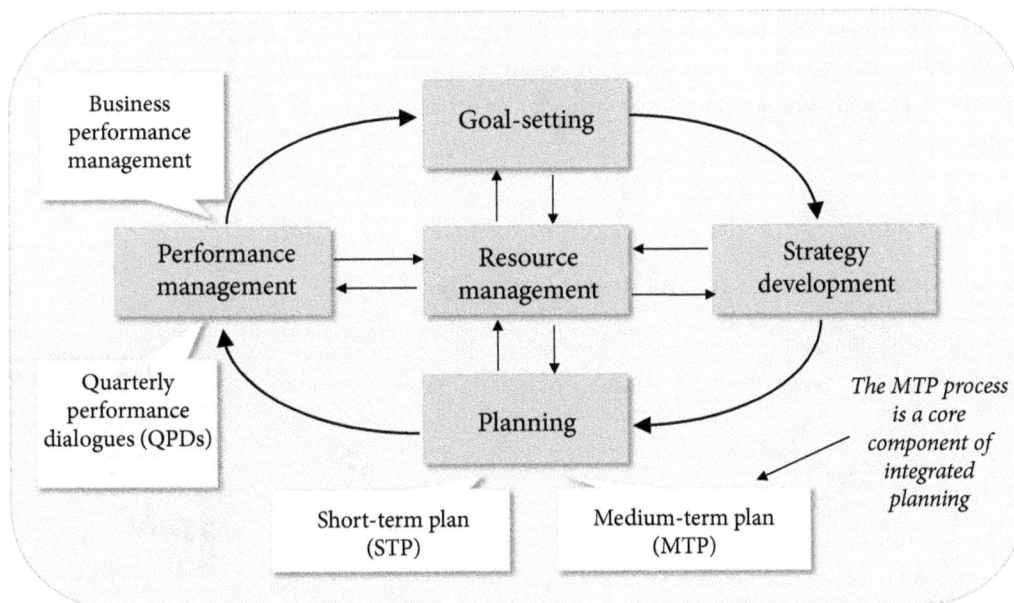

Figure 5.32: Integrated planning and its component parts

The annual flow of activities to facilitate integrated planning broadly fit together over the course of a year, as shown in Figure 5.33.

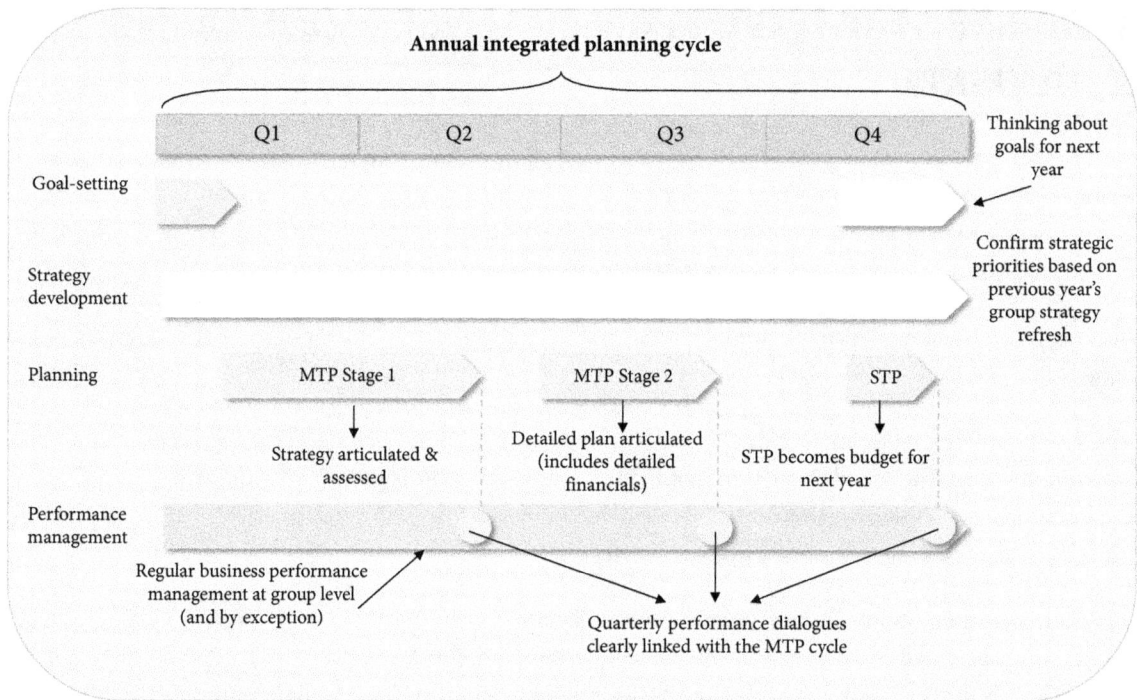

Figure 5.33: Integrated planning timeline

An integrated strategy and budget process ensures that the top strategic goals are funded over time from the strategic budget of the organisation and that operational improvement projects are catered for in the operational budgets. Strategic rhythm is created through an annual calendar that triggers key strategic activities to be formalised at specific points in time.

SUMMARY

Strategy execution implies – at least – the tasks highlighted in Figure 5.34.

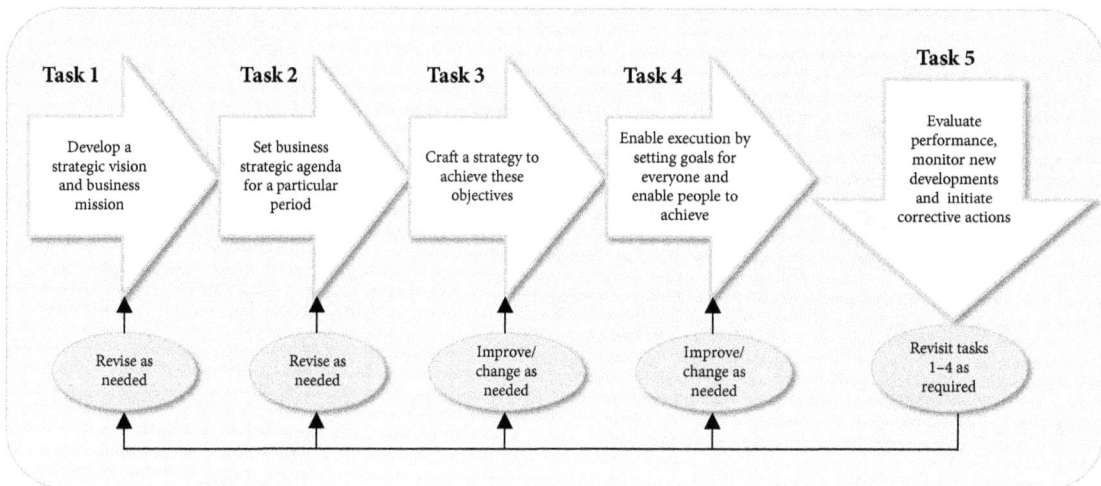

Figure 5.34: The basic tasks required for strategy execution

This chapter highlighted Task 4 of Figure 5.34. The most important element of this figure is the feedback loops from Task 5 to Tasks 1–4, keeping the whole system in touch with the ever-changing reality it operates in. This opens up the gap between what we are aiming for and where we are. Strategy execution is all about gap-closing actions.

We discussed the use of the strategy map in detail and showed many examples of how the balanced scorecard can be used to translate business goals into individual goals and objectives. This means that every job in the organisation can have a "line of sight" to the strategy, explaining the impact of that particular person on the successful implementation of the strategy.

But strategy is not only a rational, intellectual exercise. Change enablement/management highlights activities and principles aimed at touching on the more emotional – and often illogical and counter-intuitive – side of change and resistance to change. The well-known impact of culture and the resistance caused by the very tools we use during change management were also discussed.

With the principles, examples and tips of this chapter in mind, you should be able to translate company goals into individual objectives – the basis of any performance contract – and enable people to execute enterprise strategies.

Chapter 6

Strategy Renewal and Innovation 1: Strategy Innovation

"Business model innovation is not about looking back, because the past indicates little about what is possible in terms of future business models. Business model innovation is not about looking to competitors, since business model innovation is not about copying or benchmarking, but about creating new mechanisms to create value and derive revenues. Rather, business model innovation is about challenging orthodoxies to design original models that meet unsatisfied, new, or hidden customer needs." – Alex Osterwalder & Yves Pigneur[1]

LEARNING OBJECTIVES

This chapter discusses strategy renewal and innovation. The following are discussed in order to guide your understanding and assist your application of strategy renewal and innovation:

- sources of digital disruption across supply and demand
- exponential organisations
- blue ocean strategy
- sources of e-value
- overcoming stall points and decline
- portfolio of experiments and prototypes

INTRODUCTION

The biggest technology transition ever is happening – and it is happening right now. In the digital age of tomorrow, connectivity of devices will skyrocket from about 8 billion today to approximately a trillion in 2030.[2][3] The scale and impact of this digital transition is almost unfathomable. It will transform healthcare. It will transform education. It will transform science. It will transform agriculture, mining and energy. It will transform business, media and cyberspace. These changes will fundamentally transform the way we live our lives, but most of all, they will create immense opportunities – estimated at around $19 trillion in economic value over the next decade.[4]

At the same time, tectonic shifts such as these have another profound consequence – immense disruption is bound to occur. Business models will rise and fall, and the majority of companies will not exist in a meaningful way 10 to 15 years from now;[5] and the disruption is already happening. Of the Fortune 500 companies from 1955, 89 per cent are not on the 2014 list. In the next 10 years, 40 per cent of the S&P 500 companies will be gone. This means that the average lifespan of an S&P 500 company has decreased from 67 years in the 1920s to 15 years, while the average half-life of a business competency has dropped from 30 years in 1984 to five years today.[6] The implication is that businesses need to transform. They need to use technology differently. They need to change their organisational structures. They need to change their cultures and perspectives to be more customer-centric; and they need to concern themselves with speed of innovation, not doing the "right" things for too long, and actively keep reinventing themselves. Otherwise they're going to be disrupted.[7]

Executives know that digital disruption is imminent and this foresight contributes to their pervading fear and unease as disruption might be lurking around the corner. While the digitisation of processes and interfaces itself is a source of worry in the medium term, the more fundamental source of concern is not knowing when or from which direction an effective attack on one's business might come.[8] Outsourced cloud infrastructure, modular technology components and the deep pockets of venture capitalists give start-ups and incumbents alike the means necessary to launch effective and disruptive attacks. With so many possible threats, it is impossible to monitor all the different sources of disruption. Rather than identify **who** the specific disruptors are today and monitoring them (as well as the waves and waves that will follow), businesses instead need to focus on the nature of the disruption. Businesses need to understand the **why**. They need to develop a deeper understanding of the driving forces behind the digital disruption and understand why this disruption is happening.[9] Armed with these insights, instead of merely reacting to disruptors, businesses will be able to pre-empt and preferably even ride a disruptive wave of their own.

The following section illuminates various drivers of disruption. The remainder of this chapter will equip you with perspectives and tools that can be used to drive strategy innovation in an organisation.

SOURCES OF DIGITAL DISRUPTION ACROSS SUPPLY AND DEMAND

Dawson et al.[10] investigated the underlying forces that drives digital disruption from a supply-demand economics perspective, and proposed an array of instances in which businesses might be at risk of being disrupted. The authors noted that these instances can be used as early measures of a business's exposure to a threat, but inversely, they can also serve as indicators of possible opportunities.

Their six sources of digital disruption are shown in Figure 6.1. The figure is an adaptation of the original.[11] The descriptions of the sources of disruption below follow the following sequence: first the three instances reflecting a modest degree of change in supply and demand are discussed, followed by the three instances reflecting an extreme degree of change in supply and demand. Within these two sets the supply orientation is discussed first, then the demand orientation, then the connecting supply and demand orientation.

Extreme degree of change in supply and demand	**RE-IMAGINE BUSINESS SYSTEMS** Creating new means of supply	**CREATE HYPERSCALE PLATFORMS** Connecting supply and demand while blurring industry boundaries	**CREATE NEW VALUE PROPOSITIONS** Serving new (perhaps unrealised) demand	New
Modest degree of change in supply and demand	**UNCONSTRAIN SUPPLY** Unlocking the latent supply that has always existed	**CREATE MULTI-SIDED PLATFORMS** Connecting supply and demand	**UNDISTORT DEMAND** Serving under-served existing demand	Existing
	Supply	Connecting supply & demand	Demand	

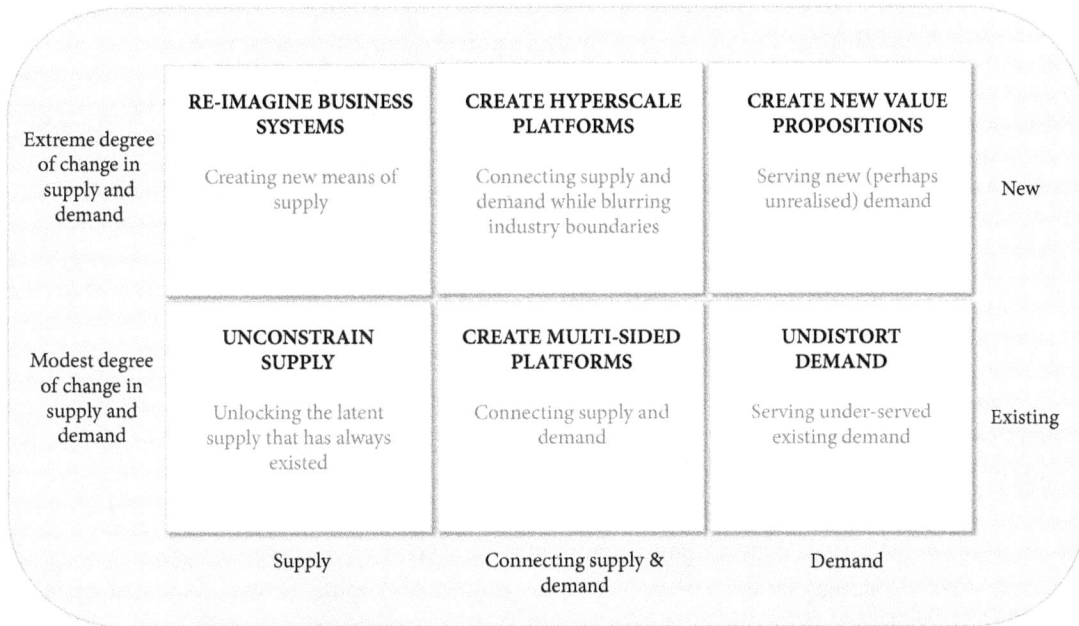

Figure 6.1: Sources of digital disruption across supply and demand

1. **Disruption can stem from digital technologies that unconstrain supply** by increasing its accessibility or by exposing sources of supply that were previously disconnected, underutilised, impossible or uneconomical to access.

- Your business model may be vulnerable if:
  - Customers utilise the offering only partially.
  - Production is inelastic to price.
  - Supply is utilised in a variable or unpredictable way.
  - Fixed or step costs are high.
- Examples include AirBnB (underutilised apartment space) and Uber (underutilised vehicles).
- Mechanisms that allow attackers to disrupt include the pooling of redundant capacity virtually, digitising physical resources or labour, tapping into the sharing economy and making capacity available in smaller increments.

2. **Disruption can stem from digital technologies that undistort demand**. This means that more efficient ways are found to give customers what they have always wanted, exactly how, where and when they want it. This is perhaps done by providing customers with more complete information or unbundling aspects of the offering.

- Your business model may be vulnerable if:
  - Your customers have to cross-subsidise other customers.
  - Your customers have to buy the whole offering to get access to the one part they want.
  - Your customers can't get what they want where and when they want it.
  - Your customers get a user experience that doesn't match global best practices.
- Examples include Spotify (unbundling music from albums into single tracks) and Netflix (binge-watching movies and TV shows).

- Mechanisms that allow attackers to disrupt include making the offering easier to use and more immediate, improving search and filtering tools, streamlining order processes to make them more user-friendly, utilising smart recommendation engines, providing custom-bundled offerings, providing digitally enhanced offerings, and utilising new business models that undercut alternatives while attaining a larger share of the market.

3. **Disruption can stem from digital technologies that create multi-sided platforms**, where the presence of the business as intermediary eases the matching of supply and demand, lowers transaction costs and reduces information asymmetry.

- Your business model may be vulnerable if:
    o Transactions are difficult for customers to conduct.
    o High information asymmetries exist between customers and suppliers.
    o High search costs exist.
    o Fees of existing intermediaries are high.
    o Transactions have long lead times.
- Examples include Wikipedia (unbundling information from volumes of encyclopaedias to searchable web pages created and consumed by the market) and Google Adwords (information-seekers and paying Adword advertisers).
- Mechanisms that allow attackers to disrupt include finding new cheaper and easier ways to connect supply and demand, making available real-time and transparent exchanges of information, disintermediation, automated transaction processing, and increased transparency through search and comparison tools.

4. **Disruption can stem from digital technologies that re-imagine business systems**. Incumbents that have long focused on perfecting their industry value chains are often amazed to discover that new entrants have found a completely different way to make money. Disruptions of this type change how value chains work, transform the scalability of cost structures and enable step-change reductions in both fixed and variable costs, and help turn products into services.

- Your business model may be vulnerable if:
    o Redundant value-chain activities exist (e.g. a high number of handovers or repetitive, nonvalue adding manual work).
    o The industry consists of well-entrenched physical distribution or retail networks.
    o Overall industry margins are higher than those of other industries.
- Examples include Netflix (digitising movies), Dropbox and Amazon Web Services (digital storage space), Walmart and Zara (digitally integrated supply chains).
- Mechanisms that allow attackers to disrupt include changing the supply-side cost structure by automating, virtualising, making use of digital channels or virtualised services that can substitute or reshape physical retail networks, and disintermediation. Disruptors are keen to disrupt as the industry's high margins are attractive, while value-chain inefficiencies invite the removal of incumbent intermediaries in order to go directly to customers.

5. **Disruption can stem from digital technologies that create new and enhanced value propositions.** This element goes beyond improving existing offerings to providing unprecedented functionalities and experiences that customers didn't realise they wanted – but soon wanted to have.

- Your business model may be vulnerable if:
  - Information or social media could greatly enrich your product or service.
  - The offering is physical and not yet digitally "connected".
  - Significant lag time exists between the point of purchase and point of delivery.
  - Customers have to physically go and retrieve the product (for instance insurance, rental cars and groceries).
- Examples include Smartphones (Internet-connected device in one's pocket) and social media (free broadcasting capability).
- Mechanisms that allow attackers to disrupt include improving the connectivity of physical devices, enriching the offering with information, layering social media on top of products and services, extending products and services through digital features, digital or automated distribution approaches, and new delivery and distribution models.

6. **Disruption can stem from digital technologies that create hyperscale platforms**. Hyperscale platforms blur the lines between traditional industries and span various product categories and customer segments. Owners of these platforms have an enhanced opportunity to upsell and cross-sell offerings and also enjoy huge operating advantages in the form of process automation, algorithms and network effects created by the interactions of their millions or billions of users, customers and devices.

- Your business model may be vulnerable if:
  - Existing business models charge customers for information.
  - No single, unified, and integrated set of tools governs the interactions between users and suppliers in an industry.
  - The potential for network effects is high.
- Examples include Apple (iPhone, iMac, iPod and iTunes etc.), Google (Google search, Gmail, Google Maps, YouTube, Android etc.) and Amazon (physical and digital retail, software-as-a-service).
- The mechanisms that allow attackers to disrupt is the development of a hyperscale platform that creates or combats network effects, and which leverages the platform's millions of customers and their information to compete. While a hyperscale platform may provide many advantages to the business, access to the millions of customers may well be one of the greatest advantages. At the same time, users and suppliers allow themselves to be locked into this relationship, partly because of the free access to information that they themselves are given.

These six perspectives clarify the sources of digital disruption and can serve to lessen the uncomfortable and terrifying feelings that accompany unseen perils. By utilising these perspectives as early indicators of disruption, executives can identify the threats and opportunities before they manifest, giving them time to prepare. The other advantage of this economic perspective is that executives can use it to analyse all their areas of concern at once, including the business itself, the supply chain, the specific industry, the broader industry, and the entire business ecosystem and its interaction with other ecosystems.[12]

Practical guideline

Use Figure 6.1 and its descriptions above and complete Table 6.1 for your business.

Table 6.1: Sources of digital disruption across supply and demand analysis

Source of Disruption	Possible Threat	Insights Regarding the Nature of the Threat	Possible Opportunity	Insight Regarding the Nature of the Opportunity	Implications? What Strategic Moves Are Required Now?
Unconstrain supply					
Undistort demand					
Create multi-sided platforms					
Re-imagine business systems					
Create new value propositions					
Create hyperscale platforms					

EXPONENTIAL ORGANISATIONS

A few examples of disruptive businesses are listed in Table 6.2. Businesses like these have recently attracted the label "exponential organisations" (ExOs), because they exhibit growth and performance patterns that are exponentially better than the industry norm. The authors of the book *Exponential Organisations*[13] define an ExO as "one whose impact (or output) is disproportionally large – at least 10X larger – compared to its peers because of the use of new organisational techniques that leverage exponential technologies."

Table 6.2: ExOs show 10X better performance[14]

Company	Industry	Performance
AirBnB	Hotel	90x more listings per employee
GitHub	Software	109x more repositories per employee
Local Motors	Automotive	1000x cheaper to produce new car model, 5–22x faster process for a car to produce (depending on vehicle)
Quirky	Consumer goods	10x faster product development (29 days vs 300 days)
Google Ventures	Investments	2.5x more investments in early start-ups, 10X faster through design process
Valve	Gaming	30x more market cap per employee
Tesla	Automotive	30x more market cap per employee
Tangerine (formerly ING Direct Canada)	Banking	7x more customers per employee, 4x more deposits per customer

What is truly astonishing about these ExOs is the speed of growth and disruption of these businesses. Where in the past it took almost 20 years for a business to grow and become a billion dollar megalith, by utilising exponential technologies the same can be achieved within 18 months or even less – the trend is gradually downwards. A few examples of these trend-setting ExOs are shown in Figure 6.2.

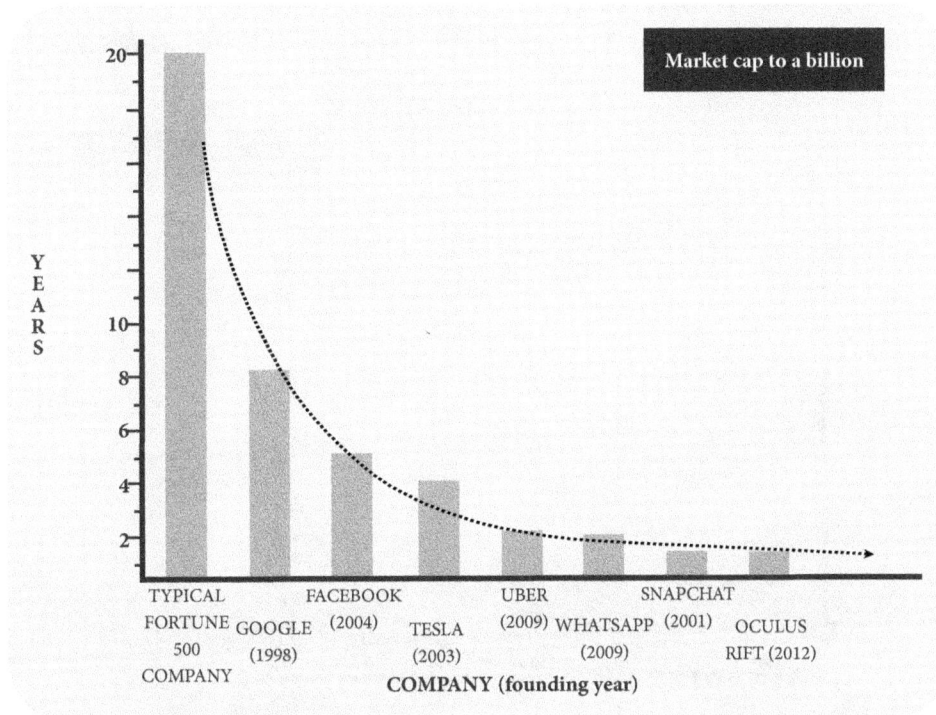

Figure 6.2: Time needed to reach a $1 billion market capitalisation[15]

Furthermore, when ExOs have reached their initial billion-dollar valuations, their growth doesn't stop. They sustain this growth pattern over several years, as seen in Table 6.3.

Table 6.3: Company valuation increase in three years (2014)[16]

Company	Age (years)	2011 Valuation	2014 Valuation	Increase
Haier	30	$19 billion	$60 billion	3x
Valve	18	$1.5 billion	$4.5 billion	3x
Google	17	$150 billion	$400 billion	2.5x
Uber	7	$2 billion	$20 billion	10x
AirBnB	6	$2 billion	$10 billion	5x
Github	6	$500 million	$7 billion	14x
Waze	6	$25 million	$1 billion (2013)	50x
Quirky	5	$50 million	$ billion	40x
Snapchat	3	0	$10 billion	10 000x +

But how do they do this? The power of ExOs is partly contained in the exponential equation and what's become known as Moore's Law. Gordon Moore, the co-founder of Intel and Fairchild Semiconductor, predicted in 1965 that "the number of transistors in a dense integrated circuit doubles approximately every two years".[17] What this implies is that during the early years, the doubling effect may seem negligible, but as soon as a certain critical mass has been reached, the subsequent jumps in the larger scheme of things become enormous – and capable of far exceeding stable linear growth. This pattern is depicted in Figure 6.3.

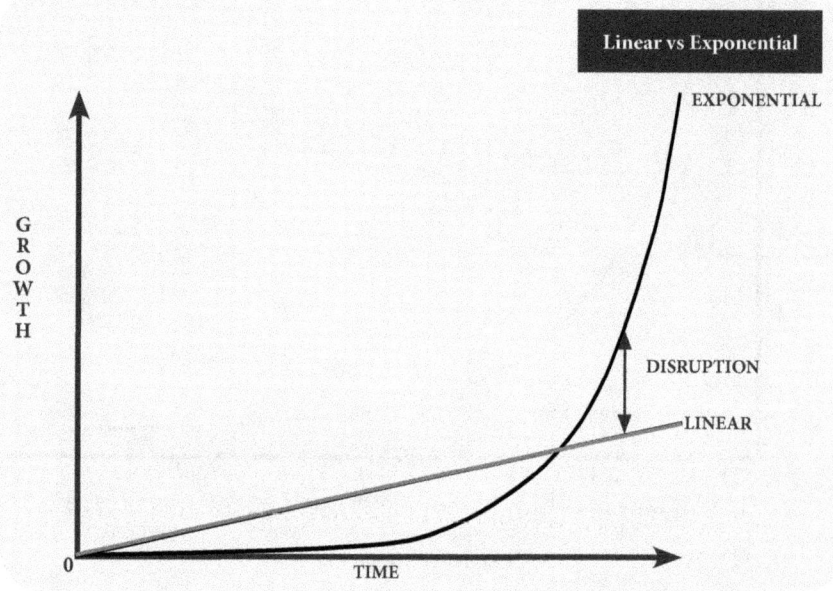

Figure 6.3: Linear growth versus exponential growth[18]

Clayton Christensen has also written extensively about the subject of disruptive innovation, and his insights concur precisely with Figure 6.3. Christensen defines disruptive innovations as those innovations that create an entirely new market by providing a new bundle of performance attributes, which existing customers do not initially value. In fact, disruptive innovations actually perform worse in the performance characteristics that existing customers value, but these innovations improve so rapidly that they ultimately address the needs of mainstream customers, at which point it allows them to disrupt and invade established markets.[19] [20]

One source of ExO's power lies in Ray Kurzweil's observation that Moore's Law applies not only to integrated circuits, but also to information technology. The extraordinary thing about information technology is that digitisation allows us take a single digital asset and make numerous copies of it to create an abundance of resources. Best of all, this reproduction and distribution of digital assets can all occur at a near zero cost.[21] [22] [23] The implication of this is that when you access resources and information-enable them, then your marginal costs (the costs added by producing one extra item of a product) are driven towards zero. When one additionally makes use of cloud infrastructure that is available on demand, rather than incurring the fixed costs of owning one's own infrastructure, it is possible to create a business whose costs are almost entirely variable – and this makes it super-scalable, even for small start-ups. ExOs therefore not only experience exponential performance increases, but also exponential cost decreases. Furthermore, as technology provides us with better performance and innovators are kept honest by competitive market dynamics, total costs to consumers also decrease exponentially. A few examples of this effect are shown in Table 6.4.

Table 6.4: Decreased costs of technologies[24]

	Cost (averages) for equivalent functionality	**Scale**
3D printing	$40 000 (2007) to $100 (2014)	400x in 7 years
Industrial robots	$500 000 (2008) to $22 000 (2013)	23x in 5 years
Drones	$100 000 (2007) to $700 (2013)	142x in 6 years
Solar	$30 per kWh (1984) to $0.16 per kWh (2014)	200x in 20 years
Sensors (3D LIDAR sensor)	$20 000 (2009) to $79 (2014)	250x in 5 years
Biotech (DNA sequencing of one whole human DNA profile)	$10 million (2007) to $1000 (2014)	10 000x in 7 years
Neurotech (BCI devices)	$4000 (2006) to $90 000 (2011)	44x in 5 years
Medicine (full body scan)	$10 000 (2000) to $500 (2014)	20x in 14 years

Many factors contribute to designing an ExO, but these five higher-level and inter-related points are key:

1. **An ExO's core trait is that it provides a minimum of 10X improvement over the status quo**. This performance is, however, the end result and not the point of departure.
2. **Every ExO has some type of innovation that drives its exponential curve**, and its curve could be fuelled by a technology innovation, a product innovation, a process innovation, a business model innovation, a management innovation or some other type of innovation.
3. **ExOs are information-enabled** and information is its greatest asset. Digitisation allows ExOs to radically reduce the marginal costs of supply, which allows the supply side of the business to scale rapidly. At the same time, when any domain, discipline, technology or industry, becomes information enabled, Moore's Law comes into effect (Kurzweill calls this phenomenon the Law of Accelerating Returns) and the price to performance ratio begins doubling approximately annually. This further supports the ExO's 10X effect.
4. **ExOs figure out how to leverage assets that they don't own**. Where the traditional organisational paradigm was concerned with the ownership of scarcity, ExOs are concerned with tapping into external abundance using technologies. Therefore, rather than assembling assets under their own control, ExOs seek to tap into valuable caches of existing assets. This allows them to scale at a tremendous pace at a fraction of the cost.
5. **EXOs succeed in creating communities around them**. ExOs have a Massive Transformative Purpose (MTP) (see below) that attracts people from outside to the cause. By building communities and doing things in public, instead of having to find the right kinds of people, the right kinds of people find the business. Communities are also crucial in building network effects, where increased scale leads to increased value or functionality for the participants. This reinforcing mechanism therefore becomes a self-fulfilling prophecy. Additionally, communities create strong customer lock-in, which supports its scaling as it allows the business to retain the customers it already has.
6. **ExOs solve a real customer problem on a frequent basis**. Larry Page, the co-founder of Google, refers to this as the "toothbrush test". Does the business do something so useful that a user would go back to it several times a day?[25] Only things that are exceptionally useful will attract the attention required to scale exponentially.

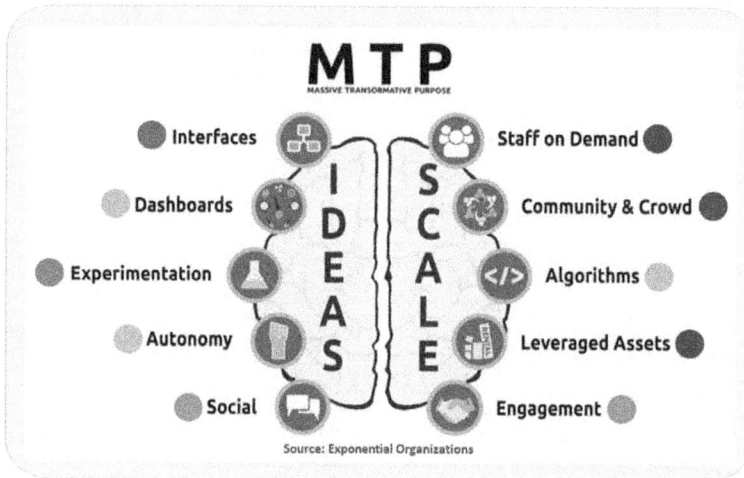

Figure 6.4: Core elements of exponential organisations[26]

Since 2008, Ismail, Malone and Van Geest have been researching the top global 100 fastest-growing start-ups and have identified a pattern of traits that many ExOs share. This pattern consists of three acronyms: (1) MTP, (2) IDEAS and (3) SCALE. These are shown in Figure 6.4.

An MTP is the higher, aspirational purpose of the organisation (see chapter 2's *Vision description*). An MTP serves to capture the hearts and minds of both those inside and (especially) outside the organisation by stating what the organisation aspires to accomplish, without stating how the organisation aims to do it. The idea of an MTP is to dream big and to compel people towards the business's journey. Examples of a few MTPs are:[27]

- TED: "Ideas worth spreading."
- Google: "Organise the world's information."
- X Prize Foundation: "Bring about radical breakthroughs for the benefit of humanity."
- Quirky: "Make invention accessible."
- Singularity University: "Positively impact one billion people."

As additional food for thought, Kahlil Gibran[28] once noted that "Work is love made visible. The goal is not to live forever; the goal is to create something that will."

SCALE reflects ExO attributes that are external to the organisation.

Staff on demand refers to the leveraging of personnel outside of the base organisation when necessary. This allows the business to scale up their capabilities on demand, providing the organisation with immense speed, flexibility and functionality – all of these vital for competing in a fast-changing world.

Community & crowd is built on the principles of open innovation: it is impossible for any organisation to contain all the knowledge in the world. It is therefore necessary to reach outside the organisation and pull ideas and resources in. The "community" of an organisation is made up of its team members, partners, vendors, staff on demand, customers, users and fans. The "crowd" is everyone else outside of those layers. The idea behind crowd and community is to tap into the creativity and innovation of entities outside of the organisation; use them for validation of experiments; or even crowd funding. The crowd aren't employees, thus they can't be commanded to take action. They have to be persuaded and pulled into the organisation. This is where an MTP is useful.

Algorithms are complex mathematical equations or "sets of rules" used in calculations or other problem-solving operations. Today, much of the world is run by algorithms. Amazon's recommendations, Google's search results, the price of your airline ticket and the posts you see on Facebook are all controlled by algorithms. With the imminent explosion of Internet-enabled devices and the Internet of things (IoT) producing more data than we could possibly make sense of, algorithms may be our only saviour for dealing with the chaos of the approaching digital data overload.

Leveraged assets refer to the renting, sharing or simply the use of assets that one does not own. Where the traditional businesses are generally concerned with the ownership of scarcity, a new wave of nonasset businesses are emerging that are fully embedding themselves in the sharing economy. This concept is known as **collaborative consumption**[29] and these ExOs are concerned with tapping into external sources of abundance by using technology. The rule of thumb is that when the asset in question is rare or extremely scarce, then ownership is the better and more secure option. However, if the asset is information-based or commoditised, then access is key.[30]

Engagement refers tomeans ways of captivating customers, users and employees and enabling their collaborative behaviour. Examples of engagement mechanisms include digital reputation systems, gamification and incentive prizes. Customer and user engagement is a core asset to any organisation, as it provides the opportunity for increased loyalty, network effects and virtuous feedback loops that result in faster growth. Employee engagement (see chapter 8) may very well be even more important. Organisations therefore have to do their best to create an organisational environment that inspires the exceptional contribution of their employees, and unlocks their boldness, creativity and zeal.[31]

When the above external SCALE elements are in place, exponential inputs will be generated for the business to deal with. ExOs' internal processes therefore need to be extremely robust in order to efficiently and effectively manage these inputs. Distinctly different internal operations in the form of IDEAS attributes are therefore required.

Interfaces are filtering and matching processes that allow ExOs to bridge SCALE externalities and internal IDEAS control frameworks. They are algorithms and automated workflows that route SCALE inputs to the right people at the right time internally. While interfaces may start out manual, being self-provisioning (completely automated and requiring no manual input) is a key feature that allows ExOs to scale seamlessly and exponentially. Most ExOs' interface processes are unique and proprietary, and at peak productivity they empower the management of the enterprise's SCALE attributes. Essentially, interfaces are what allow ExOs to cope with abundance.

Dashboards are the data collection and visualisation techniques used to display the organisation's real-time metrics. A tension has always existed in business between balancing instrumentation and data collection versus actually running the business and getting things done. ExOs minimise the burden of data collection by leveraging the Internet, automated data-mining, online analytic techniques, sensors and various forms of customer input to track and collect data in real time and share it with everyone in the organisation. This gives them the information edge and allows them to be more responsive.

Experimentation deals with using the Lean Start-up methodology (see chapter 7 in *Crystallising the Strategic Business Landscape*) and continually testing hypotheses at minimum cost and with controlled risk. Experimentation is the attribute that allows organisations to "safely" learn and adapt. A key message from the lean start-up methodology is that companies should "fail fast and fail often, while eliminating waste." With the tremendous growth that will happen in the future, the only way for organisations to survive is by becoming true learning organisations. In the words of Eric Ries,[32] "The modern rule of competition is whoever learns fastest, wins."

Autonomy is the virtue of having the freedom and independence to self-organise and self-govern. In an organisation, this essentially means decentralised or distributed authority. A term describing this form of governance is Holacracy, which is defined as "a social technology or system of organisational governance, in which authority and decision-making are distributed via fractal, self-organising teams rather than being vested at the top of a hierarchy".[33] ExOs encourage autonomy as it gives individuals the freedom to take initiative, increasing the innovation, agility and efficiency of the organisation (see chapter 8). It is important to note that autonomy does not imply a lack of accountability or a lack of hierarchy. Holacracies tend to be based on competence-based hierarchies rather than position-based hierarchies, and also rely more on peer-based accountability than on authority-based accountability.

Social technologies are technologies that are applied in some social context in order to connect individuals or for some other objective. According to J.P. Rangaswami, chief data officer at Deutsche Bank, social technologies have three key objectives: (1) To reduce the distance between obtaining information and decision-making; (2) to reduce the search costs of information by having it flow through the individual's perception; and (3) to leverage communities to expand ideas.[34] Social technologies improve an organisation's intimacy as they create new lines of communication and new information flows that create horizontal interactions in vertically oriented companies, promote cross-pollination, and enhance the chances for serendipitous innovation, transparency, engagement and trust. Furthermore, when applying social technologies, knowledge is improved and is more widely shared, information and decision-making latency is reduced (time between idea, acceptance and implementation), and the organisation is centred on its MTP, which ensures that the diverse parts of the organisation don't drift off in pursuit of different or conflicting goals.

When a business idea has assembled the above ingredients, it has a strong chance of becoming an ExO. Although Ismail, Malone and Van Geest (2014) note that the presence of all these attributes is not necessary, a minimum of four of these attributes is required.

A comparison between the characteristics of traditional linear organisations and those of ExOs is shown in Table 6.5.

Table 6.5: Linear organisations versus exponential organisations[35]

Linear organisation characteristics	Exponential organisation characteristics
Top-down and hierarchical in its organisation	Autonomy, Social Technologies
Driven by financial outcomes	MTP, Dashboards
Linear, sequential thinking	Experimentation, Autonomy
Innovation primarily from within	Community & Crowd, Staff on Demand, Leveraged Assets, Interfaces (innovation at the edges)
Strategic planning largely an exploration from the past	Experimentation
Process inflexibility	Autonomy, Experimentation
Large number of full-time employees	Algorithms, Community & Crowd, Staff on Demand
Controls/own its own assets	Leveraged assets
Strongly invested in the status quo	MTP, Dashboards, Experimentation

Armed with this blueprint of the characteristics of ExOs, the only task remaining is to embody these characteristics in your business to unleash your exponential growth potential. As further inspiration, we conclude this section with Figure 6.5.

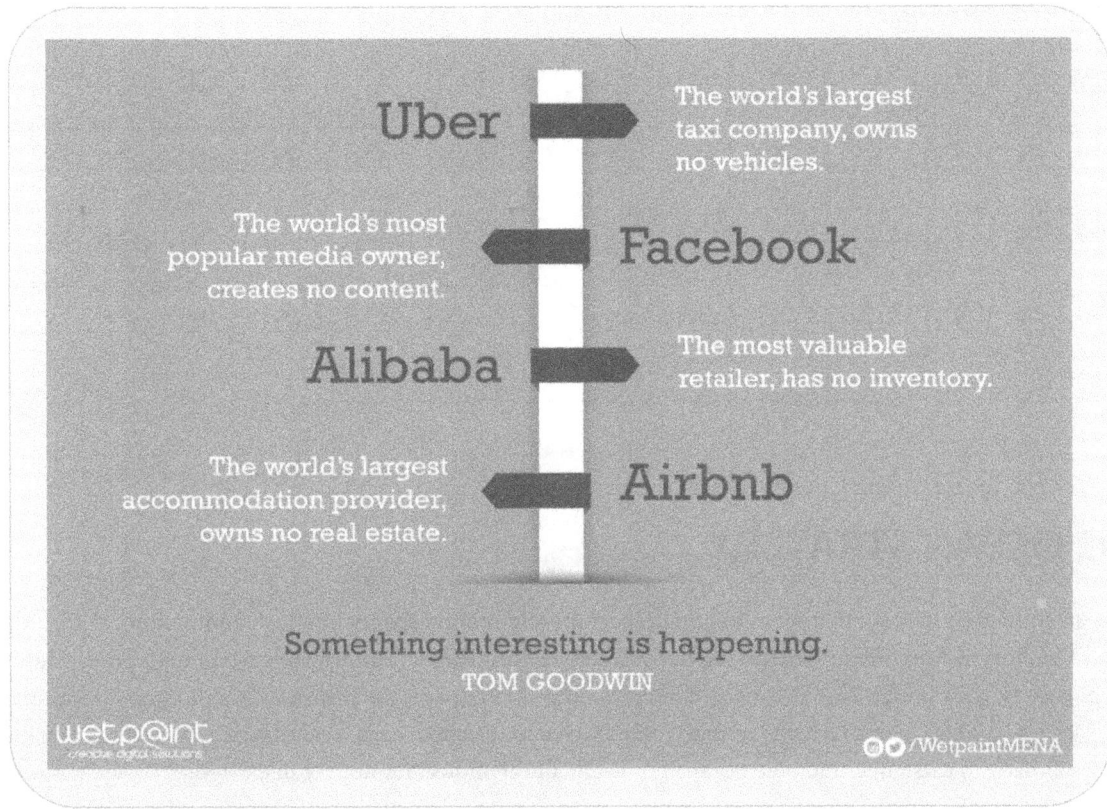

Figure 6.5: Something interesting is happening[36]

Application tool

A shorthand version and example of measuring your exponential quotient is provided in Table 6.6. In order to possibly become an ExO, the business requires at least four of the 11 attributes. A more detailed survey of the business's ExO quotient can be completed at www.exponentialorgs.com/survey. In the expanded survey, ExOs achieve a score of over 55 out of 84. How do you score in Table 6.6? How can your business be altered to achieve a higher ExO score? Use Figure 6.4 and the associated descriptions as reference.

Table 6.6: ExO idea assessment[37]

Business	MTP	S	C	A	L	E	I	D	E	A	S
AirBnB	✓		✓		✓	✓	✓				
Local Motors	✓	✓	✓		✓		✓				
Uber	✓		✓		✓	✓	✓				
Google Ventures	✓			✓			✓	✓	✓		
Valve	✓							✓		✓	✓
Your business											

BLUE OCEAN STRATEGY

Blue ocean strategy is strategy that seeks to pursue uncontested market spaces in which competitors are "irrelevant". Kim and Mauborgne[38] hold that "Competing in overcrowded industries is no way to sustain high performance. The real opportunity is to create blue oceans of uncontested market space". In Kim and Mauborgne's[39] paradigm the business universe consists of two types of space, namely red and blue oceans. Red oceans represent all the business industries already in existence, and blue oceans represent all the industries not yet in existence.

These authors argue that companies competing in red oceans try to outperform rivals in order to obtain a bigger slice of the existing demand. However, as the red ocean market becomes increasingly saturated with competitors, supply overtakes demand and competition becomes fierce. Competitors then often start to engage in benchmarking to at least stay on par with rivals, but this leads to a decline in differentiation between competitors. When this happens, customers are forced to increasingly base their buying decisions on cost, leading to price wars, the commoditisation of products and services, and ultimately abysmal profit and growth prospects.[40]

Creators of blue oceans, on the other hand, seek to create new market spaces that are untainted by competition, and that allow demand to be created rather than fought over. Blue ocean strategy assails competitors by moving around them rather than competing directly with them. This approach leads to opportunities for rapid and profitable growth, while creating clear barriers to imitation.

The evidence speaks for itself: A study by Kim and Mauborgne[41] shows that while blue ocean strategies accounted for merely 14 per cent of the 108 new business launches that they studied, they generated 38 per cent of the total revenues and 61 per cent of the profits.

One of the primary differences between red and blue ocean strategies is that red ocean strategies assume a "structuralist" view where the industry boundaries and rules of the game are well defined and accepted. Within these constraints, there is no other choice but to compete head-on with competitors to capture a larger piece of the existing market share. Blue ocean strategy, on the other hand, assumes a "reconstructionist view", where industry boundaries are seen as malleable. Blue ocean strategy therefore seeks to reconstruct and redefine the industry boundaries and the rules of the game.[42]

The main paradigmatic differences between red and blue ocean strategies are highlighted in Table 6.7.

Table 6.7: Red ocean strategy vs blue ocean strategy paradigms[43]

Red Ocean Strategy	Blue Ocean Strategy
Compete in existing market space	Create uncontested market space
Beat the competition	Make the competition irrelevant
Exploit existing demand	Create and capture new demand
Make the value and cost trade-off	Break the value and cost trade-off
Align the whole system of a company's activities with its strategic choice of differentiation or low costs	Align the whole system of a company's activities in pursuit of differentiation and low costs

Value innovation

The key driver of blue ocean strategy is value innovation. It was traditionally believed that strategy is essentially a choice between low-cost and differentiation options, and that a trade-off exists between the two. This conventional paradigm dictates that businesses can only deliver higher value by raising costs, or lower costs by delivering less value. Value innovation fundamentally rejects this trade-off and holds that it is possible for organisations to simultaneously pursue differentiation and low costs.[44]

Kim and Mauborgne[45] define customer value and organisational value as:

1. *Customer Value = Utility – Price*
2. *Organisation Value = Price – Cost*

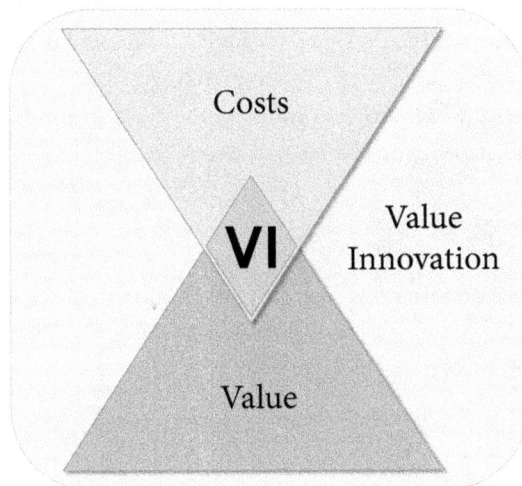

Figure 6.6: Value innovation[46]

When a business delivers more utility to customers while streamlining costs, value innovation occurs, and a leap in value is created for both customers and the business. When this leap is big enough, a blue ocean of uncontested market space is created. This is depicted in Figure 6.6.

Although the conceptual underpinnings of blue and red oceans are relatively new, these two oceans have always coexisted and always will. Just think about all the industries that didn't exist 30 years ago that exist today. The real question is therefore: which industries will exist 30 years from now and how do we go about creating them? Research by Kim and Mauborgne[47] highlights the following:[48]

1. **Creating a blue ocean is not necessarily about technology innovation.** Blue oceans seldom result from technological innovations, but rather from the linkage between existing technology and what customers find valuable.

2. **Company and industry are the wrong units of analysis.** Company and industry analysis have little explanatory power regarding how and why blue oceans are created, and the most appropriate unit of analysis is the strategic move. This refers to the set of managerial actions and decisions involved in making a major market-creating business offering.

3. **A large R&D budget does not ensure the creation of new market space.** The key to creating new markets is making the correct strategic moves. When organisations understand the drivers behind a good strategic move, they are empowered to create multiple blue oceans over time, leading to continuous growth and profits. The creation of blue oceans is therefore a product of strategy, meaning the power lies with managerial action.

4. **It is not necessary to venture into distant waters to create blue oceans.** Most often it is possible to create blue oceans within existing red oceans or within an organisation's core business.

5. **Blue ocean strategy never uses competition as a benchmark.** Benchmarking prohibits an organisation's ability to reconstruct industry boundaries as it causes organisations to be caught in the current industry paradigms of value creation.

6. **Blue ocean strategies create barriers to imitation**. Blue oceans are difficult to imitate and allow creators to experience a period without any credible challenges from would-be competitors.

    6.1. **Blue ocean strategies create economic barriers to imitation**. Blue ocean strategies allow the rapid accumulation of large volumes of customers, leading to economies of scale. This places competitors at a cost disadvantage. Imitation also requires competitors to change their whole system of activities to fit the new model, which in itself is not an easy or cheap accomplishment. Furthermore, the leap in value offered by blue oceans builds customer loyalty, and expensive marketing campaigns are usually required to overthrow a blue ocean creator.

    6.2. **Blue ocean strategies create cognitive barriers to imitation**. Blue ocean creators are first movers that are different by definition and this assists in building the brand. Almost all of the organisations studied by Kim and Mauborgne are still remembered today for the blue oceans that they created. At the same time, imitation of a blue ocean strategy is unlikely, as such imitation could lead to a conflicting brand image within the rival organisation. Additionally, the drastic changes required to imitate a blue ocean model could additionally lead to organisational politics which will impede the change to the new business model.

Principles of blue ocean strategy

Kim and Mauborgne[49] found that companies that succeeded in creating new markets or industries all had a consistent pattern of strategic thinking in common, and termed this pattern "blue ocean strategy". Blue ocean strategy consists of six key principles that are shown in in Table 6.8 and are subsequently discussed.

Table 6.8: The six principles of blue ocean strategy[50]

Principle	Risk factor each principle attenuates
Formulation principles	
1. Reconstruct market boundaries	Search risk
2. Focus on the big picture, not the numbers	Planning risk
3. Reach beyond existing demand	Scale risk
4. Get the strategic sequence right	Business model risk
Execution principles	
5. Overcome key organisational hurdles	Organisational risk
6. Build execution into strategy	Management risk

First principle: Reconstruct market boundaries

Blue ocean strategies carve out new market spaces for themselves by adapting the current market boundaries; they value innovating and disrupting the status quo. The **reconstructing market boundaries** principle attenuates the search risk associated with the challenge of identifying commercially compelling blue ocean opportunities, e.g. searching for blue oceans in the wrong places. Kim and Mauborgne created a framework called the six paths framework,[51] which can be used to challenge the fundamental assumptions that companies make in strategy formulation and thereby assist businesses in reconstructing their market boundaries. Ungerer[52] extended the six paths framework by incorporating Hamel[53] and Ungerer et al.[54] views and the resultant "10 techniques for creating new marketspace" are shown in Figure 6.7.

Looking across alternatives refers to looking across alternative offerings, which may or may not have different functions and forms, but are used to broadly achieve the same goal. Thinking in this way is useful as it can assist businesses in identifying trade-offs that customers make in choosing between different offerings. These differences then provide the opportunity for value innovation in the spaces between these different industry offerings. This approach can similarly be used to identify opportunities to embody a function in a new and better form or use the same form for a new function.[56] [57]

Looking across strategic groups within industries means looking within an industry at the different groups of company that follow a similar strategy. Generally strategic groups have preconceived ideas of the value that can be offered at a certain price point. By value innovating, a company can therefore carve out a new position for itself between the strategic groups within an industry. Breaking the value–cost ratio can therefore lead to a reconception of the product or service.[58]

Looking across the chain of buyers is evaluating all the parties that are involved in the buying process. Considering the chain of buyers, **purchasers** pay for the products or services, **users** use the products or services, and **influencers** influence the buying decision. These three user groups may overlap, but when they do not, frequently the different groups have different perceptions as to what is valuable. Looking at a product or service from these different perspectives can possibly lead to the identification of a new opportunity space.[59] This perspective is aligned with customer-centricity and the jobs-to-be-done approach previously mentioned, where users are scrutinised to identify the essence of what they really need to accomplish and then providing only that.[60]

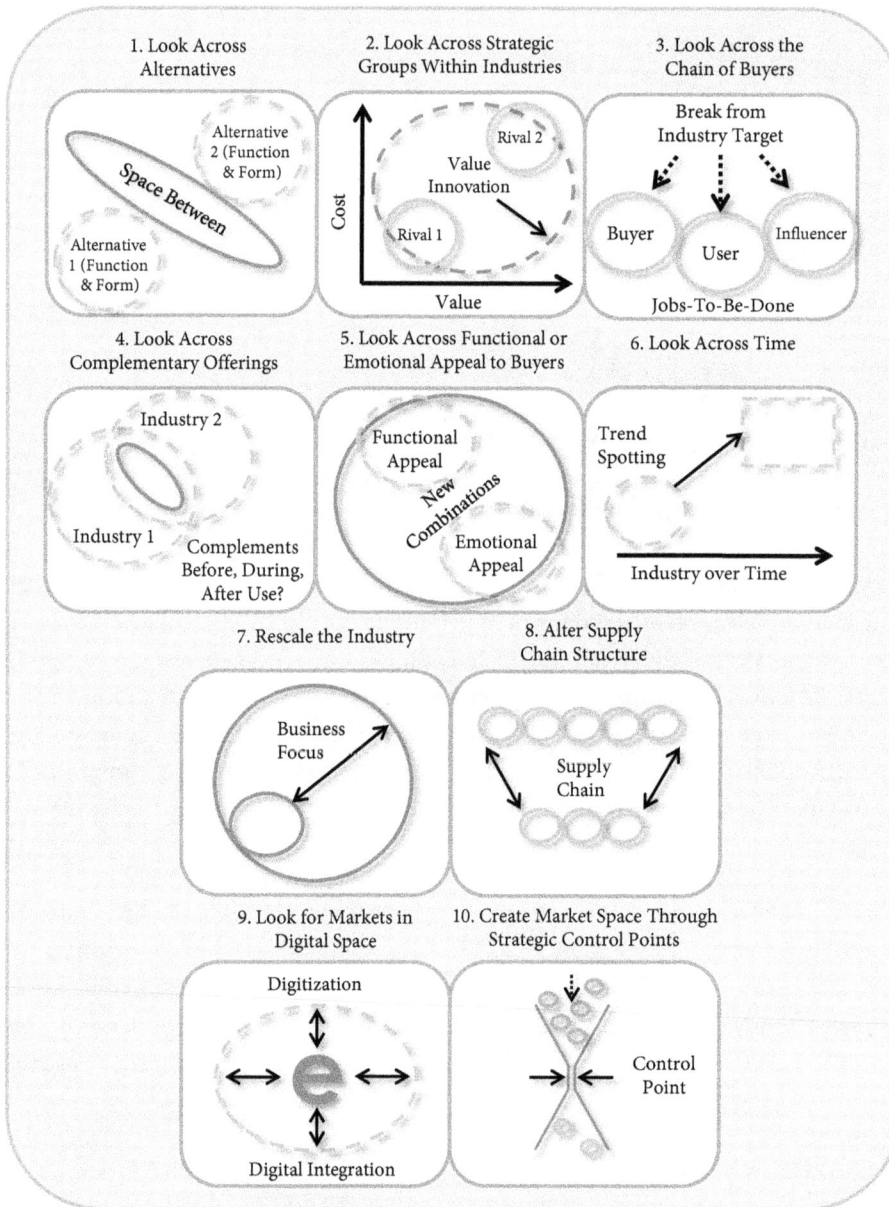

Figure 6.7: 10 techniques for creating new market space[55]

Looking across complementary product and service offerings means considering the total solution customers seek when choosing a product or service. In most cases products and services are not used in solidarity and usually rely on other products and services (possibly from other industries), which affects their value. By inspecting the context that an offering is used in, and considering what happens before, during and after a product or service is used, complementary products can often be identified that will eliminate user pains. This in effect significantly increases the value of the offering.[61]

Looking across the functional or emotional appeal to buyers is considering the conventional utility and emotional attractiveness of industry offerings. By challenging this functional or emotional orientation of an industry, value can be unlocked. In a functional industry, for instance, elements can be added to make the industry more emotional. In contrast, in an emotional industry elements can be removed to make it more functional.[62]

Looking across time means identifying how customers' perception of value changes over time and how industry trends impact a company's business model. When looking across time, one considers how value is currently being delivered, while thinking about how it might be delivered in the future. Doing this can lead to the identification of a new opportunity space. However, there are three guidelines that need to be adhered to in assessing opportunity spaces presented by trends across time: (1) the trends must be decisive to the business; (2) they must be irreversible; and (3) they must have a clear trajectory.[63]

Rescaling the industry means rescaling the size or focus of businesses in an industry. Rapid consolidation of a fragmented industry can lead to economies of scale in purchasing, capital utilisation, marketing and administration. Conversely, scaling down the size of businesses in an industry can lead to niche businesses that are able to better serve narrow or local customer segments.[64]

Altering the supply chain structure means either removing or adding intermediaries to the supply chain to either compress or lengthen it. Compressing the supply chain (vertical integration) gives companies enhanced control, increased coordination, efficiencies and cost savings.[65] On the other hand, lengthening the supply chain by adding intermediaries can also be a valuable space if it is possible to provide value to customers not obtainable otherwise. A South African example is MWeb, who positioned themselves as an intermediary between the core ADSL provider, Telkom, and thereby facilitated a smoother customer process of obtaining ADSL.

Looking for markets in digital space means digitising products or services in order to capitalise on the capabilities and features that digital provides. As previously mentioned, digital assets can be copied infinitely to create an abundance of resources. At the same time, the reproduction and distribution of digital assets can all occur at zero marginal cost. Additionally, digital space allows businesses to compete globally from day one, provides enhanced access to new channels and offerings, allows for faster and enhanced information-sharing, and better integration and coordination. These distinctive attributes of the Internet present valuable new opportunities that can be pursued.[66] Additionally, see the sources of e-value in the following section.

Creating market space through strategic control points means using control points to capture value. Control points were previously defined as the mechanisms that businesses specifically control and leverage to prevent imitation and lock competitive advantages in for themselves..[67] Fourteen types of control point were defined in chapter 3, and these mechanisms can be used to carve out blue ocean opportunity spaces when correctly applied.

Application tool

Use the 10 techniques in Figure 6.7 to challenge conventional wisdom about competing in your industry and devise ways in which your current market boundaries can be expanded or reconstructed to create a new blue ocean. Incorporate your new insights into the business model you constructed in chapter 3.

Second principle: Focus on the big picture, not the numbers

Blue ocean strategies provide unprecedented value by diverging from the industry norm in meaningful ways. The **focus on the big picture, not the numbers** principle attenuates the risk associated with the strategic planning process, e.g. analysis paralysis and an unclear course of action. Rather than investing excessive amounts of time and resources in numeric analysis, planning and "tick-box" strategy, blue ocean strategy utilises a new way of strategy formulation, namely by using a strategy canvas.

A strategy canvas is a graphical diagnostic framework that depicts a company's relative performance against competitors across the industry's critical competitive factors. On the horizontal axis all the critical factors that the

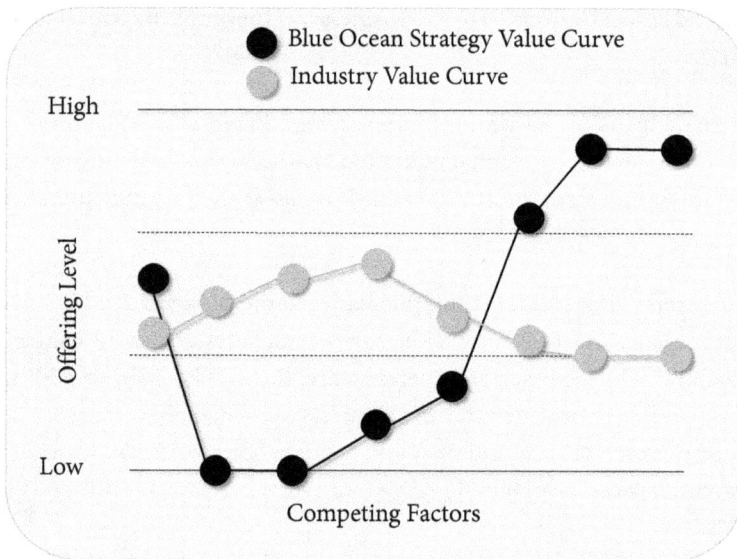

Figure 6.8: Strategy canvas[68]

industry competes on are listed, and on the vertical axis the offering levels which customers receive across these competitive factors are captured. Companies then sketch out their current value curve, as well as the value curves of competitors. Soon an industry value curve pattern should emerge. The goal is then to develop a new blue ocean value curve that meaningfully diverges from the industry norm, and that is capable of successfully competing in the market. This is depicted in Figure 6.8.

Several levers are available to businesses that can assist them in diverging from the industry norm. The first model we've introduced was that of the 10 techniques for creating new market space. The second model that Kim and Mauborgne[69] provide is the **Four Actions Framework**, shown in Figure 6.9. The four actions framework challenges the industry's strategic logic by considering the following questions:

- Which of the factors that the industry takes for granted should be eliminated?
- Which factors should be reduced well below the industry's standard?
- Which factors should be raised well above the industry's standard?
- Which factors should be created that the industry has never offered?

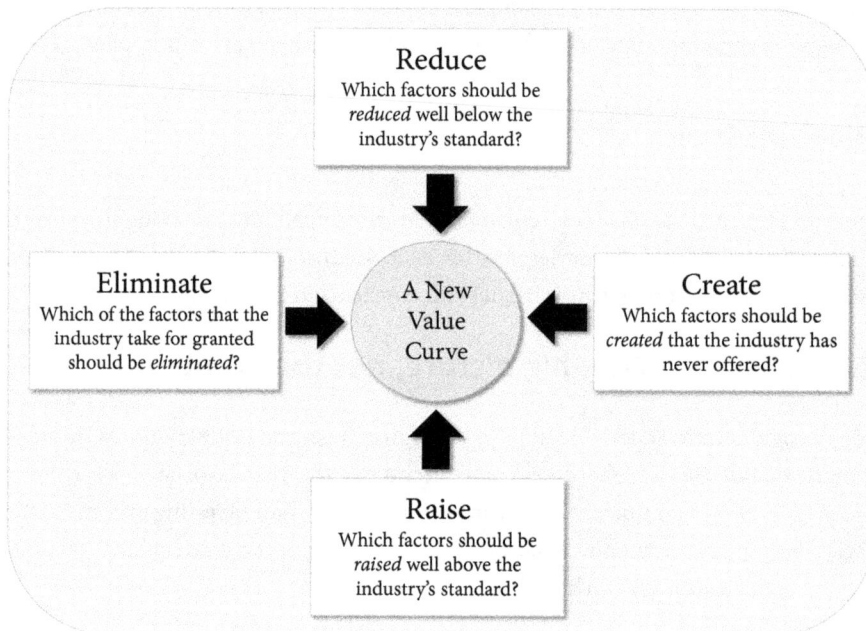

Figure 6.9: Four actions framework[70]

By applying the four actions framework to the strategy canvas, a new blue ocean value curve can be created. The third model that Kim and Mauborgne[71] provide for creating exceptional customer value is the **Buyer Utility Map**, shown in Figure 6.10. The buyer utility map consists of the stages of the **Buyer Experience Cycle** on the horizontal axis, and the six levers of utility on the vertical axis. By using the map, businesses can consider the industry utility provided to customers during each phase of the customer experience cycle, possibly leading to the identification of ways to create a new blue ocean value curve.

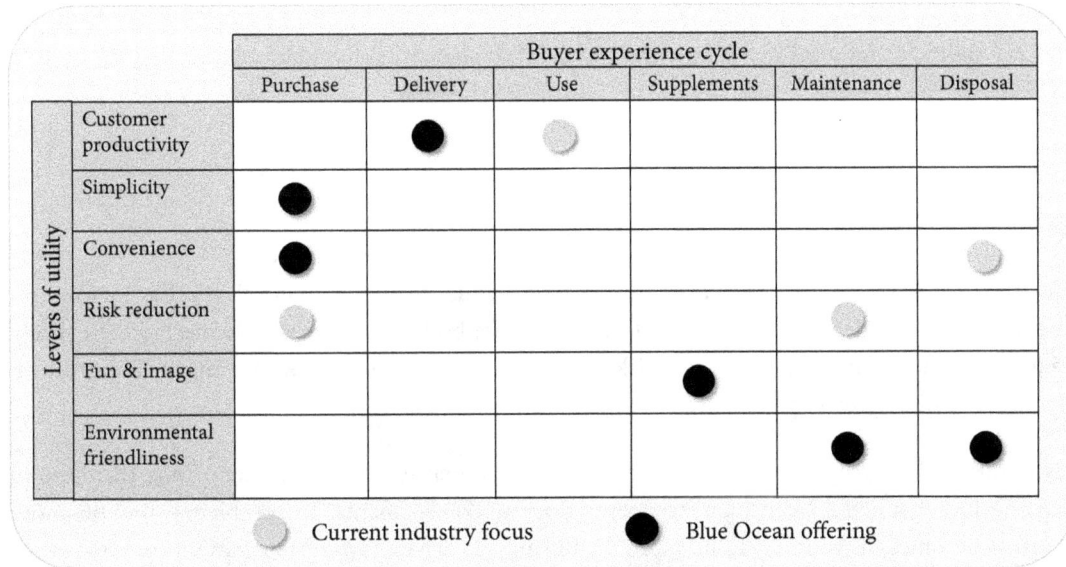

Levers of utility	Buyer experience cycle					
	Purchase	Delivery	Use	Supplements	Maintenance	Disposal
Customer productivity		●	○			
Simplicity	●					
Convenience	●					○
Risk reduction	○				○	
Fun & image				●		
Environmental friendliness					●	●

○ Current industry focus   ● Blue Ocean offering

Figure 6.10: Buyer utility map[72]

In summary, the strategy canvas serves three purposes. Firstly, it captures the current industry state of affairs of the known market space. This allows companies to understand the way in which competitors are competing and the factors on which they are competing. Secondly, it compels companies to action by re-orienting their strategic focus from **competitors** to **alternatives** and from **customers** to **noncustomers** of the industry. Thirdly, the strategy canvas shifts the focus of strategy planning from a process primarily centred on numeric analysis and document creation to a conversational process where collective wisdom is built in a creative top-down and a bottom-up fashion.[73]

Application tool

Use the strategy canvas in Figure 6.8 to sketch out your current value curve, the value curves of your three main competitors, and the resultant industry value curve. Then use the 10 techniques for creating new market space in Figure 6.7, the four actions framework in Figure 6.9 and the buyer utility map in Figure 6.10 to create a new blue ocean value curve. Table 6.9 may be useful for this process. Incorporate your insights into the business model you constructed in chapter 3.

Table 6.9: Eliminate–reduce–raise–create grid (ERRC grid)[74]

Eliminate	Raise
Which of the factors that the industry takes for granted should be eliminated? List those here…	Which factors should be raised well above the industry standard? List those here…
Reduce	**Create**
Which factors should be reduced well below the industry's standard? List those here…	Which factors should be created that the industry has never offered? List those here…

Third principle: Reach beyond existing demand

Blue ocean strategies do not merely seek to capture a piece of the existing demand that exists in a red ocean, but instead to create additional demand by offering a leap in value for both customers and themselves. The **reach beyond existing demand** principle attenuates the scale risk associated with creating a new market, e.g. a market whose size is small and offers limited growth prospects.

Businesses traditionally attempt to expand by looking towards their existing customers. They therefore introduce customised offerings that better cater to preferences of finer market segments. The problem is that the more intense the competition becomes in the market, the more the business is driven towards customised offerings that cater to an even finer market segment. The risk is therefore entering markets that are too small to profitably serve. Blue ocean strategy works in the opposite direction. Instead of segmenting, blue ocean strategy tries to maximise the number of customers that it attracts by concentrating on noncustomers and the commonalities in what they value. This approach allows the business to reach beyond the existing demand and unlock a new mass of customers that did not previously exist.[75]

Kim and Mauborgne[76] distinguish between three types of noncustomer.

First-tier noncustomers are customers who are on the verge of the company's current market. These customers occasionally purchase an industry's offerings out of necessity, but are ready to leave the industry as soon as the opportunity presents itself. Therefore, although these customers sometimes make purchases, they are mentally noncustomers. If a leap in value is presented to them however, they will fully embrace it and the frequency of their purchases will increase, unlocking a huge amount of dormant demand.

Second-tier noncustomers are customers who are consciously choosing against the industry's offerings. They know what the industry offers, but their needs or requirements are not being met and they have therefore not become customers. Better solutions can therefore unlock this mass of dormant demand.

Third-tier noncustomers are customers who are in distant markets that are far removed from the business. These customers have never been considered as a viable target group, nor have they ever considered the industry's offerings as an option. By focusing on the commonalities between these noncustomers and current customers, businesses can devise how they will pull these noncustomers into the market, unlocking another pocket of dormant demand.[77]

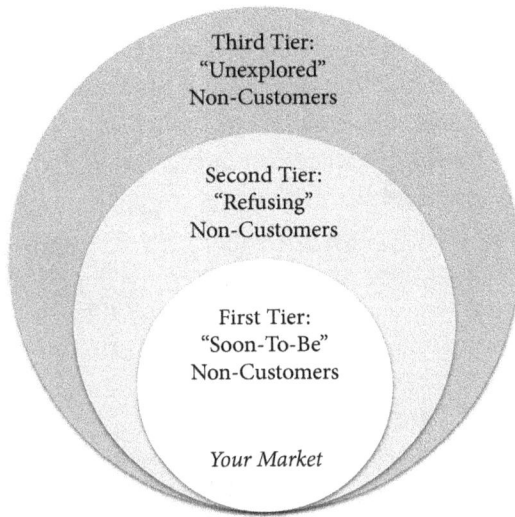

Figure 6.11:Three tiers of noncustomer[78]

The three tiers of noncustomer are depicted in Figure 6.11. Also see the Need Saturation Scale in chapter 4 of *Crystallising the Strategic Business Landscape*.

In deciding which of these noncustomers to target, the rule of thumb is to target the largest group of noncustomers first.[79] However, simply maximising the size of the blue ocean is not the goal. Market share can be gained rapidly. Whether this can be done profitably, is another question.

Fourth principle: Get the strategic sequence right

Blue ocean strategies are embedded in robust business models that allow them to generate healthy profits over a prolonged period of time. The **get the strategic sequence right** principle attenuates the risk associated with business model formulation, e.g. pursuing business ideas that are not commercially viable.

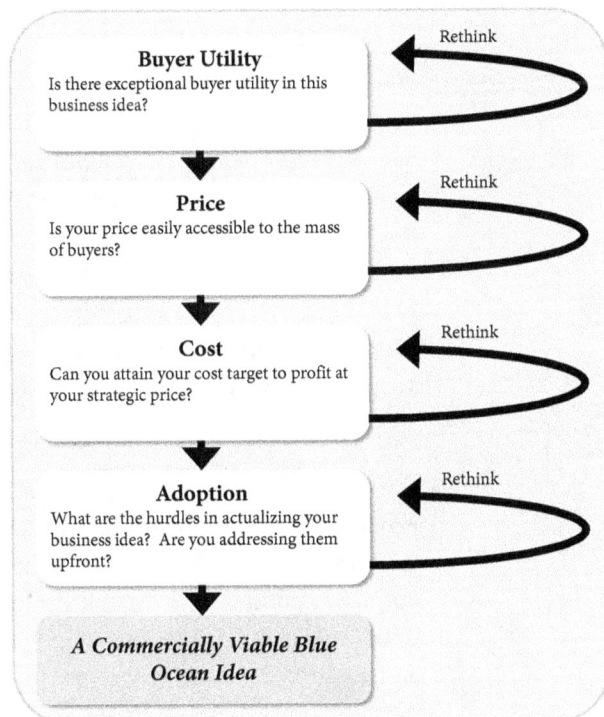

Figure 6.12: Sequence of blue ocean strategy[80]

Blue ocean strategy advocates the use of a generic strategic sequence for formulating business models along a set of key criteria that need to be met before progressing to the next stage. Following this sequence dramatically reduces the business's business model risk and enhances the odds of creating a commercially viable blue ocean. This sequence is shown in Figure 6.12.

The sequence shows that blue ocean strategy should start with an idea that delivers exceptional buyer utility (the differentiation aspect of blue ocean strategy). If the idea does not offer exceptional buyer utility, then a leap in value is not created and there is no compelling reason for noncustomers to purchase the business's offerings. The idea should therefore be rethought until it provides such value to customers. The strategy canvas, value innovation, the buyer utility map and the ERRC grid can be useful in this regard.

The second step is to determine the strategic price (the low-cost aspect of blue ocean strategy). The strategic price is the price that will not only make the offering accessible to the target mass of customers, but it is also the price that will retain customers as they are convinced that they will not find better value with an imitator.[81] The strategic price should be rethought until it meets this criterion.

299

The third step is to determine the cost target that needs to be hit, while keeping the strategic price fixed, that will still deliver a healthy profit to the company (the organisational aspect of value innovation). The cost target is calculated as the strategic price minus the profit margin. In blue ocean strategy, costs do not drive prices, as this means a decrease in customer value. At the same time, organisational value should not be reduced due to high costs.[82] If it therefore seems that the business idea will be unprofitable at the set strategic price and cost target, then efficiency innovations (key partnerships, key resources, key activities and cost structure elements) are required to hit the cost target. However, in some cases, no matter how hard the business tries, the cost target will simply remain elusive. In such cases, the strategic price needs to be re-evaluated. Successful innovators never assume that there is only one way to price a product. Expensive products can be made accessible to the mass market by leasing them; using time-share models; or using slice-share models (see chapter 3). The goal is thus not to compromise on the strategic price, but to hit the cost target through a new price model.

The fourth step is to determine the organisational hurdles to adoption and overcome them up front in order to arrive at a commercially viable blue ocean idea.[83] This is discussed further via the two remaining principles.

Interested readers can also refer to chapter 3 and scrutinise the proposed generic process of business model formulation – and see that these sequences coincide.

Fifth principle: Overcome key organisational hurdles

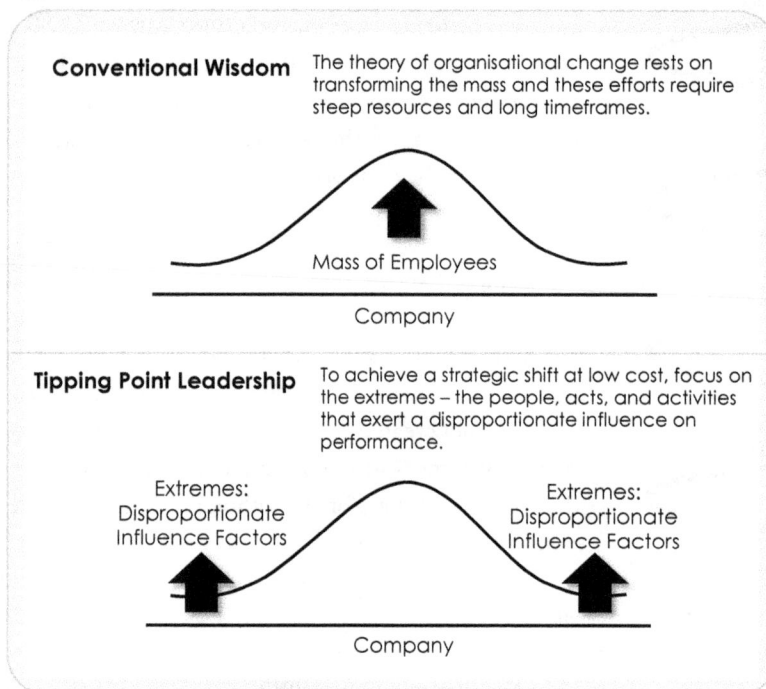

Figure 6.13: Tipping point leadership[85][86]

Blue ocean strategies overcome the adoption hurdles presented by their departure from the status quo. The **overcome key organisational hurdles** principle attenuates the organisational risk associated with executing a blue ocean strategy, e.g. cognitive barriers to adoption, resource barriers to adoption, motivational barriers to adoption, and political barriers to adoption.

Cognitive barriers to adoption are people's resistance to change because they are comfortable with the status quo and do not see the need for change. Resource barriers to adoption are resource deficiencies that prevent the execution of blue ocean strategies. Motivational barriers to adoption are staff who are unmotivated to change swiftly and purposefully. Political barriers to adoption are the opposition experienced due to powerful parties that harbour vested interests.[84] Successful blue ocean strategies overcome all these hurdles by defying conventional wisdom regarding organisational change, via tipping point leadership, shown in Figure 6.13 .

Tipping point leadership holds that fundamental change can occur quickly (and with fewer resources) in an organisation when the beliefs and energy of a critical mass of people create an epidemic movement towards an idea.[87] Rather than trying to persuade the mass of employees to change (requiring steep resources and long time-frames), tipping point leadership concentrates on the **people, acts and activities** that exercise a **disproportionate influence** on performance. By transforming the extremes, tipping point leaders are able to change the core fast and at a low cost to execute the blue ocean strategy. Key questions are therefore:[88]

What factors or acts exercise a disproportionally positive influence on
- breaking the status quo?
- getting the maximum bang out of each buck of resources?
- motivating key players to aggressively move forward with change?
- knocking down political roadblocks that crush even the best strategies?

Sixth principle: Build execution into strategy

Blue ocean strategies succeed in obtaining the trust, commitment and voluntary cooperation from all stakeholders of the organisation. The **build execution into strategy** principle attenuates the management risk associated with pursuing a blue ocean, e.g. distrust, noncooperation and sabotage. Blue ocean strategy increases the chances of successful strategy execution by using the power of fair process. Fair process is built on three pillars: engagement, explanation and expectation clarity.

Engagement means involving individuals in the strategic decisions that affect them by asking for their inputs and allowing them to refute the merits of other people's ideas and assumptions. Engagement communicates the blue ocean strategist's respect for individuals and their ideas. Not only does engagement result in better strategies and decision-making, but it also increases the commitment of those involved to execute the chosen path. **Explanation** is communicating to everyone involved and affected why strategic decisions are made as they are. Explaining to people the underlying thinking that went into decisions provides them with confidence that managers have considered their opinions and have made decisions impartially in the overall interest of the business. As such, explanation builds trust in a manager's intentions. Lastly, **expectation clarity** is clearly stating what the new rules of the game are after the strategy has been set. Employees naturally have fears regarding their place in an organisation. These fears can be diffused by being transparent about what they will be responsible for, how their performance will be judged, and what the new milestones are. It is of the utmost importance that these are clearly communicated to them so that they understand what is expected of them.[89]

When all three of these principles of a fair process are followed, voluntary cooperation in strategy execution is usually the result. Inversely, by not using a fair process, resistance and even refusal to execute the strategy are almost certain. These differences are shown in Figure 6.14 .

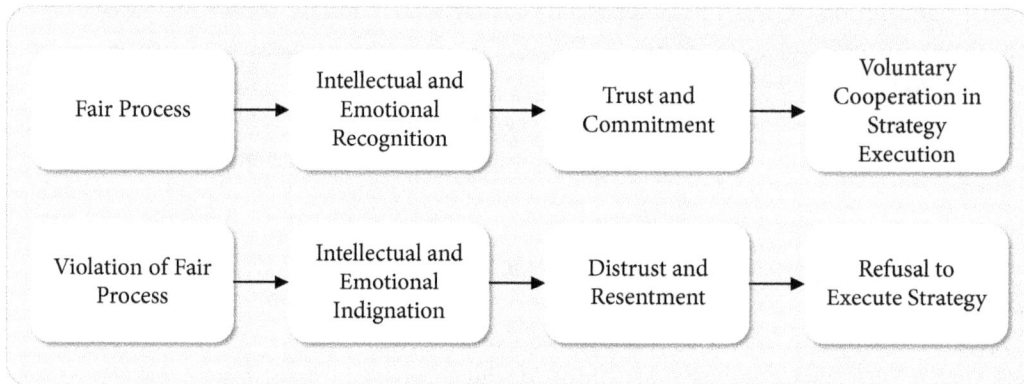

Figure 6.14: The execution consequences of the presence and absence of fair process in strategy-making[90]

🔍 Case study: Nintendo Wii [91] [92] [93] [94] [95] [96] [97]

The Wii is a home gaming console released by Nintendo in 2006. Gaming consoles are connected to a television and allow users to play audio-visual games by means of some remote control. Before the release of the Wii, Nintendo was a distant third player in a market that had been dominated by two industry giants: Sony with its PlayStation (PS1, PS2 & PS3) and Microsoft with its Xbox (Xbox and Xbox 360).

Instead of trying to outcompete its rival in a head-on battle in an industry where "hard-core" gamers value graphics, speed, detail and the most immersive sound experience, Nintendo decided to challenge long-held industry orthodoxies and released the Wii. "The consensus was that power isn't everything for a console. Too many powerful consoles can't coexist. It's like having only ferocious dinosaurs. They might fight and hasten their own extinction."[98] The Wii's value curve compared to that of the PlayStation 3 and Xbox 360 is shown in the strategy canvas in Figure 6.15.

The Wii as a console is less powerful than its industry counterparts. It has a less powerful central processing unit (CPU), a less powerful graphical processing unit (GPU) and less random access memory (RAM). It also doesn't have a DVD player, meaning that one can't use it to watch movies or TV shows like you can with the PS3 or Xbox 360. The Wii also doesn't support 5.1-channel Dolby Digital sound, has less internal storage and worse connectivity features than its rivals. The Wii cut out some of the most important features of performance that the industry always believed mattered to gamers. Pure insanity. Right?

The difference is that instead of focusing on hard-core gamers, the Nintendo Wii focused on a large mass of underserved and unexplored customers: kids, families, casual gamers and people who have always found gaming too difficult, intimidating, confusing or serious. Where the industry always believed that gamers all value the same things, Nintendo realised that casual gamers have totally different desires and behaviours to hard-core gamers.

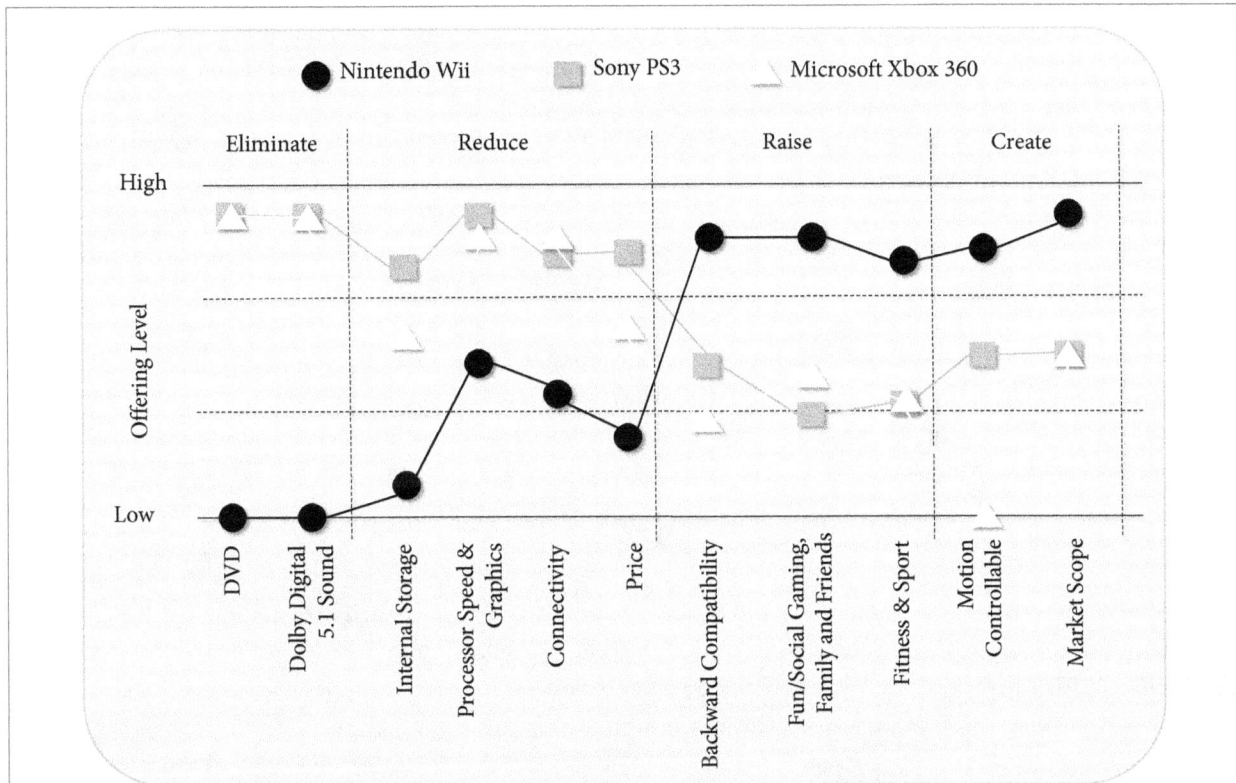

Figure 6.15: Nintendo Wii's blue ocean strategy value curve

Casual gamers tend to play less than hard-core gamers. They are therefore more reluctant to pay a lot for a gaming console as they won't use it as often. Also, because casual gamers play less and have cumulatively played less than their hard-core counterparts, they are less experienced overall. Games that are extremely difficult require complex button combinations, or deep strategies that are not appealing to them. Instead, casual gamers value simplicity and accessibility over graphics and depth – something you can just pick up and get into – something for the whole family.

Therefore, by cutting expensive features that hard-core gamers value, Nintendo was able to manufacture the Wii at lower cost than the PS3 or Xbox 360, while passing on the savings to customers and retailing the Wii at a lower price. The Wii's cost savings were so much in fact, that where the industry usually makes a loss on console sales and only makes a profit on subsequent game sales, the Wii already made profits of between $6 and $79 per console sold (depending where in the world it was sold).

The primary attraction of the Wii for casual gamers, however, lay in its innovative motion controller. The Wii remote controller has built-in accelerometers and uses infrared detection to sense the controller's position in three-dimensional space. This allows gamers to control their games with physical gestures, in addition to button-presses. Gamers can therefore swing the controller like a golf club when playing golf, or swing the control like a bat when playing baseball, or swing the controller like a sword when fencing – all movements that are much more intuitive for casual gamers, kids and parents than those presented by other gaming controls.

Still, Nintendo was facing the daunting task of having to pull a mass of untapped nongamers into the industry. It overcame this barrier to adoption by bundling the Wii Sports game with the Wii console (in all areas except Japan and South Korea). Sports like the ones mentioned above are all very familiar, even to nongamers. Therefore allowing casual gamers to socialise and compete against friends and family in games that were familiar to them made the Wii feel very "safe", and built their confidence to expand their horizons and eventually move on to other game genres. Nintendo also stated that they chose the name "Wii", because it sounds like "we". This emphasises that the console is for everyone. The "ii" further represents two people standing next to each other, highlighting its social interaction. Otherwise the "ii" can be interpreted as representing the Wii Remote and Nunchuk.

In summary, Nintendo was able to reconstruct its industry market boundaries (look across strategic groups in an industry/look across functional and emotional appeal to buyers) by reaching beyond the existing demand of the hard-core gaming community, and succeeded in creating a blue ocean for itself. Nintendo applied the principles of value innovation to produce the Wii at a lower cost, creating a leap in value for the business, but also selling the console at lower prices to create a leap in value for customers. Lastly, it differentiated itself by introducing a motion-sensing controller and aligning the whole focus of the console around being family-friendly, fun, interactive, and social.

While it is true that Microsoft and Sony have in the meanwhile also introduced their own motion-sensing controls to turn the blue ocean red, Nintendo still succeeded in profitably selling more than 100 million Wiis worldwide (31 March 2016) and making the Wii a household name to a mass of previous nongamers.

SOURCES OF E-VALUE

Over the years, various shifts have occurred in the emphasis that businesses place on their approach to entrepreneurship and competition. One of the paradigms that has recently received revived attention is the emphasis on value creation to satisfy customer needs.[99] [100] [101] [102] [103]

Value is an elusive and fickle concept, as it is a relative term that is deeply influenced by a customer's perceptions. Beauty and value both lie in the eyes of the beholder. An offering is regarded as valuable when its perceived benefit, utility or gain outweighs its price. According to Golub and Henry,[104] "A product's value to customers is, simply, the greatest amount of money they would pay for it. In other words, a product will rarely be purchased when its price exceeds its value to the customer. Conversely, whenever the value of a product exceeds its price, customers can improve their lot by buying it." It also needs to be mentioned that the price of the offering need not only be in the form of money. The price could also imply a trade of some sort, an investment in time, or the effort required to obtain the offering.[105]

Value creation and value-oriented thinking aren't new concepts and have always been a vital component of business. Edward de Bono, for instance, noted that "Companies that solely focus on competition will ultimately die. Those that focus on value creation will thrive."[106] The problem facing businesses today, however, is that given the relative newness of the Internet, research relating to value creation in e-business is still in its infancy. The result is a vague understanding of e-value, which inhibits entrepreneurs' ability to formulate value propositions that cater to customer needs and thus inhibits entrepreneurs' ability to effectively compete online.[107] In an attempt to alleviate this hindrance and provide greater clarity on the subject, Ungerer[108] studied the extant literature and proposed an integrated perspective on sources of e-value creation, as shown in Figure 6.16.

These 18 sources of e-value represent different types of value that customers find valuable online (at an almost thematic level of abstraction) and which businesses would do well to incorporate in their value propositions to maximise the potential of the Internet, and thereby enhance their potential survivability in the e-environment. Twelve of these sources were classified as being predominantly functional sources of e-value, while six of the sources were classified as being predominantly emotional sources of e-value. These 18 sources are discussed below.[111] [112]

Effectiveness refers to doing a job well and obtaining the desired result. This source of value is related to the performance quality, reliability and functionality of offerings, and can involve doing things better, faster, more accurately, more consistently, or producing fewer defects.[113] Excelling at effectiveness therefore involves creating an offering that is superior in the consequence that it produces. Examples of businesses that excel at effectiveness include AirBnB (a more effective way of finding affordable lodging), Kickstarter (a more effective way of obtaining funding for products) and Dropbox (a more effective way of ensuring that one's files are backed up).

Affordability and cost reduction refers to finding innovative ways to be more efficient to lower expenses for customers. Affordability involves creating value for customers by making the offering available at a price point that is acceptable to them. Cost reduction involves reducing customers' expenses in things that they are already doing or are necessary for them to do.[114] Cost reduction therefore does not necessarily mean that the resulting offering is low cost or affordable. It simply represents a better, lower-cost solution than current practices or products. Examples of businesses that excel at affordability and cost reduction include Skype (making long-distance video chat and voice calls affordable), Google (reducing the cost of searching for information) and Groupon (making offerings affordable via group economies of scale).

Range and complementarities refers to the variety of products and services offered[115] and the synergies or complementarities that exist between them. Range provides optionality and choice to customers, whereas complementarities are present whenever having a bundle of goods or services together provides more value than the total value of having each of these in isolation.[116] Examples of businesses that excel at range and complementarities include Amazon (offers a huge range of products – its economies of scope and scale create internal efficiencies and external customer value); Apple (seamlessly integrated proprietary closed platform and product family); and eBay (synergistic advantages gained via scale and scope of online auctions).

Reach and accessibility refers to the degree to which a company can make its offerings accessible to customers.[117] [118] Reach is the potential geographic, demographic, psychological or behavioural penetration of the company's offerings.

Accessibility on the other hand is concerned with the ways in which customers are connected with offerings.[119] Reach and accessibility essentially involve eliminating barriers to consumption and giving customers access to products, services, their data, and digital capabilities at any time or place. Examples of businesses that excel at reach and accessibility are Dropbox (data always accessible online); YouTube (video streaming always accessible online); and Spotify (music streaming always accessible online).

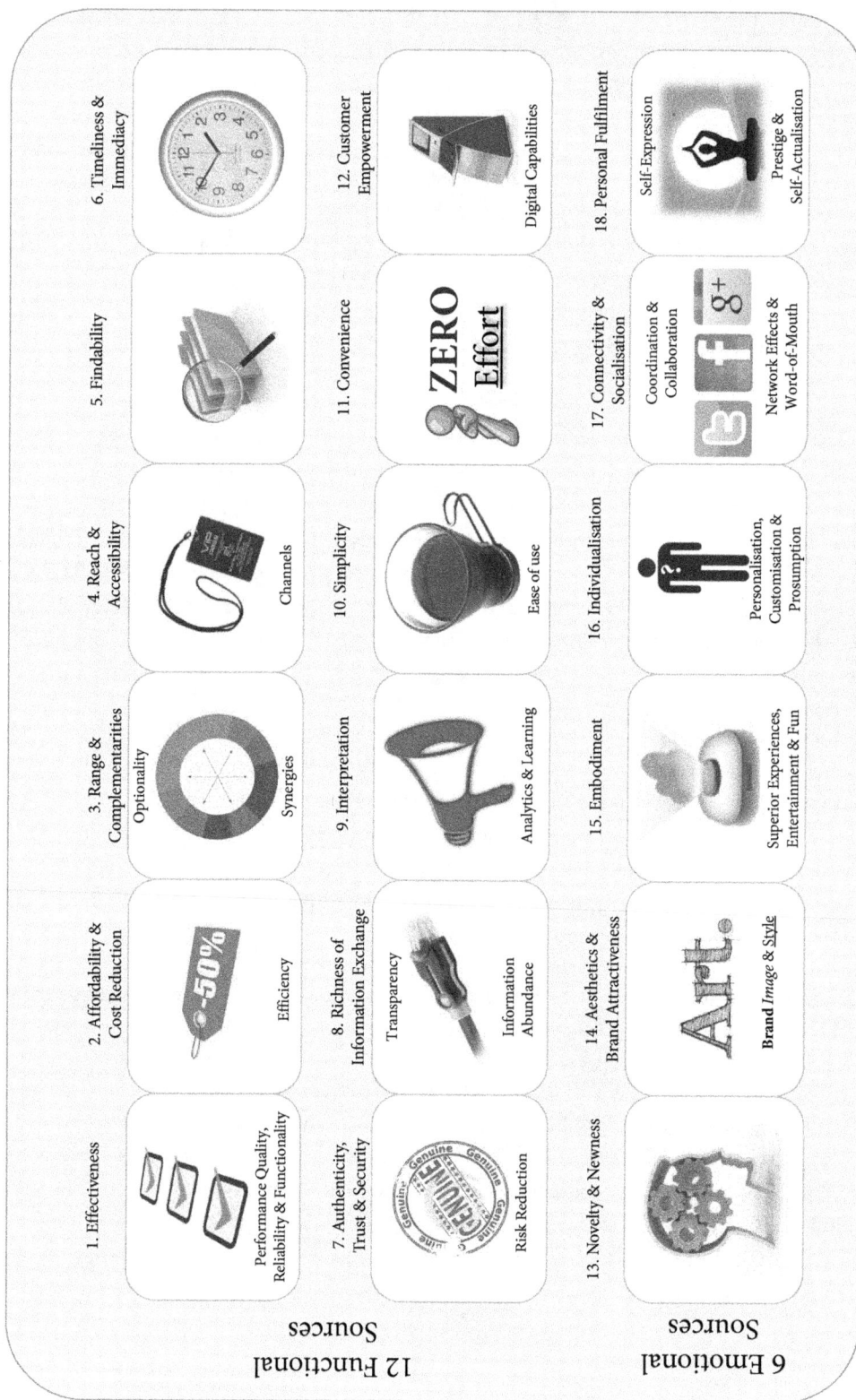

Figure 6.16: 18 sources of e-value[109][110]

Findability refers to the ability to find something or the ability to be found. Findability is related to search and filtering capabilities and is a source of value, as people's attention needs to be directed to improve their chance of finding what they really seek.[120] With millions of websites all clamouring for attention,[121] [122] findability is the only mechanism that will help businesses and users alike cope with the chaos of the approaching digital information overload. Examples of businesses that excel at findability are Google (making the world's information accessible via search and filtering); Uber (finding the nearest Uber taxi); and information aggregation sites such as Digg (Digg's slogan – "what the Internet is talking about right now").

Timeliness and immediacy refers to meeting customers' need for instant gratification.[123] Time is a scarcity[124] [125] and immediacy is valuable. This is evident as customers are often willing to pay more for something they can instantly obtain than waiting to get access to it at a later stage.[126] Examples of businesses that excel in timeliness and immediacy are Netflix (all-you-can-binge-watch series and movies, accessible at your convenience); Valve (their steam platform hosts a myriad games, which after purchase can be downloaded and played immediately); and Amazon (on some days they have same-day delivery, and books on Kindle are available instantly after purchase).

Authenticity, trust and security deal with making customers feel at ease with purchasing products online. Authenticity refers to genuineness. Trust relates to having confidence in a website's integrity and reliability. Lastly, security relates to the safety of transactions and the safeguarding of customer information.[127] [128] These two issues, transactional security and overall concerns for privacy, are two of the most significant issues that dissuade people from shopping online.[129] [130] Furthermore, as most people are risk-averse,[131] [132] it is critical to reduce buyer apprehensiveness in order to conduct business online. Examples of businesses that excel in authenticity, trust and security are Verisign (online authentication service); Avira (antivirus, e-mail and browser safety); and PayPal (secure online transactions).

Richness of information exchange relates to the quality, depth and detail of the bidirectional information exchange between a company and its customers and the company's ability to leverage captured customer information to better serve them.[133] Companies may for instance use customer information to develop individualised products, to reinvent customer relationships, or otherwise leverage a single digital asset to provide value across many different and disparate markets.[134] [135] [136] Examples of businesses that excel in the richness of information exchange are Wikipedia (the largest free encyclopaedia that anyone can edit); Amazon (mining customer behaviour data and making recommendations to individuals); and Cyber Dust (the inverse of high richness of information exchange – private encrypted disappearing messaging and networking).

Interpretation refers to the creation of clarity or understanding. It deals with explaining how something works or is intended to be used. Interpretation is a source of value, as many software solutions only become useful when the user has a thorough understanding of the package.[137] Interpretation from an expert may therefore be required and many businesses consequently make their money not from the software per se, but by providing paid support services that help customers use the software. Inversely, these interpretation services can be offered for free, raising the perceived value and attractiveness of the software. Examples of businesses that excel in the interpretation are Google Analytics (monitors and interprets your website traffic); Adobe (has a myriad multimedia/creativity software products and excellent learning support); and One Month (online courses digestible in one month).

Simplicity refers to making things simple and easy to do. Complexity by definition increases the difficulty of using and understanding something. Simplicity works in the opposite direction to erase complexity, to make things easy to use and understand. Simplicity is a source of value in e-business, as the online environment is inherently complex. From an "obliterating barriers to consumption" view, simplicity relates to breaking through the skills barrier to make offerings so simple and straightforward that they become accessible to new groups of customers.[138] Examples of businesses that excel in simplicity are SurveyMonkey (making it super-simple to create surveys); Eventbrite (making it super-simple to create and manage event registrations); and Tinder (making it super-simple to meet the love of your life).

Convenience is about making customers feel like they are exhibiting zero effort,[139] therefore making it extremely comfortable to do something. Convenience is an overarching concept that relates to many of the other sources of value and involves making things simpler, more intuitive and more user-friendly, and in e-business it also has to do with the way that information is presented, searched for and accessed.[140] [141] [142] Though convenience may seem like a redundant source of value as it is a composite of many of the other sources, it cannot be omitted as the concept embodies more than the sum of its parts, and is something that customers are willing to pay for.[143] Examples of businesses that excel in convenience are Dropbox (automatically syncs files to the cloud); SARS (e-filing); and SnapScan (making purchases by using your mobile phone's QR code scanner).

Customer empowerment refers to enabling and authorising customers. Customer empowerment is about giving customers enhanced control over interactions and business processes,[144] allowing them to help themselves. It is about enabling customers to make independent decisions and equipping them with digital capabilities to execute those decisions and preferences.[145] As a result, customer empowerment raises customer productivity,[146] increases convenience and delivers a more satisfying experience. Examples of businesses that excel in customer empowerment are ABSA (online banking); Ster-Kinekor (online movie reservations); and Lulu.com (online book publishing).

Novelty and newness refers to doing new things in new ways to entice customers. The value of novelty and newness lies in the ability to satisfy an entirely new set of needs that customers possibly didn't even perceive they had.[147] This could involve innovations in products and services, processes, distribution, marketing or markets. It can also involve novel transaction structures, transactional content and transactional participants.[148] Lastly, newness also relates to updatedness, where customers derive value from having the latest, best-functioning product version or most up-to-date content. Examples of businesses that excel in novelty and newness are Rubybox (receive monthly, randomised beauty products); Prezi (create "zooming" presentations instead of "paging" presentations); and CNN (breaking news, latest news).

Aesthetics and brand attractiveness refers to the aesthetic appeal, brand image or style of an e-business or offering. It is intuitive and research confirms that people use appearances to make judgements about realities.[149] A website's design and first impressions are therefore critical,[150] as users translate appearance into confidence about performance. Aesthetics and brand attractiveness are therefore key elements in convincing Internet users to become paying customers[151] and can aid in creating long-term e-loyalty. Examples of businesses that excel in aesthetics and brand attractiveness are Apple (premium, elegant, sleek product and software designs); Yuppiechef (South African kitchen and appliance e-retailer with more than 20 awards under its belt since 2009); and Shutterstock (selling beautiful stock images).

Embodiment refers to the way in which the digital world and people's digital interactions are embedded in different forms to create a more real, fun, entertaining or simply superior experience. People are always looking for the next best thing – high-definition display, 3D display, holographic interfaces, virtual reality, surround sound and the like. A free experience may therefore be possible, but it is the embodiment of the experience in a better form that is valuable and what people will pay for.[152] Physical examples of embodiment include books (words can be read on a screen, but sometimes it just feels good to have the same words printed on bright white cottony paper, bound in leather) and music (it can be streamed via Spotify, but it just isn't the same as seeing the band live at a concert).[153] Digital examples include online gaming (playing against the A.I. is okay, but playing with friends online and communicating via Teamspeak just makes the experience much more real and entertaining) and Skype (long-distance phone calls to relatives were good, but being able to see their expressions via video chat is just so much better).

Individualisation involves tailoring offerings to an individual customer's needs and circumstances. Personalisation, customisation and prosumption are all different ways to individualise offerings. Personalisation is initiated by the e-business (through customer data-mining) and usually involves the minor individualisation of interfaces, recommendations and ads based on customer behaviour and location. Customisation, conversely, is initiated by the customer[154] and involves tailoring of the offering itself based on customer needs. Lastly, during prosumption (also known as co-creation) the production and consumption process converges[155] [156] and customers play an active role in helping with the design or production of their final product. Examples of businesses that excel in individualisation are Facebook (personalises your newsfeed and uses targeted ads); LinkedIn (users customise their profiles to create a sleek résumé); and Lego Digital Designer (provides customers with virtual tools to create their own Lego sets, which are produced and sent to customers).

Connectivity and socialisation relate to Internet users' increased need to connect, interact, share stories and socialise with their friends, family, colleagues, companies and other people.[157] [158] All of these are enabled by the extended reach and openness of the Internet that provides a channel for information-sharing, communication and collaboration.[159] Additionally, this extended reach is very conducive to network effects and word-of-mouth communication, because as a users' network grows, they are better able to collaborate in real time, coordinate and execute tasks, and receive recommendations and advice about offerings from friends, contacts, or genuine past users. Examples of businesses that excel in connectivity and socialisation are Facebook ("Facebook's mission is to give people the power to share and make the world more open and connected. People use Facebook to stay connected with friends and family, to discover what's going on in the world, and to share and express what matters to them."); Waze (crowd sourced traffic information); and Slack (collaboration app for managing teams and projects).

Personal fulfilment relates to giving customers the opportunity to achieve a sense of happiness or satisfaction as a result of some achievement or experience that caters to an emotional need or assists in building their identity. It could also involve giving customers the opportunity to gain prestige, social recognition and self-esteem, to express themselves or self-actualise. Building virtual communities can be particularly helpful in fulfilling these desires,[160] [161] as virtual communities are places where recognition and respect can be earned, creating a sense of belonging. Examples of businesses that excel in personal fulfilment are Blizzard (games such as StarCraft and World of Warcraft are always packed with rankings and achievements that can be earned); WordPress (allows anyone to blog about what interests them); and Instagram (allows people to show off their photos to the world).

Considering its application, the 18 sources of e-value can be used in different ways. Firstly, they can act as a learning tool for informing our understanding of value creation in e-business, and hence our understanding of competition in e-business. Secondly, they can act as a brainstorming tool that guides our thinking about developing innovative and desirable e-value propositions. Finally, they can be used as an analytical tool for determining the key strengths of businesses or identifying weaknesses that require refinement.[162]

There are no prescriptions as to how many sources of value a business should focus on or pursue. These sources of value can either be pursued in isolation to develop a very focused offering, or in combination to deliver a better overall customer experience. In most cases however, businesses will have traces of the majority of these sources of value in their value propositions, but these won't necessarily be significant enough to constitute factors that the business particularly excels at. On average, businesses will therefore only have a few sources of value that will act as the core drivers of their value propositions.[163]

Although the author does not claim it is an exhaustive list (impossible task) or even that there is mutual exclusivity between the identified sources of value (because of the complex and idiosyncratic associations embedded in language), this perspective at the very least provides a good point of departure for thinking about value creation in e-business,[164] as it reflects commonly cited and ubiquitously manifested sources of e-value. More importantly, the 18 sources of e-value can serve as a sound basis for spurring further theoretical conversations about the vital topic of e-value creation.[165]

Application tool

Reflect on the 18 sources of e-value by asking yourself the following questions about your business:

- What is our unique selling proposition/value composition?
- Are we clearly articulating the value we provide?
- What types of value are the most important to our customers?
- How can we incorporate these types of value to create desirable offerings?
- What types of value can we excel at providing?
- Is there an alignment between our value creation competencies and customer value needs?
- What additional offerings or complements can we create to fully exploit our value creation competencies?
- Which value creation deficiencies do we have that need to be overcome?

OVERCOMING STALL POINTS AND DECLINE

Executives and managers are quick to blame uncontrollable external factors such as market conditions, economic cycles, government regulations and competitive rivalry when organisation performance has slowed down, plateaued or declined within a certain time frame. The harsh reality is that the bad performance of an organisation is seldom due only to external conditions outside the influence domain of decision-makers, but more the result of strategic choices and decisions that were within the power and control of senior executive teams. Research[166] indicates that most stalls in organisation performance occur for reasons that are both knowable and addressable at the time of occurrence. This of course is good news for strategists, because it indicates that organisations can do something about their own future prosperity. Both growth and decline are self-inflicted outcomes largely caused by managerial decisions.

A growth stall point is the start of material reversals in the growth fortunes of an organisation.[167] A stall point also indicates the moment when a firm's growth rate slides into a prolonged period of decline. A stall point is therefore a moment in time that best represents a turning point, or significant downturn, in corporate revenue growth. The challenge associated with stall points is that they happen suddenly, without much prior warning due to an in inability of traditional performance metrics to register that trouble is on the horizon. The reality is that most organisations experience a period or periods of slower growth and possible decline over time. The key questions are:

- What causes a stall point?
- How can it be identified earlier?

An analysis[168] of more than 500 companies over 50 years indicates that more than half of all root causes of a growth stall fall into one of four categories: premium-position captivity, innovation management breakdown, premature core abandonment, and talent bench shortfall (see Figure 6.17).

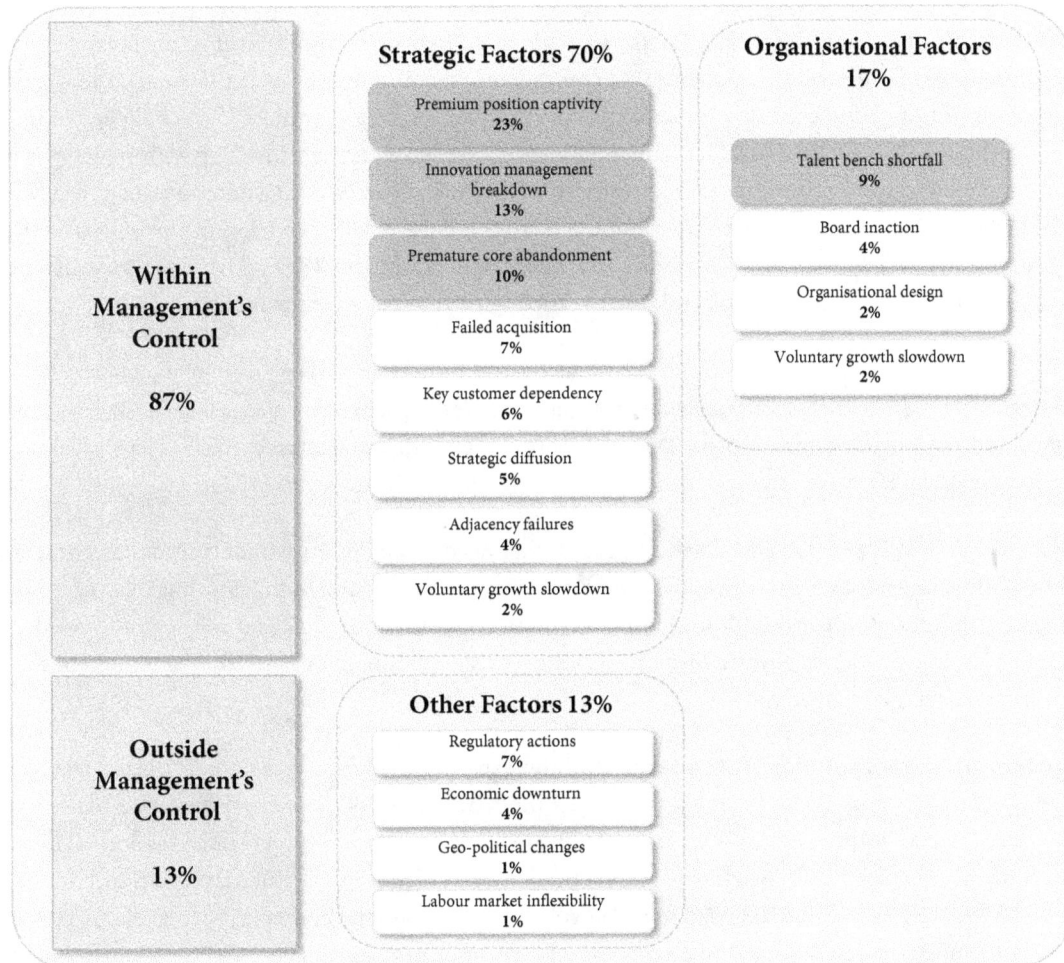

Figure 6.17: Root causes of revenue stalls[169]

The largest category of factors responsible for significant revenue stalls is called **premium-position captivity,** which is the inability of an organisation to react effectively to new low-cost competitive challenges or to significant shifts in how customers value product features. The term "captivity" indicates the tendency of management teams to hold on for too long to historical successes. The dilemma with a company that occupies a premium market position is that it gets insulated for longer than its competitors against the evolution and changes in the external environment. Successful premium position incumbents have less reason to "doubt its business model (which has historically provided its competitive advantage) and once it perceives the crisis, it changes too little too late".[170] A cruel reversal occurs when the inherent historical strengths of a firm are transformed into towering weaknesses. Eastman Kodak and Caterpillar as price and quality leaders have found themselves unable (or unwilling) to formulate a timely, effective response to the threat posed by foreign entrants. A potential premium-position captivity onset can be identified early via marketing data that shows pockets of rapid market share loss, particularly in narrow customer segments, and increasing resistance among key customers to solutions packages and other bundling of services. Other clues are customer resistance to paying price premiums for product enhancements and the unwillingness of management to accept that low-cost providers and nonpremium rivals can enter the middle and high-end markets over time. Market leaders need to scan the competitive environment on a continuous basis to pick up early clues in customer need shifts and competitor moves.

Innovation management breakdown is a failure to achieve desired or required returns on investments in new products, services and business development. This comes from a continuing problem in managing the business's internal processes for updating existing products and services and creating new ones. This challenge of innovation is not so much linked to individual product launch failures, as we have seen for instance with new types of Coke. Innovation breakdowns are attributable more to the systemic inefficiencies or dysfunctions in the new product development processes of an organisation. An example is Xerox's failure to commercialise the invention of distributed personal computing in the mid-1970s. Companies that shift the bulk of their R&D activities to their business units might be exposed to potential innovation breakdowns. The logic behind such shifts is clear:

> "The closer R&D is to markets and individual unit strategies, the higher its return on investment should be. But problems seem to arise when decentralisation is combined with an explicit (or implicit) metric that demands a high share of revenue growth from new-product introductions. The result can be an over-allocation of resources to ever smaller incremental product opportunities, at the expense of sustained R&D investment in larger, future product platforms."[171]

Innovation management is a fragile and sensitive process that needs a mix of investments in incremental and next-generation solutions as well as a coordinated balance between corporate level R&D and business unit innovation focus areas. The allocation of funding for lower-cost versions of existing products and services also needs to be on the corporate innovation radar. Innovation is part of the long-term play of an organisation and flaws in the process are slow to surface and take time to fix.

Premature core abandonment represents a failure to fully exploit growth opportunities in the existing products, customers and channels of the core business franchise. The temptation to enter far-distant opportunities diverts focus away from the core business areas. This strategic diversification move is a direct transgression of the guideline to "stick to your core business". Two beliefs drive this action: (1) the current markets are saturated and (2) the current business model impediments signal the need to start exploring new potential competitive terrains. However, giving up on a current market too early creates the opportunity for rivals or new entrants to take up the abandoned market space. In the early 1980s K-mart's diversification into cafeterias, buffet chains and pizza-video parlours created the opportunity for Walmart to expand their core business. The takeout is that business leaders should actively explore the potential to revitalise their core businesses, no matter how "mature" they are.

The last major reason for organisations to experience a period of stalled growth is related to a **talent bench shortfall**. This refers to a lack of adequate leaders and staff with the skills and capabilities required for successful strategy execution. This is not only a matter of a shortage of talent, but more about the absence of required capabilities to execute key strategic processes such as solution-selling skills or consumer-marketing expertise in key areas of a company, most visibly at the executive level. The talent shortfall manifests in the form of key person dependency, loss of key talent and a narrow experience base. The lack of talent to execute the strategic agenda is due to internal inefficiencies in the talent management process that do not produce the required variety, quality and quantity of talent. Packard's law states that no company can consistently grow revenues faster than its ability to get enough of the right people to implement that growth and still become a great company.[172]

Application tool

Consider the following questions to think proactively about potential sources of growth stalls in your current business portfolio:[173]

- What are the core assumptions about the marketplace and capabilities that are critical to executing our strategy successfully?
- What are our current market definition boundaries and who are our emerging competitors?
- What is the definition or description of our core market(s) and market share? What is the emerging pattern?
- How do we test for shifts in our key customer groups' valuation of our product/service attributes? What is the emerging pattern?
- How effective are we compared to our competition in translating customer needs into new product and service offerings?
- Do we have core customers who are increasingly unwilling to pay a premium for our superior brand reputation and performance? What is the emerging pattern?

Practical guideline

The following practices can assist organisations to raise their early warning capabilities to spot potential stall points:

- Establish a core belief identification squad. Mobilise a diverse cross-functional work group to identify and describe the organisation's most deeply held assumptions about itself and the industry in which it operates. Also explore orthodoxies associated with the industry as well as 10 things customers will never say about the business.[174]
- Conduct a premortem strategy analysis. This includes a full strategy analysis of the external and internal environment of the organisation[175] as well as the development of possible future scenarios (see chapter 4).
- Appoint a shadow cabinet. A shadow cabinet is a group of high-potential employees who complement the work of the executive committee of an organisation. They can be given the task of developing perspectives on

specific intractable challenges around core business issues or can be invited to executive committee meetings on a rotating basis. The idea is to bring fresh perspectives offered by this creditable, well-informed constituency to the executive committee. This initiative can only work, however, in a culture of openness and respect for new ideas.

- Invite a venture capitalist or industry analyst to your strategy review. This is an effective way to bring an external view into the discussion to probe core assumptions and identify potential weaknesses.

Phases of organisational decline

We now further explore the proactive identification of organisational decline through early warning signals. In his 2009 book *How the mighty fall*, Jim Collins describes institutional decline as a staged disease that is harder to detect but easier to cure in the early stages, and easier to detect but harder to cure in the later stages. Collins notes: "An institution can look strong on the outside but already be sick on the inside, dangerously on the cusp of a precipitous fall".[176]

Before the actual downfall and decline of an organisation, three stages of organisational decline can be identified – each phase with its own core features.[177] These are:

Stage 1: Hubris born of success. The decline indicators associated with this stage are:

- Success entitlement and arrogance where success is viewed as "deserved", rather than incidental, short-lived, or even hard-earned in the face of formidable odds. Here people begin to believe that success is enduring and will last forever no matter what the organisation decides to do or not to do.
- Neglect of the primary growth engine of the business by being distracted by superfluous threats, adventures, and opportunities. This leads to a failure to renew the core business with the same creative passion that made it great in the first place.
- The tendency to replace "why" with "what". Instead of continuing to create an understanding of why specific things are done and knowing under what conditions they will not work any longer, the focus shifts to explaining success as doing these specific things.
- A decline in the learning orientation in the organisation. Leaders lose the curiosity and learning orientation that characterised those genuine great individuals who, no matter how successful they become, maintain a learning curve as steep as when they first began their careers.
- Discounting the role of luck in success. Here success is explained as due to the superior qualities of the enterprise and its leadership, instead of acknowledging that luck and incidental events might have played a helpful role.

Stage 2: Undisciplined pursuit of more. Here the decline indicators are:

- An unsustainable quest for growth, where big is confused with great. Early success creates pressure for more growth, setting up a vicious cycle of expectations which strains people, the culture, and systems to a breaking point. This creates constraints on delivering tactical excellence on an ongoing basis.
- Undisciplined discontinuous leaps where the organisation enters into strategic moves that fail at least one of the following three tests: Do they ignite passion and fit with the company's core values? Can the organisation be the best in the world at these activities or in these arenas? Will these activities help drive the organisation's economic or resource engine?

- There is a decline in the proportion of the right people in key seats, because of the loss of staff and/or growing beyond the organisation's ability to get enough people to execute that growth with excellence.
- A lack of cost discipline due to a perception of easy cash. The organisation tends to respond to increasing costs by increasing prices and revenues rather than increasing cost discipline.
- The emergence of bureaucratic rules that replace the ethic of freedom and responsibility – the hallmarks of a culture of discipline. Gradually people start to think in terms of "jobs" rather than responsibilities.
- A problematic succession of power as the organisation experiences leadership-transition difficulties. It shows up in poor succession planning, failure to groom excellent leaders from within, political turmoil, bad luck, or an unwise selection of successors.
- Personal interests are placed above organisational interests as the people in power allocate more to themselves or their constituents. This can include more money, more privileges, more fame, or more of the spoils of success. Here individuals try to capitalise as much as possible in the short term, rather than investing in building the business towards greatness for decades into the future.

Stage 3: Denial of risk and peril. The decline indicators are as follows:

- Any negative data are discounted whilst positives are amplified. There is a tendency to discount or explain away negative data rather than presume that something is wrong with the company. Leaders also tend to highlight, amplify and concentrate on external praise and publicity. This artificially positive image is also reflected in the risk practices, where potential down-side risks are underplayed.
- Big bets are made and bold goals are set without empirical validation. Leaders tend to set audacious goals and/ or make big bets that aren't based on accumulated experience or facts.
- There is a gradual erosion of healthy team dynamics as shown in a marked decline in the quality and amount of dialogue and debate. There is a shift toward either consensus or dictatorial management, rather than a process of argument and disagreement followed by unified commitment to execute decisions.
- Blame is externalised as leaders point to external factors or other people to pin blame on rather than accepting full responsibility for setbacks and failures.
- Obsessive reorganisations are used as a quick fix for deep business challenges. The brutal realities of the organisation are not confronted; instead the enterprise is chronically reorganised. People become more preoccupied with internal politics than external conditions.
- An arrogant detachment by those in power becomes evident. It manifests in outrageous symbols and perks of executive-class status, which amplify detachment. A plush new office building may disconnect executives even more from daily realities.

Application tool

Use Table 6.10 to evaluate your organisation's manifestation of potential decline indicators.

Table 6.10: Organisational decline indicators

Stage 1: Hubris born of success	Indicators	Comments on current status
	Success entitlement and arrogance	
	Neglect of the primary growth engine	
	Replacing "Why" with "What".	
	A decline in the learning orientation	
	Discounting the role of luck in success	
Stage 2: Undisciplined pursuit of more	**Indicators**	**Comments on current status**
	Unsustainable quest for growth	
	Undisciplined discontinuous leaps	
	Declining proportion of the right people in key seats	
	Lack of cost discipline	
	Bureaucratic rules replacing ethic of freedom and responsibility	
	Problematic succession of power	
	Personal interests placed above organisational interests	
Stage 3: Denial of risk and peril	**Indicators**	**Comments on current status**
	Negative data are discounted whilst positives are amplified	
	Bets and goals lack empirical evidence	
	Erosion of healthy team dynamics	
	Externalising blame	
	Obsessive reorganisations	
	Arrogant detachment	

In the last part of this chapter the aspect of creating and maintain a portfolio of innovation experiments is described as a key capability for winning organisations.

PROTFOLIO OF EXPERIMENTS AND PROTOTYPES

Growing and expanding the core business in current, related and new markets will eventually run up against a growth limit. Somewhere on the growth path of an organisation there will be a need for new product and service offerings. To create this organisational capacity to generate new business opportunities on a regular basis, one needs to maintain a portfolio of experiments and prototypes. Ongoing and continuous efforts are necessary to maintain and improve the competitive position of an organisation. The creation of a portfolio of business model experiments and product/service prototypes and concepts is a pragmatic way to increase the sustainability potential of an organisation.

A portfolio of experiments is dependent on an innovation process that stimulates idea generation. Innovation is a process where new combinations or connections between variables are created for new insights to emerge in the form of new technologies, applications, markets and organisational practices resulting in business value creation.[178] In an internal innovation process, external market efficiencies should be replicated through an internal venture capital process. An internal market for ideas creates a pull for innovative ideas. The internal innovation processes shown in Figure 6.18 enable the flow of ideas to create a portfolio of ideas, experiments and new ventures.

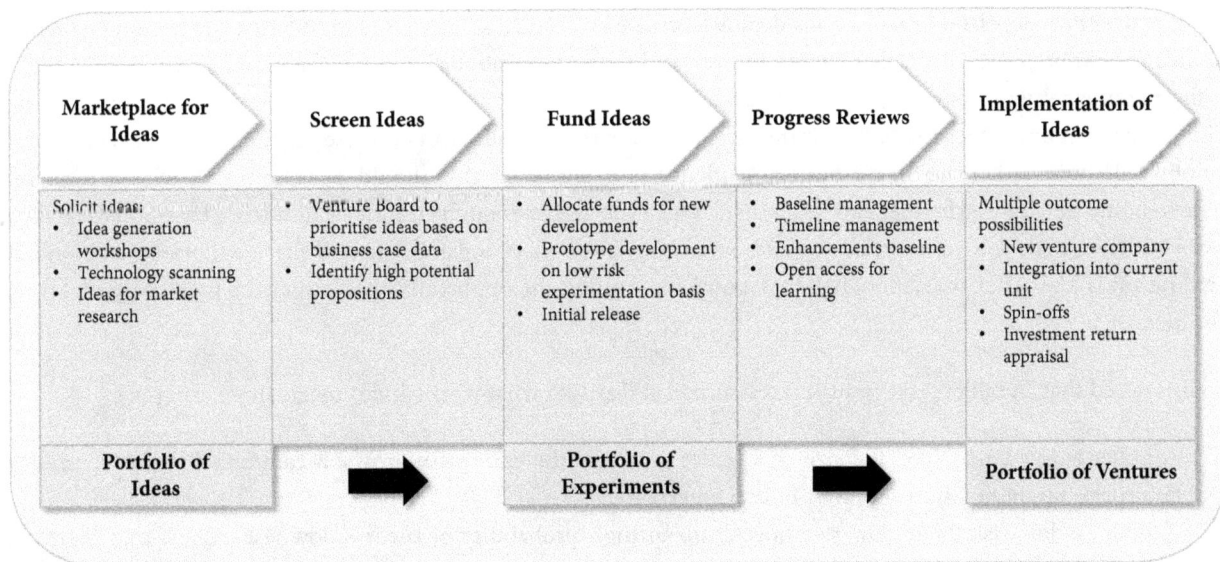

Figure 6.18: Innovation funnel[179]

Embedding innovation as a key organisation process creates a practice where it is reinforced in every area of the business and energy is focused and supported through an internal venture funnel idea management system. This is needed because sustainable innovation requires a consistent flow of a lot of ideas. Hamel's Law on innovation[180] states that for every 1 000 ideas, only 100 will have enough commercial value to merit a small-scale experiment, only ten of those will warrant a significant financial investment, and of those, only a couple will turn out to be unqualified successes. Gillette, that celebrated 100 years of being on the cutting edge of innovation in 2001, is an example of evolving innovation in the razor arena. Nokia's orientation towards constant innovation has similarly allowed them to deliver 15 significant market firsts since 1992.

The process of hypothesis testing to determine which business concept can work or not can be done by applying the lean start-up process.[181] The lean start-up process begins in the idea phase where (1) hypotheses are generated. These hypotheses are then (2) built into minimum viable products that (3) are tested in the market against real customers. This process of testing new product and service concepts in a fast and efficient low-cost manner is useful for creating and maintaining a portfolio of business experiments. In doing so, possible alternative product and service futures for an organisation are created to stimulate reinvention and agility.

Jim Collins[182] notes that the ability to generate internal empirical evidence for use in decision-making is the hallmark of successful organisations. Collins described high-performing organisations with the moniker "10X", where every 10X organisation beats its industry index by at least 10 times. Instead of looking for external expertise or advice – authority figures, peers, group norms – for their primary cues on how to proceed in time of uncertainty, 10X organisations favour empiricism as the foundation for their decisions and action. They use direct observation, practical experiments, and engage directly with evidence "rather than relying upon opinion, whim, conventional wisdom, authority, or untested ideas. Having an empirical foundation enables 10Xers to make bold, creative moves and bound their risk."[183]

The practice that successful organisations deploy to create an empirical fact-based foundation for deciding whether an idea should be pursued is called **"firing bullets and then cannonballs"**.[184] First, the organisation fires "bullets" to figure out what will work. Bullets are low-cost, low-risk experiments. These bullets are used to check what is hit with the current aim. Does the bullet hit the target – or anything at all? And do these hits merit conversion to a big cannonball? Bullets that show no empirical evidence of eventual success should be terminated, while promising bullets should be explored further and "calibrated". Once you gather enough empirical confidence based on the bullets that you have fired, you concentrate your resources on the most promising one and fire a calibrated cannonball. Calibration is key. After the cannonball hits, you keep mining the opportunity to extract the most potential from this idea.

Collins noted that "A bullet is an empirical test aimed at learning what works and it meets three criteria:

- A bullet is low cost. Note: the size of a bullet grows as the enterprise grows; a cannonball for a $1 million enterprise might be a bullet for a $1 billion enterprise.
- A bullet is low risk. Note: low risk doesn't mean high probability of success; low risk means that there are minimal consequences if the bullet goes awry or hits nothing.
- A bullet is low distraction. Note: this means low distraction for the overall enterprise; it might be very high distraction for one or a few individuals."[185]

The practice of firing bullets and then cannonballs is aimed at low-cost experimentation to test the viability of new innovative ideas. It aims at preventing a loss of time and money spent on nonstarter ideas. The discipline to accept the feedback results and to use this input creatively for tinkering with and adapting the original idea is part of an ongoing experimental process.

Application tool

Evaluate your organisation's innovation process against the to above guidelines to create a portfolio of experiments and prototypes. What evidence is there that a portfolio of ideas, experiments and ventures exists? Is there evidence of fast and low-cost experiment practices such as the lean start-up methodology of firing bullets and then cannonballs? Which of the following behaviours[186] do you most need to increase?

- Firing enough bullets.
- Resisting the temptation to fire uncalibrated cannonballs.
- Committing, by converting bullets into cannonballs once you have empirical validation.

CONCLUSION

This chapter discussed various perspectives and tools that can be used to drive strategy renewal and innovation in an organisation. Different sources of digital disruption from a supply and demand perspective were firstly discussed, which provides executives with a deeper understanding of the driving forces behind digital disruptions. These sources are therefore intended to be used as indicators to identify (perhaps otherwise unseen) threats and opportunities before they manifest, giving executives time to prepare. Exponential organisations were introduced as businesses whose impact is 10X that of their industry and the various ingredients required to build such an organisation were highlighted.

Blue ocean strategy, which seeks to create new market space where competitors are irrelevant, was discussed next. It was mentioned that three benefits of blue oceans include rapid and profitable growth and the opportunity to establish barriers that make it difficult for others to follow. Given our digital context, various sources of e-value were discussed next. These sources highlight elements that customers find valuable online, and which organisations would do well to integrate into their value propositions.

The causes and indicators of business stall points and decline were also discussed, which provided insights on how to prevent or overcome these. Lastly, the process of setting up a portfolio of experiments and prototypes for business renewal and innovation was discussed.

In conclusion, the modern age we live in is wonderful and at the same time frightening. This chapter sheds some light on the immense disruption that technology will still bring about in the times ahead. It also discussed the immense opportunities that are available to those conscious enough to spot them, and bold enough to pursue them. What is apparent is that strategy innovation has become an even more vital organisational capability than ever before, as the rapid pace of change is only accelerating – spurring the need for faster and more severe organisational renewal. In this sense, every organisation has to become a learning organisation that is as dynamic and adaptable as the environment it operates in.

Chapter 7

Strategy renewal and innovation 2: Inorganic Growth Strategies

"Joint Ventures, Alliances, and other Corporate Partnerings are fuelling the growth of the world's most successful companies. The demand to deliver more new products, more quickly, and at lower prices has never been greater. Joint Ventures and other collaborative business arrangements are revolutionizing how winning companies compete. They permit companies to enter new markets and field new products that they otherwise couldn't do on their own. They are the quickest way to grow your company, particularly in times of change." – Curtis E. Sahakian [1]

"Treating M&A as a strategic capability can give companies an edge that their peers will struggle to replicate." – McKinsey & Company[2]

LEARNING OBJECTIVES

This chapter focuses on inorganic growth strategies for an organisation. Guidelines and processes are described in order to engage in these business growth options. At the end of this chapter, you will be able to use the following perspectives and tools as basis for developing insights and guidance on choosing and leading inorganic growth strategies:

- Describe the different inorganic growth options for an organisation.
- Understand the dynamics and processes involved in creating a successful strategic alliance.
- Explain the rationale, benefits and formats for different types of strategic alliance.
- Explain the critical success factors for executing a successful strategic alliance.
- Understand the dynamics and processes involved in creating a successful merger and acquisition (M&A).
- Explain the critical success factors for executing a successful M&A.
- Understand the place and role of restructuring a business portfolio as a strategic performance improvement option.

INTRODUCTION AND KEY CONCEPTS

This chapter is part of the strategy renewal and innovation options of a firm as part of the strategic architecture landscape (see Figure 7.1). The focus is on inorganic growth approaches for an organisation. The following specific inorganic growth approaches are described:

- strategic alliances and partnership
- M&As

Restructuring as a strategic option to change the business portfolio or financial structure of a business is also discussed as an alternative to improve the performance of an organisation.

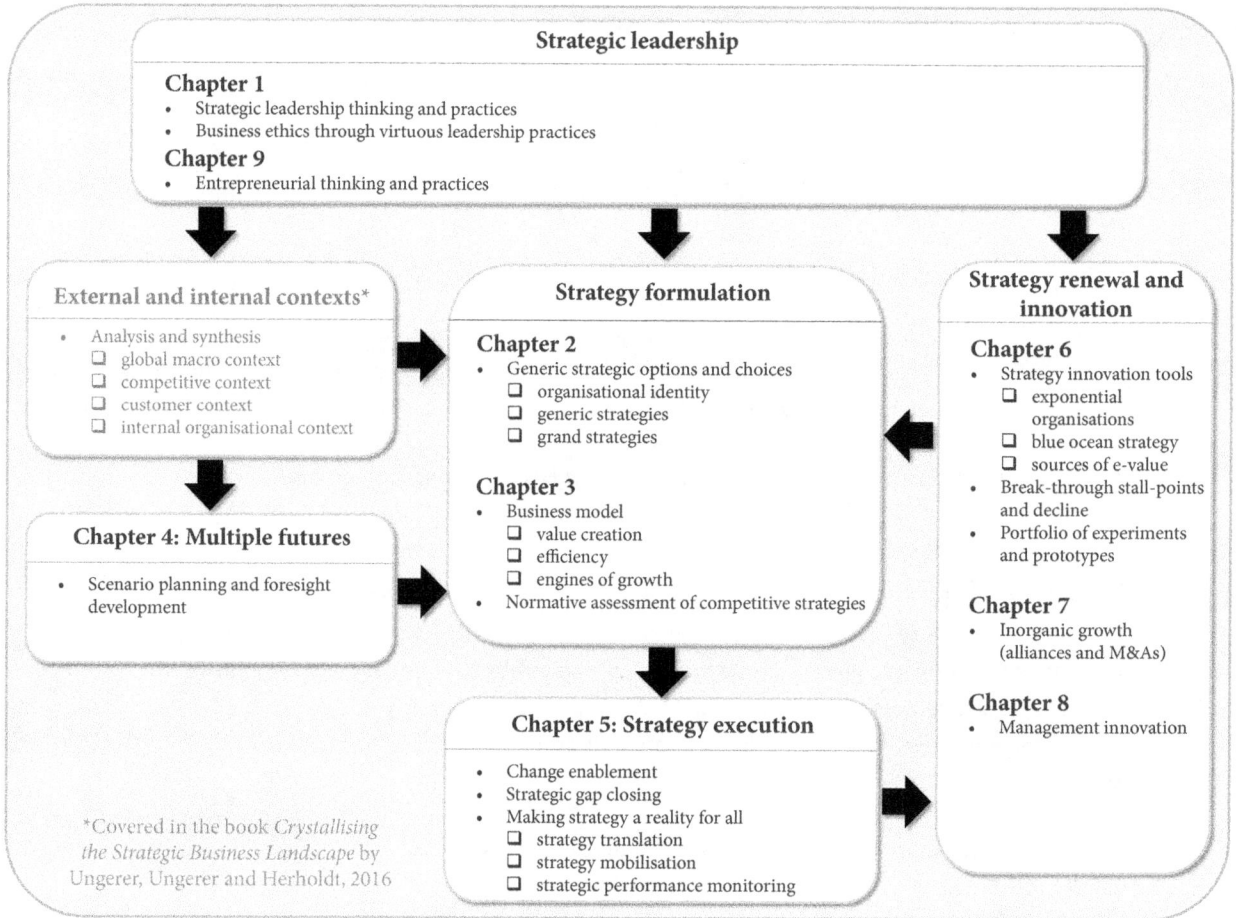

Figure 7.1: The strategic architecture landscape

In general there are two business growth approaches a firm can follow, namely organic growth and inorganic growth. Organic growth is the maintenance and acceleration of the current portfolio momentum of an organisation by leveraging the current product, service and market scope to increase current market share. Inorganic growth strategies focus on expanding the product, service and market scope of an organisation by either partnering with other firms or by acquiring new firm assets to complement and expand the current business portfolio to grow the performance basis and potential of the enterprise. Firm growth can therefore be stimulated by portfolio momentum, market share growth and direct or indirect asset expansion strategies. Research[3] indicates that firms that realise two or more out of these three growth approaches have compound annual growth rates (CAGR) that are on average far better than those who only focus on one growth approach (see Figure 7.2). McKinsey[4] indicates that "the top-quartile companies in our database on two or more of the three drivers of growth – portfolio momentum, M&A, and market share gain – stood out as relative winners. Before the downturn, they enjoyed a 24 percentage-point differential in their compound annual growth rate (CAGR) against the poor performers. During the downturn, outperformers boasted a more than 3-point advantage".

Companies' performance[1] on three drivers of growth (portfolio momentum, M&A, and market share gain)	Revenue growth, compounded annual growth rate (CAGR), %		
	1999–2007	2007–08	2008–09
Executed well on 2 or 3 (n=66)	30.7	20.3	2.9
Executed well on 1 (n=135)	16.9	14.9	1.3
Did not execute well on any and/or executed poorly on 1 to 3 (n=391)	6.5	3.8	-0.2
Difference between top and bottom performers, percentage points	+24.2	+16.5	+3.1

[1] Based on growth decomposition analysis of 592 companies. Analysis spanned different time frames for some companies between 1999 and 2007. Data for 2010 is not yet available for majority of companies analysed.
Source: Bloomberg; McKinsey analysis

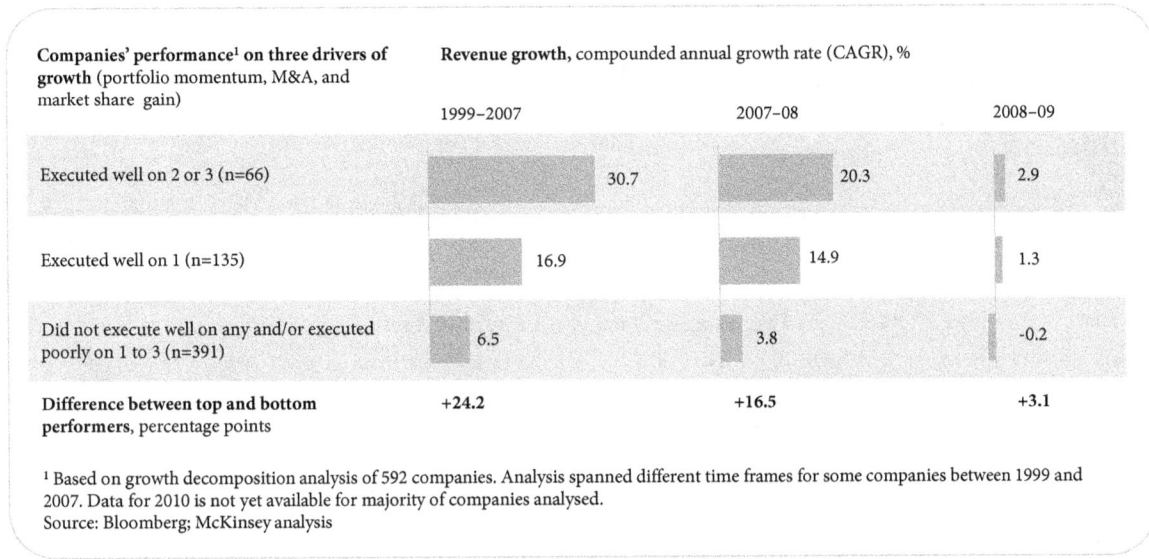

Figure 7.2: Multiple growth avenues pay off in good and bad times

A strategic alliance is based on the willingness of two or more organisations to work together by pooling resources in order to supply to a market what they could not do independently. In a strategic alliance the parties can keep their individual identity, but pool their resources and capabilities in a new shared joint venture. An organisation can use strategic alliances or collaborative partnerships to complement its own strategic initiatives and strengthen its competitiveness. Such cooperative strategies go beyond normal company-to-company dealings (e.g. supply chain activities) but fall short of merger or full equity joint venture partnership.

In an acquisition one firm (the acquirer) is buying a controlling stake in another firm (the acquired) with the intention of making the acquired firm a subsidiary business in the business portfolio of the acquirer.[5] Acquisitions can focus on either horizontal expansion or vertical expansion. Horizontal expansion is the acquisition of competitors with the aim of eliminating competition or entering new channels and markets. Vertical integration is the acquisition of suppliers or customers with the intent to control raw materials (especially where suppliers are few and buyers many) or to own the channel to the consumer. Related acquisitions are the acquisition of a firm in a highly related industry. A reverse merger is the action of a private company that takes over a publicly traded one – often in order to gain a stock exchange listing. The term is also used when a company takes over another company or entity that is larger.[6]

The distinction between a merger and an acquisition is in the area of control.[7] In an acquisition, there is a clear passing of control from the acquired company to the acquiring company. However, in a merger, it is merely a uniting of interests and control does not pass firmly from one company to another.

In the next part of this chapter we discuss strategic alliances and M&As as inorganic growth choices for a firm. We also explore restructuring as an approach to improve the performance of an organisation.

STRATEGIC ALLIANCES AND PARTNERSHIPS IN STRATEGY RENEWAL AND INNOVATION

Introduction

A strategic alliance can be described as a formal inter-enterprise cooperative agreement where two or more separate companies acknowledge their shared dependency by collaborating for mutual benefits, shared risks, shared control and jointly contributing resources and capabilities to gain access to new markets and new technology and to reduce cost. In a strategic alliance the two or more parties who pursue a set of agreed-upon objectives can remain independent organisations. This form of cooperation can be seen as a position between M&As and organic growth. Alliances often involve a variety of collaborate arrangements is the form of joint marketing, joint sales or distribution, joint production, design collaboration, joint research and projects to jointly develop new technologies or products. See Table 7.1 for different forms of strategic alliance.

Table 7.1: Types of strategic alliance

Partnership type	Description
Research	The focus is on generating new ideas and innovations to support business growth.
Product/service development	The intent is to accelerate the pace of incorporating new products and service concepts into the current enterprise portfolio.
Manufacturing	Manufacturing partnerships produce products more cost-effectively and reduce time-to-market.
Distribution	Distribution partnerships avoid the cost and complexities involved in creating new distribution channels and networks in new markets.
Sales and Marketing	Partners with complementary sales forces gain sales coverage benefits and prevent additional investments in expanding the current capacity.

Global strategic alliances are working partnerships between enterprises (often more than two) across national boundaries and increasingly across industries.[8] McDonald's and Coca-Cola collaborate globally, where McDonald's buys its soft drinks exclusively from Coca-Cola. Coca-Cola is also the sole supplier of soft drinks to Disney's theme parks.[9]

Strategic alliances are used more and more by organisations to maintain a competitive advantage in the global economy[10] [11] due to increased competitive intensity, risk and uncertainty. Increasingly leaders in organisations recognise they need to collaborate in order to compete locally and globally. It has become very difficult for an organisation to create and maintain a competitive advantage in every value chain activity it participates in and to be able to excel in a wide range of technologies required in the design, development, manufacturing and marketing of new products and services.[12]

The following five criteria could be used to see if an alliance meets the requirements of a strategic alliance:[13]

- The venture is critical to the success of a core business goal or objective of the parties. A truly strategic relationship would have a great bearing on the prospects for achieving revenue growth or cost-saving targets.
- The venture is critical to the development or maintenance of a core competency or other source of competitive advantage for the parties.

- The venture blocks a competitive threat to the parties. An example of strategic alliances that block competitive threats are airline alliances that permit route-sharing among carriers. Cost and routing are the two primary determinants that customers use for flight selection. By adopting a route-sharing alliance, airlines blocks the competitive threat of preferential routing in the specific markets in which the airline chooses to compete.
- The venture creates or maintains strategic choices for the parties. Longer-term options are created through the alliance, e.g. market expansion options.
- The venture mitigates a significant risk to the business of the parties. An example is dual sourcing strategies for critical production components or processes to mitigate risks as part of supply-side strategic alliances.

The different alliance and partnership options, from a deal-structuring viewpoint, and the associated requirements, advantages and disadvantages are reflected in Table 7.2.

Table 7.2: Alliance partnership options

Partnership format	Success criteria	Advantages	Disadvantages
Cooperative alliance: Encapsulates all forms of cooperative agreements between parties to create and unlock joint value.	• Clear shared intent and goals • Strong relationships • Strong communication	• Low cost in establishing alliance • Fast implementation	• Can be viewed as temporary • Culture challenges • Work practices alignment challenges
Minority equity: This represents a noncontrolling interest in a venture.	• Clear shared vision • Top executive support • Clarity on value creation elements	• Arms-length relationship not disruptive for core business	• Alignment over time on intent • Benefit realisation • Risk management challenges
Joint venture: Can be either the creation of a new jointly owned entity by parties or the minority ownership in a new entity.	• Scope alignment • Culture alignment • Resource allocation rules	• Pooling of resources • Shared opportunity space	• Complex to manage • High set-up costs • Human capital alignment
Consortia: A form of industry collaboration to complete major projects e.g. Bombela consortium* to create and run the Gautrain.	• Clear governance structure	• Access to wide range of partner capabilities • Risk sharing	• Bureaucracy challenges • Alignment challenges

*The Bombela consortium consists of Murray & Roberts Ltd, Bouygues Travaux Publics SA, Bombardier Transportation UK Ltd, SPG Concessions Ltd and J&J Group.[14]

The success rate of strategic alliances to produce the required results, as set out in the beginning by the parties, are however not that high. Some researchers[15][16] indicate that up to 70% of alliances fail or fall short on delivering on expectations or are disbanded. Other researchers[17] show failure rates of 50–54 per cent, which indicates that alliance success is difficult to achieve and needs to be planned and managed in a specific way.

In the following sections we explore the advantages of strategic alliances, the management thereof and the critical success factors.

Advantages of strategic alliances

Strategic alliances are attractive strategic moves for a number of reasons. Some of the most frequently mentioned motivations are:[18]

- Market expansion: The possibility of gaining market entry opportunities in new geographical areas locally and globally.
- Product and service expansion: Assisting to broaden a product line or fill product-line gaps.
- Economies of scale: By joining forces, alliance firms create cost savings through economies of scale benefits in research and development, production and/or marketing.
- Competence and innovation enhancement: Alliance partners fill gaps in their current expertise and knowledge base by learning from each other.
- Shared distribution and networks: This strengthens access to buyers in a cost-competitive way.
- Competitive benefits: By pooling resources alliance partners can close the gap on leading competitors.
- Access to relationship capital: Access to new relationship networks (government, society, industry, interest groups) is facilitated through partnering with local and global players.
- Standard-setting to enhance interoperability of products and solutions: Alliance partners can be influential in setting standards for an industry, e.g. standards for technologies in the areas of computers, Internet-related technologies, high-definition televisions, mobile phones.
- Risk mitigation: Alliances allow for the sharing of risks, whether political or commercial.
- The cost of a full acquisition may be too high.

A strategic alliance is a way to preserve the independence of the cooperative partners without losing out on the shared benefits that offers a real alternative to M&As.

Management of strategic alliances

Research[19] shows that alliance outcome and failure can be attributed to a number of strategic and operational factors such as:

- lack of strategic fit in terms of complementary resources
- lack of organisational fit in terms of compatible cultures, decision-making processes and systems
- lack of trust
- inappropriate choice of governance structure
- inability to manage conflict
- lack of adaptable interorganisational exchange processes
- impact of sudden major environmental shocks

A lack of experience and organisational capability on the part of the alliance partners is also frequently mentioned as a reason for alliance failures. Successful strategic alliance organisations focus deliberately on ways to capture, integrate, and disseminate alliance-management know-how. One way of doing this is to create a separate, dedicated organisational unit charged with the responsibility to capture prior alliance experiences. Examples of these dedicated alliance functions are firms such as Hewlett-Packard, General Motors, Eli Lilly and Pfizer, who have appointed a "Vice-President or Director of Strategic Alliances" with his or her own staff and resources. This dedicated function coordinates all alliance-related activity within the firm and can enhance the firm's ability to generate high returns from alliances.[20] An investment in a dedicated alliance function can enhance a firm's alliance capability by: "(1) acting as a focal point for learning and leveraging both explicit and tacit lessons from prior and ongoing alliances; (2) keeping numerous stakeholders, including investors, apprised of new alliances and successful events in ongoing alliances; (3) improving internal coordination and resource support of alliances; and (4) monitoring and evaluating alliance performance".[21] Research confirms that firms that invest in a capability to manage strategic alliances are able to enhance the probability of success – both in the short run (generating a positive market response) and in the long run (meeting the alliance objectives).[22]

The set-up phase of a strategic alliance needs to be carefully planned through a variety of inter-related process steps, as shown in Figure 7.3.

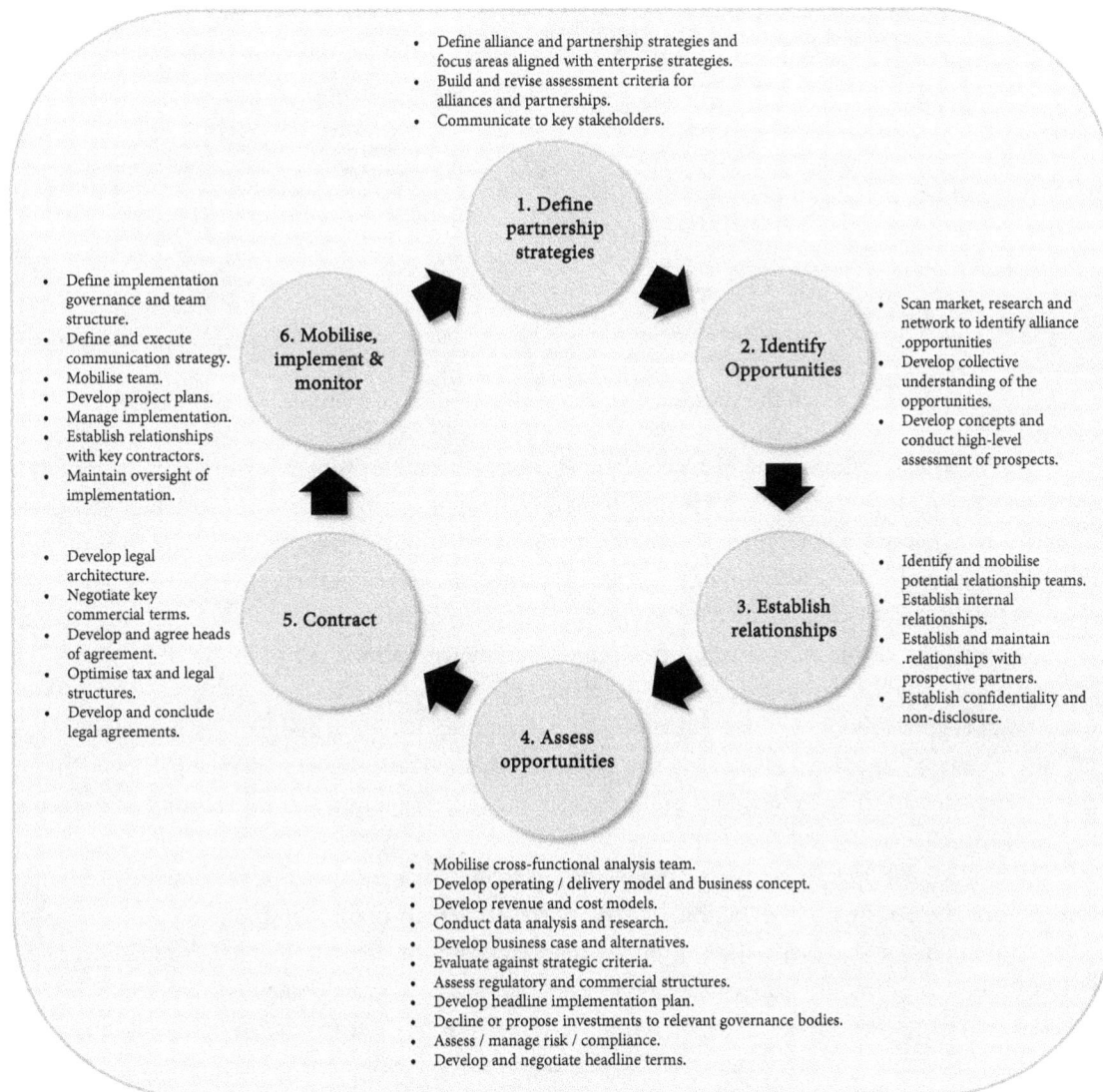

Figure 7.3: Generic strategic alliance and partnership development cycle

The "run" or execution phase of a strategic alliance also needs specific ongoing strategic attention, as indicated in Figure 7.4.

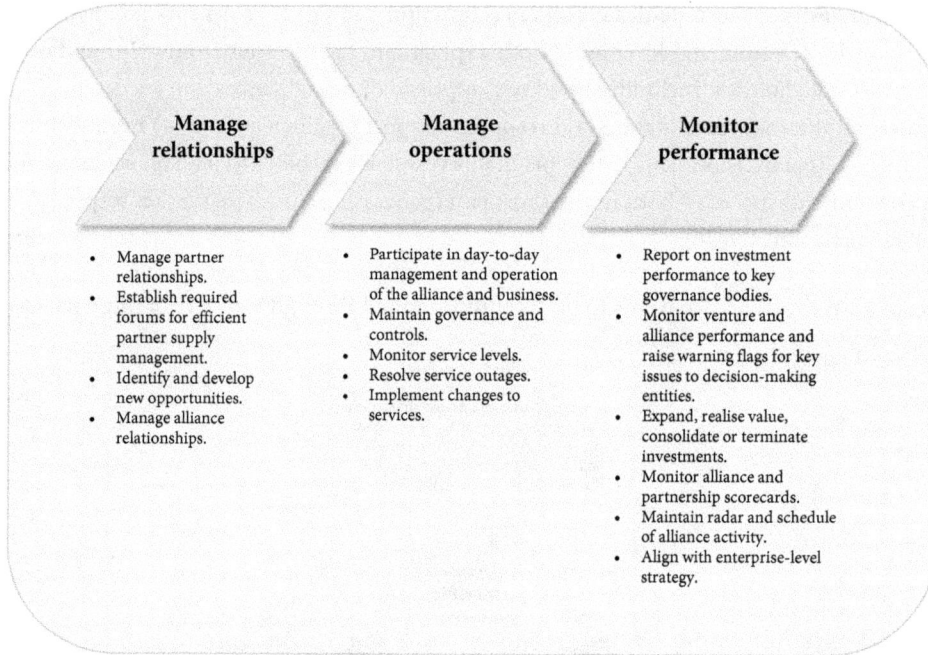

Figure 7.4: Generic strategic alliances and partnerships operations and investment monitoring cycle

The following best practices[23] can aid the success of strategic alliances, joint ventures and partnerships.

- Ensure "sound strategic alignment" between the partners. Strategic sponsorship from the top for an alliance venture is essential for the success of such an endeavour. The sponsorship needs to be visible to stakeholders of both parties and it needs to be clear who is taking ultimate responsibility for the venture. If there is disalignment at the top it will hamper the execution of the venture somewhere down the line.
- A clear scorecard and appropriate metrics ensure that alliance parties watch "the same game and scoreboard". Making the progress visible on mutually agreed-upon parameters focuses the attention of players and creates alignment on required actions to ensure continued success.
- The creation of appropriate and functional governance structures with clear mandates is an essential ingredient of an alliance management capability. The pairing of representatives from the alliance parties in appropriate alliance forums to ensure both technical and managerial cooperation and control is required to increase the potential of the alliance.
- The creation of regular interaction opportunities for the cooperating parties helps the flow of information and the building of relationships – both building blocks for creating trust in the venture.
- The departure points and associated assumptions that underpin the creation of strategic alliances need to be tested from time to time within the context of an ever-changing macro external environment. Sometimes the intent and scope of a venture needs to be renegotiated to fit a new set of external circumstances. Strategic alliance ventures can never be static and need re-alignment and repositioning as time passes.

A sample of tools that alliance teams use to enhance success is reflected in Table 7.3.

Table 7.3: Alliance management tools[24]

Alliance planning	Partner selection	Alliance negotiation	Alliance management	Alliance termination
• Value Chain Analysis • Needs Analysis Checklist	• Partner Screening Criteria • Cultural Fit Evaluation	• Negotiations Matrix. • Needs v/s Wants Checklist • Alliance Contract Template • Alliance Metrics Framework	• Trust-building worksheet • Alliance Communication • Infrastructure	• Relationship Evaluation Criteria • Annual Status Report • Termination Checklist

Partnering and alliances key success factors

The key factors associated with alliance and partnership success[25] are summarised in Figure 7.5.

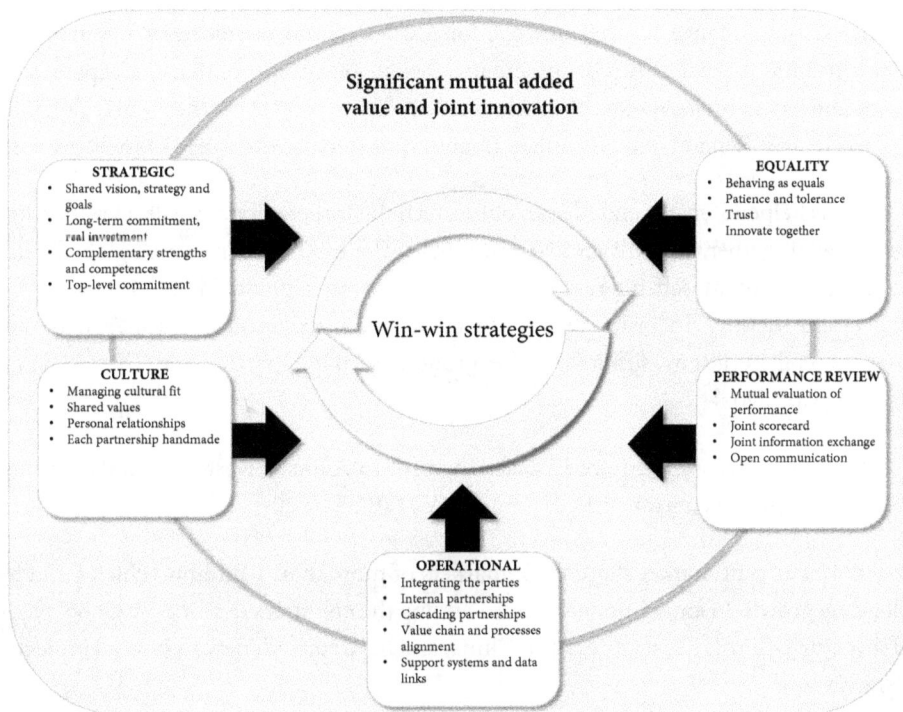

Figure 7.5: Major factors associated with strategic alliance and partnership success[26]

Application tool

When you plan to initiate a strategic alliance venture option, use the following guidelines to plan and execute this:

- evaluation of possible types of strategic alliance (Table 7.1) and alliance partnership option (Table 7.2)
- steps in planning a strategic alliance (Figure 7.3) and monitoring actions (Figure 7.4). Also see alliance management tools in Table 7.3
- factors to imbed in an alliance approach to increase alliance success potential (Figure 7.5)

Next we describe a case study on the Renault–Nissan alliance as an example of a global alliance in the vehicle manufacturing industry.

Case study of Renault–Nissan alliance[27]

Background

The Renault–Nissan alliance was signed on 27 March 1999.

> The Renault–Nissan Alliance has built a unique business model that has created significant value for both companies. For over 15 years, employees at Renault and Nissan have worked as partners with an attitude of mutual respect and company pride while keeping brands and corporate identities.[28]

> The Renault–Nissan Alliance has become the longest-lasting cross-cultural combination among major carmakers. This unique partnership is a pragmatic, flexible business tool that can expand to accommodate new projects and partners worldwide. The Alliance is a buffer to protect partners during regional downturns, and it has accelerated Renault and Nissan's momentum in some of the world's fastest growing economies.

> The Alliance has helped Renault and Nissan outperform historic regional rivals, elevating both companies into an elite tier. Together, Renault and Nissan rank in the top four car groups globally. Based on cross-shareholding and mutual self-interest, the Alliance business platform maximises synergies without destroying brand identity. In order to achieve competitive economies of scale, many automakers are embarking on collaborations similar to the ground-breaking partnership that Renault and Nissan established 15 years ago.[29]

AVTOVAZ: In 2012, Renault–Nissan acquired a majority stake in Alliance Rostec Auto BV, a joint venture with Russian Technologies which will control 74.5 per cent of AVTOVAZ by 2014.

The Alliance targets 10 per cent market share in all markets of more than 1 million vehicles. On top of that, the Alliance is accelerating growth in emerging markets, including the countries that will be global engines of growth in the twenty-first century: Brazil, Russia, India and China, and beyond, with new industrial projects in Indonesia, Myanmar and Nigeria.

Principles for the alliance

> The Alliance is based on trust and mutual respect. Its organisation is transparent. It ensures: Clear decision-making for speed, accountability and a high level of performance; Maximum efficiency by combining the strengths of both companies and developing synergies through common organisations, Cross-Company Teams and shared platforms and components.

> The Alliance attracts and retains the best talents, provides good working conditions and challenging opportunities: it grows people to have a global and entrepreneurial mindset. It generates attractive returns for the shareholders of each company and implements the best established standards of corporate governance. It contributes to global sustainable development.

Figure 7.6a: Cross company teams

Structure of the alliance

Renault holds a 43.4% stake in Nissan, while Nissan owns 15% of Renault shares. Each company has a direct interest in the results of its partner. Renault–Nissan B.V.*, the common strategic management structure of the Renault–Nissan group, was founded on March 28, 2002. Incorporated under Dutch law, Renault–Nissan B.V. is equally owned by Renault and Nissan. Renault–Nissan B.V. is the registered office of the Alliance Board, which meets regularly in Paris and Tokyo.

* B.V. (Besloten vennootschap) is a closed limited liability company under Dutch law.

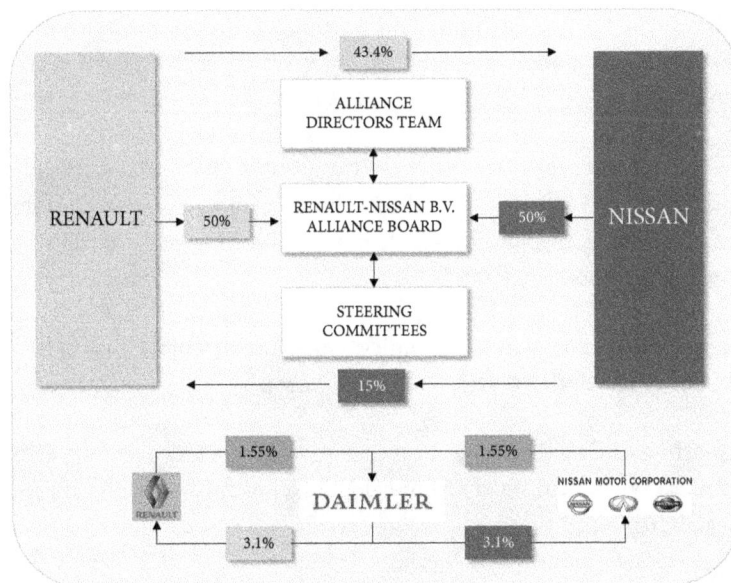

Figure 7.6b: Renault–Nissan alliance structure

Governance: Renault–Nissan B.V. Alliance Board

The Alliance Board is the common governance body of the Alliance, held by Renault–Nissan BV, headquartered in Amsterdam, with 50% shareholdings by both companies. It is formally composed of three Renault senior executives and three Nissan senior executives, and it is supported by the full Executive Committee of both companies. It is chaired by Renault–Nissan Alliance Chairman and CEO Carlos Ghosn.

The board focuses on strategic direction, significant new opportunities for collaboration, and the progress of the Alliance relative to industry benchmarks. Alliance Board meetings typically include a focus on: Mid-term plan progress; Validation of product plans; Commonality of products and powertrains; Strategic investments impacting the Alliance; and Strategic cooperation with third parties.

The Alliance Directors Team: In May 2009, in the midst of the global economic slowdown, the Renault–Nissan Alliance created a small team of dedicated Alliance directors to accelerate synergies and best-practice sharing. The directors foster deeper, broader cooperation to enhance performance of all partners. The Alliance Managing Directors are responsible for the operations of Alliance functions for both partners. Alliance Directors advise teams in partner companies and accelerate best practice sharing across the Alliance to help increase synergies. They may oppose any measures taken by Renault or Nissan that run counter to the development of synergies, referring the matter to the executive committee of the company concerned or even, ultimately, the Alliance Board.

Sales results from the alliance: 2013 and 2015

The Renault–Nissan Alliance sold a record 8,264,821 vehicles in 2013, representing one in 10 new cars sold worldwide. Calendar-year sales increased 2.1% from 2012, propelled by record sales in the car group's two largest markets, China and the United States. 2013 was the fifth straight year of sales growth for the Renault–Nissan Alliance.

Together, Renault and Nissan ranked as the No. 4 car group in terms of worldwide sales. Nissan sold 5.1 million units worldwide, up 3.3%. Renault sold 2.6 million units, up 3.1%, despite a 1.7% decline in the European market. AVTOVAZ, owner of the Lada brand, sold 533,634 units, down 12.1% from 2012 amid the economic slowdown in Russia.

The Renault–Nissan Alliance sold 8,528,887 vehicles in 2015, up almost 1 percent from the previous year, thanks to record sales in the United States, China and Europe.

Combined sales for the world's fourth largest car group, which includes Renault Group, Nissan Motor Co., Ltd., and Russia's AVTOVAZ, held steady from calendar-year 2014 – despite sharp declines in the overall Russian and Brazilian markets.[30]

Management for synergies

Value of other synergies realised by 2013: It is estimated the realised synergies from the Renault–Nissan alliance is €2.8B against a 2016 target of €4.3B.

PURCHASING

Renault–Nissan Purchasing Organisation, or RNPO, is the Alliance's largest common organisation. It negotiates prices among suppliers on behalf of both Renault and Nissan. Since 2009, joint purchasing represents 100% of Alliance commodity purchases, compared to 30% in 2001.

RESEARCH AND DEVELOPMENT

Common Module Family (CMF): The Next Step in Integration Common Module Family is a modular architecture system that dissects the vehicle into five components – known as the "4+1 Big Modules" concept. The modules include four basic body units (engine compartment, cockpit, front underbody and rear underbody), plus the vehicle's electrical and electronic systems. Product developers "mix and match" components for a larger variety of vehicles – from urban subcompacts to compacts, mid-size sedans, crossovers and SUVs.

CMF has three segments: CMF-A: small, fuel-efficient vehicles for high-growth markets; CMF-B: mid-sized vehicles; CMF-C/D: larger vehicles, including many SUVs and crossovers

Exchanges of powertrains and common powertrains: To capitalise on powertrain expertise of both partners, the Alliance co-develops common engines and gearboxes. Centers of excellence stem from the companies' historic areas of expertise: Renault specialises in diesel engines and manual transmissions, while Nissan specialises in gasoline engines and automatic transmissions. Powertrain synergies represented €709 million in 2012.

In addition to synergies on parts, platforms and purchasing, the Renault–Nissan Alliance has created numerous teams that have unlocked cost savings strategies around the world, including:

Logistics: A unified team has commonised packing, shipping and other functions that are completely invisible to the consumer, achieving €176 million in synergies in 2012.

Customs & Trade: A dedicated team has reduced customs duties and administrative costs that each company incurred separately. The team has also negotiated better terms and implemented economic policies to establish best practices for regions around the globe. Customs & Trade represented a level of synergies of €400 million in 2012.

IS/IT: Renault and Nissan share common information systems infrastructure, data centres and licenses, and generated €60 million in synergies in 2012.

Sales and Marketing: In 2012, the Alliance won its first fleet contracts to supply at least 15,000 vehicles on multiple continents for global food company Danone. In 2013, Alliance fleet also signed sales contracts with IT group ATOS and pharmaceutical company Merck.

Strategic cooperation with Daimler

Daimler AG, maker of Mercedes, is one of the world's largest luxury car manufacturers. In April 2010, the Renault–Nissan Alliance and Daimler AG announced a strategic partnership based on three "pillar projects" with the expectation that the relationship could deepen as the teams discovered specific new projects. The scope of the partnership has expanded substantially in four years. Under the cooperation, teams are working together on the following projects:

FOR RENAULT AND DAIMLER:

A new common architecture for Daimler's smart and Renault Twingo successors (New Twingo revealed in February 2014). Citan, a new light commercial vehicle under the Mercedes-Benz brand, based on Renault technology and produced in Renault's plant in Maubeuge, France. Ultra-low-consumption diesel and gasoline engines, including a 1.5 litre diesel engine, manufactured by Renault in Valladolid (Spain), for the Mercedes A and B Class.

FOR NISSAN AND DAIMLER:

Production of Mercedes-Benz 4-cylinder gasoline engines at Nissan's new powertrain assembly facility in Decherd, Tennessee. A Daimler 2.2 litre turbo diesel engine, coupled with a 7-speed automatic or 6-speed manual gearbox for the Q50, Infiniti's new flagship Sedan. Cross supply of Mercedes Canter – Nissan Atlas trucks in Japan. A future luxury entry-level Infiniti compact car co-developed on the Mercedes front Wheel Drive architecture used for Class A and Class B models. Research and development on next-generation Fuel-Cell Electric Vehicle. Daimler also granted Nissan a license to manufacture automatic transmissions (9 speed) with its latest technology for use in Nissan and Infiniti vehicles.

FOR RENAULT, NISSAN AND DAIMLER:

Renault–Nissan and Daimler are jointly developing a new family of three- and four cylinder gasoline engines with turbo-charging and direct fuel injection. The engines feature advanced technology with significantly improved fuel efficiency.[31]

Case questions:

- Use the best practice guidelines as described in this chapter and indicate how they were applied in the Renault–Nissan alliance.
- Use Figure 7.5 to identify how the Renault–Nissan alliance meets the success factors. Describe the application of the factors in detail.

MERGERS AND ACQUISITIONS (M&As)

Introduction

This section reviews the various reasons and objectives why companies look at M&As to grow their own portfolio. The key pre- and postmerger factors are also described as part of the features of successful M&As. Takeovers as a special type of acquisition are also covered.

From a financial perspective, a merger or acquisition can be defined as two companies that come together where the shareholders gain value in excess of the sum created when the two companies join forces.[32] As already indicated earlier, an acquisition can be described as "a strategy through which one firm buys a controlling interest in another firm with the intent of making the acquired firm a subsidiary business within its portfolio".[33] In the case of an acquisition, one firm, the acquirer or buyer, purchases and absorbs the operations of another, the acquired or seller.

A merger represents, at least in theory, the intent to combine and pool the assets of two equals in a newly created entity.[34]

Mergers and acquisitions (M&As) have become a frequently used strategic option to expand the portfolio of a business. M&As are specifically suited to situations where alliances do not provide a firm with the required resource capabilities or cost-reducing opportunities and where ownership of assets allows for a more tightly integrated operation, creating more control, autonomy and efficiencies than alliances.

Despite the perceived support for M&As, the performance scorecard of M&As does not look good. A study from Bloomberg Business in 2002 showed that "61% of buyers destroyed their own shareholders' wealth. A year after their deals, the losers' average return was 25 percentage points below their industry peers. The study further showed that the buyers lost largely because they paid too much, transferring wealth to the sellers' shareholders.[35] A KPMG report concluded that 83 per cent of mergers did not actually add value at all.[36]

McKinsey report in 2011 that their data shows that big M&A deals can create significant value for the acquirer, but success takes time to unfold and is dependent on an appropriate M&A strategy and execution practices. McKinsey states: "Indeed, in our analysis of such deals over the past decade, half had created excess returns to shareholders when measured two years after the deal's completion. In one-third, returns were significantly higher relative to the industry average".[37]

Reasons for M&As

The key reasons for engaging in an M&A as part of the strategy of an organisation[38] can be summarised as follows and are discussed in more detail:

Growth and increase in shareholder value:[39] The departure point of classic economic theory is that the primary economic goal of a business is to maximise returns to shareholders, and therefore acquisitions should be expected to cause positive gains in the shareholder wealth of the acquiring firm.[40] The opposite can however also happen, where studies indicate that acquisitions do not always cause positive gains for shareholders of the acquiring firm.[41]

Growth through portfolio momentum and organic growth are not always an internal growth option for all organisations. Organisations are also not always willing to take the risk associated with internal growth.[42] These companies rather choose to grow through M&As. However, in some instances merger and acquisition transactions only lead to sales growth and do not always result in value growth.[43]

Increased market power and control:[44] Researchers[45] indicate that the intent to increase market power and control within a targeted competitive space is often mentioned as a reason for acquisitions and mergers. Through M&As a businesses can acquire other competitors in the same industry and create substantial dominance or market power in that industry. One test of market power is a before-and-after comparison of the merging firm's prices.[46] Market power exists when a firm can sell its offerings above competitive levels or when the value chain activities are executed at a lower cost than those of competitors.[47] Market leadership is associated with market power.

Pursuing market power[48] can be a strategic motive for acquisitions along with other reasons to gain more control in a market through creating barriers to entry, synergy and acquiring a competitor. Researchers[49] argue that increased market power can enable businesses to benefit from higher prices, but at the same time reduces market efficiency because there is less competition.

Increased diversification and conglomeration:[50] Diversification and conglomeration through M&As were popular during the 1960s and 1970s. Conglomeration[51] occurs when a business invests in several firms in seemingly unrelated industries or product lines. The objective of conglomeration is to achieve growth and to spread risks by branching into several different business areas at the same time. There are many reasons why firms consider conglomeration. The first is synergism, which suggests that consolidations are made to achieve economies of scale, and implies that mergers are more than merely the sum of individual companies. The second reason is diversification, which suggests that by branching into different types of activity a business can reduce its risks. Other reasons are better external financing rates and costs through scale benefits, debt capacity and creditworthiness and internal shifting of funds to avoid transactions costs and taxation.[52]

Although diversification reduces the risk of a business it does not necessarily add value. Research[53] indicates that companies that invest in their core line of business gain added benefits, while companies that invest in peripheral lines of business do not. Focused acquisitions, therefore, lead to greater synergies and operating efficiencies rather than diversifying acquisitions. It is clear that conglomerate diversification only adds value to a merger or acquisition when there are synergistic reasons.[54] There are, however, still benefits from diversification for some firms. Conglomerate diversification is the optimal strategy for less profitable firms.[55] However we need to remember that no more than 50 per cent of diversification through M&A strategies are successful.[56]

International expansion can be seen as a form of diversification by entering new geographical country markets through an M&A strategy. Companies gain direct access to these markets by acquiring existing operational businesses in the target market.

Overcoming entry barriers:[57] Barriers of entry are the expenses and difficulties a firm encounters when it wants to enter an industry or market for the first time. Examples of entry barriers are economies of scale, established customer relationships and brand loyalty. A new entrant overcomes some of the entry barriers by acquiring an incumbent market player. This facilitates immediate market access for the buyer. Cross-border acquisitions are a way to overcome country-entry barriers and fast-track new market entry. However this is never a risk-free strategic move.

Learning and developing new capabilities:[58] Sometimes organisations do an acquisition to gain access to competences and capabilities they do not have, for example specific technological capabilities. The guideline is that firms should seek acquisitions to complement their existing capabilities and to enhance their current knowledge base. By broadening the knowledge base of a firm it becomes more flexible to deal effectively with rapidly changing situations.

Hubris and self-interest of management:[59] We have already indicated that M&As are a risky growth strategy, with overwhelming empirical evidence[60] that suggests that mergers are break-even situations at best and, at worst, failures. Therefore, there must be other reasons why businesses pursue acquisitions. It may be that managers pursue goals other than shareholder wealth maximisation, or they are overly optimistic. In many M&As managers increase their own power without considering the effect on shareholder wealth. This is called self-interest empire-building.[61]

Hubris,[62] [63] as excessive pride or self-confidence, is acknowledged as a reason why managers overpay for acquisitions. Hubris by management is also linked to the agency problem, where managers pursue excessive growth to promote personal interests. Other personal motives include the personal agenda of chief executive officers, who wish to boost their own egos but, sadly, at the expense of the shareholders. These executives seem to fall in love with the acquisition and then do not walk away when they should.[64] Other personal motives for pushing an M&A deal are managerial prestige, a personal challenge to grow sales and the acquisition of inefficient management to execute a turnaround challenge. In addition, the challenge to integrate a new business or to oversee larger operations might also fuel personal ambition for more power and status. Whatever the personal motive, it mostly leads to failed M&As.[65]

Synergistic benefits:[66] Synergy benefits are a big driver for pursuing an M&A. There are three different types of synergy[67], namely financial synergy, managerial synergy and operational synergy.

Financial synergy is an increase in financial advantages after a merger. The improved financial performance relates to aspects such the net earnings, return on capital employed, and return on total assets of the firms.[68]

Managerial synergy is realised when the acquirer's management works cooperatively with the target's management and does not replace them. Managerial synergy occurs where the acquirer's management believes that the target's management can complement its own skills and experience. Managerial synergy occurs where the acquirer provides capital-raising skills and the target is responsible for product development and manufacturing skills. Research[69] indicates that the market reacts positively to acquirers who retained the target's management.

Operational synergy is achieved by sharing and integrating resources and activities, especially in horizontal M&As. Examples of these shared resources and activities are procurement and outbound logistics. Lower cost of new products and increased speed to market are some of the envisaged benefits.

Consolidation:[70] A consolidation can be the result from a merger between two companies. A consolidation implies reduction of costs, leveraging of synergies and the realisation of the benefits of economies of scale and improved time to market.[71] Economies of scale tend to lead to a decrease in production costs and/or a reduction of the inefficiencies within a business. Improved time to market allows the acquirer faster or cheaper entry into a new market. Economies of scale exist when costs tend to increase at a less than proportionate rate from the increase in output.[72] To achieve this, fixed costs are spread over a larger volume of output.

Market timing:[73] Some acquisitions are stock market-driven, where overvalued companies use stock to buy undervalued targets, even though both companies can be overvalued. Research[74] found that the market considers high-valued acquirers more likely to have market timing motives. The term "industry shocks" also describes market timing. Many M&As occurred during the 1980s where numerous industries experienced deregulations and fundamental changes. Market timing motives are considered to be value-decreasing.

Asset stripping:[75] Another reason why companies are acquired is because buyers focus on businesses that they deem to be undervalued, sell off all the assets and generate a sizeable profit on the transaction. This realisation of company assets and redistribution of cash is known as asset stripping.[76] Companies also consider asset-stripping part of the target company in order to generate immediate cash flows to assist with decreasing the finance used to acquire the target. This practice reduces the gearing risk associated with the acquisition.[77]

Various reasons for M&As have been discussed. Some of these reasons result in an increase in shareholder wealth while others do not. In conclusion, companies should only consider M&As when they will increase shareholder wealth, and should avoid those that do not.[78]

Challenges associated with M&As

"The main reasons for the failure of M&A strategies can largely be summarised as:

- a lack of clarity on the strategic reasons or rationale for the proposed transaction
- the egos of executives with an excessive involvement in a deal-making state of mind
- an overestimation of the cost savings and synergies
- a poor integration process, due in particular to the management of cultural differences"[79]

An acquisition growth strategy will add little value to shareholders or will fail if the rationale is not clearly defined. Such strategies should be to accelerate growth or increase market share, rather than adopt an "everyone else is doing it" approach.[80]

M&As are done in two clear phases, namely a premerger and a postmerger phase. Whereas a lot of energy is normally spent on the premerger phase, researchers[81] emphasised the importance of postmerger integration and stated that unsuccessful integrations contributed to approximately 53 per cent of all unsuccessful deals. It is clear that the real value realisation is in the postmerger phase and not all the focus should be only on the deal-making phase.

A variety of other possible reasons exist for value destruction within an M&A context.[82] [83] These include an overestimation of the potential gains (financial) because of the size of the offerer (normally larger) compared to the offeree; the percentage gains for the acquirer's shareholders are much lower than for the offerees'; management may not be acting in the best interests of its shareholders when trying to increase in size but reducing the value per share; sellers capturing all the gain if the net present value (NPV) used is zero when acquired; high debt financing to pay for the acquisition later constrains funding for product innovation; and lastly, by the time of announcing a takeover, the share price already reflects the potential gains through earlier announcements and the strategy shared with the markets.

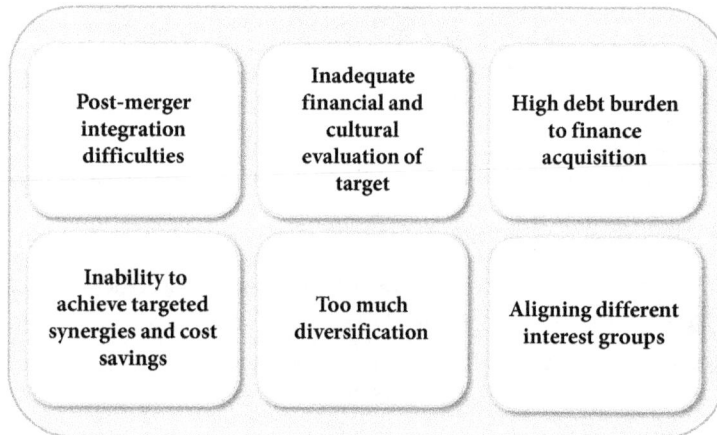

Figure 7.7: Generic M&A challenges[86]

Lastly, experts and advisers can make or break a deal.[84] Expert advisers are a valuable resource if one knows how to manage them. However, "expert advisers, when they have a floor or an audience, can run amok. When someone recognises that they are considered to be an expert, there is often the danger of their ego going haywire. Keep them on a tight leash".[85] The main challenges associated with M&As are summarised in Figure 7.7.

Features of effective M&As

In this part we describe the practices associated with effective acquisitions and make a distinction between the premerger and postmerger phases. Successful acquirers develop an internal M&A capability over time and reap competitive benefits. Below is a description of this internal strategic competitive capability.

> "Even some of the largest and most complex organisations are perceived as attractive buyers by small and nimble targets, largely due to the way they present themselves and manage M&A. The best among them tend to lead with deep industry insight and a business case that is practical and focused on winning in a marketplace instead of on synergies or deal value. They let target company managers see how they fit into a broader picture. They also have scalable functions and a predictable, transparent M&A process that targets can easily navigate. Finally, they are purposeful about how they present themselves, supporting executives with consistent and compelling materials that demonstrate the best of the organisation. As a result, they are able to use their position in the market to succeed in dimensions that go beyond price – and are often approached by targets that aren't even yet "for sale." This is a real competitive advantage ..."[87]

When planning a merger the following questions need to be addressed:[88]

- Does the merger make sense?
- What are the people-related issues? How will we integrate and retain talent?
- How will we integrate cultures and transfer knowledge?
- How will we maintain commitment and performance during the merger process?
- How will we align people-related systems, processes and organisation?
- How will we integrate operational systems to ensure efficiency?
- How will we implement the merger quickly and effectively?

Management should be able to answer the following questions when a board is assessing an M&A proposal.[89]

Does the reward potential warrant the risk and management distraction?

- Can the M&A deliver shareholder returns equal to top quartile performance in the industry?
- How risky are the value-creation opportunities that underpin the deal?
- How much top management time will be consumed?
- Are there other high-potential initiatives that will receive less attention or be slowed?

Is the strategic rationale well grounded?

- Does the M&A build upon a successful business model?
- Will the acquisition significantly improve the profitability or growth of the acquirer's market?
- How will management use the acquisition to develop competitive advantage?
- Are the projected competitive advantages and corresponding financial improvements realistic relative to competitive performance?

Is the integration plan well designed?

- Does clarity exist around the high-value opportunities that management should pursue?
- Is there sufficient specificity around what needs to be done to capture the high-value opportunities?
- Is there clear management accountability for delivering the high-value opportunities?

Are top managers establishing a common management model to drive long-term success?

- Do the two top management teams agree on the definition of success?
- Is there agreement on the best metric(s) for measuring performance?
- Is there a process for agreeing and resolving the high-value opportunities in the future?

Premerger planning

The success factors associated with the premerger planning phase can be summarised as follows and are discussed further:

Target-hunting[90]

Creating an acquisition target pool is the first step in the premerger planning phase. Successful acquirers identify up to 200 opportunities to investigate. Of the 200, approximately 40 targets will be approached, resulting in 12 target opportunities having further discussions. Of these 12 targets, three will be front runners to finally conclude one deal. Figure 7.8 is a visual representation of this opportunity-funnelling process.

It is necessary to invest in creating and maintaining an acquisition target database to continuously capture opportunities. However no database is final and up to date, and it is best to collate information from different sources on a continuous basis.

Porter[92] recommends that at least two of the following conditions should be favourable for acquisitions to be profitable:

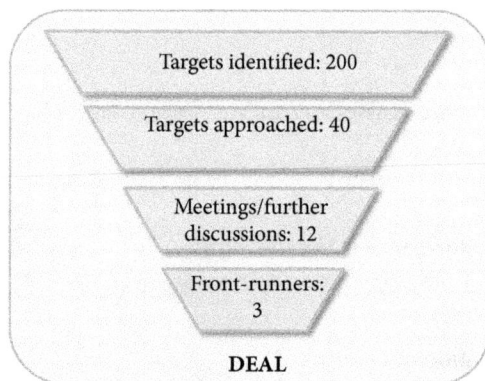

Figure 7.8: Typical target hunting statistics[91]

1. The seller is likely to accept a low minimum price. This may be the case when the seller is anxious to sell the business, has cash flow problems or has lost its key management.
2. The market for companies is imperfect, which could lead to above-average returns. This will be the case when the buyer has superior information, the number of buyers is low, economic conditions are poor, the company to be acquired is "sick" or when noneconomic objectives such as the retention of its employees are a problem.
3. The buying firm has the distinct ability to improve the acquired firm and will thus be able to manage it far more effectively than the sellers. This ability should be distinctive enough for the buyer to outbid its competitors and still have the ability to earn above-average profits.
4. The acquisition will strengthen the buying firm's position in its existing business. Even though the return on the acquisition may be average, it may result in a total above-average return for the buyer. For instance, this will be the case if the existing business could benefit from the distribution channels of the acquired company, or if it could gain entry to international markets through the company.

Strategic fit

A clear strategic rationale on its own is no guarantee of a successful merger, but the absence of it is disastrous. An important factor in achieving success is a good strategic fit between the acquiring company and the target company. To achieve this requires identifying and quantifying potential synergies for the acquirer.

There are ultimately only two reasons for an acquiring management to extract greater returns for shareholders. Firstly, they may be better managers; secondly, they may bring the so-called synergy effect. These synergies can come from both competitive cost benefits and differentiation advantages.[93] The focus is on motivating additional competitive benefits and value-adds that the merger will create.

Due diligence

M&As are inherently risky, because the acquirer has limited knowledge about the target.[94] Usually, some details will be deeply buried in the books or records of the target. Therefore, the acquirer may not base the acquisition decision entirely on the information provided by the target, but may seek to investigate the target further. Such an investigation is known as "due diligence". A careful and thorough due diligence lays the foundation for postacquisition success.[95] The more the acquirer learns about the target firm, the greater the chances of success.

Research[96] shows that the activities of due diligence become more important as the complexity of M&As increases. The danger is not that companies fail to do a due diligence, but that they fail to do it well. If a due diligence is done well it can reduce the risk. A proper due diligence goes beyond performing a traditional financial-orientated due diligence only. It needs to include financial, legal, human resources, operations, business culture and strategic aspects.[97]

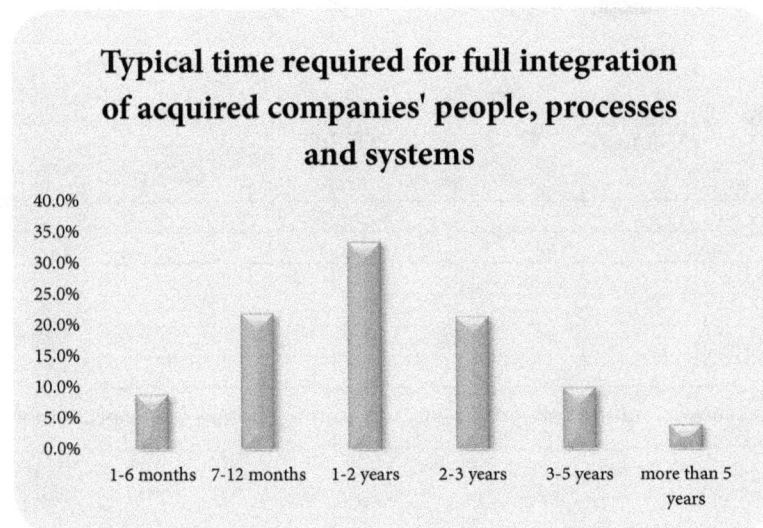

Figure 7.9: M&A value realisation periods[98]

The value that can be created for shareholders when performing an acquisition depends on the quality and rigour of the due diligence process. Realising the potential value of an M&A can take up to five years to achieve (see Figure 7.9), with an average of two to three years for most acquirers.

Deal structure

A proper deal's structure is also important for successful M&As. A deal's structure includes the price paid and type of financing. Many M&As fail simply because the acquiring firm paid too much for the acquisition.[99] When high-priced acquisitions hit the news, the transaction value gets most of the attention.[100] However, closer scrutiny reveals that the deal structure, how the price ultimately gets turned into cash, often matters more than the reported valuation.

Crucial aspects of a deal structure are the form of the transaction, form of payment, allocation and timing. The form of the transaction describes what the buyer is paying for and includes sale of stock, sale of assets etc. The form of payment describes the payment method and includes cash, stock, options and debt. Allocation is the allocation of the purchase price to different assets such as patents and licences. Timing is when the sellers receive their money.[101] Other considerations can include shareholder structure, insurance considerations, tax strategies and preparations for regulatory requirements.

The key processes that form part of the premerger phase are highlighted in Figure 7.10. It is clear that the value potential of a successful M&A is created in this phase, but the value creation is part of the postmerger integration phase.

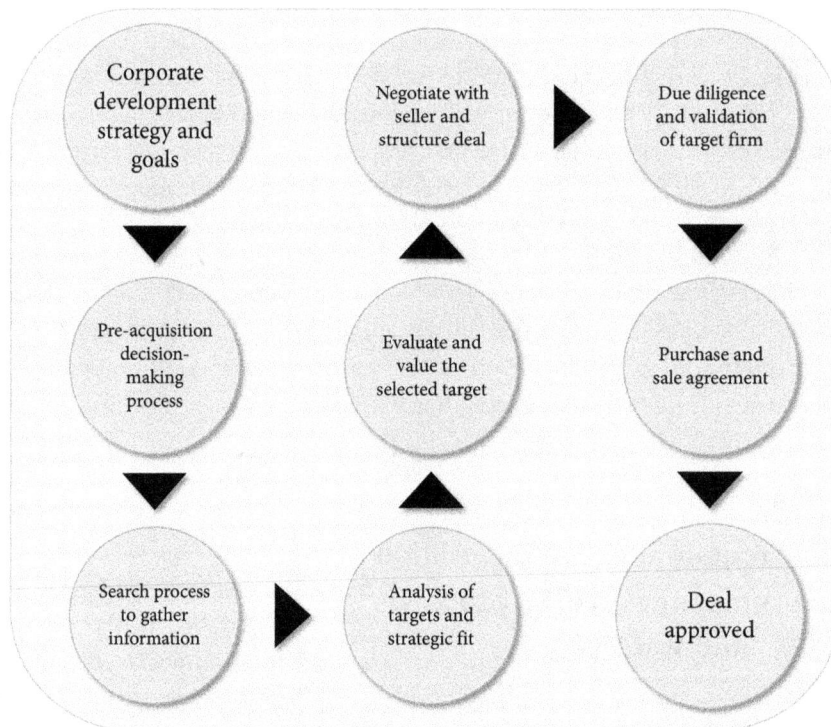

Figure 7.10: Generic premerger process[102]

Postmerger integration

Here we look at team selection, integration execution, culture integration and communication as key aspects that contribute to integration success.[103]

Team selection and talent retention

Team selection includes various elements such as the appointment of suitable leadership,[104] the selection of an appropriate management team, and the retention and integration of talent.[105] A key role to fill with the appropriate talent is a dedicated postmerger integration manager to take responsibility for extracting the envisaged value from the acquisition and to lead the integration project. An effective integration manager creates and tracks the progress of the integration team. A large part of an integration manager's role also involves project management. Effective integration managers do not merely track whether synergies are being captured, but they also assist in realising those synergies by breaking deadlocks that inevitably occur when two organisations merge.[106] Other key roles are an experienced integration team and support from key executives. The integration team should perform a full-time function with ample resources and strong leadership. It should follow a project-management approach, where integration project teams are separate from the core business. Most team members should be dedicated full-time to the postmerger integration. The integration team should be balanced and include members of both companies.[107]

Leadership played a major role in the successes of the Renault–Nissan alliance and in the failure of the DaimlerChrysler–Mitsubishi merger.[108] The difference in the leadership styles centred on the use of teams. In Renault–Nissan the CEO, Ghosn, focused on the implementation of permanent and temporary teams as the main intervention for change. In contrast, Eckrodt, the CEO of DaimlerChrysler–Mitsubishi, used few teams and failed to empower them.

What differentiates superb deals from the rest is that the CEO acts quickly to put in place a strong, unified management team to move the organisation forward.[109] Leaders of successful M&As assess the top executives of both firms against the mission and business scope of the new entity. They do this before the merger instead of waiting for fault lines to emerge. This early move to redeploy senior leadership has a powerfully positive impact on the economic performance of the target organisation.

Buyers need to identify the critical and high-potential employees who will keep the business at the top.[110] Underperformers and toxic individuals should be removed. To help keep the top talent in place, businesses should establish long-term incentives and remunerate their employees at market-related rates. The selection and recognition of executives is also cited as a key factor, as well as the ability to provide top management for the acquired company. Regular staff surveys to sense the mood of employees from the target firm is an essential feedback mechanism to evaluate the progress of the postmerger integration process.

Integration execution

The integration process is a multistage process which should be planned in phases to deliver value over time. An important factor during the execution of the integration is the quick and effective or speedy execution of the integration.[111] The success of M&As tends to decline over time.[112] The assessment of the success of an acquisition needs to be sensitive to the treatment of time. Speed in postacquisition integration has become best practice amongst practitioners and manifests in cycles of 100-day execution periods. This ensures momentum and focus in each period and progress is measured after each 100-day cycle.

Experts argue that a company has just two years to make a deal work.[113] After year two, the window of opportunity for forging merger synergies has largely closed. Companies that squabble over the details of the integration only frustrate customers and employees and delay the process. When integration takes longer than two years, there is a distinct and quantifiable loss. Not only do these companies fail to maximise the potential synergies, they often destroy shareholder value. Companies that achieve momentum early are more apt to produce successful acquisitions. Momentum is gained as a natural by-product of a sound strategy and the personal energy and involvement of the executive team.

With the two-year frame established, leading acquirers turn their focus towards the execution. The way in which a merger or acquisition is executed can make or break the deal. The overwhelming reason for failed mergers lies in flawed executions. A solid execution depends on management's priorities: how they are balanced, delivered, and communicated.[114]

There is no way to avoid the inevitable dislocation within the target company, and the best way to integrate is to move as rapidly as possible and finalise all integration efforts. This mindset of integration will limit the amount and duration of discomfort experienced by the target company's employees. Research[115] indicates three key aspects to consider when implementing an integration process: speed of implementation; key employees of the acquired company should be involved in the process; and goals and objectives should be clearly defined for "early wins". Indecision and delay of implementation increase speculation and uncertainty, the enemies of integration success. It is clear that crisp decision-making and speed of implementation cannot be overemphasised.[116] Studies[117] show that fast integration has a positive effect on the motivation of employees to stay with the company, and that the more the leadership style is relational, supportive and inspirational, the stronger the effect of the fast integration.

The creation of an integration strategy[118] and plan[119] is key for integration success and for creating shareholder wealth. To keep the value of a merger from evaporating, leaders need to manage the integration process actively and map a path between the integration and strategic intent. Once the leaders have considered the particular challenges posed by the strategic rationale behind the merger, they can move ahead with active management of the three phases of the integration (see Figure 7.11). Phase 1 sets the stage by articulating the vision and naming key leaders. Phase 2 designs the new company's organisation and operating plans. Finally, phase 3 makes the integration happen by aggressively implementing plans that bring the vision to life.

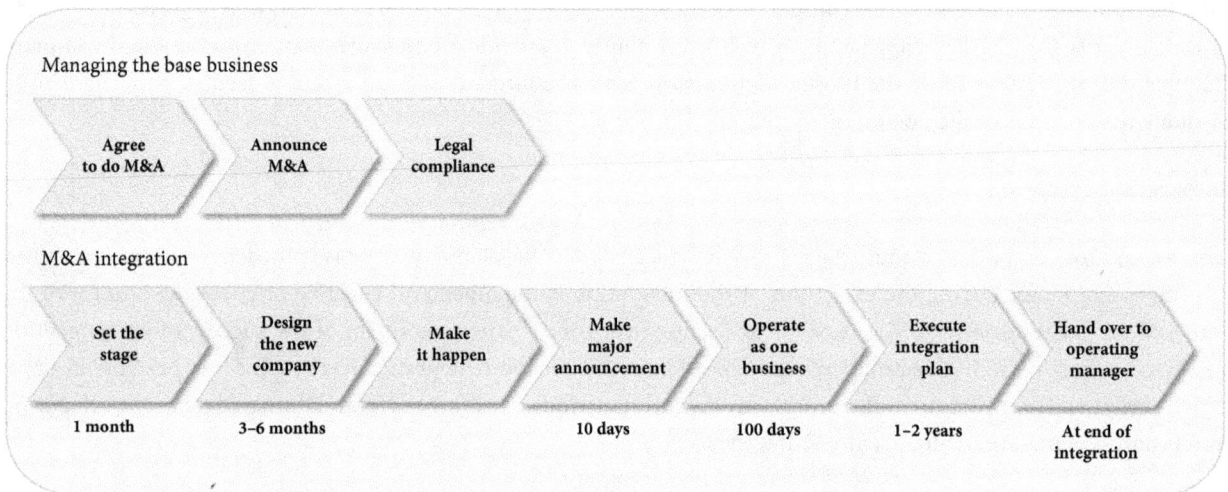

Figure 7.11: Phases of integration[120]

A study[121] of 270 mergers in various countries and regions found that in most cases sales growth had slowed dramatically after the merger – on average, it had dropped six percentage points. To avoid this trap, successful acquirers consciously focus from the start of the integration process on growing sales by strengthening sales and marketing in order to sustain profitable revenue growth and initially place deliberately less focus on cost-cutting initiatives. That's because revenue growth is necessary for earnings growth, the most reliable engine for driving total shareholder returns over the long term.

Another important focus area during the postmerger integration phase is devoting sufficient resources to retaining current customers and gaining new ones.

> "That typically involves improving the customer experience by streamlining processes; creating consistent marketing messages on how the merger will improve offerings; minimising changes in sales-account managers; ensuring that the formerly distinct companies present a single face to the customer; and attending to trivial-sounding but important matters like making sure the merged sales force has the correct name for each contact."[122]

Aligned measurements are a key success factor for a successful postmerger integration. These measurements must be balanced both in terms of financial and nonfinancial indicators and between leading and lagging measures. It is important to implement performance measurements to track the progress and success of the postmerger integration.

Culture integration

Culture integration and knowledge transfer are critical elements for successful M&As.[123] The culture created in the target organisation must be both satisfying and challenging to attract top people.[124] Companies with a closed and uniform culture often have trouble in taking over companies or even managing employees that have worked outside their own company for some time. To overcome the risk of a culture clash, it is important to create integration projects on which employees from both the acquiring and acquired firm can work together.[125] By using new shared tasks, the employees are inhibited from using the full extent of their culture that is familiar from old tasks, and are able to compromise on a new, shared way of doing things.

It is very likely that the acquiring and acquired firms will have different corporate cultures, which must be merged effectively for business success.[126] The challenge is to help the two distinct groups work productively together. The new culture must represent the best of both worlds and be driven by business considerations. To achieve this, managers can be trained for cultural integration, with an emphasis on interpersonal skills and diversity of cognitive abilities. Managers can use these skills to empower employees to take responsibility for the merger targets and to accept change as the new reality. The most important thing is for the employees of the acquired company to feel that they are a part of the acquiring company as quickly as possible.[127] If during the transitional period of postmerger integration employees believe that their leaders care about them, they develop a positive attitude to the change and commit to greater involvement in the integration.[128] A study[129] on organisation change during an acquisition integration shows that transformational leadership is related to improved subordinate performance, job satisfaction and acquisition acceptance. Transformational leadership is defined as a relationship between a leader and followers based on a set of leader behaviours perceived by subordinates as exhibiting idealised influence, motivational inspiration, intellectual stimulation, and individual consideration.[130]

Successful acquirers focus hard on overcoming the challenges associated with cultural misalignment, key talent defection and problems with target management teams. For unsuccessful integrators, culture and talent issues are the greatest sources of value loss. Others are defection of the target's existing customers, an unattractive market, too much difference between target business processes, overly ambitious revenue synergy assumptions, over-ambitious cost take-out assumptions, integration costs exceeding expectations and supply-chain problems.

Communication

Communication to all stakeholders, including employees, is very important during the postmerger integration phase. Research[131] indicates that managers who convince their people to believe in a vision fare much better in a merger integration. Yet despite a vast array of communication technologies and capabilities, inadequate communication continues to bring down otherwise successful deals. Communication does not just happen – managers must take responsibility, plan it carefully, and then control it over time. If customers, suppliers and key employees do not fully understand the strategic intent of the merger, they will leave. Communication is critical, even if it becomes clear that synergies do not exist. Whether the plan is to re-integrate or, in rare cases, to isolate and potentially divest the target company, the company should move quickly to communicate problems.

The creation of a "master questions and answers workbook" is part of an integrated communication plan that reflects the key messages and summary of the features and progress with a merger. The aim of this document is to anticipate and deal with all possible scenarios or questions that could be raised by internal or external stakeholders. It is a reference to be used by the key role-players such as executive management, internal communications, media liaison and customer care line executives.

Regular communication is key to successful postmerger integration.[132] If employees receive initial word of a merger or acquisition without immediate follow-up information, they will suspect that management is trying to hide bad news such as layoffs. Even if you do not yet have all the facts, discuss all that you are allowed to reveal. When you do have news to report, be honest and direct, and inform people immediately. Group meetings are best for matters that affect everyone on your team. Informing all employees at the same time will reduce the potential for gossip and spread of misinformation. Use personal discussions for private issues.[133]

Regular performance review results on progress with the postmerger integration should also be communicated to stakeholders. This ensures alignment and transparency based on shared information – both essential ingredients for positive stakeholder relationships. New learning from the integration should also be shared to foster both acquisition-specific and broader organisational learning as a result of the acquisition.

Practical guideline

To conclude this section we summarise and integrate the key success factors relevant in the postmerger phase in Table 7.4.

Table 7.4: Key postmerger integration success factors[134]

Theme	Key success factor	Description
Leadership	The acquiring company should provide relational, supportive and transformational leadership.	The directors of the acquiring company need to be involved in the integration and inspire trust. Employees who believe that their leaders care about them develop a positive attitude towards the change and commit to greater involvement in the integration.
	The vision and goals between the acquiring and target companies should be aligned.	The company should have a vision of how the combined company should look and function. Defining the desired end state supplies the people running the integration process with a more specific picture of the destination.
Planning	The acquiring company should determine an integration strategy.	The integration strategy should articulate how the target company will be integrated and includes decisions on changes in the target to manage the integration in a systematic way.
	The acquiring company should compile an integration project plan that is focused on the areas where the integration can capture the most value.	The integration project plan contains the practical implementation of the integration strategy and should include the following components: roles and decision lines, short-term administrative actions, communication plans (immediate and ongoing), management of the process for achieving the targeted benefits of the acquisition, and a progress dashboard.
	The acquiring company should appoint a full-time integration manager who is responsible for the integration.	An effective integration manager creates and tracks the progress of the integration team. A large part of an integration manager's role involves project management. An effective integration manager also helps to capture the synergies between the acquiring and target companies.
	The acquiring company should appoint a strong full-time integration team to conduct the integration.	The integration team must be a discrete, full-time function with ample resources. It should follow a project-management approach where integration teams are separate from the core business. The integration team should be balanced with employees of both companies.
Execution	The integration project plan needs to be implemented as quickly as possible to realise synergies and mitigate the risk of failure.	The speed of the integration is important because the chances for success decline over time. When integration takes longer than two years, there is a distinct and quantifiable loss. Companies that achieve momentum early are more apt to produce successful acquisitions. To achieve early momentum, companies identify and celebrate early wins.

Theme	Key success factor	Description
Execution (continued)	Strategic changes at the target company need to be executed right away.	The integration should start with effecting the radical changes that can add the most value and only then manage the easier parts of the integration. Some things, such as management appointments and other political calls, need to be settled right away.
	The culture of the target firm needs to be integrated with the culture of the acquiring firm.	The acquiring company needs to be aware of cultural issues and differences. The challenge with culture integration is to help the two distinct cultures of the acquirer and target to work together. It is important to let the employees of the acquired company feel that they are a part of the acquiring company as quickly as possible.
	Communication from senior management must be significant, constant and consistent throughout the integration process.	Communication does not just happen; managers must take responsibility, plan it carefully, and then control it over time. Communication is critical, even if it becomes clear that synergies do not exist. When you do have news to report, be honest and direct and inform people immediately.
	Continued focus on customers and sales throughout the integration process.	The challenge is to keep sales and customer service from getting hurt by the turmoil of the integration. From the customer's perspective, the integration should be seamless. Management should focus employees' eyes on the ball, that is, carrying on the base business.
Performance measurement	The integration team should implement performance measurement metrics to track and measure the progress of the integration.	Implementing performance measurement metrics and monitoring progress against these generates evidence of 'quick wins' and successes. These measurements must be balanced both in terms of financial and nonfinancial indicators and between leading and lagging measures and include measures such as staff satisfaction, sales-related and other financial targets.

Next the regulatory landscape in South Africa related to M&As is described in support of responsible corporate governance.

Regulatory requirements of a public listed company during an M&A[135]

A public listed company on the JSE in South Africa needs to comply with various regulatory requirements and Acts. These are the JSE Listings Requirements, the Companies Act, the Takeover Code, the Competitions Act and exchange control regulations[136].

The JSE Listings Requirements govern, amongst other things, all corporate actions undertaken by listed companies. Primarily the JSE fulfils a compliance function to ensure appropriate disclosure and the application of the listings requirements in relation to a listed company and any related party issues. Options, derivatives, issuing of shares for cash or share repurchases are often utilised for innovative and tax-efficient structuring of M&As. This requires the involvement and approval of the JSE.

In South Africa there is a dedicated and defined set of laws and regulations to facilitate and regulate M&As. These laws and regulations are defined within the Companies Act and the Code on Takeovers and Mergers, which applies to all publicly listed and large private companies (Act No. 71 of 2008; Government Notice, R. 29 of 1991). This code is overseen by the Securities Regulatory Panel (SRP)[137]. The Takeover Code exists principally to ensure the fair and equal treatment of all holders of securities in relation to an affected transaction.

The Takeover Code stipulates that the boards of an offerer and the offeree company and their respective advisers have a duty to act in the best interests of the holders of the respective securities. The general principles and the code will inevitably impinge on the freedom of action of boards and persons involved in affected transactions. Each director of an offerer and offeree company has a responsibility to ensure, so far as he or she is reasonably able to, that the code has been complied with in the conduct of an affected transaction. An affected transaction is defined in section 440A (s440A) of the Companies Act as a transaction that would result in a change in control of the company or someone becoming the sole holder of all the securities in a company (Act No. 61 of 1973)[138]. In the case of an affected transaction, the SRP is the primary regulator.

There are two means of acquiring the interests of a company: either acquiring the company's assets or its shares. The first method is to acquire all its assets. In terms of the Companies Act, the sale of all – or a substantial part of – the assets of a firm requires shareholder approval and cannot be decided by a board of directors alone or unilaterally. Shareholder approval by means of a special resolution in terms of Section 228 (s228) of the Companies Act No. 61 of 1973 is required. It should be noted that a firm does not cease to exist after selling all of its assets, and can become a cash shell with no assets. The SRP and the JSE regulate the sale of assets by listed entities.

The second method is to purchase all of a firm's voting shares from its owners in exchange for cash, securities or shares. An acquisition can be done by means of two mechanisms, either a takeover offer in terms of Section 440 (s440) of the Companies Act or a scheme of arrangement as per Section 311 (s331) of the Companies Act. A scheme of arrangement implies the cooperation of the board of directors of the offeree company. The offeree will propose a scheme of arrangement in terms of Section 311 of the Companies Act between the offeree company and its shareholders (Act No. 61 of 1973). A scheme meeting should then be convened at which a 75 per cent majority of scheme members (present in person or represented by proxy at the scheme meeting) will have to approve the scheme. Following approval of the scheme at the scheme meeting, an application will be made to the High Court of South Africa for the sanctioning of the scheme.

The Competition Commission (CC) defines a merger or acquisition as follows: "In terms of Section 12 of the Competition Act, 1998 (Act No. 89 of 1998), as amended, a merger occurs when one or more firms directly or indirectly acquire or establish direct or indirect control over the whole or part of the business of another firm" (Competition Commission South Africa (CC SA), 2011).[139]

The Mergers and Acquisitions Division (MAD) of the CC conducts merger reviews in terms of Chapter 3 of the Competition Act 89 of 1998. Firms entering into intermediate or large mergers are required in terms of Section 13A of the Competition Act 89 of 1998 to notify the commission of such mergers in a prescribed manner and form and may not implement that merger until it has been approved, with or without conditions, by either the commission (intermediate mergers) or the tribunal (large mergers) or the Competition Appeal Court.

After the MAD has been notified it will investigate and analyse the likely effects of the merger and decide what impact the competition will have on local markets. The MAD will consider the expected influence that the transaction is likely to have on the following:[140] A particular industrial sector or region; Employment; The ability of small businesses, or firms controlled or owned by historically disadvantaged persons, to become competitive; and The ability of national industries to compete in international markets.

Exchange controls have gradually been relaxed but the South African Reserve Bank's approval is required if the proceeds of the transaction or part of it are to exit the country to pay nonresident shareholders.

From this section, it is clear that a public listed company embarking on an M&A is subject to and needs to comply with various stringent regulatory requirements.[141]

Takeovers

A takeover is a special type of acquisition strategy where the target firm (the acquired) does not solicit the acquiring firm's bid.[142] Unsolicited takeovers are therefore unfriendly acquisitions or hostile takeovers.

Hostile takeovers would be relatively insignificant if business managers did their job properly by making a company so efficient and profitable that a raider simply cannot afford to pounce. Historically, companies that are at risk of becoming a possible target of a hostile takeover share certain characteristics from a trio of perspectives: managerial, strategic and financial.[143] From a **management perspective,** these characteristics can be: unfocused leadership, shareholders being uninformed in relation to their business and a loss of external focus. From a **financial perspective** an underperforming share price, or a valuation that does not measure up to its peers, weaker profitability and a balance sheet that is overleveraged may contribute to it being an "at-risk" company. The factors contributing to the **strategic perspective** are, amongst other things, synergistic benefits, economies of scale, strong brands and a lack of clear controlling shareholders.

Proactive measures or tactics are the most effective measures in preventing a hostile bid due to lack of warning, and create the time to respond to a hostile bid once it has been launched. These measures and tactics can also make any unwanted takeover prohibitively expensive to a predator. The most common proactive measures that can be used are:[144]

- Voting agreements between shareholders can be established. These are also known as a "voting pool". In order to avoid a hostile takeover, shareholders can form a voting pool that has the aim of voting against a resolution that may seek to accept any hostile offer for the company. Shareholders must, however, take cognisance of the definitions for acting in concert and affected transactions contained in section 440 A (1) of the Companies Act and also set out in Section B of the Code on Takeovers and Mergers.
- "Shark repellents" are used in conjunction with "poison pills" and include measures such as staggered boards, restrictions on shareholder actions, and the right of a shareholder to appoint additional directors to the board – as could be the case in a hostile bid scenario.
- Surplus cash could be distributed by paying a large dividend or by committing the company to a major new project. Shareholder approvals are always required if a firm wishes to eliminate excess cash, increase borrowings or propose the payment or distribution of special dividends. This also applies if the sale of assets, or the re-issue of shares/options or convertible instruments to friendly parties, are being considered.
- Employee severance contracts can be entered into with employees triggering so-called "golden parachutes" – a situation that often occurs when a hostile offer is received or a change of control occurs. These contracts can be entered into with any level of employee in a company, but more so with the senior executives of the firm.

- Poison pills provide an effective means of blocking attempts at a hostile takeover and effectively give existing management sufficient time to affect changes and improve the company's performance. The following items are examples of poison pill strategies:[145]
  - Bonus issues: In the case where the company has sufficient reserves, a bonus issue of new shares can be offered to existing shareholders. This can have the effect of reducing the earnings per share and thus raising the price earning (P/E)[146] multiple of the shares. As a result of the increased number of shares in issue it can also result in an increase in the total purchase consideration payable by the bidder.
  - Share splits can have a similar effect, as the combined share price after the split is normally higher than before the split occurred.
  - Share options: An option to acquire a certain number of shares at a discount can be issued to a third party. The third party would normally be a friendly party or one of the "white knight"[147] identified. The issue of the option has to be approved by shareholders and is therefore a measure that should be put in place long before the start of any hostilities. This option will also only be exercisable in the event of a hostile bid being received or other actions as determined in the option agreement taking place. This is a highly successful method of making hostile bids prohibitively expensive to a predator.
  - Flip in rights: This is normally a rights option awarded to all existing shareholders of the target company, giving them the right to acquire additional shares in the target company at a substantial discount. The shares that the predator acquires are excluded from this right. As this is a kind of share option, it will normally be triggered by the same events as mentioned under share options.
  - Lock-up options are largely similar to share options. The difference is that they give one selected bidder the right to purchase shares in the target company at a discount on the price that the shares could be purchased at by a rival bidder. It effectively restricts the takeover to one selected party. A lock-up clause means that shareholders forming part of a voting pool agreement are prevented from selling their shares for a number of years, locking them into the voting pool agreement until the voting pool agreement lapses.
  - Convertible instruments, preference shares or debentures can be issued to existing shareholders or a friendly party. These instruments can take two forms: the first is that the instruments convert into ordinary shares in the event that a hostile bid for the company is launched. The conversion will normally be done on favourable terms for the holders of the convertible instruments. The second is where the instruments are redeemable at a premium – as in the case of a hostile takeover. This will have the effect of increasing the cost of the bid to the predator.

From a strategic perspective a company can prevent its lack of unpreparedness by adopting a thoroughly proactive approach. Being prepared will ensure that all elements of the business and its financial strategy are aligned to deliver optimal shareholder value. Then, should an unsolicited or hostile approach ultimately occur, the company will be able to focus on putting the core elements of its defence strategy in place and prevent decisions from being taken under pressure or in a rash and irresponsible manner.[148]

Application tool for M&As

Use the information about M&A premerger and postmerger challenges and success factors to develop a broad plan for a target acquisition you want to develop a strategy for. Include the following in the plan:

- strategic rationale for the deal and strategic fit
- deal enablers and deal-breakers
- main premerger activities and approach
- main postmerger plan to ensure value realisation

Next we describe a case study on the context, events, process and strategy for the 1995 M&A between Barclays plc and Absa and the 2016 unfolding events of an intended portfolio rationalisation by Barclays.

Case study of Barclay's M&A of ABSA in 2005 and the unfolding events

Background

The seeds for "an international partner of reference" and a bigger role in the rest of Africa for Absa were sown in 2002 as part of a scenario development process of possible futures for Absa.

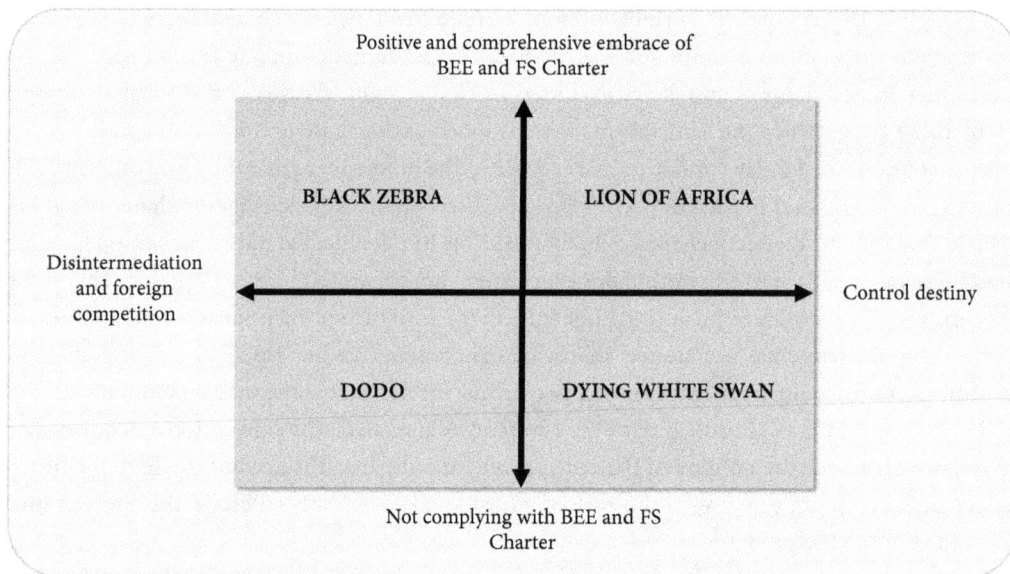

Figure 7.12: Absa 2002 future scenario possibilities

The "Lion of Africa" scenario described a possible future with the following features:[149]

> "Absa is the leading South African Financial Services (FS) player and dominates the growing emergent market while retaining and growing its traditional markets as reflected in measures such as market share, profitability, asset size and brand positioning because of its passion and obsession for the customer. Absa is always driven to deliver a perfect match between value proposition promise and actual customer experience. Absa's footprint and reach is appropriate for its market. Absa's innovative, approachable, "global but local appeal" with internationally experienced leadership and progressive attributes becomes a magnet for talent. Black shareholding in Absa is representative of the demographic diversity of South Africa which increases Absa's legitimacy and relevancy in the South African society.

Because of this, Absa becomes a prime influencer on development policy to government and other key players in the economic and social development of the country. As the economy grows, Absa has the largest profitable share of the FS industry. Absa's success and significance in the South African economy enables it to expand into the rest of Africa and has a preferred partner status with the South African government in championing NEPAD as a vehicle for economic transformation of Africa and in the process masters the art of doing business on the African continent. Such presence and gravitas makes Absa attractive as an alliance partner for local retailers and foreign banks."[150]

The above scenario stimulated the strategic repositioning of Absa as a key financial sector role-player on the African continent. The 2005 Annual Report of Absa states:

"Absa views partnering with a significant global player as key to the creation of long-term shareholder value and to the delivery of its strategic vision of becoming the leading financial services business in South Africa and the pre-eminent bank on the African continent. Barclays, as a major global bank with extensive interests in Africa, is an ideal partner and shares Absa's vision.

The acquisition accelerates the strategic objective of Barclays – to build its retail and commercial banking, investment banking and credit card presence in selected international markets. ... Absa is an excellent partner for Barclays in expanding its interests in South Africa, given Absa's strong market position across major market and product segments, distribution capabilities in South Africa and its operations and footprint in Africa."[151]

The 2005 deal

Barclays to buy £2.9bn Absa stake

by John Reed in Johannesburg and Jane Croft and Paul J Davies in London, *Financial Times*, 9 May 2005.[152]

"Barclays announced on Monday that it would buy a majority stake in South African bank Absa for up to £2.9bn in what will be the largest overseas investment into South Africa since apartheid ended 11 years ago. Trevor Manuel, South Africa's finance minister, said on Sunday he had given his approval for the deal subject to certain conditions.

Barclays, which was the biggest bank in South Africa before it pulled out 18 years ago during the apartheid era, said it would pay R82.50 plus a dividend of R2.0. The bank added it had received letters of support from shareholders representing 63 per cent of Absa. Absa is South Africa's third-largest bank by assets, but is the country's largest retail bank with a customer base of 6.3m and about 670 branches.

The deal is also highly significant for Barclays, the UK's third-largest bank, which has been negotiating for eight months to do the transaction. It is the bank's largest acquisition since it bought Woolwich for £5.6bn in 2000 and is the first deal for new chief executive John Varley, who took over last September. It also marks a return to South Africa for Barclays, which was forced to pull out of the country in 1986 by anti-apartheid protests.

Barclays has sweetened its offer marginally to win over three minority shareholders – believed to include Investec – who were holding out for a better price than the R79 first indicated. The price represents a premium of more than 36.4 per cent to Absa's share price when the talks were first announced eight months ago. Barclays will also set up a scheme of arrangement to enable the minority shareholders to sell about one-third of their stakes enabling them to benefit from some upside. Absa's biggest shareholders, insurer Sanlam and investment holding company Remgro with a total of about 30 per cent of shares are expected to sell out completely.

Barclays has given assurances that Absa will remain publicly listed in South Africa and that it would retain its local identity. Danie Cronje and Steve Booysen will also retain their posts as chairman and chief executive respectively. Mr Manuel also asked Barclays to furnish the South African Reserve Bank with a letter of comfort confirming it will "maintain the financial soundness of Absa".[153]

2005–2007

The Barclays plc Annual Report of 2005 states:

"The strategy we pursue of diversifying both our portfolio of businesses and the geographies in which we compete has proved to be sound. The growing contribution of our global businesses and of our International Retail and Commercial Banking businesses has reduced our dependence on the home market. This shift is evident in this year's results. It continues to be our goal to generate at least 50% of our earnings from outside the UK while improving the contribution from our UK-based businesses. We are making very good progress towards this goal. Our overall strategy remains unchanged."[154]

The Absa Annual Report of 2006 states:

"All of the business areas delivered strong growth in attributable earnings. The retail, business, corporate and investment banking segments benefited from a buoyant operating environment and the earnings uplift was assisted by the Absa-Barclays integration benefits."[155]

In 2007 the following comments emerged:

"The local banking community is mystified by Reserve Bank governor Tito Mboweni's attack on UK bank Barclays for its shareholder role in Absa. Barclays took a 56.4 per cent stake, worth R29.8 billion, in Absa in 2005 – the first major acquisition by an offshore investor of one of the big four local banks. London's Financial Times reported yesterday that Mboweni had described Barclays' stewardship of Absa as "discouraging". And he had complained to the *Financial Times* that he "had yet to see the benefits of Barclays' management of Absa". The newspaper commented that "such criticism is highly unusual for a central banker" and came at a sensitive time for the UK bank."[156]

The Absa Annual Report of 2007 states:

"Achieving the targets set by the Absa–Barclays integration programme

The objective of this programme was to improve profit before tax by R1,4 billion by implementing best practices applied by Barclays. The Group achieved this target by year-end, 18 months ahead of plan. Actual sustainable synergies as at 31 December 2007 were R1 428 million."[157]

"Actual sustainable synergies as at 31 December 2007 were R1 428 million comprising R698 million of revenue generated synergies and R730 million in cost savings. The benefits were achieved in the following areas:

- Customer value interventions in the retail operations;
- The creation of a competitive investment bank;
- Best-practice sourcing, which includes leveraging off the global supplier contracts of Barclays; and
- The implementation of a new customer-centric operating model in ACBB, improving the quality and speed of credit decisions and enabling relationship managers to improve the profitability of customers by focusing on the provision of more appropriate solutions.

Absa and Barclays will continue to share ideas and best practices to deliver further benefits to shareholders to improve the competitiveness of the franchise."[158]

Next we explore the evolving relationship between Absa and Barclays as reported in the business press.

The relationship between Absa and Barclays

by Phakamisa Ndzamela, *Financial Mail*, 2 September 2013[159]

"Behind the Absa-Barclays tie-up is a rich and colourful history of two institutions that at first glance appear strange bedfellows. Barclays disinvested from SA in 1987 amid criticism for doing business in the country under apartheid. It was also embroiled in controversy when its MD, Chris Ball, approved an overdraft facility for businessman Yusuf Surtee, a sympathiser of the United Democratic Front, a coalition opposing apartheid. The money was used to pay for newspaper advertisements calling for the unbanning of the ANC, which was then illegal."

Barclays left Africa only to return via Absa

"Barclays' British parent company pulled out and its assets were taken over by First National Bank. The eagle had flown, only to return two decades later to acquire a stake in Absa. Absa itself had evolved from being Volkskas bank, the "bank for the people", with its roots in agriculture, to being part of the Amalgamated Banks of SA (Absa), a merger of Volkskas, the United Building Society, Allied Bank and some assets of the Sage Group. By the time Barclays came wooing Absa in 2005 for a 55% stake for US$5,5bn, Absa had grown into the largest retail bank on the continent. In the deal Barclays acquired the shares of Sanlam, Remgro and some minorities. Barclays, which was started in 1690 in the City of London to cater for goldsmiths, and is now among the world's top banks and keen on expanding in Africa. This year Barclays increased its Absa stake to 62,3%, raising questions about its intentions and whether it would buy out minorities. Absa bought eight of its African assets and agreed to change its name and branding to Barclays Africa Group."

The formation of Absa

"Commenting on the formation of Absa, nonexecutive director Louis von Zeuner says Volkskas would not have been able to survive on its own. "It was good at the time that they could be part of a consolidation exercise, as I believe it was good for Absa to be ready when Barclays looked at opportunities on the continent." Von Zeuner, who joined Volkskas in 1981, says historically financial services were limited to white people. Volkskas had a strong agricultural brand. As its customer base grew younger, it had to cater for student loans and more sophisticated products, including electronic banking.

Later, insurance and bank assurance were added to its offerings. "The more banking opened to the broader population, so more and different services became necessary," says Von Zeuner. Whereas the United Building Society and Allied had links to building societies dating back to the late 1800s, Absa's roots are deeply entrenched in Afrikaner *volkskapitalisme*, which loosely translated means "people's capitalism". It was this ideology that led to the creation of Volkskas by the Broederbond in 1934 to meet the needs of Afrikaner farmers who grappled with getting credit from established banks after the Great Depression. Volkskas was launched as a co-operative bank but soon transformed into a fully fledged bank in the 1940s."

Afrikaner intellectuals get into business

"Afrikaner intellectuals in the 1900s believed that the source of Afrikaner poverty was not capitalism as an economic system, but the fact that Afrikaners did not have a stake in capitalism, hence the formation of companies such as Volkskas and Sanlam. Volkskas's merger into Absa gave it a new image and helped it make the transition into a democratic SA. But by the early 2000s it continued to be dominated by male Afrikaner executives; it was led by Danie Cronje and then Nallie Bosman, who was succeeded by Steve Booysen. Santie Botha, who in 1998 was appointed as the first female executive director at Absa, says Absa "was a very Afrikaans bank" in those days. The management and leadership was male-dominated and Afrikaans-dominated. The need for transformation became apparent, says Botha. The emphasis was to get black people and women into the executive committee. The strategy's success became apparent as government contracts grew. "In 1997 we had zero out of nine government contracts in provinces. By 2001 we had seven out of nine. We also deliberately went into sports. We sponsored soccer. The strategy here was to say: we are a South African bank. Black economic empowerment (BEE) was top of the agenda when I was in exco," she says."

Absa the first bank to do a BEE deal

"In 2004 Absa was the first big-four bank to do a BEE deal. It sold 10% of its shares to the Batho Bonke consortium led by former Umkhonto we Sizwe soldier and political prisoner turned businessman Tokyo Sexwale. In 2007, Absa, which was now controlled by Barclays, appointed former deputy finance minister and deputy reserve bank governor Gill Marcus as chair. In 2009 Maria Ramos, a former director-general of national treasury and Transnet CEO, was appointed group chief executive of Absa. Ramos's first job was in the then Barclays-owned First National Bank in the 1970s and her studies at Wits University were later sponsored by the bank. Barclays Africa's leadership is now more representative – it is chaired by Wendy Lucas-Bull and has at least four women directors.

The bank has grown steadily. In 1992 Absa had 140 branches and assets worth over R80bn. By the time Barclays made the 2005 acquisition, Absa had total assets of R313,9bn. In 2006 the total assets had jumped to R453bn.

With the acquisition of eight of Barclays' African operations, it has close to 1400 branches and will be a leading franchise, ranking in the top four by revenue, in seven African countries. The new acquisitions will add more than R80bn to the R788bn of assets reported in the six months to June. Assets include loans and advances to customers, investments in associates and cash.

Slowly, the blue of the Barclays brand is starting to replace the red of the Absa brand, though management says branches will not change. Whatever the colour scheme, the bank once known as Volkskas has undergone a fundamental change to meet the challenges of doing business in the 21st century."[160]

Absa's share price performance

Absa share price growth up to 2013 is reflected in Figure 7.13. The graph normalises the different competitors to 100 per cent in 2003 to show the relative growth in share price over the last decade. Absa's share price has grown steadily from R33 back in May 2003 to R146.75 in May 2013 – an increase of 344.69%. For Standard Bank (R30.84 to R111.15) that increase is 260.3%. Nedbank (R81.9 to R177.10) clocks 116.22%. For FirstRand it is 407.55% (R5.9 to R30.14).[161]

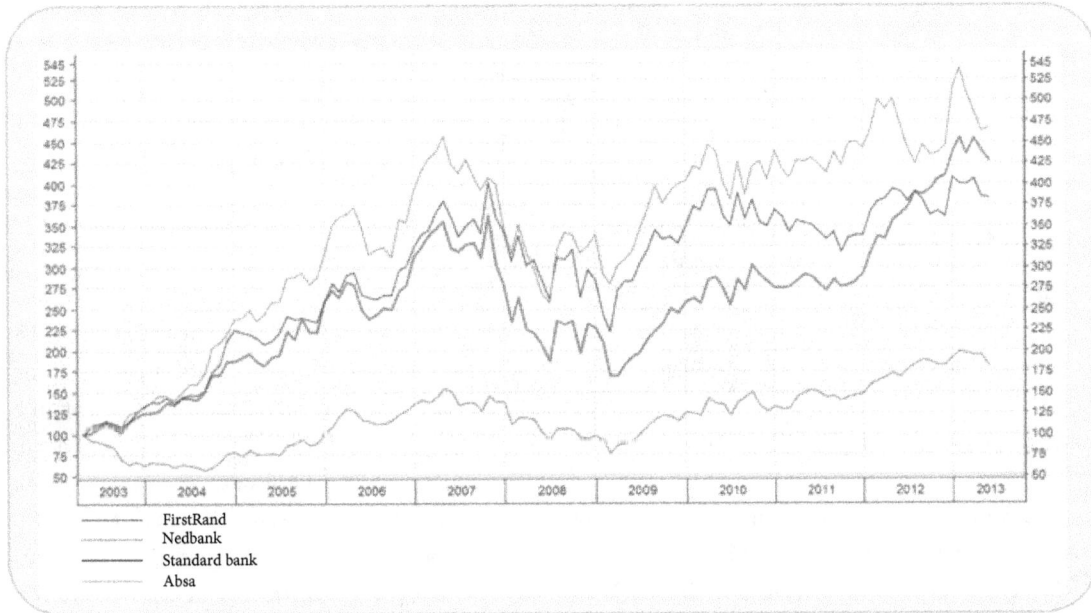

Figure 7.13: Share price growth across banks: 2003–2013

More corporate action in 2013

Absa and Barclays get green light for Africa
by Sasha Planting, *Moneyweb*, 22 July 2013[162]

"After warning investors of looming delays, Absa Bank announced on Monday that African regulators have given Absa the go-ahead to acquire the majority of Barclays Plc's African assets. Absa (JSE:ASA) will acquire Barclays' banking operations in Botswana, Ghana, Kenya, Mauritius, Seychelles, Tanzania, Uganda and Zambia, as well as Barclays' Africa Regional Office in South Africa. These operations will be merged with Absa's Africa operations. The transaction excludes Barclays' operations in Egypt and Zimbabwe.

In a conference call on Monday morning, Absa CEO Maria Ramos called the deal transformational and a milestone for both companies. "We have created one of the leading banking groups in Africa. Our goal is to assist in accelerating Africa's true global potential and to become the go-to bank on the continent."

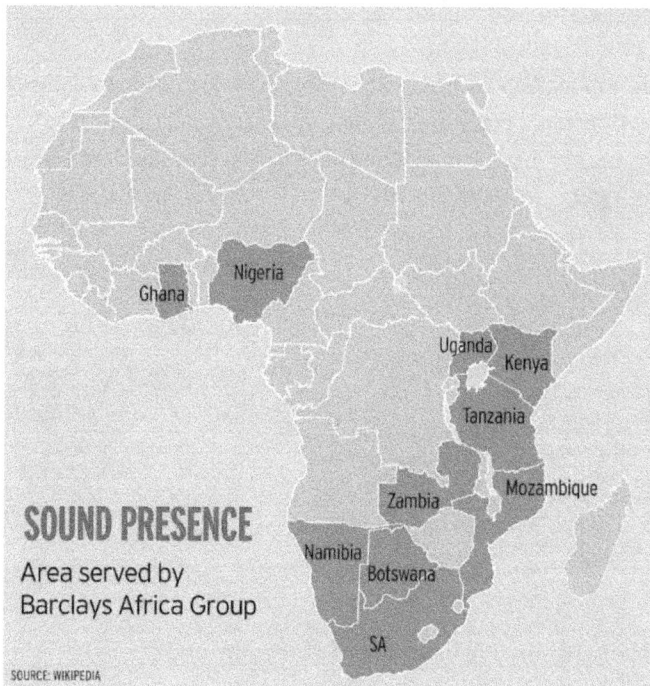

Figure 7.14: Barclays Africa 2016 footprint

The transaction is worth R18.2bn, and will be settled with 129.5m Absa shares. The deal becomes effective at the end of July, at which point Barclays' stake in Absa will increase from 55.5% to 62.3%. The new entity will be known as the Barclays Africa Group and will be listed on the JSE under that name. Barclays Bank Kenya and Barclays Bank Botswana will retain their respective listings. However Absa will retain the use of the Absa name and brand in South Africa. This is simply playing to its brand strengths. "Barclays has a strong brand on the continent, while Absa has a strong brand in SA, so we will keep that brand here," Ramos said.

The combined organisation will employ one third of all the Barclays Group employees and will contribute almost 15% of the bottom line to the Barclays Group and almost 25% to the global retail and business bank, chief executive of Barclays Africa Kennedy Bugane told Moneyweb recently. "But even more important, it currently contributes the third biggest geography to the group after the UK and the US. It is the fastest growing region and it will increasingly reflect that in the contribution to the group's bottom line." "As part of Barclays global strategy Africa remains core," says Ramos. "Africa's is a fast growing region and we believe we have a great platform for growth."

Absa's share price does not reflect its CEO's excitement on the deal. The share has declined 15% this year, and 1.6% today, to reach R140.06. It is one to watch."[163]

A new turn in 2016

Barclays Africa exit: On the block
by Hillary Joffe, *Financial Mail*, 11 March 2016[164]

"BARCLAYS Plc's announcement last week that it would sell down its stake in Barclays Africa comes nearly 11 years after the British bank confirmed it had struck a deal to buy a controlling stake in the then Absa in May 2005. And though Johannesburg's financial community has been astounded and appalled at the way Barclays has handled its exit, the UK banking group arguably didn't handle its entrée that well either. Talk was that it did itself no favours by approaching then-president Thabo Mbeki to gain his blessing on the deal, which was then presented to the regulators as a done deal late in 2005. It emerged later that SA's banking regulator had barred Barclays from implementing a key part of its plan – which was to inject its somewhat sub-par operations in the rest of Africa into Absa, perhaps in the hope that the whole thing could then be fixed up, dressed up and sold on.

It was only several years later that the regulators were won over and Absa was finally allowed to buy most of Barclays' other African operations in 2013, with Barclays raising its stake in the SA-based group to 62%. And now the UK group has put at least 40% of Barclays Africa (BAGL) on the market after a strategic review in which it decided it ought to simplify its structure to focus on two core divisions, "anchored in the two financial centres of the world, London and New York".

Johannesburg apparently wasn't part of that strategic review. One might have expected that Barclays would have worked with the SA board and management team to puzzle out how best to deal with the Barclays Africa stake – as Nedbank and its parent Old Mutual have done, according to a cautionary this week which said they were "engaging collaboratively" in the strategic review which Old Mutual is busy with. However, both CE Maria Ramos and Barclays Africa chair Wendy Lucas-Bull are adamant that the board and executive management of the SA group were told of Barclays' plans to sell only hours before Barclays sent out the strategic update with the announcement of its financial results last week. And Barclays' press office in London says governance issues prevented the Barclays board from informing the SA team before the board had made its decision.

Many find this hard to believe. If it did in fact know that its parent was contemplating a sale, Barclays Africa should have put out a cautionary notice on the JSE, certainly once rumours of Barclays' intentions began to leak into London's financial media in December. If it didn't, that makes the way Barclays has handled the move all the more bizarre. Most groups putting a US$4.5bn asset on the market would give some indication of what kind of deal they wanted to do, if they didn't have one in place already. Not so Barclays, whose announcement was frighteningly thin on detail. "If you wanted to offload an asset and you really didn't care about the price, this is the way you would do it," said one former investment banker. That Lucas-Bull resigned immediately from the Barclays Plc board "tells you exactly that these businesses are now on different paths and that there are potential conflicts of interest," says another banker.

That clearly is the thinking at rating agency Fitch, which downgraded its rating of Barclays Africa by two notches not long after Barclays announced its intention to sell, citing a lower likelihood of support from the British parent for the SA group. All of this came as Barclays Africa reported its highest return on equity since the financial crisis, raising headline earnings by 10% with its operations in the rest of Africa contributing strongly as it continued to pursue its strategy of building a great African franchise. "This is a really good business," said Ramos.

So why is Barclays so keen to sell? The official answer, from both parent and subsidiary, is about regulation. "100% of the financial responsibility with only 62.3% of the benefits," is the tagline of a slide in the Barclays presentation detailing the rationale for the sell-down "to a level which permits accounting and regulatory deconsolidation". The key is in Barclays Africa's return on equity for the year to end-March 2016, which is 17% in local SA terms, but gets diluted down to 8.7% by the time it gets to Barclays Plc. A part of that (3%) is goodwill, but most of it is to do with regulatory requirements, old and new. Banks domiciled in the UK have long had to pay a bank levy on their worldwide balance sheets, with Barclays having to pay the levy on 100% of the asset even though it owns 62% of it. The levy can't be passed on to SA shareholders in Barclays Africa, nor does any excess capital which it is holding count for regulatory purposes at Barclays Plc. In addition, much tougher new capital requirements have been imposed since the financial crisis, particularly on banks that are deemed large enough to pose risks to global financial stability. The narrative is of a series of regulatory acronyms – from G-SIB (global systemically important banks) buffer to TLAC (total loss-absorbency capacity) requirements as well as other requirements.

These present challenges to Barclays as a controlling shareholder, obliging it to hold additional overlays of capital to cover losses in its subsidiaries. … The Basel-based Financial Stability Board announced new rules in November, requiring those in Barclays' category to hold 2% additional capital to meet higher TLAC across their operations globally.

But few in the market are persuaded that new regulations were the only, or even the main, factor prompting Barclays' decision. Barclays is the most weakly capitalised of the big global banks, and selling down the SA asset would help in two ways. It would reduce the regulatory burden, so allowing the Barclays group to hold less capital, and a successful sale, or sales, would bring in some cash to boost the holdings of capital. It had to sell something big – and Barclays Africa, with its healthy growth prospects and sound capital ratios, was no doubt deemed the most saleable of its assets.

But Barclays has had a lot of other things going on in recent years. Its capital has itself been the subject of question marks, with the UK's serious fraud office investigating allegations dating back to 2007 that kickbacks were paid on Qatari investments. Then there was the Libor (London interbank rate) scandal in which Barclays was embroiled. This is a banking group which has been through three CEs in 12 months and three chairmen in nine months.

On the face of it then, its decision to sell down its BAGL holding is more about Barclays than it is about SA or Africa. Even so, the weak rand and SA's troubled politics can't have helped, and banking industry sources say the relationship between Barclays and BAGL has never been an entirely happy one, with "culture" differences persisting. And allegations of money laundering that have emerged recently will no doubt have spooked the Barclays parent, given the sanctions it could face in the US if the allegations were proved to be true.

Ramos says Barclays' decision is absolutely not a reflection on SA's political environment, or on Africa. "Barclays has been in many countries across the continent for a very long time. This is not a reflection on SA or anything else across the continent. It is genuinely a reflection of the changes in the global financial and regulatory environment since the 2008 financial crisis, which has made it very difficult for globally significant financial institutions." For Barclays Africa, the chance to be set free and gain new, more stable long-term shareholders could be as much an opportunity as a threat. Ramos emphasises that it is very early days and that the Barclays Africa management team and board will now "sit back and think carefully what this really means for us in terms of options, and what we can propose to Barclays Plc."[165]

The *Sunday Times* of March 13, 2016 report in an interview with Maria Ramos, CEO of Barclays Africa Group where she says: "Barclays plc has been an exceedingly supportive shareholder. We've had an extremely constructive relationship." "Yes we are going through tough times, but this is part of an economic cycle. I think the prospects for Africa are unbelievably good; the continent is not without its challenges but this is an exciting part of the world." "An ideal shareholder of reference would be someone committed to the long-term stability of the business and who isn't looking to generate returns on a quarter-by-quarter basis."[166]

The major shareholding of Absa as at December 31, 2015 is reflected in Figure 7.15.

MAJOR SHAREHOLDERS

Barclays Africa Group's largest 10 shareholders as at December 31 2015

	%
Barclays Bank PLC (UK)	62.32
Public Investment Corporation (SA)	5.60
Stanlib Asset Management (SA)	2.18
Old Mutual Asset Managers (SA)	1.76
Sanlam Investment Management (SA)	1.57
Dimensional Fund Advisors (US, UK, AU)	1.42
Prudential Portfolio Managers (SA)	1.37
BlackRock Inc (USA, UK)	1.28
The Vanguard Group Incorporated (SA, AU)	1.21
Abax Investments (SA)	1.16
Other	20.13

Geographic split	%
UK	64.3
SA	20.7
US and Canada	7.9
Other countries	7.2

SOURCE: BARCLAYS AFRICA

Figure 7.15: Barclays Africa major shareholders

Case questions:

- What are the main lessons about planning and executing an M&A strategy based on the Barclays –Absa case study?
- Do a stakeholder analysis to determine the satisfaction and main concerns of each stakeholder group.
- What possible future scenarios can unfold for Absa?

In the last part of this chapter we describe restructuring as an approach to changing the set of businesses or the financial structure of an enterprise.

RESTRUCTURING

Restructuring is a strategy that a business follows when it changes its business portfolio or its financial structure by divesting businesses from the company portfolio and downsizing.[167] The rationale for restructuring varies from streamlining the business to fit a new economic and global context to rationalising the product, service or market portfolio to focus more on the core business lines of the enterprise. Restructuring is also used as a way to deal with failed acquisitions.

In general, organisations deploy three types of restructuring strategy: downsizing, downscoping and leveraged buy-outs (LBOs).[168]

Downsizing is a process where the headcount of an organisation is reduced, which may or may not change the composition of the business portfolio of a company. Downsizing can also involve the reduction in the number of business units and specialist units. Downsizing represents a management intervention to cut costs by a reduction in labour or closing facilities, and can be part of an M&A strategy to realise envisaged cost synergies. The process of executing a downsizing strategy needs to meet the requirements of procedural justice and fairness. Downsizing should be a last option after longer-term alternative recourse strategies like internal staff transfers and redeployment, reskilling and entrepreneurial joint ventures have been exhausted. Downsizing causes erosion in the resource base of a firm. Management should not only think about short-term benefits, but should prevent a "revolving door syndrome" where the same people who were laid off, are rehired over time by the same organisation.

Downscoping involves the divestment or spin-out of current businesses in a company's portfolio that meet the portfolio criteria. This usually relates to selling-off unrelated businesses that do not form part of the core business of the enterprise. This process is done to increase the financial performance of a portfolio and to create more value from existing assets. The divestment of *Business Week* magazine from the portfolio of the McGraw-Hill companies in 2009 is an example of downscoping strategy. Through a downscoping strategy an organisation can refocus its efforts on its core business areas and improve its competitiveness.

An LBO is a restructuring strategy where a party (usually a private equity firm) buys all the assets of a firm to take it private. After a LBO transaction the shares of the company are no longer public tradable. An LBO strategy is not only applied to restructure distress assets but also more and more to build and expand firm resources. LBOs are associated with significant amounts of debt. To support debt payments, parts of the assets of a company can be sold to focus on the firm's core business.

Research indicates that companies that actively engaged in managing their business portfolio through divestments and acquisitions create more shareholder value than those who keep a fixed line-up of businesses.[169] GE is an example of a global enterprise that continuously managed their mix of business lines. When Jeff Immelt[170] took the reins in 2003 he refocused three areas in the GE portfolio: (1) Healthcare, with a focus on diagnostic pharmaceuticals and biosciences by acquiring British-based Amersham; (2) Media and entertainment, by merging Vivendi Universal entertainment with NBC to create a broad-based media business; and (3) divesting the insurance portfolio and spin-off remaining life and mortgage insurance businesses.[171]

Below is an example of a restructuring announcement by Anglo American plc.

Case study of Anglo American plc[172]

In February 2016 Anglo American plc announced as follows through the office of the Minister of Mineral Resources:

> The Group CEO of Anglo American plc announced earlier today that the company is undertaking a review of its portfolio of mining assets globally. The Minister of Mineral Resources, Mr Mosebenzi Zwane (MP), has had discussions with the CEO, Mr Mark Cutifani, on the company's intentions. Mr Cutifani informed Government that the current global economic environment has resulted in the company considering a strategic re-positioning with a focus on diamonds and platinum group metals and copper. The company has assured the Minister that the sale of what the company now considers to be noncore assets will take place over time and in a responsible manner. The company has committed to ensuring that assets will be sold as going concerns, where possible, and that employees will be transferred to new owners in order to maintain employment. As far as possible, any large-scale retrenchments should be avoided.

> "As I have indicated previously, I see these changes in the mining sector as an opportunity for new entrants. The sale of assets allows for new black economic empowerment champions to participate in this industry, thus further driving our broader socio-economic objectives, including economic transformation," Minister Zwane said.

> "What is of paramount importance at this time is that ongoing discussions take place between the department, organised labour and the company as well as other key stakeholders directly affected by the afore stated review. I have been assured that this will continue to take place. Open lines of communication will go a long way in ensuring a seamless transition during this time," Minister Zwane said. "South Africa remains an attractive investment destination, and as government we will continue to improve the ease of doing business and optimising the development of mineral resources, in line with the objectives of the Mineral and Petroleum Resources Development Act (MPRDA)," Minister Zwane concluded.[173]

Case questions:

- What was the market reaction on this announcement?
- Use this case to analyse the benefits and downside of restructuring as a strategy by using additional information from media sources.

CONCLUSIONS

In this chapter we looked at different strategies that an organisation can deploy to stimulate inorganic growth. The different types of strategic alliance and partnerships, the advantages, the management thereof and the success factors were described. The application of the concepts associated with strategic alliances was illustrated by the Renault–Nissan alliance case study.

M&As as a much-used inorganic growth strategy were described, covering key aspects such as reasons, challenges, features, regulatory requirements and best practices associates with pre- and postmerger processes. Takeovers as a special acquisition type were also described.

The Barclays–Absa 2005 M&A and the unfolding related events were described as a case study to demonstrate the complexities involved in M&A strategies.

Lastly, restructuring as a strategy to reposition the business portfolio or business line-up of an enterprise was described, with the associated options of downsizing, downscoping and LBOs.

Chapter 8

Strategy Renewal and Innovation 3: Management Innovation

*"Most of what we call management consists of making it difficult
for people to get their work done."* – Peter Drucker

LEARNING OBJECTIVES

This chapter discusses the why, what and how of management innovation. In particular, the following themes are discussed in order to guide your understanding and assist your application of management innovation:

- Why?
    - management in the industrial economy
    - management challenges in the new economy

- What?
    - Deming's theory of management
        - building quality into the process: theory of variation
        - joy in work (employee engagement)
    - management innovation moon shots

- How?
    - measurement of an organisation's management innovation sophistication and the process of management innovation
    - management innovation case studies
        - management innovation insights

The "who" of management innovation relates to those able to affect the change – managers and leaders initially, and all employees of the enterprise eventually. The where of management innovation relates to enterprises of all shapes, sizes and maturity that have realised that they need a new management paradigm for creating additional competitive advantages in the modern knowledge, digital and creative economies. Lastly, the when of management innovation relates to a constant and consistent application of management innovation practices at all times of the working day.

As will become apparent during this chapter however, many management innovation principles are applicable even to situations outside of one's work life, especially those situations that require leadership, collaboration and community mobilisation.

OUR INHERITED MANAGEMENT PARADIGM OF THE INDUSTRIAL ECONOMY

Management is the process of controlling things, people or systems. In an organisational context, the aim of management is to achieve cooperation and coordination among various individuals in order to create and supply a good or service,[1] in a way that creates maximum prosperity for the employer and employee.[2] Typical tasks of management include (1) establishing goals and constructing plans, (2) motivating employees and aligning their efforts, (3) coordinating and controlling activities, (4) acquiring and allocating resources, (5) accumulating and applying knowledge, (6) establishing and nurturing relationships, (7) identifying and developing talent, and (8) understanding and balancing the demands of external constituencies.[3]

Frederick Winslow Taylor (1856–1915), the father of industrial engineering, greatly influenced management as we know it today with his early practices in the 1880s and later writings in 1911 on "the principles of scientific management". Before Taylor's influence, two management forms were particularly prominent. The first is "personal management", where each individual is responsible for his or her own livelihood, daily tasks, deciding what to do, how to do it, and when and where. It is essentially self-management and self-regulation, where individuals act as entrepreneurs and craftsmen and are free to do as they please. The second management form is "management of initiative and incentive". In this paradigm, the problem that management sets before its workforce is to conduct the work at hand in the best and most economical way possible. Management relies on employees' innate knowledge, skill, and ingenuity – their initiative[i] – to yield the largest possible return to the employer. Management's primary task is therefore to persuade each employee to deliver his or her absolute best, thereby reaping the maximum amount of initiative from employees, which in combination and compounded result in superior performance.[4] However, the reality is that the average employee falls far short of giving employers their full initiative on an ordinary basis. Additional persuasion is required. Incentives are therefore set before employees in order to benefit from their initiative and can involve the promise of rapid promotion or advancement, higher wages, shorter work hours, a better work environment than ordinary employees have or other special benefits.[5] Sound familiar?

Management of initiative and incentive isn't without its flaws, however. While working at Midvale Steel Works in 1878, Taylor observed that employees were not working their machines or themselves nearly as hard as they could. The problem with management of initiative and incentive is that several factors can influence the work process and cause inefficiencies in the system. One of these factors is known as "soldiering" – deliberately working slowly in order to deceive employers about what is humanly possible. Reasons for soldiering include having an easy day of work every day and getting paid normal wages; skewing incentive schemes in one's favour so that they become easily attainable; and the fallacy that an increase in output[ii] for each person or machine would result in putting a large number of people out of work.[6] However, there are also other factors that cause those with even the best of intentions to work inefficiently, namely natural ineptitude, rule-of-thumb methods that result in waste, and poor tools and resources that are not fit for purpose. When a competent person is given insufficient resources to conduct his or her job, how can one possibly imagine that he or she will succeed? In the words of W. Edwards Deming,[7] "A bad system will beat a good person every time." Similarly, any one of these factors can cause one to falter and be inefficient. The

---

i   Taylor uses "initiative" in the broadest sense and sees it as including all the good qualities sought in good employees.

ii Increased productivity stimulates demand because of lower prices. Therefore, instead of putting people out of work, the opposite is true, and productivity actually creates jobs. Also see the explanation on the following page.

effect? Slower production, higher labour costs, lower productivity and throughput, a decrease in competitiveness, lower profitability and lower overall prosperity.

According to Taylor[8] the principal objective of management is to ensure that the maximum prosperity for the employer and the maximum prosperity for each employee is realised. This necessitates that every aspect of business is developed to its highest state of excellence. This highest state of excellence can only be achieved when the highest state of productivity[iii] and efficiency[iv] has been reached.

In the industrial economy that aimed to produce uniform products in large quantities by utilising a relatively unskilled workforce executing elementary repetitive tasks, efficiency above all else was king.

Taylor explained that productivity and efficiency are directly correlated to competitiveness. The more productive the organisation, the more goods it is able to produce. The more efficient the organisation, the cheaper the goods are to manufacture. The cheaper the goods are to manufacture, the lower their price can be, and the more competitive the organisation is in the market place. This lower price stimulates more demand for these manufactured goods and therefore grows the industry, creating more jobs (as opposed to the fallacy that efficiency destroys jobs). Having produced more goods than their competitors, the organisation is able to sell more. The more the organisation sells, the higher its profits and the higher the wages it is able to pay its staff. This in return serves as an incentive for being more productive and efficient, reinforcing the cycle.[9]

Taylor's[10] simple example is:

> "If you and your workman have become so skilful that you and he together are making two pairs of shoes in a day, while your competitor and his workman are making only one pair, it is clear that after selling your two pairs of shoes you can pay your workman much higher wages than your competitor who produces only one pair of shoes is able to pay his man, and that there will still be enough money left over for you to have a larger profit than your competitor."

Fuelled by his obsession for efficiency, and in order to rectify the shortcomings of and building on the "management of initiative and incentive" paradigm, Taylor started the process of developing his philosophy of scientific management (later known as **Taylorism**) by conducting various time and motion studies at Midvale Steel Works. By implementing his philosophy at Midvale Steel Works and later at Bethlehem Steel, Taylor was able to double the output per man on average[11] and therefore double the productivity while under his supervision – quite a feat in efficiency!

In summary, scientific management advocates the analysis of workflows and the development of rules, laws, and formulae (best practices or a "science" of sorts) that are helpful to employees in their routine tasks, and thereby improve economic efficiency through labour and machine productivity.[12] In scientific management the greatest prosperity is obtained when work is done via the expenditure of the smallest amounts of human effort, natural resources, and the cost of capital.[13]

---

iii   Productivity is the effectiveness of productive effort, and is measured as the rate of output per unit of input, e.g. producing 25 units per hour is more productive than producing 20 units per hour.

iv   Efficiency is a relative measure of resource effectiveness compared to some standard. If the standard production rate is 30 units per hour, then a process producing 25 units is only 83.33 per cent efficient.

Taylor's four principles of scientific management are outlined below:[14]

- **The development of a true science**: Replace rule-of-thumb methods and judgement of the employee with standardised best-practice methods born from the scientific analysis of the task. Employees should be observed and their actions analysed in order to uncover best practices or rules that can be enforced as the standard.
- **Scientific selection of the employee**: Scientifically select and train specific employees for certain jobs. In the past employees selected their own work and taught themselves the best they could. Some individuals are simply more adept at certain tasks than others. Employees need to be purposed to the tasks that they are more skilled at, and this requires closer managerial attention to individual capabilities.
- **His scientific education and development**: Collaborate with employees to ensure that all work is done in accordance with the new science. Those who are unable or who refuse to adopt the new methods should be repurposed, as they will otherwise not be optimally efficient. Part of the adoption of the new methods and work rate involves incentivising performance by paying each employee a large daily bonus for working fast, meticulously and doing what he or she is supposed to do.
- **Intimate friendly cooperation between the manager and employees**: Management assumes new responsibilities that in the past were left to employees. These new responsibilities include tasks that management is better fitted to do, and include planning, creating a science of tasks, selecting employees, selecting implements, providing help, encouragement, and generally making it easy for employees to do their jobs. This liberates workers from various burdens and allows them to actually perform tasks.

Taylor believed that the cure for inefficiency laid in systematic management, and that the best management was a true science that consisted of laws, rules and principles as a foundation.[15] For a range of methods for completing a certain job, there is always one method that is quicker and better than any of the rest. This method can only be discovered through the scientific study and analysis of all the possible methods, together with accurate, minute, motion and time studies.[16]

As manufactured products were becoming increasingly complex, it was inherent that workers would not necessarily be good at all the jobs required to manufacture a complete product. Rather than relying on a single person to produce a complete product, it would be more efficient if many workers could collaborate on a single product and only perform the tasks that they were particularly skilled at. This would result in increased speed of production, productivity of the system, and even enhanced quality. What better way to achieve this type of collaboration and coordination than via hierarchical systems that exhibit tight control over the resources and activities of the system, resulting in lower risk, reduced waste and increased efficiency, and leading to enhanced competitive performance and increased margins?

As opposed to some other leaders of the time who sought to procure competent people for their factories that other people had trained, Taylor had the insight that the demand for such people far exceeded their supply, and as such, they needed to be developed within the enterprise.[17] It was Taylor's[18] vision that "In future … no great man can (with the old system of personal management) hope to compete with a number of ordinary men who have been properly organised to efficiently cooperate." Similarly, Taylor[19] noted that

> "The time is fast going by for the great personal or individual achievement of any one man standing alone and without the help of those around him. And the time is coming when all great things will be done by that type of cooperation in which each man performs the function for which he is best suited, each man preserves his own individuality and is supreme in his particular function, and each man at the same time loses none of his originality and proper personal initiative, and yet is controlled by and must work harmoniously with many other men."

In order to develop an efficient organisation, each person had to be trained to achieve his or her highest state of efficiency, which meant that each one needed to be developed to do the highest grade of work possible within his or her natural abilities.[20] The selection of the right people for the right job was therefore of paramount importance. In a similar vein, management often had better education than employees, and would therefore be more efficient at certain jobs. Under management of initiative and incentive, management consisted largely of the delegation of responsibility to workers for getting jobs done, and workers were required to take full responsibility for general plans and detail of work, tools, and the actual physical work.[21] Scientific management required management to take on additional responsibilities. Management needed to turn the work process into a science that liberated workers from many technical and planning tasks and equipped them with the most efficient means for completing a task.[22]

Regarding the relationship between management and employees, Taylor[23] said:

"Each man should daily be taught by and receive the most friendly help from those who are over him, instead of being, at the one extreme, driven or coerced by his bosses, and at the other left to his own unaided devices. This close, intimate, personal cooperation between the management and the men is of the essence of modern scientific or task management."

The core differences between scientific management and management of initiative and incentive are shown in Table 8.1.

Table 8.1: Scientific management vs personal management derived from Taylor[24]

Scientific management/"Taylorism"	Management of initiative and incentive/personal management
Science	Rule of thumb
Harmony	Discord
Cooperation	Individualism
Maximum output	Restricted output
The development of each person to his or her highest level of efficiency and prosperity	Self-regulation and self-taught skills

Taylor's principles of scientific management in conjunction with inputs from various others in the industrial economy set the stage for many of the management principles and practices still in existence today. Some of these influential individuals [25] [26] [27] [28] [29] [30] are:

- Adam Smith (1723–1790): Classical economics, modern free market, division of labour
- Daniel McCallum (1815–1878): Principles of management and the modern organisational chart
- Henri Fayol (1841–1925): Components of management and principles of management
- Henry Gantt (1861–1919): Gantt chart, scheduling, production and cost control
- Henry Ford (1863–1947): Mass production via assembly lines
- Max Weber (1864–1920): Organisational structure, bureaucracy, hierarchies, lines of authority and control
- Frank (1868–1924) and Lillian Gilbreth (1878–1972): Motion studies, human factors engineering and ergonomics

- Mary Parker Follett (1868–1933): Organisational theory and organisational behaviour
- Alfred Sloan (1875–1966): Decentralised bureaucracy, divisionalisation, delegation, and planned obsolescence at General Motors
- Elton Mayo (1880–1949): Organisational behaviour, Hawthorne studies
- Frank Donaldson Brown (1885–1965): Financial administrative controls at General Motors
- Chester Barnard (1886–1961): Functions of the executive, authority and incentives
- Walter Shewhart (1891–1967): Statistical quality control
- William Edwards Deming (1900–1993): Quality management
- Kenneth Richmond Andrews (1916–2005): Deliberate strategy
- Alfred DuPont Chandler, Jr (1918–2007): Strategy and structure
- Harry Igor Ansoff (1918–2002): Strategic management
- Armand Vallin Feigenbaum (1922–2014): Total quality management.
- Philip Bayard Crosby (1926–2001): Zero defects

From these contributors, prevailing management themes include analysis, synthesis, logic, rationality, hierarchy, planning and control, quality assurance, variation minimisation, predictability, project management, empiricism, workflow optimisation, work ethic, monetary rewards, the primacy of shareholder interests, elimination of waste, efficiency, standardisation of best practices, mass production, specialisation, divisionalisation, knowledge transfer and documentation.[31] [32]

Although the principles discussed in this chapter and the themes above are a far cry from a complete management paradigm in all its richness and complexity, they do provide valuable insights into core management aspects and a way of thinking about management in the industrial economy. Hierarchy, bureaucracy, control and system-wide efficiency paved the way for organisational success. In Taylor's[33] words: "In the past the man has been first; in the future the system must be first."

Other common beliefs or assumptions that are becoming more problematic in the twenty-first century that managers in the Western world often hold are:[34] [35] [36] [37]

- Organising work
  - Hierarchy and bureaucracy are the best forms of organising.
  - Everybody needs a boss.
  - Work titles matter more than the value added.
  - If you delegate responsibility, you lose power.
  - Most people are only good at one role.
  - Optimisation of every area in an organisation leads to optimisation of the entire organisation.
  - Efficiency is the premier measure of value.

- Management of change
  - It takes a crisis to provoke change.
  - It takes a strong leader to change a big company.
  - To lead change, you need a very clear agenda.

- o   People are mostly against change.
- o   With change there are always winners and losers.
- o   Organisations can only cope with so much change.
- o   Change must start at the top.

- Motivating people
  - o   Rewards and punishments are the most effective motivators for people.
  - o   Humans are motivated by selfishness, greed and fear.
  - o   Poor people have different motivations than other people.
  - o   You can't trust people to do the right thing.
  - o   Competition is a necessary aspect of life.
  - o   Only a few people are creative.
  - o   Diversity is a problem.

- Controlling people
  - o   People work best under controls and regulation.
  - o   Authorisation is required in order to take initiative.
  - o   Quality is inversely related to quantity.

- Achieving results
  - o   Results are achieved by setting objectives.
  - o   Organisations can be improved by fighting fires.
  - o   Unconstrained growth is good.
  - o   A healthy economy leads to a healthy society.
  - o   Rational decisions can be made on the basis of guesswork and opinion.

As will become clear in later parts of this chapter, many of these assumptions are complete fallacies, whilst others contain an inkling of truth, albeit not quite complete. The assumptions that we make about the world restrict our actions in it. It is therefore necessary to have a clear understanding about the explicit, or maybe unintentional, assumptions that we carry with us, and perhaps it is time to abandon old assumptions that have done nothing but prevent us from flourishing. Possibility awaits …

Application tool

Using Table 8.2, make a list of all the management and leadership assumptions that you or your organisation consciously or subconsciously harbour. Carefully think about whether these assumptions are verified truths, or opinions with an inkling of truth to them. What has the effect of these assumptions been on the way that you conduct business? Have they been destructive or constructive to the ultimate goal you wish to achieve? What revised assumption would be a better reflection of reality, and what would the implication for business be?

Table 8.2: Management assumption analysis

Assumption	Verified/opinion	Destructive/ constructive	Revised assumption	Implication
Organising work				
Management of change				
Motivating people				
Controlling people				
Achieving results				

MANAGEMENT CHALLENGES OF THE NEW ECONOMY

Since the onset of the industrial economy and Taylor's "principles of scientific management", the world has dramatically and irreversibly changed. There have been shifts in the global and macro context, shifts in local contexts, shifts in regulation, shifts in socio-economic standards, shifts in technology, shifts in society and culture, shifts in customer needs, shifts in the competitive forces in industries, shifts in industry structure, shifts in the basis of competition, and shifts in ecology and the environment. The world is simply not the same as it once was. **Yet the grand management challenge in the new economy stays exactly the same as it was in the old economy: Keep the business relevant, secure a competitive advantage, generate profits and sustain the business to the benefit of all stakeholders.**

In this enduring pursuit, management and management thinking has slowly began to evolve. Some of the influential thinkers of that have shaped modern management perspectives[38][39][40] are:

- Robert Greenleaf (1904–1990): Servant leadership
- Douglas McGregor (1906–1964): Theory X and Theory Y
- Abraham Maslow (1908–1970): Hierarchy of human needs
- Peter Drucker (1909–2005): Management theory and practice
- James McGregor Burns (1918–2014): Transactional, transformational, aspirational and visionary schools of leadership theory
- Frederick Irving Herzberg (1923–2000): Two-factor hygiene and motivation theory
- Henry Mintzberg (1939–present): Emergent strategy, strategic management and organisation theory
- Coimbatore Krishnarao Prahalad (1941–2010): Core competence and business eco-systems
- Tom Peters (1942–present): Organisational effectiveness and the empowerment of decision–makers at different organisational levels
- Richard Rumelt (1942–present): Strategy evaluation and strategy dynamics
- Michael Eugene Porter (1947–present): Competitive strategy, strategic positioning and shared value
- Peter Senge (1947–present): The learning organisation
- Robert Chia (1949–present) and Robin Holt (1966–present): Strategy without design

- Chris Zook (1950–present): Growth via core differentiators
- W Chan Kim (1952–present) and Renée Mauborgne (1963–present): Blue Ocean strategy
- Clayton Christensen (1952–present): Disruptive innovation
- Steve Blank (1953–present): The customer development process
- Gary Hamel (1954–present): Core competencies and management innovation
- Henry Chesbrough (1956–present): Open innovation
- Rita Gunther McGrath (1959–present): Strategy in uncertain and volatile environments
- Peter Diamandis (1961–present): Abundance thinking and exponential technology
- Alexandre Havard (1962–present): Virtuous leadership
- Daniel H Pink (1964–present): The changing workplace
- Alexander Osterwalder (1974–present) and Yves Pigneur (1954–present): Business modelling and business model canvas
- Rachel Botsman (1977–present): Collaborative consumption
- Eric Ries (1978–present): Lean start-up

From these, prevailing management themes in the modern economy include psychology, human relations, appreciation for human needs, empowerment, self-actualisation, intrinsic and extrinsic motivation, visionary and virtuous leadership, natural leaders and leaders as servants, transparency, information ubiquity, openness, community and networks, sharing and shared value, value innovation, disruptive innovation, exponential growth, abundance, core competencies, sustainable competitive advantages, transient competitive advantages, emergent strategy, experimentation, learning, speed, agility and adaption.

In order to achieve the grand management challenge there are certainly many subchallenges. The creation of a competitive advantage and the generation of profits present extraordinary daily and long-term challenges by themselves. However, the last-mentioned theme – adaption – and the quest to remain relevant in an ever-changing competitive environment is undoubtedly one of the most fundamental challenges facing management, and is the core focus of this section. Businesses who don't adapt become ill-equipped and are inadequate players in the new world. Over time, these businesses stagnate and start drifting further and further away from customer needs, until one day they've drifted so far that they find themselves in a barren landscape of irrelevance, at which point they perish. In the same way that it is absolutely crucial for businesses to adapt to the changing competitive environment in order to stay relevant and survive, so too management has to adapt to a new age. *Management innovation* **is required**. Business and management therefore need to embrace the heartbeat and themes of the new economy, and align, entwine and infuse these new thoughts and ideas into current business practices in order to remain relevant. Businesses that refuse to adapt to the new normal; those stubborn and unwilling few who choose to cling to archaic management practices and ways of doing business – they have already declared themselves obsolete. In the words of W. Edwards Deming: "It is not necessary to change. Survival is not mandatory." For the rest, the winds of change provide opportunity, liberty – and hopefully, above all – better management.

In the remainder of this section, we explore four great inter-related driving forces that have played a significant role in the metamorphosis of the competitive business landscape. These driving forces are agents of change, and they themselves therefore reflect key management challenges that need to be addressed: (1) the invention, adoption and proliferation of the Internet; (2) generational shifts and the emergence of new subcultures with new values; (3) shifts in competences required to develop competitive advantages; and (4) a global yearning for the restoration of humanity in business. These driving forces are depicted in Figure 8.1.

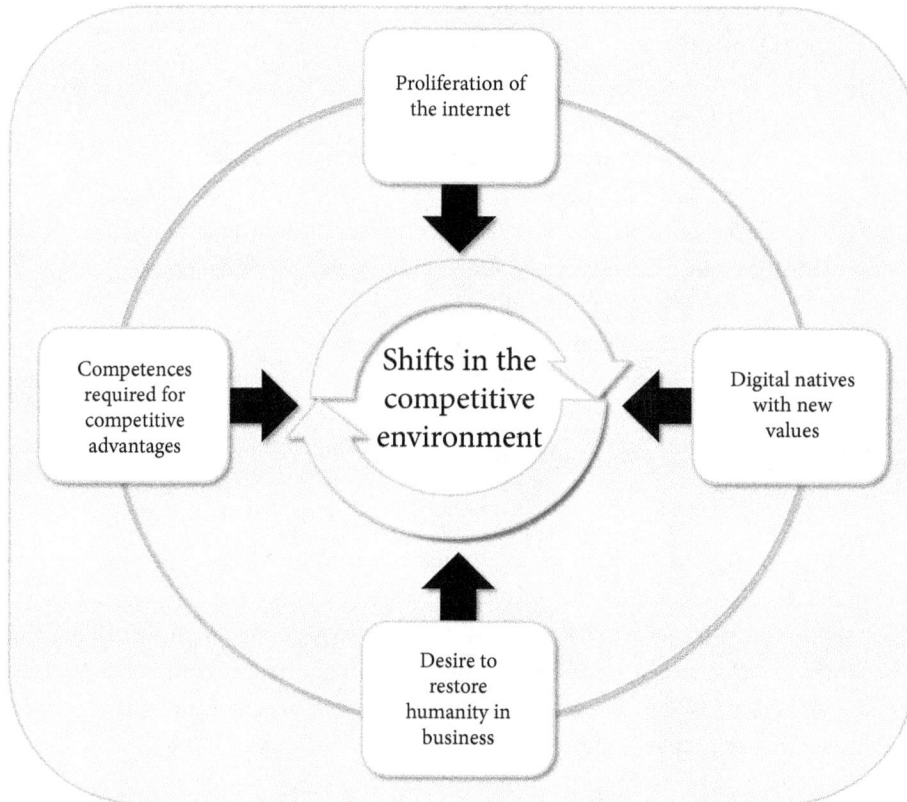

Figure 8.1: Four drivers of environmental change

The proliferation of the Internet

Alongside the discovery of fire, the wheel and electricity, the Internet is one of the most disruptive technologies ever invented. It has revolutionised a myriad industries via new digital business models: media (music, video, news, radio, publishing), entertainment (gaming, gambling, social media), finance (banking, accounting and taxes, stock markets), transportation-travel-and-tourism (airlines, taxi services, accommodation), communication (mail, phones), real estate, recruitment, healthcare, education, software, auctions, retail, art – and the list goes on; it has severely impacted practically every aspect of modern living as we know it; and almost single-handedly spawned a new age – the digital economy. The Internet opened up the world, liberated information, connected the globe and unleashed the possibility of abundance.

Fundamental benefits of the Internet are: (1) it gives people access to unprecedented amounts of relevant information; (2) it enhances transparency; (3) it equips people with countless new digitally enabled capabilities; (4) it reduces the capital required to start a business; (5) it allows even small firms to be global competitors from day one; and (6) it enhances people's ability to share, interact, socialise, communicate and collaborate in real-time, globally.[41] [42] [43]

The Internet represents a tectonic shift in the business landscape and it is a force that businesses simply can't afford to ignore. In a McKinsey survey involving over 4 800 SMEs in 12 countries and across all sectors of the economy, it was found that small businesses that have a high web technology utilisation rate grew twice as fast, brought in twice as much revenue through exports as a percentage of total sales, and created more than twice as many jobs as small businesses that had a minimal web presence.[44] Research by Goldstuck[45] similarly found that SMMEs with a website are much more likely to be highly profitable than companies without a website. From the 410 000 SMMEs in South Africa that have a website, 27 per cent were strongly profitable with only 5 per cent making a loss. This is in contrast to the 240 000 South African SMMEs that do not have a website, where only 11 per cent were strongly profitable and 16 per cent were making a loss.

The major challenge facing management is to cope with the increasingly digital and hyper-competitive world. Given the advantages of the Internet, it becomes clear that businesses that fail to adopt Internet technologies will struggle to compete against their digitally enabled counterparts. Businesses need to embrace the Internet as a major communications channel, sales channel, business catalyst, and a new form of doing business – or run the risk of becoming obsolete. Internet activities, however, should not be carelessly pursued in an indiscriminate manner, but be purposefully driven to unlock value, serve customers and thereby enhance the business's survivability in the new economy.

"Generation Y", "Generation Z" and new economy values

Computers and the Internet's influence on society itself have been immense. Together they have not only spawned new subcultures, but even entire generations of "digital natives" who have grown up alongside the Internet (1969), personal computers (1977) and the World Wide Web (1989). "Generation Y" or "Millennials" (born between approximately 1981–1995) represents the first wave of digital natives who were born before the year 2000, many of whom grew up with a personal computer at home. Following them are "Generation Z" or "Post-Millennials" (born approximately between 1996–2010), the second wave of digital natives who only know a world in which digital technology, the Internet and its applications exist.

Exposure breeds competence. Therefore having been exposed to and immersed in a digital and hyper-linked world from such young ages, Generation Y and Generation Z individuals are typically considered to be proficient with and comfortable around many forms of technology. Their constant interaction with technology, digital socialisation and increased accessibility to an abundance of information has imprinted itself on the mindsets and perspectives of these generations who literally grew up online, cultivating a new subculture with new values.

Generation Y have typically (but not absolutely) been credited with traits such as being entitled, narcissistic, having inflated views of themselves, having high expectations of themselves and others, having a desire for rapid work advancement, being ambitious, self-confident, passionate, energetic, optimistic, skilled in technology, able to multi-task, multi-dimensional, outspoken, achievement-focused, challenge-seeking, liberal, tolerant of social and cultural differences, team- and community-oriented, perceiving the world as limitless and filled with unbounded possibility, seeking ongoing feedback, resistant to negative feedback, yearning for innovative work environments that offer versatility, flexibility and work-life balance, harbouring a strong desire for social interaction, a desire for responsibility, involvement in decision-making, the ability to affect the business and making a difference in the world.[46 47 48 49 50 51 52 53 54 55 56] Research into the traits of Generation Z has been less extensive, but a general opinion exists that in many ways Generation Z will be much like Generation Y, but even "more so" in some aspects. The defining characteristics of Generation Z will still evolve as they mature, but preliminary data suggests that Generation Z is more entrepreneurial, more realistic, less entitled, less social and more multi-tasking that Generation Y. They are also very independent, instant-minded, easily distracted, ambitious, private, novelty-seeking, cynical, appreciative of order, structure and predictability, tech-savvy and comfortable with various online collaboration tools.[57 58 59]

The major challenge facing management is to cope with, attract, motivate and retain this new generations of employees and customers who have vastly different ideas, expectations and perspectives of the world and how it should work, while not alienating older generations and their beliefs or being insensitive to their technological discomfort in the process. The values and expectations of these new generations were cultivated by and have seeped into the very fabric of the Internet and have now slowly started infiltrating the modern work environment. Managers who want to fully engage the new workforce and unleash their passion will have to understand the set of social values driving them.[60] Some of these are:

1. All ideas compete on an equal footing.
2. Contribution counts for more than credentials.
3. Hierarchies are built bottom-up.
4. Leaders serve rather than preside.
5. Tasks are chosen, not assigned.
6. Groups are self-defining and self-organising.
7. Resources are attracted, not allocated.
8. Power comes from sharing, not hoarding.
9. Mediocrity is exposed.
10. Dissidents can join forces.
11. Users can refuse most policy decisions.
12. Intrinsic rewards matter most.

Hamel[61] continues to explain that the Internet compounds our passions because online

> "No one can kill a good idea. Everyone can pitch in. Anyone can lead. No one can dictate. You get to choose your cause. You can easily build on top of what others have done. You don't have to put up with bullies and tyrants. Agitators don't get marginalised. Excellence usually wins (and mediocrity doesn't). Passion-killing policies get reversed. Great contributions get recognised and celebrated."

For traditional, conservative managers adopting or partially adopting these values will be a momentous task, but no one said that management in the new economy would be easy.

Competencies for competitive advantage in the new economy

The new economy does not operate in the same way that the industrial economy operated. No longer is the aim merely the efficient execution of elementary repetitive tasks in order to mass-produce products. Where the industrial economy relied on a workforce that was relatively unskilled, the "knowledge economy" relies on knowledge workers that are highly skilled and multi-skilled. But even these skills are not enough. With the Internet providing access to the world's information, creativity and synthesis of facts are becoming increasingly important. Where the industrial economy sought to produce products based on a defined blueprint, most of what is created in the new economy has no such blueprint. Most endeavours are new, and whatever is created needs to be customised to fit the context. A whole new level of innovation and talent is required for organisations to build competitive advantages and compete successfully. Simply put, the basis of competition and the competencies required to develop competitive advantages have shifted.

In the new economy, it is not enough for businesses to merely have a workforce that are obedient and diligent drones. With rising living standards and increased education, the supply of skill and expertise has simply increased; and *any* business can purchase and acquire these skills at a moderate price. Because of this, the *productivity frontier* (as Porter calls it) has shifted outwards. There has been an overall increase in the operational efficiency shared by all competitors, and obedience, diligence and expertise are no longer sufficient foundations for building competitive advantages.[62] Rather, they are the minimum requirements. But if these are no longer sufficient, how does one now create advantages?

Hamel[63] suggests that we have moved beyond the "knowledge economy" and have entered "the creative economy", where the creation of competitive advantages depends on employee engagement. Competitiveness itself is therefore inexorably linked to a business's management innovation. "In a world where customers wake up every morning asking, "What's new, what's different, and what's amazing?" success depends on a company's ability to unleash the initiative, imagination, and passion of employees at all levels."[64]

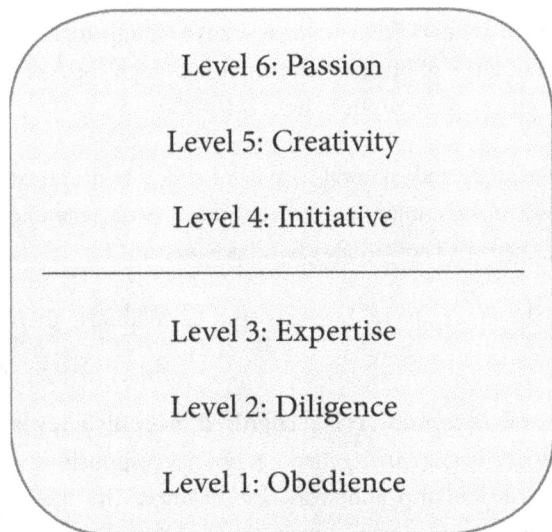

Level 6: Passion

Level 5: Creativity

Level 4: Initiative

_____

Level 3: Expertise

Level 2: Diligence

Level 1: Obedience

Figure 8.2: A hierarchy of human capabilities at work[66]

Hamel explains via his hierarchy of human capabilities at work (shown in Figure 8.2) that in the industrial economy, the first three tiers of capability (obedience, diligence, and expertise) were sufficient; however, in the creative economy employees need to bring the higher-level capabilities (initiative, creativity and passion) to work. Companies require (1) employees who are proactive and take the initiative to solve problems without being told; (2) employees who challenge conventional wisdom, are creative and always on the lookout for great ideas; and (3) employees who are passionate about their work, see it as their calling to make a positive impact in the world, and are willing to pour their heart and soul into it.[65]

The delicate part is that unlike the lower-order capabilities, the higher-order capabilities are gifts that employees choose to share and cannot be commanded by management.[67] The major challenge facing management is therefore to engage employees by creating an organisational environment that inspires their exceptional contribution and unlocks their boldness, imagination and zeal.[68] In this quest managers will need to (1) set compelling and socially relevant visions; (2) demonstrate praise-worthy values; and (3) create space and opportunities for employees to excel.[69]

Restoring humanity in business

In the industrial economy, efficiency above all else was king. The focus was on production, productivity and results; and in this pursuit, management exhibited tighter control and stricter management to improve output, reduce variation, increase predictability, enhance quality and achieve better margins. Although these results were achieved, the business practices of strict supervision, work standards, tight control and punishment for noncompliance destroy, over the lifetime of a worker, his or her inherent initiative, creativity and motivation and saps the life-force from his or her mortal body. In the words of Hamel,[70] "Tragically the technology of management frequently drains organisations of the very qualities that make us human: our vitality, ingenuity, and sense of kinship."

It is time that we recognise that people are not merely automatons of production, cogs in a machine, or resources at the system's disposal. People are human. They have souls, feelings, dreams and aspirations. Management is about people. Therefore, instead of trying to reduce people to mechanisms of function, should we not strive to make work life more humane and not less?

Not only are command-and-control management practices inhumane, but they are also ineffective in the new economy. This is because low-engagement environments fail to fully exploit the talents of people, making the business less innovative and resilient than it could be.[71] A 2007–2008 global workforce survey by Towers Perrin[72] (now Towers Watson) polled more than 90 000 workers in 18 countries and found a strong positive correlation between higher engagement, better earnings growth and bigger profit margins.[73] Yet, the same survey revealed that only 21 per cent of employees were truly engaged in their work and 38 per cent were mostly or entirely disengaged.

The truth is that business is failing employees. Employees have lost faith in the integrity of their leaders.[74] Further data from the Towers Perrin survey suggests that only 38 per cent of employees believe that senior management is sincerely interested in employee wellbeing and has their best interests at heart.[75] Even worse, a 2014 Gallup survey[76] revealed that only 17 per cent of respondents viewed the ethical standards of business executives as "high" or "very high". When a CEO bends the truth, breaks a promise, or is found guilty of corruption, trust is lost.[77]

> "Trust is not simply a matter of truthfulness, it is also a matter of amity and goodwill … When business leaders treat employees as expendable resources while pocketing huge bonuses, or hack away at employee benefits while retaining their own lavish perks, corporations will be viewed suspiciously, whether or not any laws have been broken."[78]

When trust is eroded and there is a misalignment between the interests of business and individuals, then competitiveness suffers.

In the industrial economy, efficiency above all else was king. **In the new economy, it is recognised that efficiency is important, but important alongside other factors** such as employee engagement, corporate social responsibility, environmental consciousness, transparency and fairness, virtuous leadership and work–life balance. The major challenge facing management is to reinvent command-and-control-type businesses as mobilise-and-mentor-type businesses, thereby restoring humanity in business, and over time, restoring people's faith in humanity.

Conclusion

Following from these four drivers of change, the resultant competitive environment represents a tug-of-war between traditional management practices and new economy thinking. The real and probably most difficult challenge for management is to weigh the pros and cons of the different approaches, and apply the most appropriate or a combination of both where appropriate. Some of the apparent trade-offs that are commonly believed to exist between traditional and new economy management are shown in Table 8.3. However, in reality nothing is clear-cut; a lot of complexity exists; many of the lines are blurred; and many of the trade-offs are complete fallacies. Instead of reflecting the absolute truth or a set of either–or choices, these "trade-offs" should serve as a catalyst for thinking about the dimensions of one's own management style and inherent orientation, and with this self-knowledge continually strive to improve oneself and one's management effectiveness.

Table 8.3: Traditional and new economy management trade-offs

Traditional management	New economy management
Production	Humanity
Productivity, effectiveness, performance, work standards	Engagement, joy in work, creativity, innovation, initiative
Bureaucracy, supervision, control, mistrust	Self-regulation, autonomy, freedom, responsibility, transparency
Discipline, compliance, structure, order	Self-discipline, self-determination, unstructured, fluidity, natural order
Hierarchy	Community
Position and power	Contribution and meritocracy
Top-down control	Peer-review
Authority and command	Willing participation
Dictatorship	Democracy
Employees as followers	Employees as leaders
Competition	Cooperation
Divisionalisation	Integration
Results	Process
Focus	Diversity
Politics	Fairness
Fear	Trust
Caution	Risk
Robustness	Adaptability
Extrinsic motivation	Intrinsic motivation
Mission oriented	Higher purpose
Rationality	Passion
Deliberate	Emergent

Application tool

Use the dimensions above as a point of departure and identify aspects of your organisation that can be improved. Use the template in Table 8.4.

Table 8.4: Dimensions of management improvement analysis

Management or organisational dimension	Current practice	Revised practice

As a sanity check, can you unequivocally convince five of your colleagues that the revised practice will have the desired result? If yes, talk to your key influencers about implementing the change. Otherwise gather inputs from your colleagues and devise a better solution.

DEMING'S THEORY OF MANAGEMENT

William Edwards Deming (1900–1993) was an American engineer, statistician, professor, author and management consultant best known for his quality management contributions to post-war Japan. Deming had worked at the Bell System, the company who instituted the first quality assurance department, alongside Walter Shewhart (1891–1967) who introduced statistical quality control in 1924 and George Edwards (1890–1974), the first president of the American Society for Quality Control (ASQC).[79]

After the Second World War, the Japanese were interested in rebuilding Japan, developing foreign markets, and improving Japan's reputation for producing low-quality products. In 1950 Deming was invited by the Union of Japanese Scientists and Engineers to speak to Japan's leading industrial organisations. Deming convinced the Japanese that by instituting his methods their quality would become the best in the world.[80] What followed between 1950 and 1960 has since become known as the "Japanese post-war economic miracle". Deming's management principles not only led to an increase in the quality and productivity of Japan's industry, but in part also allowed Japan to become the second most powerful economy in the world.

Although rarely credited, Deming's philosophy, which he called the "system of profound knowledge," was one of the first attempts at prescribing a new management paradigm for the modern world.

One of Deming's views, the Deming reaction chain,[81] explains why Japan experienced such rapid economic growth. Deming argued that an increase in quality led to a decrease in costs (because of reduced rework, reduced delays, reduced machine time and reduced waste of materials) and a resultant increase in productivity. Having achieved this quality standard, a company is able to better capture the market with products that are both better in quality and lower in cost. This stimulates more demand for a company's products, leads to growth, and allows more and more jobs to be created. The Deming reaction chain in systems diagram format is shown in Figure 8.3.

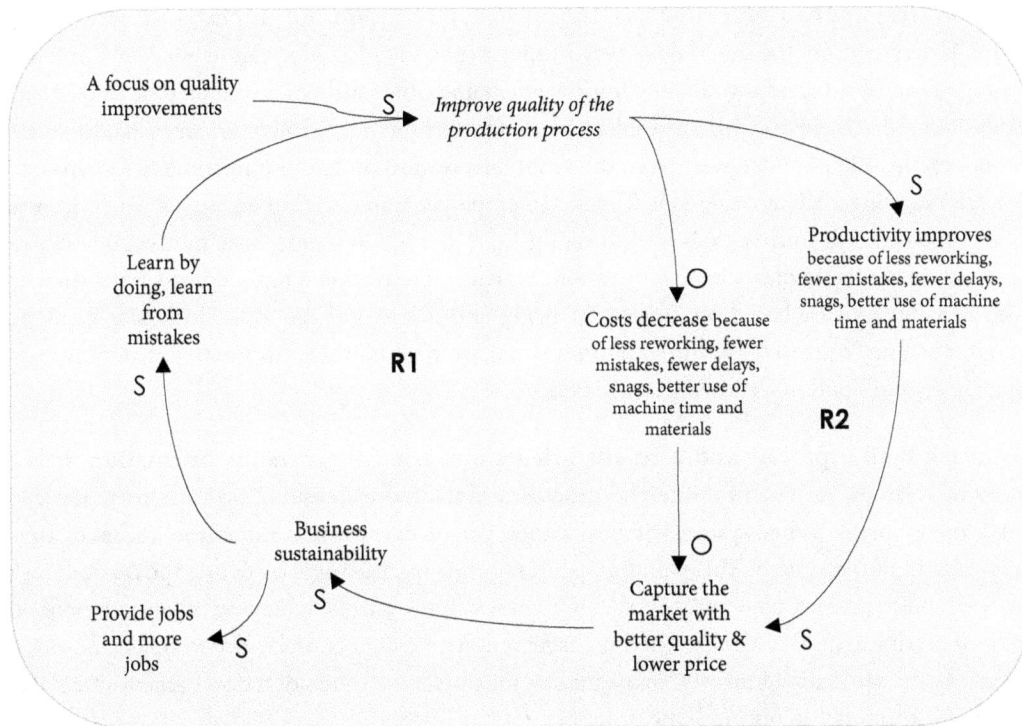

Figure 8.3: The Deming reaction chain system diagram

Deming's core teachings, however, revolved around the theory of management in which one achieves quality increases in the first place. According to George Edwards,[82]

> "Quality control exists when successive articles of commerce have characteristics more nearly like its fellows would and more nearly approximating the designer's intent, than would be the case if the application were not made … This approach recognises that good quality is not accidental and that it does not result from mere wishful thinking, that it results rather from the planned and interlocked activities of all the organisational parts of the company …"

Deming's theory of management advocated "joy in work" achieved via learning obtained from experience and coordinated by theory.[83] Deming[84] believed that joy in work is capable of "unleashing the power of human resource contained in intrinsic motivation". In Deming's view, intrinsic motivation is the motivation an individual experiences from the sheer joy of an endeavour.

Deming's belief system for increasing quality – **the system of profound knowledge** – consists of three interdependent elements: (1) paradigms of Deming's theory of management; (2) components of Deming's theory of management; and (3) Deming's 14 points for management.

Deming's paradigms reflect a shift in managerial assumptions that are needed to promote joy in work. Deming's theory of management paradigms are:[85]

1. **People are best inspired by a mix of intrinsic and extrinsic motivation, not only extrinsic motivation**. Intrinsic motivation is derived from the sheer joy of performing an act. Intrinsic motivation energises an individual, and these energies can be directed towards the improvement and innovation of a system. One of management's top responsibilities is therefore to create an atmosphere that fosters intrinsic motivation in each individual. Extrinsic motivation, on the other hand, comes from the desire of a reward or fear of punishment. Extrinsic rewards are largely hygienes – insufficient rewards will make an employee unhappy, but an excess won't necessarily cause joy in the same way that intrinsic motivation causes joy.[86] The fire lit by extrinsic motivation does not burn in the same way as the flame of intrinsic motivation. Extrinsic motivation simply doesn't resonate with the soul. Extrinsic punishments are based on judging, policing and destroying the individual. Management based on extrinsic motivation "squeeze[s] out from an individual, over his lifetime, his innate intrinsic motivation, self-esteem, dignity, and build into him fear, self-defence".[87]

2. **Manage using both a process and a results orientation, not only a results orientation**. It is the job of management to improve and innovate the processes that produce results, not just to manage results. As previously mentioned,[88] "A bad system will beat a good person every time." Sometimes mistakes aren't the fault of employees but of the system. This paradigm shift requires management to define the capabilities and limits of a process, and to predict, plan and control outcomes with the aim of achieving organisational optimisation. Crucial to this paradigm is evidence-based management where data is used for decisions, and not opinion or guesswork. At the same time however, management must take into consideration variables that are unknown and unknowable in order to optimise the process.

3. **Management's function is to optimise the entire system so that everyone wins, not only to maximise elements of the system**. Individuals, organisations, and the systems of organisations are interdependent. When one single element is optimised, it may cause suboptimisation of another element. Management's role is to optimise the entire system towards its goal, even if it means suboptimisation of various elements in this pursuit.

4. **Cooperation works better than competition**. In a cooperative environment, everybody wins. Customers win quality products and services that they enjoy; the firm wins profits and job-security for employees; suppliers win long-term customers; and the community wins an excellent corporate citizen. In a competitive environment, there are many losers. Head-on competition mostly ends in price wars, which lead to diminishing profit margins for both businesses. Porter suggests that instead of competing to be the best, companies should compete to be different.[89] Although this is still competition, there is an underlying flavour of cooperation by not merely copying the products and services of rivals.

The second aspect of Deming's theory of management is its four interdependent major components:[90]

1. **Appreciation of a system**

   A system is a collection of interacting elements that share a common purpose or aim. It is management's role to promote the aim of the entire system and to optimise the entire system, not just the subelements, towards its aim.

2. **Theory of variation**

   Variation is inherent to all processes. There are two causes of variation: (1) special and (2) common. Special causes of variation occur due to influences external to the system. It is the role of employees and engineers to identify and resolve special causes of variation. A system free of special causes of variation is stable and predictable in the variation that it produces. The remaining variability, the common causes of variation, occur due to the inherent design and structure of the system itself and are sometimes referred to as the "voice of the system". It is the role of management to isolate and reduce these common causes of variation, for instance by replacing certain machines in the manufacturing process with superior machines that produce more uniform products.

Two common errors that occur in managing variation are (1) treating a common cause of variation as a special cause of variation, and (2) treating a special cause of variation as a common cause of variation. In the first case, management **tampers with** the system and invariably increases its variability; while in the second case management allows a **special cause of variation** to persist, thereby continuing to produce nonuniform products. Both these errors need to be avoided, while reducing the variability of the system, in order to increase the quality of outputs.

3. **Theory of knowledge**
    Information, no matter how quick or complete, is not knowledge. "Knowledge is indicated by the ability to predict future events with a quantifiable risk of being wrong and the ability to explain past events without fail."[91] Knowledge accumulates when a theory is stated: the theory is used to predict a future outcome; an experiment is run; the observed outcome is compared to the predicted outcome; and the results either support or refute the theory, leading to the theory's validation, revision, or abandonment. Experience is worthless without the assistance of theory. Theory allows people to understand and interpret their experience. It allows people to think, ask questions, and to learn and grow. Furthermore, the causes of success in one system do not directly translate into success in another system. The theory underlying the success in one system can be used as a basis for learning in another system, however.

4. **Psychology**
    Psychology is essential to helping us understand people, the interactions between people, and the interactions between people and the system of which they are a part. Management needs to understand the nuances between intrinsic and extrinsic motivation and apply the proper mix of the two types for each person to achieve optimum energy and work output.

The last and probably most insightful aspect of Deming's system of profound knowledge is his roadmap for pursuing quality in a system, called the 14 points for management. Deming's 14 points for management are discussed below:[92]

1.   **Create a constancy of purpose towards improvement of product and service, with the aim of becoming competitive, staying in business and providing jobs**. Argued in reverse order, the purpose of business is to create jobs that give employees the opportunity to exercise their gifts and earn a dignified living.[93] [94] The best way to assure jobs and stay in business is by building a stable, productive and profitable organisation. This is best achieved by being competitive in the market, which requires the continuous pursuit of developing quality products and services.[95] Leaders therefore need to create vision and mission statements developed from the values of the organisation to align stakeholders, provide them with purpose and aspirations for quality products and services, and give them a frame of reference for focused, consistent behaviour and decision-making.

2. **Adopt the new philosophy**. Management must accept that the world has changed and it is the dawn of a new economic age. Management must awaken to the challenge, accept its responsibilities, embrace the new paradigms (Deming's four components) and lead the change.

3. **Cease dependence on inspection to achieve quality. Eliminate the need for inspection on a mass basis by building quality into the product in the first instance**. There are three methods to pursue predictable uniformity at low cost: (1) defect detection, (2) defect prevention, and (3) continuous improvement. **Defect detection** relies on mass inspection of all products to distinguish between the conforming and defective products. Mass inspection, however, does nothing to decrease the variability of the quality characteristics of products and services.[96] It is merely a policing operation, but because it is a separate subsystem, it could create the negative impression in other departments that quality concerns are someone else's responsibility. **Defect prevention**, also known as zero defects, involves improving processes to produce outputs within specification limits. Defect prevention creates the impression that employees' jobs are complete when they achieve zero defects. However, this could tempt employees to widen specification limits and thereby achieve zero defects, rather than improving the process. **Continuous improvement** is the ongoing and relentless reduction of process (unit-to-unit) variation, even when the process is already within specification limits. It is always economical to reduce unit-to-unit variation around the nominal value, without capital investment.[97]

4. **End the practice of awarding business on the basis of price tag. Instead, minimise total cost. Move towards a single supplier for any one item via a long-term relationship of loyalty and trust**. Long-term relationships with statistical evidence of quality supplies promote continuous improvement in the uniformity and reliability of products and services, and hence lower total costs.

5. **Improve constantly and forever the system of production and service to improve quality and productivity, and thus constantly decrease costs**. One method for standardising a process and increasing the quality of its outputs is to use the **SDSA (standardise-do-study-act) cycle**. In the **standardise** step, employees study the process to define best-practice methods and key indicators for process performance. In the **do** step, employees conduct planned experiments using the best-practice methods on a trial basis. In the **study** step, employees collect and analyse data on the key indicators to determine how effective the best-practice methods were. Lastly, in the **act** step, managers institute the standardised best-practice methods and formalise them via training.

    A useful Japanese method that promotes good housekeeping and creates an environment in which quality can thrive is the **5-S movement**. "In a 5S environment there is a place for everything, and everything in its place. Time spent searching for items is essentially eliminated, and out of place or missing items are immediately obvious." [98] The 5Ss are:[99]

    - **Seiri** (sort): Simplify the process by removing unnecessary work-in-progress, tools, machinery, documents and papers.
    - **Seiton** (set in order): Label things so that they are easily identifiable, and keep things organised by creating a proper place for them.
    - **Seiso** (shine): Maintain a clean workplace and promote proactive maintenance.
    - **Seiketsu** (standardise): Be a clean and neat person, and help in the development of best-practice methods for your area.
    - **Shitsuke** (sustain): Be disciplined and adhere to best-practice methods.

Some employees at Motorola Corporation added a sixth S to the list.

- **Shituke**: Be well mannered.

Empowerment is another means through which quality can be improved. The prevailing definition of empowerment broadly relates to dropping the decision-making authority down to the lowest appropriate level in an organisation. The premise is that if people are empowered to make decisions, that they will take pride in their work and be motivated to work harder. Although this sounds ideal, employees are frequently only empowered until they make a mistake and then heads roll. The goal of empowerment in quality management, on the other hand, and in Deming's definition, is to increase joy in work for all employees. According to Deming, empowerment as a process involves giving employees:[100]

- the opportunity to define and document key systems
- the opportunity to learn about systems through training and development
- the opportunity to improve and innovate the best-practice methods
- the freedom to use their own judgement to make decisions **within the context** of the best-practice methods
- an environment of trust in which superiors will not react negatively to the judgement used by people within the context of best-practice methods

Employees in turn need to accept responsibility for:

- increasing their training and knowledge of the system
- participating in the development, standardisation and improvement of best-practice methods
- increasing their freedom in decision-making within the context of best-practice methods

6. **Institute training on the job**. Employees are an organisation's most prized assets. Organisations should therefore take a long-term interest in the development of employees and allow them to acquire new skills by training on the job. Training should include formal class work, experiential work and instructional materials. If an employee is not in statistical control of his or her job, then more training of the type that he or she is receiving will be beneficial.

7. **Institute leadership.** Leaders help people and machines to do a better job. A leader should view an organisation as a system consisting of inter-related components, each with an aim, but all focused collectively on supporting the overall aim of the organisation. Leaders pursue the creation of stable processes that function with low variation. Leaders use their knowledge of variation to know when employees are experiencing difficulties that make their performance fall outside the specification limits, and treat these cases as special causes of variation. At the same time, leaders can identify when a process itself is unstable and high in variation, and thereby seek to remove the common cause of variation and improve the process itself rather than blame the people. A leader therefore uses his or her knowledge built on theory and experience to predict future events and to plan the actions that are necessary to pursue the organisation's aim.

8. **Drive out fear so that everyone may work efficiently for the company**. A workforce subjected to fear experiences poor morale, poor productivity, reduced creativity, a reluctance to take risks, poor interpersonal relationships, emotional problems, physical ailments, behavioural disorders and reduced motivation to optimise the system of interdependent stakeholders. An environment ruled by fear is tyrannical and the economic

loss from the effect on people is huge. It is management's duty to eliminate the causes of fear such as a lack of job security, possibility of physical harm, unrealistic expectations, shortcomings in hiring and training, poor supervision and mentoring, a lack of operational definitions, blame for problems of the system, public humiliation, faulty inspection procedures and so forth.

9. **Break down barriers between departments. People in research, design, sales, and production must work as a team to foresee and reduce problems in the production and use of products and services.** Management's job is to optimise the entire organisation consisting of interdependent stakeholders. This may require suboptimisation of some aspects of the organisation. Management must therefore remove incentives for optimisation of departmental areas in favour of incentives that favour organisation-wide performance.[101]

10. **Eliminate slogans, exhortations, and targets for the workforce that ask for zero defects and new levels of productivity without providing methods.** Slogans, exhortations and targets without methods do not do anything to help to improve or innovate a process, product or service. Examples of meaningless targets are:

   - "Do it right the first time."
   - "Safety is job number 1."
   - "Zero defects."

These kinds of statement do not provide guidance for action; they just reflect management's wishes for a desired result. Such ambiguous targets without methods to achieve them offload management's responsibility for improving the system onto workers, who are often powerless to effect the required change. This causes resentment, mistrust and overall negativity.[102]

11. **Eliminate management by objective, management by numbers and numerical goals that are not based on process capability.** Work standards can have a devastating effect on the quality and productivity of a system. In a system of work standards, employees are blamed if they do not meet production schedules – often due to problems beyond their control. In an attempt to meet work standards, employees are dysfunctionally motivated to work fast to meet a production quota and thereby invariably produce more defects. Such practices rob a worker of pride in his or her workmanship and deny them the opportunity to produce high-quality goods that would contribute to the stability of their employment. *The problem is that work standards are often negotiated values that have no relationship to the actual capability of the process.* When work standards are set too high, it increases the pressure on workers to perform without giving them new methods, tools or resources to do so. This destroys worker morale. Similarly, when work standards are set too low, the company loses out on production as workers meet their quotas and spend the rest of the day doing nothing; this also destroys morale. Any goal provided should reflect the process's capability and not be just an arbitrary conjuration.

12. **Remove barriers that rob people of their right to pride in their workmanship and joy in work.** People deserve the chance to find joy in their work. Joy in work provides the impetus to excel, perform better and improve quality to the benefit of the worker's self-esteem, the company and customers. At the moment there are many barriers that prevent joy in work that management should seek to reduce:

   - employees not understanding the business's mission and what is expected of them in this regard
   - employees being forced to act as automatons who are not allowed to think or use their skills

- employees being blamed for problems of the system
- hastily designed products and inadequately tested prototypes
- inadequate supervision, training and mentoring
- faulty equipment, materials and methods
- management by objective and management systems that only focus on results
- the traditional performance appraisal process (annual merit rating)

13. **Institute a vigorous programme of education and self-improvement**. Continuous education and self-improvement are important vehicles for improving employees, both professionally and personally. It is the responsibility of leaders to educate and improve themselves and their people, in the pursuit of optimising the entire organisation. While point 6 deals with job skills, point 13 deals with education that improves the individual, regardless of his or her job. [103]

14. **Take action to accomplish the transformation**. In order to adopt the system of profound knowledge, energy and effort must be exerted. The transformation cannot occur without the backing of a critical mass of stakeholders. Leaders wanting to accomplish the transformation will need to mobilise this critical mass by understanding people's reasons for wanting (or not wanting) the transformation; understanding how these reasons interact; and devising participative ways in which the objections can be overcome to make the transformation a reality.[104]

Deming's system of profound knowledge that consists of his paradigms, components and points for management provides a vastly different perspective for management than the crude, efficiency-driven perspective of the industrial era. Even though Deming's theory of management is more than 60 years old, it already contained a subtle consideration for people – a perspective that has only recently started gaining more traction. In summary, Deming's theory of management is a systems-focused perspective that promotes joy in work and the wellbeing of employees and accounts not only for the process of producing quality goods, but also the people producing the goods, and the interactions between the people and the process.

Deming's system of profound knowledge provides a better point of departure for management, however, significant progress still needs to be made to develop a new and even more rounded management philosophy fit for the challenges of the twenty-first century. The next section discusses the management aspirations that we should strive for in the creation of such a management paradigm.

THE 25 MANAGEMENT INNOVATION MOON SHOTS

The rate of evolution of modern management practices and paradigms has largely stagnated.[105] Management 1.0 has become a mature technology that possesses many flaws that need to be remedied in order to be fit for the future.[106]

Ambition is a catalyst of achievement. Therefore, partly inspired by the 14 grand engineering challenges set by the US National Academy of Engineering,[107] a group of 35 management scholars, new-age management thinkers, progressive CEOs, consultants, entrepreneurs and venture capitalists assembled in May 2008 to debate the future of management, with the mission of laying out an agenda for reinventing management in the twenty-first century.[108]

The quest of this makeshift group of renegades was to answer the questions:[109]

- What is it about the way that large organisations are managed, structured and led that most impedes their ability to thrive in the decades ahead?
- What sorts of change will be needed in management and practices to create organisations that are truly fit for the future?
- What should the critical priorities for tomorrow's management pioneers be?
- How should management itself be innovated?
- What is management's equivalent to unpacking the human genome, inventing a cure for AIDs, reverse-engineering the brain or reversing global warming?

The result of their endeavour was a list of 25 management innovation moon shots – tremendously ambitious goals – that would serve to focus the energies of management pioneers everywhere in the combined effort to develop Management 2.0.[110]

Management innovation can be described as a marked departure from traditional management principles, processes, practices or organisational forms that significantly alters the way that the work of management is performed.[111] The 25 management innovation moon shots do not claim to be exhaustive or even mutually exclusive, but each one illuminates a critical aspect that needs to be addressed on the journey to Management 2.0.[112]

The 25 management innovation moon shots are discussed below:[113]

1. **Ensure that the work of management serves a higher purpose.**
    Businesses do not exist solely for the purpose of making money. Most businesses, and all good businesses, have some higher aspiration – they aim to achieve some type of big, hairy, audacious goal (BAHGs)[114] that serves to advance society, make the world a better place or a bit easier to live in. People strive to find meaning in their lives, and therefore also strive to find meaning in their work. Business purely for the sake of profit is emotionally uninspiring and is not specific or compelling enough to spur renewal. A higher, more fulfilling purpose is required in the businesses of tomorrow, and it is up to managers to set and strive for socially significant or otherwise noble goals.

2. **Fully embed the ideas of community and citizenship in management systems.**
    As the world opens up through new connections, great businesses will be characterised by their collaborative systems that embrace interdependence and the ethos of community and citizenship. New governance systems are needed that promote cohesion instead of adversarial win–lose relationships, to the benefit of all stakeholder groups.

3. **Reconstruct management's philosophical foundations.**
    The historical principles of management that were inherited require an overhaul in order to be relevant and effective in the new economy. Businesses of the future need to be not only operationally excellent, but also adaptable, innovative, inspiring and socially responsible. The principles of management that will be able to realise these attributes need to be uncovered, and it may be required to look for these in fields as diverse as anthropology, biology, design, political science, urban planning and theology.[115]

4. **Eliminate the pathologies of formal hierarchy.**

Hierarchies will always be a feature of human organisation, but traditional top-down hierarchies often present weaknesses that Management 2.0 should seek to overcome. Their weaknesses include (1) a tendency to give more weight to experience at the expense of new thinking; (2) not giving followers sufficient influence in choosing their leaders; (3) the vast difference in power between different hierarchical levels, which cannot be justified by differences in competence; (4) incentive structures that motivate managers to cling to authority when it actually needs to be distributed; and (5) undermining the self-worth of individuals with little formal power.[116]

This calls for the elimination of the traditional organisational pyramid in favour of a "natural" hierarchy where status and influence correspond to contribution rather than position. Hierarchies need to be dynamic to reflect the dynamism of the working environment. When new endeavours are initiated, reorganisation should be possible to allow power to flow rapidly towards those adding value and away from those who aren't. Additionally, instead of a single organisational hierarchy, multiple hierarchies should exist, each reflecting the expertise in some critical domain.

5. **Reduce fear and increase trust.**

An anxious and fearful workplace is not an environment that is conducive to helping employees flourish. Yet so many businesses are still run in a command-and-control style where threats are used as the primary means of enforcing compliance. Such systems reflect a deep mistrust of employees' commitment and competence, and discourage initiative and personal judgement. If the aim is to build organisations that are adaptable, innovative and engaging, then new management systems are required that (1) are built on trust; (2) drive out fear; (3) allow information to be widely shared; (4) allow opposing opinions to be freely expressed; and (5) encourage initiative and risk-taking.

6. **Reinvent the means of control.**

Traditional management systems focused on efficiency were obsessed with control as a means of ensuring compliance and the diligent execution of activities. Businesses of tomorrow need to extract more than this from employees, namely employee creativity, initiative, entrepreneurship and engagement. The idea of discipline-versus-innovation needs to be expelled, in favour of **self**-discipline **and** innovation. The control systems of the future will need to rely more on peer review and less on top-down supervision; and more on shared values and aspirations for providing guidance and less on constrictive rules.

7. **Redefine the work of leadership.**

Leaders in Management 2.0 will no longer be characterised as grand visionaries, all-wise decision-makers or totalitarian disciplinarians. Instead, leaders of the future will be characterised by their ability to mobilise others (even despite a lack of formal authority) and by their ability to create environments where every employee has the opportunity to collaborate, innovate and flourish. Leaders of the future will be those who thrive in the new system of natural hierarchies, and leaders will increasingly need to become social architects, constitution writers and entrepreneurs of meaning.

8. **Expand and exploit diversity.**

In biology, diversity is essential to the survival of a species. The larger the genetic diversity, the larger the likelihood that some individual organisms will possess favourable traits, such as a natural resistance to disease, cold or other hostile factors. In business, diversity is similarly advantageous to long-term sustainability. Diversity in experience, values and capabilities allows the generation of vastly different ideas, options, and experiments, which are vital for strategic renewal and survival. In the future, management systems should therefore value diversity, disagreement and divergence just as highly as they value conformance, consensus and cohesion.

9. **Reinvent strategy making as an emergent process.**
Given the turbulence and uncertainty of the fast-changing new economy, prediction is difficult and long-range planning is of limited value. Instead of seeking to uncover the "one best strategy" through analytical top-down methods, businesses of the future should increasingly focus on (1) developing a wide portfolio of strategic options; (2) making use of low-cost experiments to test critical assumptions, thereby eliminating some options and pivoting to new options; and (3) investing resources in selected strategies that are gaining the most traction in the marketplace. Strategy formulation in the future will be less forced and more fluid. Instead of trying to craft strategy, much of management's work in the future will revolve around creating the conditions in which new strategies can emerge and evolve.

10. **Destructure and disaggregate the organisation.**
In order to capitalise on fleeting opportunities, organisations need to be nimble. Organisations need to be able to rapidly reconfigure their capabilities, infrastructure and resources as projects demand. However, organisational barriers such as rigid unit boundaries, functional silos, divergent political agendas and long-fostered groupthink can hamper the rapid realignment of skills and assets. Organisations of the future need to be adaptable, which means that they will require looser structures and smaller units that can reorganise fluidly around new opportunities on the fly.

11. **Dramatically reduce the pull of the past.**
Most management processes are entwined with subtle biases that favour continuity over change. Examples are (1) long-term planning processes that reinforce outdated perspectives of the competitive environment; (2) budgeting processes that make it difficult for speculative ideas to get seed funding; (3) incentive systems that favour caretaker managers over internal entrepreneurs; (4) measurement systems that underestimate the value of new strategic options; and (5) recruitment processes that overvalue analytical skills while undervaluing conceptual skills. Although continuity is important, subtle preferences for the status quo need to be acknowledged, examined and even expelled if it is found that these biases circumvent the true goals of the business.

12. **Share the work of setting direction.**
In an increasingly complex and fast-changing business environment, the task of setting corporate direction will become increasingly challenging. It is unlikely that a small group of executives will be able to chart the organisational path to corporate renewal and success without employee inputs. Foresight and insight, rather than position and power, should be the overriding voices in setting corporate direction. Additionally, the failures of many top-down strategies in the past serve as a reminder that employee commitment can only be obtained through a participatory process where employees take ownership of the generated strategy. In Management 2.0, it is clear that the responsibility of setting the direction of the business should be broadly shared.

13. **Develop holistic performance measures.**
One common flaw of existing performance measurement systems is that they tend to overemphasise the achievements of some goals, while undervaluing the importance of other critical, but more subtle goals. Short-

term profit goals often occupy the limelight, while objectives critical to future competitiveness such as building new growth platforms and customer-driven innovation occupy a lower priority. In Management 2.0 these limitations will need to be overcome and companies will need to create more holistic measurement systems.

14. **Stretch executive time frames and perspectives.**

It is not uncommon to read about executives who favoured short-term profits over long-term sustainability. Research also suggests that most executives would not fund a viable new initiative if doing so reduced current earnings. One needs to bear in mind that executives will always have a responsibility to shareholders. However, instead of merely blaming executives for their short-sightedness, the compensation and incentive systems of the future should be reinvented to focus executive attention on creating long-term stakeholder value, thereby stretching executive time horizons and perspectives.

15. **Create a democracy of information.**

One saying that has withstood the test of time is "knowledge is power". Traditionally, managers have often hoarded information in order to "retain" more power and control, but these actions are ultimately self-defeating. Under a regime of information hoarding, employees can't do their jobs until they have asked permission or referred a decision upwards, and adaptability, a crucial organisational attribute in a volatile world, suffers. It is also more and more the case that value creation occurs at the interface between frontline employees and customers. When starved of information, employees can't act quickly or intelligently and this negatively impacts the effectiveness of the whole business. Grassroots employees therefore need to be some of the best-informed individuals in order to be able to make the right decisions for customers in a timely manner. In the future, information sharing and not its hoarding will drive organisational success. Hence, information systems that promote information transparency and give every employee access to critical performance metrics and other data are needed.

16. **Empower the renegades and disarm the reactionaries.**

Every now and again the status quo of an organisation needs to be disrupted in order to adapt to the changing environment. Although it is not impossible, management innovation is unlikely to be led by sitting monarchs who have grown fond of the current state of affairs. Change, however, is a necessity for survival. Incumbents who therefore ignore its call are likely to be defeated by new start-ups who understand and embrace the new rules of the game. The only solution to making organisations fit for such a revolution is to develop management systems that redistribute power to those who have the most emotional equity invested in the future and have the least to lose from change.

17. **Expand the scope of employee autonomy.**

Most organisations truncate the initiative and innovation of their employees via rigid policy guidelines, tight spending limits and a lack of self-directed time. These limitations on the autonomy of employees at the bottom or middle of the organisational pyramid are often demoralising and create a feeling of powerlessness. Businesses should therefore redesign their management systems in order to facilitate and encourage local experimentation and bottom-up initiatives, thereby giving employees the freedom to initiate change.

18. **Create internal markets for ideas, talent and resources.**

Getting seed funding or support for a speculative future oriented idea in a big organisation is a nightmare. The rational, analytic methods used by most well-managed companies make it nearly impossible to build a business case for diverting resources from large established markets with known customers to small emerging markets with unknown customers.[117] The effect is that companies overinvest in the past and underfund the future. The irony is that every attractive market that exists today was small and poorly defined at its inception.[118] Furthermore, funding decisions are usually made by executives at the top where decisions are heavily influenced by political factors. In order to make resource allocation more flexible, dynamic, decentralised, apolitical and ultimately fair, businesses of the future need to create internal markets for resources where established and new projects all compete on an equal footing for talent and money.

19. **Depoliticise decision-making.**
The quality of executive decision-making is often compromised by unstated biases, pride, self-confidence and incomplete data. Given the increasing complexity of the competitive landscape, the number of variables that need to be considered in decision-making is staggering. Yet, when deciding to spend millions of dollars to enter a new market or pursue a new technology, senior leaders rarely consult those on the ground who are often best suited to evaluate the issues that will make or break the new strategy. Management 2.0 requires new decision-making processes that (1) allow the capturing of a diversity of views; (2) exploit the organisation's collective wisdom; (3) are free of position-influenced biases; and (4) ultimately increase the quality of decision-making.

20. **Better optimise trade-offs.**
Trade-offs exist in every business and refer to compromises that exist between two incompatible variables. Think about how often we have heard a similar discussion between an employee and a client: "Sir, unforeseen complications have severely delayed the project. We have two choices. Either we finish the project on time or we finish the project within budget. Choose one." In reality, there is an array of options. For every scenario and every decision, there is an optimum point where the most value can be created – in this example, the point where the project is the least over-budget **and** the least delayed. In future, organisational success will depend on the ability of employees at all levels to dynamically optimise seemingly irreconcilable trade-offs. Examples include trade-offs between (1) short-term earnings and long-term growth; (2) competition and collaboration; (3) structure and emergence; (4) discipline and freedom; and (5) individual and team success. While traditional management systems have often involved crude, universal policies that favour certain goals, in Management 2.0 systems are needed that encourage healthy competition between opposing objectives in order to arrive at an optimum solution for both.

21. **Further unleash human imagination.**
A lot is known about the process of fostering human creativity. It requires organisations to (1) equip people with innovation tools; (2) allow them time to think and reflect; (3) destigmatise failure; (4) create opportunities for unexpected learning; (5) set ambitious goals that won't be achieved by business as usual; and so forth. However, very few organisations actually support employee creativity in these ways via their management systems. Far worse, many companies institutionalise a sort of creative apartheid where only a few individuals are given creative roles while it is wrongly assumed that most other employees are unimaginative. To enhance the innovation capabilities of organisations in future, management processes will need to nurture the creativity of every employee in the organisation and not only a select few.

22. **Enable communities of passion.**
Passion is a multiplier of human endeavour. When people are passionate about their tasks, they naturally excel and achieve more. One of the greatest shames of traditional business is that most employees are emotionally

disengaged at work. Apart from being a disgrace to humanity itself, organisations also underperform because of it. Eiji Toyoda once said: "A person's life is an accumulation of time – just one hour is equivalent to a person's life. Employees provide their precious hours of life to the company, so we have to use it effectively, otherwise, we are wasting their life." Management 2.0 needs to create a work environment that is radically better – a work environment that is engaging, energetic and where people can live out their passions and find meaning in their work. This can be accomplished by establishing communities of passion and better aligning the organisation's objectives with people's natural interests. It is an organisation's *duty* rather than a "*nice-to-have*" to connect employees who share similar passions and allow like-minded individuals to converge around worthy causes.

23. **Retool management for an open world.**

Emerging business models in the new economy and other phenomena such as open innovation increasingly rely on value created by individuals and entities outside the organisation. Great benefits can be gained from these value-creating networks and forms of social production, but it is unlikely that traditional management tools that make use of positional power to direct and lead will be effective. When working with communities and a network of volunteers, rather than dictating from the top, leaders will need to develop and make use of new approaches in order to energise, mobilise, and coordinate human effort.

24. **Humanise the language and practice of business.**

Key words that are usually used to describe the goal of management include "efficiency", "advantage", "value", "superiority", "focus" and "differentiation". However important these objectives may be, they lack the power to stir human hearts. Because people increasingly yearn for meaning, management pioneers need to find ways to infuse ordinary business activities with deeper, soul-inspiring ideals such as honour, truth, love, justice and beauty. These timeless virtues possess the power to inspire extraordinary accomplishment and need to be infused into daily business, rather than writing them off as silly, fluffy notions of management dreamers.

25. **Retrain managerial minds.**

The world is evolving and so must management. Managerial training has traditionally focused on a particular set of cognitive skills, such as left-brain thinking, deductive reasoning, analytical problem-solving and solutions engineering. Managers of the future will need additional skills in their toolkit, including reflective or double-loop learning, systems-based thinking, creative problem-solving and values-driven thinking. Business schools and businesses alike need to redesign their training programmes to develop these skills and additionally reorient management systems to encourage their application.

Application tool

Carefully consider the 25 management innovation moon shots. Select the moon shots that can be accomplished in the next year in your organisation (maximum five). For each moon shot, note what initiative will achieve it. The moon shots are ambitious. It is therefore better to focus on a select few than making scant progress on all of them. Similarly, select those moon shots that can be achieved within the next 5 and 10 years (as many as needed), and also note what long-term initiatives can be used to achieve them.

Table 8.5: Management innovation moon shot roster

No.	Moon shot	Initiative for achievement in 1 year
1.		
2.		
3.		
4.		
5.		
No.	Moon shot	Initiative for achievement in 5 years
No.	Moon shot	Initiative for achievement in 10 years

Practical guideline

The goal of management innovation is to overcome the limits of traditional management systems without losing the advantages that they provide. Though it is necessary for organisations to become a lot more adaptable, innovative and inspiring, it doesn't make sense to pursue these aims if it means abandoning the fundamental virtues of focus, discipline and performance.[119]

A fine line exists between management innovation and management chaos; and tension will always exist between control and freedom. Control is critical, but often it comes at the cost of initiative, creativity and passion – essential cornerstones of organisational success.[120] Some experimentation will therefore be required to uncover exactly which means of management innovation work and those that don't.

Perhaps control from within rather than from without, time frames that extend beyond the next 12 months, serving a higher purpose, and the ethos of community can serve as viable starting points for the development of an alternative management paradigm.

MEASUREMENT OF AN ORGANISATION'S MANAGEMENT INNOVATION SOPHISTICATION AND THE PROCESS OF MANAGEMENT INNOVATION

Kaplan and Norton[121] famously noted that "What you measure is what you get". This saying has the twofold meaning that (1) if you don't measure something, it doesn't exist (e.g. you don't have any data and can't make decisions or improvements); and (2) the things that you measure drive employee behaviour (e.g. employees try to perform particularly well on the indicators that they are measured on). Having the right measures and metrics is therefore crucial for understanding your business and cultivating the desired behaviour in employees.

Following from this, the measurement of a business's management innovation sophistication is of the utmost importance in (1) obtaining a management innovation baseline for the business; (2) driving management innovation; and (3) continually checking the business's management innovation progress.

A validated questionnaire that can be used to establish the level of management innovation sophistication of a business is shown in Table 8.6.

Table 8.6: Management innovation measurement questionnaire[122]

Theme	Moon shot	Questionnaire statement: Rate (1) Strongly Disagree, (2) Disagree, (3) Undecided, (4) Agree, (5) Strongly Agree
1. Mending the soul	1. Ensure that the work of management serves a higher purpose.	1. Our leader's focus is on the achievement of socially significant and noble goals that go beyond short-term profits.
		2. The actions of leaders within my organisation demonstrate a commitment to social, community and environmental goals.
		3. My organisation is making a difference in society.
	2. Fully embed the ideas of community and citizenship in management systems.	4. It is important in our organisation that employees identify with values of social awareness.
		5. The organisation expects that lower-level operations demonstrate a socially conscious approach to their work.
		6. The organisation truly considers its social and environmental impact with its financial results (i.e. triple bottom line).
	3. Humanise the language and practices of business.	7. The organisation truly cares for its employees.
		8. Our leaders genuinely value inputs from employees.
2. Unleashing capabilities	4. Reduce fear and increase trust.	9. There is a sense of trust among employees in the organisation.
		10. The organisation readily delegates decision-making authority to lower-level employees.

Theme	Moon shot	Questionnaire statement: Rate (1) Strongly Disagree, (2) Disagree, (3) Undecided, (4) Agree, (5) Strongly Agree
2. Unleashing capabilities (continued)	5. Reinvent the means of control.	11. Peer review (i.e. peers on similar levels evaluate each other's work) is used as a support and control mechanism.
		12. Information-sharing between peers in the organisation is encouraged.
	6. Further unleash human imagination.	13. The organisation provides its employees with the resources needed for innovation.
		14. The organisation tolerates failure of new ideas.
		15. Employees share information as a source of innovation.
	7. Expand and exploit diversity.	16. The organisation actively encourages constructive participation by people from diverse backgrounds.
		17. Employees feel free to put forward their differences of opinion.
		18. Management is open to the idea of trying unconventional ways of solving problems.
	8. Enable communities of passion.	19. The employees identify with the organisation's values.
		20. The employees believe in what the organisation is trying to accomplish.
		21. There are strong bonds between the organisation and its employees.
	9. Take the work out of work.	22. Employees feel comfortable discussing personal issues with other employees and management.
		23. The organisation pays a lot of attention to the general working conditions of employees.
3. Fostering renewal	10. Share the work of setting direction.	24. Before taking important decisions, management consults widely within the organisation.
		25. Leaders in the organisation seek and use input from employees in their departments.
	11. Reinvent strategy-making as an emergent process.	26. Strategic decisions about product offerings are made based on feedback from various stakeholders.
		27. New ideas are always being tried in the organisation.
		28. Management creates conditions in which changes in strategy can emerge.
	12. Destructure and disaggregate the organisation.	29. The organisation is able to reconfigure capabilities when confronted with change or opportunities.
		30. The organisation is structured using small teams to achieve its objectives.
		31. The organisation promotes open and transparent communication.
	13. Create internal markets for ideas, talents and resources.	32. New initiatives and legacy programmes compete on an equal footing for available resources.
		33. The organisation has loosely committed resources to make it easier for potential innovators to find resources.
		34. Senior leaders give the necessary support to new ideas.

Theme	Moon shot	Questionnaire statement: Rate (1) Strongly Disagree, (2) Disagree, (3) Undecided, (4) Agree, (5) Strongly Agree
3. Fostering renewal (continued)	14. Depoliticise decision-making.	35. Most employee levels within the organisation participate in decision-making.
		36. Job design permits work to overlap different tasks to broaden people's experience and exposure.
4. Distributing power	15. Eliminate the pathologies of formal hierarchy.	37. The organisation's hierarchy structure is flat.
		38. Employees are rewarded based on their value-adding contributions instead of their title or rank.
		39. The organisation often uses teams with members from different departments to accomplish objectives.
	16. Expand the scope of employee autonomy.	40. Employees have freedom to decide how to accomplish a given task.
		41. Employees are free to make appropriate decisions in their work.
		42. Management encourages employees to challenge established ways of accomplishing tasks.
	17. Redefine the work of leadership.	43. Our leaders encourage the employees to collaborate and innovate in the workplace.
		44. Leaders in the organisation are seen as mentors.
		45. Leaders mobilise others by personal influence rather than by positional authority.
	18. Create a democracy of information.	46. The organisation makes sure employees have access to the information needed to perform their work.
		47. Management communicates the organisation's performance results to employees on a regular basis.
		48. With regard to communication, the organisation has an open door policy, meaning that all levels can have access to anyone for support.
	19. Dramatically reduce the pull of the past.	49. The organisation supports new ways of doing things.
		50. Employees are free to take risks in getting their work done.
5. Seeking harmony	20. Develop holistic performance measures.	51. The organisation's measurement tools incorporate both financial and nonfinancial indicators.
		52. Employees are recognised and rewarded for meeting nonfinancial goals.
		53. Customers' feedback is used as a source of new ideas or opportunities.
	21. Better optimise trade-offs.	54. The organisation can be described as flexible by continually adapting to change.
		55. Employees have the information and freedom to optimise trade-offs between traditional methods and experimentation.
		56. Each group gets the cooperation it needs from other workgroups to achieve its goals.

Theme	Moon shot	Questionnaire statement: Rate (1) Strongly Disagree, (2) Disagree, (3) Undecided, (4) Agree, (5) Strongly Agree
5. Seeking harmony (continued	22. Stretch executive time frames and perspectives.	57. Management rewards both short-term and long-term target achievements.
		58. Rewards and incentives take into consideration the employees' contribution to long-term results.
		59. The organisation rewards and recognises innovation initiatives.
6. Reshaping minds	23. Retrain managerial minds.	60. The organisation provides opportunities for constructive reflection to learn from past successes and failures.
		61. The organisation provides a unique environment to learn and develop new management skills.
		62. The organisation makes use of programmes that teach individuals the necessary skills for creative thinking.
	24. Retool management for an open world.	63. The role of the leaders in our organisation is to energise and empower employees rather than to manage by position or title.
		64. Our leaders find new ways to mobilise and coordinate human effort to foster cooperation in value chains.
		65. Managers actively promote open communication and collaboration between employees.
	25. Reconstruct management's philosophical foundations.	66. Employees are free to try new ideas or practices without fear of failure.
		67. The organisation values freedom more than control.
		68. Management creates an atmosphere where ideas can be freely stated and evaluated.

These 68 questions can be posed to a diverse group of employees in an organisation regarding:

- The level of progress on each of the statements: "To what extent do you agree that these statements are an accurate reflection of how things are currently done in your organisation?"
- The importance of progress on each of the statements: "To what extent do you agree that it is important that your organisation makes progress in each of these practice areas over the next three years?"

The responses can then be averaged in order to obtain a corresponding progress and importance score for each of the 25 management innovation moon shots. Armed with the information obtained from this questionnaire, organisations can identify specific weaknesses, development areas or managerial practices that still need to be improved.

Although many managers are aware that management innovation is required, they are not actively encouraging or actively involved in making those changes. Being confronted with an actual status report regarding the organisation's management innovation sophistication will encourage managers to question their practices and make changes. The information gained from this questionnaire can further serve as vital early indicators of the readiness of management to deal with new global challenges that companies face due to increased globalisation, competition and advances in technology, and further encourage greater management innovation.[123]

Regarding the process of management innovation, it can in the most basic terms be reduced to three phases: (1) motivation, (2) invention, and (3) validation. These phases are depicted in Figure 8.4.

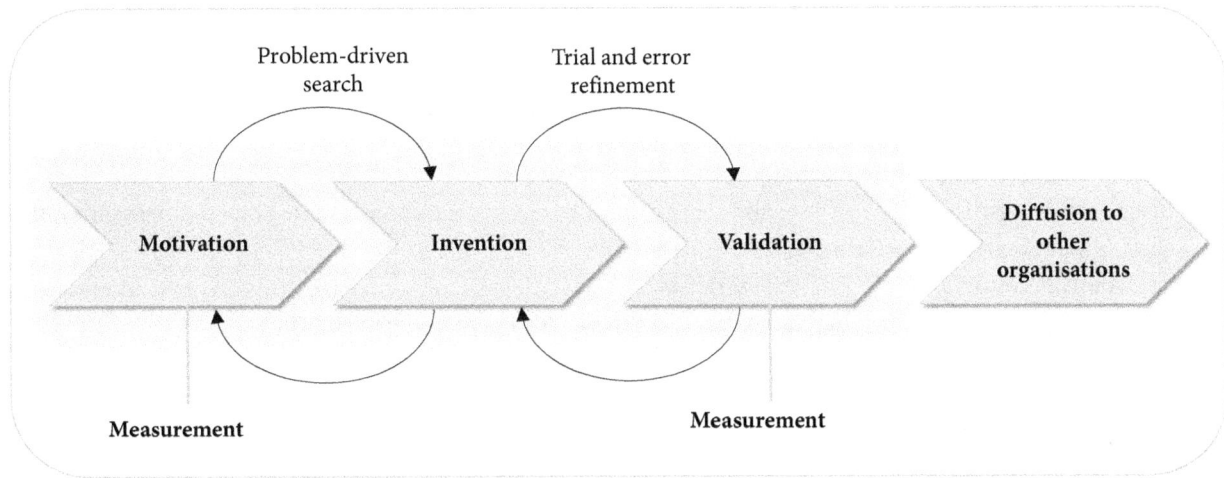

Figure 8.4: Simplified management innovation process constructed from Birkinshaw & Mol[124] and Birkinshaw, Hamel & Mol[125]

The first phase is motivation. Any new initiative requires a minimum amount of energy or motivation to propel it forward. A desire for change needs to be evoked. The motivation for pursuing management innovation usually derives from a dissatisfaction with the status quo; imminent strategic threats that need to be mitigated; the need to solve a novel problem; inspiration from management thinkers; inspiration from examples of actual management innovations that had positive effects in other companies or scenarios; and a desire to reap the benefits of management innovation such as an improved working environment, increased employee engagement, improved productivity, innovation, quality, profitability, market share and other competitive advantages.[126] [127] Measuring a business's management innovation sophistication and being explicitly confronted by weaknesses that still need to be overcome can also serve as the impetus for change.

Once the desire and motivation have been fostered, the second step deals with inventing the actual management innovation practices. This step is somewhat fuzzy – a characteristic of any type of innovation, but even more so when dealing with a severely under-researched innovation domain.[128] The broad guideline is that the developed management practices need to be context-specific and need to fit the business's specific situation. Management innovation practices are usually developed via the process of identifying a number of critical factors (the management innovation moon shots can serve as a point of departure) that need to be addressed and then devising workable solutions.[129]

The third phase involves internally and externally validating whether the proposed solutions will have the desired impact. Small-scale, low-risk and low-cost experimentation/implementation of the proposed solutions can be used to test the solutions, and based on the results (which again requires measurement) lead to the eventual refinement and full-scale implementation of the solutions.

With management innovation, like any other form of innovation, potential risks exist. The largest risk is failing to implement the innovation, which will have a negative impact on the organisation's profitability, cause inefficiencies in its processes and waste valuable resources.[130] This risk is amplified by the fact that the final version of the management innovation does not typically have a tangible form, which makes it complex and ambiguous. Employees therefore need to be convinced that proposed management changes will yield the desired advantages. This could prove difficult, as management innovation results are normally only observable after a long period of time. The external opinion of academics, consultants or experts regarding the proposed changes could therefore prove useful.

Other barriers that can hinder the implementation of management innovation are:[131] [132]

- a lack of training on innovation techniques or how to be innovators
- unsupportive organisational structures and a lack of incentive programmes for fostering management innovation
- a lack of senior management involvement
- opportunistic consultants who propose established practices instead of innovative ideas, in order to repeatedly sell the same solution, maximising their return, but to the detriment of the business
- a lack of open communication and transparency
- allocating insufficient time and resources to innovators for new ideas to develop
- pressure for short-term performance instead of long-term performance
- compensation schemes for executives or senior managers are not focused on innovation
- underdeveloped innovation metrics

Inversely, factors that are conducive to the success of management innovation are:[133] [134] [135] [136] [137]

- an active commitment and encouragement from top management
- the provision of tools and innovation training to employees
- setting exciting challenges that unleash passion
- adequate allotment of resources and organisational support
- a dedicated management innovation function
- developing a questioning or problem-solving culture
- developing an innovation culture
- discouraging a short-term profit focus and fostering a shared focus
- diverse exposure: the more employees are exposed to different ways of doing things, different industries, different environments, countries and markets, the more inspired, open and creative they will be
- building a capacity for low-risk experimentation
- making use of external change agents to explore ideas
- becoming a serial management innovator and continuously performing management innovation
- flat hierarchical structures
- small team sizes
- rewards that are both monetary and nonmonetary
- transparency, communication and the flexibility of employees in the workplace

Finally, given management innovation's ability to contribute to an organisation's long-term sustainability and competitive advantages, the question is: Can organisations afford to ignore management innovation any longer?

MANAGEMENT INNOVATION CASE STUDIES

Management innovation can manifest itself in various different forms – novel organisational structures, innovative practices or processes, embedded culture or even altered work environments that promote creativity, collaboration and energy. Hamel noted: "If your goal is to escape the straitjacket of conventional management thinking, it helps to study the practices of organisations that are decidedly unconventional. With a bit of digging, you can unearth a menagerie of exotic organisational life-forms that look nothing like the usual doyens of best practice."[138]

This section highlights a few interesting cases of successful management innovation.

Case study of Toyota

"Why has it taken America's automobile manufacturers so long to narrow their efficiency gap with Toyota? In large part, because it took Detroit more than 20 years to ferret out the radical management principle at the heart of Toyota's capacity for relentless improvement. Unlike its Western rivals, Toyota has long believed that first-line employees can be more than cogs in a soulless manufacturing machine; they can be problem solvers, innovators and change agents. While American companies relied on staff experts to come up with process improvements, Toyota gave every employee the skills, the tools, and the permission to solve problems as they arose and to head off new problems before they occurred. The result: year after year, Toyota has been able to get more out of its people than its competitors have been able to get out of theirs. Such is the power of management orthodoxy that it was only after American carmakers had exhausted every other explanation of Toyota's success – an undervalued yen, a docile workforce, Japanese culture, superior automation – that they were finally able to admit that **Toyota's real advantage was its ability to harness the intellect of "ordinary" employees** … Management orthodoxies are often so deeply ingrained in executive thinking that they are nearly invisible and are so devoutly held that they are practically unassailable. The more unconventional the principle underlying a management innovation, the longer it will take competitors to respond. In some cases, the head-scratching can go on for decades."[139]

Case study of Whole Foods Market

"It's tough for rivals to replicated advantages based on a web of individual innovations spanning many management processes and practices. That's one reason why no competitor has matched the performance of Whole Foods Market [an upscale organic and natural foods supermarket chain], which has grown during the past 25 years to 161 stores and $3.8 billion in annual sales. While other grocery chains have been slashing costs to fend off Wal-Mart, Whole Foods has been rapidly evolving an extraordinary retail model – one that already delivers the highest profits per square foot in the industry. What may not be obvious to health-conscious consumers and growth-loving investors is that the company's management model is just as distinctive as its high-margin business model. John Mackey, the company's founder and CEO, says his goal was to "create an organization based on love instead of fear" and describes Whole Foods as a "community working together to create value for other people". At Whole Foods, the basic organizational unit isn't the store but small teams that manage departments such as fresh produce, prepared foods, and seafood. Managers consult teams on all store-level decisions and grant them a degree of autonomy that is nearly unprecedented in retailing. Each team decides what to stock and can veto new hires. Bonuses are paid to teams, not to individuals, and team members have access to comprehensive financial data, including the detail of every co-worker's compensation. Believing that 100:1 salary differentials are incompatible with the ethos of a community, the company has set a salary cap that limits any executive's compensation to 14 times the company average. Just as startling is the fact that 94% of the company's stock options have been granted to non-executives. **What differentiates Whole Foods is not a single management process but a distinctive management system**."[140]

Case study of Steve Jobs at Pixar

"Despite being a denizen of the digital world, or maybe because he knew all too well its potential to be isolating, Jobs was a strong believer in face-to-face meetings. "There's a temptation in our networked age to think that ideas can be developed by e-mail and iChat," he told me. "That's crazy. Creativity comes from spontaneous meetings, from random discussions. You run into someone, you ask what they're doing, you say 'Wow', and soon you're cooking up all sorts of ideas." He had the Pixar building designed to promote unplanned encounters and collaborations. "If a building doesn't encourage that, you'll lose a lot of innovation and the magic that's sparked by serendipity," he said. "So we designed the building to make people get out of their offices and mingle in the central atrium with people they might not otherwise see." The front doors and main stairs and corridors all led to the atrium; the café and the mailboxes were there; the conference rooms had windows that looked out onto it; and the 600-seat theatre and two smaller screening rooms all spilled into it. "Steve's theory worked from day one," Lasseter recalls. "I kept running into people I hadn't seen for months. **I've never seen a building that promoted collaboration and creativity as well as this one**." Jobs hated formal presentations, but he loved freewheeling face-to-face meetings. He gathered his executive team every week to kick around ideas without formal agenda, and he spent every Wednesday afternoon doing the same with his marketing and advertising team. Slide shows were banned. "I hate the way people use slide presentations instead of thinking," Jobs recalled. "People would confront a problem by creating a presentation. I wanted them to engage, to hash things out at the table, rather than show a bunch of slides. People who knew what they're talking about don't need PowerPoint."[141]

Case study of Google

Google, the web-based search engine giant, is continually pushing the boundaries of innovation. The founders, Larry Page and Sergey Brin, understand that in a discontinuous world, it is not a company's competitive advantage at a single point in time that is important, but instead its evolutionary advantage over time.[142] The only way for Google to protect its first mover advantage in online search and web-based advertising is to innovate relentlessly. The founders therefore desire to create a fertile environment where its highly talented people can thrive and continually drive Google's evolution with out-of-the-box thinking.

What Hamel[143] calls a "brink-of-chaos" management style, really involves Google's unique product-development process that is built around a swarm of small, autonomous teams that each aims to invent the next big breakthrough for Google.[144] The logic is that small, independent teams have fewer dependencies to manage and are therefore more responsive and quicker in launching initiatives. The company firmly believes that if you can experiment more cheaply and rapidly than competitors, you can test more ideas and improve your chances stumbling upon a great idea.[145]

Google proudly fosters a just-try-it attitude and gives people supple freedom to express themselves. Google's formula for innovation is internally described as "70-20-10": 70 percent of engineering resources get allocated to improvement of the base business, 20 percent gets focused on services that extend the core business, and 10 percent gets allocated to fringe ideas.[146] Every developer further has the freedom to use 20 percent of their time to work on and experiment with whatever new ideas inspire them.[147] This drives a dual purpose: (1) it generates a portfolio of fresh strategic options, and (2) it ensures that no one has to leave Google to pursue a personal passion.[148] Employees are further motivated to generate big profit generating ideas via the quarterly "Founders Awards" where Google grants millions of dollars' worth of restricted stock to teams who have made remarkable contributions to the company's success. From Page and Brin's perspective, talented employees shouldn't have to leave Google to join a start-up to get rich.[149]

Google therefore does everything in its power to make the company feel like an intimate entrepreneurial start-up itself, instead of a big corporate bureaucracy.[150] The organisational structure of Google is flat, non-hierarchical, highly democratic and involves a dense network of horizontal communication.[151] As mentioned above, Google's management model is built around small work units and a team-focused approach that involves high internal transparency, lots of experimentation, and vigorous peer-to-peer feedback.[152] Decision-making is consultative and employees are encouraged to speak up.[153] Instead of driving strategies top-down and assigning projects, Google tries to create conversations. This allows people to get involved and commit to problems themselves, which attracts a lot of buy-in and drives execution.[154] Google also doesn't micro-manage its highly motivated and capable workforce. When employees get stuck, they will ask for help. Google's culture is meritocratic and questioning, as the founders understand that breakthroughs come not from blind obedience, but from questioning assumptions and challenging conventional paradigms.

Another core design principle for Brin and Page was that they wanted to create a company where they would like to hang out. According to Brin, "We try to provide an environment where people are going to be happy. I think that's a much better use of money than, say, hundred-million-dollar marketing campaigns or outrageously inflated salaries." Google's offices around the world, and especially the "Googleplex" (head office) in Mountain View, California therefore seem more like adult playgrounds than workplaces. Buildings are for instance fitted with quick access slides or fireman-poles to floors below, beanbags, quirky office decorations, large whiteboards in offices for sharing ideas, meeting pods, sleeping pods, stylish relaxation areas, pool- foosball- and ping-pong tables, video game stations, bowling alleys, climbing walls, beach volleyball courts, gyms, swimming pools, doctors' offices, laundry services, child care facilities, hybrid car rentals, professional masseurs, and of course, high quality free food.[155] [156] [157] But creating an enticing and engaging work space is not only spawned by physical surroundings, but also intellectual surroundings. Google only hires A-players who are curious, have wide-ranging and unconventional interests, and are idealistic and passionate about changing the world.[158] These are typically the rebels who aren't afraid to defy conventional wisdom and are brave enough to dream big. Talented people are attracted to working for Google, because the company empowers them to work on some of the world's most fascinating problems in the quest to achieve Google's mission – organise the world's information and make it universally accessible and useful.[159] [160]

Case study of Semco

Semco is a Brazilian cellular-manufacturing business that produces technologically sophisticated products such as marine pumps, digital scanners, commercial dishwashers, truck filters and mixing equipment for everything from bubble gum to rocket fuel. When Richardo Semler took over Semco from his father in 1980, the business was close to bankruptcy. Through hard work, luck and drastic management changes, Semler was able to save the company from ruin and turn it into one of the fastest growing companies in Brazil between the 1980s and 1990s, while also being named as the best company to work for in Brazil for a number of years.[161]

Semler credits three core company values to Semco's remarkable turnaround: (1) employee involvement, (2) profit sharing and (3) information.

Semler firstly sought to get employees involved and create a real democracy. His first insight was that employees would be happier if they had real control over their working conditions; and the enterprise would benefit from employees' enhanced participation.[162] His second insight was that human beings weren't designed to work in big groups. "In an immense production unit, people feel tiny, nameless and incapable of exerting influence on the way work is done and profit is made." [163] Individual involvement gets lost. Semler therefore reduced the size of their work units, and reduced the size of people working in one of their factories by splitting it into three separate plants.[164] "The first effect of the break-up was a rise in costs due to duplication of effort and a loss in economies of scale. Unfortunately, balance sheets chalk up items like these as liabilities, all with dollar figures attached, and there's nothing at first to list on the asset side but airy stuff like 'heightened involvement' and 'a sense of belonging'. Yet the longer term results exceed our expectations. Within a year, sales doubled, inventories fell from 136 days to 46, we unveiled eight new products that had been stalled in R&D for two years … overall quality improved … increased productivity let us reduce the workforce by 32% through attrition and retirement incentives."[165]

Semler[166] also dramatically flattened the organisational pyramid. "Pyramids emphasize power, promote insecurity, distort communications, hobble interaction, and make it very difficult for people who plan and people who execute to move in the same direction." He therefore instituted organisational circles that consist of three levels: the central circle at the first level consists of people who integrate the company's activities; the second level contains the heads of the different divisions; and the third circle contains all other employees.[167] In this structure, employees at the third level can earn more than employees at the levels above, given that they are specialists. At Semco people are rewarded for their expertise and knowledge instead of the titles that they hold.

In a similar fashion, people aren't hired or promoted until they've been interviewed and accepted by all future subordinates. Employees also evaluate all managers bi-annually, and fill out anonymous questionnaires about the company's credibility and management competence – among other things, asking employees about what would make them quit or go on strike.[168] Another part of employee involvement was that employees had the right to vote on long-term company decisions such as moving to a new factory or expanding the product line. This democratic approach ensured that employees take ownership of decisions and be more receptive to changes.

Semler[169] fundamentally believed in giving employees control over their lives. "We hire adults, and then we treat them like adults." Resultantly, one of the first things Semler did when he took control of Semco was to discard manuals, rules and regulations in favour of common sense.[170] Although it was admittedly a risky tactic to allow employees to use their own judgement, it eventually paid off. At Semco there were no longer rules regarding dress codes and travel expenses and the company did no security searches or audits of petty cash.[171] "Not that we wouldn't prosecute a genuinely criminal violation of our trust. We just refuse to humiliate 97% of the work force to get our hands on the occasional thief or two-bit embezzler … Some people spend $200 a day (while travelling) while others get by on $125. Or so I suppose. No one checks expenses, so there is no way of knowing. The point is, we don't care. If we can't trust people with our money and their judgement, we sure as hell shouldn't be sending them overseas to do business in our name."

By the same logic they also eliminated time clocks and employees were responsible for setting their own workhours and pay levels.[172] "We couldn't believe they would come to work day after day and sit on their hands because no one else was there. Pretty soon, we figured, they would start co-ordinating their work hours with their co-workers. And that's exactly what happened."[173] Semco also insisted that employees rotate their jobs every two to five years to prevent boredom. This further ensured that multiple employees could fulfil a job requirement, which made the entire business more flexible. Job rotation also discouraged personal empire building and allowed employees to gain a better understanding of business as a whole.[174]

Semler[175] explained that the corporate man is a very recent animal. In our hunter days, "If you had to kill a mammoth or do without supper, there was no time to draw up an organization chart, assign tasks, or delegate authority. Basically, the person who saw the mammoth from farthest away was the Official Sighter, the one who ran the fastest was the Head Runner, whoever threw the most accurate spear was the Grand Marksman, and the person all others respected and listened to was the Chief. That's all there was to it … What I'm saying is, put ten people together, don't appoint a leader, and you can be sure that one will emerge. So will a sighter, a runner, and whatever else the group needs … But getting back to that mammoth, why was it that all the members of the group were so eager to do their share of work – sighting, running, spearing, chiefing – and to stand aside when someone else could do it better? Because they all got to eat the thing one it was killed and cooked. What mattered was results, not status. Corporate profit is today's mammoth meat." The second great value at Semco was therefore profit sharing. Twice a year Semco calculated 23% of after-tax profits on each division's income statement and allowed employees to decide how to use or distribute the profits.

Where profit-sharing initiatives in other companies usually fall flat is that they make it difficult for employees to understand how their inputs relate to profits and how that profit is divided.[176] The third great value of Semco is therefore transparency. All employees were privy to the company's data. Employees were sent monthly balance sheets, income statements and cash flow statements for their various departments. Employees were also given training to allow them to understand the numbers of how the business is doing.[177] This transparency increased trust and fostered an understanding in employees that their own productivity would lead to beneficial outcomes.[178] "And that's all there is to it. Participation gives people control of their work, profit sharing gives them a reason to do it better, information tells them what's working and what isn't … We are very, very rigorous about the numbers … And because we're so strict with the financial controls, we can be extremely lax about everything else."[179]

Management innovation insights

From the chapter as a whole and the cases above, a pattern of management innovation begins to emerge. Some of the identifiable practices or themes[180] [181] [182] are shown in Table 8.7.

Table 8.7: Practices and themes of management innovation

Empowerment	Business focus, work assignment and decision-making
• Give everyone a voice. • Empower everyone. • Don't force people into roles. • Broadly define roles. • Unleash the creativity and initiative in all employees. • Experiment cheaply and experiment often.	• Make the mission the boss. • Set clear targets and provide transparent data. • All ideas compete on equal footing. • Resources are free to follow opportunities. • Resources get attracted, not allocated; tasks are chosen, not assigned. • Commitment is voluntary. • Business cases are built and peers are consulted. • Decisions are democratic, peer-based and transparent. • Communication is open, transparent and is encouraged.
Organisational structure and leadership	**Rewards, promotion and conflict**
• Flatten or remove hierarchies. • Hierarchies are built bottom-up. • Leaders serve rather than preside. • Leaders are accountable to the led. • Authority is derived from expertise. • Merit counts more than credentials and titles. • Community is emphasised over hierarchy. • Communities are self-defining and self-organising. • Work is self-directed and self-regulated. • Supervision is limited. • Team sizes are small.	• Rewards are aligned with contributions, not with power and position. • Companies have compensation committees. • There are both monetary and nonmonetary rewards. • Employees play a significant role in the promotion of peers and the recruitment of new hires. • Encourage competition for impact, not promotion. • Conflict gets resolved via a fair process. • Companies have procedures in place to analyse alternative solutions.
Power and trust	
• Power comes from sharing, not hoarding. • With power and freedom comes responsibility. • Employees are given autonomy and trusted to make the right decisions.	

Questions that may be useful for identifying where to start your organisation's management innovation journey include:[183]

• What are the difficult trade-offs that your organisation never seems to get right?
• What are big organisations bad at?
• What are the emerging challenges that the future has in store for your organisation?
• What things exhibit the attributes or capabilities that you'd like to build into your organisation? And how are these imbued in enviable quantities?
• How can more win–win situations be created for management and employees?

- What counterbalances can be instituted to ensure that people stay disciplined given their new freedom? Are these measures really worth the effort compared to the downside risk or are we better off trusting employees to do the right thing?

CONCLUSION

This chapter discussed the why, what and how of management innovation. It was argued that management innovation is essential as the business landscape has dramatically changed since the industrial era, but the evolution of modern management practices and paradigms have largely stagnated. The new economy presents a new reality for business that poses exciting new challenges; but these challenges won't be overcome if management is trapped in an archaic mindset.

Management innovation is the means by which the management domain itself will be rejuvenated in order to fit the new world. Management innovation is also the actual principles, processes, practices or organisational forms that are distinctly different from the traditional norm and which significantly alter the way that the work of management is performed. Management innovation therefore refers to both the process of innovation regarding management and the unique output of such a process. Finally, the task of performing management innovation is still largely malleable, but can be accomplished by establishing a baseline of the management innovation sophistication of the business relative to the management innovation moon shots, and then improving on this rating by developing context-specific management solutions or alternatives.

Management innovation is daunting and ambitious, but as Porter[184] once noted, the difficulty of a task contributes to the significance of the subsequent advantage.

Let this also be a solace and encouragement: those who have previously succeeded in management innovation have done so without any guidelines or clear aim; and via the 25 management innovation moon shots we are at least armed with the latter. Management is about people. Management innovation is therefore about innovating around people; cultivating an engaged workforce and making organisations genuinely human – making them adaptable, innovative and community-minded.[185] It can further be said that conducive to the process of management innovation is human virtuousness, specifically the attributes of empathy and self-knowledge. This is because management innovation revolves largely around understanding oneself and understanding the needs and feelings of others, with the goal of making people feel valued, energising them and giving them the freedom and autonomy to achieve great things. In a sentence – treat people like adults and manage the way you would want to be managed.

Chapter 9

Entrepreneurial thinking and strategy practices

"Entrepreneurship is key to the growth and development of nations" – Calá et al. (2015)[1]

LEARNING OBJECTIVES

In recent years a strong belief that "entrepreneurship" is a crucial driver of economic growth for both developed and developing nations has emerged among scholars and policy makers (see, for instance Audretsch, Keilbach and Lehmann, 2006[2] and, for a comprehensive survey, Van Praag and Versloot, 2007[3]). This chapter underwrites this belief and will therefore cover entrepreneurial strategy – not different from strategy, but a different kind of strategy-making and execution.

This chapter will therefore discuss the following:

- What (or who) is an entrepreneur?
- The entrepreneurial process
- Starting up a business
- The "entrepreneurial personality" – is there something like it?
- Entrepreneurship in South Africa
- Intrapreneurship
- Some notable South African entrepreneurs

CASE STUDY OF LILY O'BRIEN'S CHOCOLATES

Winning the British Airways chocolate contract is a high point for any chocolate business, but winning it from Lindt is a triumph. This is what happened to Mary Ann O'Brien. She tells British Airways' *Business Life* magazine[4] about starting up as an entrepreneur:

Mary Ann O'Brien, 53, is the founder of Lily O'Brien's – named after her daughter – a luxury chocolate brand whose customers include British Airways. She founded the business in her flat in County Kildare in 1992 and it now (2014) has a turnover of €20m. She became a senator in the Irish parliament in 2011.

> **"I'm from Tipperary and my father was a racehorse trainer.** To this day I still love horses. I think they're the dolphins of the earth. If you're used to them, they're just gorgeous to be around, and you can't really think of much else when you're with them.

I was a terrible troublemaker in school and academically a complete disaster. After flunking university and going travelling, I found work at the Phoenix Park Racecourse in Dublin. My board included Stavros Niarchos, Robert Sangster, Dermot Desmond, John Magnier – all men with great vision. They had stepped in to save the racecourse but they were also very ambitious. My job was to get every race sponsored and we subsequently became the only racecourse in the world to have every race sponsored every day.

When the racecourse closed down, I started an event management company and ran that successfully for years. I had a baby and just after that I started to get flu and went from being a person who could work 18 hours a day to being completely burnt out. I was down to seven stone. I'd gone from someone who could go to parties and drink all night, to someone who couldn't go outside the front door for a year and a half. But after about two years I got out of it. I found an amazing doctor and he made me do a lot of meditation and a lot of yoga and put me on a special diet. To this day I'm a great believer in the importance of business people managing their stress levels as the world gets faster and faster.

I was sitting in the reception area of a boutique hotel in South Africa on holiday soon afterwards when I spotted a chess set. I asked if I could take it out by the pool. They laughed and said, "It's made of chocolate." I met the owner's daughter, who was a similar age to me, and spent the entire holiday in the kitchen learning how to make chocolate. Before I left, I went into Cape Town and bought moulds, piping bags, palette knives and a couple of books, so when I returned to Ireland I had a baby chocolate factory in my suitcase.

At home I had a little kitchen and three saucepans and I started making stuff. My focus group was the women at the hairdressers in the local village. I started to sell to them, then I went to the local farmers' market and that first Easter I sold eggs to all my family and friends."

So far, this could be the story of many an ordinary housewife, but Mary Ann was an entrepreneur. Her story continues:[5]

To develop her skills further she attended a chocolate-making course in Belgium and continued cold calling. She'd melt and hand-pipe chocolates every night, then box them up and drive around the country in her car with them. "I was the only employee, so I used to cry when things broke because I didn't have an engineer."

With the firm gaining some traction, O'Brien borrowed £36,000 from AIB in Dublin and in 1993 also bought proper, industrial chocolate-making machinery and moved operations from her flat into a proper catering kitchen to service her growing client list.

During this time she approached the supermarket chain Superquinn. "I was a great woman for knocking on a door with a briefcase and prototypes, even though I didn't really have a factory." They liked the moulds of lion's heads and crocodiles she'd brought back from South Africa. "So they allowed me to put some of my chocolates in the chocolate section of the bakery. And within nine months, the Belgians were out and I was in." At that stage it was only me and two part time employees so I did the delivery, the accounts, the selling and the making myself. It was seven days a week.

The contract was worth £250,000 at the time. O'Brien put her daughter Lily, whose name she adopted for the business, in a crèche and took on the deliveries, production, packing and sales herself.

In 1994, Aer Lingus asked O'Brien to tender for its trans-Atlantic and European contract, making six million mint pins and three million "two-choc" boxes. I laughed and said, "Look lads, I couldn't make that in a year." But in 1995 the airline came knocking again. By then, O'Brien's sales had hit the £1m mark and she had her own purpose-built factory. She took on the Aer Lingus deal, and "went immediately to British Airways, where I won my first very large BA contract. After that, I was away like a shot from a gun." It was big business. Everyone in the business section of every plane, from noon onwards every day on every BA flight got a two-choc. "That was four million two-chocs a year, which allowed us to get into the airline catering business."

The timeline of Mary Ann's business during the early years is shown in Figure 9.1.

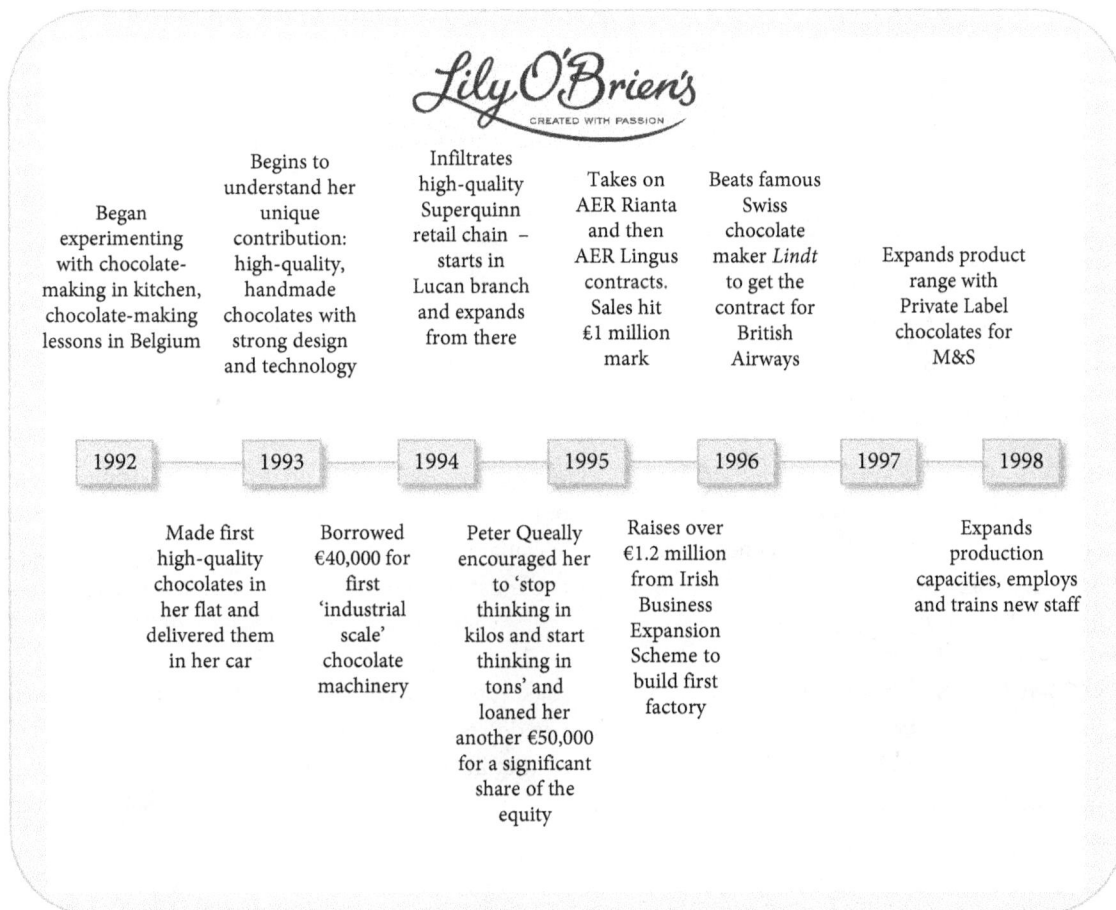

Figure 9.1: Lily O'Brien's – the early years

This might sound too much like a fairy tale, but the story of Lily O'Brien's Chocolates took a decided turn for the worse after 9/11 with the destruction of the World Trade Centre buildings. With airlines grounded in the United States and people afraid of flying, any business reliant on airlines was bound to suffer. And of course, the financial crisis years of 2007–2008 were just around the corner.

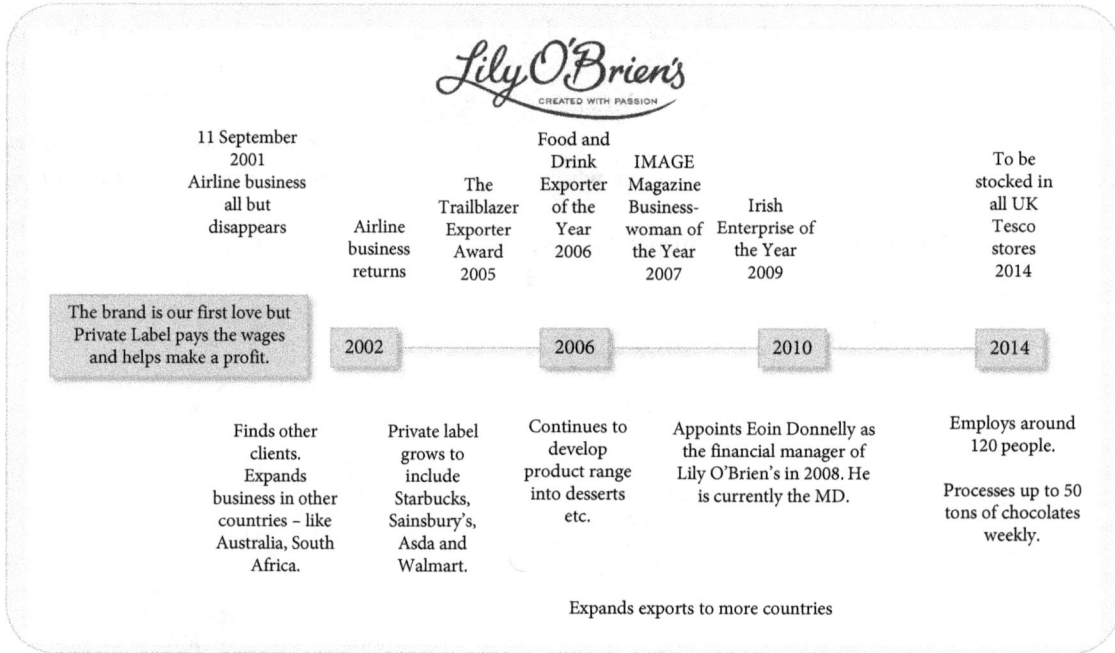

Figure 9.2: Lily O'Brien's: self-sustainability

In 2008, the group served 17 million branded Lily O'Brien's chocolates on 23 airlines around the world. Turnover hit £16m. The business had opened a store in Manhattan, and O'Brien was trying to keep a handle on the recession and a sky-high cocoa rice price. "Speculators can really push the price up, which makes me very cross because it's my livelihood. But what goes up must come down – if you're at it long enough you just hang on."

O'Brien says the recession gave them a bit of a shake-up because retailers wanted big promotions yet a premium brand like Lily O'Brien's cannot afford to go down the discount or promotional route too far. "We are a premium brand and people don't mind paying that little bit more for it. We come under a little bit of pressure from the retailer but the sell through is good and we work hard to see what they need and fulfil those needs."

As a way to reduce costs in recent years, they looked at making the chocolates smaller and the cardboard lighter but thought against it as they wanted to maintain its premium credentials. According to Eoin Donnelly: "We saw some of our competitors reengineering down and changing the boxes so they were lighter, using cheaper ingredients in the product but there is a tipping point with that, where the product is no longer something that you might even buy, never mind give as a gift. People are very quick to pick up on taste changes in products they like. We noticed during the recession that people still bought chocolate because it was an affordable luxury. It was recession resilient."

Lily O'Brien's secret is, of course, its engine room – the factory. Here is an eye-witness report of someone lucky enough to have been given a tour of the factory.[6]

The first thing which struck me as we walked through the doors of the factory was the tantalising smell of chocolate. It was a rich aroma which immediately wrapped itself around my senses. Lily's is clinical on the inside; exacting standards in production are key to the quality end result.

We started at the beginning. Three large silver vats hold superior-quality Belgian chocolate made to Lily O'Brien's own unique recipe. One milk, one dark and one white. Lily's make over 240 lines and each is made with the same high-quality chocolate.

From the vats it is piped to the factory floor where it is tempered and ready for use. Tempering is what gives the chocolate its brilliant shine and ensures you get a snap rather than a crumble when you bite into it.

The factory is set out in a linear production line, meaning the raw ingredients go in one end and the finished product comes out the other. The chocolate is filled into molds, which come in all shapes and sizes, depending on the type of chocolate being produced.

The molds are then flipped over and most of the chocolate drained out to be re-tempered again. The molds are cooled leaving a cavity ready for its filling. Depending on the type of chocolate this could be a single or double filling. The molds continue along the production line and the filling is covered with chocolate to form the bottom of the sweet. The end result is a perfectly formed chocolate.

The finished chocolates are actually placed in boxes by hand and it's that attention to detail that ensures the highest quality of product is produced.

Quality control at Lily's

Quality control is paramount at Lily O'Brien's. I asked Mary Ann if they have actual chocolate tasters on site, to which she replied: "everyone here is a chocolate taster and everyone treats the factory like they own it". There is an incredible sense of pride in the work carried out by the staff at Lily's and it was very evident from the people I met.

The factory also has the highest BRC approval rating available and taste tests are carried out every two hours to ensure the highest standards are met. I tried a few myself (for research) and I can say for certain they were perfect.

Any chocolates (seconds) not deemed suitable to make it into a box are sold in the factory shop on site. Lily O'Brien's has also worked with the very worthy Food Cloud group who work to reduce food waste and food poverty.

Meeting Mary Ann O'Brien

Warm, personable, engaging and very much with her feet on the ground is how I would describe the lady behind Lily's. She splits her time between Lily's and her work as an esteemed Senator.

She is focused and passionate about the brand and constantly on the lookout for new trends in terms of flavours and innovative ways to bring the joy of chocolate to her customers. The team at Lily's plan a year in advance. A necessity to ensure they hit their key market dates such as Easter, Valentines and Christmas.

While sitting with Mary Ann I got to sample a brand new range of desserts which were prepared for an airline tender. Mississippi Mud Pie and Key Lime Pie were on the menu. Quality, high-end desserts with incredible taste sensations.

With the quality produced in their factory, Lily O'Brien's not only survived the recession, but thrived. So much so that on 27 January 2014, Carlyle Cardinal Ireland (CCI), the Irish private equity fund founded by the Carlyle Group (NASDAQ: CG) and Cardinal Capital Group announced it had made a significant investment in Lily O'Brien's, the Irish manufacturer of premium chocolates and desserts sold in 16 countries.[7]

CCI said:

[Lily O'Brien's Chocolates] has driven strong product growth outside of the UK and Ireland, with 2012 sales to Australia increasing by 370% between 2011 and 2012, and sales to the U.S. increasing by 100% in the same period.

Robert Easton, Managing Director of CCI, said: "Lily O'Brien's is a great example of an Irish business with a world-class reputation. We are delighted to join the founder and management team to continue to grow the business. The company's growth has accelerated in recent years, thanks to their unique recipes delivering award-winning products fuelling increasing demand in the domestic and international marketplace. Our investment will help Lily O'Brien's take their chocolates and desserts to an even wider audience of consumers around the world."

Founder Mary Ann O'Brien, who will continue to play an active role within the company, said: "The success of our business is thanks to Eoin Donnelly, managing director, our management team, staff and loyal customer base. While we have grown Lily O'Brien's from a kitchen table business into an international brand, the investment from CCI, along with CCI's global network, should ensure Lily O'Brien's continues to grow to the next level. The CCI team has a proven track record of working with businesses such as ours and we are excited about what we can achieve in the coming years."

On 3 December 2015 Eoin Donnelly said:[8]

"We're going to be up again this year, which is great," Mr Donnelly told the *Irish Independent*. A joint venture between US private equity group Carlyle and Dublin-based Cardinal Capital, Carlyle Cardinal Ireland, acquired a majority stake in Lily O'Brien's (around 80pc) last year for a rumoured €15m.

Mary Ann O'Brien, the company's founder, has a significant minority shareholding and Mr Donnelly also holds a stake.

"No time has been wasted [since the deal]. Plans kicked in right away last year. We doubled our capacity last year, but the plans now are how do we fill it?" Mr Donnelly said.

"We are growing and growing significantly. We're planning to double our business over the next few years. If we've doubled our business in the next five years, then I'd be looking at expansion again."

He said Carlyle Cardinal came with a "rolling action plan" that effectively became their plan for the first 100 days.

"As soon as the deal was done, effectively we were into, 'now here's the new scenario'. We knew it was going to be that. It was what we knew it was going to be. They were difficult enough when they were across the table from us. I do remember saying, at one stage, I can wait until they're on the same side of the table as us because they have great experience and great knowledge that we would be able to add to the business," Donnelly said.

Carlyle Cardinal appointed a nonexecutive director, Steve Newiss, who is chief commercial officer with Burton's Foods – which has a number 2 position in the UK biscuit sector.

The UK is Lily O'Brien's main market, and its primary focus.

Around 20pc of business is in the US and just under 10pc in Australia.

Asked what an expanded company would be like in five years, Mr Donnelly said he would like to see the business heading towards the "magic number" of €50m.

"I would want our chocolate business to be extremely strong, but I would want our desserts business to have grown substantially. Currently it's 90pc chocolate, 10pc desserts. I would want that desserts business to have grown as well," he said.

Many of you recognise the language – this is big business "talk".

Mary Ann herself has the following advice for entrepreneurs:[9]

- The relationship between you and your financial controller is vital – but try to stop them from being "penny wise and pound foolish".
- Keep your ego in a basket under the desk and don't show it to others. Too many good little businesses are seriously harmed by megalomaniac bosses stuffing around.
- Don't let fear get the better of you, use it to your advantage. Fear, well managed, can be a creative motivator. After September 2001, with airlines floundering, Mary Ann was forced to develop other markets – and eventually the airline customers returned.
- Don't shy away from difficult conversations. If left, issues tend to become worse, but never show anger to anyone – not employees, not suppliers and never to customers.
- Stay close to your competitors and never get smug. Learn from them and co-operate wherever and whenever you can.
- Travel – and keep travelling – particularly in the USA. The number of ideas to be found there is staggering.
- If you don't know, don't be afraid to ask – and hook up with a mentor.

And also:[10]

1. First of all, take your time. Get as much advice and mentorship from people that have been there, done that, got the t-shirt and made all of the mistakes.
2. Make sure that you have some consumer insight before you start and that there really is a gap in the market for your product.
3. Be prepared for some knocks and be prepared to really garner your resilience.
4. Make sure you have a passion. Be willing to work all hours that God sends to begin with, because it does take that.

WHAT (OR WHO) IS AN ENTREPRENEUR?

There are many definitions of entrepreneurship (or an entrepreneur). The University of Stellenbosch offers a course in Entrepreneurship and Innovation Management (in the faculty of Economic and Management Sciences) aimed at:[11]

> "… assist[ing] students to obtain an orientation of possibly establishing their own business in future and not strive to achieve the so-called work security in the form of a fixed appointment. Therefore it allows the student to create own job opportunities but also to make creative contributions to other businesses."

According to the University of Pretoria's B.Com Entrepreneurship Department (part of the Faculty of Economic and Management Sciences):[12]

> "Entrepreneurs start new businesses and take on the risk and rewards of being an owner. This is the ultimate career in capitalism – putting your idea to work in a competitive economy. Some new ventures generate enormous wealth for the entrepreneur. However, the job of entrepreneur is not for everyone. You need to be hard-working, smart, creative, willing to take risks and good with people. You need to have heart, motivation and drive.

> … But there is a downside of entrepreneurship too. Your life may lack stability and structure. Your ability to take time off may be highly limited and you may become stressed as you manage cash flow on the one hand and expansion on the other.

> Think about problems that people would pay to have a solution to. It helps to know finance. It's a must to really know your product area well. What do consumers want? What differentiates you from the competition? How do you market this product? A formal business plan is not essential, but is normally a great help in thinking through the case for a new business.

> Entrepreneurs have many personalities. Some are fiery revolutionaries. Some are gentle souls with good ideas. Some are driven, but difficult. Some have grown up in the most difficult circumstances imaginable – emerging with enormous determination to strive for greatness. Others are pleasant, personable and compassionate renegades.

> Generally, there will be a life event, key motivator or a source of inspiration that causes a person to strike out on their own, rather than work inside a larger company."

Another useful way of constructing a definition is to use the definitions employed by surveys to measure entrepreneurial activity. The most used surveys are shown in Table 9.1.

Table 9.1 – Measures of entrepreneurship

Measure	Definition	Source
Nascent entrepreneurship	Percentage of adult population that have taken action to create a new business in the past year but have not paid any salaries for more than three months.	Global Entrepreneurship Monitor[13]
New business start-ups	Percentage of adult population that own or manage a new business from 3 to 42 months old.	
Total entrepreneurial activity (TEA)	Nascent entrepreneurship + New business start-ups. Also called "Early-stage Entrepreneurial Activity Index" (EA).	
Opportunity-based entrepreneurs	Entrepreneurs who have taken action to create a new venture in pursuit of perceived business opportunities.	
Necessity-based entrepreneurs	Entrepreneurs who have taken action to create a new venture because of the lack of better employment alternatives.	
Entry density	Number of newly registered limited-liability firms per 1000 working age population.	World Bank Group Entrepreneurship Survey (WBGES)[14]
Entry rate	New firms over the total number of lagged registered businesses.	
Business density	Number of existing registered companies with limited liability per 1000 working-age population.	
Entry rate	Number of new firms as a ratio of the total number of incumbent and entrant firms in a given year.	Distributed micro-data analysis (Bartelsman et al. 2004)[15]
Complex Entrepreneurship Context index	Based on 26 variables that measure entrepreneurial activity, strategy and attitudes for 54 countries across 2003–2006.	Acs et al. (2008)[16]

The Business Dictionary[17] defines an entrepreneur as follows:

> "Someone who exercises initiative by organising a venture to take benefit of an opportunity and, as the decision maker, decides what, how and how much of a good or service will be produced.
>
> An entrepreneur supplies/raises risk capital as a risk taker, and monitors and controls the business activities. The entrepreneur is usually a sole proprietor, a partner, or the one who own the majority of shares in an incorporated venture.
>
> According to economist Joseph Alois Schrumpeter (1883–1950), entrepreneurs are not necessarily motivated by profit, but regard it as a standard for measuring achievement or success."

Even if entrepreneurship (or, more difficult, the entrepreneurial spirit) is difficult to define, the entrepreneurial process is rather straightforward.

![Application tool icon] **Application tool**

Think of Mary Ann O'Brien's career as an entrepreneur as shown in our case study of Lily O'Brien's Chocolates. Which of the elements contained in the above definitions can you find in her story? Which essential elements (in your view) are missing?

Table 9.2: Lily O'Brien entrepreneurial case analysis

Definition element	Application in the case study	What (in your opinion) could she have done differently?
Definition element	Essential elements missing in the case study	What (in your opinion) could she have done differently?

THE ENTREPRENEURIAL PROCESS – THE BIG PICTURE

According to Hisrich, Peters and Shepherd,[18] the entrepreneurial strategy can be defined as "the set of decisions, actions and reactions that first generate, and then exploit over time, a new entry".

The process of entry broadly unfolds as follows (see Figure 9.3):

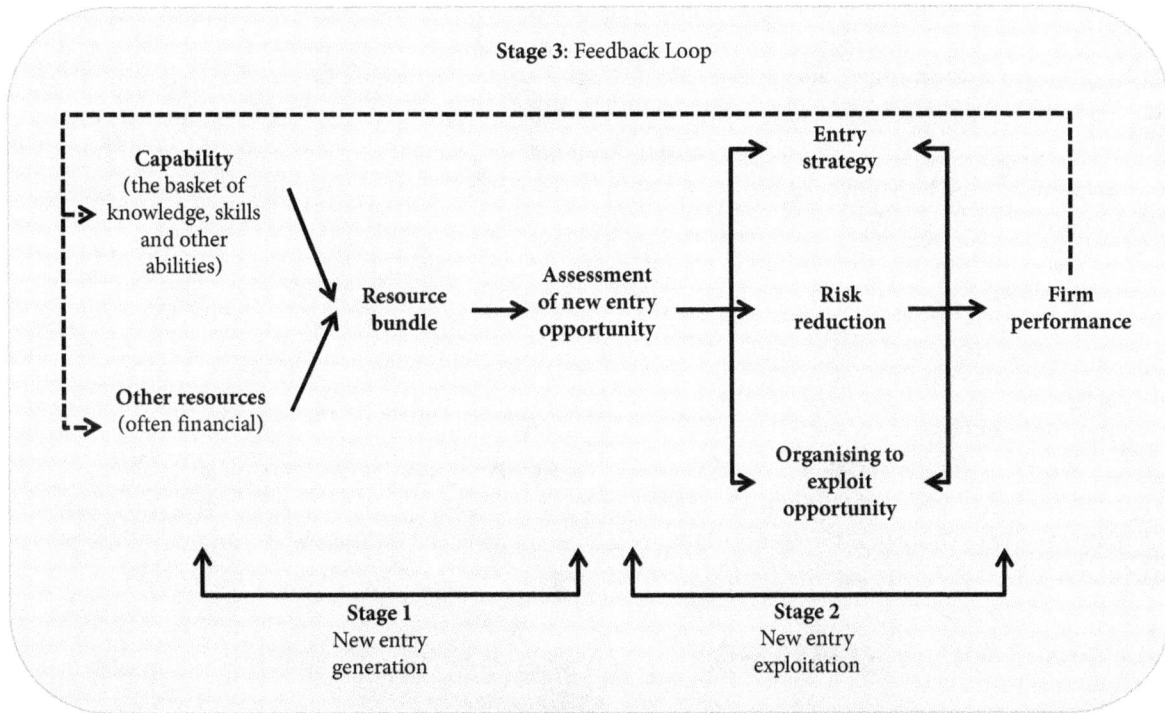

Figure 9.3: The process of entrepreneurial entry (based on Hisrich, Peters & Shepherd (2005)[19]

Stage 1 essentially consists of generating an opportunity to enter business. This entails a stock-take of yourself and your abilities – especially your ability to raise the necessary finances. To succeed you have to assemble a resource bundle that is unique, difficult to emulate and able to meet a need in the market.

A crucial part of this is assessing the entry opportunity. The companion book to this one, *Crystallising the Strategic Business Landscape: Strategy analysis practices and tools for business leaders and strategy practitioners,*[20] covers analysis practices and tools for analysing the business landscape. This can be a valuable resource for assessing the marketplace, looking for opportunities. Chapter 1 has tools for assessing yourself and your own thinking obstacles and suggestions to remedy them.

Stage 2 consists of developing an entry strategy and executing it. The chapters in this book will help you to do this, especially chapter 2 – developing options and choices (also in the e-market) and packaging them in vision and mission statements, developing a differentiation, cost, value and growth strategy as well as thoughts about entering foreign markets (amongst other ideas) .

Chapter 3 will guide you to develop a robust business model, able to withstand the challenges you will experience when implementing your strategy. Chapter 4 helps you to develop different scenarios – especially important when entering new and unknown market spaces – and chapter 5 will help you to implement your chosen strategy. Chapters 6, 7 and 8 are especially important, insofar as they deal with different ways of looking at innovation.

Much of the activity in stage 2 is aimed at minimising risk – especially the risk of business failure.

Stage 3 occurs as business results accumulate. This will give you an indication of how accurate your assessment of your resources bundle and your entry opportunity was, and also measure how well you have strategised and implemented your strategy. This will give you the opportunity to implement changes where required. The results of these changes will be fed back to you and you will be able to establish if they are causing your results to move in the desired direction.

In a nutshell, this is how any business – no matter how large or small – operates.

In summary so far:

- Entrepreneurship is a way of thinking and acting that focuses on:
  - the identification and exploitation of business opportunities from a broad general perspective
  - driven by the leadership of individuals or small groups
- Entrepreneurship strategy is the identification of the entrepreneurial business opportunity and the plans and actions to develop and exploit that opportunity

STARTING UP A BUSINESS

Broadly speaking, there are four stages (or four kinds of feedback) to a start-up:[21]

1. customer validation
2. operating process validation
3. financial validation
4. self-sustainability

Customer validation: A business idea remains just that until it is tested in the marketplace. During this stage you have to convince customers, backers/investors and employees (or partners) about the validity of your idea. At this stage it will be advisable not to cling to your original idea, but to change it as you go along. The BBC programme *Dragon's Den* has many examples of people losing backers because they refuse to change a set idea about the product or service they are trying to bring to market. The whole idea behind this phase is to develop a number of customers that are committed to buying the product or service offered.

Operating process validation: Now that you have customers, you have to deliver the product or service reliably and efficiently. There are potentially many unforeseen snags that have to be ironed out in the delivery process. It is easy to overcompensate for snags – thereby losing money – or undercompensate – thereby losing customers (or potential customers because of bad word-of-mouth). Designing your customer interface and getting it up and running is a crucial step to surviving in the marketplace. Your customers are extremely useful because they will tell you what is not working well – if you let them.

Financial validation: Your value proposition has been accepted by customers and your operating process delivers. This means that you are generating some income. It is almost never the figure you expected and planned for. Getting too much business is as challenging as getting too little. Once customers have started to experience your product or service, their needs change. They need something a little different, they want special payment options, they find ways of mangling your product or service that you never expected. This is a difficult stage and one where many entrepreneurs stumble. The initial rush of bringing the product/service to market is over and things settle into a humdrum rhythm. Even the problems are no longer fun, because they re-occur. Many entrepreneurs employ someone (or many people) to take care of the day-to-day and are not available to take decisions as needed, strangling the growth of the firm.

Self-sufficiency: To continue to be viable, enterprises need to innovate – essentially to start thinking from scratch. Many entrepreneurs are loath to do this, since it was such a struggle to turn their first idea into a success. If you manage to do this, the firm will be able to sustain itself. It usually means that you are not the sole "ideas man or woman" and that you allow the wisdom of partners, employees, customers and investors to influence the business and how it operates. At this stage you can think of appointing someone to take over the day-to-day running of the enterprise – it will get by without you.

A similar, but alternative, depiction of the start-up process based on a lean approach is depicted in the form of the customer development process in Figure 9.4. The customer development process is somewhat more linear than the lean start-up process and better clarifies the boundaries between strategy formulation and execution.

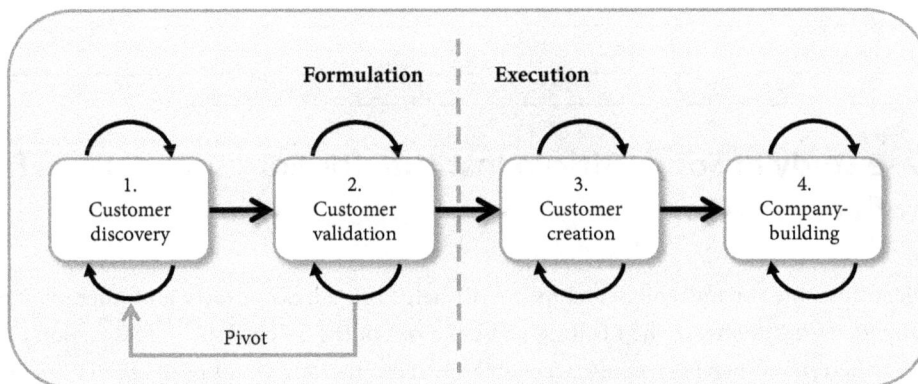

Figure 9.4 – Customer development process (adapted from Blank)[22]

The above customer development process consists of four phases. The first two phases deal with strategy formulation with the last two phases dealing with strategy execution. In the first phase, customer discovery, the start-up sketches all its hypotheses on the business model canvas. It is then necessary to "get out of the building" and establish whether the hypothesised customer need actually exists. A minimum viable product is also created as a solution to this need. In the second phase, customer validation, the start-up then proceeds to test its proposed solution and all its other hypotheses against customers. Based on the feedback gained, it is then possible to make small adjustments (iterations) or substantial adjustments (pivots) to the business model. This process continues until a need and a suitable solution with enough customer interest are determined. The third phase, customer creation, deals with scaling up the business. At this stage the product is deemed refined enough to sell, and scale is built by generating demand through marketing and sales expenditures. In the fourth phase, company-building, the business shifts from a start-up searching for an effective business model to functional departments executing its model.

The lean start-up methodology and customer development process do not claim that they will make individual start-ups more successful, though they do boast that lean methods will result in lower failure rates across a broad portfolio of start-ups.[23] Blank[24] additionally states that the basic assumption of conventional design-oriented approaches is that it is possible to figure out most of the unknowns of the business in advance, before executing the idea. He also states that start-ups do not unfold in accordance with master plans. Rather, the ones that succeed quickly test their ideas in the market, fail, learn, adapt, and iterate.

Application tool

Think about Mary Ann O'Brien in our case study. How well did she manage these stages?

Stage	Evidence in the case study	In your opinion, what could she have done differently or better?
Customer validation		
Operating process validation		
Financial validation		
Self-sufficiency		

Case study of South African Institute for Entrepreneurship (a social profit enterprise)

The South African Institute for Entrepreneurship (SAIE) helps to address poverty and unemployment through entrepreneurially focused initiatives. The institute was born out of the Triple Trust Organisation (TTO) in 1996 in recognition of the critical need for easily accessible business literacy training materials for both the small enterprise sector and for schools.

With 19 years of experience in developing innovative, experiential-based training materials, the SAIE promotes a positive mindset in youth and adults across South Africa, and assists in the creation of effective entrepreneurs and enterprises.

The SAIE trains educators, trainers, co-operatives and community-based organisations to convey business skills, uncover entrepreneurship qualities and ensure sustainable economic development and wealth creation. The institute currently works in education, agriculture, enterprise development and information technology.

Our mission is: We achieve results by creating a dynamic culture of entrepreneurship in South Africa through the development of innovative programmes and methodologies that are underpinned by key entrepreneurial drivers.

Our products and projects[25]

Business VENTURES for schools

The VENTURES system is an holistic solution to educator development because it proceeds from two complementary starting points:

- Good learning materials without development training will not transform the educator;
- yet educator development training without good learning materials will not deliver effective and efficient learning in the twenty-first century.

The VENTURES educator development system provides the tools, the techniques and the training to empower and guide the educator to take on the role of a dynamic facilitator of twenty-first-century learning. Since the content, logistics and OBE methodology are provided and driven by the VENTURES learning materials, educators can see beyond the classroom confines of the subject, and think and act entrepreneurially.

Best Game

The Best Game is in essence not a game at all. It is a carefully constructed business skills development tool masquerading as a game. The Best Game is interactive and experientially based. It simulates real market conditions and business scenarios in the training room. The process gets participants to weigh up information, make decisions and exploit opportunities. There are two versions: *Info Tech* and *Enterprise*.

SETA-accredited skills programmes

The SAIE has been providing on-site and countrywide training in entrepreneurship for 20 years. The expertise and experience developed over this period have allowed us to develop highly specialised, focused skills development courses that sharpen the knowledge, skills and understanding in specific areas of entrepreneurship. Therefore our executive programmes, which are run over two tough days, are more useful and beneficial than drawn-out months-long courses.

The SAIE Academy now offers compact, practical courses to encourage lifelong learning that can be implemented in various areas of a demanding business world. Our course materials and content are constantly upgraded to keep them fresh, relevant and effective.

We draw on the latest case studies, real-world experiences and current issues in the business sector and use training tools developed over many years to simulate business settings that imitate actual, on-the-ground and real-life situations.

Our courses are accredited with the South Africa Qualifications Authority (SAQA) through the Service Seta, and therefore qualify for the appropriate credits. Our facilitators have many years of experience in the field of entrepreneurship and, to remain relevant, constantly update their own experiences and skills.

Available courses

Entrepreneurship & Launching your Idea/Business
Business Leadership & Management
Business Strategy & Design Innovation
Writing a Successful Business Plan

Projects

Agriculture

The chronic lack of food security experienced by more than a third of the country's population highlights the severe inequalities in South African society and impacts the current and future stability of the nation. Because the current food insecurity in South Africa is not a result of large-scale commercial farming, the emphasis must be on strengthening small-scale farming and community food gardening programmes, and most importantly should provide the opportunity for these initiatives to generate income to supplement household food provision. In terms of current best practice for addressing food insecurity, it is clear that programmes must invest in training for small-scale producers, most critically by providing entrepreneurial expertise. In this way rural food gardeners will be able to be linked to the economic mainstream.

Education

Entrepreneurs look at suboptimal situations and see opportunities where others see disaster – the Institute as entrepreneur is no different. As far back as 1996 it saw the opportunity to influence the mindset of learners to think entrepreneurially. It did this by developing the Business VENTURES curriculum to be used in schools as a core part of the curriculum. Because it could not be assumed that educators would themselves be well-prepared or have access to quality materials, the institute developed innovative, interactive, fully researched materials and provided training for teachers so they were able to use the materials. Embedded into every lesson plan are the key entrepreneurial drivers that form the core values of the institute. The goal – to have every learner behave entrepreneurially.

Enterprise development

Because our human capital development is low – and if we see this as a glass half full – this provides a wonderful opportunity for improvement and growth. South Africa measures low on indices that only measure individual variables (like GEM); however the good news is that South Africa is relatively strong institutionally. So if we can develop a vibrant entrepreneurial culture – something at the core of the existence of the Institute for nearly 20 years – South Africa could become a winning nation – one that is an entrepreneurial role model to the rest of the world. The areas where we can improve the most are in start-up skills and human capital development – with only 42,7 per cent of our population perceiving that they have the capabilities for starting a business (compared to a sub-Saharan Africa average of 74 per cent). When the Institute was established in 1996 it believed that there was enormous potential, given the strength of the country institutionally and the locked up and undeveloped potential individually. Its goal is to develop an entrepreneurial culture through mindset and skill development.

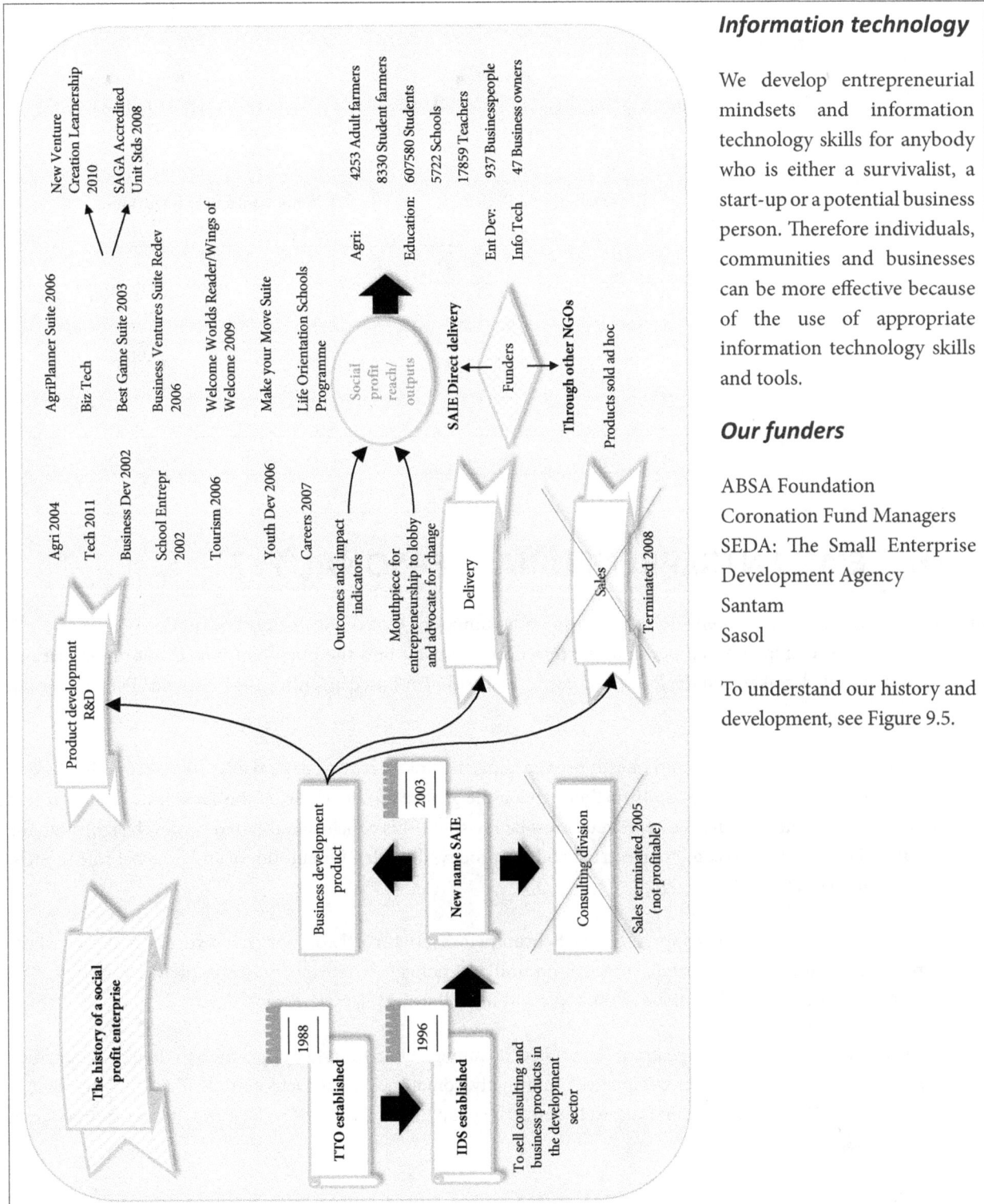

Figure 9.5: History of the South Africa Institute of Entrepreneurship[26]

Information technology

We develop entrepreneurial mindsets and information technology skills for anybody who is either a survivalist, a start-up or a potential business person. Therefore individuals, communities and businesses can be more effective because of the use of appropriate information technology skills and tools.

Our funders

ABSA Foundation
Coronation Fund Managers
SEDA: The Small Enterprise Development Agency
Santam
Sasol

To understand our history and development, see Figure 9.5.

Application tool

Clearly, SAIE is a different kind of start-up, but a start-up nonetheless. How would you evaluate their performance up to now?

Elements of entrepreneurial success (in your opinion)	How well did SAIE do?	What could they have done differently/better?
1.		
2.		
3.		
4.		
5.		
6.		
7.		

IS THERE AN ENTREPRENEURIAL PERSONALITY?

In many articles about entrepreneurship there is an assumption – often unwritten and unsaid – that there is something like an "entrepreneurial personality" that needs coaxing into the open and into action. More serious research has been undertaken and the *Journal of Economic Psychology* based an entire 2011 issue on "Personality and Entrepreneurship".[27]

The contributions are clustered around questions regarding the links between personality, socio-economic factors and entrepreneurial development. Results further explain the gender puzzle, while, at the same time, it is clear that stereotypes of what makes the ideal entrepreneur must be revisited. This conclusion is based on new insights into the effects that variables, such as risk tolerance, trust and reciprocity, the value for autonomy and external role models, have on entrepreneurial decision-making.

Most writing about entrepreneurship refers to Schrumpeter's (1942)[28] theory of "creative destruction", where innovative opportunities arise through competition and technology destroying previous market offerings. The *Economist* (2009)[29] devoted a whole issue to the topic and the following characterisation emerged:

> Entrepreneurs in the Schumpeterian sense "take advantage of any market opportunity" they discover; they are "strongly attached to their companies", "unusually, sometimes excessively, confident", "highly tolerant of risk", willing "to delegate certain tasks to trustworthy people" and they need to be able to create and maintain "social networks to succeed".[30]

Preference

This underwrites some of the stereotypes we tend to hold about entrepreneurs – and that many entrepreneurs hold about themselves, or try to live up to. Research[31] confirms that women are less likely to be entrepreneurs, but not, as feminists claim, because they are discriminated against when it comes to the distribution of opportunities and resources. Rather, the causes can be found in preference; fewer women express a wish to be entrepreneurial and fewer women choose to run young or immature businesses. More importantly, this preference seems to be influenced by factors such as industry and entrepreneurial experience, role in the household and family and skills and knowledge base.

More impactful on the decision to be an entrepreneur seems to be the availability of role models (also for women). Self-employed family members appear important for predicting involvement in entrepreneurial activity. The opinion of significant others often plays a decisive role in individual decision-making.[32] Parents shape the preferences of their children, and often provide financial support and advice in the period after start-up.

Risk tolerance and fear of failure

Entrepreneurs are often portrayed as highly risk-tolerant. Research indeed finds a link, but show that persons whose risk attitudes are in the medium range have higher chances of survival than those who have particularly low or high risk attitudes.[33] Further, a tendency to accept failure may signal that an individual is willing to search for new possibilities and learn through experimentation, whereas an antifailure attitude can obstruct entrepreneurial endeavours, as it makes individuals reluctant to experiment and does not allow them to learn from mistakes.[34, 35]

Willebrands, Lammers and Hartog (2011)[36] found that **perceptions** of risk have a positive effect on enterprise performance, because they cause risk mitigation measures to be taken.

Need for autonomy

It is generally true that most entrepreneurs could do financially better in full-time employment. It is also true that jobs that provide more autonomy are more satisfactory and motivating.[37] Entrepreneurs trade off the benefits of autonomy against the higher income traditional employment may offer. But autonomy is only one of a number of nonfinancial benefits (probably associated with autonomy) entrepreneurs experience – the ability to innovate and prompt decision-making, for instance. More research into these aspects will be beneficial.[38] It should be noted that it is only solo entrepreneurs that earn less than their salaried counterparts – as soon as the entrepreneur starts to appoint employees, his or her income outstrips the salaried person's.[39]

Other perceived barriers to entrepreneurship

There is some evidence[40] that **fear of the administrative burden** and **the lack of financial support** at crucial stages in the development of the start-up are also factors that keep qualified and motivated people in the nascent stage, in other words wanting to be an entrepreneur, but hesitant about taking the final step.

In summary, it is clear that some factors play a role in the decision to "go entrepreneurial". As soon as these factors are compared over economies – even regions in the same economy – the relative impact of these factors becomes scrambled. There is therefore no single "entrepreneurial personality". Successful entrepreneurs are as different from one another as you and I. The decision to be an entrepreneur is an individual one and – apart from the most general – few factors predispose someone to be an entrepreneur.

Anyone prepared to work hard enough – and to learn and adapt as they go – can take a good idea and successfully turn it into a need-satisfying product or service – a proposition of value.

What entrepreneurs themselves have to say

Eugene Pienaar (2013) interviewed ten entrepreneurs who have achieved exceptional financial success in more than one business. They were asked to relay their life story with emphasis on their entrepreneurial endeavours. Key questions were asked focusing on what created and drove their success.[41]

The ten entrepreneurs were:

Name	Short business biography
Nick Ferguson	Nick Ferguson is the co-owner of the award-winning Daddy Hotel Group. Nick and his partner are the creators of the Old Biscuit Mill and Woodstock Exchange. In both cases they turned old run-down buildings into theme-based, lifestyle-driven working environments. He is the co-founder of the online retailer and group buying site Daddy's Deals and co-owner of Long Range Systems SA, providing pager solutions to a variety of businesses including restaurants, hospitals, churches, entertainment venues. It is best known for its paging devices that are found in Kauai food outlets to notify customers when collections are ready.
Dale Kushner	Dale started his entrepreneurial career as a clothing distributer in the United States while still a student. He founded AFS productions in 1996 in Los Angeles and has since relocated the Head Office to Cape Town. The company produces films, stills and commercials for the international market, especially for those wanting to shoot within Africa.
Vinny Lingham	Vinny is an Internet entrepreneur who has created various businesses worth tens of millions of rand. In 2003 he founded incuBeta, an investment holding company that engages in the ownership, management and support of online marketing companies in various stages of development, with offices in the United States, the United Kingdom and Cape Town. In 2003, Lingham founded Clicks2Customers, a subsidiary of incuBeta that provides search engine marketing software and services. He is also co-founder of the Silicon Cape Initiative, a South African-based organisation that aims to turn the Western Cape into a high-tech start-up hub. Vinny's latest business is called Gyft, which is a digital gift card platform that enables users to buy, store, send and redeem their gift cards conveniently from their mobile devices.
Greg Anderson	Greg is the founder of CFS-Europe, a technology company that developed their own proprietary hardware and software that captures customer and patient feedback at the point of service. CFS-Europe holds a 65 per cent market share in the national healthcare service in the United Kingdom. He is also the founder of Uvuko Solar, a Cape Town-based solar and electrical company specialising in the low-cost housing market within the Western and Eastern Cape, and the founder and CEO of the V&A Market on the Wharf. It houses more than 50 local vendors that include local arts and crafts as well as an array of fresh and organic foods.
Huenu Solsona	Heunu started Adventure Boot Camp (ABC) in September 2005, training 30 women at Kirstenbosch Gardens. The four-week outdoor exercise programme offers fitness instruction, nutritional counselling and motivational training. Today ABC trains approximately 3 500 women in over 100 camps across South Africa. In 2012, Huenu co-founded *The Galileo*, an open-air cinema, with its first venue at Kirstenbosch Gardens and later expanded the concept to other venues.
Malcolm Hall	Malcolm Hall is the President and CEO of Open Box, which was started in 2001. He also started various small entrepreneurial businesses, including an export company taking local arts and crafts to the international market.

Dayne Falkenberg	Dayne and his brother have founded various software companies during the course of their careers. Their current company, Clevva (an expert system which empowers salespeople with information about complex products) has recently received the Industry Award for Best Innovation for 2012.
Daniel Nel	Daniel founded Nebula in 1997 – a leading telecommunications solutions firm.
Christo Davel	Christo, former dentist and hotelier, launched 20twenty online bank in 2001 before any bank in South Africa had such an offering, but after six months 20twenty lost its banking licence when Saambou went into curatorship. Since then he has started 22seven – a financial aggregation service helping people start over with their money: to see new things about it, get to know it better, keep it simpler, and grow it smarter.
Carlos Gomes	Carlos built up De La Rey hardware store, achieving hundreds of millions of rands' worth of turnover before being acquired by Massmart in 2005. Carlos thereafter founded Wellness Warehouse.

Based on the interviews, Eugene Pienaar developed the following framework (Figure 9.6) to explain the entrepreneurial successes of his interviewees. The framework pulls together much of our information so far and adds some useful insights.

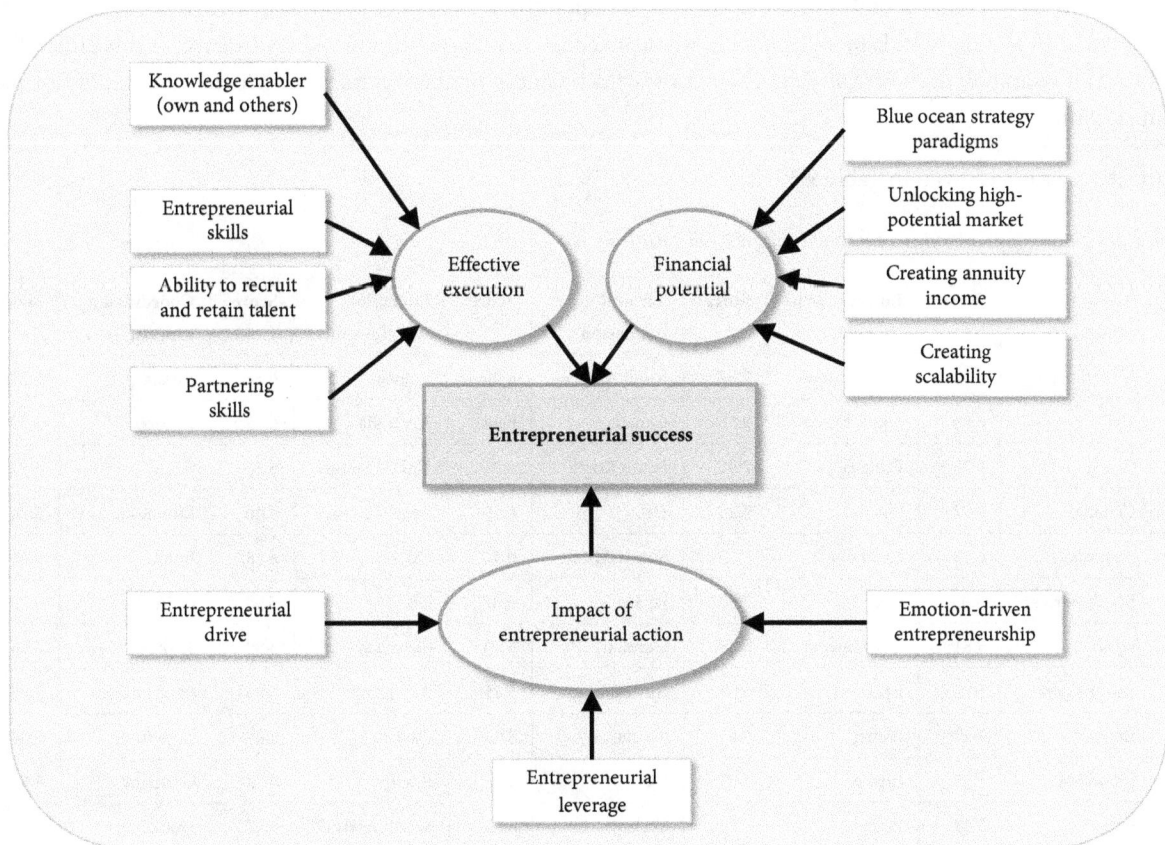

Figure 9.6: Framework for entrepreneurial success (based on Pienaar, 2013)

The following subfactors apply:

- Knowledge enabler: field-specific knowledge, start-up knowledge
- Entrepreneurial skills: ability to sell, leadership skills, innovation skills, ability to develop untapped resources
- Entrepreneurial drive: need for achievement, business-ownership as career choice
- Emotion-driven entrepreneurship: absolute focus on business creation and product/service creation
- Entrepreneurial leverage: limiting downside, risk perception, no Plan B, maintaining momentum, entrepreneurial confidence

THE STATE OF ENTREPRENEURSHIP IN SOUTH AFRICA

The most authoritative, recent research about entrepreneurship has been the publication of the EY G20 Entrepreneurship Barometer 2013.[42] The model is composed of qualitative information (from their survey of more than 1 500 entrepreneurs) and quantitative data based upon entrepreneurial conditions across the G20 economies. For each pillar of entrepreneurship, excluding coordinated support, this information is weighted 50–50 between qualitative and quantitative inputs. For coordinated support, only qualitative survey responses are used.

The advantage of integrating both the survey results and quantitative data is the ability to provide an assessment of the current level and the trends in a G20 entrepreneurial ecosystem based upon local sentiment. To this end, official statistics (for example, the average time taken to start a business or the tax burden) provide a baseline for each member country.

South Africa's rank is given in Table 9.3:

Table 9.3: South Africa's ranking relative to other G20 countries

	Access to funding	Score	Entrepreneur-ship culture	Score	Tax and regulation	Score	Education and training	Score	Coordinated support	Score
1	United States	7.12	United States	7.67	Saudi Arabia	6.40	France	6.58	Russia	6.23
2	UK	6.86	South Korea	7.53	Canada	6.34	Australia	6.53	Mexico	5.89
3	China	6.75	Canada	7.45	South Korea	6.34	United States	6.50	Brazil	5.87
4	Canada	6.62	Japan	7.28	UK	6.19	South Korea	6.40	Indonesia	5.84
5	Australia	6.48	Australia	7.18	**South Africa**	**6.10**	EU	6.25	India	5.76
6	**South Africa**	**5.95**	UK	7.00	Japan	6.07	UK	5.98	China	5.75
7	Japan	5.81	Germany	6.88	Germany	5.84	Germany	5.89	Turkey	5.66
8	South Korea	5.75	EU	6.07	Australia	5.75	Argentina	5.85	**South Africa**	**5.65**
9	Brazil	5.67	France	5.68	Russia	5.65	Canada	5.81	Argentina	5.64
10	Indonesia	5.53	Russia	5.05	EU	5.48	Brazil	5.78	Germany	5.53
11	India	5.48	India	4.95	Turkey	5.45	**South Africa**	**5.67**	France	5.41
12	EU	5.41	Brazil	4.88	Indonesia	5.38	Saudi Arabia	5.66	Saudi Arabia	5.39
13	Saudi Arabia	5.25	Italy	4.67	United States	5.33	Italy	5.47	EU	5.37
14	Germany	5.23	**South Africa**	**4.33**	Mexico	5.21	Russia	5.46	South Korea	5.36

	Access to funding	Score	Entrepreneur-ship culture	Score	Tax and regulation	Score	Education and training	Score	Coordinated support	Score
15	Russia	5.04	Turkey	4.30	France	5.12	Mexico	5.32	Australia	5.31
16	France	4.74	Argentina	4.06	China	5.07	Japan	4.72	Canada	5.29
17	Turkey	4.57	Mexico	3.96	Brazil	4.83	Turkey	4.39	UK	5.19
18	Mexico	4.42	China	3.88	Italy	4.76	China	4.35	Japan	5.04
19	Italy	4.03	Indonesia	3.80	India	4.39	Indonesia	3.88	Italy	4.97
20	Argentina	3.27	Saudi Arabia	3.38	Argentina	4.31	India	3.49	United States	4.85

Access to funding

According to the report, 75 per cent of local entrepreneurs say that access to funding is difficult (although our ranking shows that it is more difficult in many other countries). Also, many believe that funding conditions are deteriorating, in terms of bank lending, angel investors or initial public offerings. More positively, some 69 per cent have seen an improvement in microfinance, while 53 per cent report improvements in government funding. The last two sources are viewed as vital to create more entrepreneurs. Microfinance is particularly ideal for millions of poor, unskilled and unemployed South Africans who, despite their disadvantages, often have the talent to develop successful businesses. Local entrepreneurs point to microfinance as a key funding instrument for the long-term growth of entrepreneurship locally.

Merger and acquisition (M&A) deal activity in South Africa, on the rise through the early 2000s, has slowed since the financial crisis. But South Africa still has a very high rate of M&A investment relative to the national GDP. Worryingly, while figures show that venture capital availability is better than the average for rapid-growth economies, perceptions of those surveyed are considerably worse than average. Therefore, access to funding is an obstacle of our own making.

Overall, South Africa has a highly mature financial sector but, although funds are available, they are not made easily accessible to entrepreneurs. Further, much of the capital is often too expensive, which limits the growth of promising ventures. To counter this, entrepreneurs look to the government. In the opinion of survey participants, public aid and government lending could make the biggest difference in improving the long-term growth of entrepreneurship. Government will need to play a supporting role, to complement the country's financial services sector.

Entrepreneurship culture

The area where South Africa fares worst. The country's performance overall is weighed down by below-average scores on innovation metrics, such as the number of scientific and engineering articles published, spending on research and development (R&D) and the number of researchers in this area. Patent applications, which provide another measure of innovation activity, fell by 24 per cent in South Africa between 2008 and 2011, but have since increased by more than 20 per cent.[43] This still implies that South Africa's research institutions will not produce enough innovations with a commercial application in the near term, undermining prospects for South Africa's innovation-led start-ups.

Despite these weaknesses, 70 per cent of South Africa's entrepreneurs believe their culture encourages entrepreneurship. Possibly a high level of media attention to a few successful entrepreneurs, rather than academic, corporate or institutional strengths, has fuelled this impression. Still, exceptionally high proportions of local entrepreneurs indicated that measures such as promoting their role as job creators and getting more start-up success stories publicised could have a strong impact on cultural perspectives of entrepreneurship.

Some interventions to consider:

Government
- Promote the power and value of entrepreneurship as the engine of economic growth.
- Remove the stigma of failure.
- Create networking opportunities.

Entrepreneurs
- Share your story.
- Help the next generation of entrepreneurs.

Corporations
- Sponsor incubators and accelerators.
- Recognise the contributions and success of entrepreneurs.

Tax and Regulation

South Africa's best position. South Africa has strong start-up and taxation compliance procedures, in contrast to other members of the so-called "BRICS club" of rapid-growth markets. In terms of tax and regulation, the country puts in a good performance against both mature and rapid-growth G20 economies. Although difficulties and bureaucracy remain, it is relatively easy, quick and cheap to start a business, and the time spent on taxes is in line with mature economies, making this a relative strength for the country's entrepreneurial ecosystem. Nevertheless, local entrepreneurs are still keen for greater support in complying with regulations, and 42 per cent point to the need for an agency to assist in this area.

The biggest challenge to emerge after start-up is the cost of firing workers, highlighting the ongoing need for labour-law reform in the country. Out of the 140 countries tracked by the World Economic Forum (WEF) in 2015,[44] South Africa is 107th on **labour market flexibility**. In more detail, South Africa is at 140 (stone last) on **cooperation in labour-employer relations**, 137th on **flexibility of wage determination** and 138th on **hiring and firing practices**.

These are the most worrying features of the South African economy for entrepreneurs. New businesses cannot afford to comply with burdensome labour laws, therefore many businesses will remain small or in the informal sector to avoid them. Regulatory reforms or tax credits could relatively easily help ease hiring terms, especially for the previously unemployed or for young workers, while incentivising firms to hire more freely.

Education and Training

South Africa spends more on education (as a percentage of GDP) than most G20 countries and significantly more than most other rapid-growth economies. However, this funding is not effectively deployed. South Africa's education system is in clear need of reform. According to the WEF, South Africa is 120th out of the 140 countries surveyed on **quality of education**,[45] pointing to serious skills supply problems in the longer term.

Based on the Entrepreneurship Barometer, South Africa has low tertiary education enrolment and a low proportion of the workforce has a degree. This means many more advanced entrepreneurial ventures simply don't have access to the skills they require. In the shorter term more could be done to bolster informal learning and training schemes. Based on the sentiment from the survey, the private sector is helping to pick up the slack, for example through stronger corporate engagement with start-ups – 62 per cent of those polled think access to such schemes has improved in recent years, compared with 36 per cent across the G20 overall.

Coordinated support

South Africa's entrepreneurs report improved access to various support structures, including business incubators, mentor programmes, industry-specific training programmes, entrepreneurial workshops and corporate engagement with start-ups. All this is encouraging, particularly in terms of business incubators, as local entrepreneurs consider them to be the single most important tool for strengthening the future of entrepreneurship in South Africa.

Only a minority of entrepreneurs note improvements in network-related elements of coordinated support, such as clubs, associations, chambers of commerce and small business administration. This is less encouraging.

Among G20 countries, access to educators has dropped most sharply in South Africa, with 30 per cent of respondents reporting a deterioration in the past three years. This contrasts with competing rapid-growth markets that are reporting strong improvement. This again highlights the need for wider educational reform, while suggesting that informal learning and mentorship opportunities will remain vital in the years ahead.

Of the G20, South Africa does seem significantly more enthusiastic about tailored support for female entrepreneurs. As far back as 1998, for example, the government set up the Technology for Women in Business initiative to help empower women within the technology sector.[46] This shows recognition of the value of more targeted entrepreneurial support.

Intrapreneurship

It took Healey Cypher less than a year to realise his company, eBay, was missing out on a huge business opportunity.

While 75% of all consumer purchases happen within 15 miles of someone's home in physical stores, the company only offered e-commerce services for clients. As chief of staff of global product management, he met a lot of retailers, and he knew they would want products for physical retail as well.

With a slight nod from the CEO, he assembled a team of engineers to come up with ways to use tech to enhance physical stores. In their free time (and in addition to their regular jobs), they created an interactive storefront and convinced Toys 'R' Us to install one. Over the next two years they did the same for TOMS, Sony and Rebecca Minkoff. eBay never asked Cypher to do this, but his success became the centrepiece of the company and a new, formal division.[47]

Cypher worked for a start-up before joining eBay and has since left to start his own venture. He could easily have left eBay and introduced the idea outside, but like more and more employees called **intrapreneurs**, he chose to start something new in his existing company – innovating from within.

This is a recent example of entrepreneurship – someone inside an organisation acting entrepreneurially. To recognise, research, resource and implement a valuable proposition is possible everywhere. The only difference is that eBay took the financial risk and now rakes in the financial rewards. The principles in this chapter (and this book) can be applied by anyone spotting a business opportunity and moving to occupy that space.

Increasingly firms, mindful of the money to be made, are encouraging employees to act entrepreneurially. The biggest difference is that your possible backers are also employed by the company and they need convincing that your scheme won't harm the existing brand and that it is compatible with the firm's strategy. Companies (like Nokia) support these activities with company policies that encourage entrepreneurial activity and risk-taking. These policies will cover aspects such as:

- **Ownership rights:** where individuals or groups gain recognition for new opportunity development
- **Profit centres:** where investments are made according to possible income and performance is tracked throughout the lifecycle of the new product/service
- **Entrepreneurial team-building:** to overcome interpersonal barriers and get project teams up and running sooner
- **Systems for settling disputes** and unhealthy rivalry between intrapreneurial groups

In recent years companies such as Deloitte, GFK, Accenture, Ashoka and Barclays have instituted formal programmes to encourage their employees to create new projects and roles. They provide conferences, webinars, even career coaches to teach important skills.

According to Fast Company: "The future belongs to individuals and companies who embrace the entrepreneurial spirit, whether that is inside or outside a company."[48]

Some notable South African entrepreneurs

Such a list would (besides the ones already mentioned) include the following:

Anton Rupert (4 October 1916–18 January 2006): He started his global empire with a personal investment of just £10 in 1941 when he, together with two fellow investors, started manufacturing cigarettes in his garage, which he eventually built into the tobacco and industrial conglomerate Rembrandt Group, overseeing its transition to the industrial and luxury branded goods sectors, with Rembrandt eventually splitting into Remgro (an investment company with financial, mining and industrial interests) and Richemont (a Swiss-based luxury goods group). Richemont merged all their tobacco interests under Rothmans International, which became part of the giant British American Tobacco in 1999, giving the Rupert family a stake of 35 per cent in BAT. Currently, the family's interests are managed by Johann Rupert, himself a serial entrepreneur.

As a young man leaving school in 1948 with no vocational direction, **Renier van Rooyen's** career began with a clerkship in a magistrate's office, then co-ownership of the Bargain Shop in Upington, to the establishment of his first company, Bargain Stores (Pty) Ltd. in 1957. He went on to found Pep Stores as a retail clothing company in 1965 and saw it listed on the Johannesburg Stock Exchange in 1972. Christo Wiese said about him:

"Right at the outset Renier van Rooyen, founder of PEP, who is one of South Africa's great entrepreneurs, said we had to articulate our values, or our philosophy, very clearly so that everybody would know the kind of drumbeat to which we march. We used five words: faith, positive thinking, hard work, enthusiasm and compassion. Faith can mean many things – faith in yourself, faith in your fellow man, faith in a higher being, in your country. Hard work speaks for itself."

Well-known for her string of beauty queen titles, former Miss South Africa and Miss World runner-up **Basetsana Kumalo** (Bassie to her friends) started out by selling sandwiches at local soccer games. During her reign as Miss South Africa in 1990, Bassie became a TV presenter on a popular local show, *Top Billing*. It was then that she quickly turned her fame into fortune by beginning to build her brand. In 1995, she became a joint shareholder of Tweselopele Productions, the production company that housed *Top Billing* and later went on to become JSE-listed, making her one of the youngest black female directors in South Africa. She went from strength to strength when she launched her own clothing, eyewear and cosmetics range that reached over 250 stores in the subSaharan region.

Christo Wiese, in 2016 number 214 on the Forbes top 500 rich list,[49] took up an executive directorship at PEP (which his parents helped found) after practising law. He left to make his fortune in diamond mining, but returned, became the largest individual shareholder and Pepkor's chairman in 1981 and took the company public in 1986. By then Pepkor had taken over Shoprite and he had started investing in industries as diverse as consumer brand distribution, mining, industrial supplies and financial services. Along the way he has also taken positions in the liquor, technology and property sectors.

"I was fortunate in that I grew up in a business home. My father had a farm but he also had a business in town. Eventually my mother had her own business. And so I learned about those things, in a way, almost subconsciously. Today I notice how many people there are that are well educated but simply have no idea as to how a business works. Sitting around the dinner table while things are discussed – you become aware of the very basic principles. You know that the customer is king and you've always got to be ready to render the best possible service. So for me it came very naturally."[50]

Herman Mashaba's academic dream was shattered in 1980 in his second year of a B. Admin at the University of the North when the University was shut down due to political unrest. He found himself a clerical job at Spar and later at Motani Industries. He saved enough to buy a car and started selling products on a commission basis from the boot of his car – including hair products. It took him 19 months to make up his mind to start his own hair care manufacturing business. In February 1985 the first bottle of *Black Like Me* products hit the South African market. In 1997 he sold his business to Colgate Palmolive, but bought it back in 1999 and in 2001 launched it in the UK. To date he has invested in various sectors: mining, construction, exhibitions, real estate, security, aviation and information technology, and in 2005 sold 49.9 per cent of *Black Like Me* to Amka Products. He will stand as mayor of Johannesburg in the 2016 elections for the Democratic Alliance.

In 1993 **Ronnie Apteker** co-founded Internet Solutions, South Africa's first Internet service provider (ISP). With thousands of employees, it became one of the country's most successful post-apartheid businesses, winning numerous technology awards. Since 2000, Apteker has been one of the leading independent film producers in South Africa.

Cyril Ramaphosa launched the National Union of Mineworkers after completing his articles and joining the legal department of the Council of Unions of South Africa. He started the Shanduka Group, which has interests in the resources sector, energy sector, real estate, banking, insurance and telecoms. He is also known for the role he played during the negotiations to bring a peaceful end to apartheid and for steering the country to its first democratic elections in 1994. In early 2011 Ramaphosa took over the McDonald's franchise in South Africa and is currently the deputy president of South Africa.

Elon Musk developed an interest in computing with the Commodore VIC-20. He taught himself computer programming and at age 12, sold the code for a BASIC-based video game he created called *Blastar* to a magazine called *PC and Office Technology* for approximately $500. After finishing school at Pretoria Boys' High, he went to live with his mother in 1989 and went to university in Canada and the University of Pennsylvania and finished his PhD at Stanford. In 1995 Elon and his brother started Zip2 (with a loan from their father) which developed and marketed an Internet "city guide" for the newspaper publishing industry. When he sold the application to Compaq, his share of the sale came to $22 million. He used this money to co-found X-com, which eventually developed and sold PayPal. His share was $165 million. He used this money to become involved in Solar City (hiring out solar systems for less than your current electricity bill), Tesla (developing electric cars and a support system to keep them on the road) and SpaceX (which is sending reusable rockets to the international space station, with plans to conquer space through affordable space flight).

Ludwick Marishane started businesses as a teenager in Limpopo. Many failed, like his own brand of biodiesel, healthy cigarettes and a security magazine. In 2009, he started HeadBoy Industries, a business that designs and commercialises new products and services in South Africa. He is South Africa's youngest patent-holder after having invented DryBath – the world's first bath-substitute solution, which he presented at a TED Conference in Johannesburg in 2012.

Colin Thornton dropped out of a degree in computer science at the University of the Witwatersrand, and began raising funds for what is now the million-dollar computer repair company, Dial a Nerd. Colin founded Dial a Nerd in 1998 at the age of 19. His first computer repair room was in the garage of his parents' home and clients were close friends and family. By focusing on home users and offering a high level of service, he occupied a niche, which helped Dial a Nerd grow into the business it is today. His company has a presence in most major South African cities, with five branches and over 70 staff members countrywide. It has over 40 000 customers consisting of home-based computer users and small to medium-sized businesses.

Patrice Motsepe is a South African magnate who is the founder and executive chairperson of African Rainbow Minerals. Motsepe first became a lawyer specialising in business and mining law. He soon founded a mining services venture to clean gold dust from inside mine shafts, implementing a system of worker remuneration that combined a low base salary with a profit-sharing bonus. Forbes listed him at no. 1577 on their rich list in 2016, worth $1.48 Billion.

In 2009, **Vuyokazi Ngalo** began designing and sewing her own clothes in her spare time. Two years later she started her own business, but her monthly revenue was seldom more than R1 000. Today, with the help of the Awethu Project, she has hired her first full-time employee and is generating revenue of about R20 000 per month. Vuyokazi's progress is set to continue, with her designs showcased at the 2013 International Fashion Sale at the Gallagher Conference Centre. She has also secured financing from the Small Enterprise Finance Agency (SEFA) to assist with a new marketing campaign for her business, Wonga Designs. She now employs six people – who often work through the night to make deadlines.

Lise Butler and **Amanda Haupt** registered DT Designs (trading as Design Team) in 2002, after showing their first ideas at Decorex 2000. They are a textile design business focusing on the design, print and conversion of South African-inspired textiles. Contemporary, topical designs form the basis of their fabric collections, rather than the already well-represented ethnic approach. Emphasis is placed on quality and uniqueness of design, keeping in touch with global trends and design styles.[51] They currently employ around 60 people, many of them starting as unskilled labourers in the factory.

This list can go on and on, but these entrepreneurs are enough to demonstrate that entrepreneurship is alive and well in South Africa.

CONCLUSION

In this chapter we looked at entrepreneurial thinking and strategy practices. Our case studies (Lily O'Brien's Chocolates and the South African Institute of Entrepreneurship) guided us through the process of trying to understand entrepreneurship. Along the way we discovered that there are no secret personality traits or business recipes behind successful entrepreneurs. There are maybe two aspects that consistently distinguish successful entrepreneurs from unsuccessful ones (of which there are many more). Both of these aspects have been highlighted by Mary Ann O'Brien:

- The founder's ego often destroys a good business. Successful entrepreneurs are passionate, charming, likeable people, many with an excellent sense of humour. They all have a drive to succeed but never at the cost of their stakeholders.
- Founders are not lazy. Successful entrepreneurs work harder than anyone in their enterprises. Their strategy is to be enterprising and energetic, even (often especially) when things are not going well. Their optimism makes them "good to be around".

Our Figure 9.5 (based on Pienaar's 2013 research) is as good a summary as any to explain what makes entrepreneurs successful.

After looking at the state of entrepreneurship in South Africa, we ended with a short list of some notable South African entrepreneurs. This list is not meant to be exhaustive, or even to list the most important entrepreneurs. They are merely examples of what can be achieved by ordinary people – people like you and me.

There are, of course, entrepreneurs that will not appear on any list such as this – people who saw and exploited a business opportunity, like the drug dealer in your suburb, the illicit trade in alcohol and cigarettes, chop-shops that reassemble stolen cars, buyers and sellers of stolen goods, government officials who accept bribes to "grease the wheels of bureaucracy", international people-smuggling cartels – a whole economy of shady and criminal dealings. From time to time, even the affairs of fêted business leaders show them up to be crooks. The most dramatic example might be Bernie Madoff, the convicted conman who ran a $64 billion Ponzi scheme since the early 1990s and was only arrested after he confessed to his sons. He recently said that his victims "had themselves to blame".[52]

437

What makes the difference? As we said in chapter 1 of this book:

> The core departure point we take is that all human beings, which include business and organisation leaders, inherently have the capacity and potential to do both good and evil. If we however continue to project organisations as characterised only by cut-throat competition, greed and selfishness, we end up feeding a corruptible monster. On the other hand, if we focus on the bright side of organisations, we "aim to increase the possibilities that organisational virtuousness will be self-fulfilling".[53]

In this paradigm both business and their leaders serve as forces for good.

CHAPTER 1 ENDNOTES

1. Strategic Leadership Institute. (n.d.). Leadership Quotes. [Online] Available: http://www.strategicleadershipinstitute.net/articles/leadership-quotes/ [Accessed 21 November 2015].
2. Ibid.
3. Rosenzwigh, P. 2007. *The halo effect: ... and the eight other business delusions that deceive managers.* New York: Free Press, p. 156.
4. For a detailed description on strategy analysis and synthesis see Ungerer, M., Ungerer, G.D. and Heroldt, J. 2016. *Crystallising the strategic business landscape: Strategy analysis practices and tools for business leaders and strategy practitioners.* Randburg: Knowres Publishing.
5. Rumelt, R.P. 2011. *Good strategy. Bad strategy: The difference and why it matters.* New York: Krown Business, p. 5.
6. Rosenzwigh, 2007.
7. Collins, J. 2001. *Good to great: Why some companies make the leap and others don't.* New York: Random House.
8. Lawrence, K. 2013. Developing leaders in a VUCA environment. [Online]. Available: http://www.kenan-flagler.unc.edu/executive-development/about/~/media/Files/documents/executive-development/developing-leaders-in-a-vuca-environment.pdf [Accessed 3 November 2015].
9. Sullivan, J. 2012. VUCA: the new normal for talent management and workforce planning. [Online]. Available: http://www.eremedia.com/ere/vuca-the-new-normal-for-talent-management-and-workforce-planning/ [Accessed 3 November 2015].
10. Lawrence, 2013.
11. Ibid.
12. Horney, N., Pasmore, B. & O'Shea, T. 2010. Leadership agility: A business imperative for a VUCA world. *People & Strategy,* 33:4.
13. Lawrence, 2013.
14. When asked by Forbes contributor Avi Dan why they changed their business model, Keith Weed, chief marketing and communication officer for Unilever, gave the response as in the text. From Lawrence, ibid.
15. Lawrence, 2013.
16. Sullivan, 2012.
17. Impact International 2012. Vuca: Volatility, Uncertainty, Complexity, Ambiguity. Internal discussion document.
18. Ibid.
19. Ibid.
20. Ibid.
21. Horney, Pasmore & O'Shea, 2010. 33(4):32–38.
22. Williams, T., Worsley, T.W., & Lawler III, E.E. 2013. The agility factor. *Strategy+business,* April.
23. See http://www.impactinternational.com/blog/2012/01/leadership-vuca-world [Accessed 4 November 2015].
24. Lawrence, 2013. p. 5.
25. Vedanta Limited. 2010. 'Focused on delivery longterm value people a sustainable future'. *Vedanta Resources Annual Report 2010.* [Online]. Available: http://www.vedantaresources.com/media/11705/vedantaar2010.pdf [Accessed 4 July 2015].
26. Vedanta Limited. 2010. 'Vision & Values'. [Online]. Available: http://ar2010.vedantaresources.com/overview/glance.html [Accessed 4 July 2015].
27. Woodman, J. 2014. 'India's rejection of Vedanta's bauxite mine is a victory for tribal rights'. *The Guardian.* [Online]. Available: http://www.theguardian.com/global-development/poverty-matters/2014/jan/14/india-rejection-vedanta-mine-victory-tribal-rights [Accessed 4 November 2015].
28. Eccles, R. G., & Nohria, N. 1992. *Beyond the hype: Rediscovering the essence of management.* Boston: Harvard Business School Press, p. 29.
29. Rego, A., Cunha, M.P.E. & Clegg, S. 2012. *The virtues of leadership.* Oxford: Oxford University Press, p. 19.
30. Ferraro, F., Pfeffer, J. & Sutton, R.I. 2005. Economic language and assumptions: How theories can become self-fulfilling. *Academy of Management Review,* 30(8):8–24.
31. Ghosal, S. 2005. Bad management theories are destroying good management practices. *Academy of Management Learning and Education,* 4(1):75–91.
32. Rego et al, p. 20.
33. Zander, R.S. & Zander, B. 2002. *The art of possibility.* New York: Penguin Books, p. 61 and 63.
34. Gore, A. 2009. Discovery Invest Leadership Summit, Sandton, Johannesburg, 22 July. [Online]. Available: http://www.bizcommunity.com/Article/196/40/38201.html [Accessed 16 November 2015].
35. Drucker, P.F. 1999. *Management challenges for the 21st century.* London: HarperCollins, p. 43.
36. Zander & Zander, 2002, p. 108.
37. Ibid, p. 101.
38. Kahneman, D. 2011. *Thinking fast and slow.* New York: Macmillan.
39. Petersen, C. 2000. The future of optimism. *American Psychologist,* 55: 44–55.
40. Cameron, K. 2008. *Positive Leadership: Strategies for extraordinary performance.* San Francisco, CA: Berrett Koehler.
41. Kahane, A. 2010. *Power & love: Solving tough social and organisational problems.* Cape Town: Tafelberg.
42. Rego et al, pp. 23–24.
43. Chia, R.C.H. and Holt, R. 2011. *Strategy without design.* Cambridge: Cambridge University Press.
44. Novak, M. A. 2012. Why we help. *Scientific American,* July, 30 (1):20–25.
45. Ibid.
46. Gosling, J. & Mintzberg, H. 2003. The five minds of a manager. *Harvard Business Review,* November:1–9. Reprint version.
47. Diamandis, P.H. & Kotler, S. 2012. *Abundance: The future is better than you think.* New York: Free Press.
48. Ibid.

49. Spreitzer, G. M. & Sonenshein, S. 2003. *Positive deviance and extraordinary organising*, p. 209. In Cameron, K.S., Dutton, J.E. & Quinn, R.E. (Eds.), *Positive organisational scholarship*. San Francisco,CA: Berrett Koehler.

50. Cameron, K.S. 2003. Organisational virtuousness and performance, p. 53. In Cameron, Dutton & Quinn, 2003.

51. Jaworski, J. 1996. *Synchronicity: The inner path of leadership*. San Francisco, CA: Berrett Koehler.

52. Drucker, P.F. 1993. *The post-capitalist society*. London: Routledge, p. 1.

53. Nel, C. & Beudeker, N. 2009. *(R)evolution: How to create a high-performance organisation*. Cape Town: Village of Leaders Products, p. 23.

54. Ibid.

55. This view is reflected in a presentation by Christo Nel with the title (R)evolution: Creating the high-performance organisation, USB Leader's Angle, 2009.

56. Hamel, G. 2012. *What matters now*. San Francisco: Jossey-Bass, pp. 30–31.

57. Ioannou, I. & Hancock, H. 2013. Changing the world. *Business Strategy Review*, London Business School, Special Edition, p. 6.

58. Drucker, 1999, p. 135.

59. Nel & Beudeker, 2009, p. 21.

60. Ibid, p. 23.

61. Rego et al, p. 24.

62. Kanter, R.M. 2008. The corporate conduct continuum: From "do no harm" to "do lots of good", in C.C. Manz, K.S. Cameron, K.P. Manz & R.D. Marx (Eds.), *The virtuous organisation: Insights from some of the world's leading management thinkers* Singapore: World Scientific, pp. 279–286.

63. This insight is based on Roedinger, B. 2012. Self-reflective report on business in India. July, USB, Unpublished.

64. Collins, J. & Hansen, M.T. 2011. *Great by choice*. London: Random House, pp. 190–191.

65. Ibid. Also see Ungerer et al, 2016, Chapter 1 for more strategy-related paradoxes.

66. De Wit, B. & Meyer, R. 2014. *Strategy: An international perspective*. Hampshire: Cengage Learning, 5th ed, p. 71.

67. Mintzberg, H. 1987. The strategy concept I: Five Ps for strategy. *California Management Review*, 30(1):11–24.

68. Mintzberg, H., Ahlstrand, B., & Lampel, J. 2009. *Strategy Safari*. Edinburgh Gate: Prentice Hall, pp. 16–17.

69. For a more expanded description on thinking about strategy also see Ungerer et al, 2016, chapter 1.

70. Mintzberg, 1987.

71. Mintzberg, H. 1994. Rethinking strategic planning Part I: Pitfalls and fallacies. *Long Range Planning*, 27(3):12–21.

72. Montgomery, C.A. 2012. *The strategist*. London: HarperCollins, p. 72.

73. Porter, M.E. 1996. What is strategy? *Harvard Business Review*, 74 (6): 61–78.

74. Ibid.

75. See Porter, 1996; also Porter, M. & Kramer, M. 2011. Creating shared value. *Harvard Business Review*, Issue HBR Reprint R1101C, 1–17.

76. Sisodia, R.S. 2013. Understanding the performance drivers of conscious firms. *California Management Review*, (55)3:87–96.

77. Ibid, p. 89.

78. Drucker, P.F. 1986. *Management: Tasks, responsibilities, practices*. New York: Truman Talley Books, pp. 90–92.

79. Porter, 1996.

80. Ibid, p. 64.

81. Gaiam Life. 2015. 'Stream of Consciousness. Ray Anderson'. http://blog.gaiam.com/quotes/authors/ray-anderson [Accessed 4 November 2015].

82. Adapted from Mintzberg et al, 2009, p. 12.

83. Montgomery, 2012, p. 6.

84. Montgomery, 2012, p. 103.

85. Rumelt, R.P. 2011. *Good strategy. Bad strategy: The difference and why it matters*. New York: Krown Business, p. 4.

86. Stalk, G. 2004. Playing hardball: Why strategies still matter. *Ivey Business Journal*, (69)2–8.

87. Ungerer, G.D. 2015. A competitive strategy framework for e-business start-ups. Unpublished PhD dissertation, University of Stellenbosch.

88. Rosenzwigh, 2007, pp. 145–148.

89. Whittington, R. 2012. Conference presentation. Strategic Management Society, 32nd Annual International Conference, Prague, Czech Republic.

90. Whittington, 2012.

91. Hamel, G. 1996. Strategy as revolution. *Harvard Business Review*, July–August: 78.

92. Ibid, p. 71.

93. Mintzberg, 2007.

94. For a detailed description on strategy analysis and synthesis, see Ungerer et al, 2016.

95. Montgomery, 2012, p. 110.

96. Hamel, 1996, 81.

97. Ibid.

98. Mintzberg, H. 1987. The strategy concept II: Another look at why organisations need strategies. *California Management Review*, Fall:25–31.

99. These results are from an unpublished working paper by M. Ungerer: An exploratory study on the views of internal actors' interpretation of strategy practices: Emerging trends based on a multi-case study of Southern African companies. University of Stellenbosch Business School. The eight case studies are:

    1. Esterhuyse, D. 2013. Strategy-as-Practice Perspective: A case study of a professional services provider in a regional industry context. MBA research report. South Africa: University of Stellenbosch.

    2. Geises, M.M. 2013. How we do it: Strategy-as-practice in Old Mutual Namibia. MBA research report. South Africa: University of Stellenbosch.

3. Jacobs, J. 2013. Strategy-as-practice perspective: A case study of a business unit in the mining industry. MBA research report. South Africa: University of Stellenbosch.

4. Jansen van Vuuren, M. 2011. A strategy-as-practice perspective: A case study of a business unit in a print media organisation. MBA research report. South Africa: University of Stellenbosch.

5. Maharaj, T. 2013. Strategy-as-practice perspective: A case study of a company in the financial services industry. MBA research report. South Africa: University of Stellenbosch.

6. Mingeli, B. 2012. Exploratory research on strategy-as-practice at Namibia Power Corporation. MBA research report. South Africa: University of Stellenbosch.

7. Myburgh-van Reenen, G.M. 2012. Strategy-as-practice: A case study of a South African fruit export company. MBA research report. South Africa: University of Stellenbosch.

8. Simelane, S.N. 2013. Strategy-as-practice: A case study of a company in the sugar and renewable energy industry in Swaziland. MBA research report. South Africa: University of Stellenbosch.

100. Hendry, J. & Seidl, D. 2003. The structure and significance of strategic episodes: Social systems theory and the routine practices of strategic change. *Journal of Management Studies*, 40(1):175–196.

101. Mintzberg,, H. 2009. *Management*. San Francisco, CA: Berret Koehler.

102. Ibid, p. 8.

103. Montgomery, 2012, p. 133.

104. Mintzberg, 2009, pp. 9 & 66.

105. Mackey, A. 2008. The effect of CEOs on firm performance. *Strategic Management Journal*, 29: 1357–367.

106. Montgomery, 2012, p. 77.

107. Based on the conceptual idea of Volberda, H.W., Morgan, R.E., Reinmoeler, P., Hitt, M.A., Ireland, R.D. & Hoskisson, R.E. 2011. *Strategic management: Competitiveness and globalisation*. Andover: Cengage, p. 402.

108. This definition is partly based on a description in Ireland, R.D., Hoskisson, R.E. & Hitt, M.A. 2011. *The management of strategy concepts*. 9th ed. London: Cengage, p .308.

109. Management and Business Studies Portal. Henry Mintzberg. [Online]. Available: http://www.mbsportal.bl.uk/taster/subjareas/busmanhist/mgmtthinkers/mintzberg.aspx [Accessed: 30 July 2012]; and Mintzberg, H. 1973. *The nature of managerial work*. New York: Harper & Row, p. 59.

110. Mintzberg, 2009, pp. 48–91.

111. Ibid, pp. 89–90.

112. Based on Hoskisson, R.E., Hitt, M.A. and Ireland, R.D. 2008. *Business Strategy Theory*. Hampshire: Cengage Learning.

113. Watkins, M.D. 2012. How managers become leaders: The seven seismic shifts of perspective and responsibility. *Harvard Business Review*, June: 65–72.

114. Ibid, pp. 6-67.

115. Porter, M.E., Lorsch, J.W. & Nohria, N. 2004. Seven surprises for new CEOs. *Harvard Business Review*, October:1–10, Reprint.

116. Bottger, P.C. & Barsoux, J. 2009. What new general managers must learn and forget in order to succeed, *Strategy & Leadership*, 37(6):25–32.

117. Finkelstein, S. 2004. The seven habits of spectacularly unsuccessful executives. *Ivey Business Journal*. (68)3, Jan/Feb: 1–6.

118. Montgomery, 2012, p. 134.

119. Drucker, P.F. 2005. Managing oneself. *Harvard Business Review*, January: 100–109.

120. Based on article by Drucker, 2005.

121. Mintzberg, 2009, p. 91.

122. Hamel, G. & Prahalad, C.K. 1990. The core competence of the corporation. *Harvard Business Review*, May–June, 1–15.

123. Ungerer, M., Pretorius, M. & Herholdt, J. 2011. *Viable business strategies: A fieldbook for leaders*. 3rd updated ed. Johannesburg: Knowres Publishing, p. 141.

124. Hamel, G., & Prahalad, C.K. 1989. Strategic intent. *Harvard Business Review* (May/June): 63–76.

125. For a detailed description see chapters 2–5 in: Ungerer et al, 2016, chapters 2–5.

126. Buckingham, M. 2012. Leadership development in the age of the algorithm. *Harvard Business Review*, June, 86–94.

127. Rego et al, 2012, p. 183.

128. Some parts of the view reflected here are based on a book chapter by M Ungerer with the title *Virtuous Leadership*, in Velddsman, T. & Johnson, A. *The Leadership Handbook*, to be published in 2016.

129. Bass, B.M., Waldman, D.A., Avolio, B.J. & Bebb, M. 1987. Transformational leadership and the falling dominoes effect. *Group and Organisation Studies*, 12(1):73–87. Also see Pearce, C.L. & Sims, H.P. Jr. 2002. Vertical versus shared leadership as predictors of the effectiveness of change management teams: An examination of aversive, directive, transactional, transformational, and empowering leader behaviors. *Group Dynamics: Theory, Research, and Practice*, 6(2):172–197.

130. Brenner, S.N. & Molander, E.A. 1977. Is ethics of business changing? *Harvard Business Review*, 55(1):57–71.

131. Wang, D. & Hackett, R.D. 2015. Conceptualisation and measurement of virtuous leadership: Doing well by doing good. *Journal of Business Ethics*, DOI 10.1007/s10551-015-2560-18 February. [Online]. Available: http://link.springer.com/article/10.1007%2Fs10551-015-2560-1#/page-1 [Accessed 3 November 2015].

132. Cameron, K. 2011. Responsible leadership as virtuous leadership. *Journal of Business Ethics*, 98(1):25–35.

133. Stanford Encyclopedia of Philosophy. 2014. Virtue Ethics. [Online] Available: http://plato.stanford.edu/entries/ethics-virtue/ [Accessed 26 November 2015].

134. Flynn, G. 2008. The virtuous manager: A vision for leadership. *Journal of Business Ethics*, 78(3):359–372.

135. De Araújoa, M.S.G. & Lopes, P.M.P.R. 2014. Virtuous leadership, organisational commitment and individual performance. *TÉKHNE – Review of Applied Management Studies*, 12(1):3–10.

136. Flynn, G. 2008. The virtuous manager: A vision for leadership. *Journal of Business Ethics*, 78(3):359–372. Also see Cameron, 2011, 25–35.

137. Rego et al, 2012, pp. 25–26.

138. Ibid, p. 28.

139. Wang & Hackett, 2015.

140. Cameron, 2011, pp. 25–35.

141. Pearce, G.L., Waldman, D.A. & Csikszentmihaly, M. 2006. Virtuous leadership: A theoretical model and research agenda. *Journal of Management, Spirituality & Religion*, 3(1–2):60–77, DOI: 10.1080/14766080609518611.

142. Hackett, R.D. & Wang, Q. 2012. Virtues and leadership: An integrating conceptual framework founded in Aristotelian and Confucian perspectives on virtues. *Management Decision*, 50(5), 868–899.

143. Wang & Hackett, 2015.

144. Kelley, H.H. 1972. Attribution in social interaction. In E. Jones, D. Kanouse, H. Kelley, N. Nisbett, S. Valins & B. Weiner (Eds), *In attribution: Perceiving the causes of behavior*. Morristown, NJ: General Learning Press.

145. Wang & Hackett, 2015.

146. Ibid.

147. Ibid.

148. Peterson, C. & Seligman, M. 2004. *Character strengths and virtues: A handbook and classification*. New York: Oxford Press.

149. Ungerer, M., Herholdt, J. & Le Roux, J. 2013. *Leadership for all: Virtue practices to flourish*. Randburg: Knowres Publishing.

150. De Vries, M.K. 2001. *The leadership mystique: A user's manual for the human enterprise*. London: Prentice-Hall, p. 219.

151. Peterson, C. & Seligman, M. 2004. *Character strengths and virtues: A handbook and classification*. New York: Oxford Press.

152. Via Institute on Character. 2016. 'VIA Classification of Character Strengths' [Online]. Available: http://www.viacharacter.org/www/Character-Strengths/VIA-Classification [Accessed 5 July 2015].

153. Wang & Hackett, 2015.

154. Ungerer et al, 2013.

155. Wang & Hackett, 2015.

156. The view is reflected in a TED video by Barry Schwartz, 2009.

157. Thompson Jnr, A.A., Strickland lll, A.J. & Gamble, J.E. 2010. *Crafting and executing strategy: Text and readings*, 17th ed. Berkshire: McGraw-Hill, p. 290.

158. Rego et al, 2012, p. 93.

159. Thompson et al, 2010, p. 298.

160. Ibid, p. 299–303.

161. Ibid, p. 304.

162. Volberda et al, 2011, p. 419.

163. Rossouw, G.J. & Van Vuuren, L.J. 2003. Modes of managing morality: A descriptive model of strategies for managing ethics. *Journal of Business Ethics,* 46(4): 392–393. Also based on Thompson et al, 2010, p. 308.

164. Rossouw & Van Vuuren, 2003. Also based on Thompson et al, 2010, p. 308.

165. Rego et al, 2012, p. 183.

166. Ibid.

167. Drucker, P. 2004. What makes an effective executive? *Harvard Business Review,* 82(6):58–63.

168. Information for this part of the case is available from: http://www.biography.com/people/howard-schultz-21166227#birth-of-the-modern-starbucks [Accessed 7 December 2015].

169. Information for this part of the case comes from Ignatius, 2010.

170. Ibid.

171. Starbucks Company Profile. 2015. Starbucks. [Online]. Available: http://www.starbucks.com/about-us/company-information/mission-statement [Accessed 7 December 2015].

172. Starbucks. 2014. 'What is the Role and Responsibility of a For-Profit Public Company?' [Online]. Available: http://www.starbucks.com/responsibility/global-report [Accessed 7 December 2015].

173. Starbucks. 2016. 'Environment: Pioneering Sustainable Solutions' [Online]. Available: http://www.starbucks.com/responsibility/environment [Accessed 7 December 2015].

174. Starbucks. 2016. 'Working at Starbucks' [Online]. Available: http://www.starbucks.com/careers/working-at-starbucks [Accessed 7 December 2015].

CHAPTER 2 ENDNOTES

1. Google. 'Quotes on strategic choices. [Online]. Available: https://www.google.co.za/search?q=quotes+on+strategic+choices&espv=2&biw=1920&bih=979&tbm=isch&imgil=O0mGN9FAhZHorM%253A%253BxA2_GscK1a9osM%253Bhttp%25253A%25252F%25252Fquotesgram.com%25252Fmichael-porter- [Accessed 6 January 2016].

2. Ibid.

3. For a detailed description on strategy analysis and synthesis see Ungerer, Ungerer & Herholdt, 2016. *Crystallising the strategic business landscape: Strategy analysis practices and tools for business leaders and strategy practitioners*. Randburg: Knowres Publishing.

4. Gallup. 'The Competitive Advantage of Aligning Purpose, Brand and Culture: Organizational Identity'. www.gallup.com/services/170918/organizational-identity.aspx [Accessed 8 January 2016].

5.   Senge, P. 1990. *The fifth discipline – the art and practice of the learning organisation.* London: Random House.
6.   Henry, A.E. 2011. *Understanding strategic management.* New York: Oxford Press, p. 8.
7.   Fritz, R. 1989. *The path of least resistance: Learning to become the creative force in your own life.* New York: Fawcett Columbine.
8.   Ungerer, M., Pretorius, M & Herholdt, J. 2011. *Viable business strategies.* Randburg: Knowres Publishing.
9.   Lipton, M. 2004. Walking the talk (really!): Why visions fail. *Ivey Business Journal,* 68 (3): 358–364.
10. Kotter, J.P. 1996. *Leading change.* Boston: Harvard Business Press, p. 72.
11. Boardman, T. 2006. Nedbank Annual Report. Nedbank Group.
12. Volberda, H.W., Morgan, R.E., Reinmoeller, P.R., Hitt, M.A., Ireland, R.D. & Hoskinsson, R.E. 2011. *Strategic management: Competitiveness and globalization.* Hampshire: Cengage, p. 23.
13. This description is based on Ungerer, Pretorius & Herholdt, 2011, pp. 168–173.
14. Louw, L. & Venter, P. (Eds.) 2006. *Strategic management. Winning in the Southern African workplace.* Cape Town: Oxford University Press.
15. Pine, B.J. and Gilmore, J.H. 2008. The eight principles of strategic authenticity. *Strategy & Leadership,* 36(3):35 –40.
16. Gilmore, J.H. & Pine, B.J. 2007. *Authenticity: What consumers really want.* New York: Harvard Business Press, p. 198.
17. Kanter, R.M. 2011. How great companies think differently. *Harvard Business Review,* 89(11): HBR Reprint 1–11.
18. Volberda et al, 2011, pp. 23–25.
19. Ibid, p. 26.
20. Description based on Thompson Jnr, A.A., Strickland lll, A.J. & Gamble, J.E. 2010. *Crafting and executing strategy: Text and readings,* 17th ed. Berkshire: McGraw-Hill, p. 29.
21. Malone, M.S. 2007. *Bill & Dave: How Hewlett and Packard built the world's greatest company.* New York: Penguin.
22. Hamel, G. 2012. *What matters now.* San Francisco, CA: Jossey-Bass, p. 34.
23. Brazzoli, F. 2013. Strategic Management individual assignment as part of MPhil in emerging country leadership. University of Johannesburg. Unpublished.
24. Koorts, C. 2014. Woolworths Holdings Limited: Strategic framework critique. MBA Strategic Management Individual Assignment. University of Stellenbosch Business School. Unpublished.
25. Porter, M.E. 1996. What is strategy? *Harvard Business Review,* 74 (6): 5.
26. Ibid, p. 10.
27. Porter, M.E. 1998. *Competitive advantage: Creating and sustaining superior performance.* New York: Free Press.
28. Porter, M. 1980. *Competitive strategy: Techniques for analyzing industries and competitors.* New York: Free Press, p. 39.
29. Ibid, pp. 35–37.
30. Ungerer, G.D. 2015. *A competitive strategy framework for e-business start-ups.* Stellenbosch: University of Stellenbosch.
31. Ibid, pp. 37–38.
32. Ibid.
33. Ibid.
34. Thompson Jnr et al, 2010, p. 141.
35. Porter, 1996.
36. Ibid, p. 10–11.
37. Ibid, p. 11.
38. Ibid, p. 13–15.
39. Ibid, p. 15–16.
40. Ibid, p. 16–17.
41. Ibid, p. 12.
42. Gonzales-Benito, J. & Suarez-Gonzalez, I. 2011. A study on the role played by manufacturing strategic objectives and capabilities in understanding the relationship between Porter's generic strategies and business performance. *British Journal of Management,* 21(4):1027–1043.
43. Porter, 1996, pp 61–78.
44. These views are based on Thompson Jnr et al, 2010; Volberda et al, 2011; Pearce, J.A. & Robinson, R.B. 2009. *Competitive strategy: Formulation, implementation & control* (11th ed.). New York: McGraw-Hill/Irwin.
45. Beeslaar, M., Fraser, C., Moodley, S., Pienaar, G. & Schoeman, R. 2015. A strategic architecture perspective on ZARA. MBA strategic management group assignment. University of Stellenbosch Business School. Unpublished.
46. Ungerer, 2015.
47. Case study information based on company website. [Online]. Available: http://www.shopriteholdings.co.za/OurBrands/Pages/Group-Composition.aspx [Accessed 14 January 2016].
48. Treacy, M & Wiersema, F. 1993. Customer intimacy and other value disciplines. *Harvard Business Review,* 71(1):84–94.
49. Pearce & Robinson, 2009.
50. The Enterprise Advocate. 2012. 'The Tracey & Wiersema Value Discipline Model – Part 1'. [Online]. Available: http://www.enterprise-advocate.com/2012/02/the-tracey-wiersema-value-discipline-model-part-1/ [Accessed 6 January 2016].
51. Pearce & Robinson, 2009, p. 207.
52. Ungerer, 2015.
53. Ibid.
54. Ibid.
55. Ibid.
56. Hagiu, A. & Wright, J. 2013. Do you really want to be on e-bay? *Harvard Business Review,* 91(3):103–108.
57. Ibid.

58. Ibid.
59. Gummerus, J. 2011. *Customer value in e-service: Conceptual foundation and empirical evidence.* Helsinki: Hanken School of Economics.
60. Porter, M. E. 2001. Strategy and the internet. *Harvard Business Review,* 79(3):62–79.
61. Lee, C.-S. & Vonortas, N.S. 2004. Business model innovation in the digital economy. In G. Doukidis, N. Mylonopoulos, & N. Pouloudi, *Social and economic transformation in the digital era.* Hershey, PA: Idea Group Publishing, pp. 164–181.
62. Tapscott, D., Ticoll, D., & Lowy, A. 2000. *Digital capital: Harnessing the power of business webs.* (1st ed.). Boston: Harvard Business School Press.
63. Rayport, J., & Sviokla, J. 1995. Exploring the virtual value chain. *Harvard Business Review,* 73(6):75–85.
64. Lee & Vonortas, 2004.
65. Hagiu & Wright, 2013.
66. Porter, 2001.
67. Hagiu & Wright, 2013.
68. Baker, W., Marn, M., & Zawada, C. 2001. Price smarter on the net. *Harvard Business Review,* 29(2):122–127.
69. Porter, M.E. 2001. Strategy and the internet. *Harvard Business Review,* 79(3):62–79.
70. Cusumano, M.A. 2013. Technology strategy and management: Evaluating a startup venture. *Communications of the ACM,* 56(10):26–28.
71. Barsh, J., Crawford, B., & Grosso, C. 2000. How e-tailing can rise from the ashes. *McKinsey Quarterly* (3):98–109.
72. Ibid.
73. Lee & Vonortas, 2004.
74. Porter, 2001.
75. Teece, D. (2010). Business models, business strategy and innovation. *Long Range Planning,* 43(2):172–194.
76. Zhou, L., Dai, L., & Zhang, D. (2007). Online shopping acceptance model – A critical survey of consumer factors in online shopping. *Journal of Electronic Commerce Research,* 8(1):41–62.
77. Barsh et al, 2000.
78. Porter, 2001.
79. Barsh et al, 2000.
80. Zhou, Dai & Zhang, 2007.
81. Porter, 2001.
82. Lee & Vonortas, 2004.
83. Ibid.
84. Barsh et al, 2000.
85. Ibid.
86. Zhou et al, 2007.
87. Jones, G.R. 2007. *Amazon.com Case.* Texas: A&M University.
88. Reeves, M., Love, C. & Tillmanns, P. 2012. Your strategy needs a strategy. *Harvard Business Review,* September: 76–83.
89. Ibid.
90. Ibid, p. 78.
91. Ibid, pp. 78–80.
92. Ibid, p. 81.
93. Ibid.
94. Reeves, M., Haanaes, K. & Sinha, J. 2015. *Your strategy needs a strategy.* Boston, MA: Harvard Business Review Press.
95. Reeves et al, 2012.
96. Radder, L. & Louw, L. 1998. The SPACE matrix: A tool for calibrating competition. *Long Range Planning,* 31(4):549–559.
97. Ibid, p. 550.
98. Ibid, p. 551.
99. Ibid.
100. Ibid.
101. Ibid, p. 553.
102. Simister, P. 2011. SPACE Analysis – Strategic Position and Action Evaluation Matrix. [Online]. Available: http://www.differentiateyourbusiness. co.uk/space-analysis-strategic-position-and-action-evaluation-matrix [Accessed 16 January 2016].
103. For more factors per dimension to consider, see Radder et al, 1998.
104. Volberda et al, 2011.
105. Schaan, J. 2008. International strategy elective class interaction. Bellville, Cape Town: University of Stellenbosch Business School (USB). July.
106. Volberda et al, 2011, p. 331.
107. Shankar, S., Ormiston, C., Bock, N. & Shaus, R. 2008. How to win in emerging markets. *MIT Sloan Management Review,* 49(3): 19–23; Raymond, A, Kim J. & Shao, A.T. 2001. Export strategy and performance: A comparison of exports in a developed and an emerging market. *Journal of Global Marketing,* 15(2):5–29.
108. Lin, X. & Wang, C.L. 2008. Enforcement and performance: The role of ownership, legalism and trust in international joint ventures. *Journal of World Business,* 43(3):340–351; Huff, L & Kelly, L. 2003. Levels of organisational trust in individualist versus collectivist societies: A seven-nation study. *Organisation Science,* 14(1): 81–90.
109. Volberda et al, 2011, p. 337.
110. Ibid, p. 336.
111. Ibid, p. 337.

112. Bio-Oil. Products. https://www.bio-oil.com/en/product/introduction [Accessed 23 January 2016].
113. Letschert, J. 2008. *Taking a local brand to the global arena: Lessons from an SA entrepreneur.* USB Leader's Angle, 27 June.
114. Ibid.
115. Ibid.
116. Pearce & Robinson, 2009, pp. 211–236.
117. Ibid, p. 266 (adapted).
118. Christensen, C.M. & Overdorf, M. 2000. Meeting the challenge of disruptive change. *Harvard Business Review,* 78(2):66–76.

CHAPTER 3 ENDNOTES

1. Magretta, J. 2002. Why business models matter. *Harvard Business Review,* 80(5):87, 90.
2. Ungerer, M., Ungerer, G., & Herholdt, J. 2016. *Crystallising the Strategic Business Landscape: Strategy Analysis Practices and Tools for Business Leaders and Strategy Practitioners.* Randburg: Knowres Publishing, pp. 250–256.
3. Mansfield, G.M., & Fourie, L.C. 2004. Strategy and business models – strange bedfellows? A case for convergence and its evolution into strategic architecture. *South African Journal of Business Management,* 35(1):35–44.
4. Magretta, 2002, pp. 86–93.
5. Zott, C., Amit, R., & Massa, L. 2011. The business model: Recent developments and future research. *Journal of Management,* 37(4):1019–1042.
6. Ibid.
7. Mansfield & Fourie, 2004, p. 35–44.
8. Osterwalder, A. 2004. *The business model ontology – A proposition in a design science approach.* Switzerland: University of Lausanne.
9. Ungerer, G.D. 2015. *A competitive strategy framework for e-business start-ups.* Stellenbosch: University of Stellenbosch.
10. Osterwalder, A., & Pigneur, Y. 2009. *Business Model Generation.* Self-published.
11. Ungerer et al, 2016, p. 251.
12. Mansfield & Fourie, p. 35.
13. Ibid, p. 42.
14. Zott, C., & Amit, R. 2008. The fit between product market strategy and business model: Implications for firm performance. *Strategic Management Journal,* 29(1):1.
15. Ungerer 2015, p. 41.
16. Ungerer et al, 2016, p. 247.
17. Teece, D. 2010. Business models, business strategy and innovation. *Long Range Planning,* 43(2):173.
18. Rumelt, R. P. 1998. Evaluating business strategy. In H. Mintzberg, J.B. Quinn, & S. Ghoshal, *The strategy process* (revised ed., pp. 1–11). Prentice Hall Europe, pp. 4–6.
19. Porter, M. 1980. *Competitive strategy: Techniques for analyzing industries and competitors.* New York: Free Press, pp. xxiv, 4.
20. Ungerer, 2015, pp. 65–69.
21. Mansfield & Fourie, 2004, p. 42.
22. Linder, J.C., & Cantrell, S. 2000. *Changing business models: Surveying the landscape.* Cambridge: Accenture Institute for Strategic Change, p. 2.
23. Ungerer, 2015.
24. Ibid, p. 67.
25. Markides, C. 1999. A dynamic view of strategy. *Sloan Management Review,* 40(3):56.
26. Porter, 1980.
27. Ungerer, 2015, p. 248.
28. Ibid, p. 248.
29. Ibid, p. 248.
30. Osterwalder & Pigneur, 2009.
31. Ibid.
32. Ungerer, 2015.
33. Ungerer et al, 2016, pp. 251–257.
34. Osterwalder & Pigneur, 2009.
35. Ibid.
36. Ibid.
37. Ibid.
38. Ibid.
39. Ibid.
40. Ibid, p. 30.
41. Porter, M.E. 2001. Strategy and the internet. *Harvard Business Review,* 79(3):71.
42. Ungerer, 2015. p. 208.
43. Ibid.
44. Osterwalder & Pigneur, 2009, p. 31.
45. Ibid.
46. Ibid.
47. Kim, W., & Mauborgne, R. 2005. *Blue Ocean strategy.* Boston: Harvard Business School Press, p. 135.

48. Osterwalder & Pigneur, 2009, p. 31.
49. *Ryanair's Business Model.* 2011. Air-Scoop: [Online]. Available: http://www.air-scoop.com/pdf/Ryanair-business-model_Air-Scoop_2011.pdf [Accessed 18 April 2013]
50. Hagiu, A., & Wright, J. 2013. Do you really want to be on e-bay? *Harvard Business Review,* 91(3):104.
51. Osterwalder & Pigneur, 2009, pp. 104–05.
52. Ibid, pp. 92–105.
53. Ibid, p. 32.
54. Ibid, pp. 92–105.
55. Kim & Mauborgne, 2005, p. 135.
56. Ungerer, 2015.
57. Ibid.
58. Ibid, p. 295.
59. Osterwalder & Pigneur, 2009. p. 33.
60. Osterwalder, 2004. p. 100.
61. Barney, J.B. 1991. Firm resources and sustained competitive advantage. *Journal of Management,* 17(1):99–120.
62. Thompson, A.A., Strickland, A.J., & Gamble, J.E. 2008. *Crafting & executing strategy: The quest for competitive advantage: concepts and cases* (16th ed.). New York: McGraw-Hill Irwin.
63. Volberda, H.W., Morgan, R.E., Reinmoeller, P., Hitt, M. A., Ireland, R.D., & Hoskisson, R.E. 2011. *Strategic management: Competitiveness and globalisation.* Hampshire: Cengage Learning EMEA.
64. Thompson et al, 2008.
65. Ibid.
66. Weill, P., Malone, T.W., D'Urso, V. ., Herman, G., & Woerner, S. 2005. Do some business models perform better than others? A study of the 1000 largest US firms. *MIT Sloan School of Management,* Working paper 226, pp. 1–39.
67. Osterwalder & Pigneur, 2009.
68. Tilles, S. 1963, Jul/Aug. How to evaluate corporate strategy. *Harvard Business Review*: 115–116.
69. Porter, M. 1996, Nov/Dec. What is strategy? *Harvard Business Review,* 61–78:5.
70. Ibid, p. 5.
71. Ibid, pp. 10–17.
72. Ibid, p. 17.
73. Ibid, p. 16.
74. Osterwalder & Pigneur, 2009.
75. Ibid.
76. Ibid.
77. Ibid.
78. Ibid.
79. Ibid.
80. *Business model canvas.* 2011. Business Model Generation. [Online]. Available: http://www.businessmodelgeneration.com/canvas [Accessed 1 Oct 2012].
81. Maurya, A. 2012. *Running lean* (2nd ed.). Sebastopol: O'Reilly Media.
82. Reis, E., 2011. *The lean startup.* New York: Crown Business.
83. Blank, S. 2013. Why the lean start-up changes everything. *Harvard Business Review,* 91(5):65–72.
84. Maurya, 2012.
85. Ibid, p. 5.
86. Ungerer, 2015.
87. Van der Heijden, K. 2001. Back to basics: Exploring the business idea. *Strategy & Leadership,* 29(3):16.
88. Clarke, K. 2001. What price on loyalty when a brand switch is just a click away? *Qualitative Market Research: An International Journal,* 4(3):161.
89. Reichheld, F., & Schefter, P. 2000. E-loyalty. *Harvard Business Review,* 78(4):106.
90. Anderson, R., & Srinivasan, S. 2003. E-satisfaction and e-loyalty: A contingency framework. *Psychology & Marketing,* 20(2):123.
91. Newell, F. 1997. *The new rules of marketing: How to use one-to-one relationship marketing to be the leader in your industry.* New York: McGraw-Hill.
92. Valvi, A., & Fragkos, K. 2012. Critical review of the e-loyalty literature: A purchase-centred framework. *Electronic Commerce Research,* 12(3):3.
93. Anderson & Srinivasan, 2003, p. 123.
94. Srinivasan, S., Anderson, R., & Ponnavolu, K. 2002. Customer loyalty in e-commerce: An exploration of its antecedents and consequences. *Journal of Retailing,* 78(1):41.
95. Clarke, 2001, p. 161.
96. Reichheld & Schefter, 2000.
97. Srinivasan et al, 2002, p. 41.
98. Clarke, 2001, p. 161.
99. Anderson & Srinivasan, 2003.
100. Clarke, 2001, p. 161.
101. Reichheld & Schefter, 2000, p. 106.
102. Ungerer, 2015.

103. Ibid.
104. Slywotzky, A. 2002. *The art of profitability*. New York: Mercer Management Consulting, p. 108.
105. Slywotzky, A., & Morrison, D. 1997. *The profit zone: How strategic business design will lead you to tomorrow's profits*. New York: Times Books.
106. Ungerer et al, 2011, p. 187.
107. Oliver, C. 1997. Sustainable competitive advantage: Combining institutional and resource-based views. *Strategic Management Journal*, 18(9):704.
108. Ibid, p. 679.
109. Barney, 1991.
110. Hough, J., Thompson Jr, A.A., Strickland III, A.J., & Gamble, J.E. (2011). *Crafting and executing strategy: Creating sustainable high performance in South Africa: Text, readings and cases* (2nd ed.). Berkshire: McGraw-Hill Higher Education, p. 117.
111. Volberda et al, 2011, p. 107.
112. Pearce, J., & Robinson, R. 2011. *Strategic management: Formulation, implementation & control* (12th ed.). McGraw-Hill Higher Education, p. 173.
113. Carlton, D., & Perloff, J. 1994. *Modern industrial organization*. New York: HarperCollins College Publishers, p. 110.
114. Ungerer, 2015. p. 301.
115. Ibid.
116. Lee, C.-S., & Vonortas, N.S. 2004. Business model innovation in the digital economy. In G. Doukidis, N. Mylonopoulos, & N. Pouloudi, *Social and economic transformation in the digital era* (pp. 164–181). Hershey, PA: Idea Group, p. 171.
117. Ungerer et al, p. 188.
118. Lee & Vonortas, 2004, p. 171.
119. Amit, R., & Zott, C. 2001. Value creation in e-business. *Strategic Management Journal*, 22(6–7):493–520.
120. Arthur, W. 1996. Increasing returns and the new world of business. *Harvard Business Review*, 74(4):100.
121. Amit & Zott, 2001, p. 508.
122. Van der Heijden, 2001, p. 16.
123. Ibid.
124. Slywotzky & Morrison, 1997, p. 53.
125. Ungerer et al, 2011, pp. 188, 189.
126. Porter, 1996, pp. 13–15.
127. Ungerer et al, 2011, p. 188.
128. Van der Heijden, 2001, pp. 14, 15.
129. Slywotzky & Morrison, 1997, p. 53.
130. Hess, M., & Ricart, J. 2002. *Managing customer switching costs*. Pamplona: University of Navarra, p. 1.
131. Lee & Vonortas, 2004, pp. 172, 174.
132. Van der Heijden, K. 2001. Back to basics: Exploring the business idea. *Strategy & Leadership*, 29(3):15.
133. Magretta, 2002, p. 91.
134. Ungerer, 2015.
135. Slywotzky & Morrison, 1997, p. 53.
136. Ungerer, 2015.
137. Ibid.
138. Porter, 1980, pp. 10, 11.
139. Slywotzky & Morrison, 1997, p. 53.
140. Kelly, K. 2008, January 31. *Better than free*. The Technium: [Online]. Available: www.kk.org/thetechnium/archives/2008/01/better_than_fre.php [Accessed 16 August 2012].
141. Mansfield & Fourie, 2004, p. 38.
142. Van der Heijden, 2001, p. 14.
143. Porter, 1996, p. 5.
144. Ungerer, 2015.
145. Pearce & Robinson, 2009, pp. 174, 175.
146. Slywotzky & Morrison, 1997, p. 52.
147. Hess & Ricart, 2002, p. 1.
148. Ibid.
149. Kotler, P. 1997. *Marketing managment: Analysis, planning, implementation, and control* (9th ed.). New Jersey: Prentice Hall.
150. Rumelt, R. 1987. Theory, strategy, and entrepreneurship. In D. Teece, *The competitive challenge: Strategies for industrial innovation and renewal*. Cambridge, MA: Ballinger.
151. Porter, 1980.
152. Porter, M. 1985. *Competitive advantage*. New York: The Free Press.
153. Kotler, 1997.
154. Edlin, A., & Harris, R. 2013. The role of switching costs in antitrust analysis: A comparison of Microsoft and Google. *Yale Journal of Law and Technology*, 15:9.
155. Yang, Z., & Peterson, R. 2004, Oct. Customer perceived value, satisfaction, and loyalty: The role of switching costs. *Psychology & Marketing*, 21(10):806.
156. Ungerer, 2015.
157. Ibid, p. 338.
158. Burnham, T.A., Frels, J.K., & Mahajan, V. 2003. Consumer switching costs: A typology, antecedents, and consequences. *Journal of the Academy of Marketing Science*, 31(2):111, 112.

159. Hess & Ricart, 2002, p. 2.
160. Hax, A., & Wilde II, D. 2001. The delta model – discovering new sources of profitability in a networked economy. *European Management Journal,* 19(4):379–391.
161. Lee & Vonortas, 2004, pp. 170, 172.
162. Hess & Ricart, 2002, p. 8.
163. DeVine, J., & Gilson, K. 2001. Using behavioral science to improve the customer experience. *Harvard Business Review,* 79(6):2.
164. Yang & Peterson, 2004, p. 805.
165. Ungerer, 2015.
166. Shapiro, C., & Varian, H. 2009. *Locked in, not locked out.* Mariott School: [Online]. Available: http://marriottschool.net/emp/Bryce/manec387_old/handouts/locked_in.pdf, p. 1. [Accessed 25 Feb 2013].
167. Ibid.
168. Edlin & Harris, 2013, p. 9.
169. Ungerer, 2015.
170. Burnham et al, 2003, pp. 111, 112.
171. Edlin & Harris, 2013, p. 12.
172. Hagel, J.I., & Singer, M. 1999. Unbundling the corporation. *Harvard Business Review,* 77(2):139.
173. Shapiro & Varian, 2009, p. 1.
174. Edlin & Harris, 2013, p. 13.
175. Porter, 1980, p. 120.
176. Coyles, S., & Gokey, T. 2002. Customer retention is not enough. *McKinsey Quarterly* (2):88.
177. Edlin & Harris, 2013, p. 12.
178. Riggins, F.J., & Rhee, H. 1998. Toward a unified view of electronic commerce. *Communications of the ACM,* 41(10):88–95.
179. Edlin & Harris, 2013, p. 14.
180. Porter, 1980, p. 120.
181. Lee & Vonortas, 2004, pp. 170, 172.
182. Ibid.
183. Burnham et al, 2003, pp. 111, 112.
184. Edlin & Harris, 2013, p. 11.
185. Ibid.
186. Shapiro & Varian, 2009, p. 2.
187. Edlin & Harris, 2013.
188. Ibid, pp. 15, 16.
189. Ibid, p. 9.
190. Yang & Peterson, 2004, Oct. p. 806.
191. Ungerer, 2015.
192. Edlin & Harris, 2013, p. 15.
193. Ibid, p. 15.
194. Ibid, p. 12.
195. Hess & Ricart, 2002, p. 8.
196. Srinivasan et al, 2002, p. 42.
197. Yang & Peterson, 2004, Oct. p. 802.
198. Zhou, L., Dai, L., & Zhang, D. 2007. Online shopping acceptance model – a critical survey of consumer factors in online shopping. *Journal of Electronic Commerce Research,* 8(1):55.
199. Yang & Peterson, 2004, p. 802.
200. Gommans, M., Krishnan, K., & Scheffold, K. 2001. From brand loyalty to e-loyalty: A conceptual framework. *Journal of Economic and Social Research,* 3(1):43.
201. Reichheld, F., & Schefter, P. 1996. *The Loyalty Effect.* Boston: Harvard Business School Press.
202. Gommans et al, 2001, p. 43.
203. Reichheld & Schefter, 1996.
204. Yang & Peterson, 2004, Oct. p. 802.
205. Srinivasan et al, 2002, p. 41.
206. Gommans et al, 2001, p. 46.
207. Reichheld & Schefter, 2000, p. 106.
208. Ibid.
209. Ibid.
210. Gommans et al, 2001, p. 8.
211. Ungerer, 2015, p. 303.
212. Arya, S., & Srivastava, S. 2012. Acquiring e-loyalty: Competition is just one click away: a literature review. *International Journal of Research Management, Economics and Commerce,* 2(11):148.
213. Ibid, p. 151.
214. Yang & Peterson, 2004, pp. 802, 803.
215. Valvi & Fragkos, 2012, pp. 33.
216. Anderson & Srinivasan, 2003, pp. 132, 133.

217. Gustafasson, A., Johnson, M., & Roos, I. 2005. The effects of customer satisfaction, relationship commitment dimensions, and triggers on customer retention. *Journal of Marketing, 69*(4):210.
218. Yang & Peterson, 2004, pp. 804, 805.
219. Ibid.
220. Valvi & Fragkos, 2012.pp. 31, 32.
221. Balabanis , G., Reynolds, N., & Simintiras, A. 2006. Bases of e-loyalty: Perceived switching barriers and satisfaction. *Journal of Business Research*, 59(2):221.
222. Oliver, R. 1999. Whence consumer loyalty? *Journal of Marketing*, 63:33.
223. Clarke, 2001, p. 160.
224. Arya & Srivastava, 2012, p. 150.
225. Reichheld & Schefter, 2000, p. 112.
226. Valvi & Fragkos, 2012, p. 31.
227. Ibid.
228. Mascareigne, J. 2009. *Customer retention: Case studies of agencies in the professional service sector*. Lulea: Lulea University of Technology, p. 9.
229. Ibid.
230. Anderson & Srinivasan, 2003, pp. 132, 133.
231. Gommans et al, 2001, p. 47.
232. Reichheld, F., & Schefter, P. 2000. E-Loyalty. *Harvard Business Review, 78*(4):108.
233. Levitt, T. 1981. Marketing intangible products and product intangibles. *Cornell Hotel and Restaurant Administration Quarterly, 22*(2):37–44.
234. Ibid.
235. Gommans et al, 2001, p. 51.
236. Goldstuck, A. 2012, Aug 7. *Joining the E-Party*. Fin24: [Online]. Available: http://www.fin24.com/opinion/columnists/joining-the-e-party-20120807 [Accessed 29 Jan 2013].
237. Gommans et al, 2001, pp. 47, 49.
238. Reichheld & Schefter, 2000, p. 108.
239. Srinivasan et al, 2002, pp. 44, 45.
240. Ibid, pp. 43, 44.
241. Ibid, p. 43.
242. Mascareigne, 2009, p. 65.
243. Levitt, 1981, pp. 37–44.
244. Valvi & Fragkos, 2012, p. 33.
245. Mafé, C., & Navarré, L. 2010. *Segmenting consumers by eshopping behaviour and online purchase intention*. Valencia, Spain: University of Valencia, p. 19.
246. Rohm, A., & Swaminathan, V. 2004. A typology of online shoppers based on shopping motivations. *Journal of Business Research, 57*(7):748–757.
247. Anderson & Srinivasan, 2003, pp. 132, 133.
248. Arya & Srivastava, 2012, p. 150.
249. Reichheld & Schefter, 2000, pp. 107, 110.
250. Balabanis et al, 2006, pp. 221, 222.
251. Gommans et al, 2001, p. 49
252. Reichheld & Schefter, 2000, pp. 105–114.
253. Srinivasan et al, 2002, pp. 44, 45.
254. Wolfinbarger, M., & Gilly, M. 2003. eTailQ: Dimensionalizing, measuring, and predicting etail quality. *Journal of Retailing, 79*(3):197.
255. Srinivasan et al, 2002, p. 44.
256. Vrechopoulos, A., Siomkos, G., & Doukidis, G. 2001. Internet shopping adoption by Greek consumers. *European Journal of Innovation Management, 4*(3):142–152.
257. Amit, R., & Zott, C. 2001. Value creation in e-business. *Strategic Management Journal, 22*(6–7):506.
258. Osterwalder & Pigneur, 2009, p. 23.
259. Lee & Vonortas, p. 170.
260. Srinivasan et al, 2002, p. 42.
261. Hagel, J.I., & Armstrong, A. 1997. *Net gain: expanding markets through virtual communities*. Boston: Harvard Business School Press, p. 7.
262. Mascareigne, 2009, p. ii.
263. Gommans et al, 2001.
264. Wolfinbarger & Gilly, 2003, p. 183.
265. Mascareigne, 2009, p. 21.
266. Gommans et al, 2001, p. 50.
267. Korgaonkar, P., & Wolin, L. 1999, Mar/Apr. A multivariate analysis of web usage. *Journal of Advertising Research, 39*(2):56.
268. Welch, N. 2010. A marketer's guide to behavioral economics. *McKinsey Quarterly, 47*(1):3.
269. Zhou et al, 2007, p. 54.
270. Caruana, A., & Ewing, M. 2010. How corporate reputation, quality, and value influence online loyalty. *Journal of Business Research, 63*(9–10):1104.
271. Reichheld & Schefter, 2000, p. 107.
272. Ibid, p. 110.
273. Poleretzky, K. 1999, Jan. The call center & e-commerce convergence. *Call Center Solutions*(17):76.

274. Carlson, J., Sinnappan, S., & Kriz, A. 2005. *A conceptual framework to manage e-loyalty in business-to-consumer e-commerce.* CiteSeer: [Online]. Available: http://citeseerx.ist.psu.edu/viewdoc/download?doi=10.1.1.194.3202&rep=rep1&type=pdf, p. 2 [Accessed 25 Feb 2013].

275. Zhou et al, 2007, pp. 42, 43.

276. Goldstuck, A. 2012. *Internet matters: The quiet engine of the South African economy.* World Wide Worx: [Online]. Available: http://internetmatters.co.za/report/ZA_internet_Matters.pdf, p. 20 [Accessed 31 July 2012].

277. Valvi & Fragkos, 2012. p. 29.

278. Zhou et al, 2007, pp. 4 2, 43.

279. Mafé & Navarré, 2010.

280. Sen, S., Padmanabhan, B., Tuzhilin, A., White, N., & Stein, R. 1998. The identification and satisfaction of consumer analysis-driven information needs of marketers on the WWW. *European Journal of Marketing,* 32(7/8):688–702.

281. Zhou et al, 2007, pp. 42, 43.

282. Ibid.

283. Ungerer, G.D. 2015, p. 137.

284. Schaffer, E. 2000, May. A better way for web design. *InformationWeek,* 784(1):174.

285. Mafé & Navarré, 2010, pp. 19, 20.

286. Gommans, M., Krishnan, K., & Scheffold, K. 2001. From brand loyalty to e-loyalty: A conceptual framework. *Journal of Economic and Social Research,* 3(1):50–52.

287. Hutt, E., Le Brun, R., & Mannhardt, T. 2001. Simplifying web segmentation. *McKinsey Quarterly,* 38(3):12.

288. Lociacono, E., Watson, R., & Goodhue, D. 2002. WebQual: A measure of website quality. *Marketing Theory and Applications,* 13(3):432–438.

289. Gommans et al, 2001, p. 50–52.

290. Balabanis et al, 2006, pp. 221, 222.

291. Gommans et al, 2001, p. 52.

292. Srinivasan et al, 2002, p. 43.

293. Herzberg, F. 1968. *One more time: How do you motivate employees.* Boston: Harvard Business Review.

294. Lechelle, P. 2014, May 26. *Pirate metrics.* PierreLechelle: [online]. Available: https://www.pierrelechelle.com/aarrr-pirate-metrics [Accessed 13 Apr 2016].

295. Magretta, J. 2012. *Understanding Michael Porter.* Boston: Harvard Business Review Press, pp. 19–33.

296. Porter, 1996, p. 10.

297. Markides, 1999, p. 56.

298. Magretta, 2012, p. 23.

299. Ibid, p. 29.

300. Mintzberg, H., Ahlstrand, B., & Lampel, J. 2009. *Strategy safari.* Edinburgh Gate: Prentice Hall, p. 26.

301. Andrews, K. 1965. *The concept of corporate strategy.* Homewood: R.D. Irwin.

302. Chandler, A.J. 1962. *Strategy and structure: Chapters in the history of the American industrial enterprise.* Cambridge, MA: MIT Press.

303. Selznick, P. 1957. *Leadership in administration: A sociological interpretation.* Evanston, IL: Row, Peterson.

304. Learned, E.P., & Christensen, C.R. 1965. *Business policy: Text and cases.* Illinois: Irwin, Homewood.

305. Rumelt, 1998, p. 1.

306. Osterwalder & Pigneur, 2009, pp. 16, 17.

307. Maurya, 2012.

308. Caroll, L. 1865. *Alice's Adventures in Wonderland.* New York: Macmillan.

309. Maurya, 2012.

310. Ibid.

311. Osterwalder & Pigneur, 2009, pp. 138, 139.

312. Ibid, pp. 138, 139.

313. Ibid, pp. 210, 211.

314. Rumelt, R. P. 1979. Evaluation of strategy: Theory and models. In D.E. Schendel & C. Hofer (Eds.), *Strategic management: A new view of business policy and planning,* pp. 196–212. Boston: Little, Brown, pp. 196–199.

315. Rumelt, 1998, pp. 1, 9, 10.

316. Rumelt, R. 2011, June. The perils of bad strategy. *McKinsey Quarterly,* 48(3):1–10.

317. Acur, N., & Englyst, L. 2006. Assessment of strategy formation: How to ensure quality in process and outcome. *International Journal of Operations & Production Management,* 26(1):70, 71.

318. Rumelt, 1979, p. 203.

319. Ungerer, 2015.

320. Acur & Englyst, 2006, p. 70.

321. Ungerer, 2015.

322. Casadesus-Masanell, R., & Ricart, J.E. 2011. How to design a winning business model. *Harvard Business Review,* 89(1–2):102.

323. Magretta, 2002, p. 90.

324. Weill, P., & Vitale, M. R. 2001. *Place to space: Migrating to ebusiness models.* Boston: Harvard Business School Press.

325. Hamel, G. 2000. *Leading the revolution.* Boston: Harvard Business School Press.

326. Rumelt, 1998, pp. 1–6.

327. Rumelt, 1979, pp. 199, 203.

328. Tilles, 1963.

329. Porter, 1996, pp. 9, 17.

330. Porter, 1980, p. xxvii.

331. Magretta, 2002. p. 90.
332. Rumelt, 1998, p. 2.
333. Tilles, 1963, p. 114.
334. Porter, 1996, pp. 9, 17.
335. Johnson, G., Scholes, K., & Whittington, R. 2005. *Exploring corporate strategy: Text and cases* (7th ed.). Edinburgh Gate: Pearson Education, pp. 356–361.
336. Rumelt, 1998, p. 3.
337. Porter, 1980, p. xxvii.
338. Tilles, 1963, p. 115.
339. Magretta, 2002, p. 90
340. Drucker, P.F. 1994. The theory of the business. *Harvard Business Review,* 72(5):100.
341. Linder, J.C., & Cantrell, S. 2001. Five business-model myths that hold companies back. *Strategy & Leadership,* 29(6):14.
342. McGrath, R.G. 2011, Jan/Feb. When your business model is in trouble. *Harvard Business Review,* 89(1–2):97.
343. Porter, 1980, p. xxvii.
344. Rumelt, 1998, p. 1.
345. Blank, 2013, p. 67.
346. Ries, 2011.
347. Collins, J., & Hansen, M.T. 2011. *Great by choice: Uncertainty, chaos and luck – why some thrive despite them all.* New York: Harper Collins, p. 96.
348. Chia, R.C., & Holt, R. 2009. *Strategy without design: The silent efficacy of indirect action.* Cambridge: Cambridge University Press.
349. Mintzberg et al, 2009, pp. 175–232.
350. Cusumano, M.A. 2013. Technology strategy and management: Evaluating a startup venture. *Communications of the ACM,* 56(10):26–28.
351. Hough et al, 2011, p. 7.
352. Zook, C., & Allen, J. 2011, November. The great repeatable business model. *Harvard Business Review,* 89(11):107–114.
353. Teece, 2010. p. 174.
354. Johnson, M.W., Christensen, C.M., & Kagermann, H. 2008, December. Reinventing your business model. *Harvard Business Review,* 86(12):60, 65.
355. Kim, & Mauborgne, 2005, p. 118.
356. Linder & Cantrell, 2001.
357. Porter, 1980, pp. 34–46.
358. Ibid., p. 11.
359. Teece, D. 2010. Business models, business strategy and innovation. *Long Range Planning,* 43(2):173.
360. Rumelt, 1998, pp. 4–6.
361. Rumelt, 1979, pp. 202, 203.
362. Teece, 2010, p. 173.
363. Johnson et al, 2008, Dec., pp. 60, 65.
364. Porter, 1996, Nov/Dec., pp. 9, 17.
365. Johnson et al, 2008, pp. 60, 62.
366. Volberda et al, 2011, pp. 187, 188.
367. Porter, 1980, p. 46.
368. Ibid, p. 4.
369. Porter, M.E. 2008. The five competitive forces that shape strategy. *Harvard Business Review,* 86(1):78–93.
370. Casadesus-Masanell & Ricart, 2011, p. 102.
371. Rumelt, 2011, June, pp. 1–10.
372. Hough et al, 2011, p. 7.
373. Teece, 2010, p. 180.
374. Casadesus-Masanell, R., & Ricart, J.E. 2007. Competing through business models. *IESE Business School-University of Navarra Working Paper,* pp. 12, 13.
375. Linder & Cantrell, 2001.
376. Van der Heijden, 2001, pp. 15, 16.
377. Casadesus-Masanell & Ricart, 2007, pp. 10–13.
378. Casadesus-Masanell & Ricart, 2011, p. 102.
379. Teece, 2010, pp. 179–181.
380. Van der Heijden, 2001, pp. 15, 16.
381. Rumelt, 1998, p. 6.
382. Casadesus-Masanell & Ricart, 2007, p. 11.
383. Ibid, pp. 8–12.
384. Casadesus-Masanell & Ricart, 2011, p. 102.
385. Ibid, p. 102.
386. Teece, 2010. pp. 179–180.
387. Porter, 1996, pp. 13–15.
388. Ansoff, H. I. 1965. *Corporate strategy: An analytical approach to business policy for growth and expansion.* New York: McGraw-Hill.
389. Johnson et al, 2005, pp. 371–373.
390. Rumelt, 1998, p. 7.
391. Rumelt, 1979, pp. 201, 202.
392. Ansoff, 1965.

393. Porter, 1980, p. xxvii.
394. Tilles, 1963, pp. 115–118.
395. Weill et al, 2005, pp. 1–39.
396. Rumelt, 1998, p. 7.
397. Tilles, 1963, pp. 115, 116.
398. Cusumano, 2013, p. 29.
399. Teece, 2010, p. 174.
400. Kim & Mauborgne, 2005, p. 118.
401. Magretta, J. 2002. Why business models matter. *Harvard Business Review,* 80(5):90.
402. Rumelt, 1998, p. 5.
403. Magretta, 2002, p. 90.
404. Teece, 2010, p. 174.
405. Johnson et al, 2005, p. 361–371.
406. Kim & Mauborgne, 2005, pp. 147–170.
407. Rumelt, 1998, p. 3.
408. Tilles, 1963, pp. 118–120.
409. Rumelt, 1998, p. 3.
410. Kim & Mauborgne, 2005, pp. 147–170.
411. Markides, C. 1999, pp. 55–63.
412. Porter, 1996, p. 10.
413. Rumelt, 1998.
414. Ibid, p. 10.
415. Alex. 2014, Aug 5. *Announcing UberPool.* Uber: [Online]. Available: https://newsroom.uber.com/announcing-uberpool/ [Accessed 16 Apr 2016].
416. Deep, A. 2015, Sept 24. *How Uber works: Insights into business & revenue model.* NextJuggernaut: [Online]. Available: http://nextjuggernaut.com/blog/how-uber-works-business-model-revenue-uber-insights/ [Accessed 16 Apr 2016].
417. Sam. 2015, Jan 7. *UberCARGO: A reliable ride for your items.* Uber: [Online]. Available: https://newsroom.uber.com/hong-kong/en/a-ride-for-your-goods-introducing-ubercargo/ [Accessed 16 Apr 2016].
418. *Uber Cape Town,* 2016, Apr 16. Uber: [Online]. Available: https://www.uber.com/cities/cape-town/ [Accessed 16 Apr 2016].
419. Voytek, 2014, Aug 11. *Optimising a dispatch system using an ai simulation framework.* Uber: [Online]. Available: https://newsroom.uber.com/semi-automated-science-using-an-ai-simulation-framework/ [Accessed 16 Apr 2016].
420. Ungerer et al, 2016, pp. 250-256.

CHAPTER 4 ENDNOTES

1. Peter Schwartz is an American futurist, innovator, author, and co-founder of the Global Business Network. He is a pioneer in the field of scenario development. Many people first learned about scenarios and their uses from his famous book, *The art of the long view.* See Schwartz, P. 1996. *The art of the long view.* New York: Currency Doubleday.
2. Kahn, H. 1962. *Thinking about the unthinkable: Scenarios and metaphors.* New York, NY: Horizon Press.
3. Hiltunen, E. 2013. *Foresight and innovation: How companies are coping with the future.* New York, NY: Palgrave Macmillan.
4. Fahey, L., & Randall, R. 1998. *Learning from the future: Competitive foresight scenarios.* New York, NY: John Wiley.
5. Walton, J. 2008. Scanning beyond the horizon: Exploring the ontological and epistemological basis. *Advances in Developing Human Resources* 10:147–165.
6. Mietzner, D., & Reger, G. 2005. Advantages and disadvantages of scenario approaches for strategic foresight. *International Journal of Technology Intelligence Planning,* 1(2):220–239.
7. Ringland, G. 2002. *Scenarios in business.* Chichester, UK: Wiley.
8. Walton, 2008.
9. Wilson, I. 1999. Mental maps of the future. *Scenario building: A suitable method for strategic property planning, the cutting edge 1999:* pp. 5–7. September 1999. Cambridge, United Kingdom: The Property Research Conference of the RICS, St. John's College.
10. NDT (National Department of Tourism), 2012. *Shaping the future of tourism: 2030 tourism.* Pretoria: NDT.
11. Börjeson, L.H., Hojer, M., Dreborg, K-H., Ekvall, T. & Finnveden, G. 2006. Scenario types and techniques: towards a user's guide. *Futures* 38(7):723–739.
12. Börjeson et al, 2006.
13. Ungerer, M., Ungerer, G. and Herholdt, J. 2016. *Crystallising the strategic business landscape: Strategy analysis practices and tools for business leaders and strategy practitioners.* Randburg: KR Publishing.
14. Meissner, P. & Wulf, T. 2012. Cognitive benefits of scenario planning: Its impact on biases and decision quality. *Technological Forecasting and Social Change,* 80(4):801–814.
15. Bradfield, R. 2008. Cognitive barriers in the scenario development process. *Advances in Developing Human Resources,* 10(2):198–215.
16. Schoemaker, P. 1993. Multiple scenario development: Its conceptual and behavioral foundation. *Strategic Management Journal,* 14(3):193–213.
17. Chermack, T.J. 2013. Drivers and outcomes of scenario planning: A canonical correlation analysis. *European Journal of Training and Development,* 37(9):811–834.
18. Varum, C.A. & Melo, C. 2010. Directions in scenario planning literature. A review of the past decades. *Futures,* 42(4):355–369.

19. Office of the Presidency. 2008. [Online]. Available: www.thepresidency.gov.za/docs/pcsa/planning/**scenario**/welcome.pdf [Accessed 20 November 2015].

20. Ibid.

21. Ibid.

22. Cronje, F. 2014. *A time traveller's guide to our next 10 years*. South Africa: Tafelberg. ISBN 10: 0624068668

23. Institute of Race Relations (with Moneyweb) (21 November 2014). [Online]. Available: http://irr.org.za/reports-and-publications/articles-authored-by-the-institute/time-travelling-to-2014-2013-moneyweb-21-november-2014 [Accessed 21November 2015].

24. 702 Live (Weekend breakfast with Africa and Sam) (9 October 2014). [Online]. Available: http://www.702.co.za/articles/385/the-surprising-future-of-south-africa [Accessed 21 November 2015].

25. Schwartz, 1996, p. 4.

26. Hamel, G. 2000. *Leading the revolution*. Harvard Business School Press. p137. ISBN 978-0-452-28324-4

27. For a full discussion of Industry Analysis see chapter 3 in Ungerer et al, 2016.

28. Fahey & Randall, 1998.

29. Hamel, 2000.

30. Mietzner & Reger, 2005.

31. Vorster, S., Ungerer, M., & Volschenk, J. 2013. 2050 Scenarios for long-haul tourism in the evolving global climate change regime. *Sustainability*, 5(1): 1–51. ISSN 2071-1050. [Online]. Available: www.mdpi.com/2071-1050/5/1/1 [Accessed 11 February 2016].

32. Ringland, 2002.

33. Some of the sources were: Talwar, R. 2010. Forecasting the future of travel and tourism: Scanning the horizon In *Trends and issues in global tourism 2010*. Conrady, R., & Buck, M., Eds. Heidelberg, Germany: Springer; Varum, C.A.; Melo, C.; Alvarenga, A.; & De Carvalho, P.S. 2011. Scenarios and possible futures for hospitality and tourism. *Foresight* 13:19–35; NDT, 2012; United Nations World Tourism Organisation (UNWTO) 2011; *Policy and practice for global tourism*. Madrid, Spain: UNWTO 2011; Goldin, I. 2010. *Tourism and the G20: T20 Strategic Paper*. Background Paper: T20 Tourism Ministers' Meeting, Buyeo, Republic of Korea, October 2010; Euromonitor. 2009. World travel market trends. December. [Online]. Available: http://www.euromonitor.com/World_Travel_Market_Trends [Accessed 14 September 2010]; Conrady & Buck, 2010; Stupnytska, A. 2010. *Global economy, the BRICS and beyond*. Presentation. WTTC Global Summit, Beijing, China, May.

34. Eg Intergovernmental Panel on Climate Change (IPCC). 2007. *Climate change 2007: synthesis report*: Report of the Intergovernmental Panel on Climate Change: Geneva, Switzerland: IPCC; Scott, D. 2012. Towards climate compatible travelism. In *Green growth and travelism – letters from leaders*. Lipman, G , DeLacy, T., Vorster, S., Hawkins, R., & Jiang, M., Eds. London: Goodfellows.

35. Eg World Economic Forum (WEF). 2009. *Towards a low carbon travel & tourism sector*. Report. Geneva, Switzerland: Booz & Company, May; World Economic Forum (WEF). 2011. *Policies and collaborative partnership for sustainable aviation*. Project White Paper. Geneva, Switzerland: WEF, January; International Air Transport Association (IATA). 2010. *Aviation and climate change*. Geneva, Switzerland: IATA; United Nations World Tourism Organisation, United Nations Environment Programme, World Meteorological Organisation (UNWTO-UNEP–WMO). 2008. Climate change and tourism: Responding to global challenges, 2008. [Online]. Available: http://www.unwto.org/sdt/news/en/pdf/climate2008.pdf [Accessed 23 December 2011].

36. Eg Scott, D.; Peeters, P.; Gössling, S. 2009. *Can tourism 'seal the deal' of its mitigation commitments? The challenge of achieving 'aspirational' emission reduction targets*. September. [Online]. Available: http://www.cstt.nl/userdata/documents/can%20tourism%20'seal%20the%20deal'%20of%20its%20mitigation%20commitments,%20paul.pdf [Accessed 19 November 2012].

37. Dubois, G.; Peeters, P.; Ceron, J.P.; & Gössling, S. 2011. The future tourism mobility of the world population: Emission growth *versus* climate policy. *Transport. Res. Pol. Pract. A*, 45:1031–1042.

38. Air Transport Action Group (ATAG). 2012. *Aviation: benefits beyond borders*. Geneva, Switzerland: ATAG.

39. United Nations World Tourism Organisation (UNWTO). 2008. International recommendations for tourism statistics 2008, ST/ESA/STAT/SER.M/83/Rev.1. [Online]. Available: http://unstats.un.org/unsd/tradeserv/tourism/0840120%20IRTS%202008_WEB_final%20version%20_22%20February%202010.pdf [Accessed 20 March 2011].

40. Eg Dietz, T. & Stern, P.C. 2002. Exploring new tools for environmental protection. In *New tools for environmental protection: education, information, and voluntary measures*. Dietz, T., & Stern, P.C., Eds.; Washington, DC: National Academy Press. [Online]. Available: http://www.nap.edu/chapterlist.php?record_id=10401&type=pdf_chapter&free=1 [Accessed 26 March 2012].

41. NDT, 2012.

42. Hichert, T. 2012. *The future of tourism in South Africa: A horizon scan*. Background Paper. National Department of Tourism's scenario-building process. Bellville, South Africa: Institute for Futures Research.

43. Lipman, G. 2012. *Report on macro-level drivers that will impact future tourism scenarios*. Background Paper. National Department of Tourism's scenario-building process. Brussels, Belgium: greenearth.travel.

44. Saunders, G. 2012. *NDT tourism scenario planning to 2030/2050: Selected key drivers*. Background Paper: National Department of Tourism's scenario-building process. Sandton, South Africa: Grant Thornton.

45. World Economic Forum (WEF). 2012. Outlook on the Global Agenda 2012. [Online]. Available: http://www3.weforum.org/docs/GAC11/WEF_GAC11_OutlookGlobalAgenda.pdf [Accessed 23 December 2011].

46. McKinsey & Company. 2011. *Global economic scenarios 2010–2020: Volatility in a multi-speed world*. McKinsey Quarterly Global Executive Survey. Boston, MA: McKinsey. [Online]. Available: http://www.amchamsineurope.com/file/613/competitiveness%20of%20EU%20and%20US%20companies.pdf [Accessed 27 May 2012].

47. Earth Negotiations Bulletin (ENB). 2012. *Summary of the Bonn climate change conference*. Bonn, Germany, 14–25 May 2012. Geneva, Switzerland: International Institute for Sustainable Development 12:1–23.

48. International Air Transport Association (IATA). 2011. *Report of the Board of Governors*. Agenda item 6, Document 1. Report presented at the 67th Annual General Meeting. Singapore, June.

49. United Nations Framework Convention on Climate Change (UNFCCC). 1997. *Kyoto Protocol to the United Nations Framework Convention on Climate Change*. Bonn: UNFCCC Secretariat. [Online]. Available: http://unfccc.int/kyoto_protocol/items/2830.php [Accessed 6 March 2011].

50. Lyle, C. *Breaking the surly bonds of economic regulation*. 2011. Québec: Air Transport Economics.

51. United Nations World Tourism Organisation (UNWTO). 2011. *Provisional Agenda Item 5*. Report of the Secretary-General, General Assembly, 19th session, Gyeongju, Republic of Korea, 8–14 October. [Online]. Available: https://s3-eu-west-1.amazonaws.com/storageapi/sites/all/files/pdf/a19_05_report_sg_e.pdf [Accessed 3 October 2011].

52. World Travel and Tourism Council (WTTC). 2011. *Travel and tourism 2011*. London: WTTC.

53. Scowsill, D. 2011. Speech by David Scowsill, President and CEO of the World Travel and Tourism Council. [Online]. Available: http://www.onecaribbean.org/content/files/WTTCDavidScowsill.pdf [Accessed 22 May 2012].

54. International Air Transport Association (IATA). 2011. *International Air Transport Association Annual Report 2011*. Singapore: IATA, June.

55. World Travel and Tourism Council (WTTC). 2011. *Travel and tourism economic impact 2011*. London: WTCC.

56. Dray, L., Evans, A., & Schäfer, A. 2011. Fleet renewal policies – initial estimations. Paper prepared for the World Economic Forum Aviation, Travel and Tourism Industry Agenda Council. Geneva: WEF, p. 1.

57. WEF, 2011.

58. O'Hanlon, S. 2011. Aviation biofuels: From fields to wheels up (R&D to Commercialization). Presentation at a World Biofuels Conference, London, UK. [Online]. Available: http://library.greenpowerconferences.com/abm/presentation.pdf [Accessed 14 November 2011].

59. International Air Transport Association (IATA). 2009. *A global approach to reducing aviation emissions*. Montreal: IATA, p. 4. [Online]. Available: http://www.iata.org/SiteCollectionDocuments/Documents/Global_Approach_Reducing_Emissions_251109web.pdf [Accessed 12 December 2010].

60. Air Transport Action Group (ATAG). 2009. *Beginner's guide to aviation efficiency*. Geneva: ATAG.

61. Aviation Global Deal Group (AGD group). 2011. *A coordinated pathway towards a global sectoral agreement for international aviation emissions*. AGD Group Discussion Paper. London: AGD Group.

62. Gössling, S., Peeters, P., & Scott, D. 2008. Consequences of climate policy for international tourist arrivals in developing countries. *Third World Q.* 29:874.

63. Meinshausen, M. 2005. *On the risk of overshooting 2°C*. Paper presented at the Scientific Symposium on avoiding dangerous climate change. MetOffice, Exeter, UK, 1–3 February.

64. Organization for Economic Cooperation and Development (OECD). 2011. *Climate change and tourism policy in OECD countries*. CFE/TOU (2010)10/FINAL. Paris: OECD.

65. Hichert, T. 2012. *The future of tourism in South Africa: Trends and driving forces*. Background Paper. National Department of Tourism's scenario-building process. Bellville, South Africa: Institute for Futures Research.

66. UN World Trade Organization. 2011. Provisional Agenda Item 5. Report of the Secretary-General, General Assembly, 19th session, Gyeongju, Republic of Korea, 8–14 October. [Online]. Available: https://s3-eu-west-1.amazonaws.com/storageapi/sites/all/files/pdf/a19_05_report_sg_e.pdf [Accessed 3 October 2011].

67. World Travel and Tourism Council (WTTC). 2010. Climate change: A joint approach to addressing the challenge. [Online]. Available: http://www.wttc.org/bin/pdf/original_pdf_file/climate_change_final.pdf [Accessed 2 December 2010].

68. Lyle, 2011.

69. Williams, K. 2011. Speech by British Airways CEO. Caribbean Tourism Organization Conference, Marigot, Saint-Martin, 16 September. [Online]. Available: http://www.eturbonews.com/25264/british-airways-ceo-provides-world-view-state-tourismindustry [Accessed 19 September 2011].

70. Beaverstock, J., Derudder, B., Faulconbridge, J., & Witlox, F. 2010. International Business Travel in the Global Economy 2010. [Online]. Available: http://books.google.co.za/books?id=Z4wiZsqvm3sC&pg=PA118&lpg=PA118&dq=virtual+technology+video+conferencing+business+travel+substitute&source=bl&ots=23BjCBgxuP&sig=VImPFmxtFOqbNa0BXYC2XQsZbA0&hl=en&sa=X&ei=SyLFT-6vGDsrBhAfH69zvCQ&redir_esc=y#v=onepage&q=virtual%20technology%20video%20conferencing%20business%20travel%20substitute&f=false [Accessed 29 May 2012].

71. Mullich, J. 2010. The new face of face-to-face meetings efficiencies, technology, and better metrics bring greater ROI. *Wall St. J.* [Online]. Available: http://online.wsj.com/ad/article/globaltravel-face [Accessed 29 May 2012].

72. United Kingdom Climate Change Committee (UKCCC). 2011. *Government response to the committee on climate change report on reducing CO^2 emissions from UK aviation to 2050*. London: UK Department of Transport.

73. Karlitekin, C. 2010. Forecasting the future of travel and tourism: Future of global aviation. In *Trends and Issues in Global Tourism 2010*; Conrady, R., Buck, M., (Eds). Heidelberg: Springer.

74. Scott et al, 2009.

75. Scott, D., & Lemieux, C. 2009. *Weather and climate information for tourism*. Report. World Meteorological Organisation and United Nations World Tourism Organization. Geneva, Switzerland, August 2009. [Online]. Available: http://www.unwto.org/climate/support/en/pdf/WCC3_TourismWhitePaper.pdf [Accessed 20 March 2011].

76. WEF, 2011.

77. Organization for Economic Cooperation and Development (OECD). 2011. *Climate change and tourism policy in OECD countries*; CFE/TOU(2010)10/FINAL; OECD: Paris, France.

78. Yeoman, I. Our sustainable future – looking back from 2050. 2012. In *Green Growth and Travelism—Letters from Leaders*; Lipman, G., DeLacy, T., Vorster, S., Hawkins, R., Jiang, M., Eds.. London, UK: Goodfellows.

79. Strong, M. 2009. Facing down Armageddon: Our environment at a crossroads. *World Pol. J.*, 26:25–32.

80. Sivell, P.M., Reeves, S.J., Baldachin, L., & Brightman, T.G. 2008. *Climate change resilience indicators*. Berkshire, UK: South East United Kingdom Regional Assembly, Transport Research Laboratory.

CHAPTER 5 ENDNOTES

1. Buffett, W. 1930. Goodreads. [Online]. Available: http://www.goodreads.com/quotes/226056-in-the-business-world-the-rearview-mirror-is-always-clearer [Accessed 13 July 2016].
2. Slywotsky, A. 2004. *The art of profitability.* (Updated edition). Boston: Little, Brown. ISBN 10: 0446692271 / ISBN 13: 9780446692274
3. Reported in Neilson, GL, Martin, KL & Powers, E. 2008. The secrets to successful strategy execution. *Harvard Business Review* 86(6): pp. 60–70 (June 2008).
4. Turning great strategy into great performance. [Online]. Available: http://www.marakon.com/insights-and-ideas/article/turning-great-strategy-into-great-performance#.VsdBvlT5i00 [Accessed 19 February 2016].
5. Kaplan, R.S. & Norton, D.P. 2008. *The execution premium.* Boston: MA: Harvard Business School Publishing Corporation.
6. For a full description of Reinforcing (R) loops and Balancing (B) loops see Ungerer, M., Ungerer, G. & Herholdt, J. 2016. *Crystallising the strategic business landscape: Strategy analysis practices and tools for business leaders and strategy practitioners.* Johannesburg, KR publishing.
7. PricewaterhouseCoopers (2014) Research on the strategy-execution gap. [Online]. Available: http://www.strategyand.pwc.com/global/home/what-we-think/cds_home/the_concept/research-strategy-execution-gap
8. Getting it done! 2000. Fast Company [Online]. Available: http://www.fastcompany.com/39491/getting-it-done [Accessed 20 February 2016].
9. Based on: Diaz, I. 2010. Strategic execution plan and monitoring mechanisms for Corporate Clients SBU. MBA strategic management assignment. University of Stellenbosch Business School. Unpublished.
10. Kaplan, Robert S. & Norton, David, P. 2005. Focusing your organisation on Strategy — with the Balanced Scorecard (3rd ed.) *Harvard Business Review* (On Point Collection), includes the following: 1. The Office of Strategy Management; 2. Putting the Balanced Scorecard to Work; 3. Measuring the strategic readiness of intangible assets; 4. Using the Balanced Scorecard as a strategic management system; 5. Having trouble with your strategy? Then Map it.
11. Sasol is an international integrated energy and chemicals company that leverages the talent and expertise of our more than 31 000 people working in 37 countries. We develop and commercialise technologies, and build and operate world-scale facilities to produce a range of high-value product streams, including liquid fuels, chemicals and low-carbon electricity.
12. Opperman, S. 2013. Strategy execution plan – Synfuels technical support. MBA strategic management assignment. University of Stellenbosch Business School. Unpublished.
13. USBS Management team (2015) Example of a strategy map of the University of Stellenbosch Business School (USBS). Unpublished.
14. Ibid.
15. Ibid.
16. Kaplan, R. 2000. The balanced scorecard – making strategy happen. Public Conference, Vodaworld, Johannesburg, May 8.
17. USBS, 2015.
18. Opperman, S. 2013. Strategy execution plan – Synfuels technical support. MBA strategic management assignment. University of Stellenbosch Business School. Unpublished.
19. Diaz, I. 2010. Strategic execution plan and monitoring mechanisms for Corporate Clients SBU. MBA strategic management assignment. University of Stellenbosch Business School. Unpublished.
20. Kafidi, P.L. 2013. Strategic execution plan and monitoring mechanisms for the NAMFISA strategy utilizing guidelines for a strategic map and a balanced scorecard. MBA strategic management assignment. University of Stellenbosch Business School. Unpublished.
21. Ibid.
22. Diaz, 2010.
23. Ibid.
24. Hammer, M., & Champy. J. 1993. *Reengineering the corporation: A manifesto for business revolution.* London: Harper Collins.
25. Sull, D., Holmes, R. & Sull, C. 2015. Why strategy execution unravels – and what to do about it. *Harvard Business Review* 93(3):58–66.
26. Bossidy, L., Charan, R. & Buck, C. 2002. *Execution: The discipline of getting things done.* New York, NY: Crown Business. ISBN 0-609-61057-0
27. Sull et al, 2015, p. 65.
28. Ibid, p. 66.
29. Trompenaars, F. & Hampden-Turner, C. 2012. *Riding the waves of culture: Understanding diversity in global business* (3rd ed.) New York: McGraw-Hill.
30. Ungerer, M., Herholdt, J. & Le Roux, J. 2013. *Leadership for all — Virtue practices to flourish.* Johannesburg: KnowRes Publishing.
31. Godin, S. 2008. *Tribes: We need you to lead us.* Portfolio: The main idea of the book is that lasting and substantive change can be best effected by a tribe: a group of people connected to each other, to a leader and to an idea. Smart innovators find or assemble a movement of similarly minded individuals and get the tribe excited by a new product, service or message, often via the internet (consider, for example, the popularity of the Obama campaign, Facebook or Twitter). Tribes, Godin says, can be within or outside a corporation, and almost everyone can be a leader; most are kept from realising their potential by fear of criticism and fear of being wrong.
32. Bunker, BB & Alban, BT. 2006. *The handbook of large group methods: Creating systemic change in organizations and communities.* San Francisco: Jossey-Bass. Large Group Interventions are methods used to gather a whole system together to discuss and take action on the target agenda. That agenda varies from future plans, products, and services, to redesigning work, to discussion of troubling issues and problems. *The Handbook of Large Group Methods* takes the next step in demonstrating through a series of cases how Large Group Methods are used to address twenty-first century challenges in organisations and communities.
33. Bos, A.H. 1974. Oordeelsvorming in groepen: Polariteiten riture als sleutel tot ontwikkeling van sociale organisenen. Wageningen: Veenman & Zonen BV. University of Wageningen. Doctoral thesis.
34. Scharmer, C. Otto 2007. *Theory U: Leading from the future as it emerges.* Cambridge, MA: The Society for Organizational Learning.
35. Ballreich, R. & Glasl, F. 2001. *Team development and organisation development as a means for conflict prevention and conflict resolution.* Berghof Handbook for Conflict Transformation. ISSN 1616-2544. [Online]. Available: http://www.berghof-handbook.net [Accessed 20 May 2016].

36. Senge, PM., Scharmer, C. O., Jaworski, J., & Flowers, B.S. 2005. *Presence: Exploring profound change in people, organizations and society.* London: Nicholas Brealey.
37. Otto Scharmer Homepage [Online]. Available: http://www.ottoscharmer.com/publications/executive-summaries [Accessed 16 March 2016].
38. Kotter, J.P. 1996. *Leading change.* Harvard Business School Press. ISBN 978-0-87584-747-4. In this book he perfected the 8-step process for leading change.
39. Keller, S. & Aiken, C. 2009. The inconvenient truth about change management. *McKinsey Quarterly,* 1–18. April.
40. Lottery tickets study as described in Langer, E.J. 1982. "Chapter 16: The illusion of control" in Kahneman, D. Slovic, P. & Tversky, A. eds., *Judgment under uncertainty: Heuristics and biases.* Cambridge: Cambridge University Press.
41. Gladwell, M. 2000. *The tipping point: How little things can make a big difference.* Boston:Little, Brown.
42. Deci, E.L. 1971. Effects of externally mediated rewards on intrinsic motivation. *Journal of Personality and Social Psychology,* 18:105–115.
43. Plant, R.W., & Ryan, R.M. 1985. Intrinsic motivation and the effects of self-consciousness, self-awareness, and ego-involvement: An investigation of internally controlling styles. *Journal of Personality,* 53:434–449.
44. Harackiewicz, J.M. 1979. The effects of reward contingency and performance feedback on intrinsic motivation. *Journal of Personality and Social Psychology,* 37:1352–1363.
45. Amabile, T. ., DeJong, W., & Lepper, M.R. 1976. Effects of externally imposed deadlines on subsequent intrinsic motivation. *Journal of Personality and Social Psychology,* 34:92–98.
46. Deci, E.L., Betley, G., Kahle, J., Abrams, L., & Porac, J. 1981. When trying to win: Competition and intrinsic motivation. *Personality and Social Psychology Bulletin,* 7:79–83.
47. Ariely, D. 2008. *Predictably irrational: The hidden forces that shape our decisions.* New York, NY: Harper Collins: p. 71.
48. The seminal ultimatum game study is by Guth Werner, Rolf Schmittberger & Bernd Schwarze, 1982. An experimental analysis of ultimatum bargaining. *Journal of Economic Behaviour and Organization,* 3(4):367–388. Note that new ultimatum game research in the field of neuro-economics shows us exactly what part of the brain operates the bilateral anterior insula (not part of the prefrontal cortex) in rejecting small offers (as reported by Sanfey et al, 2003. The neural bias of economic decision-making in the ultimatum game. *Science 300*:1755–1758.
49. Cameron, L. 1999. Raising the stakes in the ultimatum game: Experimental evidence from Indonesia. *Economic Inquiry,* 37(1):47–59. This assumption was also tested by having US participants play the game for $100. They found no difference between play for $100 and play for $10, as reported in Hoffman, E.K., McCabe, K.A. and Smith, V.L. 1996. On expectations and the monetary stakes in ultimatum games. *International Journal of Game Theory* 25:289–301.
50. Kim, W.C. & Mauborgne, K. 2003. Fair process: Managing in the knowledge economy. [Online]. Available: hbr.org. January. https://hbr.org/2003/01/fair-process-managing-in-the-knowledge-economy/ [Accessed 12 April 2016].
51. Ibid.
52. Ungerer, Ungerer & Herholdt, 2016 *Crystallising the strategic business landscape: Strategy analysis practices and tools for business leaders and strategy practitioners.* Johannesburg: KR Publishing.
53. Ghosh, P. 2013. How many people did Joseph Stalin kill? *International Business Times,* 3 May. [Online]. Available: http://www.ibtimes.com/how-many-people-did-joseph-stalin-kill-1111789 [Accessed 29 March 2016].

CHAPTER 6 ENDNOTES

1. Osterwalder, A., & Pigneur, Y. 2009. *Business model generation.* Self-published, p. 136.
2. Chambers, J. 2016. Cisco's John Chambers on the digital era. (R. Kirkland, Interviewer). [Online]. Available: http://www.mckinsey.com/industries/high-tech/our-insights/ciscos-john-chambers-on-the-digital-era?cid=other-eml-nsl-mip-mck-oth-1604 [Accessed 18 Apr 2016].
3. Ismail, S., Malone, M., & Van Geest, Y. 2014. *Exponential organisations.* New York: Diversion Books.
4. Chambers, 2016.
5. Ibid.
6. Van Geest, J. 2014, Oct 20. *Exponential organisations – Why new organisations are 10X better, faster and cheaper than yours.* [Online]. Available: Slideshare: http://www.slideshare.net/vangeest/exponential-organizations-h [Accessed 24 April 2016].
7. Chambers, 2016.
8. Dawson, A., Hirt, M., & Scanlan. 2016, Mar. *Economic essentials of digital strategy.* McKinsey & Company: [Online]. Available: http://www.mckinsey.com/business-functions/strategy-and-corporate-finance/our-insights/the-economic-essentials-of-digital-strategy?cid=other-eml-nsl-mip-mck-oth-1604 [Accessed 18 April 2016].
9. Ibid.
10. Ibid.
11. Ibid.
12. Ibid.
13. Ismail et al, 2014, p. 18.
14. Ibid, p. 46.
15. Ibid, p. 15.
16. Ibid, p. 293.
17. Moore, G.E. 1965, Apr 19. Cramming more components onto integrated circuits. *Electronics Magazine,* 38(8):114–117.
18. Ibid, p. 20.
19. Bower, J.L., & Christensen, C.M. 1995. Disruptive technologies: Catching the wave. *Harvard Business Review,* 73(1):44, 45.
20. Christensen, C.M., & Overdorf, M. 2000. Meeting the challenge of disruptive change. *Harvard Business Review,* 78(2):72.

21. Lee, C.-S., & Vonortas, N.S. 2004. Business model innovation in the digital economy. In G. Doukidis, N. Mylonopoulos, & N. Pouloudi (eds), *Social and economic transformation in the digital era*. Hershey, PA: Idea Group Publishing, p. 168.

22. Rayport, J., & Sviokla, J. 1995. Exploring the virtual value chain. *Harvard Business Review*, 73(6):75–85.

23. Tapscott, D., Ticoll, D., & Lowy, A. 2000. *Digital capital: Harnessing the power of business webs*. (1st ed.). Boston: Harvard Business School Press, p. 5.

24. Ismail et al, 2014, p. 30.

25. Ibid, p. 161.

26. Ibid, p. 53.

27. Ibid, p. 54.

28. Ibid, p. 157.

29. Botsman, R., & Rogers, R. 2010. *What's mine is yours: The rise of collaborative consumption*. London: HarperCollins.

30. Ismail et al, 2014, p. 76.

31. Hamel, G. 2012. *What matters now*. San Francisco: Jossey-Bass, p. 142.

32. Ismail et al, 2014, p. 99.

33. Ibid, p. 104.

34. Ibid, p. 110.

35. Ibid, p. 113.

36. Goodwin, T. 2015, Mar 3. *The battle is for the customer interface*. [Online]. Available: TechCrunch: http://techcrunch.com/2015/03/03/in-the-age-of-disintermediation-the-battle-is-all-for-the-customer-interface/ [Accessed 24 Apr 2016].

37. Ismail et al, 2014, p. 173.

38. Kim, W., & Mauborgne, R. 2004, Oct. Blue Ocean strategy. *Harvard Business Review*, 82(10):69.

39. Ibid, p. 72.

40. Ibid, pp. 70–73.

41. Ibid, p. 73.

42. Ibid, p. 77.

43. Ibid, p. 76.

44. Ibid, p. 76.

45. Ibid, p. 77.

46. Ibid, p. 77.

47. Ibid, p. 75–78.

48. Ungerer, G.D. 2015. *A competitive strategy framework for e-business start-ups*. Stellenbosch: University of Stellenbosch.

49. Kim & Mauborgne, 2004, p. 72.

50. Kim, W., & Mauborgne, R. 2005. *Blue ocean strategy*. Boston: Harvard Business School Press, p. 21.

51. Ibid, pp. 47, 48.

52. Ungerer, G.D. *A competitive strategy framework for e-business start-ups*. Stellenbosch: University of Stellenbosch, p. 187.

53. Hamel, G. 1996. Strategy as revolution. *Harvard Business Review*, 74(4):72, 73.

54. Ungerer et al, 2011, p. 94.

55. Ungerer, 2015, p. 187.

56. Kim & Mauborgne, 2005, p. 49.

57. Hamel, 1996, pp. 72, 73.

58. Kim & Mauborgne, 2005, p. 56.

59. Ibid, p. 61.

60. Johnson, M.W., Christensen, C.M., & Kagermann, H. 2008, Dec. Reinventing your business model. *Harvard Business Review*, 86(12):57–68.

61. Kim & Mauborgne, 2005, p. 56.

62. Ibid, pp. 69, 70.

63. Ibid, pp. 75, 76.

64. Hamel, 1996, p. 73.

65. Ibid, p. 73.

66. Ungerer et al, 2011, p. 94.

67. Ungerer, 2015, p. 217.

68. Kim & Mauborgne, 2005, p. 86.

69. Ibid, p. 29.

70. Ibid, p. 29.

71. Ibid, p. 121.

72. Ibid, p. 121.

73. Ibid, pp. 82, 83.

74. Ibid, p. 35.

75. Ibid, pp. 101, 102.

76. Ibid, p. 104.

77. Ibid, pp. 105, 109.

78. Ibid, p. 104.

79. Ibid, pp. 114, 115.

80. Ibid, p. 118.

81. Kim, W., & Mauborgne, R. 2000, Sept/Oct. Knowing a winning business idea when you see one. *Harvard Business Review,* 78(5):132.
82. Kim & Mauborgne, 2005, p. 119.
83. Ibid, pp. 118, 119.
84. Ibid, pp. 147–149.
85. Ibid, p. 169.
86. Kim, W., & Mauborgne, R. 2016. *Tipping point leadership.* Blue Ocean Strategy: [Online]. Available: https://www.blueoceanstrategy.com/tools/tipping-point-leadership/ [Accessed 27 Apr 2016].
87. Kim & Mauborgne, 2005, p. 151.
88. Ibid, p. 151.
89. Ibid, p. 175.
90. Ibid, p. 183.
91. Osterwalder, A. 2007, Jan 5. *Nintendo's Blue Ocean strategy: Wii.* Business Model Alchemist: [Online]. Available: http://businessmodelalchemist.com/blog/2007/01/nintendos-blue-ocean-strategy-wii.html [Accessed 4 May 2016].
92. Kim, W., Mauborgne, R., & Hunter, J. 2007. *Lessons learned from noncustomers.* [Online]. Available: Blue Ocean Strategy: https://www.blueoceanstrategy.com/teaching-materials/nintendo-wii/# [Accessed 4 May 2016].
93. Dob, S. 2010, Jun 23. 'Case Study: Blue Ocean Strategy - Nintendo Wii'. [Online]. Available: http://samidob.blogspot.co.za/2010/06/casetudy-blue-ocean-strategy-nintendo.html [Accessed May 4, 2016].
94. Dare Start Business (DSB). 2015, Jan 7. *Nintendo Wii business innovation strategy.* Dare Start Business: [Online]. Available: http://www.darestartbusiness.com/nintendo-wii-business-innovation-strategy/ [Accessed 4 May 2016].
95. Thurrott, P. 2010, Oct 6. *Xbox 360 vs. Playstation 3 vs. Wii: A technical comparison.* [Online]. Available: SuperSite for Windows: http://winsupersite.com/product-review/xbox-360-vs-playstation-3-vs-wii-technical-comparison [Accessed 4 May 2016].
96. O'Gorman, P. 2008. Wii: Creating a Blue Ocean the Nintendo way. *Palermo Business Review* (2):97–107.
97. Nintendo. *Hardware and Software Unit Sales.* 2016, Mar 31. [Online]. Available: Nintendo: https://www.nintendo.co.jp/ir/en/sales/hard_soft/ [Accessed 4 May 2016].
98. Hall, K. 2006, Nov 16. The big ideas behind Nintendo's Wii. *Bloomberg Business Week, Special Report.*
99. Johnson et al, 2008, pp. 57–68.
100. Bettencourt, L.A., & Ulwick, A.W. 2008. The customer-centered innovation map. *Harvard Business Review,* 86(5):109–114.
101. Kim & Mauborgne, 2005.
102. Lee & Vonortas, 2004.
103. Amit, R., & Zott, C. 2001. Value creation in e-business. *Strategic Management Journal,* 22(6–7):493–520.
104. Golub, H., & Henry, J. 2000. Market strategy and the price-value model. *McKinsey Quarterly,* 37(3):47.
105. Ungerer, 2015.
106. Prifti, E. 2013, Aug 3. *Edward de Bono Quotes.* [Online]. Available: http://www.slideshare.net/eridaprifti/edward-de-bono-quotes [Accessed 20 May 2016].
107. Ungerer & Schutte, 2015, pp. 1082–1101.
108. Ungerer, 2015.
109. Ibid, p. 290.
110. Ungerer & Schutte, 2015.
111. Ibid.
112. Ungerer, 2015.
113. Osterwalder & Pigneur, 2009, p. 23.
114. Ibid, pp. 24, 25.
115. Wells, J.D., & Gobeli, D.H. 2003, Mar/Apr. The 3R framework: Improving e-strategy across reach, richness, and range. *Business Horizons,* 46(2):7.
116. Amit & Zott, 2001, p. 504.
117. Wells & Gobeli, 2003, p. 6.
118. Osterwalder & Pigneur, 2009, p. 25.
119. Kelly, K. 2008, Jan 31. *Better than free.* The Technium: [Online]. Available: www.kk.org/thetechnium/archives/2008/01/better_than_fre.php [Accessed 16 Aug 2012].
120. Ibid.
121. Gommans, M., Krishnan, K., & Scheffold, K. 2001. From brand loyalty to e-loyalty: A conceptual framework. *Journal of Economic and Social Research,* 3(1):46.
122. Srinivasan, S., Anderson, R., & Ponnavolu, K. 2002. Customer loyalty in e-commerce: An exploration of its antecedents and consequences. *Journal of Retailing,* 78(1):41.
123. Kelly, 2008.
124. Koiso-Kanttila, N. 2005. Time, attention, authenticity and consumer benefits of the web. *Business Horizons,* 48(1):64.
125. Gummerus, J. 2011. *Customer value in e-service: conceptual foundation and empirical evidence.* Helsinki: Hanken School of Economics, p. 47.
126. Kelly, 2008.
127. Valvi, A., & Fragkos, K. 2012. Critical review of the e-loyalty literature: A purchase-centred framework. *Electronic Commerce Research,* 12(3):31, 32.
128. Arya, S., & Srivastava, S. 2012. Acquiring e-loyalty: Competition is just one click away: A literature review. *International Journal of Research Management, Economics and Commerce,* 2(11):151.
129. Korgaonkar, P., & Wolin, L. 1999, Mar/Apr. A multivariate analysis of web usage. *Journal of Advertising Research,* 39(2):57.

130. Gommans et al, 2001, p. 50.
131. Zhou, L., Dai, L., & Zhang, D. 2007. Online shopping acceptance model – a critical survey of consumer factors in online shopping. *Journal of Electronic Commerce Research,* 8(1):54.
132. Welch, N. 2010. A marketer's guide to behavioral economics. *McKinsey Quarterly,* 47(1):3.
133. Wells & Gobeli, 2003, p. 7.
134. Rayport & Sviokla, 1995, pp. 75–85.
135. Tapscott et al, 2000.
136. Lee & Vonortas, 2004, pp. 166, 168, 171.
137. Kelly, 2008.
138. Johnson et al, 2008, pp. 61–62.
139. Arya & Srivastava, 2012, p. 150.
140. Osterwalder & Pigneur, 2009, p. 25.
141. Srinivasan et al, 2002, p. 44.
142. Arya & Srivastava, 2012.
143. Reichheld, F., & Schefter, P. 2000. E-loyalty. *Harvard Business Review,* 78(4):110.
144. Ungerer et al, 2011, pp. 104–106.
145. Ibid.
146. Kim & Mauborgne, 2000, p. 133.
147. Osterwalder & Pigneur, 2009, p. 23.
148. Amit & Zott, 2001, pp. 494, 508.
149. Levitt, T. 1981. Marketing intangible products and product intangibles. *Cornell Hotel and Restaurant Administration Quarterly,* 22(2):37–44.
150. Gommans et al, 2001, p. 51.
151. Goldstuck, A. 2012, Aug 7. *Joining the e-party.* [Online]. Available: Fin24: http://www.fin24.com/opinion/columnists/joining-the-e-party-20120807 [Accessed 29 Jan 2013].
152. Kelly 2008.
153. Ibid.
154. Amit & Zott, 2001, p. 506.
155. Lee & Vonortas, 2004, p. 170.
156. Osterwalder & Pigneur, 2009, p. 23.
157. Seybold, P. 2001. *The customer revolution.* New York: Crown Business.
158. Korgaonkar & Wolin, 1999.
159. Lee & Vonortas, 2004, p. 166.
160. Hoegg, R., Martignoni, R., Meckel, M., & Stanoevska-Slabeva, K. 2006. *Overview of business models for web 2.0 communities.* St. Gallen: University of St. Gallen, p. 10.
161. Gummerus, 2011.
162. Ungerer & Schutte, 2015, pp. 1082–1101.
163. Ibid.
164. Ungerer, 2015.
165. Ibid.
166. Olson, M.S., Van Bever, D. & Verry, S. 2008. When growth stalls. *Harvard Business Review,* Mar:51–61.
167. Ibid, p. 52.
168. Ibid, p. 53.
169. Ibid, p. 55.
170. Ibid, p. 54.
171. Ibid, p. 56.
172. Collins, J. 2009. *How the mighty fall and why some companies never give in.* New York: HarperCollins.
173. Olson et al, 2008, p. 59.
174. For more ideas on assumptions testing see chapter 7 in Ungerer et al, 2016. See chapters 2–6 on external and internal strategy analysis practices.
175. Ungerer et al, 2016.
176. Collins, 2009.
177. Ibid.
178. Ungerer et al, 2011, p. 125.
179. Based on Hamel, G. 2000. *Leading the revolution.* Boston: Harvard Press, pp. 299–306.
180. Hamel, G. 2001, Jul 9. Innovation's New Math. *Fortune,* 72(7):66–67.
181. For a detailed description on hypothesis testing see chapter 7: Ungerer et al, 2016.
182. Collins, J. & Hansen, M.T. 2011. *Great by choice.* London: RH Business Books.
183. Ibid, p. 25–26.
184. Ibid, p. 78–86.
185. Ibid, p. 81.
186. Ibid, p. 98.

CHAPTER 7 ENDNOTES

1. Sahakian, C.E. 2010. 'Strategic Alliance Quotes'. *Strategic Alliance Management & Social Media*. [Online]. Available: http://sgbmedia.typepad.com/blog/2010/11/strategic-alliance-quotes.html [Accessed 11 March 2016].

2. Ferrer, C., Uhlaner, R. & West, A. 2013. M&A as competitive advantage. *McKinsey Quarterly*, August: 1.

3. Dora, D., Smit, S. & Viguerie, P. 2011. Drawing a new road map for growth. *McKinsey Quarterly*, April. [Online]. Available: http://www.mckinsey.com/global-themes/employment-and-growth/drawing-a-new-road-map-for-growth [Accessed 11 March 2016].

4. Ibid.

5. Volberda, H.W., Morgan, R.E., Reinmoeller, P.R., Hitt, M.A., Ireland, R.D. & Hoskinsson, R.E. 2011. *Strategic management: Competitiveness and globalization*. Hampshire: Cengage, pp. 280–281.

6. Kariithi, N.K. 2007. *Longman dictionary of financial terms*. Johannesburg: Pearson Education.

7. De Wit, P.G.S. 2015. *Postmerger and acquisition implementation strategies: A case study within an aggregates firm*. Unpublished MBA research, University of Stellenbosch Business School, p. 6.

8. Deresky, H. 2002. *International management: managing across borders and cultures*. 4th ed. Upper Saddle River: Prentice Hall.

9. Thompson, J. & Martin, F. 2010. *Strategic management: Awareness and change*. New Hampshire: Cengage, p. 537.

10. Townsend, J.D. 2003. Understanding alliances: a review of international aspects in strategic marketing. *Marketing Intelligence and Planning*, 21(3):143–155.

11. Gonzalez, M. 2001. Strategic alliances: The right way to compete in the 21st century. *Ivey Business Journal*, 66(1): 47–51.

12. Kauser, S. & Shaw, V. 2004. The influence of behavioural and organisational characteristics on the success of international strategic alliances. *International Marketing Review*, 21(1):17–52.

13. Wakeam, J. 2003. The five factors of a strategic alliance. *Ivey Business Journal*, May/June.

14. Bombela Concession Company (Pty) Ltd. 'About Bombela'. [Online]. Available: http://www.bombela.com/shareholding.asp [Accessed 22 March 2016].

15. Gonzalez, 2001, pp. 47–51.

16. Klein, S. & Dev, C. 1997. Partner selection in market-driven strategic alliances. *South African Journal of Business Management*, 28(3):97–105.

17. Kale, P., Dyer, J.H. & Singh, H. 2002. Alliance capability, stock market response, and long-term alliance success: The role of the alliance function. *Strategic Management Journal*, 23:747–767.

18. Thompson Jnr, A.A., Strickland lll, A.J. & Gamble, J.E. 2010. *Crafting and executing strategy: Text and readings*. 17th ed. Berkshire: McGraw-Hill, p. 217.

19. Kale et al, 2002.

20. Ibid.

21. Ibid, p. 752.

22. Ibid, p. 762.

23. Wakeam, 2003.

24. Kale et al, 2002.

25. Pudney, R. 2002. Collaborating to compete. *The Ashridge Journal*. Winter:16–23. [Online]. Available: http://tools.ashridge.org.uk/website/IC.nsf/wFARATT/Collaborating%20to%20Compete/$file/CollaboratingToCompete.pdf [Accessed 21 March 2016].

26. Ibid

27. The information for this case is based on the following two sources: [Online]. Available: http://www.nissan-global.com/EN/COMPANY/PROFILE/ALLIANCE/RENAULT01/index.html and http://www.nissan-global.com/EN/DOCUMENT/PDF/ALLIANCE/HANDBOOK/2014/BookletAlliance2014_GB.pdf [Accessed 21 March 2016].

28. The information for this part of the case is [Online]. Available: http://www.nissan-global.com/EN/COMPANY/PROFILE/ALLIANCE/RENAULT01/index.html [Accessed 21 March 2016].

29. Source for case study: [Online]. Available: http://www.nissan-global.com/EN/DOCUMENT/PDF/ALLIANCE/HANDBOOK/2014/BookletAlliance2014_GB.pdf [Accessed 21 March 2014].

30. Nissan Motor Corporation website. [Online]. Available: http://www.nissan-global.com/EN/NEWS/2016/_STORY/160204-03-e.html [Accessed 22 March 2016].

31. Nissan Motor Corporation website. [Online]. Available: http://www.nissan-global.com/EN/DOCUMENT/PDF/ALLIANCE/HANDBOOK/2014/BookletAlliance2014_GB.pdf [Accessed 21 March 2014].

32. Lee, C.F. & Lee, A.C. 2006. *Encyclopedia of finance*. New York: Springer Science.

33. Hoskisson, R.E., Hitt, M.A., Ireland, R.D. & Harrison, J.S. 2008. *Competing for advantage*. 2nd ed. Ann Arbor: Edwards Brothers, p. 245.

34. Thompson et al, 2010, p. 171.

35. Henry, D. 2002. Mergers: Why most big deals don't pay off. *Bloomberg Business,* October:14.

36. KPMG Survey. 2001. *Survey: World class transactions*. India: KPMG.

37. Agrawal, A., Ferrer, C. & West, A. 2011. When big acquisitions pay off. *McKinsey Quarterly,* May. [Online]. Available: http://www.mckinsey.com/business-functions/strategy-and-corporate-finance/our-insights/when-big-acquisitions-pay-off [Accessed 22 March 2016].

38. De Wit, 2015, pp. 7–11.

39. Cummins, J.D. & Weiss, M.A. 2004. Consolidation in the European insurance industry: Do mergers and acquisitions create value for shareholders? *Brookings–Wharton Papers on Financial Services*, 217–258.

40. Carper, W.B. 1990. Corporate acquisitions and shareholder wealth: A review and exploratory analysis. *Journal of Management*, 16(4):807–823.

41. Ibid.

42. Trautwein, F. 1990. Merger motives and merger prescriptions. *Strategic Management Journal*, 11(4):283–295.
43. Carper, 1990.
44. Oberg, C. & Holstrom, J. 2006. Are mergers and acquisitions contagious? *Journal of Business Research*, 59(12):1267–1275.
45. Cummins & Weiss, 2004.
46. Borenstein, S. 1990. Airline mergers, airport dominance and market power. *American Economic Review*, 80(2):400–404.
47. Volberda et al, 2011, p. 281.
48. Brouthers, K.D., Van Hastenburg, P. & Van den Ven, J. 1998. If most mergers fail why are they so popular? *Long Range Planning*, 31(3):347–353.
49. Southwick, L. 2005. Economies of scale and market power in policing. *Managerial and Decision Economics*, 26(8):461–473.
50. Matsusaka, J.G. 1993. Takeover motives during the conglomerate merger wave. *RAND Journal of Economics*, 24(3), 357–379.
51. Melnik, A. & Pollatschek, M.A. 1973. Debt capacity, diversification and conglomerate mergers. *Journal of Finance*, 28(5):263–1273.
52. De Wit, B. & Meyer, R. 2014. *Strategy: An international perspective*. 5th ed. Hampshire: Cengage, p. 245.
53. Doukas, J.A., Holmen, M. & Travlos, N.G. 2001. *Corporate diversification and performance: Evidence from Swedish conglomerate and nonconglomerate acquisitions*. New York: Department of Finance, Stern School of Business, pp. 281–314.
54. Barragato, C.A. & Markeleviech, A. 2007. Earnings quality following corporate acquisitions. *Managerial Finance*, 34(5):304–315.
55. Sinha, P.K. 1999. On conglomerate diversification, anthology. *Atlantic Economic Journal*, 27(1):115.
56. Thompson & Martin, 2010, p. 509.
57. Volberda et al, 2011, pp. 284–285.
58. Ibid, p. 290.
59. Morck, R., Shleifer, A. & Vishny, R. 1990. Do managerial objectives drive bad acquisitions? *Journal of Finance*, 45(1):31–48.
60. Brouthers et al, 1998.
61. Oberg & Holstrom, 2006.
62. Ibid.
63. Nguyen, H.T., Yung, K. & Sun, Q. 2012. Motives for mergers and acquisitions: Ex-post market evidence from the US. *Journal of Business Finance & Accounting*, 39(9/10):1357–1375.
64. Bower, J.L. 2001. Not all M&As are alike – and that matters. *Harvard Business Review*, March:1–21.
65. Brouthers et al, 1998.
66. Bradley, M., Desai, A. & Kim, E.H. 1988. Synergistic gains from corporate acquisitions and their division between the stockholders of target and acquiring firms. *Journal of Financial Economics*, 21(1):3–40.
67. Trautwein, F. 1990. Merger motives and merger prescriptions. *Strategic Management Journal*, 11(4):283–295.
68. Kumar, S. & Bansal, L.K. 2008. The impact of mergers and acquisitions on corporate performance in India. *Management Decision*, 46(10):1531–1543.
69. Matsusaka, 1993.
70. Evripidou, L. 2012. M&As in the airline industry: Motives and systematic risk. International Journal of Organisational Analysis, 20(4):435–446.
71. Miller, E.L. 2008. *Mergers and acquisitions: A step-by-step legal and practical guide*. Hoboken, NJ: John Wiley and Sons.
72. Evripidou, 2012.
73. Vishny, R. 2003. Stock market driven acquisitions. *Journal of Financial Economics*, 70(3):295–311.
74. Nguyen et al, 2012.
75. Slorach, S. 2004. *Corporate finance, mergers & acquisitions*. New York: Oxford University Press.
76. Hawkes, V. 1999. *ACT companion to treasury management*. Cambridge: Woodhead Publishing.
77. Ray, K.G. 2010. *Mergers and acquisitions: Strategy, valuation and integration*. New Delhi: Asoke K Ghosh.
78. De Wit, 2015.
79. Pudney, 2002.
80. Potgieter, P. 2013. *Premerger and acquisition strategies: A multiple case study of unsolicited takeover attempts in South Africa since 2004*. Unpublished MBA research, University of Stellenbosch Business School, p. 43.
81. Ficery, K., Herd, T. & Purche, B. 2007. Where has all the synergy gone? *Journal of Business Strategy*, 28(5):29–35.
82. Firer, C., Ross, S.A., Westerfield, R.W. & Jordan, B.D. 2008. *Fundamentals of corporate finance*. Maidenhead: McGraw-Hill Education.
83. Potgieter, 2013, p. 44.
84. Meredith, K. 2012. *The devil in the deal*. Cape Town: Zebra Press, p. 168.
85. Ibid, p. 172.
86. Based on Volberda et al, 2011, p. 293
87. Ferrer et al, 2013, pp. 2–3.
88. De Wit, 2015, p. 21.
89. Armour, E. 2002. How boards can improve the odds of M&A success. *Strategy & Leadership*, 30(2):13–20.
90. Sweeting, M. 2008. *Approaching partners and targets in mergers and acquisitions: A practical guide for private companies and their UK and overseas advisers*. London: Kogan Page, pp. 119–126.
91. Ibid.
92. Porter, M.E. 2004. *Competitive strategy*. New York: Free Press, p. 352.
93. Clark, C.J. 1987. Acquisitions – techniques for measuring strategic fit. *Long Range Planning*, 20(3):12–18.
94. Ahammad, M.F. & Glaister, K.W. 2013. The pre-acquisition evaluation of target firms and cross-border acquisition performance. *International Business Review*, 22(5):894–904.

95. De Wit, 2015, p. 23.
96. Perry, J.S. & Herd, T.J. 2004. Reducing M&A risk through improved due diligence. *Strategy and Leadership*, 32(2):12–19.
97. Ahammad & Glaister, 2013.
98. Galpin, T.J. & Herndon, M. 2007. *The complete guide to mergers and acquisitions*. 2nd ed. San Francisco, CA: Jossey-Bass, p. 63.
99. Eccles, R.G., Lanes, K.L. & Wilson, T.C. 1999. Are you paying too much for that acquisition? *Harvard Business Review*, 77(4):136–146.
100. Reed, M. 2009. *The devil is in the deal structure. Softletter Financial Handbook*, Softletter. p. 178.
101. Ibid.
102. Based on Pudney, R. 2003. 2+2=5, Directions. *The Ashridge Journal*, Summer:16–23.
103. De Wit, 2015, pp. 24–28.
104. Lafforet, C. & Wageman, R. 2009. Successful mergers and acquisitions: Beyond the financial issues. *Leader to Leader*, 54:44–51.
105. Walker, J.W. & Price, K.F. 2000. Why do mergers go right? *Human Resource Planning*, 23(2):6–8.
106. Shelton, M.J. 2003. Managing your integration manager. *McKinsey Quarterly*. Special Edition: 81.
107. Epstein, M.J. 2004. The drivers of success in postmerger integration. *Organizational Dynamics*, 33(2):174–189.
108. Gill, C. 2012. The role of leadership in successful international mergers and acquisitions: Why Renault–Nissan succeeded and DaimlerChrysler–Mitsubishi failed. *Human Resource Management*, 51(3):433–456.
109. Lafforet & Wageman, 2009.
110. Bonney, T. & Kehoe, K. 2011. Recruiting and retaining talent: Certain steps are required before and after a deal. *Mergers and Acquisitions: The dealmaker's journal*, 46(5):34.
111. Walker & Price, 2000.
112. Angwin, D. 2004. Speed in M&A integration: The first 100 days. *European Management Journal*, 22(4):418–430.
113. Bert, A., MacDonald, T. & Herd, T. 2003. Two merger integration imperatives: urgency and execution. *Strategy and Leadership*, 31(3):42–49.
114. De Wit, 2015, pp. 24–28.
115. Gole, W.J. & Morris, J.M. 2007. *Mergers and acquisitions: business strategies for accountants*. Hoboken: John Wiley and Sons, pp. 215–216.
116. Loubser, L.R. 2012. Investigating and evaluating the merit of a strategic acquisition: A case study in the aggregate industry. Unpublished MBA research, University of Stellenbosch Business School, p. 20.
117. Schweizer, L. & Patzelt, H. 2012. Employee commitment in the post-acquisition integration process: The effect of integration speed and leadership. *Scandinavian Journal of Management*, 28(4):298–310.
118. Epstein, 2004.
119. Carr, R., Elton, G., Rovit, S. & Vestring, T. 2004. Beating the odds: A blueprint for successful merger integration. *European Business Journal*, 16(4):161–166.
120. Based on: Gadiesh, O., Ormiston, C. & Rovit, S. 2003. Achieving an M&A's strategic goals at maximum speed for maximum value. *Strategy & Leadership*, 31(3):35–41.
121. Rothenbuecher, J. & Schrottke, J. 2008. Merger, grow sales. *Harvard Business Review*, May.
122. Ibid.
123. Walker & Price, 2000.
124. Bert et al, 2003.
125. Weber, R.A. & Camerer, C.F. 2003. Cultural conflict and merger failure: An experimental approach. *Management Science*, 49(4):400–415.
126. Fern, B.N. 1992. Managing the culture clash in mergers. *American Banker*, 157(161):August, 4.
127. Tarba, S. & Weber, Y. 2011. Exploring integration approach: Postmerger integration in the high-tech industry. *International Journal of Organizational Analysis*, 19(3):202–221.
128. Zhang, J., Ahammad, M.F., Tarba, S., Cooper, C.L., Glaister, K.W. & Wang, J. 2015. The effect of leadership style on talent retention during merger and acquisition integration: Evidence from China. *International Journal of Human Resource Management*, 26(7):1021–1050.
129. Nemanich, L.A. & Keller, R.T. 2007. Transformational leadership in an acquisition: A field study of employees. *Leadership Quarterly*, 18(2007):49–68.
130. Ibid.
131. Bert et al, 2003.
132. Messmer, M. 2006. Leadership strategies during mergers and acquisitions. *Strategic Finance*, 87(7):15–16.
133. De Wit, 2015, pp. 24–28.
134. Ibid., pp. 36–38.
135. This part is largely based on Potgieter, 2013, pp. 26–31.
136. JSE Limited. 2007a. *Section 7: Listing Particulars. Listing Requirements*. [Online] Available: http://www.jse.co.za/docs/listings_requirements/SECT07.DOC [Accessed: 11 October 2009]; JSE Limited. 2007b. *Section 8: Financial Information. Listing Requirements*. [Online] Available: http://www.jse.co.za/docs/listings_requirements/SEC08.DOC [Accessed: 11 October 2009]; Republic of South Africa. 1998b. *Competition Act*, No. 89 of 1998; Republic of South Africa. 1991. *Securities Regulation Code on Take-overs and Mergers and the Rules, Government Notice*, R. 29 of 1991; Republic of South Africa. 1973. *Companies Act*, No. 61 of 1973.
137. Ibid.
138. Republic of South Africa. 1973. *Companies Act*, No. 61 of 1973.
139. Loubser, 2012; Competition Commission South Africa (CC SA).
140. CC SA, 2011
141. Potgieter, 2013, pp. 26–31.
142. Volberda et al, 2011, p. 281.
143. Potgieter, 2013, p. 31.
144. Ibid, pp. 35–37.

145. Ibid.
146. The price-to-earnings ratio (P/E) is a valuation method used to compare a company's current share price to its per-share earnings. [Online]. Available: http://www.investinganswers.com/financial-dictionary/ratio-analysis/price-earnings-ratio-pe-459 [Accessed 30 May 2016].
147. A white knight is an individual or company that acquires a corporation on the verge of being taken over by forces deemed undesirable by company officials (sometimes referred to as a "black knight"). While the target company doesn't remain independent, a white knight is viewed as a preferred option to the hostile company completing their takeover. Unlike a hostile takeover, current management typically remains in place in a white knight scenario, and investors receive better compensation for their shares. [Online]. Available: http://www.investopedia.com/terms/w/whiteknight.asp [Accessed 30 May 2016].
148. Potgieter, 2013, pp. 35–37.
149. Absa Strategy Team, 2002. Absa internal strategy document on Possible Future Scenarios. Unpublished.
150. Ibid.
151. ABSA Annual Report. 2005. [Online]. Available: http://www.southafrica.to/Banks/ABSA/financials/ABSA-20051231.pdf [Accessed 27 March 2016.].
152. Reed, Croft and Davies. *Financial Times*, 9 May 2005. [Online]. Available: http://www.ft.com/cms/s/0/11c1560c-bfe4-11d9-b376-00000e2511c8.html#axzz43zMrFW7s [Accessed 26 March 2016].
153. Ibid. Also see Circular to Absa Shareholders for details on the scheme of arrangements. [Online]. Available: http://www.absa.co.za/deployedfiles/Absa.co.za/PDF's/About%20Absa/Barclays%20Transaction/Barclays%20transaction.pdf [27 March 2016].
154. Barclays plc Annual Report. 2005. [Online]. Available: https://www.home.barclays/content/dam/barclayspublic/docs/InvestorRelations/AnnualReports/AR2005/barclays-plc-annual-report-2005.pdf [Accessed 27 March 2016].
155. ABSA Annual Report 2006. [Online]. Available: http://www.absa.co.za/deployedfiles/Absa.co.za/PDFs/About%20Absa/Annual%20Reports/Bank%20Reports/2006/Annual%20Report.pdf [Accessed 27 March 2016].
156. Barclays plc Annual Report. 2005. [Online]. Available: https://www.highbeam.com/doc/1G1-161250139.html [Accessed 26 March 2016].
157. Absa Annual Report. 2007. [Online]. Available: http://www.sharedata.co.za/Data/002337/pdfs/ABSABANK-P_fin_dec07.pdf [Accessed 27 March 2016].
158. Ibid.
159. Ndzamela, P. 2013. 'The relationship between Absa and Barclays'. Financial Mail 29 August 2013. [Online]. Available: http://www.financialmail.co.za/fm/CoverStory/2013/08/29/the-relationship-between-absa-and-barclays [Accessed 26 March 2016].
160. Ibid.
161. Moneyweb. 2013. [Online]. Available: http://www.moneyweb.co.za/archive/which-bank-share-has-performed-best/ [Accessed 26 March 2016].
162. Planting, S. 2013. 'Absa and Barclays get green light for Africa. Moneyweb. 22 July 2013. [Online]. Available: http://www.moneyweb.co.za/archive/absa-and-barclays-get-green-light-for-africa/ [Accessed 26 March 2016].
163. Ibid.
164. Joffe, H. 2016. *Financial Mail*, March 11. [Online]. Available: http://www.financialmail.co.za/coverstory/2016/03/10/barclays-africa-exit-on-the-block [Accessed 26 March 2016].
165. Ibid.
166. Crotty, A. 2016. A Barclays sell-off plot? It's fiction, says Ramos. *Sunday Times*, *Business Times*, March 13, p. 3.
167. Volberda et al, 2011, pp. 299–303.
168. Ibid.
169. Thompson et al, 2010, p. 278.
170. Ibid.
171. Ibid.
172. Department of Mineral Resources, Republic of South Africa, 2016, February 16. [Online]. Available: http://www.angloamerican.com/~/media/Files/A/Anglo-American-PLC-V2/presentations/2016pres/sa-dmr-statement.pdf [Accessed 24 March 2016].
173. Ibid.

CHAPTER 8 ENDNOTES

1. Grant, R.M. 2008. The future of management: Where is Gary Hamel leading us? *Long Range Planning*, 41(5): 474.
2. Taylor, F.W. 1911. The principles of scientific management. *American Society of Mechanical Engineers*: 3–4.
3. Hamel, G. 2006. The why, what and how of management innovation. *Harvard Business Review*, 84(2):74.
4. Taylor, 1911, p. 15.
5. Ibid, p. 16.
6. Ibid, p. 6.
7. Deming, W.E. 1993, February. Deming Four-day Seminar. (M. Stoecklein, Interviewer). Phoenix, Arizona.
8. Taylor, 1911, pp. 3–4.
9. Ibid, p. 4–7.
10. Ibid, p. 4.
11. Ibid, p. 26.
12. Ibid, p. 17, 44.
13. Ibid, p. 4.
14. Ibid, p. 17, 44, 69.

15. Ibid, p. 2.
16. Ibid, p. 11.
17. Ibid, p. 1–2.
18. Ibid, p. 2.
19. Ibid, p. 75.
20. Ibid, p. 3.
21. Ibid, p. 18.
22. Ibid, p. 12.
23. Ibid, p. 12.
24. Ibid, p. 75.
25. Hamel, G. 2009. Moon shots for management. *Harvard Business Review,* 87(2):92.
26. McGrath, R. 2014, July 30. *Management's three eras: A brief history. Harvard Business Review*: [Online]. Available: https://hbr.org/2014/07/managements-three-eras-a-brief-history# [Accessed 16 December 16, 2015].
27. Tanz, J. 2003, October 1. *A brief history of management.* CNN Money: [Online]. Available: http://money.cnn.com/magazines/fsb/fsb_archive/2003/10/01/353427/ [Accessed 16 Dec 2015].
28. Aziz, K. 2012, August 22. *A brief history of the management field.* Slideshare: [Online]. Available: http://www.slideshare.net/khalid1173/a-brief-history-of-management-field [Accessed 16 Dec 2015].
29. Bosman, M. 2009, Jan 15. *Strategic Leadership Institute.* The historical evolution of management theory from 1900 to present: The changing role of leaders in organisations. [Online]. Available: http://www.strategicleadershipinstitute.net/news/the-historical-evolution-of-management-theory-from-1900-to-present-the-changing-role-of-leaders-in-organizations-/ [Accessed 16 Dec 2015].
30. Gitlow, H., Oppenheim, A., Oppenheim, R., & Levine, D. 2005. *Quality management* (3rd ed.). New York: McGraw-Hill, p. 33.
31. Hamel, 2006.
32. Hamel, 2009, p. 92.
33. Taylor, 1911, p. 2.
34. Gitlow et al. 2005, p. 34.
35. Hamel, 2006, p. 79.
36. Hamel, G. 2011. First let's fire all the managers. *Harvard Business Review,* 89(12):51.
37. Wheatley, M. J. 2007. *Finding our way: Leadership for an uncertain time.* San Francisco, CA: Berett-Koehler.
38. Dearlove, D., & Crainer, S. 2015. *Distinguished Achievement Awards (2011–2015).* Thinkers 50: [Online]. Available: http://thinkers50.com/ [Accessed 25 Jan 2016].
39. Robinson, D. 2005, January. Management theorists: Thinkers for the 21st century. *Training Journal.* [Online]. Available: http://www.gdufs.biz/theorists.pdf 30–36 [Accessed 28 May 2016].
40. Kiechel, W. 2012. The management century. *Harvard Business Review,* 90(11):62–75.
41. Ungerer, G.D. 2015. *A competitive strategy framework for e-business start-ups.* Stellenbosch: University of Stellenbosch.
42. Dean, D., Digrande, S., Field, D., Lundmark, A., O'Day, J., Pineda, J., & Zwillenberg, P. 2012, March. *The connected world: The $4.2 trillion opportunity.* Boston Consulting Group: [Online]. Available: https://publicaffairs.linx.net/news/wp-content/uploads/2012/03/bcg_4trillion_opportunity.pdf [Accessed 7 June 2012].
43. Manyika, J., & Roxburg, C. 2011, October. *The great transformer: The impact of the internet on economic growth and prosperity.* McKinsey Global Institute: [Online]. Available: http://www.mckinsey.com/Insights/MGI/Research/Technology_and_Innovation/internet_matters [Accessed 8 May 2012].
44. Ibid, p. 4.
45. Goldstuck, A. 2012. *Internet matters: The quiet engine of the South African economy.* World Wide Worx: [Online]. Available: http://internetmatters.co.za/report/ZA_internet_Matters.pdf [Accessed 31 July 2012].
46. Twenge, J. 2006. *Generation Me.* New York: Free Press (Simon & Shuster).
47. Alsop, R. 2008, October 21. The trophy kids go to work. *Wall Street Journal*: [Online]. Available: http://www.wsj.com/articles/SB122455219391652725 [Accessed 2 February 2016].
48. Urban, T. 2013, September 11. *Why Generation Y yuppies are unhappy.* Wait but why: [Online]. Available: http://waitbutwhy.com/2013/09/why-generation-y-yuppies-are-unhappy.html [Accessed 2 February 2016].
49. Harvey, P. 2010, May 17. *As college graduates hit the workforce, so do more entitlement-minded workers.* University of New Hampshire Media Relations: [Online]. Available: http://www.unh.edu/news/cj_nr/2010/may/lw17gen-y.cfm[Accessed 2 February 2016].
50. Strauss, W., & Howe, N. 2000. *Millennials rising: The next great generation.* New York: Vintage Original.
51. *The Economist.* Generation Boris. 2013, June 1. *The Economist*: [Online]. Available: http://www.economist.com/news/britain/21578666-britains-youth-are-not-just-more-liberal-their-elders-they-are-also-more-liberal-any[Accessed 2 February 2016].
52. Korn Ferry. 2015. *Futurestep survey finds compensation one of the least important factors for recruiting Millennial talent.* 2015, March 5. Los Angeles, CA: Korn Ferry: [Online]. Available: http://www.kornferry.com/press/futurestep-survey-finds-compensation-one-of-the-least-important-factors-for-recruiting-millennial-talent/ [Accessed 2 February 2016].
53. Gilbert, J. 2011, September. *The millennials: A new generation of employees, a new set of engagement policies.* Iveys Business Journal: [Online]. Available: http://iveybusinessjournal.com/publication/the-millennials-a-new-generation-of-employees-a-new-set-of-engagement-policies/ [Accessed 2 February 2016].
54. Roberts, K. 2015, April 8. *Millennial workers want free meals and flex time.* [Online]. Available: http://www.lwdirect.com/millennial-workers-want-free-meals-and-flex-time/[Accessed 2 February 2016].
55. Furlong, A. 2013. *Youth studies: An introduction.* New York: Routledge.
56. Burstein, D. 2013. *Fast future: How the millennial generation is shaping our world.* Boston, MA: Beacon Press.

57. Knoll, Inc. 2014. *What comes after Y? Generation Z: Arriving to the office soon.* [Online]. Available: https://www.knoll.com/media/938/1006/What-Comes-After-Y.pdf [Accessed 2 February 2016].
58. Montini, L. 2014, September 2. *Generation Z: 5 Things to know about your future hires* Inc.com: [Online]. Available: http://www.inc.com/laura-montini/meet-you-future-hires-5-characteristics-of-generation-z.html [Accessed 2 February 2016].
59. Elmore, T. 2015, September 3. *Six defining characteristics of Generation Z.* Growing Leaders: [Online]. Available: http://growingleaders.com/blog/six-defining-characteristics-of-generation-z/ [Accessed 2 February 2016].
60. Hamel, G. 2012. *What matters now.* San Francisco: Jossey-Bass, pp. 173–175.
61. Ibid, p. 176–177.
62. Ibid, p. 141.
63. Ibid, p. 140.
64. Ibid, p. 140.
65. Ibid, p. 141.
66. Ibid, p. 141.
67. Ibid, p. 142.
68. Ibid, p. 142.
69. Ibid, p. 143.
70. Hamel, 2009, p. 98.
71. Hamel, 2012, p. 150.
72. Towers Perrin, 2007–2008. *Closing the engagement gap: A road map for driving superior business performance. Towers Perrin Global Workforce Study Global Report.* Towers Perrin. [Online]. Available: https://c.ymcdn.com/sites/www.simnet.org/resource/group/066D79D1-E2A8-4AB5-B621-60E58640FF7B/leadership_workshop_2010/towers_perrin_global_workfor.pdf [Accessed 1 February 2016].
73. Hamel, 2012, pp. 138–139.
74. Ibid, p. 147.
75. Ibid, p. 143.
76. Riffkin, R. 2014, December 18. *Americans rate nurses highest on honesty, ethical standards.* Gallup.com: [Online]. Available: http://www.gallup.com/poll/180260/americans–rate-nurses-highest-honesty-ethical-standards.aspx [Accessed 1 February 2016].
77. Hamel, 2012, p. 147.
78. Ibid, p. 147.
79. Gitlow et al. 2005, p. 32.
80. Ibid, p. 32.
81. Skousen, M. 2013. *Economic logic* (4th ed.). Regnery, p. 94.
82. Gitlow et al, 2005, p. 31.
83. Ibid, p. 34.
84. Deming, W. E. 1986. *Out of the crisis.* Cambridge, MA: Massachusetts Institute of Technology Center for Advanced Engineering Studies.
85. Gitlow et al. 2005, p. 35.
86. Herzberg, F. 1968. *One more time: How do you motivate employees.* Boston: Harvard Business Review.
87. Deming, W. E. 1993. *The new economics for industry, government, education.* Cambridge, MA: Massachusetts Institute of Technology.
88. Ibid.
89. Magretta, J. 2012. *Understanding Michael Porter.* Boston: Harvard Business Review Press, pp. 21–28.
90. Gitlow et al. 2005, pp. 36–37.
91. Ibid, p. 36.
92. Ibid, p. 37–50.
93. Carter, J. 2015, November 2. *Should we strive for business instability? A systems view.* LinkedIn: [Online]. Available: https://www.linkedin.com/pulse/should-we-strive-business-instability-systems-view-jason-carter [Accessed 22 Jan 2016].
94. Brook, M. 2014. *New dimensions in health: Simple secrets to creating optimal health.* Bloomington: Balboa Press, p. 297.
95. Ibid, p. 297.
96. Gitlow et al. 2005 Hill, p. 38.
97. Ibid, p. 38.
98. Bullington, K.E. 2003. 5S for Suppliers. *Quality Progress.* Vol 56, no. 9: 56–59.
99. Gitlow et al. 2005, p. 41.
100. Ibid, p. 43.
101. Ibid, p. 46.
102. Ibid, p. 47.
103. Ibid, p. 49.
104. Ibid, p. 49.
105. Hamel, 2009, p. 91.
106. Ibid, p. 92.
107. National Academy of Engineering. 2008. 'Grand Challenges for Engineering in the 21st Century'. Washinton, DC: The National Academics of Sciences, Engineering, Medicine. http://www.engineeringchallenges.org/challenges.aspx [Online]. Available: engineerinchallenges.org [Accessed 22 Jan 2016].
108. Ibid, pp. 91, 92, 94.
109. Ibid, pp. 92, 94.
110. Ibid, p. 94.

111. Hamel, 2006, p. 74.
112. Hamel, 2009, p. 92.
113. Ibid.
114. Collins, J.C., & Porras, J. I. 1994. *Built to last: Successful habits of visionary companies.* New York: Harper Business.
115. Hamel, 2009, pp. 91–98.
116. Ibid.
117. Bower, J.L., & Christensen, C.M. 1995. Disruptive technologies: Catching the wave. *Harvard Business Review,* 73(1):44.
118. Christensen, C.M., Johnson, M.W., & Rigby, D. K. 2002. Foundations for growth: How to identify and build disruptive new businesses. *MIT Sloan Management Review,* 43(3):23, 34.
119. Hamel, 2009, p. 98.
120. Ibid, p. 98.
121. Kaplan, R., & Norton, D. 1992. The balanced scorecard – measures that drive performance. *Harvard Business Review,* 70(1):71.
122. Da Silva, M. 2014. *The development of a management innovation measurement tool.* Bellville: University of Stellenbosch.
123. Ibid.
124. Birkinshaw, J., & Mol, M. 2006. How management innovation happens. *MIT Sloan Management Review,* 47(4):81–88.
125. Birkinshaw, J., Hamel, G., & Mol, M. 2008. Management innovation. *Academy of Management Review,* 33(4): 825–845.
126. Birkinshaw & Mol, 2006, pp. 81–88.
127. Da Silva, 2014.
128. Birkinshaw et al, 2008, pp. 825–845.
129. Da Silva, 2014.
130. Ibid.
131. Ibid.
132. Mol & Birkinshaw, 2006, pp. 24–29.
133. Birkinshaw & Mol, 2006, pp. 81–88.
134. Mol, M., & Birkinshaw, J. 2009. The sources of management innovation: When firms introduce new management practices. *Journal of Business Research,* 62(12):1269–1280.
135. Amabile, T. 1998. How to kill creativity. *Harvard Business Review,* 76(5):76–87.
136. Project Leaders International. 2008. White Paper: An integrated approach to managing innovation. [Online]. Available: http://www.rcc.gov.pt/SiteCollectionDocuments/Integrated_Innovation_PLI2008.pdf [Accessed 12 Feb 2016].
137. Da Silva, 2014.
138. Hamel, 2006, p. 81.
139. Ibid, p. 73.
140. Ibid, p. 74.
141. Isaacson, W. 2012. The real leadership lessons of Steve Jobs. *Harvard Business Review,* 90(4):99–100.
142. Hamel, G. 2007. *The future of management.* Harvard Business Press, p. 103.
143. Ibid, p. 102, 105.
144. Ibid, p. 104.
145. Ibid, p. 113.
146. Ibid, p. 106.
147. Ibid, p. 112.
148. Ibid, p. 113.
149. Ibid, p. 116.
150. Ibid, p. 112.
151. Ibid, p. 102, 109.
152. Ibid, p. 102, 107, 116, 117.
153. Ibid, p. 110.
154. Ibid, p. 110, 112.
155. Google Office Zurich (CH). 2008. 'How work could be'. [Online]. Available: Google Office Zurich: http://www.swiss-miss.com/wp-content/uploads/legacy/weblog/files/google_office_zurich.pdf [Accessed 15 February 2016].
156. Google office around the world. Mar 11, 2010. *Google offices around the world.* 2010. YouTube: [Online]. Available: https://www.youtube.com/watch?v=LB5utwRnfH4 [Accessed 15 February 2016].
157. Dunn, C. 2014, October 4. *8 of Google's craziest offices.* Fastcompany Design: [Online]. Available: http://www.fastcodesign.com/3028909/8-of-googles-craziest-offices [Accessed 15 February 2016].
158. Hamel, 2007, pp. 107, 108.
159. Ibid, p. 119.
160. Google Company. 'Google's mission is to organize the world's information and make it universally accessible and useful.' *Google Company Overview.* 2016. Google: [Online]. Available: https://www.google.co.za/about/company/ [Accessed 15 February 2016].
161. Semler, R. 1989. Managing without managers. *Harvard Business Review,* 67(5):76.
162. Ibid, p. 77.
163. Ibid, p. 77.
164. Ibid, p. 78.
165. Ibid, p. 78.
166. Ibid, p. 78.

167. Ibid, p. 78.
168. Ibid, p. 79.
169. Ibid, p. 79.
170. Ibid, p. 80.
171. Ibid, p. 80.
172. Ibid, p. 80.
173. Ibid, p. 80.
174. Ibid, p. 80.
175. Ibid, p. 81.
176. Ibid, p. 81.
177. Ibid, p. 82.
178. Ibid, p. 84.
179. Ibid, p. 84.
180. Hamel, 2007, pp. 253–254.
181. Hamel, 2012, pp. 151, 212–222.
182. Da Silva, 2014, p. 29.
183. Hamel, 2006, p. 76.
184. Porter, M.E. 2001. Strategy and the internet. *Harvard Business Review,* 79(3):74.
185. Hamel, 2009, p. 98.

CHAPTER 9 ENDNOTES

1. Calá, C.D., Arauzo-Carod, J-M. & Manjón-Antolín, M. 2015. *The determinants of entrepreneurship in developing countries.* (Documento de Trabajo No. 1). Reus: Universitat Rovira i Virgili. Departament d'Economia. See their Footnote 1: Entrepreneurship can promote growth and development through a variety of channels. We should mention, among others, **the role of new firms in enhancing regional job growth** (Ghani, E., Kerr, W.R., & O'Connell, S. 2011. *Promoting entrepreneurship, growth, and job creation.* Ch. 7, 166–199); **commercialising innovations** (Audretsch, D.B., Keilbach, M.C., & Lehmann, E.E. 2006. *Entrepreneurship and economic growth.* [Oxford: Oxford University Press; **discovering the competitive advantages of a nation** (Hausmann, R., & Rodrik, D. 2003. Economic development as self-discovery. *Journal of Development Economics,* 72(2):603–633); **increasing structural transformation by absorbing surplus labour from traditional sectors, providing innovative inputs, promoting specialization, raising productivity and employment** (Gries, T., & Naudé, W. 2010. Entrepreneurship and structural economic transformation. *Small Business Economics,* 34(1):13-29); and leading to **gap-filling and input- and output-completing activities** (Acs, Z.J., & Amorós, J.E. 2008. Entrepreneurship and competitiveness dynamics in Latin America. *Small Business Economics,* 31(3):305–322). [Emphasis our own].
2. Audretsch et al, 2006.
3. Van Praag, M.C. & Versloot, P.H. 2007. What is the value of entrepreneurship? A review of recent research. *Small Business Economics,* 29:351-82.
4. Interview conducted by Dominic Midgley, published April 14, 2014. [Online]. Available: http://businesslife.ba.com/People/What-Ive-Learnt/What-Ive-learnt-chocolatier-Mary-Ann-OBrien.html [Accessed 1 May 2016].
5. Clarke, J. 2015. Mary Ann O'Brien: how I made my fortune from airline chocolates. *MoneyWeek.* [Online] Available: http://moneyweek.com/profile-of-entrepreneur-mary-ann-obrien-47730/ [Accessed 28 May 2016].
6. O'Brien, L. Chocolate Heaven at Lily O'Brien's. 18 May 2015. [Online]. Available: http://eatdrinkrunfun.com/?p=3913 [Accessed 4 May 2016].
7. Carlyle News Release. [Online]. Available: https://www.carlyle.com/news-room/news-release-archive/carlyle-cardinal-ireland-invests-lily-o%E2%80%99brien%E2%80%99s-irish-manufacturer [Accessed 1 May 2016].
8. Kelpie, C. 2015. Lily O'Brien boss aims to double business following Carlyle Cardinal move. *Irish Independent, Business Irish (*Business Newsletter). [Online]. Available: http://www.independent.ie/business/irish/lily-obrien-boss-aims-to-double-business-following-carlyle-cardinal-move-34254058.html [Accessed 1 May 2016].
9. Lynch, R.L. 2009. *Strategic management.* (5th ed). Harlow: Financial Times Prentice Hall, p. 627
10. Hinde, N. *Huffington Post,* 17 October 2014. [Online]. Available: http://www.huffingtonpost.co.uk/2014/10/17/mary-ann-obrien-lily-obriens-chocolate_n_5965462.html [Accessed 4 May 2016].
11. University of stellenbosch. entrepreneurship & innovation Management. [Online]. Available: http://www.sun.ac.za/english/faculty/economy/business-management/academic-programmes/undergraduate/entrepreneurship-innovation-management [Accessed 16 May 2016].
12. University of Pretoria. 2016. *BCom Entrepreneurship brochure.* [Online]. Available: http://www.up.ac.za/business-management/article/42179/chair-in-entrepreneurship [Accessed 3 May 2016].
13. The Global Entrepreneurship Monitor is one of the world's foremost study centres of entrepreneurship. Through a vast, centrally coordinated, internationally executed data collection effort, GEM is able to provide high-quality information and comprehensive reports and interesting stories, which greatly enhance the understanding of the entrepreneurial phenomenon – but it is more than that. It is also an ever-growing community of believers in the transformative benefits of entrepreneurship. Their current data dates back to 1998.
14. The World Bank Group Entrepreneurship Survey (WBGES) started collecting datasets in 2000. It is a source of data that facilitates the measurement of entrepreneurial activity across countries and over time. The data also allows for a deeper understanding of the relationship between new firm registration, the regulatory environment, and economic growth. This ongoing work produces entrepreneurship snapshots on various themes that continue to illustrate the importance of entrepreneurship for the dynamism of the modern economy. This project is

joint effort by the Kauffman Foundation, World Bank Development Research Group, and the International Finance Corporation. [Online]. Available: http://www.kaufman.corp [Accessed 16 May 2016].

15. Bartelsman, E., Haltiwanger, J., & Scarpetta, S. 2004. *Microeconomic evidence of creative destruction in industrial and developing countries.* Institute for the Study of Labor, IZA. Discussion Paper no. 1374. The World Bank, Policy Research Working Paper no. 3464. [Online] Available: http://ssrn.com/abstract=612230 [Accessed 27 May 2016].

16. Acs, Z.J., Desai, S., & Klapper, L. F. 2008. What does "entrepreneurship" data really show? *Small Business Economics*, 31(3):265–281.

17. Business Dictionary. 2016. [Online]. Available: http://www.businessdictionary.com/definition/entrepreneur.html [Accessed 4 May 2016].

18. Hisrich, R. D., Peters, M.P. & Shepherd, D.A. 2005. *Entrepreneurship.* 6th ed. New York: McGraw-Hill Irwin.

19. Hisrich et al, 2005, chapter 3.

20. Ungerer, M., Ungerer, G. & Herholdt, J. 2016. *Crystallising the strategic business landscape: Strategy analysis practices and tools for business leaders and strategy practitioners,* Johannesburg: KR Publishing.

21. Lidow, D. 2014. *Startup leadership: How savvy entrepreneurs turn their ideas into successful enterprises.* San Francisco, CA: Jossey-Bass. For an interview and overview see http://www.strategy-business.com/article/00261?gko=4b6bf [Accessed 16 May 2016].

22. Blank, S. 2013. Why the lean start-up changes everything. *Harvard Business Review,* 91(5):65–72.

23. Ibid, p. 69.

24. Ibid, p. 67.

25. For more detail see http://www.entrepreneurship.co.za/

26. SA Institute for Entrepreneurship. 2016. Who are we? [Online]. Available] http://www.entrepreneurship.co.za/contents/who-are-we/ [Accessed 5 May 2016].

27. Caliendo, M., & Kritikos, A. 2012. Searching for the entrepreneurial personality: New evidence and avenues for further research. *Journal of Economic Psychology* 33(2):319–324.

28. Schumpeter, J.A. 1942. *Capitalism, socialism and democracy.* New York: Harper and Brothers.

29. *Economist.* 2009. Global heroes: A special report on entrepreneurship. 14 March.

30. *Economist,* 2009, pp. 4ff.

31. See, for instance, Verheul I., Thurik R., Grilo I. & Van der Zwan, P. 2011. Explaining preferences and actual involvement in self-employment: New insights into the role of gender. *Journal of Economic Psychology.* 33:325–341. DOI: 10.1016/j.joep.2011.02.009

32. Van der Zwan, P., Verheul, I., Thurik, R. & Grilo, I. 2013. Entrepreneurial progress: Climbing the entrepreneurial ladder in Europe and the US. *Regional Studies,* 47(5):803-825. DOI: 10.1080/00343404.2011.598504

33. Caliendo M., Fossen F. & Kritikos A. 2010. The impact of risk attitudes on entrepreneurial survival. *Journal of Economic Behavior & Organization,* 76:5–63.

34. Shepherd, D.A. 2003. Learning from business failure: Propositions about the grief recovery process for the self-employed, *Academy of Management Review* 28(2):318–329.

35. Politis, D. 2005. The process of entrepreneurial learning: A conceptual framework. *Entrepreneurship: Theory & Practice* 29(4):399–424.

36. Willebrands, D., Lammers, J. & Hartog, J. 2011. A successful businessman is not a gambler. Risk attitude and business performance among small enterprises in Nigeria. *Journal of Economic Psychology.* [Online]. Available: doi:10.1016/j.joep.2011.03.006 [Accessed 5 May 2016].

37. See, for instance, Carter, N.M., Gartner, W.B., Shaver, K.G., & Gatewood, E.J. 2003. The career reasons of nascent entrepreneurs. *Journal of Business Venturing,* 18:13–39.

38. Caliendo & Kritikos, 2012, p. 8.

39. Sorgner, A., Fritsch, M. & Kritikos, A. 2014. Do entrepreneurs really earn less? *Jena Economic Research Papers,* # 029-2014:21.

40. Van der Zwan et al, 2013.

41. Pienaar, E.B. 2013. The most prevalent features impacting on significant financial success amongst repeat entrepreneurs. Unpublished MBA Dissertation, University of Stellenbosch Business School. [Online]. Available: http://www.usb-ed.com/content/Knowledge%20Centre%20Documents/The%20Constituents%20of%20Entrepreneurial%20Success.pdf [Accessed 5 May 2016].

42. The EY G20 Entrepreneurship Barometer. 2013. The power of three: governments, entrepreneurs and corporations [Online]. Available: http://www.ey.com/GL/en/Services/Strategic-Growth-Markets/The-EY-G20-Entrepreneurship-Barometer-2013 [Accessed 6 May 2016].

43. The World Bank. 2016. Patent applications, residents. [Online]. Available: http://data.worldbank.org/country/south-africa [Accessed 6 May 2016].

44. Schwab, K. 2015. *The Global Competitiveness Report 2015–16.* (World Economic Forum Insight Report, 2015, where South Africa ranks 49th out of 140 economies measured). [Online]. Available: http://reports.weforum.org/global-competitiveness-report-2015-2016/ [Accessed 6 May 2016].

45. Schwab, 2015.

46. Technology for Women in Business (TWIB). TWIB – Empowering Women Through Tech. [Online]. Available: http://www.twib.co.za/ [Accessed 6 May 2016].

47. Krueger, A. 2015. The rise of the intrapreneur. *Fast Company,* 18 May. [Online]. Available: http://www.fastcompany.com/3046231/the-new-rules-of-work/the-rise-of-the-intrapreneur [Accessed 6 May 2016].

48. 'What Is The Role Of A Workplace After A Tragedy?' *Fast Company.* 2005. [Online]. Available: http://www.fastcompany.com/ [Accessed 6 May 2016].

49. http://www.forbes.com/billionaires/list/5/#version:static [Accessed 8 May 2016].

50. Top 500 Companies. 2015. The Wiese factor: an iconic South African success story. [Online] Available: http://www.top500.co.za/the-wiese-factor-an-iconic-south-african-success-story/ [Accessed 8 May 2016].

51. Design Team. 2011. Design Team: Creating inspiration print by print. [Online] Available: http://www.designteamfabrics.co.za/ [Accessed 10 May 2016].

52. ABC News. 2016. [Online]. Available: http://abcnews.go.com/topics/business/CEOs/bernard-madoff.htm [Accessed 9 May 2016].

53. Rego, A., Cunha, M.P.E. & Clegg, S. 2012. *The virtues of leadership.* Oxford: Oxford University Press, p. 20.

CHAPTER 1 REFERENCES

Bass, B.M., Waldman, D.A., Avolio, B.J. & Bebb, M. 1987. Transformational leadership and the falling dominoes effect. *Group and Organisation Studies*, 12(1):73–87.

Bottger, P.C. & Barsoux, J. 2009. What new general managers must learn and forget in order to succeed. *Strategy & Leadership*, 37(6):25–32.

Brenner, S.N. & Molander, E.A. 1977. Is ethics of business changing? *Harvard Business Review*, 55(1):57–71.

Buckingham, M. 2012. Leadership development in the age of the algorithm. *Harvard Business Review,* June, 86–94.

Cameron, K. 2008. *Positive Leadership: Strategies for extraordinary performance*. San Francisco: Berrett-Koehler.

Cameron, K. 2011. Responsible leadership as virtuous leadership. *Journal of Business Ethics*, 98(1):25–35.

Cameron, K.S. 2003. Organisational virtuousness and performance. In In Cameron, K.S., Dutton, J.E., and Quinn, R.E., editors, *Positive Organizational Scholarship: Foundations of a New Discipline*, 328-342. Berrett-Koehler Publishers Inc., San Francisco, CA.

Chia, R.C.H. & Holt, R. 2011. *Strategy without design*. Cambridge: Cambridge University Press.

Collins, J. & Hansen, M.T. 2011. *Great by choice*. London: Random House.

Collins, J. 2001. *Good to great: Why some companies make the leap and other don't*. New York: Random House.

De Araújoa, M.S.G. & Lopes, P.M.P.R. 2014. Virtuous leadership, organisational commitment and individual performance. *TÉKHNE – Review of Applied Management Studies*, 12(1):3–10.

De Vries, M.K. 2001. *The leadership mystique: A user's manual for the human enterprise*. London: Prentice-Hall.

De Wit, B. & Meyer, R. 2014. *Strategy: An international perspective*. Hampshire: Cengage Learning, 5th edition.

Diamandis, P.H. & Kotler, S. 2012. *Abundance: The future is better than you think*. New York: Free Press.

Drucker, P. 2004. What makes an effective executive? *Harvard Business Review,* 82(6):58–63.

Drucker, P.F. 1986. *Management: Tasks, responsibilities, practices*. New York: Truman Talley Books.

Drucker, P.F. 1993. *The post-capitalist society*. London: Routledge.

Drucker, P.F. 1999. *Management challenges for the 21st century*. London: HarperCollins.

Drucker, P.F. 2005. Managing oneself. *Harvard Business Review,* January: 100-109.

Eccles, R.G., & Nohria, N. 1992. *Beyond the hype: Rediscovering the essence of management*. Boston: Harvard Business School Press.

Esterhuyse, D. 2013. Strategy-as-practice perspective: A case study of a professional services provider in a regional industry context. MBA research report. South Africa: University of Stellenbosch.

Ferraro, F., Pfeffer, J. & Sutton, R.I. 2005. Economic language and assumptions: How theories can become self-fulfilling. *Academy of Management Review,* 30(8):8–24.

Finkelstein, S. 2004. The seven habits of spectacularly unsuccessful executives. *Ivey Business Journal* (68)3, Jan/Feb.

Geises, M.M. 2013. How we do it: Strategy-as-practice in Old Mutual Namibia. MBA research report. South Africa: University of Stellenbosch.

Ghosal, S. 2005. Bad management theories are destroying good management practices. *Academy of Management Learning and Education*, 4(1):75–91.

Gore, A. 2009. Discovery Invest Leadership Summit, Sandton, Johannesburg, 22 July. [Online]. Available: http://www.bizcommunity.com/Article/196/40/38201.html [Accessed 16 November 2015].

Gosling, J. & Mintzberg, H. 2003. The five minds of a manager. *Harvard Business Review,* November:1–9. Reprint version.

Hackett, R.D. & Wang, Q. 2012. Virtues and leadership: An integrating conceptual framework founded in Aristotelian and Confucian perspectives on virtues. *Management Decision*, 50(5):868-899.

Hamel, G. & Prahalad, C.K. 1990. The core competence of the corporation. *Harvard Business Review*, May-June, 1-15.

Hamel, G. 1996. Strategy as revolution. *Harvard Business Review*, July-August, 78.

Hamel, G. 2012. *What matters now*. San Francisco: Jossey-Bass.

Hamel, G., & Prahalad, C.K. 1989. Strategic intent. *Harvard Business Review*, May/June: 63–76.

Hendry, J. & Seidl, D. 2003. The structure and significance of strategic episodes: Social systems theory and the routine practices of strategic change. *Journal of Management Studies*, 40(1):175–196.

Horney, N., Pasmore, B. & O'Shea, T. 2010. Leadership agility: A business imperative for a VUCA world. *People & Strategy*, 33:4.

Impact International 2012. Vuca: Volatility, Uncertainty, Complexity, Ambiguity. Internal discussion document.

Ioannou, I. & Hancock, H. 2013. Changing the world. *Business Strategy Review*, London Business School, Special Edition.

Jacobs, J. 2013. Strategy-as-practice perspective: A case study of a business unit in the mining industry. MBA research report. South Africa: University of Stellenbosch.

Jansen van Vuuren, M. 2011. A strategy-as-practice perspective: A case study of a business unit in a print media organisation. MBA research report. South Africa: University of Stellenbosch.

Jaworski, J. 1996. *Synchronicity: The inner path of leadership*. San Francisco: Berret-Koehler.

Kahane, A. 2010. *Power & love: Solving tough social and organisational problems*. Cape Town: Tafelberg.

Kahneman, D. 2011. *Thinking fast and slow*. New York: Macmillan.

Kanter, R.M. 2008. The corporate conduct continuum: From "do no harm" to "do lots of good", in C.C. Manz, K.S. Cameron, K.P. Manz & R.D. Marx (Eds.), *The virtuous organisation: Insights from some of the world's leading management thinkers*. Singapore: World Scientific.

Kelley, H.H. 1972. Attribution in social interaction. In E. Jones, D. Kanouse, H. Kelley, N. Nisbett, S. Valins & B. Weiner (Eds.), *In attribution: Perceiving the causes of behavior*. Morristown, NJ: General Learning Press.

Lawrence, K. 2013. Developing leaders in a VUCA environment. [Online]. Available: http://www.kenan-flagler.unc.edu/executive-development/about/~/media/Files/documents/executive-development/developing-leaders-in-a-vuca-environment.pdf [Accessed 3 November 2015].

Mackey, A. 2008. The effect of CEOs on firm performance. *Strategic Management Journal,* 29: 1357–1367.

Maharaj, T. 2013. Strategy-as-practice perspective: A case study of a company in the financial services industry. MBA research report. South Africa: University of Stellenbosch.

Mingeli, B. 2012. Exploratory research on strategy-as-practice at Namibia Power Corporation. MBA research report. South Africa: University of Stellenbosch.

Mintzberg, H. 1973. Management and Business Studies Portal. [Online]. Available: http://www.mbsportal.bl.uk/taster/subjareas/busmanhist/mgmtthinkers/mintzberg.aspx [Accessed: 30 July 2012].

Mintzberg, H. 1973. *The nature of managerial work*. New York: Harper & Row.

Mintzberg, H. 1987. The strategy concept I: Five Ps for strategy. *California Management Review*, 30(1):11–24.

Mintzberg, H. 1987. The Strategy Concept II: Another look at why organisations need strategies. *California Management Review*, Fall:25–31.

Mintzberg, H. 1994. Rethinking strategic planning Part I: Pitfalls and Fallacies. *Long Range Planning*, 27(3):12–21.

Mintzberg, H., Ahlstrand, B., & Lampel, J. 2009. *Strategy Safari*. Edinburgh Gate: Prentice Hall.

Mintzberg,, H. 2009. *Management*. San Francisco: Berret-Koehler.

Montgomery, C.A. 2012. *The strategist*. London: HarperCollins.

Myburgh-van Reenen, G.M. 2012. Strategy-as-practice: A case study of a South African fruit export company. MBA research report. South Africa: University of Stellenbosch

Nel, C. & Beudeker, N. 2009. *(R)evolution: How to create a high-performance organisation*. Cape Town: Village of Leaders Products.

Novak, M.A. 2012. Why we help. *Scientific American*, July, 307(1):20–25.

Pearce, C.L. & Sims, H.P. Jr. 2002. Vertical versus shared leadership as predictors of the effectiveness of change management teams: An examination of aversive, directive, transactional, transformational, and empowering leader behaviors. *Group Dynamics: Theory, Research, and Practice*, 6(2):172–197.

Pearce, C.L., Waldman, D.A. & Csikszentmihaly, M. 2006. Virtuous leadership: A theoretical model and research agenda. *Journal of Management, Spirituality & Religion*, 3(1-2):60–77, DOI: 10.1080/14766080609518611.

Petersen, C. 2000. The future of optimism. *American Psychologist*, 55: 44–55.

Peterson, C. & Seligman, M. 2004. *Character strengths and virtues: A handbook and classification*. New York: Oxford Press.

Porter, M.E. 1996. What is strategy? *Harvard Business Review*, 74(6): 61–78.

Porter, M.E., Lorsch, J.W. & Nohria, N. 2004. Seven surprises for new CEOs. *Harvard Business Review*, October:1–1. Reprint.

Rego, A., Cunha, M.P.E. & Clegg, S. 2012. *The virtues of leadership*. Oxford: Oxford University Press.

Rosenzwigh, P. 2007. *The halo effect: … and the eight other business delusions that deceive managers*. New York: Free Press.

Rossouw, G.J. & van Vuuren, L.J. 2003. Modes of managing morality: A descriptive model of strategies for managing ethics. *Journal of Business Ethics*, 46(4): 392–393..

Rumelt, R.P. 2011. *Good strategy. Bad strategy: The difference and why it matters*. New York: Krown Business, p. 5.

Simelane, S.N. 2013. Strategy-as-practice: A case study of a company in the sugar and renewable energy industry in Swaziland. MBA research report. South Africa: University of Stellenbosch.

Sisodia, R.S. 2013. Understanding the performance drivers of conscious firms. *California Management Review*, (55)3:87-96.

Spreitzer, G.M. & Sonenshein, S. 2003. *Positive deviance and extraordinary organising*, p. 209. In Cameron, K.S., Dutton, J.E. & Quinn, R.E. (Eds.), *Positive organisational scholarship*. San Francisco: Berret-Koehler.

Stalk, G. 2004. Playing hardball: Why strategies still matter. *Ivey Business Journal*, (69):2–8.

Stanford Encyclopedia of Philosophy. 2014. Virtue ethics. [Online] Available: http://plato.stanford.edu/entries/ethics-virtue/ [Accessed 26 November 2015].

Strategic Leadership Institute. (n.d.). *Leadership quotes*. [Online] Available: http://www.strategicleadershipinstitute.net/articles/leadership-quotes/ [Accessed 21 November 2015].

Sullivan, J. 2012. VUCA: the new normal for talent management and workforce planning. [Online] Available: http://www.eremedia.com/ere/vuca-the-new-normal-for-talent-management-and-workforce-planning/ [Accessed 3 November 2015].

Thompson Jnr, A.A., Strickland lll, A.J. & Gamble, J.E. 2010. Crafting and executing strategy: Text and readings. 17th edition. Berkshire: McGraw-Hill.

Ungerer, G.D. 2015. A competitive strategy framework for e-business start-ups. Unpublished PhD dissertation, University of Stellenbosch.

Ungerer, M., Herholdt, J. & Le Roux, J. 2013. *Leadership for all: Virtue practices to flourish*. Randburg: Knowres Publishing.

Ungerer, M., Pretorius, M. & Herholdt, J. 2011. *Viable business strategies: A fieldbook for leaders*. 3rd updated edition. Johannesburg: Knowres Publishing.

Wang, D. & Hackett, R.D. 2015. Conceptualisation and measurement of virtuous leadership: Doing well by doing good. *Journal of Business Ethics*, 1-25. DOI 10.1007/s10551-015-2560-1. [Online] Availabel: http://link.springer.com/article/10.1007%2Fs10551-015-2560-1 [Accessed 20 June 2016].

Watkins, M.D. 2012. How managers become leaders: The seven seismic shifts of perspective and responsibility. *Harvard Business Review*, June: 65–72.

Whittington, R. 2012. Conference presentation. Strategic Management Society, 32nd Annual International Conference, October 6-9, 2012. Prague, Czech Republic.

Williams, T., Worsley, T.W., & Lawler III, E.E. 2013. The agility factor. *Strategy+business*, 15 April 2013. [Online] Available: http://www.strategy-business.com/article/00188?gko=6a0ba [Accessed 20 June 2016].

Zander, R.S. & Zander, B. 2002. *The art of possibility*. New York: Penguin Books.

CHAPTER 2 REFERENCES

Baker, W., Marn, M., & Zawada, C. (2001). Price smarter on the net. *Harvard Business Review*, 29(2):122–127.

Barsh, J., Crawford, B., & Grosso, C. (2000). How e-tailing can rise from the ashes. *McKinsey Quarterly* (3):98–109.

Beeslaar, M., Fraser, C., Moodley, S., Pienaar, G. & Schoeman, R. 2015. A strategic architecture perspective on ZARA. MBA strategic management group assignment. University of Stellenbosch Business School. Unpublished.

Boardman, T. 2006. *Nedbank Annual Report*. Nedbank Group. [Online] Available: https://www.nedbank.co.za/content/dam/nedbank/site-assets/AboutUs/Information%20Hub/Integrated%20Report/2006/2006_Nedbank_Group_Annual_Report.pdf [Acccessed 20 June 2016].

Brazzoli, F. 2013. Strategic Management individual assignment as part of MPhil in emerging country leadership. University of Johannesburg. Unpublished.

Christensen, C.M. & Overdorf, M. 2000. Meeting the challenge of disruptive change. *Harvard Business Review*, 78(2):66–76.

Cusumano, M.A. (2013). Technology strategy and management: Evaluating a startup venture. *Communications of the ACM*, 56(10):26–28.

Fritz, R. 1989. *The path of least resistance: Learning to become the creative force in your own life.* New York: Fawcett Columbine.

Gilmore, J.H. & Pine, B.J. 2007. *Authenticity: What consumers really want.* New York: Harvard Business Press.

Gonzales-Benito, J. & Suarez-Gonzalez, I. 2011. A study on the role played by manufacturing strategic objectives and capabilities in understanding the relationship between Porter's generic strategies and business performance. *British Journal of Management*, 21(4):1027–1043.

Gummerus, J. 2011. *Customer value in e-service: Conceptual foundation and empirical evidence.* Helsinki: Hanken School of Economics.

Hagiu, A. & Wright, J. 2013. Do you really want to be on e-bay? *Harvard Business Review*, 91(3):103–108.

Hamel, G. 2012. *What matters now.* San Francisco: Jossey-Bass

Henry, A.E. 2011. *Understanding strategic management.* New York: Oxford Press.

Huff, L & Kelly, L. 2003. Levels of organisational trust in individualist versus collectivist societies: A seven-nation study. *Organisation Science,* 14(1): 81–90.

Jones, G.R. 2007. *Amazon.com Case.* Texas: A&M University.

Kanter, R.M. 2011. How great companies think differently. *Harvard Business Review*, 89(11): HBR Reprint 1–11.

Koorts, C. 2014. Woolworths Holdings Limited: Strategic framework critique. MBA Strategic Management Individual Assignment. University of Stellenbosch Business School. Unpublished.

Kotter, J.P. 1996. *Leading change.* Boston: Harvard Business Press.

Lee, C.-S., & Vonortas, N.S. (2004). Business model innovation in the digital economy. In G. Doukidis, N. Mylonopoulos, & N. Pouloudi, *Social and economic transformation in the digital era.* Hershey, PA: Idea Group.

Letschert, J. 2008. *Taking a local brand to the global arena: Lessons from an SA entrepreneur.* USB Leader's Angle, 27 June. Cape Town: USB Thought Print

Lin, X. & Wang, C.L. 2008. Enforcement and performance: The role of ownership, legalism and trust in international joint ventures. *Journal of World Business,* 43(3):340–351.

Lipton, M. 2004. Walking the talk (really!): Why visions fail. *Ivey Business Journal*, 68 (3):358–364.

Louw, L. & Venter, P. (Eds.) 2006. *Strategic management. Winning in the Southern African workplace.* Cape Town: Oxford University Press, SA.

Malone, M.S. 2007. *Bill & Dave: How Hewlett and Packard built the world's greatest company.* New York: Penguin.

Pine II, B.J. and Gilmore, J.H. 2008. The eight principles of strategic authenticity. *Strategy & Leadership*, 36(3):35–40.

Porter, M. 1980. *Competitive strategy: Techniques for analyzing industries and competitors.* New York: Free Press.

Porter, M.E. 2001. Strategy and the internet. *Harvard Business Review*, 79(3), 62–79.

Porter, M.E. 1996. What is strategy? *Harvard Business Review*, 74 (6): 5.

Porter, M.E. 1998. *Competitive advantage: Creating and sustaining superior performance.* New York: Free Press.

Radder, L. & Louw, L. 1998. The SPACE matrix: A tool for calibrating competition. *Long Range Planning*, 31(4):549–559.

Raymond, A, Kim J. & Shao, A.T. 2001. Export strategy and performance: A comparison of exports in a developed and an emerging market. *Journal of Global Marketing*, 15(2):5–29.

Rayport, J., & Sviokla, J. (1995). Exploring the virtual value chain. *Harvard Business Review*, 73(6):75–85.

Reeves, M., Haanaes, K. & Sinha, J. 2015. *Your strategy needs a strategy.* Boston, MA: Harvard Business Review Press.

Reeves, M., Love, C. & Tillmanns, P. 2012. Your strategy needs a strategy. *Harvard Business Review*, September: 76–83.

Schaan, J. 2008. International strategy elective class interaction. Cape Town: USB. July.

Senge, P. 1990. *The fifth discipline – the art and practice of the learning organisation.* London: Random House.

Shankar, S., Ormiston, C., Bock, N. & Shaus, R. 2008. How to win in emerging markets. *MIT Sloan Management Review*, 49(3):19–23. Simister, P. 2011. SPACE Analysis – Strategic Position and Action Evaluation Matrix. [Online]. Available: http://www.differentiateyourbusiness.co.uk/space-analysis-strategic-position-and-action-evaluation-matrix [Accessed 16 January 2016].

Tapscott, D., Ticoll, D., & Lowy, A. (2000). *Digital capital: Harnessing the power of business webs.* (1st edition.). Boston: Harvard Business School Press.

Teece, D. (2010). Business models, business strategy and innovation. *Long Range Planning*, 43(2):172–194.

Treacy, M & Wiersema, F. 1993. Customer intimacy and other value disciplines. *Harvard Business Review*, 71(1): 84–94.

Ungerer, G.D. 2015. *A competitive strategy framework for e-business start-ups.* Stellenbosch: University of Stellenbosch.

Ungerer, M., Pretorius, M & Herholdt, J. 2011. *Viable business strategies.* Randburg: Knowres Publishing.

Volberda, H.W., Morgan, R.E., Reinmoeller, P.R., Hitt, M.A., Ireland, R.D. & Hoskinsson, R.E. 2011. *Strategic management: Competitiveness and globalization.* Hampshire: Cengage.

Zhou, L., Dai, L., & Zhang, D. (2007). Online shopping acceptance model – A critical survey of consumer factors in online shopping. *Journal of Electronic Commerce Research*, 8(1):41–62.

CHAPTER 3 REFERENCES

Acur, N., & Englyst, L. 2006. Assessment of strategy formation: How to ensure quality in process and outcome. *International Journal of Operations & Production Management,* 26(1):70, 71.

Alex. 2014, Aug 5. *Announcing UberPool.* [Online]. Available: Uber: https://newsroom.uber.com/announcing-uberpool/ [Accessed on 16 April 2016].

Amit, R., & Zott, C. 2001. Value creation in e-business. *Strategic Management Journal,* 22(6-7):493–520.

Anderson, R., & Srinivasan, S. 2003. E-satisfaction and e-loyalty: A contingency framework. *Psychology & Marketing,* 20(2):123.

Andrews, K. 1965. *The concept of corporate strategy.* Homewood: R.D. Irwin.

Ansoff, H.I. 1965. *Corporate strategy: An analytical approach to business policy for growth and expansion.* New York: McGraw-Hill.

Arthur, W. 1996. Increasing returns and the new world of business. *Harvard Business Review,* 74(4):100.

Arya, S., & Srivastava, S. 2012. Acquiring e-loyalty: Competition is just one click away: a literature review. *International Journal of Research Management, Economics and Commerce,* 2(11):148.

Balabanis , G., Reynolds, N., & Simintiras, A. 2006. Bases of e-loyalty: Perceived switching barriers and satisfaction. *Journal of Business Research,* 59(2):221.

Barney, J.B. 1991. Firm resources and sustained competitive advantage. *Journal of Management,* 17(1):99–120.

Blank, S. 2013. Why the lean start-up changes everything. *Harvard Business Review,* 91(5):65–72.

Burnham, T.A., Frels, J.K., & Mahajan, V. 2003. Consumer switching costs: A typology, antecedents, and consequences. *Journal of the Academy of Marketing Science,* 31(2):111, 112.

Carlson, J., Sinnappan, S., & Kriz, A. 2005. *A conceptual framework to manage e-loyalty in business-to-consumer e-commerce.* [Online]. Available: CiteSeer: http://citeseerx.ist.psu.edu/viewdoc/download?doi=10.1.1.194.3202&rep=rep1&type=pdf [Accessed 25 February 2013].

Carlton, D., & Perloff, J. 1994. *Modern industrial organization.* New York: HarperCollins College Publishers.

Caroll, L. 1865. *Alice's Adventures in Wonderland.* New York: Macmillan.

Caruana, A., & Ewing, M. 2010. How corporate reputation, quality, and value influence online loyalty. *Journal of Business Research,* 63(9–10):1104.

Casadesus-Masanell, R., & Ricart, J.E. 2007. *Competing through business models.* Barcelona: Spain. IESE Business School-University of Navarra Working Paper.

Casadesus-Masanell, R., & Ricart, J.E. 2011. How to design a winning business model. *Harvard Business Review,* 89(1–2):102.

Chandler, A.J. 1962. *Strategy and structure: Chapters in the history of the American industrial enterprise.* Cambridge, MA: MIT Press.

Chia, R.C., & Holt, R. 2009. *Strategy without design: The silent efficacy of indirect action.* Cambridge: Cambridge University Press.

Clarke, K. 2001. What price on loyalty when a brand switch is just a click away? *Qualitative Market Research: An International Journal,* 4(3):161.

Collins, J., & Hansen, M.T. 2011. *Great by choice: Uncertainty, chaos and luck – why some thrive despite them all.* New York: HarperCollins.

Coyles, S., & Gokey, T. 2002. Customer retention is not enough. *McKinsey Quarterly* (2):88.

Cusumano, M.A. 2013. Technology strategy and management: Evaluating a startup venture. *Communications of the ACM,* 56(10):26-28.

Deep, A. 2015, Sept 24. *How Uber works: Insights into business & revenue model.* [Online]. Available: http://nextjuggernaut.com/blog/how-uber-works-business-model-revenue-uber-insights/ [Accessed 16 April 2016].

DeVine, J., & Gilson, K. 2001. Using behavioral science to improve the customer experience. *Harvard Business Review,* 79(6):2.

Drucker, P.F. 1994. The theory of the business. *Harvard Business Review,* 72(5):100.

Edlin, A., & Harris, R. 2013. The role of switching costs in antitrust analysis: A comparison of Microsoft and Google. *Yale Journal of Law and Technology,* 15:9.

Goldstuck, A. 2012. *Internet matters: The quiet engine of the South African economy.* [Online]. Available: World Wide Worx: http://internetmatters.co.za/report/ZA_internet_Matters.pdf [Accessed 31 July 2012].

Goldstuck, A. 2012. *Joining the E-Party.* Fin24, Aug 7: [Online]. Available: http://www.fin24.com/opinion/columnists/joining-the-e-party-20120807 [Accessed 29 January 2013].

Gommans, M., Krishnan, K., & Scheffold, K. 2001. From brand loyalty to e-loyalty: A conceptual framework. *Journal of Economic and Social Research,* 3(1):43–52.

Gustafasson, A., Johnson, M., & Roos, I. 2005. The effects of customer satisfaction, relationship commitment dimensions, and triggers on customer retention. *Journal of Marketing,* 69(4):210.

Hagel, J.I., & Armstrong, A. 1997. *Net gain: expanding markets through virtual communities.* Boston: Harvard Business School Press.

Hagel, J.I., & Singer, M. 1999. Unbundling the corporation. *Harvard Business Review,* 77(2):139.

Hagiu, A., & Wright, J. 2013. Do you really want to be on e-bay? *Harvard Business Review,* 91(3):104.

Hamel, G. 2000. *Leading the revolution.* Boston: Harvard School Press.

Hax, A., & Wilde II, D. 2001. The delta model – discovering new sources of profitability in a networked economy. *European Management Journal,* 19(4):379-391.

Herzberg, F. 1968. *One more time: How do you motivate employees.* Boston: Harvard Business Review.

Hess, M., & Ricart, J. 2002. *Managing customer switching costs.* Pamplona: University of Navarra.

Hough, J., Thompson Jr, A.A., Strickland III, A.J., & Gamble, J.E. (2011). *Crafting and executing strategy: Creating sustainable high performance in South Africa: Text, readings and cases* (2nd ed.). Berkshire: McGraw-Hill Higher Education.

Hutt, E., Le Brun, R., & Mannhardt, T. 2001. Simplifying web segmentation. *McKinsey Quarterly,* 38(3):12.

Johnson, G., Scholes, K., & Whittington, R. 2005. *Exploring corporate strategy: Text and cases* (7th ed.). Edinburgh Gate: Pearson Education.

Johnson, M.W., Christensen, C.M., & Kagermann, H. 2008, December. Reinventing your business model. *Harvard Business Review,* 86(12):60, 65.

Kelly, K. 2008, January 31. *Better than free.* The Technium: [Online]. Available: www.kk.org/thetechnium/archives/2008/01/better_than_fre.php [Accessed 16 August 2012].

Kim, W., & Mauborgne, R. 2005. *Blue Ocean strategy.* Boston: Harvard Business School Press.

Korgaonkar, P., & Wolin, L. 1999, Mar/Apr. A multivariate analysis of web usage. *Journal of Advertising Research,* 39(2):56.

Kotler, P. 1997. *Marketing management: Analysis, planning, implementation, and control* (9th ed.). New Jersey: Prentice Hall.

Learned, E.P., & Christensen, C.R. 1965. *Business policy: Text and cases.* Illinois: Irwin, Homewood.

Lechelle, P. 2014, May 26. *Pirate metrics.* PierreLechelle: [Online]. Available: https://www.pierrelechelle.com/aarrr-pirate-metrics [Accessed 13 April 2016].

Lee, C.-S., & Vonortas, N.S. 2004. Business model innovation in the digital economy. In G. Doukidis, N. Mylonopoulos, & N. Pouloudi, *Social and economic transformation in the digital era.* Hershey, PA: Idea Group.

Levitt, T. 1981. Marketing intangible products and product intangibles. *Cornell Hotel and Restaurant Administration Quarterly,* 22(2):37–44.

Linder, J.C., & Cantrell, S. 2000. *Changing business models: Surveying the landscape.* Cambridge: Accenture Institute for Strategic Change.

Linder, J.C., & Cantrell, S. 2001. Five business-model myths that hold companies back. *Strategy & Leadership,* 29(6):14.

Lociacono, E., Watson, R., & Goodhue, D. 2002. WebQual: A Measure of Website Quality. *Marketing Theory and Applications,* 13(3):432-438.

Mafé, C., & Navarré, L. 2010. *Segmenting consumers by e-shopping behaviour and online purchase intention.* Valencia: University of Valencia.

Magretta, J. 2002. Why business models matter. *Harvard Business Review,* 80(5):87, 90.

Magretta, J. 2012. *Understanding Michael Porter.* Boston: Harvard Business Review Press.

Mansfield, G.M., & Fourie, L.C. 2004. Strategy and business models – strange bedfellows? A case for convergence and its evolution into strategic architecture. *South African Journal of Business Management,* 35(1):35–44.

Markides, C. 1999. A dynamic view of strategy. *Sloan Management Review,* 40(3):56.

Mascareigne, J. 2009. *Customer retention: Case studies of agencies in the professional service sector.* Lulea: Lulea University of Technology.

Maurya, A. 2012. *Running lean* (2nd ed.). Sebastopol: O'Reilly Media.

McGrath, R.G. 2011. When your business model is in trouble. *Harvard Business Reveiw,* 89(1-2):97.

Mintzberg, H., Ahlstrand, B., & Lampel, J. 2009. *Strategy safari.* Edinburgh Gate: Prentice Hall.

Newell, F. 1997. *The new rules of marketing: How to use one-to-one relationship marketing to be the leader in your industry.* New York: McGraw-Hill.

Oliver, C. 1997. Sustainable competitive advantage: Combining institutional and resource-based views. *Strategic Management Journal,* 18(9):704.

Oliver, R. 1999. Whence consumer loyalty? *Journal of Marketing,* 63:33.

Osterwalder, A. 2004. *The business model ontology – A proposition in a design science approach.* Lausanne: University of Lausanne.

Osterwalder, A., & Pigneur, Y. 2009. *Business Model Generation.* Self-published.

Pearce, J., & Robinson, R. 2011. *Strategic management: Formulation, implementation & control* (12th ed.). McGraw-Hill Higher Education.

Poleretzky, K. 1999. The call center & e-commerce convergence. *Call Center Solutions* (17):76.

Porter, M. 1980. *Competitive Strategy: Techniques for analyzing industries and competitors.* New York: Free Press.

Porter, M. 1985. *Competitive advantage.* New York: Free Press.

Porter, M. 1996. What is strategy? *Harvard Business Review,* 61–78:5.

Porter, M.E. 2001. Strategy and the internet. *Harvard Business Review,* 79(3):71

Porter, M.E. 2008. The five competitive forces that shape strategy. *Harvard Business Review,* 86(1):78-93.

Reichheld, F., & Schefter, P. 1996. *The loyalty effect.* Boston: Harvard Business School Press.

Reichheld, F., & Schefter, P. 2000. E-loyalty. *Harvard Business Review,* 78(4):106–108.

Reis, E., 2011. *The lean startup.* New York: Crown Business.

Riggins, F.J., & Rhee, H. 1998. Toward a unified view of electronic commerce. *Communications of the ACM,* 41(10):88-95.

Rohm, A., & Swaminathan, V. 2004. A typology of online shoppers based on shopping motivations. *Journal of Business Research,* 57(7):748-757.

Rumelt, R. 1987. Theory, strategy, and entrepreneurship. In D. Teece, *The competitive challenge: Strategies for industrial innovation and renewal.* Cambridge, MA: Ballinger.

Rumelt, R. 2011, June. The perils of bad strategy. *McKinsey Quarterly,* 48(3):1-10.

Rumelt, R.P. 1979. Evaluation of strategy: Theory and models. In D. E. Schendel, & C. Hofer (Eds.), *Strategic management: A new view of business policy and planning.* Boston: Little, Brown.

Rumelt, R.P. 1998. Evaluating business strategy. In H. Mintzberg, J.B. Quinn, & S. Ghoshal, *The strategy process* (revised ed., pp. 1-11). London: Prentice Hall Europe.

Ryanair's Business Model. 2011. Air-Scoop: [Online]. Available: http://www.air-scoop.com/pdf/Ryanair-business-model_Air-Scoop_2011.pdf [Accessed 18 April 2013].

Schaffer, E. 2000, May. A better way for web design. *InformationWeek,* 784(1):174.

Selznick, P. 1957. *Leadership in administration: A sociological interpretation.* Evanston, IL: Row, Peterson.

Sen, S., Padmanabhan, B., Tuzhilin, A., White, N., & Stein, R. 1998. The identification and satisfaction of consumer analysis-driven information needs of marketers on the WWW. *European Journal of Marketing,* 32(7/8):688-702.

Shapiro, C., & Varian, H. 2009. *Locked in, not locked out.* Mariott School: [Online]. Available: http://marriottschool.net/emp/Bryce/manec387_old/handouts/locked_in.pdf [Accessed 25 February 2013].

Slywotzky, A. 2002. *The art of profitability.* New York: Mercer Management Consulting.

Slywotzky, A., & Morrison, D. 1997. *The profit zone: How strategic business design will lead you to tomorrow's profits.* New York: Times Books.

Srinivasan, S., Anderson, R., & Ponnavolu, K. 2002. Customer loyalty in e-commerce: An exploration of its antecedents and consequences. *Journal of Retailing,* 78(1):41.

Strategyzer. *Business model canvas.* 2011. Business Model Generation. [Online]. Available: http://www.businessmodelgeneration.com/canvas [Accessed 1 Oct 2012].

Teece, D. 2010. Business models, business strategy and innovation. *Long Range Planning,* 43(2):173.

Thompson, A.A., Strickland, A.J., & Gamble, J.E. 2008. *Crafting & executing strategy: The quest for competitive advantage: concepts and cases* (16th ed.). New York: McGraw-Hill Irwin.

Tilles, S. 1963. How to evaluate corporate strategy. *Harvard Business Review:* July-August:115-116.

Uber Cape Town. 2016. Uber: [Online]. Available: https://www.uber.com/cities/cape-town/ [Accessed 16 April 2016].

Uber Newsroom. 2015, Jan 7. A reliable ride for your items. Uber: [Online]. Available: https://newsroom.uber.com/hong-kong/en/a-ride-for-your-goods-introducing-ubercargo/ [Accessed 16 April 2016].

Ungerer, G.D. 2015. *A competitive strategy framework for e-business start-ups*. Stellenbosch: University of Stellenbosch.

Ungerer, M., Ungerer, G., & Herholdt, J. 2016. *Crystallising the strategic business landscape: Strategy analysis practices and tools for business leaders and strategy practitioners*. Randburg: Knowres Publishing.

Valvi, A., & Fragkos, K. 2012. Critical review of the e-loyalty literature: A purchase-centred framework. *Electronic Commerce Research,* 12(3):3.

Van der Heijden, K. 2001. Back to basics: Exploring the business idea. *Strategy & Leadership,* 29(3):15–16.

Volberda, H.W., Morgan, R.E., Reinmoeller, P., Hitt, M.A., Ireland, R.D., & Hoskisson, R.E. 2011. *Strategic management: Competitiveness and globalisation*. Hampshire: Cengage Learning EMEA.

Voytek. 2014, Aug 11. *Optimising a dispatch system using an AI simulation framework*. [Online]. Available: https://newsroom.uber.com/semi-automated-science-using-an-ai-simulation-framework/ [Accessed 16 April 2016].

Vrechopoulos, A., Siomkos, G., & Doukidis, G. 2001. Internet shopping adoption by Greek consumers. *European Journal of Innovation Management,* 4(3):142-152.

Weill, P., & Vitale, M.R. 2001. *Place to space: Migrating to eBusiness models*. Boston: Harvard Business School Press.

Weill, P., Malone, T.W., D'Urso, V.T., Herman, G., & Woerner, S. 2005. Do some business models perform better than others? A study of the 1000 largest US firms. MIT Sloan School of Management. Working paper 226.

Welch, N. 2010. A marketer's guide to behavioral economics. *McKinsey Quarterly,* 47(1):3.

Wolfinbarger, M., & Gilly, M. 2003. eTailQ: Dimensionalizing, measuring, and predicting etail quality. *Journal of Retailing,* 79(3):197.

Yang, Z., & Peterson, R. 2004, Oct. Customer perceived value, satisfaction, and loyalty: The role of switching costs. *Psychology & Marketing,* 21(10):806.

Zhou, L., Dai, L., & Zhang, D. 2007. Online shopping acceptance model – a critical survey of consumer factors in online shopping. *Journal of Electronic Commerce Research,* 8(1):55.

Zook, C., & Allen, J. 2011, November. The great repeatable business model. *Harvard Business Review,* 89(11):107–114.

Zott, C., & Amit, R. 2008. The fit between product market strategy and business model: Implications for firm performance. *Strategic Management Journal,* 29(1):1.

Zott, C., Amit, R., & Massa, L. 2011. The business model: Recent developments and future research. *Journal of Management,* 37(4):1019–1042.

CHAPTER 4 REFERENCES

Air Transport Action Group (ATAG). 2009. *Beginner's guide to aviation efficiency*. Geneva: ATAG.

Air Transport Action Group (ATAG). 2012. *Aviation: benefits beyond borders*. Geneva: ATAG.

Aviation Global Deal Group (AGD group). 2011. *A coordinated pathway towards a global sectoral agreement for international aviation emissions*. AGD Group Discussion Paper. London: AGD Group.

Beaverstock, J., Derudder, B., Faulconbridge, J., & Witlox, F. 2010. International business travel in the global economy 2010. [Online]. Available: http://books.google.co.za/books?id=Z4wiZsqvm3sC&pg=PA118&lpg=PA118&dq=virtual+technology+video+conferencing+busi-ness+travel+substitute&source=bl&ots=23BjCBgxuP&sig=VImPFmxtFOqbNa0BXYC2XQsZbA0&hl=en&sa=X&ei=SyLFT6vGDsr-BhAfH69zvCQ&redir_esc=y#v=onepage&q=virtual%20technology%20video%20conferencing%20business%20travel%20substitute&f=-false [Accessed 29 May 2012].

Börjeson, L.H., Hojer, M., Dreborg, K-H., Ekvall, T. & Finnveden, G. 2006. Scenario types and techniques: towards a user's guide. *Futures* 38(7):723–739.

Bradfield, R. 2008. Cognitive barriers in the scenario development process. *Advances in developing human resources,* 10(2):198-215.

Chermack, T.J. 2013. Drivers and outcomes of scenario planning: A canonical correlation analysis. *European Journal of Training and Development,* 37(9):811–834.

Cronje, F. 2014. *A time traveller's guide to our next 10 years*. South Africa: Tafelberg. ISBN 10: 0624068668

Dietz, T. & Stern, P.C. 2002. Exploring new tools for environmental protection. In *New tools for environmental protection: education, information, and voluntary measures*. Dietz, T., & Stern, P.C., Eds.; Washington, DC: National Academy Press. [Online]. Available: http://www.nap.edu/chapterlist.php?record_id=10401&type=pdf_chapter&free=1 [Accessed 26 March 2012].

Dray, L., Evans, A., & Schäfer, A. 2011. Fleet renewal policies – initial estimations. Paper prepared for the World Economic Forum Aviation, Travel and Tourism Industry Agenda Council. Geneva: WEF.

Dubois, G., Peeters, P., Ceron, J.P., & Gössling, S. 2011. The future tourism mobility of the world population: Emission growth *versus* climate policy. *Transport. Res. Pol. Pract. A,* 45:1031–1042.

Earth Negotiations Bulletin (ENB). 2012. *Summary of the Bonn climate change conference*. Bonn, Germany, 14–25 May 2012. Geneva, Switzerland: International Institute for Sustainable Development.

Fahey, L., & Randall, R. 1998. *Learning from the future: Competitive foresight scenarios*. New York, NY: John Wiley.

Gössling, S., Peeters, P., & Scott, D. 2008. Consequences of climate policy for international tourist arrivals in developing countries. *Third World Q.* 29:874.

Hamel, G. 2000. *Leading the revolution*. Harvard Business School Press. ISBN 978-0-452-28324-4

Hichert, T. 2012. *The future of tourism in South Africa: A horizon scan*. Background Paper. National Department of Tourism's scenario-building process. Bellville, South Africa: Institute for Futures Research.

Hiltunen, E. 2013. *Foresight and Innovation: How companies are coping with the future*. New York, NY: Palgrave Macmillan.

IATA, United Nations World Tourism Organisation, United Nations Environment Programme, World Meteorological Organisation (UNWTO-UNEP-WMO). 2008. Climate change and tourism: Responding to global challenges, 2008. [Online]. Available: http://www.unwto.org/sdt/news/en/pdf/climate2008.pdf [Accessed 23 December 2011].

Institute of Race Relations (with Moneyweb)2014. 'Time travelling to 2024 – Moneyweb, 21 November 2014'. [Online]. Available: http://irr.org.za/reports-and-publications/articles-authored-by-the-institute/time-travelling-to-2014-2013-moneyweb-21-november-2014 [Accessed 21 November 2015].

Intergovernmental Panel on Climate Change (IPCC). 2007. *Climate change 2007: synthesis report.* Geneva, Switzerland: IPCC.

International Air Transport Association (IATA). 2009. *A global approach to reducing aviation emissions.* Montreal: IATA. [Online]. Available: http://www.iata.org/SiteCollectionDocuments/Documents/Global_Approach_Reducing_Emissions_251109web.pdf [Accessed 12 December 2010].

International Air Transport Association (IATA). 2011. *International Air Transport Association Annual Report 2011.* Singapore: IATA, June.

International Air Transport Association (IATA). 2011. *Report of the Board of Governors.* Agenda item 6, Document 1. Report presented at the 67th Annual General Meeting. Singapore, June.

Kahn, H. 1962. *Thinking about the unthinkable: Scenarios and metaphors.* New York, NY: Horizon Press.

Karlitekin, C. 2010. Forecasting the future of travel and tourism: Future of global aviation. In *Trends and Issues in Global Tourism 2010*; Conrady, R., Buck, M., Eds. Heidelberg: Springer.

Lipman, G. 2012. *Report on macro-level drivers that will impact future tourism scenarios.* Background Paper. National Department of Tourism's scenario-building process. Brussels, Belgium: greenearth.travel.

Lipman, G., DeLacy, T., Vorster, S., Hawkins, R., & Jiang, M., Eds. 2012. *Green Growth and travel Letters from Leaders.* Oxford: Goodfellow.

Lyle, C. *Breaking the surly bonds of economic regulation.* 2011. Québec: Air Transport Economics.

McKinsey & Company. 2011. *Global economic scenarios 2010–2020: Volatility in a multi-speed world.* McKinsey Quarterly Global Executive Survey. Boston, MA: McKinsey. [Online]. Available: http://www.amchamsineurope.com/file/613/competitiveness%20of%20EU%20and%20US%20companies.pdf [Accessed 27 May 2012].

Meinshausen, M. 2005. *On the risk of overshooting 2°C.* Paper presented at the Scientific Symposium on avoiding Dangerous Climate Change. MetOffice, Exeter, UK, 1–3 February.

Meissner, P. & Wulf, T. 2012. Cognitive benefits of scenario planning: Its impact on biases and decision quality. *Technological Forecasting and Social Change,* 80(4):801–814.

Mietzner, D., & Reger, G. 2005. Advantages and disadvantages of scenario approaches for strategic foresight. *International Journal of Technology Intelligence Planning,* 1(2):220–239.

Mullich, J. 2010. The new face of face-to-face meetings efficiencies, technology, and better metrics bring greater ROI. *Wall St. J.* [Online]. Available: http://online.wsj.com/ad/article/globaltravel-face [Accessed 29 May 2012].

NDT (National Department of Tourism). 2012. *Shaping the future of tourism: 2030 tourism.* Pretoria: NDT.

O'Hanlon, S. 2011. Aviation biofuels: From fields to wheels up (R&D to Commercialization). Presentation at a World Biofuels Conference, London, UK. [Online]. Available: http://library.greenpowerconferences.com/abm/presentation.pdf [Accessed 14 November 2011].

Organization for Economic Cooperation and Development (OECD). 2011. *Climate change and tourism policy in OECD countries;* CFE/TOU(2010)10/FINAL. Paris: OECD.

Ringland, G. 2002. *Scenarios in business.* Chichester, UK: Wiley.

Saunders, G. 2012. *NDT Tourism scenario planning to 2030/2050: Selected key drivers.* Background Paper: National Department of Tourism's scenario-building process. Sandton: Grant Thornton.

Schoemaker, P. 1993. Multiple scenario development: Its conceptual and behavioral foundation. *Strategic Management Journal,* 14(3):193–213.

Scott, D. & Lemieux, C. 2009. *Weather and climate information for tourism.* Report. Geneva: World Meteorological Organisation and United Nations World Tourism Organization. [Online]. Available: http://www.unwto.org/climate/support/en/pdf/ WCC3_TourismWhitePaper.pdf [Accessed 20 March 2011].

Scott, D. 2012. Towards climate compatible travelism. In G. Lipman, T. DeLacy, S. Vorster, R Hawkins, R and M Jiang (eds) *Green growth and Travelism – letters from leaders.* London: Goodfellows.

Scott, D., Peeters, P., & Gössling, S. 2009. *Can tourism 'seal the deal' of its mitigation commitments? The challenge of achieving 'aspirational' emission reduction targets.* September. [Online]. Available: http://www.cstt.nl/userdata/documents/can%20tourism%20'seal%20the%20deal'%20of%20its%20mitigation%20commitments,%20paul.pdf [Accessed 19 November 2012].

Scowsill, D. 2011. Speech by David Scowsill, President and CEO of the World Travel and Tourism Council. [Online]. Available: http://www.onecaribbean.org/content/files/WTTCDavidScowsill.pdf [Accessed 22 May 2012].

Sivell, P.M., Reeves, S.J., Baldachin, L., & Brightman, T.G. 2008. *Climate change resilience indicators.* Berkshire, UK: South East United Kingdom Regional Assembly, Transport Research Laboratory. Workingham: Berkshire

Strong, M. 2009. Facing down Armageddon: Our environment at a crossroads. *World Pol. J.,* 26:25–32.

UN World Trade Organization. 2011. Provisional Agenda Item 5. Report of the Secretary-General, General Assembly, 19th session, Gyeongju, Republic of Korea, 8–14 October. [Online]. Available: https://s3-eu-west-1.amazonaws.com/storageapi/sites/all/files/pdf/a19_05_report_sg_e.pdf [Accessed 3 October 2011].

Ungerer, M., Ungerer, G. & Herholdt, J. 2016. *Crystallising the strategic business landscape: Strategy analysis practices and tools for business leaders and strategy practitioners.* Randburg: KR Publishing.

United Kingdom Climate Change Committee (UKCCC). 2011. *Government response to the committee on climate change report on reducing CO^2 emissions from UK aviation to 2050.* London: UK Department of Transport.

United Nations Framework Convention on Climate Change (UNFCCC). 1997. *Kyoto Protocol to the United Nations Framework Convention on Climate Change.* Bonn: UNFCCC Secretariat. [Online]. Available: http://unfccc.int/kyoto_protocol/items/2830.php [Accessed 6 March 2011].

United Nations World Tourism Organisation (UNWTO). 2008. International recommendations for tourism statistics 2008, ST/ESA/STAT/SER.M/83/Rev.1. [Online]. Available: http://unstats.un.org/unsd/tradeserv/tourism/0840120%20IRTS%202008_WEB_final%20version%20_22%20February%202010.pdf [Accessed 20 March 2011].

United Nations World Tourism Organisation (UNWTO). 2011. *Provisional Agenda Item 5*. Report of the Secretary-General, General Assembly, 19th session, Gyeongju, Republic of Korea, 8–14 October. [Online]. Available: https://s3-eu-west-1.amazonaws.com/storageapi/sites/all/files/pdf/a19_05_report_sg_e.pdf [Accessed 3 October 2011].

Varum, C.A. & Melo, C. 2010. Directions in scenario planning literature. A review of the past decades. *Futures*, 42(4):355–369.

Vorster, S., Ungerer, M., & Volschenk, J. 2013. 2050 Scenarios for long-haul tourism in the evolving global climate change regime. *Sustainability*, 5(1):1–51. ISSN 2071-1050 [Online]. Available: www.mdpi.com/2071-1050/5/1/1 [Accessed 11 February 2016].

Walton, J. 2008. Scanning beyond the horizon: Exploring the ontological and epistemological basis. *Advances in Developing Human Resources* 10:147–165.

WEF, January & International Air Transport Association (IATA). 2010. *Aviation and climate change*. Geneva: Switzerland: WEF.

Williams, K. 2011. Speech by British Airways CEO. Caribbean Tourism Organization Conference, Marigot, Saint-Martin, 16 September. [Online]. Available: http://www.eturbonews.com/25264/british-airways-ceo-provides-world-view-state-tourismindustry [Accessed 19 September 2011].

Wilson, I. 1999. Mental maps of the future. *Scenario building: A suitable method for strategic property planning, the cutting edge*. September 1999. Cambridge, United Kingdom: The Property Research Conference of the RICS, St. John's College, September.

World Economic Forum (WEF). 2009. *Towards a low carbon travel & tourism sector*. Report. Geneva, Switzerland: Booz & Company, May.

World Economic Forum (WEF). 2011. *Policies and collaborative partnership for sustainable aviation*. Project White Paper. Geneva: Switzerland: WEF.

World Economic Forum (WEF). 2012. Outlook on the Global Agenda 2012. [Online]. Available: http://www3.weforum.org/docs/GAC11/WEF_GAC11_OutlookGlobalAgenda.pdf [Accessed 23 December 2011].

World Travel and Tourism Council (WTTC). 2010. *Climate change: A joint approach to addressing the challenge*. [Online]. Available: http://www.wttc.org/bin/pdf/original_pdf_file/climate_change_final.pdf [Accessed 2 December 2010].

World Travel and Tourism Council (WTTC). 2011. *Travel and tourism economic impact 2011*. London: WTCC.

Yeoman, I. Our sustainable future – looking back from 2050. 2012. In *Green growth and travelism – letters from leaders*. In Lipman, G., DeLacy, T., Vorster, S., Hawkins, R., Jiang, M., Eds. London: Goodfellows.

CHAPTER 5 REFERENCES

Amabile, T.M., DeJong, W., & Lepper, M.R. 1976. Effects of externally imposed deadlines on subsequent intrinsic motivation. *Journal of Personality and Social Psychology*, 34:92–98.

Ariely, D. 2008. *Predictably irrational: The hidden forces that shape our decisions*. New York, NY: HarperCollins.

Ballreich, R. & Glasl, F. 2001. *Team development and organisation development as a means for conflict prevention and conflict resolution*. Berghof Handbook for Conflict Transformation. ISSN 1616-2544. [Online]. Available: http://www.berghof-handbook.net [Accessed 20 May 2016].

Bos, A.H. 1974. Oordeelsvorming in groepen: Polariteiten riture als sleutel tot ontwikkeling van sociale organisenen. Wageningen: Veenman & Zonen BV. University of Wageningen. Doctoral thesis.

Bossidy, L., Charan, R. & Buck, C. 2002. *Execution: The discipline of getting things done*. New York, NY: Crown Business. ISBN 0-609-61057-0

Bunker, BB & Alban, BT. 2006. *The handbook of large group methods: Creating systemic change in organizations and communities*. San Francisco: Jossey-Bass.

Buffett, W. 1930. Goodreads. [Online]. Available: http://www.goodreads.com/quotes/226056-in-the-business-world-the-rearview-mirror-is-always-clearer [Accessed 13 July 2016].

Cameron, L. 1999. Raising the stakes in the ultimatum game: experimental evidence from Indonesia. *Economic Inquiry*, 37(1):47–59.

Deci, E.L. 1971. Effects of externally mediated rewards on intrinsic motivation. *Journal of Personality and Social Psychology*, 18:105–115.

Deci, E.L., Betley, G., Kahle, J., Abrams, L., & Porac, J. 1981. When trying to win: Competition and intrinsic motivation. *Personality and Social Psychology Bulletin*, 7:79–83.

Diaz, I. 2010. Strategic execution plan and monitoring mechanisms for Corporate Clients SBU. MBA strategic management assignment. University of Stellenbosch Business School. Unpublished.

Fast Company. Getting it done! 2000. [Online]. Available: http://www.fastcompany.com/39491/getting-it-done [Accessed 20 February 2016].

Ghosh, P. 2013. How many people did Joseph Stalin kill? *International Business Times*, 3 May. [Online]. Available: http://www.ibtimes.com/how-many-people-did-joseph-stalin-kill-1111789 [Accessed 29 March 2016].

Gladwell, M. 2000. *The tipping point: How little things can make a big difference*. Boston: Little, Brown.

Godin, S. 2008. *Tribes: We need you to lead us*. New York: Portfolio.

Hammer, M., & Champy. J. 1993. *Reengineering the corporation: A manifesto for business revolution*. London: HarperCollins.

Harackiewicz, J.M. 1979. The effects of reward contingency and performance feedback on intrinsic motivation. *Journal of Personality and Social Psychology*, 37:1352–1363.

Hoffman, E.K., McCabe, K.A. & Smith, V.L. 1996. On expectations and the monetary stakes in ultimatum games. *International Journal of Game Theory* 25:289–301.

Kafidi, P.L. 2013. Strategic execution plan and monitoring mechanisms for the NAMFISA. Strategy utilising guidelines for a strategic map and a balanced scorecard. MBA strategic management assignment. University of Stellenbosch Business School. Unpublished.

Kaplan, R S. & Norton, D P. 2005. *Focusing your organization on strategy – with the Balanced Scorecard* (3rd Ed.). Boston: Harvard Business Review.

Kaplan, R. 2000. The balanced scorecard – making strategy happen. Public Conference, Vodaworld, Johannesburg, May 8.

Kaplan, R.S. & Norton, D.P. 2008. *The execution premium*. Boston: MA: Harvard Business School Publishing Corporation.

Keller, S. & Aiken, C. 2009. The inconvenient truth about change management. *McKinsey Quarterly*, 1-18. April.

Kim, W.C. & Mauborgne, K. 2003. Fair process: Managing in the knowledge economy. hbr.org. January. [Online]. Available: https://hbr.org/2003/01/fair-process-managing-in-the-knowledge-economy/ [Accessed 12 April 2016].

Kotter, J.P. 1996. *Leading Change*. Boston: Harvard Business School Press. ISBN 978-0-87584-747-4.

Langer, EJ. 1982. *Chapter 16: The illusion of control*. In Kahneman, D. Slovic, P. & Tversky, A. eds., *Judgment under uncertainty: Heuristics and biases*. Cambridge: Cambridge University Press.

Mankins, MC & Steele, R. 2005.Turning great strategy into great performance. July–August 2005. Harvard Business Review. [Online]. Available: https://hbr.org/2005/07/turning-great-strategy-into-great-performance [Accessed 19 February 2016].

Opperman, S. 2013. Strategy execution plan – Synfuels technical support. MBA strategic management assignment. University of Stellenbosch Business School. Unpublished.

Plant, R.W., & Ryan, R.M. 1985. Intrinsic motivation and the effects of self-consciousness, self-awareness, and ego-involvement: An investigation of internally controlling styles. *Journal of Personality*, 53:434–449.

PricewaterhouseCoopers (2014) Research on the strategy-execution gap. [Online]. Available: http://www.strategyand.pwc.com/global/home/what-we-think/cds_home/the_concept/research-strategy-execution-gap [Accessed 20 February 2016].

Scharmer, C.O. 2007. *Theory U: Leading from the future as it emerges*. Cambridge, MA: The Society for Organizational Learning.

Scharmer, O.Homepage [Online]. Available: http://www.ottoscharmer.com/publications/executive-summaries [Accessed 16 March 2016].

Senge, PM., Scharmer, C.O., Jaworski, J., & Flowers, B.S. 2005. *Presence: Exploring profound change in people, organizations and society*. London: Nicholas Brealey.

Slywotsky, A. 2004. *The art of profitability*. (Updated edition). Boston: Little, Brown. ISBN 10: 0446692271 / ISBN 13: 9780446692274

Sull, D., Holmes, R. & Sull, C. 2015. Why strategy execution unravels – and what to do about it. *Harvard Business Review* 93(3):58-66.

Trompenaars, F. & Hampden-Turner, C. 2012. *Riding the waves of culture: Understanding diversity in global business* (3rd ed.) New York: McGraw-Hill.

Ungerer, M., Herholdt, J. & Le Roux, J. 2013. *Leadership for all — Virtue practices to flourish*. Johannesburg: KnowRes Publishing.

Ungerer, M., Ungerer, G. & Herholdt, J. 2016. *Crystallising the strategic business landscape: Strategy analysis practices and tools for business leaders and strategy practitioners*. Johannesburg: KR Publishing.

USBS Management team. 2015. Example of a strategy map of the University of Stellenbosch Business School (USBS). Unpublished.

CHAPTER 6 REFERENCES

Amit, R., & Zott, C. 2001. Value creation in e-business. *Strategic Management Journal*, 22(6–7):493–520.

Arya, S., & Srivastava, S. 2012. Acquiring e-loyalty: Competition is just one click away: a literature review. *International Journal of Research Management, Economics and Commerce*, 2(11):151.

Bettencourt, L.A., & Ulwick, A.W. 2008. The customer-centered innovation map. *Harvard Business Review*, 86(5):109–114.

Botsman, R., & Rogers, R. 2010. *What's mine is yours: The rise of collaborative consumption*. London: HarperCollins.

Bower, J.L., & Christensen, C.M. 1995. Disruptive technologies: Catching the wave. *Harvard Business Review*, 73(1):44, 45.

Chambers, J. 2016. Cisco's John Chambers on the digital era. (R. Kirkland, Interviewer). [Online]. Available: http://www.mckinsey.com/industries/high-tech/our-insights/ciscos-john-chambers-on-the-digital-era?cid=other-eml-nsl-mip-mck-oth-1604 [Accessed 18 Apr 2016].

Christensen, C.M., & Overdorf, M. 2000. Meeting the challenge of disruptive change. *Harvard Business Review*, 78(2):72.

Collins, J. & Hansen, M.T. 2011. *Great by choice*. London: RH Business Books.

Collins, J. 2009. *How the mighty fall and why some companies never give in*. New York: HarperCollins.

Dar Start Business (DSB). 2015, Jan 7. *Nintendo Wii business innovation strategy*. Dar Start Business: [Online]. Available: http://www.darestartbusiness.com/nintendo-wii-business-innovation-strategy/ [Accessed 4 May 2016].

Dawson, A., Hirt, M., & Scanlan. 2016. *Economic essentials of digital strategy*. McKinsey & Company: [Online]. Available: http://www.mckinsey.com/business-functions/strategy-and-corporate-finance/our-insights/the-economic-essentials-of-digital-strategy?cid=other-eml-nsl-mip-mck-oth-1604 [Accessed 18 April 2016].

Goldstuck, A. 2012, Aug 7. *Joining the e-party*. Fin24: [Online]. Available: http://www.fin24.com/opinion/columnists/joining-the-e-party-20120807 [Accessed 29 Jan 2013].

Golub, H., & Henry, J. 2000. Market strategy and the price-value model. *McKinsey Quarterly*, 37(3):47.

Gommans, M., Krishnan, K., & Scheffold, K. 2001. From brand loyalty to e-loyalty: A conceptual framework. *Journal of Economic and Social Research*, 3(1):46.

Goodwin, T. 2015, Mar 3. *The battle is for the customer interface*. TechCrunch: [Online]. Available: http://techcrunch.com/2015/03/03/in-the-age-of-disintermediation-the-battle-is-all-for-the-customer-interface/ [Accessed 24 April 2016].

Gummerus, J. 2011. *Customer value in e-service: conceptual foundation and empirical evidence*. Helsinki: Hanken School of Economics.

Hall, K. 2006. The big ideas behind Nintendo's Wii. *Bloomberg Business Week, Special Report*. Nov 16.

Hamel, G. 1996. Strategy as revolution. *Harvard Business Review*, 74(4):72, 73.

Hamel, G. 2000. *Leading the revolution*. Boston: Harvard Press.

Hamel, G. 2001, Jul 9. Innovation's New Math. *Fortune*, 72(7):66–67.

Hamel, G. 2012. *What matters now*. San Francisco: Jossey-Bass.

Hoegg, R., Martignoni, R., Meckel, M., & Stanoevska-Slabeva, K. 2006. *Overview of business models for web 2.0 communities*. St. Gallen: University of St. Gallen.

Ismail, S., Malone, M., & Van Geest, Y. 2014. *Exponential organisations*. New York: Diversion Books.

Johnson, M.W., Christensen, C.M., & Kagermann, H. 2008, Dec. Reinventing your business model. *Harvard Business Review*, 86(12):57–68.

Kelly, K. 2008, Jan 31. *Better than free*. The Technium: [Online]. Available: www.kk.org/thetechnium/archives/2008/01/better_than_fre.php [Accessed 16 Aug 2012].

Kim, W., & Mauborgne, R. 2000. Knowing a winning business idea when you see one. *Harvard Business Review*, 78(5):132.

Kim, W., & Mauborgne, R. 2004, Oct. Blue Ocean Strategy. *Harvard Business Review*, 82(10): 69.

Kim, W., & Mauborgne, R. 2005. *Blue Ocean Strategy.* Boston: Harvard Business School Press.

Kim, W., & Mauborgne, R. 2016. *Tipping point leadership.* Blue Ocean Strategy: [Online]. Available: https://www.blueoceanstrategy.com/tools/tipping-point-leadership/ [Accessed 27 Apr 2016].

Kim, W., Mauborgne, R., & Hunter, J. 2007. *Lessons learned from noncustomers.* Blue Ocean Strategy: [Online]. Available: https://www.blueoceanstrategy.com/teaching-materials/nintendo-wii/# [Accessed 4 May 2016].

Koiso-Kanttila, N. 2005. Time, attention, authenticity and consumer benefits of the web. *Business Horizons,* 48(1):64.

Korgaonkar, P., & Wolin, L. 1999. A multivariate analysis of web usage. *Journal of Advertising Research,* 39(2):57.

Lee, C.-S., & Vonortas, N.S. 2004. Business model innovation in the digital economy. In G. Doukidis, N. Mylonopoulos, & N. Pouloudi (eds), *Social and economic transformation in the digital era.* Hershey, PA: Idea Group.

Levitt, T. 1981. Marketing intangible products and product intangibles. *Cornell Hotel and Restaurant Administration Quarterly,* 22(2):37–44.

Moore, G.E. 1965, Apr 19. Cramming more components onto integrated circuits. *Electronics Magazine,* 38(8:114-117.

Nintendo. 'Hardware and Software Unit Sales'. 2016, Mar 31. Nintendo: [Online]. Available: https://www.nintendo.co.jp/ir/en/sales/hard_soft/ [Accessed 4 May 2016].

O'Gorman, P. 2008. Wii: Creating a Blue Ocean the Nintendo way. *Palermo Business Review* (2):97–107.

Olson, M.S., Van Bever, D. & Verry, S. 2008. When growth stalls. *Harvard Business Review,* Mar:51–61.

Osterwalder, A. 2007, Jan 5. *Nintendo's Blue Ocean strategy: Wii.* Business Model Alchemist: [Online]. Available: http://businessmodelalchemist.com/blog/2007/01/nintendos-blue-ocean-strategy-wii.html [Accessed 4 May 2016].

Osterwalder, A., & Pigneur, Y. 2009. *Business model generation.* Self-published.

Prifti, E. 2013, Aug 3. *Edward de Bono Quotes.* [Online]. Available: http://www.slideshare.net/eridaprifti/edward-de-bono-quotes [Accessed 20 May 2016].

Rayport, J., & Sviokla, J. 1995. Exploring the virtual value chain. *Harvard Business Review,* 73(6):75–85.

Reichheld, F., & Schefter, P. 2000. E-loyalty. *Harvard Business Review,* 78 (4):110.

Seybold, P. 2001. *The customer revolution.* New York: Crown Business.

Srinivasan, S., Anderson, R., & Ponnavolu, K. 2002. Customer loyalty in e-commerce: An exploration of its antecedents and consequences. *Journal of Retailing,* 78 (1):41.

Tapscott, D., Ticoll, D., & Lowy, A. 2000. *Digital capital: Harnessing the power of business webs.* (1st ed.). Boston: Harvard Business School Press.

Thurrott, P. 2010, Oct 6. *Xbox 360 vs. Playstation 3 vs. Wii: A technical comparison.* [Online]. Available: SuperSite for Windows: http://winsupersite.com/product-review/xbox-360-vs-playstation-3-vs-wii-technical-comparison [Accessed 4 May 2016].

Ungerer, G.D. 2015. *A competitive strategy framework for e-business start-ups.* Stellenbosch: University of Stellenbosch.

Valvi, A., & Fragkos, K. 2012. Critical review of the e-loyalty literature: A purchase-centred framework. *Electronic Commerce Research,* 12(3):31, 32.

Van Geest, J. 2014, Oct 20. *Exponential Organisations – Why new organisations are 10X better, faster and cheaper than yours.* Slideshare: [Online]. Available: http://www.slideshare.net/vangeest/exponential-organizations-h [Accessed 24 April 2016].

Welch, N. 2010. A marketer's guide to behavioral economics. *McKinsey Quarterly,* 47(1):3.

Wells, J.D., & Gobeli, D.H. 2003, Mar/Apr. The 3R framework: Improving e-strategy across reach, richness, and range. *Business Horizons,* 46(2):7.

Zhou, L., Dai, L., & Zhang, D. 2007. Online shopping acceptance model – a critical survey of consumer factors in online shopping. *Journal of Electronic Commerce Research,* 8(1):54.

CHAPTER 7 REFERENCES

ABSA Annual Report 2006. [Online]. Available: http://www.absa.co.za/deployedfiles/Absa.co.za/PDFs/About%20Absa/Annual%20Reports/Bank%20Reports/2006/Annual%20Report.pdf [Accessed 27 March 2016].

ABSA Annual Report. 2005. [Online]. Available: http://www.southafrica.to/Banks/ABSA/financials/ABSA-20051231.pdf [Accessed 27 March 2016].

Absa Annual Report. 2007. [Online]. Available: http://www.sharedata.co.za/Data/002337/pdfs/ABSABANK-P_fin_dec07.pdf [Accessed 27 March 2016].

ABSA strategy team. 2002. Absa internal strategy document on Possible Future Scenarios. Unpublished.

Agrawal, A., Ferrer, C. & West, A. 2011. When big acquisitions pay off. *McKinsey Quarterly,* May. [Online]. Available: http://www.mckinsey.com/business-functions/strategy-and-corporate-finance/our-insights/when-big-acquisitions-pay-off [Accessed 22 March 2016].

Ahammad, M.F. & Glaister, K.W. 2013. The pre-acquisition evaluation of target firms and cross border acquisition performance. *International Business Review,* 22(5):894–904.

Angwin, D. 2004. Speed in M&A integration: The first 100 days. *European Management Journal,* 22(4):418–430.

Armour, E. 2002. How boards can improve the odds of M&A success. *Strategy & Leadership,* 30(2):13–20.

Barclays plc Annual Report. 2005. [Online]. Available: https://www.home.barclays/content/dam/barclayspublic/docs/InvestorRelations/AnnualReports/AR2005/barclays-plc-annual-report-2005.pdf [Accessed 27 March 2016].

Barclays plc Annual Report. 2005. [Online]. Available: https://www.highbeam.com/doc/1G1-161250139.html [Accessed 26 March 2016].

Barragato, C.A. & Markeleviech, A. 2007. Earnings quality following corporate acquisitions. *Managerial Finance,* 34(5), 304–315.

Bert, A., MacDonald, T. & Herd, T. 2003. Two merger integration imperatives: urgency and execution. *Strategy and Leadership,* 31(3):42–49.

Bonney, T. & Kehoe, K. 2011. Recruiting and retaining talent: Certain steps are required before and after a deal. *Mergers and Acquisitions: The Dealmaker's Journal,* 46(5):34.

Borenstein, S. 1990. Airline mergers, airport dominance and market power. *American Economic Review,* 80(2):400–404.

Bower, J.L. 2001. Not all M&As are alike – and that matters. *Harvard Business Review,* March:1–21.

Bradley, M., Desai, A. & Kim, E.H. 1988. Synergistic gains from corporate acquisitions and their division between the stockholders of target and acquiring firms. *Journal of Financial Economics,* 21(1):3–40.

Brouthers, K.D., Van Hastenburg, P. & Van den Ven, J. 1998. If most mergers fail why are they so popular? *Long Range Planning,* 31(3):347–353.

Carper, W.B. 1990. Corporate acquisitions and shareholder wealth: A review and exploratory analysis. *Journal of Management,* 16(4):807–823.

Carr, R., Elton, G., Rovit, S. & Vestring, T. 2004. Beating the odds: A blueprint for successful merger integration. *European Business Journal,* 16(4):161–166.

Circular to Absa Shareholders for details on the scheme of arrangements. 20 May 2005. [Online]. Available: http://www.absa.co.za/deployed-files/Absa.co.za/PDF's/About%20Absa/Barclays%20Transaction/Barclays%20transaction.pdf [Accessed 27 March 2016].

Clark, C.J. 1987. Acquisitions – techniques for measuring strategic fit. *Long Range Planning,* 20(3):12–18.

Clark, J. 2013. 'Which bank share has performed best?' *Moneyweb.* 24 May 2013. [Online]. Available: http://www.moneyweb.co.za/archive/which-bank-share-has-performed-best/ [Accessed 26 March 2016].

Crotty, A. 2016. A Barclays sell-off plot? It's fiction, says Ramos. *Sunday Times,* Business Times, March 13, p. 3.

Cummins, J.D. & Weiss, M.A. 2004. Consolidation in the European insurance industry: Do merger and acquisitions create value for shareholders? *Brookings–Wharton Papers on Financial Services,* 217–258.

De Wit, B. & Meyer, R. 2014. *Strategy: An international perspective.* 5th ed. Hampshire: Cengage.

De Wit, P.G.S. 2015. *Postmerger and acquisition implementation strategies: A case study within an aggregates firm.* Unpublished MBA research, University of Stellenbosch Business School.

Deresky, H. 2002. *International management: managing across borders and cultures.* 4th ed. Upper Saddle River: Prentice Hall.

Dora, D., Smit, S. & Viguerie, P. 2011. Drawing a new road map for growth. *McKinsey Quarterly,* April. [Online]. Available: http://www.mckinsey.com/global-themes/employment-and-growth/drawing-a-new-road-map-for-growth [Accessed 11 March 2016].

Doukas, J.A., Holmen, M. & Travlos, N.G. 2001. *Corporate diversification and performance: Evidence from Swedish conglomerate and nonconglomerate acquisitions.* New York: Stern School of Business Department of Finance.

Eccles, R.G., Lanes, K.L. & Wilson, T.C. 1999. Are you paying too much for that acquisitions? *Harvard Business Review,* 77(4):136–146.

Epstein, M.J. 2004. The drivers of success in postmerger integration. *Organizational Dynamics,* 33(2):174–189.

Evripidou, L. 2012. M&As in the airline industry: Motives and systematic risk. *International Journal of Organisational Analysis,* 20(4), 435–446.

Fern, B.N. 1992. Managing the culture clash in mergers. *American Banker,* 157(161):4.

Ferrer, C., Uhlaner, R. & West, A. 2013. M&A as competitive advantage. *McKinsey Quarterly,* August: 1.

Ficery, K., Herd, T. & Purche, B. 2007. Where has all the synergy gone? *Journal of Business Strategy,* 28(5):29–35.

Firer, C., Ross, S.A., Westerfield, R.W. & Jordan, B.D. 2008. *Fundamentals of corporate finance.* Maidenhead: McGraw-Hill Education.

Gadiesh, O., Ormiston, C. & Rovit, S. 2003. Achieving M&A strategic goals at maximum speed for maximum value. *Strategy & Leadership,* 31(3):35–41.

Galpin, T.J. & Herndon, M. 2007. *The complete guide to mergers and acquisitions.* 2nd ed. San Francisco: Jossey-Bass.

Gaughan, P.A. 2000. *Mergers, acquisitions and corporate restructurings.* 2nd ed. Hoboken: John Wiley & Sons.

Gill, C. 2012. The role of leadership in successful international mergers and acquisitions: Why Renault–Nissan succeeded and DaimlerChrysler-Mitsubishi failed. *Human Resource Management,* 51(3):433–456.

Gole, W.J. & Morris, J.M. 2007. Mergers and acquisitions: business strategies for accountants. Hoboken: John Wiley and Sons.

Gonzalez, M. 2001. Strategic alliances: The right way to compete in the 21st century. *Ivey Business Journal,* 66(1):47–51.

Hawkes, V. 1999. *ACT companion to treasury management.* Cambridge: Woodhead Publishing.

Henry, D. 2002. Mergers: Why most big deals don't pay off. *Bloomberg Business,* October: 14.

Hoskisson, R.E., Hitt, M.A., Ireland, R.D. & Harrison, J.S. 2008. *Competing for advantage.* 2nd ed. Ann Arbor: Edwards Brothers.

Joffe, H. 2016, March 11. Barclays Africa Exit: On the block. *Financial Mail.* [Online]. Available: http://www.financialmail.co.za/coverstory/2016/03/10/barclays-africa-exit-on-the-block [Accessed 26 March 2016].

JSE Limited. 2007a. *Section 7: Listing Particulars. Listing Requirements.* [Online]. Available: http://www.jse.co.za/docs/listings_requirements/SECT07.DOC [Accessed 11 October 2009].

JSE Limited. 2007b. *Section 8: Financial Information. Listing Requirements.* [Online]. Available: *http://www.jse.co.za/docs/listings_requirements/SEC08.DOC* [Accessed: 11 October 2009].

Kale, P., Dyer, J.H. & Singh, H. 2002. Alliance capability, stock market response, and long-term alliance success: The role of the alliance function. *Strategic Management Journal,* 23:747–767.

Kariithi, N.K. 2007. *Longman's Dictionary of financial terms.* Johannesburg: Pearson Education.

Kauser, S. & Shaw, V. 2004. The influence of behavioural and organisational characteristics on the success of international strategic alliances. *International Marketing Review,* 21(1):17–52.

Klein, S. & Dev, C. 1997. Partner selection in market-driven strategic alliances. *South African Journal of Business Management,* 28 (3):97–105.

KPMG Survey. 2001. *Survey: World class transactions.* India: KPMG.

Kumar, S. & Bansal, L.K. 2008. The impact of mergers and acquisitions on corporate performance in India. *Management Decision,* 46(10):1531–1543.

Lafforet, C. & Wageman, R. 2009. Successful mergers and acquisitions: Beyond the financial issues. *Leader to Leader,* 54:44–51.

Lee, C.F. & Lee, A.C. 2006. *Encyclopedia of finance.* New York: Springer Science.

Loubser, L.R. 2012. Investigating and evaluating the merit of a strategic acquisition: A case study in the aggregate industry. Unpublished MBA research, University of Stellenbosch Business School.

Matsusaka, J.G. 1993. Takeover motives during the conglomerate merger wave. *RAND Journal of Economics*, 24(3):357–379.

Melnik, A. & Pollatschek, M.A. 1973. Debt capacity, diversification and conglomerate mergers. *Journal of Finance*, 28(5):1263–1273.

Meredith, K. 2012. *The devil in the deal*. Cape Town: Zebra Press.

Messmer, M. 2006. Leadership strategies during mergers and acquisitions. *Strategic Finance*, 87(7):15–16.

Miller, E.L. 2008. Mergers and acquisitions: *A step-by-step legal and practical guide*. Hoboken, NJ: John Wiley and Sons.

Morck, R., Shleifer, A. & Vishny, R. 1990. Do managerial objectives drive bad acquisitions? *Journal of Finance*, 45(1):31–48.

Ndzamela, P. 2013. 'The relationship between Absa and Barclays'. August 29, 2013. *Financial Mail*. [Online]. Available: http://www.financialmail. co.za/fm/CoverStory/2013/08/29/the-relationship-between-absa-and-barclays [Accessed 26 March 2016].

Nemanich, L.A. & Keller, R.T. 2007. Transformational leadership in an acquisition: A field study of employees. *Leadership Quarterly*, 18(2007):49–68.

Nguyen, H.T., Yung, K. & Sun, Q. 2012. Motives for mergers and acquisitions: Ex-post market evidence from the US. *Journal of Business Finance & Accounting*, 39(9/10):1357–1375.

Nissan Global. 'Alliance Facts & Figures'. 2014. [Online]. Available: http://www.nissan-global.com/EN/DOCUMENT/PDF/ALLIANCE/HAND-BOOK/2014/BookletAlliance2014_GB.pdf [Accessed 21 March 2014].

Nissan Motor Corporation website. [Online]. Available: http://www.nissan-global.com/EN/NEWS/2016/_STORY/160204-03-e.html [Accessed 22 March 2016].

Oberg, C. & Holstrom, J. 2006. Are mergers and acquisitions contagious? *Journal of Business Research*, 59 (12), 1267–1275.

Perry, J.S. & Herd, T.J. 2004. Reducing M&A risk through improved due diligence. *Strategy and Leadership*, 32(2):12–19.

Porter, M.E. 2004. *Competitive strategy*. New York: Free Press.

Potgieter, P. 2013. *Premerger and acquisition strategies: A multiple case study of unsolicited takeover attempts in South Africa since 2004.* Unpublished MBA research, University of Stellenbosch Business School.

Pudney, R. 2002 Collaborating to compete. [Online]. Available: http://tools.ashridge.org.uk/website/IC.nsf/wFARATT/Collaborating%20to%20 Compete/$file/CollaboratingToCompete.pdf [Accessed 21 March 2016].

Pudney, R. 2002. Collaborating to compete. *The Ashridge Journal,*Winter:16–23.

Pudney, R. 2003. 2+2=5, Directions. *The Ashridge Journal*, Summer:16–23.

Ray, K.G. 2010. *Mergers and acquisitions: Strategy, valuation and integration*. New Delhi: Asoke K Ghosh.

Reed, J., Croft, J., & Davies, PJ. 2005. Barclays to buy £2.9bn Absa stake. *Financial Times*, 9 May 2005. [Online]. Available: http://www.ft.com/ cms/s/0/11c1560c-bfe4-11d9-b376-00000e2511c8.html?ft_site=falcon&desktop=true#axzz4COL288he[Accessed 26 March 2016].

Reed, M. 2009. *The devil is in the deal structure*. Softletter Financial Handbook.

Republic of South Africa. 1973. *Companies Act*, No. 61 of 1973. Pretoria: Government Printer.

Republic of South Africa. 1991. *Securities Regulation Code on Take-overs and Mergers and the Rules, Government* Notice, R. 29 of 1991. Pretoria: Government Printer.

Republic of South Africa. 1998. *Competition Act*, No. 89 of 1998. Pretoria: Government Printer.

Republic of South Africa: Department of Mineral Resources. 2016, February 16. [Online]. Available: http://www.angloamerican.com/~/media/ Files/A/Anglo-American-PLC-V2/presentations/2016pres/sa-dmr-statement.pdf [Accessed 24 March 2016].

Rothenbuecher, J. & Schrottke, J. 2008. Merger, grow sales. *Harvard Business Review*, 86 (5), 24-25.

Sahakian, C.E. Strategic Alliance Quotes. [Online]. Available: http://sgbmedia.typepad.com/blog/2010/11/strategic-alliance-quotes.html [Accessed 11 March 2016].

Schweizer, L. & Patzelt, H. 2012. Employee commitment in the post-acquisition integration process: The effect of integration speed and leadership. *Scandinavian Journal of Management*, 28(4):298–310.

Shelton, M.J. 2003. Managing your integration manager. *McKinsey Quarterly*. Special Edition.

Sinha, P.K. 1999. On conglomerate diversification, anthology. *Atlantic Economic Journal* 27(1):115.

Slorach, S. 2004. *Corporate finance, mergers & acquisitions*. New York: Oxford University Press.

Southwick, L. 2005. Economies of scale and market power in policing. *Managerial and Decision Economics*, 26(8):461–473.

Sweeting, M. 2008. *Approaching partners and targets in mergers and acquisitions: A practical guide for private companies and their UK and overseas advisers*. London: Kogan Page.

Tarba, S. & Weber, Y. 2011. Exploring integration approach: Postmerger integration in the high-tech industry. *International Journal of Organizational Analysis*, 19(3):202–221.

Thompson Jnr, A.A., Strickland lll, A.J. & Gamble, J.E. 2010. *Crafting and executing strategy: Text and readings*. 17th ed. Berkshire: McGraw-Hill.

Thompson, J. & Martin, F. 2010. *Strategic management: Awareness and change*. New Hampshire: Cengage.

Townsend, J.D. 2003. Understanding alliances: a review of international aspects in strategic marketing. *Marketing Intelligence and Planning*, 21(3):143–155.

Trautwein, F. 1990. Merger motives and merger prescriptions. *Strategic Management Journal*, 11(4):283–295.

Vishny, R. 2003. Stock market driven acquisitions. *Journal of Financial Economics*, 70(3):295–311.

Volberda, H.W., Morgan, R.E., Reinmoeller, P.R., Hitt, M.A., Ireland, R.D. & Hoskinsson, R.E. 2011. *Strategic management: Competitiveness and globalization*. Hampshire: Cengage.

Wakeam, J. 2003. 'The five factors of a strategic alliance'. *Ivey Business Journal*, May/June. [Online] Available: http://iveybusinessjournal.com/ publication/the-five-factors-of-a-strategic-alliance/ [Accessed 20 June 2016].

Walker, J.W. & Price, K.F. 2000. Why do mergers go right? *Human Resource Planning*, 23(2):6–8.

Weber, R.A. & Camerer, C.F. 2003. Cultural conflict and merger failure: An experimental approach. *Management Science*, 49(4):400–415.

Zhang, J., Ahammad, M.F., Tarba, S., Cooper, C.L., Glaister, K.W. & Wang, J. 2015. The effect of leadership style on talent retention during merger and acquisition integration: Evidence from China. *International Journal of Human Resource Management*, 26(7):1021–1050.

CHAPTER 8 REFERENCES

Alsop, R. 2008, October 21. The trophy kids go to work. *Wall Street Journal*: [Online]. Available: http://www.wsj.com/articles/SB122455219391652725 [Accessed 2 February 2016].

Amabile, T. 1998. How to kill creativity. *Harvard Business Review*, 76(5):76–87.

Aziz, K. 2012, August 22. *A brief history of the management field*. Slideshare: [Online]. Available: http://www.slideshare.net/khalid1173/a-brief-history-of-management-field [Accessed 16 Dec 2015].

Birkinshaw, J., & Mol, M. 2006. How management innovation happens. *MIT Sloan Management Review*, 47(4):81–88.

Birkinshaw, J., Hamel, G., & Mol, M. 2008. Management innovation. *Academy of Management Review*, 33(4):825–845.

Bosman, M. 2009, Jan 15. *Strategic Leadership Institute*. The historical evolution of management theory from 1900 to present: The changing role of leaders in organisations. [Online]. Available: http://www.strategicleadershipinstitute.net/news/the-historical-evolution-of-management-theory-from-1900-to-present-the-changing-role-of-leaders-in-organizations-/ [Accessed 16 Dec 2015].

Bower, J.L., & Christensen, C.M. 1995. Disruptive technologies: Catching the wave. *Harvard Business Review*, 73(1):44.

Brook, M. 2014. *New dimensions in health: Simple secrets to creating optimal health*. Bloomington: Balboa Press.

Bullington, K.E. 2003. 5S for Suppliers. *Quality Progress*, 33(7): 56-59.

Burstein, D. 2013. *Fast future: How the millennial generation is shaping our world*. Boston, MA: Beacon Press.

Carter, J. 2015, November 2. *Should we strive for business instability? A systems view*. LinkedIn: [Online]. Available: https://www.linkedin.com/pulse/should-we-strive-business-instability-systems-view-jason-carter [Accessed 22 Jan 2016].

Christensen, C.M., Johnson, M.W., & Rigby, D.K. 2002. Foundations for growth: How to identify and build disruptive new businesses. *MIT Sloan Management Review*, 43(3):23, 34.

Collins, J.C., & Porras, J.I. 1994. *Built to last: Successful habits of visionary companies*. New York: Harper Business.

Da Silva, M. 2014. *The development of a management innovation measurement tool*. Bellville: University of Stellenbosch.

Dean, D., Digrande, S., Field, D., Lundmark, A., O'Day, J., Pineda, J., & Zwillenberg, P. 2012, March. *The connected world: The $4.2 trillion opportunity*. Boston Consulting Group: [Online]. Available: https://publicaffairs.linx.net/news/wp-content/uploads/2012/03/bcg_4trillion_opportunity.pdf [Accessed 7 June 2012].

Dearlove, D., & Crainer, S. 2015. *Distinguished Achievement Awards (2011–2015)*. Thinkers 50: [Online]. Available: http://thinkers50.com/ [Accessed 25 Jan 2016].

Deming, W.E. 1986. *Out of the crisis*. Cambridge, MA: Massachusetts Institute of Technology Center for Advanced Engineering Studies.

Deming, W.E. 1993, February. Deming Four-Day Seminar. (via the notes of Mike Stoecklein). Phoenix, AZ.

Deming, W.E. 1993. *The new economics for industry, government, education*. Cambridge, MA: Massachusetts Institute of Technology.

Dunn, C. 2014, October 4. 8 of Google's craziest offices. Fastcompany Design: [Online]. Available: http://www.fastcodesign.com/3028909/8-of-googles-craziest-offices [Accessed 15 February 2016].

Elmore, T. 2015, September 3. *Six defining characteristics of Generation Z*. Growing Leaders: [Online]. Available: http://growingleaders.com/blog/six-defining-characteristics-of-generation-z/ [Accessed 2 February 2016].

Furlong, A. 2013. *Youth studies: An introduction*. New York: Routledge.

Gilbert, J. 2011, September. The millennials: A new generation of employees, a new set of engagement policies. *Ivey Business Journal*: [Online]. Available: http://iveybusinessjournal.com/publication/the-millennials-a-new-generation-of-employees-a-new-set-of-engagement-policies/ [Accessed February 2, 2016].

Gitlow, H., Oppenheim, A., Oppenheim, R., & Levine, D. 2005. *Quality management* (3rd ed.). New York: McGraw-Hill.

Goldstuck, A. 2012. *Internet matters: The quiet engine of the South African economy*. World Wide Worx: [Online]. Available: http://internetmatters.co.za/report/ZA_internet_Matters.pdf [Accessed 31 July 2012].

Google Company Overview. 2016. Google: [Online]. Available: https://www.google.co.za/about/company/ [Accessed February 15, 2016].

Google Office Zurich. 2008. [Online]. Available: Google Office Zurich: http://www.swissmiss.com/wp-content/uploads/legacy/weblog/files/google_office_zurich.pdf [Accessed 15 February 2016].

Google Offices around the World. 2010. YouTube: [Online]. Available: https://www.youtube.com/watch?v=LB5utwRnfH4 [Accessed February 15, 2016].

Grant, R.M. 2008. The future of management: Where is Gary Hamel leading us? *Long Range Planning*, 41(5):474.

Hamel, G. 2006. The why, what and how of management innovation. *Harvard Business Review*, 84(2):74.

Hamel, G. 2007. *The future of management*. Harvard Business Press.

Hamel, G. 2009. Moon shots for management. *Harvard Business Review*, 87(2):92.

Hamel, G. 2011. First let's fire all the managers. *Harvard Business Review*, 89(12):51.

Hamel, G. 2012. *What matters now*. San Francisco: Jossey-Bass.

Harvey, P. 2010, May 17. As college graduates hit the workforce, so do more entitlement-minded workers. University of New Hampshire Media Relations: [Online]. Available: http://www.unh.edu/news/cj_nr/2010/may/lw17gen-y.cfm [Accessed 2 February 2016].

Herzberg, F. 1968. *One more time: How do you motivate employees*. Boston: Harvard Business Review.

Isaacson, W. 2012. The real leadership lessons of Steve Jobs. *Harvard Business Review*, 90(4):99–100.

Kaplan, R., & Norton, D. 1992. The balanced scorecard – measures that drive performance. *Harvard Business Review*, 70(1):71.

Kiechel, W. 2012. The management century. *Harvard Business Review*, 90(11):62–75.

Knoll, Inc. 2014. *What comes after Y? Generation Z: Arriving to the office soon*. [Online]. Available: https://www.knoll.com/media/938/1006/What-Comes-After-Y.pdf [Accessed 2 February 2016].

Magretta, J. 2012. *Understanding Michael Porter*. Boston: Harvard Business Review Press.

Manyika, J., & Roxburg, C. 2011, October. *The great transformer: The impact of the internet on economic growth and prosperity.* McKinsey Global Institute: [Online]. Available: http://www.mckinsey.com/Insights/MGI/Research/Technology_and_Innovation/internet_matters [Accessed 8 May 2012].

McGrath, R. 2014, July 30. Management's three eras: A brief history. *Harvard Business Review*: [Online]. Available: https://hbr.org/2014/07/managements-three-eras-a-brief-history# [[Accessed 16 December 2015].

Mol, M., & Birkinshaw, J. 2009. The sources of management innovation: When firms introduce new management practices. *Journal of Business Research,* 62(12):1269–1280.

Montini, L. 2014, September 2. *Generation Z: 5 Things to know about your future hires.* Inc.com: [Online]. Available: http://www.inc.com/laura-montini/meet-you-future-hires-5-characteristics-of-generation-z.html [Accessed 2 February 2016].

Porter, M.E. 2001. Strategy and the internet. *Harvard Business Review,* 79(3):74.

Project Leaders International. 2008. White Paper: An integrated approach to managing innovation. [Online]. Available: http://www.rcc.gov.pt/SiteCollectionDocuments/Integrated_Innovation_PLI2008.pdf [Accessed 12 Feb 2016].

Riffkin, R. 2014, December 18. *Americans rate nurses highest on honesty, ethical standards.* Gallup.com: [Online]. Available: http://www.gallup.com/poll/180260/americans-rate-nurses-highest-honesty-ethical-standards.aspx [Accessed 1 February 2016].

Roberts, K. 2015, April 8. *Millennial workers want free meals and flex time.* [Online]. Available: http://www.lwdirect.com/millennial-workers-want-free-meals-and-flex-time/[Accessed February 2, 2016].

Robinson, D. 2005, January. Management theorists: Thinkers for the 21st century. *Training Journal.* [Online]. Available: http://www.gdufs.biz/theorists.pdf 30–36 [Accessed 28 May 2016].

Semler, R. 1989. Managing without managers. *Harvard Business Review,* 67(5):76.

Skousen, M. 2013. *Economic logic* (4th ed.). Regnery Publishing.

Strauss, W., & Howe, N. 2000. *Millennials rising: The next great generation.* New York: Vintage Original.

Tanz, J. 2003, October 1. *A brief history of management.* CNN Money: [Online]. Available: http://money.cnn.com/magazines/fsb/fsb_archive/2003/10/01/353427/ [Accessed 16 Dec 2015].

Taylor, F.W. 1911. The principles of scientific management. New York, NY: American Society of Mechanical Engineers.

The Economist. Generation Boris. 2013, June 1. The Economist: [Online]. Available: http://www.economist.com/news/britain/21578666-britains-youth-are-not-just-more-liberal-their-elders-they-are-also-more-liberal-any[Accessed 2 February 2016].

Towers Perrin, 2007–2008. *Closing the engagement gap: A road map for driving superior business performance. Towers Perrin Global Workforce Study Global Report.* Towers Perrin. [Online]. Available: https://c.ymcdn.com/sites/www.simnet.org/resource/group/066D79D1-E2A8-4AB5-B621-60E58640FF7B/leadership_workshop_2010/towers_perrin_global_workfor.pdf [Accessed 1 February2016].

Twenge, J. 2006. *Generation Me.* New York: Free Press (Simon & Shuster).

Ungerer, G.D. 2015. *A competitive strategy framework for e-business start-ups.* Stellenbosch: University of Stellenbosch.

Urban, T. 2013, September 11. *Why Generation Y yuppies are unhappy.* Wait But Why: [Online]. Available: http://waitbutwhy.com/2013/09/why-generation-y-yuppies-are-unhappy.html [Accessed 2 February 2016].

Wheatley, M.J. 2007. *Finding our way: Leadership for an uncertain time.* San Francisco: Berett-Koehler.

CHAPTER 9 REFERENCES

ABC News. 2016. [Online]. Available: http://abcnews.go.com/topics/business/CEOs/bernard-madoff.htm [Accessed 9 May 2016].

Acs, Z.J., Desai, S., & Klapper, L.F. 2008. What does "entrepreneurship" data really show? *Small Business Economics,* 31(3):265-281.

Bartelsman, E., Haltiwanger, J., & Scarpetta, S. 2004. Microeconomic evidence of creative destruction in industrial and developing countries. Institute for the Study of Labor, IZA. Discussion Paper no. 1374. The World Bank, Policy Research Working Paper no. 3464. [Online] Available: http://ssrn.com/abstract=612230 [Accessed 27 May 2016].

Blank, S. 2013. Why the lean start-up changes everything. *Harvard Business Review,* 91(5):65-72.

Business Dictionary. 2016. [Online]. Available: http://www.businessdictionary.com/definition/entrepreneur.html [Accessed 4 May 2016].

Calá, C.D., Arauzo-Carod, J-M. & Manjón-Antolín, M. 2015. *The determinants of entrepreneurship in developing countries.* (Documento de Trabajo No. 1). Reus: Universitat Rovira i Virgili. Departament d'Economia.

Caliendo M., Fossen F. & Kritikos A. 2010. The impact of risk attitudes on entrepreneurial survival. *Journal of Economic Behavior & Organization,* 76:5–63.

Caliendo, M., & Kritikos, A. 2012. Searching for the entrepreneurial personality: New evidence and avenues for further research. *Journal of Economic Psychology* 33(2):319-324.

Carlyle News Release. [Online]. Available: https://www.carlyle.com/news-room/news-release-archive/carlyle-cardinal-ireland-invests-lily-o%E2%80%99brien%E2%80%99s-irish-manufacturer [Accessed 1 May 2016].

Chocolate Heaven at Lily O'Brien's. 18 May 2015. [Online]. Available: http://eatdrinkrunfun.com/?p=3913 [Accessed 4 May 2016].

Clarke, J. 2015. Mary Ann O'Brien: how I made my fortune from airline chocolates. *MoneyWeek.* [Online] Available: http://moneyweek.com/profile-of-entrepreneur-mary-ann-obrien-47730/ [Accessed 28 May 2016].

Design Team. 2011. 'Design Team Creating Inspiration print by print'. [Online] Available: http://www.designteamfabrics.co.za/ [Accessed 10 May 2016].

Economist. 2009. Global heroes, a special report on entrepreneurship. 12 March. [Online] Available: http://www.economist.com/node/13216025 [Accessed 20 June 2016].

Fast Company. 2005. 10 Ways to make slack simpler, safter and less annoying. [Online] Available: http://www.fastcompany.com/ [Accessed 6 May 2016].

Hinde, N. *Huffington Post*, 17 October 2014. [Online]. Available: http://www.huffingtonpost.co.uk/2014/10/17/mary-ann-obrien-lily-obriens-chocolate_n_5965462.html [Accessed 4 May 2016].

Hisrich, R.D., Peters, M.P. & Shepherd, D.A. 2005. *Entrepreneurship*. 6th ed. New York: McGraw-Hill Irwin.

Kelpie, C. 2015. Lily O'Brien boss aims to double business following Carlyle Cardinal move. *Irish Independent, Business Irish* (Business Newsletter) [Online]. Available: http://www.independent.ie/business/irish/lily-obrien-boss-aims-to-double-business-following-carlyle-cardinal-move-34254058.html [Accessed 1 May 2016].

Krueger, A. 2015. The rise of the intrapreneur. *Fast Company*, 18 May. [Online]. Available: http://www.fastcompany.com/3046231/the-new-rules-of-work/the-rise-of-the-intrapreneur [Accessed 6 May 2016].

Lidow, D. 2014. *Startup leadership: How savvy entrepreneurs turn their ideas into successful enterprises*. San Francisco, CA: Jossey-Bass.

Lynch, R.L. 2009. *Strategic management*. (5th ed). Harlow: Financial Times Prentice Hall.

Midgley, D. Interview. Published April 14, 2014. [Online]. Available: http://businesslife.ba.com/People/What-Ive-Learnt/What-Ive-learnt-chocolatier-Mary-Ann-OBrien.html [Accessed 1 May 2016].

Pienaar, E.B. 2013. The most prevalent features impacting on significant financial success amongst repeat entrepreneurs. Unpublished MBA Dissertation, University of Stellenbosch Business School. [Online]. Available: http://www.usb-ed.com/content/Knowledge%20Centre%20Documents/The%20Constituents%20of%20Entrepreneurial%20Success.pdf [Accessed 5 May 2016].

Politis, D. 2005. The process of entrepreneurial learning: A conceptual framework. *Entrepreneurship: Theory & Practice* 29(4):399–424.

Rego, A., Cunha, M.P.E. & Clegg, S. 2012. *The virtues of leadership*. Oxford: Oxford University Press.

SA Institute for Entrepreneurship. 2016. Who are we? [Online] Available] http://www.entrepreneurship.co.za/contents/who-are-we/ [Accessed 5 May 2016].

Schumpeter, J.A. 1942. *Capitalism, socialism and democracy*. New York: Harper and Brothers.

Schwab, K. 2015. *The Global Competitiveness Report 2015–16*. (World Economic Forum Insight Report, 2015). [Online]. Available: http://reports.weforum.org/global-competitiveness-report-2015-2016/ [Accessed 6 May 2016].

Shepherd, D.A. 2003. Learning from business failure: Propositions about the grief recovery process for the self-employed. *Academy of Management Review* 28(2):318-329.

Sorgner, A., Fritsch, M. & Kritikos, A. 2014. Do entrepreneurs really earn less? *Jena Economic Research Papers*, # 029-2014:21.

The EY G20 Entrepreneurship Barometer. 2013. The power of three: governments, entrepreneurs and corporations [Online]. Available: http://www.ey.com/GL/en/Services/Strategic-Growth-Markets/The-EY-G20-Entrepreneurship-Barometer-2013 [Accessed 6 May 2016].

The World Bank. 2016. Patent applications, residents. [Online]. Available: http://data.worldbank.org/country/south-africa [Accessed 6 May 2016].

Top 500 Companies. 2015. The Wiese factor: An iconic South African success story. [Online] Available: http://www.top500.co.za/the-wiese-factor-an-iconic-south-african-success-story/ [Accessed 8 May 2016].

TWIB (Technology for Women in Business) 'TWIB – Empowering Women through Tech'. [Online]. Available: http://www.twib.co.za/ [Accessed 6 May 2016].

Ungerer, M., Ungerer, G. & Herholdt, J. 2016. *Crystallising the strategic business landscape: Strategy analysis practices and tools for business leaders and strategy practitioners*. Johannesburg: KR Publishing.

University of Pretoria. 2016. *BCom Entrepreneurship brochure*. [Online]. Available: http://www.up.ac.za/business-management/article/42179/chair-in-entrepreneurship [Accessed 3 May 2016].

University of Stellenbosch. Entrepreneurship & innovation management. [Online]. Available: http://www.sun.ac.za/english/faculty/economy/business-management/academic-programmes/undergraduate/entrepreneurship-innovation-management [Accessed 16 May 2016].

Van der Zwan, P., Verheul, I., Thurik, R. & Grilo, I. 2013. Entrepreneurial progress: Climbing the entrepreneurial ladder in Europe and the US. *Regional Studies*, 47(5):803-825. DOI: 10.1080/00343404.2011.598504

Van Praag, M.C. & Versloot, P.H. 2007. What is the value of entrepreneurship? A review of recent research. *Small Business Economics*, 29:351–82.

Willebrands, D., Lammers, J. & Hartog, J. 2011. A successful businessman is not a gambler. Risk attitude and business performance among small enterprises in Nigeria. *Journal of Economic Psychology*. [Online]. Available: doi:10.1016/j.joep.2011.03.006 [Accessed 5 May 2016].

INDEX

www.ingramcontent.com/pod-product-compliance
Lightning Source LLC
Chambersburg PA
CBHW082120210326
41599CB00031B/5822